South Florida

South Florida

Includes the Tampa Bay Area, Miami & the Florida Keys

Sandra Friend & Kathy J. Wolf

The Countryman Press ✳ Woodstock, Vermont

We welcome your comments and suggestions. Please contact Explorer's Guide Editor, The Countryman Press, P.O. Box 748, Woodstock, VT 05091, or e-mail countrymanpress@wwnorton.com.

ISBN-13: 978-0-88150-626-6
ISBN-10: 0-88150-626-5
ISSN Data has been applied for.

Maps by Mapping Specialists, Madison, WI
Cover and interior design by Bodenweber Design
Text composition by PerfecType, Nashville, TN
Front cover photograph of a lifeguard station at South Beach
    by James Randklev Photography

Published by The Countryman Press, P.O. Box 748, Woodstock, Vermont 05091

Distributed by W. W. Norton & Company, 500 Fifth Avenue, New York, NY 10110

Printed in the United States of America

10 9 8 7 6 5 4 3 2 1

DEDICATION

To my husband, Rob, for his love and support.
—Sandra Friend

For my dear friend Mary Ellen Carey, who joined me on many excursions, filling me full of laughter every step of the way.
—Kathy Wolf

"Certainly, travel is more than the seeing of sights; it is a change that goes on, deep and permanent, in the ideas of living."
—Miriam Beard

Also by Sandra Friend and Kathy Wolf
Orlando, Central & North Florida: An Explorer's Guide

Also by Sandra Friend
50 Hikes in North Florida
50 Hikes in Central Florida
50 Hikes in South Florida
Along the Florida Trail
Florida
The Florida Trail: The Official Hiking Guide
Florida in the Civil War: A State in Turmoil
Hiker's Guide to the Sunshine State
Sinkholes

EXPLORE WITH US!

Welcome to the first edition of *South Florida: An Explorer's Guide,* the most comprehensive travel guide you'll find covering this region. We've included attractions, accommodations, restaurants, and shopping on the basis of merit (primarily close personal inspection by your authors) rather than paid advertising. The following points will help you understand how we've organized the guide.

WHAT'S WHERE

The book starts out with a thumbnail sketch of the most important things to know about traveling in South Florida, from which beaches you should head to first to how to deal with hurricane season. We've included important contact information for state agencies and advice on what to do when you're on the road.

LODGING

All selections for accommodations in this guide are based on merit; most of them were inspected personally or by a reliable source known to us. No businesses were charged for inclusion in this guide. Many bed & breakfasts do not accept children under 12 or pets, so if there is not a specific mention in their entry, ask them about their policy before you book a room. Some places have a minimum-stay requirement, especially on weekends or during the high season (winter).

Rates: All rates quoted are for double occupancy, one night, before taxes. When a range of rates is given, it spans the gamut from the lowest of the low season (which varies around the state) to the highest of the high season. A single rate means the proprietor offers only one rate. Rates for hotels and motels are subject to further discount with programs like AAA and AARP and may be negotiable depending on occupancy. Many places offer reduced rates for Florida residents.

RESTAURANTS

Our distinction between *Eating Out* and *Dining Out* is based mainly on price, secondarily on atmosphere. Dining in Florida is more casual than anywhere else in the United States—you'll find folks in T-shirts and shorts walking in to the dressiest of steakhouses. If a restaurant has a dress code, we note it. Expect *Dining Out* choices in urban areas to require business casual dress.

Smoking is no longer permitted within restaurants in Florida, if the bulk of the business' transactions are in food rather than drink. Many restaurants now provide an outdoor patio for smokers.

KEY TO SYMBOLS

⚜ **Special value.** The special value symbol appears next to lodgings and restaurants that offer quality not usually enjoyed at the price charged.

&. **Handicapped access.** The wheelchair symbol appears next to lodgings, restaurants, and attractions that provide handicapped access, at a minimum with assistance.

✐ **Child-friendly.** The crayon symbol appears next to places or activities that accept children or appeal to families.

✿ **Pets.** The pet symbol appears next to places that accept pets, from bed & breakfasts to bookstores. All lodgings require that you let them know you're bringing your pet; many will charge an additional fee.

▼ **Gay-friendly.** The inverted triangle symbol indicates establishments that make an extra effort to cater to a gay clientele.

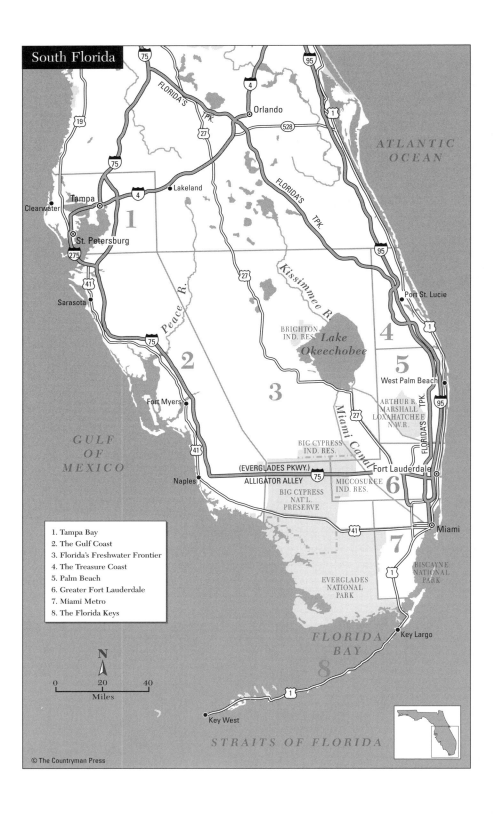

South Florida

1. Tampa Bay
2. The Gulf Coast
3. Florida's Freshwater Frontier
4. The Treasure Coast
5. Palm Beach
6. Greater Fort Lauderdale
7. Miami Metro
8. The Florida Keys

ATLANTIC OCEAN

GULF OF MEXICO

GULF OF MEXICO

FLORIDA BAY

STRAITS OF FLORIDA

N

0   20   40
Miles

Orlando
Tampa
Clearwater
St. Petersburg
Lakeland
Sarasota
Fort Myers
Naples
Port St. Lucie
West Palm Beach
Fort Lauderdale
Miami
Key Largo
Key West

Lake Okeechobee
Kissimmee R.
Peace R.
Miami Canal

BRIGHTON IND. RES.
ARTHUR R. MARSHALL LOXAHATCHEE N.W.R.
BIG CYPRESS IND. RES.
MICCOSUKEE IND. RES.
BIG CYPRESS NAT'L. PRESERVE
EVERGLADES NATIONAL PARK
BISCAYNE NATIONAL PARK

(EVERGLADES PKWY.)
ALLIGATOR ALLEY

FLORIDA'S TPK.
FLORIDA'S TPK.

© The Countryman Press

CONTENTS

CONTENTS

INTRODUCTION

Sometimes, life throws you a curveball, and for Kathy and me, it was the most active hurricane season in recent memory right in the middle of our research on this book. It's our custom to research during the off-season, when the roads are less crowded, you're guaranteed to find downtown parking, and innkeepers are happy to see you. So to be forced to evacuate a hotel in the middle of a research weekend or to be trapped in Key West as a hurricane made landfall made this one of the more memorable books I've ever written, and one of the toughest. It was tough to visit the lush nurseries and historic sites of Pine Island and beautifully canopied Punta Gorda one weekend, only to see them ripped up by a hurricane a week later. It was tough to drive home past the wreckage of houses and motels in the path of Hurricane Frances, knowing what these folks would be going through putting their lives and businesses back together. And it was tough to watch the Weather Channel and other news media replay the same hurricane scenes over and over again, scaring thousands of people away from Florida when, in fact, many Florida destinations remained untouched by any hurricane damage and were welcoming tourists with open arms. Folks tend to forget that Florida is a very big state. It takes at least 13 hours to drive from Pensacola to Key West! Florida's hurricanes are no newer than the nor'easters of New England and the blanketing blizzards of the Great Lakes states. Weather happens, and the only thing within a traveler's control is where to wait it out. It's an ironic twist, then, that what draws most people to Florida *is* the weather. We have more than our fair share of sunshine and blue skies, especially in South Florida.

South Florida has captured the imagination of explorers since the Spanish set foot on these shores in the 1500s in search of gold. The farther south you travel, the clearer and bluer the oceans become. South Florida is on the tropical fringe, with native flora originating in the Caribbean growing as far north as West Palm Beach and Pine Island. It is where rare indigenous species roam, including the elusive Florida panther and the reclusive American crocodile. While the coastal regions are heavily populated, the central portion of the peninsula has rural towns, cattle ranches, and citrus groves until you reach the mighty swamps of South Florida, the Everglades and Big Cypress.

South Florida is also an amalgam of cultures, from the Greeks who settled Tarpon Springs in 1882 and the Scots who founded Dunedin in 1852 to the Seminoles, descendents of Creeks who migrated into Florida in the 1700s. The Amish established a community near Sarasota, and a group of Japanese pine-apple farmers formed the Yamato farming colony at Delay Beach in 1905. Cuban cigar workers followed Don Vicente Martinez Ybor to Ybor City in 1886, and Cuban refugees flooded Miami after Fidel Castro's coup of Cuba in 1953. Seeking investment properties, South and Central Americans have flocked to cosmopolitan Miami and Miami Beach, as have celebrities from around the world. Many South Florida cities are the termini of highways starting in the Northeast and Midwest, and so it is here that many people end when looking for a retirement home or a getaway from fierce winter weather, which is why the "snowbird" population swells tremendously during the winter months.

With its arts communities and historic sites, seaside resorts and forests to roam, rural retreats, urban chic, and some of the best fishing and diving in the United States, South Florida is a destination worth your time to explore.

Prices for lodgings and restaurants are subject to change, and shops come and go. Your feedback is essential for subsequent editions of this guide. Feel free to write us care of the Countryman Press or Explorer's Guide, P.O. Box 424, Micanopy 32667, or e-mail ExploreFLA@aol.com, with your opinions and your own treasured finds.

ACKNOWLEDGMENTS

A project this big requires numerous helping hands, so we'd like to thank the many, many folks who came to our aid by setting up press trips, hosting us, and showing us around their towns and cities; we can't possibly list you all. We offer special acknowledgment to those who went out of their way to introduce us to their communities:

Rebecca Allen, Charlotte County Visitor's Bureau; Enid Atwater, Ann Margo Peart, and Julie Sylvester, Palm Beach County CVB; Jeff Barwick, Clewiston Chamber of Commerce; Bill and Sherri Barzydlo, Spring Bayou Inn, Tarpon Springs; Robert Belott, The Cypress, Sarasota; Becky Bragg, Peace River Outfitters; Rachel Bray-Stiles and Leon Corbett, Visit Florida; Susan Brustman and Alisah Jeffries, Susan Brustman & Associates; Lori Burns, Indian River Chamber of Commerce; Kelly Earnest, Tampa Bay Convention & Visitors Bureau; Mike Eden, Eden House, Key West; Roderick Gill, Pieces Restaurant, Key West; Veronica Gobin and Hilda Varela, Cauley Square Historic Village; Josie Gulliken and Carol Shaughnessy, Stuart-Newman Associates, Florida Keys; Maria Hayworth, Hayworth Creative; Nancy Hamilton, Jessica Fairbanks, and Lee Rose, Lee Island Coast CVB; Zaneta Hubbard and Wit Tuttell, Pinellas County CVB; Sid Kalmans and Charlene Loke, Lemon Tree Inn, Naples; Karen Krugel, Lou Hammond & Associates; Jose Lima, Bal Harbour Village; Joanne and Clift McMahon, Tropical Paradise B&B; Vanessa Menkes, The Opium Group; Judy Micelle, Naples Historical Society; Dale Nelson, Sea Castle, Siesta Key; Jane Phelan, Siesta Key Chamber of Commerce; Patty Register and Rhoda Planty, Glades County TDC; Michelle Revuelta and Jennifer Haz, Miami-Dade CVB; Lori Rosso, Sea Breeze Manor, Gulfport; Reagan Rule, JoNell Modys, and Jack Wert, Naples Marco Island Everglades CVB; Lois and Jon Steckney, Horse and Chaise B&B, Venice; Rob Wells, Tarpon Lodge, Pineland; Pat Taras and Elaine and Larry Levey, Highlands County Tourist Development Council; Jessica Taylor, Greater Fort Lauderdale CVB; Carole Stevens, The Lower Keys Chamber of Commerce; Gayle Tippett and Mary Threlkeld, Strike Zone Charters, Big Pine Key; and the fine folks at Hotel Place St. Michel, Coral Gables, and Essex House, South Beach.

In addition, Sandra would like to acknowledge a little help from friends Clyde and Niki Butcher and Jackie Obendorf; Ruth Gardner, Surfside; cartoonists Anne Sabo, Dan Smith, and Ron Johnson, who helped with picks for Pinellas;

Sandy and Bill Huff, who shared their Safety Harbor; Chuck and Betty Wilson, longtime Naples residents who showed me around town; Ethel Palmer, my favorite Clearwater Beach native; and my husband, Rob Smith, who continues to delight me with his knowledge and love of Old Florida.

Kathy would like to thank daughter, Sherri Lemon, and son, Jaime Jimino, who have been touring South Florida with me since moving here in 1987; Sherri's husband, Chris, who kept my car in check as it topped 100,000 miles; Larry and Elaine Levey, who adopted me for several days while touring Highlands County; Owhnn of Everglades Hostel and Tours in Florida City, who showed me a gorgeous part of Florida I never knew existed; Susan Scott of Siquier, Scott & Associates, who hand delivered me to the trendiest hot spots in South Beach; Dave Taylor, Schipperkes Ben and Gabi, and Lady Bug the Cat of Cypress House, who, by their very nature, supercharged me with energy after each hot August day in Key West; and, finally, Ron Mercer, who continues to show me the way.

WHAT'S WHERE IN SOUTH FLORIDA

ADMISSION FEES If an admission fee is $5 or less, it's simply listed as "fee." Fees greater than $5 are spelled out. Although fees were accurate when this book went to press, keep in mind that yearly increases are likely, especially for the larger attractions and theme parks.

AIRBOAT RIDES Airboats are an exciting way to get out in the backcountry of Florida. These shallow boats can skim over only a few inches of water. Boat sizes range from small four-seaters to massive floating buses holding up to 30 people and dictate the type of experience you can expect. The smaller intimate boats will be more one-on-one, will get into tighter places, and may be more expensive. Most of the larger boats provide

handicapped assistance. All airboats require hearing protection, which is provided by the operators.

AIR SERVICE Major international airports in the region covered by this book include Tampa International Airport, Southwest Florida International Airport in Fort Myers, Palm Beach International Airport in West Palm Beach, Fort Lauderdale–Hollywood International Airport in Fort Lauderdale, and Miami International Airport. Smaller regional airports served by commuter flights are listed in their respective chapters.

ALLIGATORS AND CROCODILES No longer an endangered species, the **American alligator** is a ubiquitous resident of Florida's lakes, rivers, streams, and retention ponds. Most alligators will turn tail and hit the water with a splash when they hear you coming—unless they've been fed or otherwise sensitized to human presence. Do not approach a sunning alligator, and never, ever, feed an alligator (it's a felony, and downright dangerous to do) in the wild. Nuisance alligators should be reported to the **Florida Fish and Wildlife**

Greater Naples Marco Island Everglades CVB

Conservation Commission (352-732-1225; www.floridaconservation.org). South Florida is also home to the endangered **American crocodile,** a reclusive species that prefers the mangrove swamps and open shallows of Biscayne Bay and Florida Bay. Individuals have been spotted as far north as Pine Island South on the west coast and Fort Lauderdale on the east coast, and chances are you'll see at least one at the Flamingo Marina in Everglades National Park.

AMTRAK One daily AMTRAK (1-800-USA-RAIL; www.amtrak.com) train makes its way from New York to South Florida: the **Silver Service/ Palmetto,** ending in either Tampa or Miami. Stops are noted in *Getting There.*

ANTIQUES The antiques districts are particularly hot in **Arcadia, Delray Beach, Plant City,** and **Sarasota,** each worth a full day for browsing. You'll find nice clusters of antiques shops in **Fort Myers, St. Petersburg,** and **Venice** as well. Since 1985 the free magazine *Antiques & Art Around Florida* (352-475-1336; www.aarf.com) has kept up with the trends throughout the Sunshine State; pick up a copy at one of the antiques stores you visit, or browse their web site to do a little pretrip planning.

ARCHEOLOGY Florida's archeological treasures date back more than ten thousand years, including temple mound complexes on the Gulf Coast such as those found at **Emerson Point, Spanish Point, Terra Ceia,** and **Weedon Island.** Remnants of the Calusa culture have been unearthed all along Pine Island Sound; you can walk through the

remains of a Calusa city in **Pineland.** In the middle of Estero Bay, **Mound Key** was once the capital of the Calusa culture. Even out in the sugarcane fields of **Belle Glade** and the hammocks of **Ortona,** mounds have been discovered, evidence of the Calusa's travels. On the Atlantic Coast, remnants of the Ais, Jeaga, and Tequesta remain, including the **Miami Circle** and burial mounds at the **Deering Estate at Cutler.** And the reefs of the Florida Keys provide a treasure trove of **shipwrecks** for divers. For more information about archeological digs and shipwrecks, contact the **Florida Division of Historical Resources, Bu- reau of Archaeological Research** (850-245-6444; http://dhr.dos.state.fl.us).

AREA CODES As Florida's population grows, its area codes continue to fragment. In general, in urban areas you must dial the area code with every local call. The need for the area code varies depending where you are in any particular county since the phone systems do not correspond to county lines.

ART GALLERIES Florida is blessed with many creative souls who draw their inspiration from our dramatic landscapes, working in media from copper sculpture and driftwood to fine black-and-white photography, giclee, and watercolor. Many artists gravitate into communities; look for clusters of art galleries in places like **Bradenton, Coconut Grove, Delray Beach, Islamorada, Matlacha, Sanibel Island, Sarasota,** and **Key West. Naples** offers the finest of the fine arts, with dozens of galleries downtown and two major art museums.

ARTS COUNCILS Many cities and counties have public art displays (such as the pigs of Venice) thanks to their local arts councils. The **Florida Cultural Affairs Division** (www.florida-arts.org/index.asp) offers resources, grants, and programs to support the arts throughout Florida. Its Florida Artists Hall of Fame recognizes great achievements in the arts.

AVIATION Florida's aviation history includes many World War II training bases and the birth of naval aviation in 1914, as well as the first scheduled commercial airline flight from St. Petersburg to Tampa. Visit the **St. Petersburg Museum of History** (727-894-1052; www.stpetemuseum ofhistory.org) for a full rundown on the history of commercial aviation.

BASEBALL Florida is home to Major League Baseball's annual spring training, so baseball fans flock down south every spring to catch the action when the **Boston Red Sox** and the **Minnesota Twins** play in **Fort Myers;** the **Cincinnati Reds** in **Sarasota;** the **New York Yankees** in **Tampa;** the **Pittsburgh Pirates** in **Bradenton;** the **Philadelphia Phillies** in **Clearwater;** and the **Toronto Blue Jays** in **Dunedin.** The **Tampa Bay Devil Rays** don't leave home for their spring training—you can catch them at Tropicana Field in **St. Petersburg.**

BEACHES Where to start? Florida's 2,000-mile coastline means beaches for every taste, from the busy social scene at **South Beach** to the remote serenity of **Caladesi Island.** Public lands are your best places to enjoy pristine dunes and uncluttered beach-

Sandra Friend

fronts—our favorites include **Bahia Honda State Park, Cayo Costa State Park, Caspersen Beach,** and the remote **Bowman's Beach** on **Sanibel Island.**

BED & BREAKFASTS Because of the sheer number of bed & breakfasts throughout Florida, we don't list every one in the region covered by this book, but we have given you selections from what we feel are the best we've encountered. There is a mix of historical bed & breakfasts, working ranches, rustic lodges, and easygoing family homes. Some of our choices, but not all, are members of associations such as **Superior Small Lodging** (www.superiorsmalllodging .com) or the **Florida Bed & Breakfast Inns** (281-499-1374 or 1-800-524-1880; www.florida-inns.com), both of which conduct independent inspections of properties. All the bed & breakfast owners we stayed with were eager to tell their stories; most have a great love for the history of their homes and their towns. We find bed & breakfast travel to be one of the best ways to connect with the *real* Florida, and we strongly encourage you to seek out the experiences we've listed throughout the book. Some motels will offer breakfast so that they can list their establishment as a bed & breakfast, and we have tried to note this wherever possible as Internet sites can be misleading.

BICYCLING Check with **Bike Florida** (www.bikeflorida.org) for bicycling opportunities in Florida, where regional groups have done a great job of establishing and maintaining both on-road bike routes and off-road trails suitable for mountain biking. Information on these routes and trails is listed in the text. The **Office of Greenways and Trails** (see *Greenways*) can provide maps and specific information on rail-trail projects throughout the state.

BIG CYPRESS NATIONAL PRESERVE Established by Congress in 1974 as the first National Preserve in the United States, **Big Cypress National Preserve** (239-695-1201; www.nps .gov/bicy), between Naples and Miami along the Tamiami Trail, protects more than 900 square miles of cypress and sawgrass habitats dependent on seasonal rains. Stop in at the **Oasis Visitor Center,** Ochopee, for an orientation to the preserve. **Friends of the Big Cypress Preserve** (239-695-0376; www. friendsofbigcypress.org), 52388 Tamiami Trail, has an excellent web site with extensive information on the natural habitat and where you can access it.

BIG CYPRESS SWAMP The Big Cypress National Preserve is only one in a network of public lands protecting the **Big Cypress Swamp,** more than a million acres of gently sloping watery wilderness fed by summer rainfall that moves slowly south in a shallow river through cypress strands and sloughs. Other public lands protecting this fragile environment are **Collier-Seminole State Park, Corkscrew Swamp Sanctuary, Fakahatchee Strand Preserve State Park, Florida Panther National Wildlife Refuge, Picayune Strand State Forest,** and the **Ten Thousand Islands National Wildlife Refuge,** where the fresh water mingles with the mangrove fringe of the Gulf of Mexico. Most of these preserves provide exploration of the habitat via boardwalks, paddling trails, or hiking trails—expect to wade them most of the year.

BIRDING As the home of millions of winter migratory birds, Florida is a prime destination for bird-watching. The **Great Florida Birding Trail** (www.floridabirdingtrail.com), supported by the Florida Fish and Wildlife Conservation Commission, provides guidance to birders on the best overlooks, hiking trails, and waterfront parks to visit and which species you'll find at each location. Sites listed in the regional Great Florida Birding Trail brochures are designated with brown road signs displaying a stylized swallow-tailed kite. Certain sites are designated "Gateways" to the Great Florida Birding Trail, where you can pick up detailed information and speak to a naturalist. In the region covered by this guidebook, these sites include Fort De Soto Park in St. Petersburg and Corkscrew Swamp Sanctuary east of Naples. The Florida Game and Fresh Water Fish Commission (850-414-7929; www.floridaconservation .org) also has a bird-watching certificate program called "Wings Over Florida."

Kathy Wolf

BOAT AND SAILING EXCURSIONS

Exploring our watery state by water is part of the fun of visiting Florida, from the blasting speed of an airboat skipping across the marshes to the gentle toss of a schooner as it sails along the Intracoastal Waterway. Many ecotours rely on quiet electric-motor pontoon boats to guide you down Florida's rivers. With South Florida's multitude of islands and massive Lake Okeechobee, boat tours and charter boats can be found out of almost every major marina.

BOOKS To understand Florida, you need to read its authors, and none is more important to read than **Patrick Smith,** whose *A Land Remembered* is a landmark piece of fiction tracing

Sandra Friend

Florida's history from settlement to development. A good capsule history of Florida's nearly five hundred years of European settlement is *A Short History of Florida,* the abbreviated version of the original masterwork by **Michael Gannon.** To understand Florida's frenetic development over the past century, *Some Kind of Paradise: A Chronicle of Man and the Land in Florida* by **Mark Derr** will offer serious insights.

South Florida's settlers had a much harsher time of homesteading than their North Florida brethren, since mosquito-borne diseases, Indian attacks, and ravaging hurricanes were common. To introduce yourself to the hardships of these early days, seek out *Their Eyes Were Watching God* by novelist **Zora Neale Hurston** for a touching fictionalization of the 1928 hurricane that decimated the southern communities along Lake Okeechobee, and *Crackers in the Glade* by **Rob Storter,** a memoir and history of his family's settlement of the Ten Thousand Islands. **Peter Matthiessen** wrote a trilogy of fiction using the true tales of early settlers in the Ten Thousand Islands, which kicks off with *Killing Mr. Watson,* a fictionalized account of the events that led up to one fateful day in Chokoloskee. And although it's well out of print, *The Mangrove Coast* (1942) by **Karl Bickel** is one of the best books written on the settlement of southwest Florida.

No discussion of the Everglades is complete without *The Everglades: River of Grass* by **Marjory Stoneman Douglas.** By putting pen to paper to write "There are no other Everglades in the world," she spearheaded a conservation effort in the 1940s to preserve the unique Everglades habitat and establish Everglades National Park. Also of note are the classic history *Man in the Everglades* by **Charlton Tebeau** and the recent *Liquid Land* by **Ted Levin. David McCally** gives an informative account of how the original Everglades ecosystem has been razed by agriculture in *The Everglades: An Environmental History*, and **Alex Wilkinson** explains the way of life for sugarcane workers in *Big Sugar.* The chronicler of Okeechobee lore is **Lawrence Will,** who wrote *Cracker History of Okeechobee* and *Okeechobee Hurricane.* Moving on to the wonders of the Big Cypress Swamp, explore this watery region through the words of **Jeff Ripple** and photos by **Clyde Butcher** in *Southwest Florida's Wetland Wilderness: Big Cypress Swamp and the Ten Thousand Islands.* **Connie Bransilver** and **Larry Richardson** collaborated on a beautiful coffee-table book, *Florida's Unsung Wilderness: The Swamps.* And to connect the dots between the swamp and the orchid growers of Redland, seek out *The Orchid Thief* by **Susan Orlean.** The natural history of the Florida Keys is thoroughly explained by **Jeff Ripple** in *The Florida Keys: Natural Wonders of an Island Paradise. Last Train to Paradise* by **Les Standiford** gives a thorough picture of Flagler's Folly, the Overseas Railroad, while *Charlotte's Story: A Florida Keys Diary* by **Charlotte Niedhauk** is a memoir of living as the caretaker on Lignumvitae Key in the 1930s.

Key West authors are known for their fine literature and plays, headed up by **Ernest Hemingway** and closely followed by **Tennessee Williams, Truman Capote, John Hershey,** and **Alison Lurie** among many others. But South Florida fairly bubbles over with mystery writers, and most of their settings take place within the cities covered in this book. Best beloved is **John D. MacDonald,** whose Travis McGee is a model for many modern sleuths. **Carl Hiaasen** and **Tim Dorsey** are known for madcap mysteries, while **Randy Wayne White, James W. Hall, Edna Buchanan,** and **Barbara Parker** tend more toward the mainstream. These folks are only the tip of the iceberg; ask around at any South Florida independent bookseller to find many more.

BUS SERVICE Greyhound (1-800-229-9424; www.greyhound.com) covers an extensive list of Florida cities; see their web site for details and the full schedule. Stops are noted in the text under *Getting There.*

CAMPGROUNDS Rates are quoted for single-night double-occupancy stays. All campgrounds offer discounts for club membership (Good Sam, etc.) as well as weekly, monthly, and resident (six months or more) stays, and they often charge more for extra adults. If pets are permitted, keep them leashed. Also see the *Parks* section of each chapter for campgrounds at state and county parks. Florida State Parks uses **Reserve America** (1-800-326-3521) for all campground reservations; a handful of sites are kept open for drop-ins. Ask at the gate.

CHILDREN, ESPECIALLY FOR The crayon symbol 𝄡 identifies activities and places of special interest to children and families.

CITRUS STANDS, FARMER'S MARKETS, AND U-PICKS Citrus stands associated with active groves are typi-

Visit Florida

(http://extlab1.entnem.ufl.edu/Olustee/
related/fl-cw.htm) for the full calendar
of events held throughout the state.

CORAL In the Florida Keys, avoid
stepping on coral. You'll damage the
living organisms, and they'll damage
you with dangerous cuts that can
quickly become infected. Washed up
on beaches or embedded in sandy
soil, dead coral can cut bare feet as
easily as broken glass.

CORAL REEFS The coral reefs paralleling the Florida Keys are the only living
coral reefs in the continental United
States. The most extensive reefs
formed along Key Largo and from
Big Pine Key west to Key West. The
coral reefs of Florida are similar to
those in the Caribbean, sharing many
species of fish and crustaceans. There
are several types of reefs in the Keys,
including bank reefs, which, heavily
affected by wave action on one side
and protected by the coral structure on
the other, harbor a great diversity of
species; patch reefs, which form on little fossil reef outcrops at 6 to 30 feet
deep and are surrounded by seagrass;
and spur-and-groove reef, where the
reef grows around eroded limestone
formations, as it does at Looe Key.

cally open seasonally from November
through April. We've listed permanent stands as well as places you're
likely to see roadside fruit and vegetable sales (often out of the backs of
trucks and vans) from local growers.
All U-pick is seasonal, and Florida's
growing seasons run year-round,
with citrus in winter and spring,
strawberries in early spring, blueberries in late spring, and cherries in
early summer. If you attempt U-pick
citrus, bring heavy gloves and wear
jeans: Citrus trees have serious
thorns. Also, don't pick citrus without
permission: It's such a protected crop
in Florida that to pluck an orange
from a roadside tree is a felony. For a
full listing of farmer's markets around
the state, visit the **USDA Florida
Marketing Services** web site
(www.ams.usda.gov/farmersmarkets/
States/Florida.htm).

CIVIL WAR As the third state to
secede from the Union, Florida has a
great deal of Civil War history to
explore, even in South Florida. For
instance, did you know that Fort
Myers was the site of the southernmost engagement of the war? For
reenactment information, visit the
Florida Civil War Events web site

Sandra Friend

CRABBING From mid-October through May, it's perfectly legal for you to dive offshore to collect **stone crab claws**—if you can stand the thought of removing them from their owners. The good news is, the crabs grow them back, so take only one from each critter. Limits set by the Florida Fish and Wildlife Conservation Commission (www.floridaconservation.org) are 1 gallon of claws per person (2 gallons per vessel), and all claws must be a minimum of 2¾ inches from elbow to tip. Divers must fly a diver-down flag.

CRABS Florida can lay claim to some of the freshest crabs in its seafood restaurants, thanks to fishermen who set crab traps in the shallows to catch stone crabs in season in such places as Chokoluskee, Cortez, Matlacha, and the Keys. Eat your crab legs with melted butter for optimum effect.

DIVE RESORTS Dive resorts cater to both open-water and cave divers, with an on-site dive shop. They tend toward utilitarian but worn accommodations—wet gear can trash a room! Lodgings categorized as such will appeal to divers because of their location.

DIVING South Florida divers focus on the sea, for there are shipwrecks to be explored, stone reefs to follow, and the wondrous beauty of the living coral reefs of the Florida Keys to experience. A diver-down flag is a must when diving off a boat, even in relatively shallow water.

THE DIXIE HIGHWAY Conceptualized in the 1910s by Carl Graham Fisher and the Dixie Highway Association as a grand route for auto touring, the

Sandra Friend

Dixie Highway had two legs that ran along the East Coast of the United States into Florida, both ending in Miami. Since it ran along both coasts of Florida, you'll find OLD DIXIE HIGHWAY signs on both US 1 and US 17 on the east coast and along US 19, 27, and 41 on the west coast, and even US 441 in the middle.

EMERGENCIES Hospitals with emergency rooms are noted at the beginning of each chapter. Dial 911 to connect to emergency service anywhere in the state. For highway accidents or emergencies, contact the **Florida Highway Patrol** at ✱FHP on your cell phone or dial 911.

THE EVERGLADES When rainfall lands on the prairies and lakes of Central Florida, it starts a southward journey down its creeks and rivers to the Kissimmee River and Fisheating Creek, which empty into **Lake Okeechobee.** Prior to the construction of the Herbert Hoover Dike, the waters of Okeechobee seeped south into creeks and the "river of grass" known as the Everglades. Decades of flood control and irrigation and drainage for agricultural development have disrupted this natural system, flushing phosphates and other chemicals into Everglades National Park. The congressionally approved **Everglades Restoration Plan** (www.everglades plan.org) seeks to undo the damage by returning water flow to its natural course and by forcing the agricultural industry to clean its water before releasing it into natural systems. The Everglades are a complex environment. Fifty miles wide, only a few inches to a few feet deep in places, the natural sheet flow of rainwater moves slowly southward to nourish sawgrass prairies punctuated by tree islands, with cypress sloughs forming where the water is deepest. As it flows into the Gulf of Mexico and Florida Bay, the water mingles with the saline mangrove estuaries, nourishing these important nurseries for marine life. During the dry season (December through April), the jagged limestone karst bedrock becomes evident, and animals cluster around deep ponds dug by alligators. The remainder of the year, it's a watery landscape as far as the eye can see.

EVERGLADES NATIONAL PARK Now protecting 1½ million acres of the Everglades ecosystem, **Everglades National Park** (www.nps.gov/ever) was dedicated on December 6, 1947,

Sandra Friend

by President Harry Truman. It was the culmination of years of effort by devoted activists concerned about drainage projects in South Florida and how they were affecting the landscape. Among those who most visibly contributed to the cause of protecting the Everglades were **Ernest Coe,** a landscape architect who founded the Tropical Everglades Park Association in 1928 with the intent of establishing a national park in South Florida, and **Marjory Stoneman Douglas,** an outspoken conservationist who rallied the public with *The Everglades: River of Grass* in 1947 and continued to fight for the natural Everglades sheet flow to be restored until her death in 1988 at age 108. The park enjoys the highest visitation of any public land in Florida, with more than 1.1 million visitors a year. There are three major gateways to the park: the **Everglades National Park Gulf Coast Visitor Center** in Everglades City, **Shark Valley** along the Tamiami Trail in the Miccosukee Reservation, and the main public-access portion of the park in South Dade County along Main Park Rd, starting at the **Ernest Coe Visitor Center.** Recreational pursuits in the park include paddling, fishing, camping, nature walks and hiking, and bicycling the park roads. Keep in mind that this is a wild natural environment and is home to numerous species of mosquitoes. To avoid tampering with the habitat, no mosquito-control spraying is done within the park. Mosquitoes are at their peak during the summer months but can be a problem almost any month of the year. January and February are when the mosquito population ebbs and are the best months for outdoor activities. In addition to your insect repellent, consider carrying a mosquito head net for those unexpected swarms at dusk and after a sudden rain—I'm happy I did.

EVERGLADES TRAIL With 20 stops along the route, this new driving tour introduces you to the flow of water through South Florida, starting at its northernmost headwaters in the Shingle Creek basin outside Orlando and moving down into Lake Okeechobee and the Everglades "river of grass" itself. Visit www.evergladestrail.com for a map and guide.

FACTORY OUTLETS You've seen the signs, but are they really a bargain? Several factory outlets offer brand and designer names for less, but you may also get a great deal at smaller shops and even the local mall. We've listed some factory outlets that we found particularly fun to shop at that also had a nice selection of eateries and close access to major highways.

FISH CAMPS Rustic in nature, fish camps are quiet retreats for anglers and their families to settle down along a lake or river and put in some quality time fishing. Such accommodations tend to be older cabins, mobile homes, or concrete-block structures, often a little rough around the edges. If the cabins or motel rooms at a fish camp are of superior quality, we say so.

FISHING The **Florida Fish and Wildlife Conservation Commission** (www.floridaconservation.org) regulates all fishing in Florida, offering both freshwater and saltwater licenses in short-term, annual, five-year, or lifetime options. To obtain a license, visit any sporting goods store or call 1-888-FISH-FLO for an instant license. You can also apply

online at www.floridafisheries.com. No fishing license is required if you are on a guided fishing trip, are fishing with a cane pole, are bank fishing along the ocean (varies by county), or are 65 years or older.

FLORIDA TRAIL The **Florida Trail** is a 1,400-mile footpath running from the Big Cypress National Preserve north of Everglades National Park to Fort Pickens at Gulf Islands National Seashore in Pensacola. With its first blaze painted in 1966, it is now one of only eight congressionally designated National Scenic Trails in the United States and is still under development— but you can follow the orange blazes from one end of the state to the other. The Florida Trail and other trails in state parks and state forests, known as the Florida Trail System, are built and maintained by volunteer members of the non-profit **Florida Trail Association** (352-378-8823 or 1-877-HIKE-FLA; www.floridatrail.org), 5415 SW 13th St, Gainesville 32608. The association is your primary source for maps and guidebooks for the trail.

FORESTS, STATE The Florida Division of Forestry (www.fl-dof.com) administers **Florida State Forests,** encompassing thousands of acres of public lands throughout Florida. There are fewer state forests in South Florida than the rest of the state, but you'll find solitude on the trails at **Myakka State Forest** and **Picayune Strand State Forest.** Most (but not all) developed state forest trailheads charge a per-person fee of $2–3 for recreational use. For $30 you can purchase an annual day-use pass good for the driver and up to eight passengers: a real bargain for families! If you're a hiker, get involved with the **Trailwalker** program, in which you tally up miles on hiking trails and receive patches and certificates. A similar program for equestrians is the **Trailtrotter** program. Information on both programs can be found at trailhead kiosks or on the Florida Division of Forestry web site.

GAS STATIONS Gas prices fluctuate wildly around the state—and not in proportion to distance from major highways, as you might think. You'll find your best bargains for filling your tank near Tarpon Springs, Fort Pierce, North Miami, Key Largo, and Okeechobee. The highest prices seem to be in Palm Beach County and Sarasota.

GOLFING Golfing is a favorite pastime for many Florida retirees, and there are hundreds of courses across the state, impossible for us to list in any detail. A good resource for research is **Play Florida Golf** (www.playfla.com/pfg/index.cfm), the state's official golf course web site. We've covered courses that are particularly interesting or feature exceptional facilities. Florida is home to both the PGA and LPGA headquarters.

Sandra Friend

GREENWAYS Florida has one of the nation's most aggressive greenway programs, overseen by the **Office of Greenways and Trails** (850-245-2052 or 1-877-822-5208; www.dep.state.fl.us/gwt/), which administers the state land acquisition program under the Florida Forever Act and works in partnership with the Florida Trail Association, Florida State Parks, water management districts, and regional agencies in identifying crucial habitat corridors for preservation and developing public recreation facilities.

HANDICAPPED ACCESS The wheelchair symbol ♿ identifies lodgings, restaurants, and activities that are, at a minimum, accessible with minor assistance. Many locations and attractions provide or will make modifications for persons with disabilities, so call ahead to see if they can make the necessary accommodations.

HERITAGE SITES If you're in search of history, watch for the brown signs with columns and palm trees that mark official Florida Heritage Sites—which cover everything from historic churches and graveyards to entire historic districts. According to the **Florida Division of Historical Resources** (http://dhr.dos.state.fl.us/bhp/markers/markers_map.html), to qualify as a Florida Heritage Site, a building, structure, or site must be at least 30 years old and have significance in the areas of architecture, archeology, Florida history, or traditional culture or be associated with a significant event that took place at least 30 years ago.

HIKING The best hiking experiences in each region are under the *Hiking* section, and you can find additional

Sandra Friend

walks mentioned under *Green Space.* Your most comprehensive hiking guides for this portion of Florida include Sandra Friend's *50 Hikes in Central Florida* and *50 Hikes in South Florida* (Backcountry Guides) and both *The Florida Trail: The Official Guide* (Westcliffe Publishing) and *Hiker's Guide to the Sunshine State* (University Press of Florida), also by Sandra Friend.

HISTORIC SITES With nearly five centuries of European settlement in Florida, our historic sites are myriad—so our coverage of Florida history is limited to sites of particular interest. For the full details on designated historic sites in Florida, visit the state-administered **Florida's History Through Its Places** web site (http://dhr.dos.state.fl.us/HistoricPlaces/Atlas.html). Historic sites that belong to the **Florida Trust for Historic Preservation** (850-224-8128; www.floridatrust.org), P.O. Box 11206, Tallahassee 32302, honor the **Florida's Historic Passport** program, in which you can purchase a pass-port for $35 ($50 family) that offers special access to member sites—some for free, others for discounted admissions.

HUNTING The **Florida Fish and Wildlife Conservation Commission** (www.floridaconservation.org) regulates hunting statewide, with general gun season falling between October and February in various parts of the state. Check the web site for specific hunt dates, the wildlife management areas (WMAs) open to hunting, and hunting license regulations.

HURRICANES While hurricanes can strike anywhere in Florida, South Florida has, over the decades, borne the brunt of the damage, especially in 2004, when our state suffered a historic four hurricanes in just six weeks. The record-breaking 2005 hurricane season roughed up South Florida as well. While traveling during hurricane season (June through October), be aware of hurricane evacuation routes from coastal areas and keep daily tabs on the weather forecasts. If a landfall is predicted, do not wait until the last minute to evacuate the area: Be proactive and get out fast. Better safe than sorry, even if it means a radical change to your vacation plans.

INFORMATION Numerous kiosks and roadside billboards will taunt you to come in for vacation deals. Most are tied to time-shares or are operating in their own interest. True visitors centers will offer information without trying to sell you something. At the beginning of each section under *Guidance* we have listed the visitors bureaus and chambers with no commercial affiliation.

INSECTS Florida's irritating insects are myriad, especially at dawn and dusk during the summer months. We love our winters when they get chilly enough to kill the little buggers off. If

IGUANAS

Currently there are hundreds of thousands of feral iguanas from the Florida Keys upward to Palm Beach County, with a sizable population in Broward and Miami-Dade Counties. An invasive species not native to Florida, they are often spotted on the side of the highway or on boat docks, basking in the sun. You'll even see cautionary road signs in Key Biscayne. Three members of the Iguanidae family, the green iguana, the Mexican spiny-tailed, and the black spiny-tailed, are causing quite a ruckus with the locals as they breed like rabbits and munch vegetation faster than a locust. If you had told me in 1999 that I would have a green iguana for a pet, I would have said you were off your rocker. But when neighbors threw one out their front door, my son couldn't resist rescuing the then-tiny creature so unprepared for the wild. (The illegal release of exotic species in Florida is punishable by a $1,000 fine and up to one year in jail.) Arguably the most spoiled iguana in South Florida, my beloved Shakespeare is now over 5 feet long and spends his days languishing in his own tropical paradise on my side patio. But for those who consider capturing one, take heed. A whip from a tail or a bite will certainly require medical attention. Iguanas, like all reptiles, carry salmonella and require special handling. Hand feeding my Godzilla-like lizard fruits, vegetables, and hibiscus blossoms (cotton candy to an iguana) has kept him healthy, happy, and very tame. Should you decide to adopt one, be prepared to provide a large enclosure and dedicate 10 or more years to caring for it.

you don't like DEET and you can't stand citronella, you'll spend 99 percent of your time indoors. Flying annoyances include the mosquito (which comes in hundreds of varieties), gnat, and no-see-um; troublesome crawling bugs are the chigger (also known as redbug), a microscopic critter that attaches itself to your ankles to feed; the tick, which you'll find in deeply wooded areas; and red ants, invaders that swarm over your feet and leave painful bites if you dare step in their nest. Bottom line—use insect repellent, and carry an antihistamine with you to counter any reactions you have to communing with these native residents.

JELLYFISH At almost any time of the year you will find jellyfish in the ocean and washed up on the shore. Take particular care with the blue Man O' War jellyfish; the sting from this marine creature is excruciatingly painful. Do not touch the dead ones on the beach, as their venom is still potent. Contrary to popular belief, they won't chase you down; but in case you get stung, consider carrying a small bottle of white vinegar in your beach bag, as this seems to help alleviate some of the pain. Then seek

Sandra Friend

medical attention, as reactions vary, just like with bee stings.

LOBSTERING August 6 through March 31 marks the annual Florida lobster season, when you're welcome to scuba or snorkel for your own dinner. Limits are six per day or 24 per boat, and specific areas, such as the waters of John Pennekamp Coral Reef State Park and Everglades National Park, are excluded. For the full list of rules and regulations, contact the Florida Marine Patrol (1-800-342-5367 or 1-800-ASK-FISH) or the National Marine Fisheries Service (813-570-5305 or 305-743-2437).

MANGROVES The mangroves that grow along South Florida's barrier islands and coastline provide a natural anchor for the buildup of sand and sediment to expand the land. During a storm they serve as a buffer between the raging water and the coastal habitats. Three types of mangroves grow in Florida: black, white, and red. **Red mangroves** have a distinct network of prop roots, roots that look like arches holding up the tree, and tend to be the "island builders." **Black mangroves** are broader and are surrounded by a network of short breathing roots protruding from the soil under the plant that look like miniature cypress knees. **White mangroves** look the most treelike, with oval light green leaves (the other mangroves have dark green, elliptical leaves).

MARITIME HERITAGE In a state where many still pull their living from the sea, it's appropriate that we have a **Florida Maritime Heritage Trail** (http://dhr.dos.state.fl.us/maritime/index.html) that ties together the ele-

Greater Fort Lauderdale CVB

ments of our maritime heritage. Visit the web site for a virtual travel guide to Florida's maritime heritage.

MOTELS, HOTELS, AND RESORTS
We've included resorts with motels and hotels for this guide since many properties in South Florida refer to themselves as resorts but do not offer everything you need to stay put on the property, such as an on-site restaurant, shopping, and tours. In general, chain motels and hotels are not listed in this guide because of their ubiquitous nature; however, we've included a handful that are either the only lodging options in a particular area or happen to be outstanding places to stay. Rest assured

Sandra Friend

that we have either set foot on each property or talked directly to an unbiased source to recommend the lodgings listed in this book.

MUSEUMS You can explore our centuries of history through the **Florida Association of Museums** (850-222-6028; www.flamuseums .org), which provides a portal to more than 340 museums throughout the state, from Heritage Village in Largo to Fort Zachary Taylor in Key West. Its web site also provides a calendar of exhibits in museums around the state.

NATIONAL WIDLIFE REFUGES
Founded by President Theodore Roosevelt on March 21, 1903, with the dedication of **Pelican Island National Wildlife Refuge** in Florida's Indian River Lagoon, the National Wildlife Refuge system protects lands used by migratory birds and vanishing species. With nine refuges in South Florida, the U.S. Fish and Wildlife Commission manages a significant chunk of the South Florida landscape. Some National Wildlife Refuges (such as **Crocodile Lakes National Wildlife Refuge** in the Florida Keys) are entirely closed to public access. Others, like **Ding Darling, Loxahatchee,** and the **National Key Deer Refuge,** provide public access on a limited basis. When visiting a National Wildlife Refuge, keep in mind that all animals *and* plants are protected—visitors have been arrested and fined for removing tree snails, orchids, and bromeliads from preserves in South Florida.

ORCHIDS South Florida is an orchidlovers' paradise. In addition to viewing them in the wild on many public lands, you can purchase your own to take home from growers ranging down the Atlantic Coast from **Boynton Beach** to **Coral Gables** and **Redland** into the Keys. There is a particularly high concentration of orchid growers along **Krome Avenue** in **South Dade County.** The international headquarters of the **American Orchid Society** (www.orchidweb .com) is in **Delray Beach.**

Visit Florida

PADDLING Canoeing and kayaking are extraordinarily popular activities in Florida, especially during the summer months, with sea kayaking a favorite along the barrier islands and the Keys. Most state parks have canoe livery concessions, and private outfitters are mentioned throughout the text.

PARKS, STATE **Florida State Parks** (850-245-2157; www.floridastate parks.org) is one of the United States's best and most extensive state park systems, with more than 150 parks. New ones open all the time! All Florida State Parks are open from 8 AM to sunset daily. If you want to watch the sunrise from a state park beach, you'll have to camp overnight. Camping reservations are centralized through **Reserve America** (1-800-326-3521),

8–8 EST, and can be booked through the Florida State Parks web site. Walk-in visitors are welcome on a first-come, first-served basis. An annual pass is a real deal if you plan to do much traveling in the state: Individual passes are $40 plus tax, and family passes are $80 plus tax, per year. The family pass is good for up to a maximum of eight people in one vehicle. Vacation passes are also available in seven-day increments for $20 plus tax, covering up to eight people in your vehicle. These passes are honored in all South Florida state parks except the Sunshine Skyway Fishing Pier, where they are good for a 33 percent discount. Pick up a pass at any state park ranger station, or order through the web site.

PARROTS A favorite pet of the early 1990s, Quaker parrots were thrown into the eco-mix after Hurricane Andrew in 1992. The loud, lime green birds put on an impressive and often humorous display, and are frequently seen in flocks of a dozen or more throughout Southeast Florida and in the Tampa Bay area. Former pet macaws have also been spotted, now breeding fifth and sixth generations of wild birds.

Kathy Wolf

PETS The dog-paw symbol 🐾 identifies lodgings and activities that accept pets. Always inform the front desk that you are traveling with a pet, and expect to pay a surcharge.

POPULATION According to the 2000 federal census, Florida's population is closing in on 16 million people. What's scary to those of us who live here is that there is a net gain of eight hundred people moving into Florida *every day*—which means an increasingly serious strain on our already fragile water resources. Ironically, more than half of that population lives south of Polk County, in the area covered by this book—despite the fact nearly 3 million acres of South Florida are unpopulated, protected wetlands in the Big Cypress Swamp and the Everglades.

PYTHONS Pet snakes are notorious for escaping their cages, so it's no wonder that Burmese pythons have

Sandra Friend

been seen in and around Everglades National Park—more than 60 were removed in 2004. Feeding off rats, squirrels, and birds, the giant pythons, some as large as 15 feet, have even been seen battling alligators. Although biologists feel the once-threatened American alligator stands a pretty good chance of keeping the invasive python population under control, there is enough evidence to support that the actively breeding pythons are enjoying their new habitat.

RAILROADIANA Florida's railroad history dates back to 1836 with the St. Joe & Lake Wimico Canal & Railroad Company, followed shortly thereafter in 1837 with the opening of the mule-driven Tallahassee & St. Marks Railroad, bringing supplies from the Gulf of Mexico to the state capital. Railroad commerce shaped many South Florida towns, with Henry Plant's **Plant System** (later the Seaboard Air Line) on the west coast and Henry Flagler's **Florida East Coast** line on the Atlantic coast changing the course of history for South Florida and especially the Florida Keys. This category notes sites of interest to railroad-history buffs.

RATES The range of rates provided spans the lowest of low season to the highest of high season (which varies from place to place) and does not include taxes or discounts such as AARP, AAA, and camping club discounts.

RESERVATIONS The Seminole and Miccosukee tribes have reservations scattered throughout South Florida as sovereign lands granted to them by the U.S. government. The Seminoles hold

Kathy Wolf

The Florida
Department of Transportation has
designated nine scenic highways
throughout the state. In South Florida, enjoy a drive on the **Gulf Coast
Heritage Trail,** which leads you
from Bradenton south along the barrier islands to Venice; the most scenic
segment (in my opinion) is the lushly
canopied narrow road on Manasota
Key. The **Big Water Heritage Trail**
leads you on a loop around Lake
Okeechobee to explore historic and
scenic sites. But nothing else in the
Southeast compares to driving the
Overseas Highway, as US 1 jumps
from island to island through the
Keys, with expanses of ocean stretching off to both horizons. The **Tamiami Trail** through Big Cypress
National Preserve leads you through
the heart of South Florida's watery
southern wilderness, where you'll see
flocks of rare white pelicans on the
salt flats and hundreds of wood storks
roosting in the cypresses.

more than 90,000 acres in South Florida and in recent times have served as
hosts with grand casinos and hotels.
For an understanding of tribal culture,
visit the **Big Cypress Seminole
Reservation** to walk through the **Ah-
Tah-Thi-Ki Museum,** the world's
largest museum devoted to Seminole
culture and heritage.

RIVERS Unfortunately, most of South
Florida's rivers vanished in the early
1900s as part of the "Everglades Reclamation" spearheaded by Governor
Napoleon Bonaparte Broward and
later carried forward by the Army
Corps of Engineers under the banner
of flood control and water management. Instead, you'll see hundreds of
canals. But there are still a few rivers
that run free, and as you can imagine,
they are extraordinarily popular for
kayaking, among them the wild and
scenic **Loxahatchee River** in Palm
Beach County, the **St. Lucie River**
in St. Lucie County, and the **Peace,
Little Manatee, Myakka, Hillsborough,** and **Estero rivers** on the
Gulf Coast. The **Kissimmee River** is
undergoing a restoration effort to undo
the damage done, but **Fisheating
Creek** is the only wild waterway that
still flows into Lake Okeechobee.

Sandra Friend

Visit Florida

SEASONS South Florida's temperate winter weather makes it ideal for vacationers, but we do have a very strong tropical delineation of wet and dry seasons. Daily afternoon thundershowers are an absolute from June through September. Winter is generally dry and crisp, with nighttime temperatures falling as low as the 40s, with rare dips into the 20s.

SEMINOLE WARS Two years into the **Second Seminole War,** Col. Zachary Taylor led U.S. Army troops south from Fort Basinger on the Kissimmee River toward the coast, running into a large Seminole ambush along the shores of Lake Okeechobee on Christmas Day, 1837, led by medicine man Abiaka, known as "Sam Jones." The **Battle of Okeechobee** raged nearly three hours, felling more than a hundred men with injuries and leaving 26 dead. Although the Seminoles were outnumbered two to one, the heavy army casualties prevented them from following the Seminoles's retreat into the Everglades.

Several months after a trading post opened on the northern boundary of Seminole Territory near the Peace River in 1849, five Seminoles attacked the trading post and killed officers

stationed there, precipitating unrest between the settlers and the Seminoles. The U.S. Army moved back in and continued to build new forts along the reservation boundary. On December 20, 1855, Billy Bowlegs (Holata Micco) led a band of Seminoles who attacked and killed federal soldiers surveying within the Seminole lands. Seminole raiding parties then attacked the Braden plantation and others near the Manatee River, and the U.S. Army sent soldiers into the Everglades to attack Seminole settlements. The **Third Seminole War** was under way. By 1858 Billy Bowlegs agreed to leave Florida with his family and be relocated to reservation lands in the west—the ultimate goal of the Seminole Wars, so the Federal Government could open up all of Florida to settlement. After the U.S. Army departed South Florida, Abiaka was the only remaining Seminole leader in the state, and fewer than three hundred Seminoles remained in Florida, all deeply hidden in the Everglades. The Seminoles never signed a peace treaty to end this war. It was not until 1957 that the U.S. Congress recognized the Seminole tribe and permitted them to apply for reservation lands in Florida. (For the Seminole tribe's description of the wars and their aftermath, please visit www.seminoletribe.com/history/index.shtml.)

SHARKS Yes, they are in the water. At any given time there are a dozen or more just offshore, but for the most part they will leave you alone. To avoid being bitten, stay out of the water if there is a strong scent of fish oil in the air, which means that fish are already being eaten and you may be bitten by mistake. You will also want to avoid swimming near piers and jetties, which are active feeding zones.

SHRIMP South Florida is a shrimp-lovers' dream, with fresh shrimp in virtually every seafood restaurant, especially on the Gulf Coast. Look for shrimp fried, broiled, sautéed, and blackened in creative recipes by Florida chefs.

STINGRAYS On the Gulf of Mexico, wading in the sea calls for the "stingray shuffle." Set each foot down on the ocean floor with a resounding *stomp* on each step, which alerts the stingrays to stay clear. As you'll discover by visiting aquarium touch tanks in South Florida, stingrays are relatively docile and don't mind being touched—but they do react to being stepped on.

THE SUNSHINE STATE The moniker **Sunshine State** was an effective 1960s advertising slogan that was required on motor vehicle tags; it became the state's official nickname in 1970 by a legislative act.

TAXES Florida's base **sales tax** is 6 percent, with counties adding up to another 1.5 percent of discretionary sales tax. In addition, a **tourist development tax** of up to 10 percent may be levied on hotel accommodations in some cities and counties, including Miami-Dade and Hillsborough.

THEME PARKS South Florida doesn't cater to the same crowd that heads to the theme parks to the north. Down here, attractions tend more toward the classics—look to **Sunken Gardens** in St. Petersburg or **Monkey Jungle** in Homestead as exam-

Sandra Friend

ples, since the parks of South Florida focus on wildlife and flora. **Busch Gardens** in Tampa is the only mega–theme park of note in the region.

TOADS The Bufo Marinus toad (or cane toad), growing as large as 9 inches in length and more than 2 pounds in weight, is usually spotted at night catching bugs under lights. In the 1960s it was originally released in sugarcane fields to control rats and mice, and now it can be seen in almost every residential neighborhood. When attacked or threatened, the nuisance species secretes a milky toxin from the back of its head. Con-

Kathy Wolf

Sandra Friend

tact with the poison will cause a nasty rash and is lethal enough to kill even large dogs within a few hours, so make sure to keep kids and Fluffy away from these critters.

TRAIL RIDING Bringing your own horses? Under state law, riders utilizing trails on state land must have proof with them of a negative Coggins test for their horses. If you're interested in riding, hook up with one of the many stables listed in the text. Under state law, equine operators are not responsible for your injuries if you decide to go on a trail ride.

VISIT FLORIDA **Visit Florida** (www .visitflorida.com), the state's official tourism bureau, is a clearinghouse for every tourism question you might have. Their partners cover the full range of destinations, from quaint small towns like Okeechobee to the snazzy new hotels on Miami Beach. Utilize their web site resources to preplan your trip, from the interactive map that lets you explore destination possibilities in regions to Sunny, the online vacation planner that assists you in compiling your itinerary.

WEATHER Florida's weather is perhaps our greatest attraction. Balmy winters are the norm, with daytime temperatures in the 80s and evenings in the 60s common for South Florida. And don't even think about snow—it's the rare freeze that reaches south of Lake Okeechobee (although we've seen it happen!). Summers are hot and wet, with temperatures soaring up to the 90s. In the Florida Keys the trade winds help keep summer temperate, but you won't avoid the rains. Florida thunderstorms come up fast and carry with them some of the world's most violent and dangerous lightning. It's best to get inside and out of or off the water should you see one coming. Contrary to popular belief, you are not safe in an automobile due to the rubber tires. One woman barely missed being struck in 2006 when a bolt entered her car and blew out the rear window. And watch for approaching storms. Even if the sky looks clear, a lightning bolt may still strike if thunder is rumbling nearby. My son was walking home from school one particularly clear day when lightning struck a tree within a few feet of him, singeing his arm and throwing him 20 feet across the road.

WHERE TO EAT We've limited our choices to local favorites and outstanding creative fare, avoiding the chains seen everywhere across America. Several Florida-based chains deserve a mention, however; you'll enjoy their cuisine when you find them. **Flanigans,** known for its excellent burgers and diverse menu, started in Pompano Beach in 1985, and now there are nearly 20 locations along the Atlantic Coast. **Hooters** got its start in Clearwater, and **Fred Fleming's Barbecue** hails from

Hawks Kay Resort

St. Petersburg, as does **Outback Steakhouse. Shells** is a family seafood restaurant serving ample portions for reasonable prices; **R.J. Gators** appeals to the sports-bar crowd with great Florida seafood on tap. **Buddy Freddy's,** based in Plant City, serves up the fine, farm-fresh, country-style food for which that town is famous, and **Leverocks** is a popular fine-dining seafood chain found all along the Gulf Coast. **TooJay's,** a New York–style deli, shines with big breakfasts, stellar sandwiches, and its yummy Mounds Cake. You'll also find the Stuart-based **Ice Cream Churn,** with 28 flavors of homemade ice cream, tucked away inside convenience stores throughout the state.

WINERIES Florida's wineries run the gamut from small family operations to large production facilities, and some partner together to provide a storefront in a high-traffic region while the growing, fermenting, and bottling is done in an area more favorable for agriculture. Native muscadine grapes are the cornerstones of the state's wines. For an overview of Florida wineries, contact the **Florida Grape Growers Association** (941-678-0523; www.fgga.org), 343 W Central Ave, #1, Lake Wales 33853.

Tampa Bay

TAMPA AND HILLSBOROUGH
COUNTY

ST. PETERSBURG

FLORIDA'S BEACH: PINELLAS
COUNTY

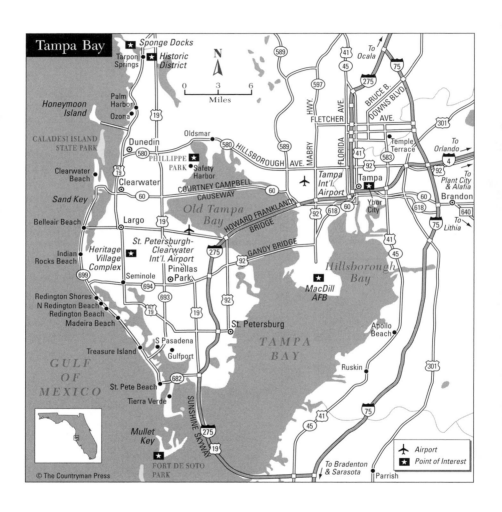

Tampa Bay

Sponge Docks
Tarpon Springs
Historic District

N

0 3 6
Miles

589
To Ocala
41
45
75
275
597
BRUCE B. DOWNS BLVD
301

Honeymoon Island

Palm Harbor
Ozona

HWY.
MABRY
FLORIDA AVE.
FLETCHER AVE.

Temple Terrace

To Orlando

CALADESI ISLAND STATE PARK

19

Oldsmar

580
HILLSBOROUGH AVE.
589

Dunedin

580

PHILLIPPE PARK
Safety Harbor

41
92
583
4

To Plant City & Alafia

Clearwater Beach

ALT 19

Clearwater

60

COURTNEY CAMPBELL CAUSEWAY

60

Tampa Int'l. Airport

Tampa
Ybor City

60

Brandon

Sand Key

Old Tampa Bay

HOWARD FRANKLAND BRIDGE

92
618
60

618

640

Belleair Beach

Largo

19

To Lithia

Indian Rocks Beach

Heritage Village Complex

St. Petersburgh-Clearwater Int'l. Airport

Seminole

699

694

693

275

GANDY BRIDGE

92

Hillsborough Bay

41

45

Pinellas Park

Redington Shores
N Redington Beach
Redington Beach
Madeira Beach

19

92

MacDill AFB

Apollo Beach

Treasure Island

S Pasadena
Gulfport

St. Petersburg

TAMPA BAY

Ruskin

301

GULF OF MEXICO

682

St. Pete Beach
Tierra Verde

SUNSHINE SKYWAY

275

41

45

75

Mullet Key

19

To Bradenton & Sarasota

FORT DE SOTO PARK

Parrish

© The Countryman Press

✈ Airport
★ Point of Interest

TAMPA BAY

From land, air, or sea, there is no missing Tampa Bay. It is one of Florida's most distinctive geologic features, the largest open-water estuary in the state, a shallow basin 12 feet deep on average, yet covering 400 square miles. Its barrier islands showcase a 35-mile ribbon of white-sand beaches on the Gulf of Mexico. Ancient tribes settled on its shores, building ceremonial and village mounds in protected coves from which they could launch their longboats to ply the bounteous waters for fish. Europeans first reached its waters in the early 1500s—Panfilo de Narvaez, Hernando de Soto, and others, Spanish conquistadors intent on discovering gold. As the Dutch and English followed, they explored and mapped the channels and rivers flowing into the bay. After the American Revolution, the United States purchased Florida from Spain in 1821, and European settlers began to trickle into the region, founding a settlement around Fort Brooke.

In the 1850s Tampa served as the end of the line for cattle drovers in North and Central Florida, who brought their herds to the docks for Capt. James McKay to supervise shipping to Cuba in exchange for gold. As a result, Tampa Bay was a major target for the Union Blockading Squadron during the war, as many successful Confederate blockade runners hid their ships in the countless channels and estuaries, seeking the opportunity to break for open water and escape to Cuba for free trade. Bringing goods back to the region, they helped support Florida's war effort. Union gunboats shelled downtown Tampa on several occasions, damaging the hotel and surrounding shopping district. The region's growth accelerated in 1884 when industrialist Henry Plant extended his railroad to Tampa Bay, determining it would make a perfect port for his export operations. Jules Verne foresaw Florida's future in space travel when he set *From the Earth to the Moon* along the shores of Tampa Bay.

As in most parts of Florida, World War II air and naval bases accelerated the region's population growth when servicemen decided to settle their families near the bases after their tour of duty was complete. The advent of television showcased vibrant downtown St. Petersburg and the sparkling sands of Clearwater and Treasure Island, enticing visitors to the region. Best known for its beach destinations, the Tampa Bay area has much to offer the traveler eager to explore.

TAMPA AND HILLSBOROUGH COUNTY

Covering more than 1,000 square miles of Florida's west coast, Hillsborough County forms an arc around the northern and eastern sides of Tampa Bay. Dutch cartographer Bernard Romans named this region and its major river in 1772 in honor of Lord Willis Hills, secretary of state for the British colonies. Soon after Florida became a U.S. territory, the federal government established Fort Brooke as a frontier outpost, and the surrounding settlement became the town of **Tampa** in 1855.

After Henry Plant brought his railroad to the region, he invested heavily in Tampa. He started a steamship line from Tampa to Key West and Havana and opened a grand $3-million-dollar, 511-room Moorish-themed hotel downtown in 1891. This grand structure is topped with distinctive minarets and is now a museum honoring Plant's legacy and a National Historic Landmark. Plant continued his rail line east through the county, where **Plant City** was founded. Now known as the Strawberry Capital of the World, this bustling city is worth a visit for its excellent fresh produce, fine family restaurants, and distinctive historic downtown shopping district.

In 1885 Don Vincente Martinez Ybor, an exiled Spanish cigar manufacturer from Cuba, moved his business from Key West to a hammock east of Tampa; soon, many factories and workers followed. The surrounding settlement became **Ybor City** (pronounced EE-bore), a community of Spanish, German, Italian, and Cuban families with nearly twelve thousand people working in more than two hundred factories. Ybor City remained the Cigar Capital of the World until Cuban tobacco was embargoed when Fidel Castro came to power.

Tampa's first developer, O. H. Platt, created **Hyde Park** in 1886. It's a neighborhood of bungalows and Princess Anne–style architecture that retains its old-time charm today within **South Tampa.** Since then, it seems that the land boom around the bay never stopped. Where the Hillsborough River flows into Tampa Bay, in 1924 David P. Davis "rebuilt" two natural islands at the mouth of the river to create the **Davis Islands.** A similar fill project connects **Rocky Point** to Clearwater via the Courtney Campbell Causeway. With the coming of two major airfields, MacDill Air Force Base and Drew Airfield, during World War II came

a huge influx of residents that expanded the population density, creating **Brandon** to the east and **Town & Country** and **Temple Terrace** surrounding
North Tampa. Standing alone against encroaching residential sprawl is **Lutz,**
a community to the northwest established by German immigrants.

Farming is still an important part of life on the eastern side of the county,
which has thus far escaped rapid development. There are the rural communities
of **Thonotosassa** along the Hillsborough River on US 301, **Alafia** and **Lithia**
along the Alafia River on FL 39 south of Plant City, and **Mango** and **Ruskin,**
known worldwide for its tomatoes, on US 301 south. Also in the southeastern
section of the county are the residential communities of **Riverview** and **Sun
City Center** along US 301. South on US 41, **Apollo Beach** provides waterfront
access for visitors, and **Gibsonton** has a storied history as a "carny village" where
many off-season circus performers have lived.

GUIDANCE In downtown Tampa you'll find all of your questions answered at the
large **Tampa Bay Visitor Information Center** (813-223-2752 or 1-800-44-
TAMPA; www.VisitTampaBay.com), 615 Channelside Dr, Suite 108A. In Ybor
City stop by the **Ybor City Visitor Information Center** (813-248-3712 or
1-877-9-FIESTA), 1600 E Eighth Ave, Suite B104; and in Plant City pick up
information (including a walking tour brochure) at the **Greater Plant City
Chamber of Commerce** (813-754-3707 or 1-800-760-2315; www.plantcity.org),
1702 N Park Rd.

GETTING THERE *By car:* Most major regional highways intersect in Tampa. **I-4**
provides an eastern connection from Orlando, while **I-75** links the region to
North Florida and the remainder of the Gulf Coast. **I-275** leads drivers down
into the heart of the city and over to St. Petersburg. The **Veterans Expressway,**
heading north from Tampa International Airport, becomes the **Suncoast Parkway,** which ties into Pasco, Hernando, and Citrus Counties to the north.

By air: **Tampa International Airport** (813-870-8700 or 1-800-767-8882; www
.TampaAirport.com) offers continual flights to national and international destinations, with major carriers such as AirTran, America, Delta, Frontier, Song, Spirit,
United, US Airways, British Airways, AirCanada, and more. Located at the intersection of FL 60 and the Veterans Expressway, the airport borders Tampa Bay
just west of downtown.

By rail: **AMTRAK** (813-221-7600) has a passenger station in the historic Union
Station in downtown Tampa.

By bus: **Greyhound** (813-229-2174 or 1-800-231-2222) stops in downtown
Tampa at 610 Polk St.

GETTING AROUND *By car:* Finding your way around downtown Tampa can be a
bit confusing. Thankfully, there are many directional signs to guide you toward
Channelside and Ybor City.

US 41 and **US 92** (Dale Mabry) slice right through the city's neighborhoods,
while **US 301** keeps to the city's rural eastern fringe, paralleling both **I-75** and

Central Tampa

US 41, which stays close to the bay as it heads south through Gibsonton, Apollo Beach, and Ruskin. FL 60 provides access between Brandon through South Tampa and the Airport/Westside Area, becoming the Courtney Campbell Causeway to Clearwater, and CR 39 ties together the rural communities of Plant City and Alafia on the county's eastern border.

By bus: **HARTline** (Hillsborough Area Regional Transit Authority, 813-975-2160; www.hartline.org) runs 207 buses on 26 city routes. The rubber-tired "In Town Trolley" runs north–south through downtown (50 cents) and connects to the electric streetcar system.

By streetcar: Great for a downtown tour, the **TECO Line Streetcar System** (813-254-4278; www.tecolinestreetcar.org) offers 11 stops that link downtown to the Port of Tampa at Channelside and Ybor City. Fares are cash only ($2 per trip), but you can buy a day pass ($4) or multiday pass; seniors and kids are half-price. It's a fun trip, too! See *Streetcar Rides.*

By taxi: **United Cab of Tampa** (813-251-5555) and **Yellow Cab Company of Tampa** (813-253-3590). Taxis must be called in advance from your location. The average cost of a taxi fare from the airport to downtown is $17. Most of the major hotels offer shuttles to the airport and attractions.

PARKING There is metered street parking throughout **downtown Tampa,** but finding a space can be downright difficult except on Sunday. Try one of the many parking garages, including those on Ashley St and at Channelside. In **Ybor City** you'll find parking garages, flat lots, and metered street parking on most of the in-town streets; fee.

MEDICAL EMERGENCIES For emergency care visit **Tampa General Hospital** (813-844-7000), One Davis Blvd, downtown; they have a trauma unit.

✳ To See

AQUARIUMS ♿ ✐ **The Florida Aquarium** (813-273-4000 or 1-800-FL-FISH1; www.flaquarium.org), 701 Channelside Dr. For more than a decade, this downtown landmark has entertained and educated families as it tells the story of Florida's unique water cycle, involving aquifers and springs, freshwater and saltwater. The multistory complex starts with an eerie entrance through a cave, where fish swim far above your head. You walk past alligators, turtles, and other freshwater creatures from our rivers and streams, reaching the mangrove estuary where native birds flit above salt water teeming with fish. Climb up to the lookout to learn about exotic plants and animals in Florida, and then follow the path into the heart of the building for a nose-to-nose encounter with stingrays, massive grouper, and spiny lobsters. Descend into a coral reef grotto, with picture windows making you feel like you're under the sea. Special exhibits house unusual sea creatures such as sea dragons and cuttlefish. Walk through a tunnel of sea turtles and sharks before you reach the lobby, where a massive touch tank lets you feel invertebrate sea life, and the outdoors "Explore A Shore" provides a wet playground for kids to let off steam. A large gift shop and restaurant round out the experience. Open 9:30–5 daily; closed Thanksgiving and Christmas. Adults $17.95, seniors 60+ $14.95, children 3–12 $12.95, under 3 free.

AMBER FRIEND GETS TO KNOW A STINGRAY UP CLOSE.

Sandra Friend

ARCHEOLOGICAL SITES Fort Brooke was the end of the line on the Fort King Military Trail from Ocala to Tampa Bay, and a crucial outpost during the Seminole Wars of the early 1800s at the confluence of the Hillsborough River with the bay. Unfortunately, it and other archeological sites in downtown Tampa vanished under centuries of building. Walk up Franklin St and through the plazas to see many blue signs that explain what was once there and is now buried beneath concrete and steel.

ART GALLERIES

Ruskin
A mural of blue ibises by Craig Todd will entice you to stop at the **Blue Ibis Art Gallery** (813-645-2906), 205 S US 41, featuring signed and numbered limited editions of wildlife art.

Tampa—Airport/Westside
At the **Tampa International Airport** (see *Getting There*), visitors enjoy a diverse mix of tapestries, sculptures, and paintings throughout the high-traffic areas. Airside E is the home of seven original historic Works Progress Administration murals painted by George Snow Hill in 1939, depicting mythical and historic figures that contributed to the history of human-powered flight, from Icarus and Daedalus to Tony Jannus, the pilot who made the world's first commercial flight between St. Petersburg and Tampa in 1914.

Tampa—Downtown and Vicinity
Artists Unlimited (813-229-5958; www.artistsunlimited.org), 223 N 12th St, encompasses working studios and gallery space, as well as a sculpture garden. Open Mon–Fri 9–6, Sat by appointment.

Tampa—Ybor City
In the artists' village (see *Selective Shopping*), watch Arnold Martinez perfect his craft at the **Arnold Martinez Art Gallery** (813-248-9572), 1909 N 19th St. He paints striking scenes of Tampa and Tampa history using media unique to Ybor City culture—Cuban coffee and tobacco juice.

The **Brad Cooper Gallery** (813-248-6098), 1712 E Seventh Ave, offers fine art and custom framing. Look for whimsical creations at **Creatures of Delight** (813-248-4167; www.creaturesofdelight.com), 1901 N 15th St. **Dean James Glassworks** (813-248-3132; www.deanjamesglass.com), 1315 E Fifth Ave, features blown-glass art.

ATTRACTIONS & ✇ **Busch Gardens Tampa Bay** (813-987-5805 or 1-888-800-5447; www.buschgardens.com), 3605 E Bougainvillea Ave, Temple Terrace, is the region's only theme park and one I remember fondly from my youth when it was just a bird garden and a brewery tour. The brewery is long gone, but the expansions and renovations over the decades have transformed this 335-acre park into one of Florida's most fun family theme park destinations, mingling a zoological experience with thrill rides and elaborate stage productions. I loved it years ago when they added the Stanley Falls log flume and Congo River Rapids rides, and now the park is really hopping with three of the world's top-rated roller coasters—Kumba, Montu, and Gwazi (a mammoth wooden coaster), as well as a brand-new one as of 2005: SheiKra, the first dive coaster in the United

BABY BONGO TWINS AT BUSCH GARDENS

States, twisting and turning on its half-mile track like an African hawk at speeds up to 70 miles per hour. If rides aren't for you, never fear—the Serengeti Plain, the core of this park, has always made it an attraction to those who love to view wildlife. Seen from walkways, the Serengeti Express train ride, or the Skyride, this 65-acre habitat features hundreds of free-roaming African animals in open landscapes. The Myombe Preserve re-creates a rain forest habitat for a tribe of great apes. The Bird Gardens are still here, too, with more than five hundred tropical birds in aviaries and enclosures. And yes, you can still pose with the famous Budweiser Clydesdale team. The little ones will love Land of the Dragons, a wet and dry playground with fanciful rides and a three-story treehouse; the Egypt area has a replica of King Tut's tomb and an archeological dig for kids. Combine this all with spectacular shows such as "KaTonga: Musical Tales From the Jungle," a Broadway-quality spectacle with massive puppets, vibrant music, and African storytelling, and you'll see why a single day just isn't enough to take it all in. Adults $57.95, ages 3–9 $47.95, with multiday offers sometimes available. Parking fees of $8–12, depending on vehicle size.

✐ Every time I pass **Dinosaur World** (813-717-9865; www.dinoworld.net), 5145 Harvey Tew Rd, Plant City, on my drive down I-4, I think about the Sinclair Dinoland exhibit I visited at the 1964 World's Fair. Today there's no larger exhibit of model dinosaurs in the world than you'll find here, towering over the pathways of a 12-acre forest. The irony, of course, is that dinosaurs never roamed Florida—it was under water at the time. After visiting the museum for some background on the Age of Dinosaurs, wander around and marvel at these massive, scientifically accurate models. Open 9–6 daily. Adults $9.75, seniors $8.95, children 3–12 $7.75.

BASEBALL Each March, the **New York Yankees** (813-879-2244 or 1-800-96-YANKS; www.legendsfield tampa.com), One Steinbrenner Dr, take over Legends Field for spring training, followed by their farm team affiliate, the **Tampa Yankees,** Apr–Aug.

HISTORIC SITES Downtown **Ybor City** is a piece of Florida frozen in time from more than a century ago, with beautiful Spanish architecture. At Bird Ave and Florida Ave, River

CENTRO YBOR, THE HAPPENING PLACE FOR SHOPPING AND DINING

Tower Park (not currently open to the public) contains one of the region's oldest landmarks, the **Sulphur Spring Water Tower** along the Hillsborough River. Drive the streets of **Hyde Park** to enjoy homes ranging from Victorian gingerbread to 1920s bungalows, and do not miss the classic **Tampa Bay Hotel** (see *Museums*), the region's largest and most grandiose historic site, circa 1891.

MUSEUMS

Tampa—Downtown and Vicinity

✒ The SS *American Victory* is a floating slice of history, a World War II merchant marine ship under restoration as the **American Victory Mariners Memorial & Museum Ship** (813-228-8766; www.americanvictory.org), 705 Channelside Dr, adjoining the Florida Aquarium (see *Aquariums*). Restoration tours are available Mon–Sat 10–5, Sun noon–5. Adults $6, seniors $5, children 6–13 $3, under 6 free.

& ✒ At the **Tampa Bay History Center** (813-228-0097; www.tampabayhistory center.org), 225 S Franklin St, browse through rolling collection cases and drawers with interpreted artifacts from the many periods of the city's history, such as the keel pin from the *Scottish Chief,* Captain McKay's blockade runner during the War Between the States, and Cuesta Ray cigar boxes from Ybor City's past. In addition to a Cracker homestead with computer stations, there are numerous hands-on activities and workstations for kids. Open Tue–Sat 10–5. Free.

& Stroll the galleries at the **Tampa Museum of Art** (813-274-8130; www .tampamuseum.com), 600 N Ashley Dr, and enjoy a view of the Hillsborough River and the Tampa Bay Hotel from the sunny Riverside Gallery, where sculpture from the permanent collection is rotated on display. I particularly enjoyed the glass art, including Louis Sclafani's *Shards,* where the texture of the rough surfaces is like layers of hard candy. Several galleries near the entrance offer rotating exhibits, but the central permanent collection is The Classical World, featuring vases and amphorae from ancient Greece as well as Roman and Etruscan art. Open Tue–Sat 10–5, Sun 11–5. Adults $7; seniors, military, and students $6; children $3. Free on weekends, except during special events.

Tampa—North Tampa

& ✒ The largest science center in the Southeast, the **Museum of Science & Industry** (813-987-6000 or 1-800-995-MOSI; www.mosi.org), 4801 E Fowler Ave, has an impressive array of hands-on science exhibits. Want to know what hurricane season is like? Step into the Gulf Coast Hurricane Chamber for a dose of 74-mile-per-hour winds. Or dare yourself to pedal the high-wire bicycle 30 feet above the ground. If you love dinosaurs, the two Diplodocus skeletons that stand three stories tall won't disappoint you. In addition to numerous permanent and rotating exhibits, MOSI offers a unique IMAX dome movie theater for a separate admission. Open Mon–Fri 9–5, Sat–Sun 9–7. Adults $15, seniors $13, children 2–12 $11, under 2 free.

University of South Florida Contemporary Art Museum (813-974-4133; www.usfcam.usf.edu), 4202 E Fowler Ave, showcases scholarly exhibitions of

THE TAMPA BAY HOTEL

& A glimpse into the Gilded Age, the **Henry B. Plant Museum** (813-254-1891; www.plantmuseum.com), 401 W Kennedy Blvd, is the world's only railroad hotel museum, celebrating Plant's Tampa Bay Hotel that opened in 1891 as a destination point for travelers on his new Plant System railroad. While most of the building and grounds now house Tampa University, the museum's niche allows them to showcase what travelers experienced back in Florida's first tourism boom. It is the only historical railroad museum in the United States, with the distinctive mix of Moorish architecture and Victorian gingerbread that makes this a one-of-a-kind historic building. Built specifically to draw tourists to Florida, it had five hundred rooms and sprawled over 6 acres, with numerous outbuildings, such as a boathouse and casino, over the years. Plant furnished his hotel with 41 trainloads of French furnishings from Paris, and his wife sought out exotic tropical plants for the hotel's botanical garden along the river—still there for you to freely stroll through today. The hotel had Florida's very first elevator and an indoor pool when it opened on February 4, 1891. Serving nearly four thousand guests the first year, it put the tiny city of Tampa on the map. But Plant's magical destination never quite caught on, and as it continued to lose money, he used his political influence to draw the base of operations for the Spanish-American War on-site. In 1898 troops camped around the hotel, and luminaries such as Teddy Roosevelt, Clara Barton, and Frederic Remington strode the grounds. After Plant died, his heirs sold the building to the city of Tampa. The first Florida State Fair was held on the grounds in 1904.

Start your tour with a 14-minute video that lays the backdrop for this grand hotel, and then walk the halls to immerse yourself in European opulence and to peek into rooms with original furniture in place. Notice the attention to detail, even in the balustrades and period lighting with Edison electric filament bulbs. In the Reading Room, almost every piece is original to the hotel, from the ebony woodwork to the inkwells and ceramic tile fireplace. The Museum Store offers original art, history books, and reproductions of the hotel's plates and coasters. As one of only two remaining Plant System hotels (the other, the Belleview Biltmore, is still in operation in Belleair—see *Florida's Beach*), it is a grand reminder of an era long past and well worth a visit. Open Tue–Sat 10–4, Sun noon–4. Fee; free parking at the garage at North Blvd and North B St. You are also welcome to walk the ground-level halls of Tampa University to see more of the hotel's intriguing Moorish architecture; free.

contemporary art, hosts workshops and lectures, and organizes visiting artist presentations. Permanent holdings include an exquisite collection of African art as well as graphics and sculpture by acclaimed artists Roy Lichtenstein and James Rosenquist. Open Mon–Fri 10–5, Sat 1–4. Free admission; parking $2.50.

Tampa—Ybor City

& ✐ At the **Ybor City Museum State Park** (813-247-1434; www.ybormuseum .org), 1818 E Ninth Ave, learn about this tight-knit community of cigar workers and their families by immersing into the past. A preserved half block includes three restored *casitas,* the traditional shotgun-style homes of cigar workers, with more undergoing restoration. The main museum is in the historic Ferlita Bakery building and focuses on the colorful history of the area. Walking tours of the city (see *Walking Tours*) depart the museum on Sat at 10:30 AM. Fee.

RAILROADIANA Henry Bradley Plant opened a new frontier when he brought the **Plant System** railroad into Tampa in 1884, linking his freight and passenger lines with a steamboat to Havana. All of the region's railroad history is tied to Plant, from the stately **Atlantic Coast Line depots** in Dunedin and Tarpon Springs to the amazing **Tampa Bay Hotel** (see *Museums*), which Plant built as a tourist destination. As compensation for laying railroad track in Florida, the state gave Plant more than 750,000 acres of land, which was developed into cities such as **Plant City,** where the depot, **Union Station,** 102 N Palmer St, is on the National Register of Historic Places. In 1901 the Plant System encompassed 1,196 miles of main line valued at $7.4 million, versus East Coast railroad magnate Henry Flagler's 466 miles of main line worth $2.7 million.

ZOOLOGICAL PARKS & ANIMAL REHAB & ✐ At **Big Cat Rescue** (813-920-4130; www.bigcatrescue.org), 12802 Easy St, the focus is on the care of exotic felines. After visiting a fur farm where wild cats were bred for slaughter à la *1001 Dalmatians,* founder Carole Baskin bought them all and brought them home, then became a strong voice against the breeding of exotic cats for the pet, fur, and entertainment industry, bringing in photographers and stars such as Jack Hanna to promote the need for caring for these abandoned and abused creatures. Staffed by eager volunteers, this nonprofit organization now cares for more than two hundred cats, including tigers, lynx, bobcats, servals, snow leopards, and more, and must turn away more than three hundred more abused cats a year. They run entirely on donations and will awaken your sense of responsibility toward the Pandora's Box of the exotic pet trade. Tour cost varies as to length and interactive nature of the tour; call or see their web site for details.

& ✐ Visit the **Lowry Park Zoo** (813-935-8552; www.lowryparkzoo.com), 1101 Sligh Ave, and marvel at the many themed sections radiating out from the wildlife carousel—it will take quite a while to explore them all. In Australia kids can romp through the squirt ponds, ride ponies, or climb through the Woolshed; the entire family can walk through the Kangaroo Walkabout or past emus and fruit bats. Descend into Africa through a broad tunnel or take the Skyfari ride to see large open enclosures with warthogs and antelopes, and savannas where giraffes, zebras, and elephants roam. My family's favorite part of the zoo is Florida, a more traditional boardwalk through enclosures where you'll see our favorite neighbors—Florida panthers, roseate spoonbills, sandhill cranes, gopher tortoises, American bison, and more. You'll walk past one of only three manatee rehabilitation hospitals in Florida and into an aquarium where you can stand nose to snout with these massive mammals and stroke a stingray at Stingray Bay. Finally, the Asia exhibit transports you above enclosures where tigers lurk beneath a waterfall, lemurs and chimps chatter, and rhino ramble along rocky cliffs. Open 9:30–5 daily except Thanksgiving and Christmas. Adults $14.95, seniors $13.95, children 3–11 $10.50; special combination tickets for the River Odyssey Ecotour (see *Ecotours*) available.

❋ To Do

AGRICULTURAL TOURS Thousands of acres of strawberries, potatoes, tomatoes, corn, and other critical crops make Hillsborough County one of the leading agricultural producers in the state. For a firsthand look at local farms, join the **Hillsborough Farm Bureau** (813-685-9121) on their monthly first Thursday tours held Sep–Nov and Jan–May. Call for details, as the tour changes each time.

BALLOONING For a bird's-eye view of Tampa Bay, **18th Century Aviation** (813-969-3345; www.18thCenturyAviation.com), 11520 River Country Dr, Riverview, lifts off at dawn.

BEHIND-THE-SCENES TOURS Tampa offers several eclectic behind-the-scenes tours of real-life businesses. **The Port of Tampa Tour** (813-905-5131), departing from the Main Port office on Wynkoop Rd, showcases the inner workings of the largest port in the Southeast, with more than 1 million passengers departing on cruise ships each year. If theater is your love, try a backstage tour of the largest performing-arts center in the Southeast, the **Tampa Bay Performing Arts Center** (see *Entertainment*), or the **Tampa Theatre** (see *Entertainment*), one of the last remaining grand movie palaces in the United States. Sports fans can take a trip behind the scenes at **Raymond James Stadium** (813-350-6576), Dale Mabry Hwy, on Tues, Wed, and Thu each week; tour highlights include the locker room, the press box, and a walk on the field where the Tampa Bay Buccaneers play. Reservations required; call in advance for times.

BICYCLING Off-road biking is at its best along the river wilderness areas of Hillsborough County. Launch your trip along the Hillsborough River basin at **Wilderness Trail** (813-987-6200), 12550 Morris Bridge Rd, Thonotosassa, and follow 20 miles of winding singletrack through pine flatwoods and oak scrub. At **Alderman's Ford Park** (813-757-3801), CR 39, Lithia, a maze of shady paved and unpaved trails strings together developed picnic areas along the Alafia River.

BIRDING The islands and shoreline of Tampa Bay are an important stopping point for migratory birds headed to Central and South America in fall and spring. Viewable only by boat, piping plovers and flocks of red knots can be seen on **Shell Key** and **Three Rooker Island,** both important refuges in the south part of the bay. Flocks of white pelicans pass through in the fall and can be seen at **McKay Bay Nature Park** (813-274-8615), 134 N 34th St; and **Apollo Beach Nature Park,** Apollo Beach, is a popular bird-watching site at the mouth of the Alafia River on the eastern shore of Tampa Bay.

BOATING Live large with a charter yacht or sailboat from **Tampa Bay Yacht Charters** (813-263-9341; www.tbyc.biz), 909 Bahia Del Sol Dr, Ruskin, or talk to them about a sight-seeing tour along the rim of Tampa Bay. Fishing charters available, too.

CRUISES The **Port of Tampa** (813-905-PORT; www.tampaport.com) is departure central for dozens of popular cruises, which take you on a slow boat to paradise in Mexico, the Caribbean, and Key West. **Carnival Cruise Lines** (305-599-2600; www.carnival.com) offers six ships weekly with four-, five-, and seven-night Caribbean cruises, while **Celebrity Cruises** (1-800-437-3111; www.celebrity.com) sends out four ships weekly with 8- to 13-day cruises heading as far as Norfolk, Virginia. **Holland America Line** (206-281-3535; www.hollandamerica.com) offers the most choices, with 7–18 nights on 13 ships each week. **Royal Caribbean International** (1-800-327-6700; www.royalcaribbean.com) whisks you away to Grand Cayman and Belize on a weekly seven-day cruise, Nov–Apr. Terminal parking is $10/day, and most of the terminals are at Channelside. See the port's web site for specific directions to each terminal.

ECOTOURS ⌖ **DolphinQuest** (813-273-4000), offered by the Florida Aquarium (see *Aquariums*), takes passengers out on the *Bay Spirit,* a 64-foot catamaran ideal for spotting bottlenose dolphins and West Indian manatees in the shallow waters of Tampa Bay. Adults $19.95, seniors 60+ $14.95, children under 12 $12.95. Lowry Park Zoo offers **River Odyssey Ecotour** (see *Zoological Parks & Animal Rehab*), a one-hour narrated tour along the Hillsborough River, with a naturalist pointing out wildlife. The *Sirenia* makes five cruises a day, Wed–Sun. Adults $14, seniors $13, children $10.

FAMILY ACTIVITIES � ⌖ **Kid City** (813-935-8441; www.flchildrensmuseum.com), 7550 North Blvd, North Tampa, is a miniature outdoor city for young children to explore, from City Hall to a doctor's office and apartments. Children are encouraged to role-play along the city streets and in the buildings while parents tag along or relax in the shade at a picnic table. Open daily; fee.

⌖ At **Malibu Grand Prix** (813-977-6272; www.malibugrandprix.com), 14320 N Nebraska Ave, enjoy miniature golf with the entire family or let the kids challenge each other on the Grand Prix racecourse. There are batting cages, go-carts, and video games, too.

⌖ After you're done with city exploration, get out in the country and take the kids to **Old McMicky's Farm** (813-920-1948), 19215 Crescent Rd, Lutz, for some hands-on country fun. Milk a cow, play in the treehouse, ride a pony: Learn about the fun of growing up on a farm. Tours 9:30–1:45; closed Sun. $8 per person.

FISHING **Tightlines Tackle Charter Service** (813-932-4721; www.tightlines fishingcharters.com), part of Tightlines Tackle Store (see *Selective Shopping*) offers private, group, and corporate charters for full and half days. Take your own tackle down to the reservoir at **Edward Medard Park** (813-757-3802), off FL 60 west of Plant City, or hit one of the fishing piers at one of the many parks on Tampa Bay (see *Parks*).

GAMING The new **Seminole Hard Rock Hotel & Casino** (see *Hotels, Motels, and Resorts*) is a top destination for Las Vegas–style action with video gaming, poker, and high-stakes bingo 24 hours a day. The complex includes several outstanding restaurants, a food court, shops, and row upon row of popular slot machines. With the only regularly scheduled horse racing on Florida's west coast, **Tampa Bay Downs Thoroughbred Racing** (813-855-4401 or 1-800-200-4434; www.tampabaydowns.com) hosts live races Dec–May. For greyhound racing, head to the **Tampa Greyhound Track** (813-932-4313; www.tampadogs .com), 8300 N Nebraska Ave, where races are held Mon–Sat and jai alai is scheduled year-round.

GENEOLOGICAL RESEARCH

Plant City
Housed in the historic 1914 Plant City High School, the **Quintilla Geer Bruton Archives Center** (813-754-7031; www.rootsweb.com/~flqgbac), 605 N Collins St, offers researchers a treasure trove of more than 3,500 books on genealogy as well as census records, family history, genealogical files, and old newspapers for Hillsborough County.

GOLF With dozens of choices, we offer a sampling. The top challenge in Hillsborough County is purportedly **The Golf Club at Cypress Creek** (813-634-8888; www.golfclubcypresscreek.com), 1011 Cypress Village Rd, Ruskin, a semiprivate 18-hole course winding around more than 600 acres of protected wetlands. Wildlife sightings are common just up the road at the public **Apollo Beach Golf Club** (813-645-6212; www.apollobeachgolf.com), 801 Golf and Sea Blvd, Apollo Beach. On the county's northwest edge in Lutz, visit the rambling cypress-edged greens of **Heritage Harbor Golf & Country Club** (813-949-4886; www.heritageharborgolf.com), 19502 Heritage Harbor Pkwy, and the **Tournament Players Club of Tampa Bay** (1-866-PLAY-TPC; www.tpc.com), 5300 W Lutz Lake Fern Rd, the only PGA tour–owned and –operated course in the region. In Temple Terrace, **The Claw at USF** (813-632-6893; www.theclaw atUSF.com) offers long, tight fairways with towering moss-draped trees. And near the airport, tee off at the scenic **Rocky Point Golf Course** (813-673-4316; www.tampasportsauthority.com/golf/rockypoint.htm), 4151 Dana Shores Dr, where water is a hazard on 12 of the 18 holes.

HIKING There are numerous parks in the county that offer short hikes and boardwalks, but one of my favorite leg-stretchers is the **Little Manatee Hiking Trail** at **Little Manatee River State Park** (see *Parks*). Stop at the ranger station for a trail map, gate combination, and directions to the hiker's entrance, which is on the north side of the river. The 6-mile loop traverses an incredible variety of habitats, including beautiful Cypress Creek, and offers a 3-mile loop for those less inclined for a long walk. A primitive campsite beckons campers out for a quiet weekend. Other great hikes in the area include the Florida Trail system in **Hillsborough River State Park** and the network of trails in **Alderman's Ford Park** in Alafia.

ICE SKATING Those Stanley Cup hopefuls had to skate somewhere, and you can, too. **The Ice Sports Forum** (813-684-7825; www.icesportsforum.com), 10222 Elizabeth Pl, offers an NHL regulation rink for figure skating and hockey practice. ✣ Or take the kids to **Countryside Mall** (727-796-1079), 27001 US 19 N in nearby Clearwater, for fun on the ice.

MANATEE WATCHING ✣ During the manatee's winter migration into Tampa Bay, you can see them by the dozens at the **TECO Big Bend Power Station Manatee Viewing Center** (813-228-4289), off Big Bend Rd at Dickman Rd, from an observation platform with exhibits, murals, videos, and other educational materials. Open Nov–Apr. Free.

PADDLING Join **Kayak Tampa Bay** (813-986-2067; www.kayaktampabay.com), based at the Tampa Marriott Waterside Hotel & Marina, and enjoy a leisurely paddle along the estuaries and channels of Hillsborough Bay. Visit **Canoe Escape** (813-986-2067; www.canoeescape.com), 9335 E Fowler Ave, to arrange a wilderness paddling trip along the Hillsborough River, where alligator sightings are guaranteed. Trips run from two hours to a full day.

SCENIC DRIVES **Bayshore Boulevard** is one of the prettiest drives in the region and should not be missed for its extensive waterfront views. The views from the **Courtney Campbell Causeway** (FL 60) are pretty incredible, too.

SCENIC WALKS How about a waterfront view for 4.5 miles? That's what you'll get walking the **world's longest continuous sidewalk** along **Bayshore Boulevard,** overlooking the sparkling waters of Tampa Bay. Or walk *over the water* on the old Gandy Bridge, now called the **Friendship Trail Bridge,** which links Picnic Island Park in Hillsborough County to Weedon Island Preserve near St. Pete, a 12-mile paved trek with 2.6 miles over the bay.

TRAIL RIDING At **In the Breeze Horseback Riding Ranch** (813-264-1919; www.breezestables.hypermart.net), 7514 Gardner Rd, near the airport, the trails wind through 300 acres of real Florida hammocks, hardwood forests, and scrub. Trail rides are offered all day, and hayrides and bonfires at night. There is a petting zoo and swimming hole on the premises, making this a great family outing. Trail rides start at $29; hayrides for $3. ♿ In Lutz, the **Bakas Equestrian Center** (813-264-3890) at Lake Park, 17302 N Dale Mabry, offers special facilities for wheelchair-bound riders.

STREETCAR RIDES

&. ♪ When I took my dad, a lifelong streetcar aficionado, down to Channel-side to ride the **TECO Line Streetcar System** (www.tecolinestreetcar.org), little did I suspect there would be dozens of tourists there doing the same exact thing. The original line existed from 1892 through 1946; the new line opened several years ago on a much more limited scale. Staffed by operators in vintage uniforms, these replica Birney Safety Cars transport you into the past, offering a 20-minute ride with 11 stops that link downtown to the Port of Tampa at Channelside and end in Ybor City, with a rare railroad-streetcar crossing along the way. Fares are cash only, but you can buy a pass ($4) good for the day, which gives you the opportunity to enjoy the ride *and* utilize the streetcar for what it's meant to be, after all—clean, comfortable, eco-friendly public transportation. And if you ask and they have the staff to handle your request, you may be able to tour the streetcar barn in Ybor City, where one of the restored Birneys is on display.

Bringing your own horse? An extensive network of equestrian trails crisscrosses **Alfia River State Park** (813-987-6771), accessed from CR 39 southeast of Brandon, and you can also take to the trails on the south side of **Little Manatee River State Park** (see *Parks*).

WALKING TOURS **Ybor City Walking Tours,** departing from Ybor City Museum State Park (see *Museums*) at 10:30 AM each Sat, include admission to the museum and a guided stroll along Seventh Ave. Fee. Self-guided tour brochures are available at the museum. In Plant City grab a **Downtown Walking Map** from the chamber of commerce to explore the city's many historic sites, including the 1914 High School & Museum at 605 N Collins St.

WATER PARKS &. Immerse into a Key West theme at **Adventure Island** (813-987-5600 or 1-888-800-5447; www.adventureisland.com), 4500 Bougainvillea Ave, a 30-acre wet playground adjoining Busch Gardens, where tropical plantings accent swimming pools and waterfalls, the wave pool, and slides that will have your heart pounding. Open daily late Mar–early Sep; weekends mid-Feb to Mar and mid-Sep through late Oct. Adults $34.95, children $32.95, plus $5 parking fee.

✳ Green Space

BEACHES While the region's best beaches are in Pinellas County (see *Florida's Beach*), Hillsborough County beaches (813-931-2121) still provide a few miles on Tampa Bay to catch some rays. Along FL 60 west of the airport, the Courtney Campbell Causeway, crowds gather on weekends to enjoy the slender strips of bayside beach at **Ben T. Davis Beach.** Over on the Davis Islands you'll find

Davis Islands Beach, open during daylight hours. At **Picnic Island Park,** 7409 Picnic Island Blvd, the bay surrounds you, with a connecting trail (see *Scenic Walks*) to Weedon Island, as well as a fishing pier, picnic shelters, and playgrounds.

BOTANICAL GARDENS It's an oasis in this urban area: Meander the boardwalks and trellised walks through 31 acres of woodlands at **Eureka Springs** (813-744-5536), 6400 Eureka Springs Rd. The springs are not open to swimming, but you can walk around the rim and follow the boardwalk off into a lush wetland filled with ferns, tall bay trees, maples, and cypresses; enjoy the fernery and orchid room along the pond. To find this little-known park, exit I-4 at US 301 and go north to the first traffic light, Sligh Ave. Turn right, then right at the T, and follow the signs. Free.

More than 3,000 species of flora are packed into just 7 acres at the **University of South Florida Botanical Gardens** (813-974-2329), 4202 E Fowler Ave at Alumni Dr and Pine Dr, just off Bruce B. Downs Pkwy. Enter through the archway and follow meandering pathways past well-identified plants in a variety of habitats from an oak hammock with a lush floor of ferns to a sunny formal garden, an orchid room, and a bamboo walkway lined with bonsai. Open 9–5 Mon–Fri, 9–4 Sat, noon–4 Sun. Free.

GREENWAYS The **Town & Country Greenway** (813-264-8511), 7311 Baseball Ave, is a paved path with trailhead access on the east side of Hanley Rd, between Hillsborough Ave and Waters Ave. The **Upper Tampa Bay Trail,** along Ehrlich Rd, runs from Wilsky Rd north.

PARKS One of the most popular state parks in Florida, **Hillsborough River State Park** (813-987-6771), protects a beautiful section of the river, including the state's southernmost stretch of rapids. Paddlers ply the short stretch of whitewater, hikers trek miles of backcountry trails in shady river hammocks, and campers appreciate the two full-service campgrounds tucked in the woods. There's even a giant swimming pool! **Little Manatee River State Park** (813-671-5005), US 301, south of Sun City Center, offers horse trails, hiking trails, and river access for paddling.

Literature fanatics—head to South Tampa to see **Ballast Point Park & Pier** (813-274-8615), 5300 Interbay Rd, the setting for Jules Verne's classic *From the Earth to the Moon.* Most folks stop here to picnic along the bay or fish on the pier, but there's also a "Jules Verne Park" historical marker and a mural blending Jules Verne's fantasy with the wildlife along the bay. 🐾 Dogs can romp free in the dog park at **Al Lopez Park,** 4810 N Himes, a 120-acre city park with nature trails, playgrounds, a fishing pier, paved walking trails, and dozens of picnic tables and grills for a nice family outing. **Centennial Park,** 1800 Eighth Ave, Ybor City, is a gathering place with picnic tables, home to the Saturday-morning farmer's market. **Cotanchobee Park,** 601 Ice Palace Dr, downtown, sits along Garrison Channel. It has a fishing pier and playground, and centers on a memorial to the Seminole Wars. **Plant Park,** on the University of Tampa campus, protects 6.9 acres along the Hillsborough River. In Ybor City the tiny **Parque**

Amigos de Marti is a sliver of Cuba in the United States. Cuba owns title to this piece of land, which contains a statue of Jose Marti and soil from all of the provinces of Cuba—considered the only free Cuban soil in the world. For City of Tampa parks information, call 813-274-8615.

In the county, **E. G. Simmons Park** (813-671-7655), 2401 19th Ave NW, Ruskin, encompasses nearly 500 acres on Tampa Bay, perfect for boating, swimming, bird-watching, and fishing. There is also a campground on-site. This park hosts many regional festivals. At **Lettuce Lake Park** (813-987-6204), 6920 Fletcher Ave, a series of boardwalks leads you out along the Hillsborough River to an observation tower, and the picnic pavilions provide scenic views. **Upper Tampa Bay Park** (813-855-1765) protects more than 2,100 acres and has walking trails, an environmental study center, and picnic groves along the shores of Tampa Bay.

SPRINGS A swim's the thing at **Lithia Springs** (813-744-5572), 3932 Lithia Springs Rd, a 200-acre park surrounding a second-magnitude spring edged with cypresses and bay trees. A small swimming beach and roped-off area for the kids provide access to the 72°F waters. Open 8–7 Mon–Fri, 8–8 weekends. Fee.

WILD PLACES North of Tampa along the Hillsborough River, **Wilderness Park** includes a chain of parks connected by a ribbon of protected land, where hikers, bicyclists, and paddlers can explore miles of unbroken wilderness. Trailheads are at **Flatwoods Wilderness Park & Trail** (813-987-6211), 16400 Morris Bridge Rd, Thonotosassa, and Bruce B. Downs Blvd, New Tampa; **Trout Creek Wilderness Park** (813-987-6200), 12550 Morris Bridge Rd; and **Morris Bridge Wilderness Park** (813-987-6209), 13330 Morris Bridge Rd. Paddlers can also access the river's tributaries via wilderness parks off US 301: **Dead River Wilderness Park** (813-987-6210), 15098 Dead River Rd; **John B. Sargeant Sr. Memorial Wilderness Park** (813-987-6208), 12702 US 301; and **Veteran's Memorial Wilderness Park** (813-744-5502), 3602 US 301.

✳ Lodging

BED & BREAKFASTS

Brandon 33511

❦ An unexpected find in Florida: A shaker saltbox evoking New England at **Behind the Fence Inn** (813-685-8201), 1400 Viola Dr, provides a touch of Amish hospitality in a relaxing setting. Innkeeper Larry Yoss was raised in an Amish home but left the community when he married his wife, Carolyn, who had been raised on a historic farm. Together, they bring rural hospitality to the fringe of the big city, their home artfully decorated with treasured finds from their days in the antiques business. The house has three guest rooms with shared bath, and two cottage rooms next to the pool each have private facilities. Rates, $69–89, include continental breakfast with fresh Amish sweet rolls. At Christmas, stop by to enjoy traditional crafts-making demonstrations by local artisans.

Tampa—Ybor City 33605

A fully equipped 1908 bungalow, the **Casita de la Verdad** (813-654-6087;

www.yborcityguesthouse.com), 1609 E Sixth Ave, offers the comforts of home with a location central to the nightlife that Ybor City is famous for. The bungalow has two bedrooms, each with a queen-size bed, and a restored claw-foot tub in the marble-floored bath, as well as a full kitchen and outdoor grilling space. Rates run $180 Sun–Thu, $250 Fri–Sat, and $350 during special events.

CAMPGROUNDS

Dover 33527

Green Acres Campground & RV Travel Park (813-659-0002), 12720 E US 92, offers seven hundred grassy sites, from full hookup to primitive, and amenities including a heated swimming pool, playground, laundry room, recreation hall, and golf course.

Ruskin 33570

🐾 Enjoy gorgeous natural scenery along the Little Manatee River at **Hide-A-Way RV Resort** (813-645-6037 or 1-800-607-2532), where it costs $26 daily (water and electric) for you to pull your trailer or RV under the oaks. Enjoy the RV lifestyle with clubhouse, scheduled activities, heated pool, and great access to the river for fishing.

🐾 Enter through the red barn at **Manatee RV Park** (813-645-7652), 6302 US 41 S, to discover a nicely forested campground with its own mini-golf course, shuffleboard, clubhouse and pool, and a large pond busy with birds. Sites include water and electric for $22.50; dump station available. Pets permitted in designated areas.

Thonotosassa 33592

Sheltered by massive live oaks, **Spanish Main RV Resort** (813-986-2415),

12110 Spanish Main Resort Trl, US 301 N, is an appealing place to set up camp for the night, with a playground, pool, and shuffleboard. RV sites are $24 and include full hookups.

HOTELS, MOTELS, AND RESORTS

Tampa—Airport/Westshore 33607

For a romantic escape head to the **Renaissance Tampa Hotel** (813-877-9200 or 1-800-644-2685; www .marriott.com/property/propertypage/ TPAIM), 4200 Jim Walter Blvd, where delightful Mediterranean decor will sweep you off your feet thanks to the influence of Gabriella and Sergio Pesce. Gabriella, who inherited her family's Ybor City cigar business, fell in love with Sergio while vacationing on the Spanish Riviera. The faux turn-of-the-20th-century architecture is enchanting, and who can resist the tray of fresh olives available to guests in the lobby? In this relatively new Marriott property, the rooms (starting at $159) and suites reflect the overall elegance of the theme. It's a short walk to shopping at International Plaza (see *Selective Shopping*). The hotel offers both complimentary on-site parking and valet parking.

Overlooking the sparkling expanse of Tampa Bay, the **Sailport Waterfront Suites** (813-281-9599 or 1-800-255-9599; www.sailport.com), 2506 N Rocky Point Dr, provides all the comforts of home. One- and two-bedroom suites ($89–169) include a full kitchen, making this an ideal location for long-term stays. Business travelers will appreciate the high-speed wireless Internet access. A pool and sunning beach let you soak in some bayside rays. Complimentary covered parking and free airport shuttle.

Tampa—Downtown 33602

In the heart of the busy Channelside district, the **Tampa Marriott Waterside Hotel & Marina** (813-221-4900 or 1-888-268-1616; www.marriott .com/property/propertypage/TPAMC), 700 S Florida Ave, adjoins the St. Pete Times Forum and has one end of the TECO streetcar line out front. The spacious rooms have luxurious cherrywood furnishings and classy art, dedicated work space with high-speed Internet access, and fabulous views across the Hillsborough River. There is an on-site spa, several restaurants, and concierge floors with upscale suites, including the Presidental Suite. Standard rooms start at $159; on-site (fee) and valet parking.

▼ At the **Sheraton Tampa Riverwalk Hotel** (813-223-2222; www .tampariverwalkhotel.com), 200 N Ashley Dr, settle into a comfortable room that evokes the city's Spanish heritage, with muted earth tones, wrought-iron lamps, and a marble coffee table. Towering over the Hillsborough River, the hotel offers great views of Henry Plant's classic 1891 Tampa Bay Hotel. Standard rooms $139–159; the spacious suites ($235 and up) are larger than most one-bedroom apartments and include a massive walk-through closet/vanity area, microwave, mini fridge, and large writing desk. Valet parking only.

Tampa—East 33610

Having attended a business meeting at the **Seminole Hard Rock Hotel & Casino** (1-866-502-PLAY; www .hardrockhotelcasinotampa.com), 5223 N Orient Rd, I can attest to the "wow" factor of their hotel rooms—I felt like I'd slipped into a chic version of the *Jetsons*. Each spacious room ($169 and up) comes with its own stereo system (I was supplied a CD upon check-in; others can be purchased in the stores of the casino complex), massive television, ultramodern furnishings, mini bar, comfortable bed, and roomy bath area with separate tub and shower. Guests enjoy a tropical art deco pool area, fitness center, and spa on the hotel side of this massive entertainment complex.

Tampa—North Tampa 33612

While **Embassy Suites USF** (813-977-7066; www.embassysuitesusf .com), 3705 Spectrum Blvd, caters to business travelers with all the usual amenities, it is also an excellent place to stay on a visit to Busch Gardens (see *Attractions*), which is 2 miles away; special package deals and complimentary shuttle available. One- and two-bedroom suites ($144–239) include a cooked-to-order breakfast.

Tampa—Ybor City 33605

🕸 In a building constructed in 1895 by the founder of Ybor City as a clinic and hospital, the **Don Vicente de Ybor Historic Inn** (813-241-4545; www.donvicenteinn.com), 1915 Republica de Cuba, offers a step back in time through its 16 boutique rooms ($119–219). The common areas evoke the splendor of Renaissance Europe, with gilded paneling and lush draperies, while each room offers elegant furnishings, floor-to-ceiling windows, and writing desks. Breakfast and parking are complimentary.

Adjoining the historic village at the Ybor City Museum State Park (see *Museums*), the **Hilton Garden Inn Tampa Ybor Historic District** (813-769-9267), 1700 E Ninth Ave, blends in seamlessly with its Latin Quarter surroundings. Rooms $149–159. From here it's an easy walk to

Centro Ybor, or you can catch a street-car to Channel-side and downtown.

Temple Terrace 33637

Set in a quiet nature preserve near a bustling business district, **Hilton Garden Inn Tampa North** (813-342-5000; www.tampanorth.garden inn.com), 600 Tampa Oaks Blvd, provides everything a business traveler needs: The clean, comfortable rooms ($84–119) include a large work desk and high-speed Internet. Families will appreciate this location as a getaway for visiting local attractions—Busch Gardens and the Museum of Science & Industry are only a few miles away.

❋ Where to Eat

DINING OUT

Tampa—Airport/Westshore

The classy **Tampa Bay Palm Restaurant** (813-849-7256; www.the palm.com), 205 Westshore Dr, is a spinoff of the original New York City steakhouse that opened in 1926, but with its own Tampa twist: The walls are decorated with caricatures of local celebrities, from newspaper colum-nists to politicians and business execu-tives. Featuring jumbo Nova Scotia lobsters and prime Angus steaks as well as nearly a dozen choices of fresh veggies served family-style, it's a seri-ous place for fine dining. Open for lunch and dinner, with entrées start-ing at $18.

Tampa—Downtown and Vicinity

Dine along the Hillsborough River at the **Ashley Street Grille** (813-226-4400), 200 N Ashley Ave, inside the Tampa Riverwalk Hotel (see *Hotels, Motels, and Resorts*), where Chef Mike Pagliari presides over a well-pedigreed kitchen, which has won various awards from *Wine Spec-*

tator magazine over the past decade. Entrées ($14–32) showcase fresh local vegetables and seafood in creations such as chile-rubbed salmon, seafood St. Jacques, and my selection, the Mediterranean penne, a garden-fresh mix of veggies, kalamata olives, and goat cheese reminiscent of the Greek islands. If you're tempted by the dessert tray, don't hesitate—the Key lime pie is just the right measure of tart. Serving breakfast, lunch, and dinner, and offering menu items via room service throughout the hotel.

Donatello (813-875-6660; www .donatellorestaurant.com), 232 N Dale Mabry, is a favorite of *Wine Spectator* magazine for the extensive wine list that complements their Northern Italian cuisine as well as their other innovative cuisine, includ-ing fresh oysters cooked with cream and spinach, fresh salmon with aspara-gus, and Angus beef with homemade pâté. Open for dinner at 6 PM daily, lunch 11:30–2:30 Mon–Fri.

Tampa—South Tampa

♞ A Tampa legend, **Bern's Steak House** (813-251-2421; www.berns steakhouse.com), 1208 S Howard Ave, doesn't do anything by halves. Their famous cut-to-order steaks come with the world's largest wine list (the size of a small laptop computer—and how can they help it, with a half million bottles of wine in stock?) and a 65-page dessert menu to complement their dessert room. Stepping into the restaurant, you feel as if you've entered a medieval castle, and each of the themed dining rooms are named for European wine districts, such as Bordeaux and Rhone. The intimate murmur of conversation flows throughout the room as you savor the art of dining. Our waiter,

Jim, along with his peers, trained for at least a year before being permitted to work alone. He took the time to explain the different cuts of meat and how they are prepared. I settled on a New York strip from the hundreds of choices on the menu. Every entrée comes with French onion soup, salad, baked potato, and fresh onion rings. If you think you'll want dessert (and you will), ask your waiter to reserve your space *before* you begin your main course. The vegetables come straight from the family farm near north Tampa Bay and are perfectly crisp; the macadamia nut–vanilla dressing gave the salad a uniquely sweet twist. As for the steak, the rarer the better! After dinner, we took the kitchen and wine cellar tour offered to all guests and marveled at the massive aquariums and the walls of fine wine in the wine cellar. Ushered upstairs to the dessert room, we enjoyed intimate seating in a giant wine vat, each a soundproof booth with your choice of music. It was tough to settle between vanilla bean crème brûlée, orange chocolate-chip pecan pie, and Grand Marnier chocolate mousse among dozens of choices, but we did our best. Our luxurious dining experience took about four hours—this is not a place you want to hurry through—and the bill for two topped $150, with a minimal amount of alcohol included. The Laxer family has nurtured their business from its humble beginnings as a sandwich shop in 1956 into a destination in itself. Reservations recommended. Free self-parking, or valet.

Tampa—Ybor City

At **Bernini of Ybor** (813-248-0099; www.berniniofybor.com), 1702 E Seventh Ave, in the grand old Bank of Ybor City, "Taste is a Matter of Art."

With a menu that changes constantly, this popular innovative Italian restaurant receives rave reviews on a national level. One evening's entrées included pork *saltimbocca, cioppino,* and veal lasagna ($15–24) and a selection of wood-fired pizzas ($10–15).

🎵 The original **Columbia Restaurant** (813-248-4961; www.columbia restaurant.com), 2117 E Seventh Ave, a tradition for more than a century, is Florida's oldest continually operating restaurant. It defines the standard to which Spanish cooking in America is held. I was honored to be present at an awards ceremony where Joe Roman, "the Singing Waiter," received a lifetime achievement award for customer service. Enjoy a flamenco dance show every night while you nibble on their incredible selection of tapas, and settle into a classic slow-cooked paella for dinner, or tender *ropa vieja* (a Cuban beef dish—one of my favorites) served with plantains and rice. While you'll find spinoffs of the original all across Florida, nothing compares to sitting in the grand interior courtyard of the original. Open for lunch and dinner; children's menu available.

The **Don Vicente de Ybor Restaurant** (813-241-4545; www.donvicente inn.com), 1915 Republic de Cuba, features contemporary cuisine in an old-world setting, serving entrées such as nut-crusted salmon and sandwiches such as the Ybor Reuben.

EATING OUT

Plant City

🍴🎵 No Floridian should miss **The Branch Ranch** (813-752-1957; www .branchranchdiningroom.com), Branch Forbes Rd, a regional favorite since 1956 located right on the Branch family farm. Family-style meals ($11–19) include your entrée (featuring choices such as country ham and catfish); a salad tray; buttermilk biscuits with fresh preserves and marmalade; fresh squash, yams, pole beans, and eggplant; and a chicken potpie. Now *that's* a dinner! I love their home-cooked macaroni and cheese, too. One quirk about this family-owned restaurant: They shut down all summer, so don't come knocking between mid-May and mid-September. Open for lunch and dinner 9–8, Sun until 6, closed Mon–Tue. Reservations recommended for holidays.

🍴 Right in the regional farmer's market, **Fred's Market Restaurant** (813-752-7763), 1401 W Martin Luther King Jr Blvd, offers some of the best country cooking in the state. Southern fried chicken, perfect mashed potatoes, and flaky biscuits are all part of an extensive buffet for less than $9 per person, or you can order from the menu, $7–12. Open 6 AM–8:30 PM, closed Sun and holidays.

Ruskin

A roadside stand with Old Florida appeal, the **Fish House** (813-641-9451), 1900 Shell Point Rd, features down-home seafood dinners ($7–11) such as smoked mullet and grits, fried oysters, and soft-shell crab. Take it to go, or eat outdoors at the shaded picnic tables. Open 11–8 Thu–Sat.

Tampa—Downtown and Vicinity

An Irish sports pub in a historic downtown building, **Hattricks** (813-225-HATT), 107 S Franklin St, shows off hockey jerseys up on the old brick walls and has the best wings in Tampa—but try the offbeat, too, such as sweet potato fries with maple syrup

or lemon-pepper grouper nuggets ($4–9). Lunch and dinner options include salads, classic sandwiches and burgers, and pub fare such as shepherd's pie, fish-and-chips, and meat loaf ($9–11).

Kick back on the palm-canopied deck at **Newk's Lighthouse Café** (813-307-6395; www.newks.com), 514 Channelside Dr, where seafood is the main event. Try a crunchy grouper sandwich, their unique shrimp and grouper gumbo, or she-crab and shrimp quiche ($8 and up). Not a seafood fan? Hot wings, chicken tenders, and Greek salad make the menu, too.

It's not your ordinary dining experience. **Splitsville** (813-514-2695; www .splitsvillelanes.com), 615 Channelside Dr, is a funky, retro bowling alley and billiards hall where sushi sits side by side with ninepins. And it's fun! Choose from gourmet tapas or classics such as chicken wings and sandwiches ($8 and up), or entrées such as pork tenderloin Waikiki ($13 and up).

Tampa—Hyde Park

America's only thatched-roof Irish pub is in a Tampa neighborhood! Get your potato-leek soup and shepherd's pie while listening to traditional Irish musicians at **Four Green Fields** (813-254-4444; www.fourgreenfields .com), 205 W Platt St, 11–3 daily.

Tampa—North Tampa

🍴 A taste of real Florida, **Skipper's Smokehouse and Oyster Bar** (813-971-0666; www.skipperssmokehouse .com), 910 Skipper Rd, serves up gator ribs, mudbugs (crawfish), conch chowder, and one heck of a black bean gator chili. No frills here—the digs are authentic, and it seemed fitting that the day I stopped by, Tampa author Tim Dorsey was hanging out signing his latest madcap novel. Enjoy live music most evenings in the "Skipperdome" under moss-draped live oaks.

Tampa—South Tampa

The trendy "SoHo" district along South Howard Avenue is the perfect place to hit the pavement to select from more than 30 independent restaurants with a full range of cuisines.

Step back into a more genteel era in the **House of Two Sisters Tea Room** (813-258-8220; www.houseof twosisters.com), 204 S Howard Ave, where formal tea is served at 11, 1, and 3 by reservation Thu–Sat ($12.95 per person).

🍴 Under a canopy of ancient live oaks, **Kojaks House of Ribs** (813-837-3774; www.kojaksbbq.com), 2808 Gandy Blvd, offers lip-smackin' ribs and barbecue—and *fast!* I'm picky about ribs and must declare these some of the best I've ever had, and on my husband's choice of a combo dinner, the fresh sausage was kickbutt spicy and good. Entrées start at $8, and the best seating is out on the porch. These folks have been around for nearly 30 years, and with the great service and killer food, I can see why.

Tampa—Ybor City

With homemade Spanish bean soup and Cuban sandwiches, **La Tropicana Café** (813-247-4040), 1822 E Seventh Ave, is an authentic Cuban café with lunches less than $10.

🍴 **The Spaghetti Warehouse** (813-248-1720; www.meatballs.com) is a fun family Italian restaurant where you can dine inside a streetcar. No matter whether you order spaghetti,

lasagna, or a salad, the portions are big, but the prices make this a great family choice: lunch and dinner less than $10.

BAKERIES, COFFEE SHOPS, AND SODA FOUNTAINS

Lithia

A bright and cheery ice cream parlor, **Katie Jean's Ice Cream & Deli** (813-650-0359), 10433 S CR 39, offers homemade sandwiches and salads ($5 and up) and, even better yet—homemade ice cream!

Tampa—Downtown and Vicinity

🍴 One of my favorite places in Tampa is **Alessi Bakeries** (813-879-4544), 2909 W Cypress St, where it still looks and smells like the bakeries of my youth. A century's worth of loving care brings forth goodies like Napoleons, éclairs, and banana bread. The deli sandwiches, salads, and entrées are world-class, too. Stop here for lunch. You'll keep coming back.

It's hard to pass by a French bakery, so don't pass up **Au Rendezvous** (813-221-4748), 200 E Madison St, when you're downtown—quiches, croissants, ooh la la! My picks are the rustic olive bread and aromatic rosemary bread.

Joffrey's Coffee (www.joffreys.com) is a local chain with numerous locations around Tampa Bay. The one I've hung out at is in Channelside, where you can grab a deli sandwich to go with your java or order up a dessertlike frozen coffee drink.

Tampa—Ybor City

All of Ybor City, it seems, gets its fresh bread and rolls from **La Segunda Central Bakery** (813-248-1531), 2512 N 15th St, where you can pick up tasty pastries, too.

✳ Entertainment

FINE ARTS Tampa Bay Performing Arts Center (813-229-7827 or 1-800-955-1045; www.tbpac.org), 1010 W. C. MacInnes Pl N, is the largest performing-arts center in the Southeast and offers a broad range of fine-arts entertainment, from the Florida Orchestra to Opera Tampa, Broadway shows, and dance. See their web site for details and ticketing.

THEATER ♿ An intimate Actor's Equity venue, the 76-seat **Gorilla Theatre** (813-879-2914; www.gorilla -theatre.com), 4419 N Hubert Ave, offers original works and classics, as well as workshops for young playwrights. Schedule varies by performance.

Enjoy movies as they were meant to be seen in the 1920s elegance of the **Tampa Theatre** (813-274-8982; www .tampatheatre.org), 711 Franklin St, where seasonal film festivals showcase the classics: Imagine watching *Casablanca* on the big screen in this plush venue from the past, replete with a pre-show Wurlitzer organ introduction. They also feature avant-garde films and documentaries you won't see at mainstream theaters, shown nightly.

NIGHTCLUBS Head to Channelside (see *Selective Shopping*) for a dose of downtown nightlife at **Banana Joe's Island Party** (813-228-7300; www .bananajoestampa.com), a Caribbean-themed dance club with music from the 70s, 80s, and 90s, or opt for more traditional entertainment in Ybor City at **Amphitheater** (813-248-2331; www.amphitheaterybor.com), with live DJs and the only revolving dance floor on Florida's west coast, and

Club Hedo (813-248-4336; www .clubhedo.com), a party bar with local radio DJs.

SPORTS The **Tampa Bay Buccaneers** (813-879-BUCS or 1-800-795-BUCS; www.buccaneers.com) play football each fall at Raymond James Stadium, and the recent winners of the Stanley Cup, the **Tampa Bay Lightning** (813-301-6500; www .tampabaylightning.com), compete in fast-paced games on ice at the St. Pete Times Forum downtown.

✳ Selective Shopping

Plant City

The historic downtown is an antiques shopper's dream—you'll easily spend a day browsing the many shops. Here's a sampling.

Look for primitives and tools at **Antiques & Treasures** (813-752-4626), 107 N Collins St; the back room is filled with furniture and glassware.

Aunt Nancy's Antiques & Gifts (813-752-8558), 108 NE Drane St, has lovely pink rose primitives by a Venice artist, vintage pottery, and Fenton glass.

You'll find an eclectic selection of dealer booths in an old McCrory's building at **Collins Street Junction** (813-659-2585), 117 N Collins St, with collectibles, ephemera, and glass.

Get lost in the maze at **Frenchman's Market** (813-754-8388), 102 N Collins St, where the jam-packed narrow aisles of this two story ex–department store are bursting with garage-sale items.

At **Pieces of Olde** (813-717-7731), 113 W Reynolds St, there is a room of tins and kitchenware, quilts, some primitives and books, and a "Mad Hatter" room.

At **Sisters & Co.** (813-754-0990), 104 E Reynolds St, I found some great books and toys to give as gifts and browsed the fun and colorful selection of clothing and purses.

At **Yesterday's Attic** (813-752-6095), 110 S Collins St, gleaming white wicker and painted primitives are accented by floral arrangements and collectibles.

Tampa—Airport/Westshore

Adjacent to the airport, **International Plaza and Bay Street** (813-342-3790; www.shopinternationalplaza .com), 2223 N Westshore Blvd, has more than two hundred shops anchored by Neiman Marcus, Nordstrom, and Dillard's, as well as an open-air village of boutique shops, Bay Street, and popular restaurants such as Blue Martini, the Cheesecake Factory, and TooJay's. Older, but still popular with shoppers, nearby **Westshore Plaza** (813-286-0790; www .westshoreplaza.com), 250 Westshore Plaza, has more than one hundred specialty stores, including Banana Republic as well as several upscale chain restaurants.

Tampa—Downtown and Vicinity

Step into a historic Victorian home just outside downtown to enter the world of **Artsiphartsi** (813-348-4838; www.artsiphartsi.com), 2717 Kennedy Blvd, where more than five hundred nationally acclaimed artists are represented in various media, from contemporary quilts to fine furniture, metalwork, jewelry, and glass. Don't miss the sculpture garden! Closed Sun.

Set right along the waterfront, where docked cruise ships dwarf the plaza,

Channelside (813-223-4250; www .channelside.com), 615 Channelside Dr, combines dining and shopping with a quick walk to attractions like the Florida Aquarium. Browse streetfront shops such as **White House Gear** and **Cigars by Antonio,** or work your way into the complex for the cinema and more shops such as **Hurricane Pass Outfitters** and **Bob the Fish Sportswear.**

A don't-miss stop for books on art and artists is the **Guilders Museum Store** at the Tampa Museum of Art (813-274-8130; www.tampamuseum .com), 600 N Ashley Dr, which also features topical gifts related to their special exhibits, playful mugs and mobiles, and a large children's section with books and toys to delight (and teach) the youngsters.

A top-notch independent bookstore, **Inkwood Books** (813-253-2638; www .inkwoodbooks.com), 216 S Armenia, has a great selection in my favorite

SHOP AND DINE AT CHANNELSIDE

Sandra Friend

niches—recent travel narrative, travel guides, and Florida authors, as well as the best modern trade paperbacks and Book Sense picks. They regularly host author visits.

Downtown, the **Old Tampa Book Company** (813-209-2151), 507 N Tampa St, offers more than forty thousand used and collectible tomes—talk about some serious browsing! Owners Ellen and David Brown should be applauded for breathing some life into Tampa's downtown, as theirs is one of few places to shop. Featuring Florida books, fine-art collectibles, and more.

Tampa—Hyde Park
Touting themselves as a "cure for the common mall," **Old Hyde Park Village** (813-251-3500; www.oldhydepark.com), 748 S Village Cir, offers upscale favorites such as Restoration Hardware, Williams-Sonoma, Pottery Barn, and Crabtree & Evelyn in a parklike setting, with on-site theaters, coffee shops, and the popular Wine Exchange. For unique gifts with a local touch, seek out **Nicholson House** (813-258-3991), 1605 Snow Ave, filled with whimsical functional art; **The Wild Orchid** (813-258-5004; www.wildorchidshop.com), 1631 W Snow Cir, a lush rain forest with live orchids, tropical home decor, garden ornaments, and gifts; and **A Source for the Home** (813-259-9999; www.asourceforthehome.com), where you'll find the perfect art glass, dinnerware, and lighting for your home. Free parking provided in several garages.

Tampa—North Tampa
For the avid angler a stop is necessary at **Tightlines Tackle Store** (813-932-4721; www.tightlinesfishingcharters.com), 6924 N Armenia Ave, where you'll find a full range of gear for the fishing possibilities around Tampa Bay—inshore, offshore, flats, and saltwater—as well as clothing, gifts, and specialty items.

Tampa—Ybor City
Rather than demolish a neighborhood of early-1900s bungalows, the city moved them from the path of I-4 to face Centennial Park (see *Parks*) as part of the Ybor City Museum State Park (see *Museums*). Painted in cheery colors, the homes are now an artists' village of shops and galleries, among them the **Arnold Martinez Art Gallery** (see *Art Galleries*) and the **Ybor City Museum Store** (813-241-6554), 1820 E Ninth Ave, where you'll find cigar art, history books, and a unique line of "Trolley Kat" books and dolls for the kids.

Cigar-making is a fine art perfected in Ybor City, so aficionados have several spots to pause, sample, and enjoy a tour. At **Gonzales y Martinez Cigar Company** (813-248-8210; www.gonzalesymartinez.com), 2103 E Seventh Ave (in the Columbia Restaurant building), learn about the area's tradition of cigar rolling. Visit the **King Corona Cigar Factory** (813-241-9109; www.kingcoronacigars.com), 1523 Seventh Ave, to sample the product of five generations of cigar crafters. You'll find Arturo Fuente products at the **Tampa Sweetheart Cigar Company** (813-247-3880; www.tampasweetheart.com), 1310 N 22nd St, and the **Ybor Tabacalera** (813-241-0326), 1805 N 22nd St, is a hand-rolled cigar factory.

Centro Ybor (813-242-4660; www.centroybor.com), 1600 E Eighth Ave, is the central shopping, dining, and entertainment district within historic

Ybor City, anchored by the Centro Español social club. Retail favorites such as Victoria's Secret and Urban Outfitters stand side by side with the Muvico 20 Cinema, nightclubs, and the **Big City Tavern** (www.bigtime restaurants.com), a vibrant jazz bar that provides a comfy place to kick back and visit with friends in a transformed 80-year-old ballroom. For souvenirs of the Ybor lifestyle, visit **Ybor Ybor** (813-247-4255), 1600 E Eighth Ave, #111.

Thonotosassa

Head east for bargains at the **Big Top Flea Market** (813-986-4004; www.bigtopfleamarket.com), 9250 E Fowler Ave, where more than a thousand dealer booths give you a choice of everything from cheap Asian goods to farm fresh local produce, fishing tackle, puppies, and garage-sale type items.

PRODUCE STANDS, FARMER'S MARKETS, SEAFOOD MARKETS, AND U-PICK

Plant City

Plant City is best known for its fabulous annual strawberry crop, and where better to buy strawberries than direct from the farm? At **Parkesdale Farm Market** (813-754-2704 or 1-888-311-1701; www.parkesdale.com), 3702 W Baker St, stop in for luscious strawberry shortcake and milk shakes, fresh strawberries, preserves, and more. Closed Sun–Mon. Driving south on CR 33 from Plant City to Alafia, you'll encounter dozens of roadside stands, most open during the winter growing season. Open daily 9–6.

Sun City

Follow the signs from US 41 to **Dooley Groves** (813-645-3256 or

1-800-522-6411; www.dooleygroves .com), 1651 Stephens Rd, where citrus is as fresh as it comes, right at the packing plant. Watch fresh orange juice being squeezed and breathe in the sweet aroma of orange blossoms. In addition to citrus, they have a gift shop full of Florida goodies. Open seasonally for nearly 40 years.

Tampa—South Tampa
Linda's Garden Fresh Produce offers farm-fresh goodies at a stand at the corner of MacDill and Interbay.

Tampa—Ybor City
Ybor City Fresh Market (813-241-2442; www.yborfreshmarket.city search.com) at Centennial Park (see *Parks*) offers fresh local produce, baked goods, and arts and crafts vendors every Sat 9–3.

✳ Special Events
February: One of Florida's wildest invasions, the **Gasparilla Pirate Fest** (813-353-8108; www.gasparillapirate fest.com), held the first Sat, celebrates the taking of Tampa—by pirates. For more than a century, Ye Mystic Krewe of Gasparilla has sailed their pirate ship into downtown, swarming the city with more than a hundred other krewes before tossing beads and doubloons to the crowd in a colorful parade. The revelry continues all weekend at parties private and public and spills over to other special events—arts festival, marathon, road race, and more—throughout the remainder of the month.

Florida Strawberry Festival (813-754-1996; www.flstrawberryfestival .com), Plant City, is the world's largest celebration of strawberries right at the peak of harvest season. The exhibition halls are filled with everything

FLORIDA STATE FAIR

The state's largest celebration of rural bounty is in an ironically urban set-ting at the **Florida State Fair** (813-621-7821 or 1-800-345-FAIR; www.florida statefair.com), 4800 US 301 N, Tampa, just off I-4 near I-75. For more than a century, it's been a statewide showcase for agriculture, with exhibits on Florida wildlife (from the Fish & Wildlife Commission) and Florida's forestry industry (from the Department of Forestry), covering historic turpentine tap-ping, cypress logging, pine straw, and careers in modern forestry. Antique steam engines are shown off in their own barn. Inside the grand exhibit hall, see the "best of," from cakes to tapestries to rag dolls, from all over Florida. There's also a giant midway to keep the kids busy, and concerts (extra fee) on some evenings during the 12-day gala. Although the fair is open in Febru-ary only, the permanent **Cracker Country** folk life museum at the fairgrounds celebrates rural Florida history and is open all year, with living-history exhibits and buildings from 1870 to 1912. See old-fashioned toys and can-dies, Octagon soap, and glass minnow traps at J. R. Terry Dry Goods, or visit the model railroad inside the Seaboard Air Line depot. Fee.

LIVING HISTORY AT CRACKER VILLAGE ON THE FLORIDA STATE FAIRGROUNDS

Sandra Friend

from art to cakes, and livestock gets its own judging in the big tents. The festival offers concerts almost every night, but it's packed on weekends, so try to visit on a weekday—and be sure to get a ticket for strawberry short-cake! $10 admission.

History comes alive at the **Fort Fos-ter Rendezvous** at Fort Foster State Historic Site, Hillsborough River State Park (see *Parks*), where an encampment and skirmishes recall the days when soldiers attempted to keep the Seminoles from migrating north of the Hillsborough River in the early 1800s. Fee.

March: Enjoy arts, crafts, food, and a celebration of one of Tampa Bay's most beloved creatures at the **Apollo Beach Manatee Arts Festival** (813-645-1366; www.apollobeachchamber .com), Apollo Beach.

At the **Tampa Heritage Cigar Festival** (813-247-1434), Centennial Park, Ybor City, cigar vendors celebrate the city's rich tradition with demonstrations showcasing the history and cultural behind the business.

May: At the **Tampa Bay International Dragon Boat Races** (813-962-7163; www.TampaBayDragon Boats.com), corporate and community rowing teams race colorful dragon-decorated boats on the Hillsborough River downtown near Cotanchobee Park, by Channelside.

Celebrate the bounty of the earth at the **Ruskin Tomato Festival** (813-645-3808; www.ruskinchamber.org), held the first weekend, with musical entertainment, fresh produce, a Cinco de Mayo celebration, and all the sliced tomatoes you can eat. The festival is held at E. G. Simmons Park off US 41.

September: The **Mainstreet Arts & Crafts Series** (813-621-7121; www .cc-events.org/msartcraft), held mid-month in Ybor City at Centennial Park, features local and national artists, musical entertainment, and local produce and baked goods vendors. Free admission and parking; repeated in November.

October: One of the country's largest rallies of vintage autos, the **NSRA Southeast Street Rod Nationals** (303-776-7841; ww.nsra-usa.com) brings together more than 1,400 pre-1949 street rods from around the U.S. at the Florida State Fairgrounds.

Guavaween (www.cc-events.org/gw), celebrated the Sat before Halloween, brings together Tampa's nickname of "The Big Guava" with a Latin approach to this day of the dead, with outlandish costumes in a late-night street parade in Ybor City, overseen by "Mama Guava," who's taking the "bore" out of Ybor.

November: **Ruskin Seafood and Arts Festival** (813-645-3808; www .ruskinchamber.org), held the first weekend at E. G. Simmons Park, sates seafood appetites with dozens of vendors serving up Florida shrimp, conch, grouper, and more. Arts and crafts vendors and live entertainment round out a weekend of fun.

December: The **Victorian Christmas Stroll** (813-254-1891; www.plant museum.com) is a genteel walk through the old Tampa Bay Hotel, decked out as it was in the days of railroad magnate Henry Plant, Dec 1–23. Christmas fun continues downtown on the first Sat at Curtis Hixon Park with **Santa Fest** and the **Holiday Parade,** and it continues on Saturdays up through Christmas with **Holidayfest** (813-223-7999; www.fun intampabay.com), featuring events such as a lighted boat parade.

TRADITIONAL MIDWAY RIDES AT THE FLORIDA STATE FAIR

Sandra Friend

ST. PETERSBURG
DOWNTOWN, BEACHES, AND SURROUNDING COMMUNITIES

Forever linked with the ideal of "Fun in the Sun" tourism and retirement to Florida, St. Petersburg is one of Florida's boomtown cities experiencing a modern transformation into one of the state's most vibrant downtowns. In the 1800s early settlers in the wilderness of Pinellas County carved a living out of the pine flatwoods, establishing ranches and vegetable farms. But it was Gen. John Williams from Detroit who purchased 2,500 acres of Tampa Bay waterfront in 1875 with the express intent of creating a grand city. Development commenced, but with some competition—Hamilton Disston, the Philadelphia developer who in 1881 promised to drain Florida's swamplands and make them livable, nabbed thousands of nearby acres from the state on Boca Ciega Bay. Eyeing a settlement established by Civil War veteran Mames Barnett in 1867, Disston established Disston City at the southern end of the peninsula on Boca Ciega Bay.

As railroad barons pushed south, they decided the fate of the two competing cities. In 1888 Peter Demens, a Russian immigrant, brought his Orange Belt Railway right down to Williams's development, and the fledlging city was dubbed **St. Petersburg** in honor of his hometown. When Henry Plant's railroad also bypassed Disston City for bustling St. Petersburg and its commercial shipping port, the development folded, and that area evolved into the quiet modern-day **Gulfport,** which boasts genteel neighborhoods of historic homes. St. Petersburg started booming in earnest in 1911, with planned communities sprouting off the downtown business district along the many creeks and bayous draining into the bay. On New Year's Day 1914, history was made during the world's first commercial flight: Daredevil pilot Tony Jannus flew former mayor Ed Pheil from St. Petersburg Airport to Tampa for the princely sum of $400.

After the Florida boom went bust, the city remained a major destination for "Tin Can" tourists driving their jalopies down the eastern seaboard to escape the winter weather and camp out in the many parks around the city, which welcomed the influx of tourists. As that population aged, the region became known as a snowbird haven for retirees seeking to spend their winters in an inexpensive trailer court. Like most Florida cities, St. Petersburg experienced a population explosion immediately after World War II, when airmen assigned to the local bases decided

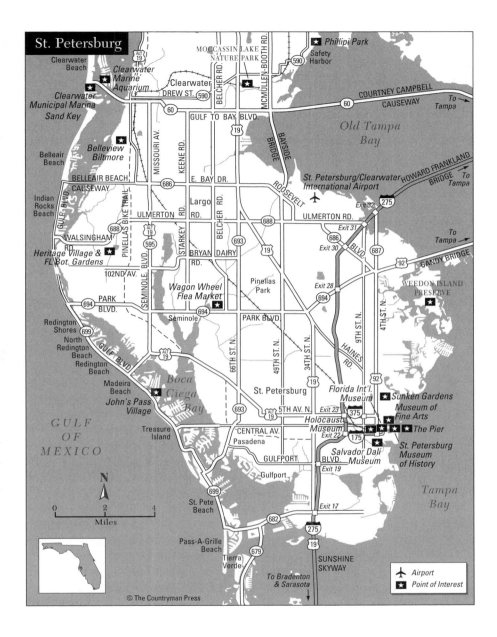

St. Petersburg

to keep their families in Florida. **St. Pete Beach** broke off from the city and merged with its oceanfront neighbors to create a separate municipality in 1957, including **Pass-A-Grille,** an Old Florida fishing village that remains mostly residential. Southwest of the city is **Tierra Verde,** a collection of islands in the unincorporated part of the county and gateway to historic Fort De Soto.

Today's St. Petersburg blends the best of old and new. Historic sites house new businesses, and the waterfront parks are still a wonderful place to walk along with your family.

GUIDANCE In downtown St. Petersburg, you'll find the **St. Petersburg Chamber of Commerce** (727-821-4069; www.stpete.com), 100 Second Ave N, in front of bustling Baywalk (see *Selective Shopping*). In Gulfport, ask for assistance at the **Gulfport Chamber of Commerce** (727-344-3711; www.gulfportchamberof commerce.com), 2808 58th St S, and at the beach, stop in the **St. Pete Beach Chamber Information Center** (www.stpetebeach.com), 6990 Gulf Blvd.

GETTING THERE *By car:* **I-275** and **US 19** provide primary access. **I-375** (exit 23A) leads you straight into downtown St. Petersburg.

By air: **St. Petersburg–Clearwater International Airport** (727-453-7800; www.fly2pie.com), 14700 Terminal Blvd, Clearwater, is off Roosevelt Blvd on the north end of the Pinellas peninsula. For a broader range of flights, check **Tampa International Airport** (see *Tampa and Hillsborough County*).

By bus: **Greyhound** (727-898-1496), 180 Ninth Ave N, St. Petersburg.

GETTING AROUND *By car:* **St. Petersburg** is laid out as a grid system, so finding your way around is a breeze. Avenues go east–west, streets go north–south. Beach Blvd follows the coastline from Vinoy Park past the Pier to the Basin. To find **Gulfport,** follow 22nd Ave S from either 54th St N or 49th St N. Keep going west to reach **St. Pete Beach.**

By bus: **Pinellas County Transit Authority** (727-530-9911; www.psta.net) offers several options, including the hourly Route 3 trolley from Treasure Island to St. Petersburg and Route 35 trolley from St. Pete Beach to St. Petersburg, and the **Official Suncoast Beach Trolley** that connects beach communities from Sand Key to Pass-A-Grille (average one hour, one way) every 30 minutes with well-marked bus stops. Daily card, $3; seven-day unlimited pass, $12.

By taxi: Local options include **Bats Taxi Company** (727-367-3702; www .BatsTaxi.com), 5201 Gulf Blvd, St. Pete Beach; and in St. Petersburg, **Independent Taxi** (727-327-3444), 4121 Fifth Ave N; **Pinellas Bay Taxi** (727-546-4955), C800 49th St N; and **St. Pete Taxi** (727-520-8831), 3160 46th Ave N.

PARKING Parking is a major issue for visitors to downtown St. Petersburg. There is a lot of free parking, especially along Beach Blvd, but it goes quickly. During the day your stay is limited to 90 minutes (8 AM–7 PM) and at night to 3 hours (7 PM–8 AM). And they *do* enforce it to the minute—you'll see the blinking golf carts of the parking authority enforcement officers zipping all over town. It's a very walkable city, so leave your car at your accommodations and hoof it, or pick one of the centrally located parking garages and keep it there while you explore. Street parking is free in Gulfport and virtually nonexistent in St. Pete Beach. Beach parking packs a per-hour metered charge, varying by location.

PUBLIC REST ROOMS The classy architecture might let you slip right past without noticing the public rest rooms at the corner of **Bayshore and Second Ave NE,** next to the Museum of History, downtown St. Petersburg.

MEDICAL EMERGENCIES **St. Petersburg General Hospital** (727-384-1414), 6500 38th Ave N, St. Petersburg.

✸ To See

AQUARIUM

St. Petersburg

A nonprofit marine education center, **The Pier Aquarium** (727-895-7437; www.pieraquarium.org), 800 Second Ave NE, is part of **The Pier** complex (see *Attractions*) and is staffed by marine science students from local colleges. Habitats represented include Tampa Bay, California's kelp forests, and coral reefs of the Caribbean and Pacific Ocean. Children and adults alike will enjoy their many hands-on programs. Fee; free admission to all on Sunday.

St. Petersburg/Clearwater Area Convention & Visitors Bureau

VIEW FROM THE TOWER AT WEEDON ISLAND PRESERVE

ARCHEOLOGICAL SITES

St. Petersburg

At **Weedon Island Preserve** (727-453-6500; www.stpete.org/weedon.htm), 1500 Weedon Island Dr, explore the ancient cultures of Florida. In 1924 a Smithsonian Institution archeological dig led by J. Walter Fawkes discovered artifacts dated between A.D. 200 and 1000. Learn the story uncovered by these early researchers at the Learning Center, which explores the ten-thousand-year history of the island's peoples, and then walk the boardwalks and trails to immerse yourself in the landscape of mangrove forests, salt flats, and upland hammocks.

Along 1620 Park St N, a large midden of oyster shells bears this large hand-lettered sign: "HERE LANDED **PANFILO DE NARVAEZ,** APRIL 15, 1528." Tucked between residential lots, this archeological site (now on private land) was once an ancient village, and from this site, the Spanish explorer Narvaez is credited with being the first European to launch an exploration of the North American continent. Please respect private property and view the site from the sidewalk. The Central Gulf Coast Archaeological Society has a detailed report online at www.cgcas.org/narvaez/1to8.htm.

ART GALLERIES

Gulfport

At **The Art Village** (727-459-1963; www.artvillagevoice.com), 2908–2914 Beach Blvd, historic cottages surround a welcoming courtyard where there's live music every weekend and working artists give classes outdoors. Call 727-344-3711 for information on Gallery Walks and Saturday Strolls. ♂ One prominent gallery in the village is **Makin' Art** (727-323-4938), 2914 Beach Blvd, where artist Nancy Gable believes that art should be hands-on. "Touch everything!" she told me, and then pointed out "celebration sticks" made from fractured art reborn anew. Her creativity shines in a combination of common items and found objects, with sticks and pottery becoming part of lamps and chairs, paintings morphing into mosaics—creativity in motion. She encourages her visitors, even the kids, to touch the art. If something breaks, no problem! It'll become part of her newest work. Down the street, bold, whimsical characters dominate the **E-Z Gallery** (727-345-9495), 3119 Beach Blvd, where the iguanas caught my eye.

St. Petersburg

St. Petersburg is truly a city of the arts, with more than 25 galleries in the downtown district. The nonprofit **Downtown Arts Association** (www.stpetearts.com) arranges gallery walks the second Saturday of each month until 9 PM. Contact the DAA for a brochure and map detailing their member galleries. Here's a sampler of what I saw while walking around downtown.

Specializing in representational art, **Alla Prima Fine Art** (727-825-0200), 695 Central Ave, showcases the best of local artists. In *Prairie Park*, plein air painter Linda Blondheim captured a striking impressionist image of palmetto-dotted Paynes Prairie; Michelle Gibson's *Sasha* brings together 4,700 hand-cut tiles to create a tiger.

Part gallery, part shop, part classroom space, **The Arts Center** (727-822-7872; www.theartscenter.org), 719 Central Ave, offers demonstrations of fine arts, hands-on workshops for members (memberships start at $45 annually), and rotating exhibits of members' work in four classy galleries.

Florida Craftsmen Gallery (727-821-7391; www.floridacraftsmen.net), 501 Central Ave, features fine art for collectors, and have showcased their members' work in all media for nearly two decades. Special exhibitions bring in fine-craft artists from around Florida.

Art glass appeals to my senses, and so I was drawn to the **Glass Canvas Gallery** (727-821-6767), 146 Second St N, a dazzling celebration of the fluid flow of this extraordinary medium, with swirls of color offered as sculpture à la Chihuly as well as more formally structured vases and bowls.

Red Cloud (727-821-5824), 208 Beach Dr NE, showcases Native American arts, from dynamic ceramics to traditional masks, Southwestern pottery, and ceremonial headdresses.

The **St. Petersburg Clay Company** (727-896-2529; www.stpeteclay.com), 420 22nd St S, is the largest working clay studio and gallery in the Southeast, where you can buy finished art or raw supplies, rent a studio, attend a workshop, or sign up for hands-on private lessons.

The Studio @ 620 (727-895-6620; www.thestudioat620.com), 620 First Ave S, brings together local artists and their audience to celebrate the creative process. Kicking off with an exhibit of 100 Years of African-American Quilting, this newcomer to the local arts scene seeks to build bridges between the visual arts, music, poetry, theater, film, dance, and dialogue.

Studio Encanto (727-821-2959), 209 First St N, showcases internationally collected artists as well as local talent such as Barry Nehr, whose painting of an egret in a cypress swamp stole my heart, and Monika Wilson with her mosaics. Owner and artist Esther M. Scott creates colorful painted tables, stained glass, and tiles.

ATTRACTIONS The Pier (727-821-6164), 800 Second Ave, St. Petersburg, is one of the city's oldest landmarks and unique in its inverted five-story design. It's been through several permutations over the years, established first by founding father Peter Demens in 1899, whose Orange Belt Railroad ran down a half-mile wharf. The first public pier opened in 1895, but most classic postcards show the "Million Dollar Pier" built in 1926, which was torn down in 1973 to create today's unusual structure. Housing a variety of shops (see *Selective Shopping*) and restaurants (see *Eating Out*), The Pier is also home to **The Pier Aquarium** (see *Aquarium*) and an observation deck with an excellent view of Tampa Bay. Parking costs $3 (valet optional for an extra charge), and a free shuttle runs between the parking lots and The Pier.

BASEBALL The region's own Major League Baseball team, the **Tampa Bay Devil Rays** (727-825-3137 or 1-888-FANRAYS; www.devilrays.com), One Tropicana Dr, plays at Tropicana Field near downtown St. Petersburg.

HISTORIC SITES

Pass-A-Grille
During the Civil War, **Egmont Key** (offshore from Fort De Soto) served as an outpost for the Union Blockading Squadron as they played cat-and-mouse with Confederate blockade runners. It also housed a refugee camp for Confederate defectors, guarded by and eventually evacuated by the Union navy. The operational lighthouse, constructed in 1848 and open for tours, is surrounded by the brick streets of the ghost town of **Fort Dade,** built during the Spanish-American War. If you're a birder, bring your binoculars—Egmont Key is also a National Wildlife Refuge for migratory species. Egmont Key is an island, however, so approach is either by your own boat or commercial ferry service. ✍ Departing from Fort De Soto Park at 10 and 11 AM daily, the **Tampa Bay Ferry** (727-867-6569; www.hubbardsmarina.com) costs $15 adults, $7.50 children. The ferry also runs snorkel trips over the underwater ruins of Fort Dade ($10); rental of snorkeling equipment available.

St. Petersburg
Many historic buildings remain in **downtown St. Petersburg** (www .stpete.org/Landmarks1.htm) as residences and businesses, including many of the shops along Central Avenue, which was the city's 1920s boom "Main Street." There are also several designated residential historic districts, including Granada Terrace around Coffee Pot Bayou, Old Southeast, and Roser Park, all developed prior to 1926. Built in 1924 and thoroughly renovated in more recent times, **The Coliseum** (727-892-5202;

EXPLORING EGMONT KEY
St. Petersburg/Clearwater Area Convention & Visitors Bureau

FORT DE SOTO

At **Fort De Soto Park** (see *Beaches*), explore the remains of Spanish-American War–era Fort De Soto, built by the federal government at the urging of railroad tycoon Henry Plant, who managed to also convince the government to use his Tampa Bay Hotel (see *Tampa* and *Hillsborough County*) as headquarters and departure point for troops headed to battles throughout the Caribbean. Built in 1898, the brick road along the battery now leads you down a historical trail, passing storehouses and living quarters completed in 1906. Stairs enable you to climb atop Battery Laidley for a sweeping view of the bay. The army post included barracks, the mess hall, and 27 other buildings. By the time men were stationed at the fort, the war was over. During World War I, the heavy mortars installed to protect Tampa were dismounted and shipped to San Diego. Twenty-four men remained on duty, never needing to fire a shot. In 1922 the army decided that the forts were no longer needed for Florida's coastal defense. The island lay fallow and wave-battered for many years, used as a quarantine station and then a bombing range before the army sold the land back to Pinellas County. The county park opened to the public in 1963.

www.stpete.org/coliseum.htm), 535 Fourth Ave, hosts major festivals and other special events. Another downtown site of interest is **Albert Whitted Municipal Airport** (www.stpete.org/air.htm), the site of the world's first commercial aviation flight in 1914, with scheduled service by National Airlines kicking off in 1934. Off the beaten path a little, look for **Admiral Farragut Naval Academy,** 501 Park St N, which started out as one of the region's original resort hotels, the Jungle Country Club, opened in 1926. Despite the exotic furnishings, it went bankrupt quickly and reopened as the academy in 1945. Despite the loss of many of the boom-era hotels, there are two nearby still in business and welcoming guests—the Don CeSar and the Renaissance Vinoy Resort and Golf Club (see *Hotels, Motels, and Resorts*).

MUSEUMS

Gulfport

At the **Gulfport Historical Museum** (727-327-0505), 5301 28th Ave S, housed in a 1912 Methodist church, learn the history of this community founded in 1867 by a Civil War veteran and incorporated 20 years later as Disston City by developer Hamilton Disston as the largest incorporated town in Florida.

St. Petersburg

& One of the nation's largest, the **Florida Holocaust Museum** (727-820-0100; www.flholocaustmuseum.org), 55 Fifth St S, humanizes the story of the 11 million who died in the Holocaust. Start your tour with a video that connects the horror of yesterday to the hate and prejudice faced by teens of today, and then follow the displays through a presentation of facts and figures to the Memory Wall, where in the open gallery you'll find the museum's centerpiece, boxcar #113 0695-5, which transported prisoners to Auschwitz. In the Court of Witnesses, experience an audiovisual presentation by survivors and liberators. Be sure to head upstairs for several changing galleries; I found the presentation Hitler's Soldiers in the Sunshine State particularly interesting since I knew very little about this chapter of Florida history—there were many POW camps in Florida, and prisoners harvested citrus and cut sugarcane during the war. As you exit, pop into the gift shop to browse history books and memorabilia. Open 10–5 Mon–Fri, noon–5 Sat–Sun. Adults $8, seniors $7, students $3. Audio wands available for an additional charge.

& ♂ A Smithsonian affiliate, the **Florida International Museum** (727-822-3693; www.floridamuseum.org), 100 Second St N, features rotating exhibits every few months. On my visit, I stepped into the 60s through a collection of vintage Barbie and her accessories, but I truly felt at home inside *The Cuban Missile Crisis: When the Cold War Got Hot*. I had chills listening to the crackly radio (". . . increases the likelihood of a nuclear war . . .") while walking through a kitchen not unlike my own from that era. The timeline swept me into a replica fallout shelter and, in an unexpected twist, a gallery of contemporary Cuban art. Open 9–5 Mon–Thu, 9–8 Fri, 9–5 Sat, and 11–5 Sun. Fee.

& Considered a top destination for lovers of the arts, the **Museum of Fine Arts** (727-896-2667), 255 Beach Dr NE, features world-class exhibitions, such as the recent Monet's London. Their comprehensive collection of more than four thousand works includes many French masters, from Cezanne to Renoir, and American artists such as Thomas Moran and Georgia O'Keeffe. Since 1965 they've showcased their masterworks in a plush setting akin to a grand home. Adults $12, seniors and students with ID $10, ages 7–18 $5, under 7 free.

& ♂ At the **St. Petersburg Museum of History** (727-894-1052; www.stpete museumofhistory.org), 335 Second Ave NE, history isn't just a thing of the past. Start your tour with a seven-minute historical overview video, and then let the interactive galleries take you on a walk through time, featuring touch-me artifacts such as a 1913 trolley car and an 1870 general store, as well as a canoe from the Tocobaga, who lived on the shores of Tampa Bay when the first Spanish conquistadors arrived in the 1500s. In the third-oldest historic museum in Florida, you'll learn a great deal about early aviation, the grand hotels of the 1920s boom, and St. Petersburg's many little-known historic neighborhoods. Open 10–5 Mon–Sat, 1–5 Sun; closed major holidays. Fee.

& Experience the master of surrealism at the **Salvador Dalí Museum** (727-823-3767 or 1-800-442-3254; www.salvadordalimuseum.org), 1000

AVIATION EXHIBIT AT THE ST. PETERSBURG MUSEUM OF HISTORY
St. Petersburg/Clearwater Area Convention & Visitors Bureau

ONE OF THE MANY PAINTINGS AT THE SALVADOR DALÍ MUSEUM

Third St S, which houses the world's largest collection of works by Dalí. Six of his 18 masterworks are housed in the museum, where curators offer detailed interpretation of the awe-inspiring canvases. There are more than 1,300 pieces in the permanent collection, displayed on a rotating basis. In a recent display of Dalí's commercial images, it was amusing to note his work appearing in 1950s advertisements for ladies hosiery and on the cover of a Jackie Gleason album. Boldly colored walls provide a backdrop to art that still surprises with sometimes delightful, sometimes disturbing, images. Open 9:30–5:30 Mon–Sat, Thu until 8 PM, noon–5:30 Sun; closed Thanksgiving and Christmas. Adults $14, seniors $10, students (with ID) $9, ages 4–9 $3.50, under 4 free.

&. ✐ One of Florida's oldest science centers, **The Science Center of Pinellas County** (727-384-0027; www.sciencecenterofpinellas.com), 7701 22nd Ave N, showcases a marine-life room with a 600-gallon touch tank, an outdoor 16th-century Indian village, and for budding stargazers, the Minolta MediaGlobe planetarium and a powerful Meade 16-inch telescope. The gift shop is fun, too! It's a perfect place to take the kids. Open 9–4 Mon–Fri, 10–4 Sat. Fee.

RAILROADIANA Were it not for the railroads, St. Petersburg might still be a sleepy little village by the bay. But the Orange Belt Railroad and Henry Plant's grand Plant System brought major commerce to the waterfront. Little remains from that era save the **Seaboard Coastline Railroad Station,** 420 22nd St S, which was built in 1926 for the Tampa and Gulf Coast Railroad, the second major player in the region.

✳ To Do

BICYCLING A green ribbon stretching from Tarpon Springs to St. Petersburg, the **Pinellas Trail** (see *Greenways*) provides bicyclists with nearly 34 miles of stress-free cruising, connecting communities and green space throughout the county. A free detailed map and guidebook can be downloaded off the web site or ordered from the county to plan your adventure. Southern trailheads are at Trail Head Park in St. Petersburg on Fairfield Ave between 37th St S and 40th St S, and north of Pasadena at Azalea Park on 72nd St N. In Gulfport, rent your bikes at **Tropical Cycles** (727-463-7602), 2908 Beach Blvd, where they also rent surreys and beach cruisers for checking out the waterfront.

BIRDING In **Granada Terrace,** herons and other wading birds flock to roost at sunset to an island off Coffee Pot Blvd. **Sawgrass Lake Park** (see *Parks*) is an excellent place to watch wading birds along the canals and osprey swooping over the lake. But the region's hot spot is **Egmont Key** (see *Historic Sites*)—it's a National Wildlife Refuge devoted to migratory birds.

BOATING The mangrove-lined shores, islands, and channels of Tampa Bay are popular with pleasure boaters throughout the region. In Gulfport, dock your craft at the **Gulfport Municipal Marina** (727-893-1071), 4630 29th Ave, an easy walk from the business district. In St. Petersburg, **Salt Creek Marina** (727-821-5482), 107 15th Ave SE, is a popular option on the south side of downtown near the Dalí Museum, but the convenient-to-everything marina is at the bayfront near **The Pier**—the **St. Petersburg Municipal Marina** (727-893-7329), 300 Second Ave SE. If you're looking to rent a boat, do it here at **Solar Surrey Boat Rentals** (727-898-2628 or 1-888-898-BOAT; www.solarsurrey.com), with electric watercraft so quiet you can slip right up behind dolphins. These 21-foot boats have a roof, CD/cassette, center dining area, and refrigerator and can be run bareboat or with a captain. Prices start at $65/hour, $195/half day, seating up to 10.

FAMILY ACTIVITIES ♿ ✐ At **Great Explorations: The Children's Museum** (727-821-8992; www.greatexplorations.org), 1925 Fourth St N, St. Petersburg, it's all about learning through exploring with play. Sail a ship, design your own robot, build a race car and race against your friends, or join in a workshop. Admission $8 ages 12 and up, $7 ages 3–11 (and seniors), under 3 free. Open 10–4:30 Mon–Sat, noon–4:30 Sun.

FISHING Recycling the old, the **Old Skyway Bridge** (727-865-0668), paralleling the Sunshine Skyway, provides a long linear state park from which to fish. Drop a line at The Pier in St. Petersburg, or join the crowd at the Fort De Soto pier. Offshore and flats fishing is hot, too—check in at the local marinas (see *Boating*) for an experienced guide.

GAMING The world's oldest continuously operating greyhound track is **Derby Lane** (727-812-3339), 10490 Gandy Blvd, established in 1925. Open Jan 2–Jun 30 for greyhound races and simulcast thoroughbred racing.

GOLF The par 72 **Mangrove Bay Golf Course** (727-893-7800; www.stpete.org/mangrove.htm), 875 62nd Ave NE, offers 18 holes of USGA championship golf on 180 well-maintained acres. Professional PGA lessons are available at this top-notch course, named one of the Top 100 most women-friendly golf courses by *Golf for Women* magazine.

HIKING In such an urban area, you wouldn't expect much hiking, but regional parks offer some beautiful boardwalks and a few natural surface trails though unspoiled habitats. At **Boyd Hill Nature Park** (see *Parks*), short nature trail loops lead from a paved path into a variety of habitats along Lake Maggiore.

Fort De Soto Park (see *Beaches*) offers three short hiking trails—the Arrowhead Nature Trail is my favorite, leading to sweeping views along the bay. **Sawgrass Lake Park** (see *Parks*) has a mile's worth of boardwalk through a lush floodplain forest. In addition to the boardwalks at **Weedon Island Preserve** (see *Archeological Sites*), you'll find nearly 4 miles' worth of trails following mangrove-lined levees and slicing through wet flatwoods.

PADDLING Launch your kayak at Soliders' Hole, **Fort De Soto Park** (see *Beaches*), for an intrepid exploration of the mangrove channels leading out to calm waters around the park's islands in Tampa Bay. A 2.3-mile marked canoe trail leads you through the maze, and rentals are available on-site.

SAILING For more than 40 years, Steve and Doris Colgate's **Offshore Sailing School** (1-800-221-4326; www.offshore-sailing.com) has trained students how to raise a sail, catch the wind, and then tack back to port, with a series of in-depth hands-on courses that turn landlubbers into live-aboards. In St. Pete the Mansion House B&B (see *Lodging*) works in conjunction with Offshore Sailing School to wean you from land to sea, combining a downtown stay with a daily workout on the water until you're ready to cast off and cruise. Offered year-round, Learn to Sail courses run from three to nine days; check the web site for seasonal pricing.

TOURS Cruise around the bay in a true military classic—the Del Mar U.S. Navy Launch, circa 1967, as piloted by Capt. Brion Kerlin on his **Bay Tours** (727-656-0700). This intimate tour seats six, and depending on your group's interest, the captain can give you a narrated tour of the St. Pete shoreline and its history, a romantic starlight cruise, a custom-tailored trip to a deserted island, a trip in search of dolphins, or a jaunt to a funky Florida waterfront restaurant. Reservations are a must. Rates are based on occupancy and time and start at $15/adult.

✳ Green Space

BEACHES **St. Pete Beach** is a destination for thousands of sun seekers, but most access the beach by stepping out the front door of their motel, condo, or cottage. There are no county parks along the beachfront, just public access points. At tiny **Gulfport,** there's a pretty public beach on Boca Ciega Bay, right along Shore Blvd, overlooking the line of condos on St. Pete Beach. **Fort De Soto Park** (727-582-2267; www.pinellascounty.org/park/05_Ft_DeSoto.htm), 3500 Pinellas Bayway S, Tierra Verde, hangs into Tampa Bay like a huge anchor on the map. Its 7 miles of isolated beachfront on five islands are considered one of the top beaches in the continental United States.

BOTANICAL GARDENS

St. Petersburg

Lose yourself among a forest of fronds at the **Gizella Kopsick Palm Arboretum** (727-893-7335; www.stpete.org/palm.htm), North Shore Dr at 10th Ave NE, a 2-acre park with more than 300 palms and cycads showcasing more than 70 species, all well labeled for botanical enthusiasts. Free; adjacent free parking.

&. ♪ **Sunken Gardens** (727-551-3100; www.stpete.org/sunken.htm), 1825 Fourth St N, is a Florida classic more than a century old, a sensory experience full of fragrances and colors, the burble of water and the play of sunlight through a virtual jungle of foliage. In 1903 local plumber George Turner Sr. began a tropical garden cascading down the slopes of an ancient sinkhole. In 1935 it officially opened as a tourist attraction, and by the 1950s it had a resident colony of flamingos, brilliant tropical macaws, and other wildlife complementing the winding paths through the lush forest. This quiet spot is still a true Florida treasure, a place to get lost under the canopy of trees and enjoy the well-maintained gardens. Best of all, the photo spots from the 1960s are still in place! Open 10–4:30 Mon–Sat, noon–4:30 Sun. Adults $8, seniors $6, children $4.

GREENWAYS The **Pinellas Trail** (727-464-8200; www.co.pinellas.fl.us/BCC/trailgd/trailgd.htm), 600 Cleveland St, Suite 750, Clearwater, is one of the busiest greenways in Florida, stretching from Tarpon Springs south to St. Petersburg and roughly paralleling the route of Alt US 19.

PARKS Stroll the trails at **Boyd Hill Nature Park** (727-893-7326), 1101 Country Club Way S, to enjoy nearly 250 acres of natural habitats and cultivated gardens along the shores of Lake Maggiore. The paved Main Trail loops around the outer edge of the park, and numerous short loops lead off it to showcase specific environments, such as a willow marsh, sand pine scrub, and floodplain forest. A former zoo, the park also showcases raptors in an aviary near the entrance and provides exhibits on native habitats at the Lake Maggiore Environmental Education Center. Closed Monday. Fee.

Protecting nearly 400 acres of wetlands, **Sawgrass Lake Park** (727-526-3020), 7400 25th St N, is an oasis of green along I-275 and the Pinellas Park border. Boardwalks lead through a red maple swamp, and you're guaranteed to see alligators and soft-shell turtles from the observation deck. A nature center at the parking area introduces the habitats and their residents.

Thanks to William L. Straub, the editor of the *St. Petersburg Times* in 1909, nearly 7 miles of Tampa Bay's waterfront has been preserved in a string of parks through St. Petersburg, with its northern anchor **Vinoy Park,** a delightful village green beneath a shady canopy of oaks.

WILD PLACES A tangled jungle of mangroves along Tampa Bay, **Weedon Island Preserve** (see *Archeological Sites*) provides this area's only place to wander into the wild, where the whine of highway traffic is replaced by the whine of mosquitoes. Nearly 4 miles of trails wind through tunnels of mangroves and sometimes-flooded flatwoods. Stop by the visitors center to get the full picture of the rich prehistory of this site, and walk the (not-so-wild) boardwalks to an observation tower that provides a panorama of Tampa Bay and views of both downtown Tampa and St. Petersburg.

✻ Lodging

BED & BREAKFASTS

Gulfport 33707

🕯 ▼ Blending the exotic with the historic, **Sea Breeze Manor** (727-343-4445 or 1-888-343-4445; www
.seabreezemanor.com), 5701 Shore
Blvd, is a place to relax. It appeals on
many sensory levels, from its globe-
trotting island decor and comfortable
beds to each room's private balcony or
porch catching the sea breeze off
adjacent Gulfport Beach on Boca
Ciega Bay. This 1923 Tudor features
five massive well-appointed rooms
with television, VCR, CD player, and
wireless Internet access, plus two cottages on the courtyard ($145–160).
Everyone in town knows innkeeper
Lori Rosso, and she delights in letting
you know the fun places to eat, drink,
and shop. Enjoy a leisurely home-
cooked breakfast on the main balcony
overlooking the waterfront, and leave
your car parked—everything you'll
want to see and do is an easy walk
down the street.

St. Petersburg 33701

▼ Offering tranquility in a quiet residential neighborhood, the **Bayboro
House** (727-823-4955 or 1-877-823-
4955; www.bayborohousebandb.com),
1719 Beach Dr SE, boasts a great
unobstructed view of Tampa Bay
along a natural waterfront where dolphins and pelicans play. Opened in
1982, it was the city's first bed &
breakfast, a grand Victorian with big
bay windows and period furnishings,
built by Charles Harvey, the developer of the neighborhood. The adjacent
cottage was the sales office for the
subdivision. Proud owners Barbara
and Charles Mattern are developing
conference center space adjoining the

pool and Jacuzzi with the intent of
offering intimate retreats and workshops. Sisters and girlfriends traveling
together will appreciate the separate
beds in the Carriage House, where a
writing desk beckons, while gentlemen traveling alone like the Harvey
Room, a grand but gentlemanly space
with a great view of the pool and bay.
Take your pick from 10 units, including the cottage, with seasonal rates
from $129 to $275.

▼ **Inn at the Bay** (727-822-1700
or 1-888-873-2122; www.innatthe
bay.com), 126 Fourth Ave NE, is
another success story of saving a historic structure—in this case, the oldest continuously occupied rooming
house in St. Petersburg, established
by Anna Morrison in 1910. Renovation wrapped up in 2001, and you
can now enjoy the results—each of
the 12 units ($145–280) has a uniquely
Florida theme, like the Siesta Key,
the Manatee, and the Lighthouse,
and most come with a whirlpool for
two. Children older than eight welcome, but with the romantic ambiance
of these rooms (and the buttery-soft
robes), you'll want to leave them at
home.

✎ 🐾 ▼ A 1920s hotel abandoned to a
crumbling neighborhood, **La Veranda B&B** (727-824-9997 or 1-800-484-
8423; www.laverandabb.com), 111
Fifth Ave N, became the phoenix that
put the surrounding community back
on its feet, thanks to the efforts of
Nancy Mayer, who took over the
building in 1995 with "a passion to
restore houses." Parts of the complex
date from the 1890s and offer vintage
charm—low doorframes and water-
glass windows. All five rooms ($99–
250) have private exterior entrances,
unique period decor, and a large

veranda for relaxing. I luxuriated in the roomy Cinnabar, enjoying a bath in the claw-foot tub—bath salts and candles included. The resident cats will join you for breakfast under the ivy trellis, and what a breakfast—I enjoyed the raisin French toast with apples and walnuts with a citrus granita.

▼ Feel pampered at the **Mansion House B&B and The Courtyard on Fifth** (727-821-9391 or 1-800-274-7520; www.mansionbandb.com), 105 Fifth Ave NE, where a comfortable bed piled with pillows awaits. The first mayor of St. Petersburg, David Moffett, lived in the Mansion House, which in 1901 anchored the development of the Northeast District, just up the street from the Vinoy Park Hotel, in which he was a partner. This home, the adjoining Kemphurst (1904), and a carriage house are clustered around a private brick courtyard with a swimming pool and hot tub. Each house has an upstairs library— and you know how we writers love libraries—plus the parlor and kitchen areas to mingle, or enjoy the intimacy of your well-appointed room with its polished hardwood floor. Original art from resident artist Marva Simpson and handmade bedding by Pat Berry grace the 12 individually themed rooms ($109–230), but I was most grateful for the antique writing desk in mine.

Now here's a charmer with an interesting story—the **Sunset Bay Inn** (727-896-6701 or 1-800-794-5133; www.sunsetbayinn.com), 635 Bay St NE, was the 1940s childhood home of Martha Bruce, who with her husband, Bob, acquired and renovated the house into a bed & breakfast in 1996. In this 1911 Colonial Revival, there are eight themed units ($150–270),

including two in the carriage house, ranging from the elegant, masculine, golf-themed Augusta Room to Marthasville, with bright candy stripes, a skylight, and a claw-foot tub, to the elegant Monterey Suite with its Jacuzzi and mini kitchen.

CAMPGROUNDS

St. Petersburg 33708

☘ Ready for your own private seaside view? Pick the right campsite at **Fort De Soto Park** (see *Beaches*), and you'll have an unimpeded view of where Tampa Bay meets the Gulf of Mexico. Each spot (water and electric) is shaded by tall Australian pines ($25). Pets accepted in certain campsites.

Hidden along a mangrove-lined bayou, the **St. Petersburg/Madeira Beach KOA Resort** (1-800-562-7714; www.koa.com/where/fl/09144 .htm), 5400 95th St N, is an appealing spot to set up camp and see the local attractions, with tent sites ($32–47), full hookup sites ($44–74), and Kamping Kabins with air-conditioning ($61–84) available.

HOTELS, MOTELS, AND RESORTS

Gulfport 33707

♿ The **Peninsula Inn & Spa** (727-346-9800; www.innspa.net), 2937 Beach Blvd, evokes the grand adventures of British explorers in the 1800s. Karen and Bob Chapman finished renovations of this century-old hospital building in 2003, and the results are stunning. Climb the staircase or use a restored original elevator to reach your room, one of 11 well-appointed units, each with a uniquely themed decor. Some, like the Serengeti, are two- or three-room suites with a sitting room and bedroom;

others, like the Nile, are smaller but just as elegant. Enjoy sleigh beds, cable television, wireless Internet, child-sitting services, two fine restaurants (see *Dining Out*), and a full-service spa on the premises, all within an easy walk of all of Gulfport. $129–245 in-season.

St. Pete Beach 33706

Enjoy your own village by the sea at **Beach Haven Villas** (727-367-8642; www.beachhavenvillas.com), 4980 Gulf Blvd, a 1950s motel with 18 units and plenty of charm. This Superior Small Lodging offers small but bright rooms with classic tiled baths in a mix of standard rooms and efficiencies ($58–147), each with a VCR in the room. The heated pool overlooks the ocean.

The **Bon-Aire Resort Motel** (727-360-5596; www.bonaireresort.com), 4350 Gulf Blvd, is a Florida classic circa 1953, an open rectangle with rooms facing the pool and beach. It's been in the same family for more than 45 years. The efficiencies and standard units ($59–144) have that 50s charm, and the baths are large for the era. Each kitchenette has a mini stove, micro fridge, coffeemaker, and dishes.

& ℐ Painted concrete pathways lead you through the appealing **Plaza Beach Resort** (727-367-2791 or 1-800-257-8998; www.plazabeach.com), 4506 Gulf Blvd, a family-owned motel where each kitchenette ($75–148) has a full fridge, and the rooms have big picture windows. The delightful patio area leading to the beach has a heated pool, shuffleboard, and life-size chess board along with a picnic area in sight of the sea. ❧ Their sister property, the **Bayview Plaza Resort** (727-367-2791 or 1-800-257-8998; www.thebay viewplaza.com), 4321 Gulf Blvd,

offers fully equipped kitchens, daily housekeeping, and a private pier with dockage for guests.

St. Petersburg 33701

& A historic landmark set right across from the waterfront at Vinoy Park, the intimate **Grayl's Hotel** (727-896-1080 or 1-888-508-4448; www.grayls hotel.com), 340 Beach Blvd NE, conveys a sense of privacy while offering rooms and suites with tasteful decor evoking both St. Pete's hip present and the past—look for the antique radio in the corner. This 1922 apartment building was once so dilapidated-looking it was almost condemned, but the Grayl family stepped in more than a decade ago and coaxed a phoenix from the ashes. The results are stunning and well worth the room rate (30 units, $89–250, most with a separate kitchen area).

Opened on New Year's Day 1926, the **Renaissance Vinoy Resort and Golf Club** (727-894-1000 or 1-888-303-4430; www.marriott.com/property/propertypage/TPASR), 501 Fifth Ave N, is a fanciful bayside destination with a blend of Mediterranean Revival and Moorish architecture. During the 1940s, soldiers occupied the hotel for rest and recuperation. The hotel has since been fully restored to its original elegance, and provide up-to-date amenities such as high-speed Internet access, fluffy robes, and VCRs. There are seven restaurants and lounges, a fitness center, day spa, and heated pool on site. A complimentary shuttle takes guests to the beach. When the hotel opened, its rates were the highest in the region ($20 back then), and they're still up there—unless you find a special discount, rates begin at more than $250 a night, with parking (valet or self) adding to the bite.

 ♿ ✿ 🐾 The **Don CeSar Beach Resort & Spa** (727-360-1881 or 1-800-282-1116; www.doncesar.com), 3400 Gulf Blvd, the pink palace on the beach, is the quintessential seaside resort, the 1926 creation of Thomas J. Rowe and a grand reminder of the Florida boom, on the register of the National Trust for Historic Preservation. But it wasn't always so. This grand dame almost ended up demolished due to neglect. Despite its parade of celebrity guests, including the New York Yankees in the 1930s trying out the new concept of spring training in Florida, and F. Scott Fitzgerald taking Zelda for a jaunt in the wilderness—for it was truly wilderness back then—this 277-room hotel didn't last long. After Rowe died in 1943 and his heirs divested themselves of the property, the Don became a rest and relaxation center for recuperating servicemen, and then a Veteran's Administration Hospital for 22 years. In 1967 the gutted building was abandoned; several years later, local resident June Hurley Brown started a "Save the Don" campaign. With $30 million in renovations, the hotel celebrated its grand reopening in 1973. Little of the original interior remains, but the re-creation of the hotel's grandeur is striking. On the fifth floor, the marble fountain that once graced the lobby was the meeting place of Rowe and the love of his life, his mistress, Maritana. Their ghosts are said to meet there still. Employees insist that Rowe, who breathed his last on the main floor, continues to watch over the hotel; his presence in a white suit and hat has been noted whenever a new set of renovations are under way.

Now part of the Loew's family, the hotel offers family- and pet-friendly amenities in a world-class setting. Enjoy afternoon tea in the lobby, or kick back poolside at the Sea Porch Café. Swim in two oceanside pools with piped-in underwater music, or relax on the beautiful beach itself. The standard rooms offer a 1920s feel with modern sensibilities, including high-speed and wireless Internet access, and rates start at a reasonable $149.

✳ Where to Eat

DINING OUT

Gulfport

Enjoy fine French cuisine at **La Cote Basque** (727-321-6888), 3104 Beach Blvd S, where veal and poultry dominate the menu in such classics as chicken Cordon Bleu, veal Piccata, and Wiener schnitzel. Entrées are $11–18, and beef lovers will enjoy the fine chateaubriand, beef Wellington, and filet mignon ($24–40).

♿ Intimate elegance reigns at **Six Tables,** the signature restaurant of the Peninsula Inn & Spa (see *Hotels, Motels, and Resorts*). Each evening at 7, Chef Thomas Rufin greets his guests and presents a selection of seven fine entrées such as chateaubriand, venison, and rack of lamb as the centerpiece of a seven-course meal with intermezzos ($70 per person; reservations required). For those with tighter budgets but refined tastes, enjoy the globetrotting British Colonial ambiance of the **Palm Terrace,** either out on the porch or in at the well-stocked bar, with live music most nights and ethnic-themed buffets several times weekly.

St. Pete Beach

Fine dining is a tradition at the **Don Cesar** (see *Hotels, Motels, and Resorts*), and in this classic resort, the place to dine is the **Maritana Grille** (727-360-1882), 3400 Gulf Blvd, named for J. Thomas Rowe's greatest love. Floribbean cuisine, that fusion of Florida Cracker and Florida Keys, is all the rage, with fresh-grilled fish prepared atop a pecan and cherry wood grill. Surrounded by thousands of gallons of saltwater aquariums, you'll feel immersed in the sea as you dine on specialties such as orange habanero barbecued Gulf fish, panseared sea scallops, and dry-aged strip steak ($28–38). Reservations recommended, especially if you'd like to dine at the Chef's Table in the kitchen. One major departure from the past: jackets not required.

St. Petersburg

One of the city's oldest restaurants, **The Garden** (727-896-3800), 217 Central Ave S, offers intimate indoor dining or a shady brick courtyard beneath a banyan tree, with creative entrées such as crab stuffed grouper or chicken Boursin ($8–17) and assorted tapas offered à la carte or as a platter of the day ($15).

EATING OUT

Gulfport

❦ ♂ Several folks suggested I try the signature crab cakes at the funky little **Backfin Blue Café** (727-343-2583), 2913 Beach Blvd; I'm glad I did—two of these big balls of flaky crab (with very little breading to hold them together and just the right amount of spice) plus a heaping mound of garlic mashed potatoes and a tasty tomato-artichoke salad filled me right up. Wine list, top-notch beers, and dressy desserts, too, if you save room. Entrées $10–19, and a kid's menu with PB&J as one of several choices. Closed Tue.

H. T. Kanes Beach Pub & Restaurant (727-347-6299), 5501 Shore Blvd, serves up Ipswitch whole-belly fried clams in a roll ($8) or as a meal ($13) as well as the "best burger in town" ($4–6, depending on toppings). Grouper, catfish, shrimp, steak, and chicken round out the dinner menu. Lunch sandwiches run $4 and up.

Hot is hot at the **Pierhouse Grill and Pepper Co.** (727-322-1741), 5401 Shore Blvd, where the "Wall of Flame" celebrates diversity in hot sauces, including Manny's Monkey Butt, the house special. Enjoy great steaks, grouper tacos, and spicy numbers such as Reuben's Crusty Balls (can you believe corned beef, Swiss, and sauerkraut deep-fried?) and Cherry Bomb Chips (yup, deep-fried hot cherry pepper rings). All these and more creative offerings for lunch and dinner ($6–15), with a killer waterfront view to boot.

Pass-A-Grille

Kick back dockside at the **Sea Critters Café** (727-360-3706; www.sea critterscafe.com), 2007 Pass-A-Grille Way, recommended by locals and visitors alike. Fresh margaritas complement tasty offerings such as risotto scallops Rockefeller, lobster pasta, crab salad, and grouper Reuben ($8–20).

Take-out's the thing at **Shaner's Land & Sea Market** (727-367-4292), 2000 Pass-A-Grille Way, with hot and cold sandwiches to go ($2–6), entrées such as crawfish and pasta or pot roast ($6–8), and platters to feed a crowd.

St. Pete Beach
With its award-winning entrées, the **Hurricane Seafood Restaurant** (727-360-9558; www.thehurricane .com), 807 Gulf Way, is sure to please. Select from crab several ways, including stone crab fresh from their own boats, snow crab flown in from Alaska, or crab cakes Maryland style, as well as hearty New York strip and filet mignon ($15–24). Enjoy sunset on the Gulf from their rooftop seating.

St. Petersburg
🦐 I enjoyed superb food and speedy service when I stopped in **Athenian Garden** (727-822-2000), 2900 Fourth St N, savoring a Greek salad and soft fresh bread in a comfortable indoor garden. Desserts are on display at the door so you'll make the proper selection to have room for them later. Entrées include Greek classics such as gyro, moussaka, pastitsio, and dolmades ($9–14), plus sandwiches, seafood, and salads.

It's where the locals go for seafood, and you'll want to follow their lead. **Mid-Peninsula Seafood** (727-327-8309), 400 49th St S, has been around for nearly 30 years, serving up fresh catches by the piece or by the pound. Nab fresh fish at their fish market, too!

St. Petersburg—Downtown
Grab a nibble at **Angie's Café** (727-823-6437), 200 First Ave N, a tiny neighborhood take-out with a handful of seats, serving up gyros, souvlaki, Greek salad, hot dogs, and hamburgers ($3–7).

🗝 You'll find **Bliss** (727-825-0373; www.floridabliss.com), 405 Central Ave, Suite 102, in the historic Snell Arcade, where you'll escape from the everyday during a leisurely fancy tea luncheon ($14 per person; 11:30–4:30) or an afternoon tea ($8; 3–4:30) with little tea cakes and sandwiches. Children are welcome to have their own tea party, too ($18 per person), with fun crafts, surprises, and tasty treats.

Several folks pointed me toward **Café Alma** (727-502-5002; www.cafealma .com), 260 First Ave S, which has taken over a historic firehouse and turned it into a happening restaurant that segues into a club atmosphere after 10 PM. You can make a fun meal just from the starters, sampling goodies such as Gorgonzola fondue, Guinness Stout–braised beef short ribs, and baked Brie encroute ($6–13), but the entrées are awesome, too—horseradish-crusted salmon, curried beef tagine, and risotto and chorizo ($13–30). Dinner served Wed–Sat until 1 AM.

At breakfast, the line was out the door at **The Dome Grill** (727-823-5090), 561 Central Ave, where you stand in line to order off the big photo menus, with selections running $2–5. Belgian waffles are a huge hit, and the daily special of eggs, home fries or grits, and toast will set you back less than $2. Served 11–2, lunch ($4–7) includes fresh pasta, ribs, gyro sandwiches, and other Greek specialties.

Voted the downtown's top sidewalk café, **Integrity Organic Restaurant** (727-824-0881), 243 Central Ave, stands out thanks to its fresh look and creative foods, such as black olive goat cheese pâté, organic pizza with roasted veggies, and hummus wrap ($4–8).

🍴 Something in the air drew me to **The Moon Under Water** (727-896-6160), 332 Beach Dr NE, and I'm glad I wandered in. The ambiance is British Colonial with a hint of London curry shop, and the menu is something this world traveler gives a thumbs-up to. Natives of Wales, the Lucases (who once owned the Mansion House B&B) mingle British isles favorites with Greek, Indian, and Middle Eastern dishes, and a few "normal" entrées (blackened salmon, pork chops, pasta Alfredo, and burgers) thrown in for good measure ($6–17). Where else can you order hummus, Greek olives, tabbouleh, raita, *and* potato-vegetable curry as sides? My soup of the night, she-crab bisque, was buttery and succulent, and the chicken tikka a mild but piquant rub. Their signature dish is curry (choose your heat wisely), and you can take a jar of the aromatic sauce home with you. It's noisy in here, and there's plenty of beer, but the locals love this tavern—and you will too.

Throughout downtown, look for distinctive **Sabrett Hot Dog** pushcarts serving up extra-long dogs with all the fixings. There's enough foot traffic around the city to warrant vendors to set up shop weekdays and Saturdays.

South Pasadena

🍴 One of my good friends grew up in Gulfport, and every time I headed down that way, she said, "Aren't you going to stop at Ted Peters?" Talk about a local institution. **Ted Peters Famous Smoked Fish** (727-381-7931), 1350 Pasadena Ave, will smoke up your catch or serve you up some of the best red snapper and mullet on earth, and they've been doing it for more than 50 years. Kick back outside and enjoy.

BAKERIES, COFFEE SHOPS, AND SODA FOUNTAINS

Gulfport

The night I happened upon **Kool Beanz Coffee & Bakery** (727-512-3131), 2908½ Beach Blvd, the courtyard was hoppin' with the brassy sounds of the Fallopian Tubes, a brash local band that packs the house with fund-raisers like these. A hangout for the sake of conversation and coffee, Kool Beanz has real appeal.

St. Pete Beach

Pause for an espresso at **La Casa Del Pane** (727-367-8322), 4393 Gulf Blvd, where their bakery offers fresh baked Italian bread, focaccia, tarilli, and biscotti.

St. Petersburg

Since 1975, **John & Noel's Central Coffee Shop** (727-550-8733), 530 Central Ave, has served up dependable breakfasts and lunches. On busy Beach Drive, **Marketplace Express** (727-894-3330), 284 Beach Dr NE, hums with java junkies and locals dropping in for a deli lunch or takeout—especially since it's right across from the Museum of Art.

✳ Entertainment

DANCING A true Florida classic, the historic **Casino Ballroom** (727-893-1070), 5500 Shore Blvd, Gulfport, overlooks Boca Ciega Bay and the twinkling lights of St. Pete Beach in the distance. Step back into the 1930s and relive the days of ballroom dancing every Sun, Tue, and Thu, or jump into the swing of swing dancing on Wednesday nights.

MUSIC Up for a jam or some cool jazz? At the **Peninsula Inn & Spa** (see *Hotels, Motels, and Resorts*), join the folks out on the **Palm Terrace** for a near-nightly jam, or wander over to the Art Village across the street to see who's hot tonight. Artists also perform on weekends at **Yabba Dew Beachside Grille,** 5519 Shore Blvd, and **H. T. Kanes Beach Pub & Restaurant** (see *Eating Out*) in Gulfport. In St. Petersburg, I caught live music on Friday night in the plaza at **Baywalk,** but for a guaranteed good time, catch the big names that play at **Jannus Landing Courtyard** (727-896-2276; www.jannuslanding .net), 16 Second St—more than 75 concerts a year!

PERFORMING ARTS

St. Petersburg

The vibrant nonprofit **American Stage Theater** (727-823-1600), 211 Third St S, offers a fresh slate of programs twice annually, with presentations ranging from classic drama such as *A Moon for the Misbegotten* to edgy comedy like the caustic *Santaland Diaries.*

The **Florida Orchestra** (813-286-2403 or 1-800-662-7286; www .floridaorchestra.org), which has performed for almost 40 seasons, puts on more than 150 concerts each year. One of their regular venues is the **Mahaffey Theater** (727-892-5767; www.stpete.org/mahaffey.htm), 400 First St S, a grand performing-arts center that also hosts Broadway musicals and other unique events.

The **Palladium Theater** (727-822-3590; www.palladiumtheater.com), 253 Fifth Ave N, a community center for the performing arts built in 1925, boasts a full-size Skinner Pipe Organ. Check their web site for a calendar of their many musical events.

✳ Selective Shopping
ANTIQUES AND COLLECTIBLES
Gulfport

I didn't expect an old-time department store, but **Beach Bazaar** (727-381-8548), 3115 Beach Blvd, is just that, with a twist—sundries on one side, antiques on the other, and an old-fashioned post office in the back.

St. Petersburg

On **Central Avenue,** dozens of shops offer up great bargains. Try **Dixiana** (727-826-5255), 625 Central Ave, for unique flax clothing; **Luna's Crafts** (727-365-0934), 649 Central Ave, for handcrafted handbags and creative jewelry; and **Juan** (727-823-5843), 601 Central Ave, to browse stacks of books and dig for collectibles. **The Flower Gallery** (727-895-6010), 531 Central Ave, features home decor with a twist—in addition to top-notch silk flowers and shrubbery, they offer art that evokes Florida and florals, including creative digital photos, fusion art glass, and ikebana arrangements. It's truly cool at **Retro World** (727-580-9669), 667 Central Ave, where you can pick up enough retro stuff to re-create a 1960s living room, complete with period furnishings, lights, and paintings. Check out the hip selection of vintage clothing in the back room, too. Also see *Art Galleries* for additional offerings.

With four floors of treasures, the **Gas Plant Antique Arcade** (727-895-0368), 1246 Central Ave, is the ultimate destination for ephemera collectors. The upper two stories are focused on fine antique furniture; on the lower floors, look for everything— from postcards and stereoscopes to Elvis memorabilia, autographs, glassware, and more.

Gulfport

Dream big at **Small Adventures Bookshop** (727-347-8732), 3107 Beach Blvd, where every nook and cranny is crammed with the literature you love, from genre paperbacks to philosophy, travel narrative, and Florida classics.

St. Petersburg

A bibliophile's pilgrimage is not complete without a visit to **Haslam's Book Store** (727-822-8616), 2025 Central Ave, a destination in itself since 1933 with room upon room upon room of books—more than three hundred thousand, they say! You'll spend countless hours browsing the neatly arranged mix of new and used books. In their fourth generation of family ownership and hands-on management, Haslam's does a great job of bringing in authors for signings and participating in the annual Suncoast Writers' Conference. Open 10–6 Mon–Sat.

Your antiquarian source in the region, **Lighthouse Books** (727-822-3278), 1735 First Ave N, offers a fine selection of rare books, prints, and maps, including a special selection of literature of the South.

Reviving "a tradition in Florida literature," **Mickler-Smith Florida Booktraders** (727-894-1565), 718 Second St N, opened in the summer of 2005 with a full stock of Florida-related books and books by Florida authors, to the delight of Florida bibliophiles and authors. Notable, too, is their growing collection of Florida folk music CDs, and videos and DVDs of Florida-focused programs.

Gulfport

Expect the eclectic at **Domain** (727-302-9299), 3129 Beach Blvd, where naughty cigarette boxes by local artists nudge up against avant-garde perfume bottles, tea towels, aromatherapy candles, and unusual creations in art glass.

I walked out of **A Tropical Gale** (727-321-9228), 2908 Beach Blvd, with bags bulging with funky Christmas gifts, from tiki mugs and faux leis to memorable Old Florida postcard designs on newfound items.

Pass-A-Grille

Vivid art catches your attention as you drive past the **Nancy Markoe Gallery** (727-360-0729), 3112 Pass-A-Grille Way. Stop and check out handmade arts and crafts by artists throughout America in a variety of media, including wood, fiber, and paper.

St. Pete Beach

Step back in time at the region's only remaining neighborhood five-and-dime store, the **Corey Avenue 5¢ and 10¢ Store** (727-360-8503; www.coreyavenue.com), 300 Corey Ave, established in 1949. Their stock includes old-fashioned items and modern sportswear, sundries, and souvenirs.

St. Petersburg

Artistreet & Co. (727-895-5347), 221 First Ave NE, stays open late on weekends and is full of whimsical items to give as gifts or take home, from sushi platters and bowls to incense, wind chimes, Aspen Bay candles, and the gift for he who has it all—monogrammed toilet paper. Nearby, arts and crafts from the islands delight the senses at **Caribbean Artworks** (727-553-9213), 203 First Ave N, including playful toys, striking large sculptures, and fine jewelry.

The **Beach Drive shopping district** tends toward the stylish, with upscale jewelers sandwiched between home-decor and fine-collectibles shops. At **Good Night Moon** (727-898-2801), 222 Beach Dr NE, *plush* plush is the rage, from adorable Lamaze for the little ones to sensual bedding for Mom and Dad. Find fun gifts at **Cherie's Eklectika** (727-821-4336), 202 Beach Dr NE, a family business with lotions and potions, funky Caribbean art, tin clocks, and goodies for cat fanciers. Victoriana reigns at **Le Chateau Michelle** (727-895-9289), 136 Beach Dr NE, where everything's soft and romantic and white. **Fanitsa's** (727-820-0091), 102 Beach Dr NE, offers classy and exotic collectibles, including Wedgwood, bisque figurines and pottery, goblets, exotic treasure chests, and fun fish and mermaid gifts. Also see *Art Galleries*.

Have your fortune told at **Heavenly Things** (727-822-8938), 216 First Ave N, where gifts run "from art to Zen," including New Age books, witch balls, and amateur musical instruments.

Chocolate fiends should stop at **Schakolad** (727-892-2400), 401 Central Ave, where the aroma will draw you in and there's always a special worth walking away with. In addition to fine handmade chocolates, they offer great fudge, too.

MALLS AND OUTLETS

St. Petersburg
Baywalk, 153 Second Ave N, has a modern Mediterranean flair and a choice of shops and restaurants reflecting today's hip urban lifestyle. Don't miss **Shapiro's** (727-894-2111; www.shapirogallery.com), 185 Second Ave N, as Michael Shapiro brings in unique American-made sculpture, pottery, fiber craft, art glass, and more from more than three hundred artists nationwide. Here you'll find Brian Andreas's endearing Story People, Alison Palmer's whimsical candlestick women, and other gifts sure to please—intarsia frames, Raku cats, even hand-dipped candles. Another intriguing shop is **Being: The Art of Urban Living** (727-922-6252), 115 Second Ave N, for chic home decor. An unusual find on the upper level is a new chain restaurant, **Dish** (727-894-5700), where diners choose buffet-style from trays of fresh veggies, seafood, and meat, and have it cooked up then and there for a heart-healthy meal (sauces optional). **Ben & Jerry's, Dan Marino's,** and **TooJay's** are some of the other popular offerings.

At **The Pier** (see *Attractions*), you'll find a variety of shops to browse, including the **Crystal Mirage Gallery** (727-895-1166), with its art glass perfume bottles, fancy stemware, and marine life cast in glass; **Rainforest Gifts** (727-821-1434), filled with tropical home decor and gift items; and **St. Petersburg Candle Gallery** (727-823-9299), where they make candles on the spot.

FARMER'S MARKET

St. Petersburg
The finest selection of produce and fresh fish in the area can be found at the **Saturday Morning Market** (727-455-4921; www.saturdaymorningmarket.com), corner Central Ave and Second St in downtown St. Petersburg, every Saturday 9–1. Live music

and crafts vendors add color to this happening scene.

✳ Special Events

February: The **St. Petersburg Grand Prix** (727-894-7749; www .gpstpete.com) brings classic autos through town on a 1.78-mile course along the waterfront and Albert Whitted Airport.

March: In its 31st year in 2006, the **International Folk Fair** (727-552-1896; www.spiffs.org) lets you explore the customs and cuisines of more than 50 cultures, with continuous folk dancing and music on the center stage.

April: Nationally known blues acts gather annually for the **Tampa Bay Blues Festival** (727-502-5000; www .tampabaybluesfest.com), held along the waterfront at Vinoy Park.

Started in 1921, the annual **Festival of the States** (727-898-3654; www .festivalofstates.com) is one of the largest civic celebrations in the South, with parades, concerts, sports, and a band competition.

✐ One of the nation's top art shows is the **Mainsail Arts Festival** (727-892-5885; www.mainsailartsfestival .org), drawing more than three hundred artists to set up their booths along the waterfront. The festival includes a lively children's arts activity center, a food court, and live entertainment.

June: The oldest African American festival in America, **Juneteenth** (727-823-5693) celebrates the Emancipation Proclamation with a candlelight vigil, inspirational music, and fun for the entire family.

October: Urban birders flock to St. Pete for the **Florida Birding & Nature Expo** (727-827-3326; www .pcef.org), hosted by local and national Audubon groups with field trips, seminars, and a festival marketplace. Proceeds go to the management of Shell Key Preserve, a pristine barrier island and nesting area in Tampa Bay.

November: Chefs strut their stuff at **Ribfest** (727-528-3828; www.ribfest .org) at Vinoy Park, and we barbecue fans benefit by the top-notch competition, accompanied not just by spicy sauces but by top country and rock bands, too.

For more than 25 years, the **St. Petersburg Boat Show** (954-764-7642; www.showmanagement.com) has taken to the waterfront with a gathering of hundreds of happy boaters swapping stories and checking out the newest manufacturers' specials.

FLORIDA'S BEACH:
PINELLAS COUNTY

*P*unta Pinal, the point of pines, is what Spanish explorer Panfilo de Narvaez
dubbed this long, thin peninsula in 1528, where he discovered a Tocobagan village on the shores of Tampa Bay and ransacked it looking for gold. Three centuries after the conquistadors moved on, settlers to the Pinellas peninsula came
from around the globe, their touch reflected in the unique communities found
to the west of Tampa and St. Petersburg along the Gulf of Mexico. After Florida
became a state, settlers sailed down the Gulf coast from outposts such as Cedar
Key to establish homesteads. Frenchman Odet Phillipe came to **Safety Harbor**
to establish a settlement in the early 1800s, centuries after Spanish explorer
Pedro Menendez de Aviles stopped in on a Native American village at the
springs. One of Florida's oldest West Coast cities, **Dunedin,** was founded in
1852 and has its roots in Edinburgh, Scotland. A thriving agricultural community
built on cotton and later citrus, it once had the largest fleet of commercial sailing
vessels in Florida. After visiting the region in 1841, James Parramore McMullen
and his six brothers settled along the "Clear Water Harbor," which evolved into
the community of **Clearwater** by the turn of the next century, thanks in large
part to developer Henry Plant, who connected the coastal cities with his railroad
and built grandiose resort hotels as destinations, including the still-operational
Belleview Biltmore (see *Lodging*) in 1897. Pinellas pioneers cleared pine flatwoods for farms in the **Seminole** and **Largo** areas, and commercially harvested
the rich fisheries off **Indian Rocks** and **Redington Beach.** Greeks seeking fortune from the rich sponge beds of the Gulf came to **Tarpon Springs** in 1882,
bringing with them hundreds of divers (and eventually their families) from
islands in the southern Dodecanese. The railroad and subsequent real estate
boom brought upper-crust residents from the Northeast who built grand homes
in neighborhoods along the bluffs overlooking the barrier islands, which were
places to raise pigs and cattle.

The county's acceleration into the tourism arena in the 1940s occurred about
the same time as a World War II population boom brought about by the station-
ing of military families throughout the region. After the war, many decided to
stay. Art deco hotels cropped up along the beachfronts, and the farms and fields
yielded to sprawling suburban communities. The advent of television showcased
the sparkling sands of Clearwater and Treasure Island, enticing more visitors to

the region. Today's Pinellas County is the most densely populated of all of Florida's counties, its tourism infrastructure primarily a ribbon along the barrier islands and major highways.

GUIDANCE Overseeing the region's tourism is the **St. Petersburg/Clearwater Area Convention & Visitors Bureau** (727-464-7200 or 1-877-352-3224; www .floridasbeach.com), 13805 58th St N., Suite 2-200, Clearwater 33760. You'll find plenty of trip-planning information on their web site. For **Clearwater Beach** (727-447-7600 or 1-888-799-3199; www.beachchamber.com), stop at either the visitors center at 333 C Gulfview Blvd at the end of the causeway or on the beach at Clearwater Beach Park for information and brochures. In **Dunedin,** the Chamber of Commerce (727-733-3197; www.dunedin-fl.com) is downtown at 301 Main Street, and in **Tarpon Springs** (727-937-6109; www.tarponsprings .com) at 11 E Orange St.

GETTING THERE *By car:* Crossing the Sunshine Skyway northbound or the Howard Frankland Bridge southbound from Tampa, **I-275** provides primary north–south access. FL 60 west from Tampa connects with US 19 and Alt US 19 on the western side of the county.

By air: **Tampa International Airport** (see *Tampa and Hillsborough County*) is the closest option with the most choices. The **St. Petersburg–Clearwater International Airport** (see *St. Petersburg*) offers additional options.

By bus: **Greyhound** (727-796-7315), 2811 Gulf to Bay Blvd, Clearwater.

GETTING AROUND *By car:* This is a long linear beachfront county with not a lot of options for major highways. I-275 slices through the eastern side of the county, south of Tampa, but most places you'll want to visit lie off either Alt US 19, US 19, or CR 699 along the beach.

By bus: In Clearwater Beach, the **Jolley Trolley** (727-445-1200; www.thejolley trolley.com), 483 Mandalay Ave, offers trips at 10 AM to Sand Key and downtown Clearwater for $1. The **Official Suncoast Beach Trolley** connects beach communities from Sand Key to Pass-A-Grille (average one hour, one way) every 30 minutes with well-marked bus stops. Daily card, $3; seven-day unlimited pass, $12.

CABANAS ON TREASURE ISLAND
St. Petersburg/Clearwater Area Convention & Visitors Bureau

PARKING Parking is at a premium in **Clearwater Beach;** there aren't enough spaces, and the beachside lots will run you a minimum of $5. **Dunedin** has lots of free street parking and several flat lots. At John's Pass Village in **Madeira Beach,** you'll pay a quarter for 30 minutes in the parking lot. If you're lucky enough to find street parking in **Tarpon Springs,** it's

free; otherwise, there are quite a few options for $3 flat-lot parking along Dode-
canese Blvd. Most shops and restaurants everywhere else offer free street parking or their own parking lots.

FLORIDA'S BEACH: PINELLAS COUNTY

PUBLIC REST ROOMS In **Clearwater** you'll find rest rooms at Clearwater
Beach Park, along the roundabout. In **Dunedin** look for them behind the
caboose on Railroad St. At **Madeira Beach** you'll find them adjacent to the
parking area at John's Pass Village. In downtown **Tarpon Springs** they are midway down the block in the heart of the shopping district, while on Dodecanese
Blvd, you'll find them in the back of the Sponge Exchange.

MEDICAL EMERGENCIES The largest medical center in the region is **Morton
Plant Hospital** (727-462-7500), 300 Pinellas St (Alt US 19), Clearwater.

✳ To See

AQUARIUMS Take a self-guided tour of the **Clearwater Marine Aquarium**
(727-441-1790; www.cmaquarium.org), 249 Windward Passage, Clearwater, with
its coral reef tanks, dolphins, and sea turtles. Trainers perform scheduled feedings. Open 9–5 Mon–Fri, 9–4 Sat, 11–4 Sun. Adults $9, children 3–12 $6.50,
under 3 free. In Tarpon Springs, the centerpiece of the **Konger Tarpon
Springs Aquarium** (727-938-5378; www.tarponspringsaquarium.com), 850
Dodecanese Blvd, is a 120,000-gallon main tank containing a living reef. Fee.

ARCHEOLOGICAL SITES More than four thousand years ago, the **Safety Harbor Culture** built their homes on the bluffs overlooking northern Tampa Bay.
The oldest park in Pinellas County, **Phillipi Park** (727-669-1947), 2525 Philippe
Pkwy, Safety Harbor, preserves the site of some of the 1930s archeological finds
that uncovered this ancient culture, as well as the site of the city and temple
complex of Tocobaga, where Spanish explorer Pedro Menendez de Aviles
stopped in 1567. The park is named for Dr. Odet Phillipi, who founded the oldest settlement on the Pinellas Peninsula here in 1823, adjacent to Espiritu Santo
Mineral Springs (on the grounds of the Safety Harbor Resort & Spa).

ART GALLERIES

Belleair Bluffs

In the airy **Art At The Plaza** (727-559-7767), 100 Indian Rocks Rd N, you'll be
enticed by works such as the marine life scenes of glassblower Chuck Boux, the
large bronzes of Joe Rotella, and whimsical welded glass sculptures by Susan
Pelish. Offering a nice mix of media, with many Florida artists represented.

Oil painting restoration is a unique art, and Laura Robinson Werner practices it
daily at **Wall Things, Etc.** (727-518-2032), 2617 Jewel Dr, her studio and
gallery space behind Traders Alley (see *Selective Shopping*). Laura also paints
vibrant watercolors and shares her space with antique glassware, glass art, the
distinctive portraiture of Edna Hibel, and an extensive collection of finely
detailed Civil War paintings by various artists.

Clearwater

I'll return soon to **The Miranda Gallery** (727-518-0071), 1764 Clearwater–Largo Rd, where Ellen Phaff's bold, bright tropical birds, fish, and palm trees shout "Florida!" and Frank Miranda's metal and wood sculptures capture the natural heart of our state. They plan to open a café out under the arbors, so stop by and visit. Since their mainstay is art shows, call ahead to ensure they're open.

Dunedin

The **Bansemer Gallery** (727-797-4658), 342 Main St, features the fine art of Roger Bansemer, known for his watercolors of Florida wildlife, landscapes, and lighthouses.

Do not miss **The Painted Fish Gallery** (727-734-5060; www.paintedfishgallery .com), 350 Main St, which features the creative spirit of Bill Renc as expressed in colorful watercolor scenes of Florida landscapes, wading birds, and fish—as paintings, drawings, and on ceramic tiles.

ATTRACTIONS Part museum, part store, all blast from the past, the **Sponge-orama** (727-938-5366), 510 Dodecanese Blvd, takes you on a trip through Tarpon Springs's century-plus history of sponge diving, kicking off with a film on Florida's unique sponge industry, patterned after the Greek tradition of diving for sponges in the Dodecanese Islands. Dioramas showcase the various sponges found on the Gulf floor and their uses, and you can purchase your own to take home from the gift shop.

BASEBALL Spring training started nearly a century ago in the area and still packs the fans in at Clearwater's Brighthouse Field, 601 N Coachman Rd, where you'll catch the **Philadephia Phillies** (727-442-8496) in action. The **Toronto Blue Jays** (727-733-0429) play in nearby Dunedin.

SPONGES HANGING UP TO DRY ON A BOAT

Sandra Friend

HISTORIC SITES

Largo

✐ The history of Pinellas County through its early architecture is collected at **Pinewood Cultural Park** (727-582-2123), 11909 125th St N, Largo, where a stroll into the piney woods takes you back in time to **Heritage Village,** a collection of original pioneer homes and early Pinellas County buildings such as the McMullen-Coachman Log Cabin, built in 1852 and the oldest existing structure in the county; the House of Seven Gables, a 13-room Victorian home from 1907; and the Safety Harbor Church from 1905. In all, there are more than 30 stops to visit, with living-history docents to help you get the feel of frontier Florida. Open daily. Free; donations appreciated.

Tarpon Springs

In the **Tarpon Springs Historic District,** visit the **Atlantic Coast Line Railroad Depot** (see *Railroadiana*) and wander down Tarpon Ave to **Spring Bayou** to see a grand array of Victorian homes, all turn-of-the-20th-century private residences. **Universalist Church** (727-937-4682), Grand Blvd and Read St, is home to the **Innis Paintings,** the world's largest collection of landscape paintings by George Innis Jr. For a step into Greece, visit the **St. Nicholas Greek Orthodox Church,** Pinellas and Orange Aves, which showcases the devotional detail of the Orthodox religion. One inscribed marble tablet was donated by settlers from Halki, an island of sponge divers near Rhodes. On Dodecanese Blvd, the **Sponge Exchange** and many of the buildings surrounding it date from 1908. In the early days, sponge boats would remain at sea for more than a month.

Built in 1883, **The Safford House** (727-937-1130), end of Parkin Ct, is a beautiful example of early Florida vernacular architecture built of virgin pine from the local sawmill. The original home was a typical dogtrot; when Anson Safford, one of the pioneering founders of Tarpon Springs, purchased it in 1887, he had it raised up and a second floor added underneath the original structure to accommodate the family's needs. In 1975 it was added to the National Register of Historic Places. The warm wooden rooms are decorated with furnishings evoking the period of Safford's residence. Docents lead tours to interpret the house's historic and architectural significance as well as the history surrounding the Safford family. Open 11–3 Wed and Fri and by appointment. Fee.

MUSEUMS

Dunedin

National Armed Services & Law Enforcement Memorial Museum (727-734-0700; www.naslemm.com), 500 Douglas Ave, commemorates the daily duties of the law enforcement and military officer, with exhibits ranging from a life-size electric chair to whiskey stills confiscated from Florida's piney woods during raids. Closed Sun and Mon. Fee.

Largo

Part of the Pinewood Cultural Park, the **Gulf Coast Museum of Art** (727-518-6833; www.gulfcoastmuseum.org), 12211 Walsingham Rd, offers nine permanent collections and several changing galleries that focus on artistic contributions from the Southeastern states, plus a gift shop, sculpture gardens, and on-site studios with regular workshops. Open 10–4 Tue–Sat, noon–4 Sun. Fee.

Safety Harbor

Filled with artifacts and exhibits interpreting the region's long history of more than ten thousand years of human occupation, the **Safety Harbor Museum of Regional History** (727-726-1668; www.safety-harbor-museum.org), 329 S Bayshore Blvd, sits on the site of a Tocabaga shell mound along Old Tampa Bay. Open 10–4 Tue–Fri, 1–4 Sat–Sun. Free.

Tarpon Springs

✒ The **Leepa-Rattner Museum of Art** (727-712-5762; www.spjc.edu/central/ museum), St. Petersburg College, 600 Klosterman Rd, is a hands-on gallery featuring the works of Abraham Rattner (1893–1978), a figurative expressionist, and Allen Leepa, Rattner's stepson, a retired professor of art. The collection includes pieces from Chagall, Picasso, Henry Miller, and other friends and contemporaries of Rattner, who is best known for his work on the Holocaust. The Challenge of Modern Art gallery is where kids (and adults) will have a blast stepping through a painting, standing within the elements of design, and working with media at a demonstration table. Closed Mon. Fee.

RAILROADIANA Depots on the **Atlantic Coast Line** in downtown Tarpon Springs and Dunedin were once part of the famous Plant System line that opened this region to commerce and tourism. Henry Plant's most famous contribution to the region, the opulent **Belleview Biltmore** (see *Lodging*), offers a daily historical tour that takes you beneath one of Florida's last of the grand railroad-era hotels to see where porters once pushed baggage carts down tracks connecting to the railroad sidings outside the building.

❋ To Do

BICYCLING A green ribbon stretching from Tarpon Springs to St. Petersburg, the **Pinellas Trail** (727-464-8200; www.co.pinellas.fl.us/BCC/trailgd/trailgd .htm), 600 Cleveland St, Suite 750, Clearwater, provides bicyclists with nearly 34 miles of stress-free cruising, connecting communities and green space throughout the county along the route of the former Atlantic Coast Line. A free detailed map and guidebook can be downloaded off the web site or ordered from the county to plan your adventure.

BIRDING Encompassing 31 acres in a heavily populated Largo, **Largo Central Park** (727-586-7415), 101 Central Park Dr, has three paved loops around manmade wetlands where you might spot roseate spoonbills from the observation tower or floating dock. In Seminole, **Boca Ciega Millennium Park** (see *Parks*) has a boardwalk along the bay, excellent for observing wading birds. Both **Caladesi Island State Park** and **Honeymoon Island State Park** (see *Beaches*) have hiking trails that bring you within binocular-sight of nesting osprey colonies. And all along the beachfront, listen for the distinctive warbles of green conures, naturalized parrots that travel in flocks and can be seen emerging from holes in palm trunks.

BOATING

Clearwater Beach

Many cruises head out from the **Clearwater Municipal Marina** (727-462-6954), 25 Causeway Blvd, including the ***Show Queen*** (727-461-3113; www.show queen.com), billed as a "tropical party cruise," and ***Southern Romance*** (727-446-5503; www.southernromance.com), a relaxing sail on a 40-foot sloop. The "world's largest speedboat," **Sea Screamer** (727-447-7200; www.seascreamer .com), spouts an enormous wake as it cruises the bay in search of dolphins. And in case you were wondering about the pirate ship, there's **Captain Memo's Pirate Cruise** (727-446-2587; www.captainmemo.com), a long-standing nautical attraction that's great for the kids (two-hour daytime cruises run $30 adults, $20 children).

ECOTOURS

Clearwater Beach
✐ On **Dolphin Encounter** (727-442-7433; www.dolphinencounter.org), cruise the Gulf of Mexico on the double-decker 125-passenger *Clearwater Express* to watch dolphins jumping in the surf and birds feeding on the shoreline. Multiple cruises daily, adults $14.95, ages 4–12 $7.50. **Sea Life Safari Nature Cruises** (727-462-2628), departing from the Clearwater Municipal Marina and the Clearwater Marine Aquarium (see *Aquariums*), offer hands-on exploration of Tampa Bay with a biologist on board who pulls a trawl net for you to pick up and examine creatures of the bay. There's also an island stop where you can pick up seashells.

Tarpon Springs
✐ Enjoy a "sea"fari adventure on **Sun Line Cruises** (727-944-4468), 776 Dodecanese Blvd, on a narrated tour of the Anclote River out to the Gulf of Mexico and surrounding bayous. A professional naturalist on board narrates local history, explains the sponge and shrimping industries, and points out wildlife along the way. Departs from the far west end of the sponge docks.

FAMILY ACTIVITIES ✐ At **Clearwater Beach Park,** One Causeway Blvd (on the roundabout), let the kids go wild on the awesome collection of playground equipment, including a tugboat and giant slides within a massive canopied sandbox. A nearby concession stand and visitors center ensure that Mom and Dad have something to check out, too. Along Gulf Blvd in both Indian Shores and Madeira Beach, **Smugglers Cove Adventure Golf** (727-398-7008) is a destination for playful mini golf. Feed the gators, too!

Dunedin
✐ An outreach of the Dunedin Fine Art Center, the **David L. Mason Children's Art Museum** (727-298-3322; www.dfac.org/childmuseum.html), 1143 Michigan Blvd, provides special exhibits for kids, interactive workshops, and family programs.

FISHING Check at the **Clearwater Municipal Marina** (see *Boating*) for numerous charter captains who'll take you on the flats or well offshore, including **Queen Fleet** (727-446-7666).

GOLF In Largo, **Bardmoor Golf Course** (727-392-1234), 7919 Bardmoor Blvd, is an 18-hole par 72 that used to host the JCPenney Classic on its well-landscaped grounds. Designed by Donald Ross, the **Belleview Biltmore Golf Club**

(727-581-5498 or 1-800-237-8947; www.belleviewbiltmore.com/golf.html), 1501 Indian Rocks Rd, is a classic Florida course dating from 1925 and part of the Belleview Biltmore (see *Lodging*) complex. Farther north in Clearwater, the **Chi Chi Rodriguez Golf Club** (727-726-4673), 3030 McMullen Booth Rd, offers a par 69 course with extensive landscaping to include more than 70 sand traps and a dozen water hazards. Built in 1908, the **Tarpon Springs Golf Course** (727-937-6906; www.gulfcoastflorida.com/tarpongolf), 1310 S Pinellas Ave, has classic styling with small, elevated greens.

HIKING One of my favorite walks in the region is the quiet 3-mile loop on **Caladesi Island** (see *Beaches*), where hikers pass through several distinct habitats, including a virgin slash pine forest, mangrove forest, and coastal dunes. Explore more than 8,500 acres of wilderness at **Brooker Creek Preserve** (see *Wild Places*) on an 11.8-mile trail system.

PADDLING Saltwater kayaking is the major attraction in this region; my friend Sandy Huff, an authority on Florida paddling, puts in her craft at **Phillipi Park** (see *Archeological Sites*) to explore the wild mangrove fringe of northern Tampa Bay. Most waterfront parks and all beaches provide launch points to hit the surf, and for offshore places like **Caladesi Island** (see *Beaches*), paddling provides a way to get there and back on your own timetable. For a day of freshwater paddling, head to **John Chesnut Sr. County Park** (see *Parks*) to explore the cypress-lined edges of massive Lake Tarpon and Brooker Creek, which flows into the lake.

✳ Green Space

BEACHES Pinellas County is well known for its famous strand stretching from **St. Pete Beach** north to **Clearwater Beach,** where white sand and aquamarine water beckons. But beauty comes at a price—if you aren't staying in a nearby hotel, you'll pay as much as $1.25/hour or $15/day (no return privileges) for beach parking. The region is a magnet for the college crowd, especially with all the nightlife available along the Clearwater Beach waterfront. So if you're looking for the quieter side of Florida's Beach, consider one of these delightful and little-known options.

ALONG THE BEACH AT CALADESI ISLAND
Sandra Friend

It takes a long walk or a ferryboat to get to **Caladesi Island State Park** (727-469-5918), but if you want solitude, there are miles of unspoiled beach to explore. **Honeymoon Island State Park** (727-469-5918), One Causeway Blvd, the launch point for Caladesi Island, also offers uncluttered sandy shores with no condos in sight. Contact Caladesi Island Connection (727-734-1501) for ferryboat times and rates.

&. In Tarpon Springs, take Tarpon Ave around Spring Bayou and follow the signs to **Fred Howard Park** (727-943-4081; www.pinellascounty.org/park/06_Howard.htm), 1700 Sunset Dr, a county park with picnic pavilions under the shade of the coastal scrub, a kayak trail, and a long, windswept causeway leading out to a palm-lined beach on the Gulf, where wheelchairs are available upon request for the physically challenged.

Sandra Friend

FLORIDA BOTANICAL GARDENS

BOTANICAL GARDENS **Florida Botanical Gardens** (727-582-2100; www.flbg.org), 12175 125th St N, Largo, part of Pinewood Cultural Park, is a place to spend a couple of hours in quiet communion with the outdoors in a peaceful venue where art meets nature. Pathways meander between tasteful plantings of both native and tropical species, through forests of palm trees, past fountains and mosaics. Numerous benches make this a great destination for all ages, and gardeners will appreciate the detailed plant identification markers complete with information on water, light, and care needs of each species. A nature trail wanders off into one of the last untouched pine forests in this area. Walkways and bridges connect with the adjacent **Gulf Coast Museum of Art** (see *Museums*) and **Heritage Village** (see *Historic Sites*). Open 7–7 daily. Free.

GREENWAYS The **Pinellas Trail** (727-464-8200; www.co.pinellas.fl.us/BCC/trailgd/trailgd.htm), 600 Cleveland St, Suite 750, Clearwater, is one of the busiest greenways in Florida, stretching from Tarpon Springs south to St. Petersburg and roughly paralleling the route of Alt US 19. The **Clearwater East-West Trail** (727-562-4167) runs about 13 miles through residential and shopping areas, connecting Tampa Bay to Clearwater Beach, crossing the Pinellas Trail.

NATURE CENTERS ✔ In addition to its nature center full of activities and critters, **Moccasin Lake Nature Park** (727-462-6531), 2750 Park Trail Ln, Clearwater, has a nice 1-mile loop trail that crosses numerous fern-lined creeks. Fee.

PARKS

Oldsmar
On the shores of Lake Tarpon, **John Chesnut Sr. County Park** (727-464-3347), 631 Chestnut Rd, offers picnicking and a boat launch, two waterfront boardwalks for exploring the shoreline, and a shady trail along Brooker Creek.

Seminole

🐾 On the shores of Boca Ciega Bay, **Boca Ciega Millennium Park** (727-588-4882), 12410 74th Ave N, has numerous picnic pavilions, a boardwalk and tall observation tower along the bay, a rugged nature trail, canoe launch, and a paw playground for your pets.

Tarpon Springs

🐾 **A L Anderson Park** (727-943-4085), 39699 US 19 N, covers more than 100 acres on the western shore of Lake Tarpon. It's a popular place for picnicking and fishing, and kids will love the playground. The Jungle and Lake Boardwalks provide great places to commune with nature.

SPRINGS With nearly 200 acres on the coast, **Wall Springs Park** (727-943-4653), 3725 De Soto Blvd, Palm Harbor, protects a small spring used as a spa until the 1960s. The park provides access to the Pinellas Trail (see *Greenways*), and construction is under way to add picnic shelters and a boardwalk along the bayou. Swimming is not permitted in the spring.

WILD PLACES Lying 3 miles offshore, **Anclote Key State Preserve** (813-469-5918) doesn't get a lot of visitors—which is what makes this barrier island extra special for beach lovers and birders alike. There are no established trails, so walking the beach is the way to spy ospreys nesting, eagles cruising along the coast, and American oystercatchers poking around for a meal. There is no formal ferry, so you must charter a boat (or pilot your own) to visit this unspoiled treasure. Easier to get to is **Brooker Creek Preserve** (727-453-6900), 3620 Sletch Haven Dr, which protects more than 8,500 acres of unspoiled forests at the northern edge of the county.

✳ Lodging

BED & BREAKFASTS

Redington Beach 33708

🐾 🐾 I'm ready to move into the unique **Park Circle B&B** (727-394-8608; www.parkcircle.com), Seven Park Circle, an intimate neighborhood of original two- and three-bedroom 1940s bungalows. Renovated in 1997, these charming homes ($145 and up) feature original tile in the kitchens and baths and original kitchen cabinets with updated appliances. Each house has its own garage, screened porch, and grassy courtyard. Host Margaret Bourgeois serves up a tasty breakfast at the office each morning, and guests can mingle at the new communal pool and cabana area or keep to themselves in their roomy, romantic bedrooms. Take a virtual tour beforehand on their web site, and choose your dream home.

Safety Harbor 34695

Conveniently located downtown within walking distance of shops and restaurants, **The Ibis** (727-723-9000; www.ibisbb.com), 856 Fifth St S, is a modern bed & breakfast that offers three pretty guest rooms ($129–165) with private baths and unique quilts in each room.

Tarpon Springs 34689

🐾 An English Tudor mansion built in 1904, the **Bavarian Inn** (727-939-

0850 or 1-800-520-4446; www.bavarian innflorida.com), 427 E Tarpon Ave, became a bed & breakfast in 2000 and continues operation under the care of innkeepers Dave and Lynn. There are nine rooms on two floors, including spacious suites such as the Edelweiss (sleeps four) and themed rooms such as the Tropical and Magnolia ($60–135). Historic touches include the original lighting system and a large common parlor, where guests can mingle and are welcome to borrow from the VHS library to watch movies in the privacy of their own room. Older children welcome.

✒ ❀ I felt like I'd stepped into my great-grandmother's house at the **Spring Bayou Inn** (727-938-9333; www.springbayouinn.com), 32 W Tarpon Ave, a 1905 Victorian in the middle of the Historic District, with tower rooms, gleaming heart pine wood floors, and a 1920s baby grand piano in the parlor. History buffs take note: The home once served as staff quarters for the long-departed Tarpon Inn. Wood crowns accent the molding around the doors and windows in the three spacious rooms and two large suites ($89–139). I found the Orchid Suite just perfect for a working writer; wireless Internet access is free—just ask! Hosts Bill and Sherri Barzydlo provide a gourmet breakfast each morning; Bill completed Le Cordon Bleu Classic Cuisine and is happy to share his expertise during a Breakfast Cooking Class (extra charge; arrange before your stay). And talk about location! It's just a minute's walk up the street to the heart of the shopping district and a short stroll down to the waterfront. Well-behaved children welcome.

Dunedin 34698

Behind the Blue Moon Inn (see *Hotels, Motels, and Resorts*), the **Dunedin RV Resort** (727-784-3719 or 1-800-345-7504; www.go camping america.com/dunedin _beach), 2920 Alt US 19 N, has a healthy winter snowbird population but offers overnight electric back-in sites for $37. Dump station available.

Palm Harbor 34683

With both shady and sunny sites, **Caladesi RV Park** (727-784-3622), 205 Dempsey Rd, has easy access to the Pinellas Trail (see *Greenways*) and an ice cream parlor out front. What more could a camper need? Nevertheless, you'll also get a heated pool and laundry room with your full-hookup site ($35).

❀ **Sherwood Forest RV Park** (727-784-4582; www.meetrobinhood.com), 175 Alt US 19, is one of the few campgrounds in the region to welcome tent campers ($25 for two people) on no-hookup spaces. Full-hookup spaces cost $38. The park has a mix of shady and sunny sites.

COTTAGES

Treasure Island 33706

Seahorse Cottages (727-367-7568 or 1-800-741-2291; www.seahorse -cottages.com), 10356 Gulf Blvd, are the way a trip to the beach used to be—peering out the windows of your little wood-frame cottage through the sea oats and sea grapes to drink in that incredible Gulf view. Natural light floods these delightful 1939 cottages, each with a full kitchen and a typical-for-the-era tiny bath and shower ($85 and up).

🦐 ♿ When it opened in 1896, it was the jewel in the crown of Henry Plant's railroad hotel empire, the "White Queen of the Gulf," the ultimate destination for wealthy northeasterners seeking a tropical paradise at the end of a direct train from New York City. The oldest operating hotel in Florida, the **Belleview Biltmore** (727-373-3000; www.belleviewbiltmore.com), 25 Belleview Blvd, Belleaire 33756, is on the National Register of Historic Places and has been the center of a maelstrom of activity recently as historic preservationists have fought to prevent an investment firm from tearing it down and replacing it with condos. While the battle isn't over yet, the preservationists have prevented any progress on the project. This is both a hotel worth visiting and a hotel worth saving, a true survivor in that it is the largest occupied wooden structure in the world—thanks to the naturally fire-resistant properties of heart pine and cypress wood used for the structural timbers. To build the hotel, Plant had nearly 1,000 acres cleared here amid palmettos and pines in 1895, using mule-powered scrapers and hundreds of laborers.

As you leave the modern lobby, step back into the Southern elegance to an era when railroad hotels defined Florida tourism: polished wood plank floors, high ceilings with chandeliers, transoms over the doors, and lavish furnishings. Down the main hall, a high-tech business lounge with complimentary Internet access sits across from Henry's Library, an intimate meeting room dominated by Plant's portrait and rows of bookshelves. The J. Harrison Smith Fine Art Gallery adjoins the Historical Museum, which contains vintage guest registers and photos, tools used around the hotel, guest history cards, and an original Istachatta Cypress Shingle Company shingle from the first roof. The Palm Grill (see *Dining Out*) is the resort-causal dining option in the hotel, with Maisie's Ice Cream Parlor down the hall serving sandwiches and sweets.

HOTELS, MOTELS, AND RESORTS

Clearwater Beach 33767

🦐 The art deco **Palm Pavilion Inn** (727-446-6777; www.palmpavilion inn.com), 18 Bay Esplanade, is one of the most appealing nonchain choices on the beach. The 29 rooms ($89 and up) range from standard to one-bedroom apartments. Every room has an in-room safe and Internet access, and my comfortable choice included retro avocado doors and trim, a tiled bath, and a refrigerator. Given its central location, I was surprised how quiet it was late at night. Enjoy the heated outdoor pool or walk between the dunes to reach the beach in moments.

Dunedin 34698

🦐 ♿ 🐾 At the **Blue Moon Inn** (727-784-3719 or 1-800-345-7504), 2920 Alt US 19 N, choose from nine luxurious suites with large picture windows and patios overlooking sweeping green

When Henry Plant died in 1899, his son Morton Plant took over the hotel's management. An avid golfer, he had the greens expanded from 6 up to 18 holes by 1909, with a Donald J. Ross course that followed the natural features of this high bluff above the Intracoastal Waterway. Two wings—East and South—were added to the hotel under Morton's direction; by 1919, the hotel became part of the Biltmore chain under John McEntee Bowman. Between the wars, times were lean, and like other major hotels throughout the country, the Biltmore was taken over by the federal government to house the Army Air Corps between 1942 and 1944. In 1947 the hotel reopened to guests. Modern improvements include the new lobby atrium; the spa, opened in 1986, with a grand indoor pool done in Greco-Roman tile under a glass atrium; and the massive outdoor swimming pool complex, an ocean of water under the sparkling sun. The links remain a top-notch destination for golfers.

You'll chuckle at the uneven upper floors, inevitable in a wooden building of this age, en route to your room. The Biltmore has 244 spacious rooms with elegant touches such as wooden chair rails and baseboards, glass doorknobs, and a large tiled bathroom. According to early advertisements for the hotel, each bedroom had "3 incandescent lights, a polished cedar mantel and tiling around the fireplace, polished floors, and oak or cherrywood furniture." Although the furnishings have been updated, I found an antique luggage stand in the walk-in closet. Choose from standard rooms, junior suites, or suites; rates start at $149. Valet or free self-parking.

Each day at 11 AM, a fascinating historical tour highlights the Queen Anne decorative pieces, the Tiffany Room, Children's Private Dining Room, Sun Parlor Suite, and the fabled Underground Railway, used to wheel in luggage on handcars directly from the railroad tracks that once sat outside the hotel (fee).

lawns, a heated pool, and a playground. The standard suites ($79) include two full-size beds; the deluxe suites ($99) offer a king-size bed, separate bedroom and living room areas, and a massive bathroom with Jacuzzi tub for two. All suites have a sleeper sofa, wet bar, microwave, coffeemaker, and numerous other amenities; a continental breakfast buffet is included.

☙ Step back into the 50s at **Seaside Artisan Motel** (727-736-4657; www.ij.net/seasideartisan), 1064 Broadway, where the nine units ($45–60) have jalousie windows and tiled floors, full kitchens, and large showers—a real old-time road-trip motel, remodeled but retaining that original Florida flair.

Indian Rocks Beach 33785
Small and appealing, the seaside **Colonial Court Inn** (727-517-0902;

www.colonialcourtinn.com), 318 Gulf Blvd, offers six different configurations of apartments (all with kitchen), a guest house, and a cottage, with rates starting at $80. Each unit is themed and has cable TV, microwave, stereo, VCR, and telephone. Pathways lead through the tropical arbor and butterfly gardens toward the beach.

The **Great Heron Inn** (727-593-5518; www.heroninn.com), 2008 Gulf Blvd, has a pool overlooking the beach, with most of the rooms centered around the pool and courtyard ($75–110). A few rooms have a direct view of the ocean ($85–135). Each unit is a small apartment with a sleeper sofa in the parlor, full kitchen, bedroom, and full bath, maximum five guests per unit. See a virtual tour of the rooms on their web site.

Madeira Beach 33708

▼ Aspiring thespians note: A stay at the **Snug Harbor Inn** (727-395-9256; www.snugharborflorida.com), 13655 Gulf Blvd, will immerse you in the stage production of your choice. Hosts T. G. and Susan Gill parlay their years in the theater to theme their eight classic units after productions such as *On Golden Pond* (complete with play props and a screen door) and *Same Time Next Year* (a piano for your pleasure). Renovated in 2000, these 1950s apartment suites ($87 and up) include a full kitchen and sitting area.

Redington Beach 33708

At the **Island House Resort Hotel** (727-392-2241; www.islandhouseresort.com), 17103 Gulf Blvd, the rooms surround a tropical pool. Built in the 1950s, these large units are a good value for the price ($46–75) and vary by size from a motel to a two-

bedroom apartment. Beach access is next to the Hilton.

Safety Harbor 34695

A destination since the 1920s, **Safety Harbor Resort and Spa** (727-237-8772 or 1-888-BEST-SPA; www.safetyharborspa.com), 105 N Bayshore Dr, offers a different take on Florida history—relax at an upscale spa with pools of mineral water emerging from springs discovered by Hernando De Soto in 1539. Fully updated with modern furnishings, the spacious guest rooms overlook Tampa Bay and have high-speed Internet access. Rates start at $129, with numerous spa and entertainment packages available.

Tarpon Springs 36750

Take the kids to the **Westin Innisbrook Golf Resort** (1-800-456-2000; www.westin-innisbrook.com), where they'll have a blast at the Loch Ness water park and miniature golf course while you're luxuriating in the view of the links—or playing on them. Rooms and suites run $125–229.

Treasure Island 33706

Relax in comfort at the intimate **Beach Side Palms** (727-360-1459; www.beachsidepalms.com), 10200 Gulf Blvd, where the six units—two studio efficiencies ($65–90), three two-room apartments ($99–145), and a five-room apartment ($138–150)—have direct access to the beach. Natural light floods each room to reveal classy furnishings and a full kitchen. Sit on the patio or play shuffleboard on an old-fashioned board. An outdoor grilling area overlooks the beach.

✳ Where to Eat

DINING OUT

Bellaire

In the Belleview Biltmore (see *Lodging*), the resort-casual **Palm Grill** offers long-standing classics in an elegant setting. The rich and creamy rock shrimp bisque has a hint of sherry, and kernels of corn to add crunch. I love the Biltmore Salad, made with mixed greens, tomatoes, goat cheese, candied pecans, and balsamic vinegar. Entrées run $13–25; sandwiches and salads, $7–13. Save room for a luxurious dessert, such as Bailey's mousse or Key lime pie.

Dunedin

Savor the view of Clearwater Harbor from your waterfront table at **Bon Appetit** (727-733-2151; www.bon appetitrestaurant.com), 150 Marina Plaza, named by *Florida Trend* magazine in 2002 as one of the state's top 250 restaurants. Enjoy lobster tail, Dover sole, filet mignon, broiled rack of lamb, and other fine entrées ($16 and up). Open for lunch and dinner; reservations recommended.

🍴 ✒ I first stumbled across **Kelly's Restaurant** (727-736-5284; www .kellyschicaboom.com), 319 Main St, while looking for breakfast en route to Honeymoon Island, and wow—what a breakfast: My platter overflowed with eggs and home fries. Parents will delight in the "pay what they weigh" option for kids. Virgel Kelly is the owner and executive chef overseeing this classy bistro with garden seating. Lunch offerings ($6–8) include grilled Brie with a baby lettuce salad, Jamaican jerk chicken, and rib-eye salad; the Gorgonzola-crusted rib eye is my dinner choice (entrées $7–20). Their adjoining Chic-a-Boom-Room

Martini Bar is a gathering place for locals, with live music 5–8 Mon–Fri and 8–11 Sun.

Palm Harbor

🍴 The decor is old school, but the food is anything but—the **Old Schoolhouse Restaurant** (727-784-2585), 3419 Alt US 19, is indeed an old schoolhouse, built in 1910 and opened as a restaurant in 1982. Under executive chef Larry Lloyd's direction, the innovative menu includes fusion foods such as sesame ginger beef short ribs and crab-crusted salmon with basil cream sauce (entrées $10–24). Specials are posted on the blackboards. I enjoyed the creamy lobster bisque and was tempted by the toasted coconut (or pecan—take your pick!) ice cream ball, but I stuck to my New Year's resolution and finished off a plate of fried oysters for dinner.

Redington Shores

At **The Lobster Pot Restaurant** (727-391-8592; www.lobsterpot restaurant.com), 17814 Gulf Blvd, shellfish is the focus of the menu, from the creamy lobster bisque to king and stone crab, escargot, and lobster delights from both Florida and Maine (entrées $14 and up). Open for dinner only; reservations recommended.

EATING OUT

Clearwater

Smokin Rib Shack BBQ (727-442-1977), 2257 Gulf-to-Bay Blvd, is the newest in a local chain of kick-butt Southern-style barbecue by Curt Luke, who serves up old-fashioned slow-smoked ribs, chicken, and pork.

Clearwater Beach

Headed out early? Catch a cheap breakfast ($2) at the **Beach Shanty**

Café (727-443-1616), 397 Mandalay Ave, where eggs, grits, and pancakes headline the menu.

✐ Right on the roundabout, **Crabby Bill's** (727-442-2163), 37 Causeway Blvd, is one location of many in a popular local chain with "fresh no-frills seafood" at cheap prices. Fresh off the local boats, nab crabs, oysters, clams, and more ($8–18), and there are also sandwiches ($6–9).

Frenchy's Rockaway Grill (727-446-4844; www.frenchysonline.com), 7 Rockaway St, is one of four Frenchy's locations on the beach and best known for its signature seafood dishes, ranging from grouper sandwiches to seafood gumbo, smoked fish spread, and the unique "grouper cheeks" (aka fish nuggets of prime grouper). My favorite is the crabby shrimp sandwich, but it's all great seafood, nothing frozen ($6–15).

Dunedin

For excellent Mexican, **Casa Tia** (727-734-9226), 369 Main St, is a top pick for vegetarian palates, and the festive Mexican atmosphere makes it an easy choice. No lard is used in their preparations, and everything is fresh. Virtually anything on the menu can be created with the vegetarian in mind. My basic fare: el burrito, the classic wet burrito slathered in melted cheese. Entrées ($8–21) include numerous fresh-fish options.

The walls are covered with covered bridge postcards at the **Covered Bridge Family Restaurant** (727-734-0808), 2070 Bayshore Blvd, where you can nab a hearty breakfast for less than $5 and check out the classic car rally every Wednesday evening. Open for breakfast and lunch daily, and dinner Wed–Sat.

Have some home brew at the **Dunedin Brewery Snug Pub** (727-736-0606; www.dunedinbrewery.com), 937 Douglas Ave, nestled in a micro-brewery providing handcrafted beers to dozens of local restaurants. They serve pub fare, including burgers, sandwiches, wings, and pizza ($6–8), and their smooth Celtic Gold Ale goes down good! Open at 5 Tue–Sat, with live music Wed–Sat.

Indian Rocks Beach

A local favorite since 1971, **Brewmaster Steak House** (727-595-2900; www.brewmastersonline.com), Gulf Blvd and Walsingham Rd, prides itself on its great steaks and the "bottomless glass" of free refills of beer and wine with your entrée, and live music on the tiki deck. Shaved prime rib, Delmonico, steak Diane, and ribs—you name it, they've got it ($10 and up for dinner).

Indian Shores

Along the travertine limestone outcroppings of Indian Shores, the **Salt Rock Grill** (727-593-7625; www.saltrockgrill.com), 19325 Gulf Blvd, offers a menu to meet the varied palate, with fine seafood and steaks, pork, tuna, and mile-high meat loaf. Dinners start at $10, and early-bird specials are offered between 4 and 5 nightly.

Largo

With the classic dark and intimate feel of an authentic Irish pub, **O'Keefe's** (727-442-9034), 1219 S Fort Harrison Ave, has delighted local residents since 1961. Their menu includes some decidedly unusual items, such as the Yuk burger (topped with peanut butter, bacon, and lettuce) and sweet potato fries sprinkled with white chocolate and cinnamon. Or how about the Seven Course Irish Dinner—one potato and six domestic draft beers? I'm not making this up, folks. Seriously eclectic entrées mingle with standards like fish-and-chips ($9–15).

Grab a filling breakfast or lunch ($2–6) at **Ted's Luncheonette** (727-584-2565), 1201 Clearwater-Largo Rd, an unpretentious family diner with big picture windows and fast, friendly service. Open 6–2:30 daily.

Widow Brown's Restaurant & Tavern (727-586-7084), 2076 Seminole Blvd, offers breakfast specials (less than $2), lunch combos ($5 and up), and all-you-can-eat fish ($6–8).

Madeira Beach
Sculley's Boardwalk Restaurant (727-393-7749), 190 Johns Pass Boardwalk, perched on John's Pass, has an old fish house atmosphere and offers up freshly caught amberjack, yellowfin, red grouper, and other house seafood favorites, including pistachio-crusted red grouper ($14–19), as well as a handful of beef, chicken, and pasta entrées.

Ozona
The good times roll at **Molly Goodhead's** (727-786-6255; www.molly goodheads.com), 400 Orange St, a popular raw bar and seafood house in this little historic village. The menu features grouper "right off the boat," steamed Gulf shrimp, calamari salad, grouper Reuben, and more. Sandwiches and salads $5–8, entrées $8–14.

The aroma of smoking meat made me walk into the **Ozona Pig** (727-773-0744), 311 Orange St, where Southern-style barbecue is the order of the day: succulent pulled pork and beef on a bun, barbecue chicken, and ribs. Hot tamales, too! Lunch and dinner

$4–16. Call a day ahead to order a picnic basket of your favorites.

Pinellas Park
For funky Louisiana fun, check out **Cajun Café on the Bayou** (727-546-6732; www.CajunCafeOnTheBayou .olm.net), 8101 Park Blvd, where you overlook the mangroves while dining on spicy favorites such as red beans and rice, Creole gumbo, crawfish étouffée, and jambalaya.

Safety Harbor
In a 1920s cottage downtown, the **Green Springs Café** (727-669-6762), 122 Third Ave N, serves up "creative American food" accompanied by music and art to delight the senses. Popular dishes include gumbo, Cajun stuffed chicken, and wild mushroom ravioli.

Tarpon Springs—Downtown
At the **Greek Pizza Kitchen** (727-945-7337; www.greekpizzakitchen .com), 150 E Tarpon Ave, a decidedly romantic interior second-floor wrought-iron terrace perches diners over the spacious main room. Serving delicious taverna food (gyros, *kefetedes*, souvlaki, *horiatiki*, and classic Greek salads, $6–8) and unique Greek-themed pizzas ($20–25), they are *the* choice for traditional food in the Historic District.

Tarpon Springs—Waterfront
A family favorite, **Hellas Restaurant** (727-943-2400), 785 Dodecanese Blvd, evokes the feel of the restaurants in the tourist districts of coastal Greece, with waiters who shout "opa!" as they serve your flaming *saganaki*, and colorful murals of the islands covering the walls. I've enjoyed everything I've ordered, from a basic gyro to *dolmades*, pastitsio, and moussaka. Entrées run $8–20.

🐚 In the Sponge Exchange, **Mama's Greek Cuisine** (727-944-2888), 735 Dodecanese Blvd #40–41, is the closest I've been to an authentic taverna in years. Their specialty is *lithrini*—whole snapper topped with olive oil, lemon, oregano, garlic, and spices, served with *horta*—but Mama's entrées ($8–17) include all the favorites, from charbroiled lamb chops to octopus, Greek shrimp, and *makaronada*.

Evoke the islands at **Mykonos** (727-934-4306), 628 Dodecanese Blvd, where Andreas and Renee Saliveras serve regional seafood favorites such as calamari stuffed with feta, a dish my sister previously enjoyed on our trip to Santorini.

Treasure Island
By the crowded parking lot early on a Sunday morning, I don't doubt the claim that **Robby's Pancake House** (727-360-4253), 10925 Gulf Blvd, has the "best pancakes on the beach," especially with the types offered—coconut, blueberry, chocolate chip, pecan, buckwheat, and more ($3–5). Open 7–2.

BAKERIES, COFFEE SHOPS, AND SODA FOUNTAINS

Belleair Bluffs
Gotta Have It (727-518-1811), 596 Indian Rocks Rd, is an ice cream parlor dishing up yummy Working Cow flavors such as raspberry truffle amid an array of whimsical gifts, kids' plush toys, tropical wear, and fancy soaps.

Dunedin
Make a whistle stop at **The Boxcar** (727-738-8550), 349A Main St, for coffee, cinnamon rolls, and the morning paper inside an authentic Orange Belt ACL boxcar, adjoining the Pinellas Trail downtown.

Palm Harbor
Dairy Rich (727-789-9285), 3109 Alt US 19, is a classic drive-up ice cream and hot dog stand where a burger basket costs $4. Just up the street, **J. J. Gandy's Famous Key Lime Pie** (727-938-PIES; www.jjgandyspies.com), 3725 Alt US 19, supplies more than a hundred local restaurants with their pies; choose from 20 tempting varieties 9–4 Mon–Sat.

Safety Harbor
A downtown landmark, the **Whistle Stop Grill & Udderly Cool Ice Cream** (727-726-1956), 915 Main St, has a giant cow out front—you can't miss it. Enjoy frozen delights, or grab a sandwich, veggie wrap, or an order of fried green tomatoes.

Tarpon Springs
You won't go wrong with a stroll down Dodecanese Blvd, where the sight of trays of tempting *pastas* (think decadent cream-filled Greek pastries, *not* spaghetti) and baklava will pull you into many storefront bakeries, including **Parthenon** (727-939-7709), 751 Dodecanese Blvd; and **Hellas** (727-943-2400), 785 Dodecanese Blvd. I've yet to be disappointed at any of the stops I've made, so explore!

✴ Entertainment
FINE ARTS

Clearwater
Ruth Eckerd Hall (727-791-7400; www.rutheckerdhall.com), 1111 McMullen Booth Rd, is a favorite stop for top-name musical acts and comedians. Check their web site for the current schedule and ticket prices.

Dunedin
At the **Dunedin Fine Art Center** (727-298-3322; www.dfac.org), 1143

Michigan Blvd, explore the galleries, visit the children's art museum (see *Family Activities*), or sign up for a hands-on workshop in the visual arts.

MUSIC One of the time-honored venues for Florida folk music, the **Ka Tiki** (727-360-2272), 8801 W Gulf Blvd on Sunset Beach (South Treasure Island), draws appreciative crowds each Thursday night for its folk night, hosted by Sunset Beach Pete and featuring troubadours such as Frank Thomas, Raiford Starke, Val Wisecracker, and Bobby Hicks. It's a don't-miss stop for serious lovers of Old Florida and of folk music.

❋ Selective Shopping

Belleair Bluffs
I'll admit it, I'm a sucker for gourmet cooking stores, so **Beans About Cooking** (727-588-3303), 100 Indian Rocks Rd N, was fun to browse, and I couldn't help but walk away with some exotic spices and sushi bowls.

At **Collectors Corner** (727-518-2771), 596 N Indian Rocks Rd, you'll find a mix of antiques and collectibles from various eras; I was thrilled to find a set of 1962 World's Fair picture flash cards!

The Galleries (727-581-9190), 100 Indian Rocks Rd, offer "distinctive gifts and home furnishings," with many decor and gift items to choose from. My favorite was the Rush Hour traffic jam puzzle for kids ($18).

Jewel Antique Mall (727-441-3036), 2601 Jewel Rd, is a rabbit warren of dealer spaces that just go on and on and on. Keep looking, and you will find *something* you like! Open daily.

Traders Alley (727-584-4799), 596 N Indian Rocks Rd, boasts a collection of more than a dozen shops, each brimming with goodies. **Victoria's Parlor** (727-581-0519) is a grandmother's attic filled with glassware. **My Little Place** (727-584-4799) offers appealing country folk art, and at **Catiques** (727-584-4799), whimsy meets antiques in a cat-lover's dream.

Clearwater
Dozens of dealers pack the **Cleveland Street Antique Mall** (727-446-3225), 1408 Cleveland St, where fine furniture, glassware, and vintage linens are just the tip of the iceberg.

Granny's Attic (727-449-9836), 1740 Drew St, has large furniture, kitschy art, and lots of ephemera to dig through.

Jam-packed with the obscure and unusual, **Greenbaum's Antiques** (727-586-4043), 1797 Clearwater/Largo Rd, had everything from an inlaid mother-of-pearl casket to hand-carved 19th-century Moorish chairs, military miniatures, and antique pottery. There's a Furniture Annex as well. Closed Sun–Mon.

It's always the holidays at **Robert's Christmas House** (727-797-1600 or 1-800-861-6389), 2951 Gulf to Bay, where a stop just before Christmas yielded both classic and whimsical ornaments, an incredible array of collectibles from Annalee dolls to Lenox, and a virtual forest, a sparkling wonderland with dozens of unique artificial trees to choose from. Gifts shipped daily. Open daily all year except major holidays.

You'll find classy glass at **Whitehouse Antiques** (727-442-4431), 603 Turner St, including Depression, ruby, cobalt, and pattern glass, as well as antique pottery and china.

Walk Mandalay Avenue to check out the beach shops. At **Key West Express** (727-461-6462), 484 Mandalay Ave, nab soft flowing dresses in bright island colors and other comfy casual wear. Searching for beach gear and boogie boards? Try **Mandalay Surf & Sport** (727-443-3884), 499 Mandalay Ave, an original on the beach since 1979. And the name says it all: **Way Cool** (727-461-1921), 433 Mandalay Ave, is a beachwear shop that catches your attention with its eye-popping aqua walls, giant parrots, and toucans.

Dunedin

Dunedin is truly a shopper's paradise, with dozens of shops lining the quaint downtown streets, informational kiosks to show you what's where, and free parking nearby. Most of the shops are open on Sunday. I spent a full afternoon whizzing through the choices; a leisurely day or weekend would be a better pace for your exploration. Here's a sampling of some of my favorites:

Browse the dealer booths at **Amanda Austin** (727-736-0778), 365 Main St, for tasteful home decor, Depression glass, vintage children's books, and craft items.

The Art and Antique Gallery (727-736-5825), 718 Broadway, features classy gifts and elegant home decor, including Victorian beaded lamps, fine soaps and candles, and a writing desk I'd love to have in my home.

I found the best purse ever at **Bohemian Pack Rat** (727-736-1933), 735 Broadway, where environmentally, economically, and socially conscious fabric items and gifts adorn this chic boutique.

Indulge yourself in the very feminine **Erika's Place** (727-733-0461), 714 Broadway, with its aromatic soaps, potpourri, and candles. I especially liked the retro powder-puff pink Christmas tree in the middle of the store, but it wasn't for sale—yet.

I love the toys at **The Kid's Corner** (727-738-0260), 346 Main St, where everything's educational and fun—and certainly not mainstream. They have a fine selection of clothing as well.

Seek out gifts from the Far East at **Kismat** (727-733-0040), 355 Main St, where I found camel bone boxes from India and Thai percussion animal carvings.

Not downtown but nearby, **Knot on Main** (727-738-8090), 2428 Bayshore Blvd, has a large number of dealer booths where you'll find antique lamps, collectible coins, ruby glass, Stubenvilleware, some crafts and gifts, and much more.

You'll find classy collectibles and fine Florida art at **Objects & Accents** (727-738-4565), 340 Main St, a different kind of home and garden shop, where I was particularly intrigued by the faux orchids and white-topped pitcher plants.

The **Old Feed Store Antiques Mall** (727-736-8115), 735 Railroad St, yields some unique gifts for friends and family. The dealer booths aren't just full of old stuff—one of my previous finds, Catch the Drift (a driftwood art shop in North Florida) shows off their wares here, too.

It's a jungle inside **Palm Latitudes** (727-733-7343), 322 Main St—you can't see the ceiling for the forest of wind chimes and ornaments! It's your one-stop Jimmy Buffet–tiki bar–surfer–tropical kitsch connection.

In a cheerfully red 1920s bungalow, **Paper Players** (727-734-4174; www.paperplayers.com), 434 Virginia Ln, has creative stationery and greeting cards, paper craft and calligraphy items, and scenes of Dunedin by local artists.

Enjoy a taste of the Old Country at **The Scottish Accent** (727-736-6618), 249 Main St, where British favorites such as Oxo, lemon curd, and Penguin bars are on the shelves.

Largo

On a back street near the Pinellas Trail, **The Amish Country Store** (727-587-9657; www.theamishcountrystore.com), 206 13th St SW, is a little grocery filled with Pennsylvania Dutch goodies, from birch beer and bulk spices, scrapple, and pretzels to homemade shoo-fly pie in the bakery. Grab a sandwich and eat it on the porch. Closed Sun–Mon.

Inside **Hidden Treasures** (727-443-6623), 118 Clearwater–Largo Rd, I unearthed unique gifts such as hand-crafted pillows, a replica Calusa mask, inlaid jewelry boxes, and lovely painted antique windows decorated by the artist-owner, Liz Rios. She takes custom orders, too.

Set under a canopy of live oak trees, **Karen's Korner** (727-581-2812), 506 First Ave SW, is a cottage filled with suites of furnishings, glassware, dishes, and collectibles at reasonable prices.

In the very roomy **Quaint Essential Antiques** (727-398-2228), 11890 Walsingham Rd, the dealer booths are nicely spaced and offer finds like antique fishing lures, McDonald's collectibles, and vintage glassware.

At **Time and Again** (727-586-3665), 904 W Bay Dr, search for a bit of everything, including stereoscope pictures, fine furniture, costume jewelry, and classy lamps.

Madeira Beach

A serious shopper's destination, **John's Pass Village** (727-397-1667; www.johnspass.com), Village Blvd, has both the typical beach shops and some truly unusual ones. Claiming more than fifteen thousand in stock, **Angel Haven** (727-399-8455), 13007 Village Blvd, is filled with angel figurines in every medium as well as angelic gifts. **The Artisan's Market** (727-394-2218), 124 John's Pass Boardwalk, has Mexican clay figurines, wall art, fountains, and more. **The Bronze Lady** (1-800-269-3412), 12955 Village Blvd, features distinctive collectibles, with their showpiece original art by Red Skelton. **Caribbean Jubilee** (727-399-0551), 13015-A Village Blvd, brims with colorful, playful plates and wall decor—just the sorts of gifts I buy for my siblings. At **Enchanted Woods From The Sea** (727-397-6715), 114 John's Pass Boardwalk, Sinbad the macaw surveys a vast array of woodcarvings, shells, and nautical items. A truly unique find, **Grandma & Grandpa's Puppets** (727-397-2446), 12801 Village Blvd, sells nothing but—but you'll find an impressive array in all sizes and shapes, animals

STROLLING THE BOARDWALK AT JOHN'S PASS

St. Petersburg/Clearwater Area Convention & Visitors Bureau

and people, marionettes to hand puppets, and priced between $3 and $50. Stop in at **John's Pass Winery** (727-362-0008; www.thefloridawinery.com), 12945 Village Blvd, for free wine tastings, gourmet foods, fudge and chocolate, and (oddly enough) Tropical Wine ice cream. Hand-painted functional glass is a classy sideline at **Peppers** (727-320-8530), 12813 Village Blvd, where their main focus is selling you heat from a huge array of hot sauces from around the world. **Tropic Shoppe** (727-397-4337), 12913 Village Blvd, has dressy tropical wear and sandals, as well as kids' clothing.

Madeira Beach Antique & Collectible Mall (727-394-8162), 15040 Madeira Way, has 45 dealer booths with a little bit of everything—coins, postcards, primitives, glassware, you name it!

Pinellas Park

For flea market bargains, browse thousands of booths at the **Mustang Flea Market** (813-544-3066; www.zipmall.com/mustang.htm), 7501 Park Blvd, and at the **Wagon Wheel Flea Market** (813-544-5319; www.zipmall.com/wagonwheel.htm), 7801 Park Blvd, on weekends.

Seminole

I love the tag line for **Seminole Books** (727-393-6707), 8701 Seminole Blvd—"more barn than noble." In fact, the building that houses more than sixty thousand used books looks like an abandoned tiki bar, and it once *was* the Porpoise Pub. I lost my sweetie for two hours in this maze of books, where shelves groan with bargains and books from the 1800s, for the discerning collector. Open 10–6 Mon–Sat.

Tarpon Springs—Downtown

Immerse in the local community through song—update your CD collection at **Greek Music Superstore & More** (727-939-8498; www.greekmusic.com), 11 Pinellas Ave, in what is likely the largest Greek-only music store in Florida. My pick: *anything* by Anna Vizzi.

Search for the unusual at **Tarpon Avenue Antiques** (727-938-0053), 161 Tarpon Ave, such as flash cards in Chinese and bookplates from the 1880s, along with many Teutonic-influenced items.

Browse the stacks at **Time Traveler Books & Antiques** (727-934-7966), 111 E Tarpon Ave, to discover historic tomes and intriguing imports from Greece. Almost immediately, I found a cookbook from the Greek island my sister loved so much.

A bright red dragonfly Tiffany lamp drew me to **Unique Designs** (727-943-0440), 218 E Tarpon Ave, where the inventory tends toward the exotic with Asian masks and elephant pedestals as well as vintage furnishings and one-of-a-kind statuary.

At the **Vintage Department Store** (727-942-4675), 167 E Tarpon Ave, discover splashy art originals and reproductions, including Peter Max, Picasso, and Monet.

Tarpon Springs—Waterfront

Dodecanese Boulevard is lined with shops, so you'll have no problem picking up something with a Greek flair. I always stop at **Gift World** (727-938-3225), 557 Dodecanese Blvd, for CDs, videos, and books in Greek. Circa 1912, the **Athens Gift Shop** (727-937-3514), 703 Dodecanese Blvd, has a unique cutaway corner that visitors like to pose at for photos.

Sandra Friend

MURAL ON THE TARPON SPRINGS SPONGE
EXCHANGE

Formerly a working sponge market,
The Sponge Exchange (727-934-
8758), 735 Dodecanese Blvd, is now a
collection of shops and restaurants,
where you can still pick up great natural sponges at the **Tarpon Sponge
Company.** At **CJ's Nature Shop,**
look for plush critters, shirts, and bags
with wildlife prints. **Miracles of the
Sea** has stained glass and sculptures
and marine art.

Luxurious handmade olive oil soap,
bath oils, and inspirational art await at
Getaguru (727-937-8193; www.geta
guru.com), 777 Dodecanese Blvd, one
of my favorite Tarpon Springs shops.

In the shopping complex near the end
of the street, **The Museum Shoppe**
(727-934-6760), 822 Dodecanese Blvd,
has a classy selection of museum
repro-ductions, the entire educational
Dover coloring book series, and statuettes of just about any deity you can
think of.

Treasure Island

A standout in a place where beach
shops are the norm, **Treasures For
Your Home** (727-360-4461), 10825
Gulf Blvd, has an excellent array of
home decor from tropical to exotic,
including imports from India, interesting garden sculptures, decorative
tiles, and decorative items with fun
seaside themes.

**PRODUCE STANDS, FARMER'S
MARKETS, SEAFOOD MARKETS,
AND U-PICK** Along Alt US 19 between Tarpon Springs and Dunedin
there are many small produce stands
to choose from, such as **Johnny's
Farm Fresh Produce** (which, like
many of the stands, sells Greek
favorites like fresh olives and feta)
and **Steve's Produce** (fresh shrimp
daily! Bananas 3 lbs for $1!).

Ward's Seafood (727-581-2640 or 1-
800-556-3761; www.wardsseafood
.com), 1001 Belleair Rd, Clearwater, a
local favorite since 1955, has the best
of the local catch. Stop by for their
succulent take-out, or have them ship
some seafood home.

✴ Special Events

January: On the sixth, **Epiphany,** in
Tarpon Springs, is an important devotional day in the Greek Orthodox faith
that includes the blessing of the fleet
and a dive for the Cross. Young men
compete for the honor of retrieving
the icon for a year of good luck.

February: **Greek Fest** (727-937-
3540), St. Nicholas Orthodox Cathe-
dral, Tarpon Springs, is a major event
featuring Greek music and dancing,
food, and children's activities. Admissions go to help families in need.

March: Just say *ohi* ("no") at the **Greek Independence Day Parade** (727-937-3540), Tarpon Springs, on the 20th at the sponge docks at 1 PM. Ask a participant why and you'll learn more about modern Greek history.

Pioneer Jamboree (727-866-6401), at the Heritage Village Pinellas Pioneer Settlement (see *Historic Sites*), Largo, on the second Saturday, is a celebration of pioneer life with folk music, antique tractors, and hayrides.

April: A major arts event for more than 30 years, the **Tarpon Springs Arts & Crafts Festival** (727-937-6109), held the second weekend, is one of the nation's top art festivals, bringing in more than two hundred artists who compete for prizes. There's also food, exhibits, and entertainment.

In the tradition of Scotland, the **Dunedin Highland Games Military Tattoo** (727-733-3197), held the first Saturday at Dunedin High School, features Massed Pipers, Drummers, Highland and Country Dancers, and the Parade of Clans. Tickets are $8 in advance, $12 at the gate, $4 children.

More than one hundred thousand people descend on the weeklong **Fun 'N Sun Festival** (727-562-4804), Clearwater, held the last weekend Apr–first weekend May. An event that's been going on annually since 1953, it features concerts, sports competition, food, arts and crafts, and the gala illuminated Fun 'N Sun Night Parade starting at Crest Lake Park.

November: For more than 26 years, the **Clearwater Jazz Holiday** (727-461-5200), held midmonth, has brought in top names from the jazz world for four days of free public concerts at Coachman Park in downtown Clearwater.

December: During **Light up the Bayou** (727-943-5523), stroll along Spring Bayou, Tarpon Springs, on Christmas Eve to enjoy the waterside luminaria in front of classic Victorian homes.

The Gulf Coast 2

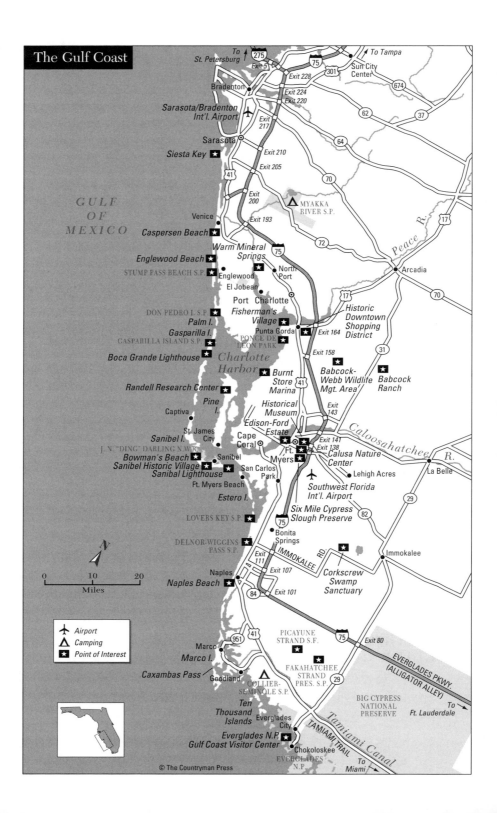

The Gulf Coast

To St. Petersburg

To Tampa

275 Exit 5

75

301 Sun City Center

Exit 228

674

Bradenton

Exit 224
Exit 220

Sarasota/Bradenton Int'l. Airport

62

37

Exit 217

Sarasota

64

Siesta Key ★

Exit 210

41

Exit 205

70

GULF OF MEXICO

Exit 200

△ MYAKKA RIVER S.P.

Peace R.

Venice

Exit 193

72

Caspersen Beach ★

75

Warm Mineral Springs

Englewood Beach ★

North Port

Arcadia

STUMP PASS BEACH S.P. ★ Englewood

El Jobean

17

70

DON PEDRO I. S.P. ★

Port Charlotte

Fisherman's Village ★

Historic Downtown Shopping District

Palm I.

Punta Gorda

Exit 164

Gasparilla I.

GASPARILLA ISLAND S.P. ★

PONCE DE LEON PARK

31

Boca Grande Lighthouse ★

Charlotte Harbor

Exit 158

Babcock-Webb Wildlife Mgt. Area ★ Babcock Ranch

Burnt Store Marina

41

Randell Research Center ★

Pine I.

Historical Museum

Exit 143

Captiva

St. James City

Edison-Ford Estate

Exit 141

Caloosahatchee R.

Sanibel I.

Cape Coral

Exit 138

Calusa Nature Center

J. N. "DING" DARLING N.W.R.

Ft. Myers

Bowman's Beach ★

Sanibel

Lehigh Acres

La Belle

Sanibel Historic Village ★
Sanibal Lighthouse ★

San Carlos Park

29

Ft. Myers Beach

Southwest Florida Int'l. Airport

Estero I.

LOVERS KEY S.P. ★

Six Mile Cypress Slough Preserve

82

DELNOR-WIGGINS PASS S.P. ★

75

Bonita Springs

★ Immokalee

Exit 111

IMMOKALEE RD.

Naples

Exit 107

Naples Beach ★

84

Exit 101

Corkscrew Swamp Sanctuary

Marco

951

PICAYUNE STRAND S.F. ★

75

Exit 80

Marco I.

EVERGLADES PKWY. (ALLIGATOR ALLEY)

Caxambas Pass

Goodland

FAKAHATCHEE STRAND PRES. S.P.

29

COLLIER-SEMINOLE S.P. △

BIG CYPRESS NATIONAL PRESERVE

To Ft. Lauderdale

Ten Thousand Islands

Everglades City

TAMIAMI TRAIL

Tamiami Canal

Everglades N.P. ★
Gulf Coast Visitor Center

Chokoloskee

To Miami

EVERGLADES N.P.

© The Countryman Press

N

0   10   20
Miles

✈ Airport
△ Camping
★ Point of Interest

THE CULTURAL COAST:
SARASOTA AND HER ISLANDS
AND MANATEE COUNTY

No one is quite sure where the name "Sarasota" came from, but it certainly is unique. It may have originated with the native peoples, who had a trading post marked "Saraxota" on early European maps. The name popped up on a Florida map in 1839, and it's been there ever since. This region has a long and storied history, with human occupation dating back thousands of years. It has a high concentration of archeological sites and is the landing site of Spanish explorer Hernando De Soto, who in 1539 arrived with his troops near the mouth of Tampa Bay in search of gold. Near the end of the Second Seminole War in 1841, Josiah Gates arrived by boat and homesteaded along the river in the area now known as **Old Manatee.** Maj. Robert Gamble established his 3,500-acre sugar plantation along the Manatee River in 1843. In 1851 William Whitaker built a log cabin at Yellow Bluffs along Sarasota Bay, the location now marked by Whitaker Gateway Park. By 1855, enough people had settled around the river for Manatee County to be formed from southern Hillsborough County. After the Civil War, settlers streamed into the interior to establish cattle ranches, citrus groves, and large farms in places such as **Parrish** and Miakka (now **Myakka**), leading to a local agricultural boom. The city of **Bradenton** grew up around the Civil War–era village of Manatee, with businesses lining downtown avenues and imposing Victorian homes built across the river in **Palmetto.** Rivers define Manatee County—Little Manatee at its northern end, the Manatee River between Ellenton and Bradenton, and the Braden River to the south.

By 1913, the small 1890s settlement of **Sarasota** that grew around the Whitaker homestead incorporated as a city, with its patterns of growth set by Mrs. Bertha Honore Palmer, wife of Chicago magnate Potter Palmer, a socialite with a winter home in **Osprey** who bought up a great deal of the county's land before the 1920s boom hit. Looking for a winter home for his circus, John Ringling came to town and threw his hat in the developer's ring by underwriting downtown skyscrapers and an artfully conceived causeway meant to open up development on his lands on the outer islands. High society flocked to this waterfront playground, with its brash new casinos and fine hotels, and established a tradition of fine arts that lives on to this day. In 1921 Sarasota broke off as its own county, including the city of **Venice,** named after the city in Italy when the post office was established in 1888. Venice is one of Florida's first planned cities, designed by noted architect John Nolan in the 1920s as an Italian Renaissance village.

The barrier islands of this region have long been a beach vacation destination for savvy Floridians. Inhabited in ancient times by Timucua and, more recently, Calusa; explored by the Spanish in the early 1500s; and permanently settled after Florida gained statehood in the 1800s, **Anna Maria Island** has three charming villages—**Anna Maria, Holmes Beach,** and **Bradenton Beach**—with a mix of old-fashioned seaside residential communities, motels and low-rise condo complexes (thanks to an ordinance prohibiting buildings from being more than three stories tall), and miles and miles of public beaches with easy access and free parking. While **Longboat Key** is primarily residential, it boasts superb beaches, resort and beach-home rentals, and some classic motels. Just off the coast of Sarasota, **St. Armands Key** is a bustling shopping district, with adjacent **Lido Key** topped with condos. Just south, **Siesta Key** is a magnet for family vacations, with dozens of excellent accommodations and their famous "baby-powder soft" beaches. Offshore from Venice (which boasts its own fabulous beaches), **Casey Key** and **Manasota Key** are primarily residential, with their narrow roads hidden beneath a tunnel of tropical vegetation.

GUIDANCE You can't miss the **Sarasota Convention and Visitor's Bureau** (941-955-0991; www.sarasotafl.org), 655 N Tamiami Trl, as it's in a large complex with the Center for the Arts and the Auditorium, right next to Boulevard of the Arts. Stop in for brochures and recommendations. The **Siesta Key Chamber of Commerce** (941-349-3800; www.siestakeychamber.com), 5118 Ocean Blvd, is in a shopping center in Siesta Village. You'll find their services very helpful when booking a room during the high season, as accommodations check in with them with availability reports. Smaller regional offices include the **Anna Maria Island Chamber of Commerce** (941-778-1541), 5313 Gulf Dr N, Holmes Beach, and the **Manatee County Tourist Information Center** (941-729-7040), 5461 Factory Shops Blvd, Ellenton, at Prime Outlet Center.

ANNA MARIA JAIL

Sandra Friend

GETTING THERE *By car:* **I-75, US 19, US 301,** and **US 41** provide primary access to the region.

By air: **Sarasota Bradenton International Airport** (941-FLY-2-SRQ; www.srq-airport.com) has regular service by six major carriers, including AirTran, Delta, and US Airways, and by two commuter airlines.

Sarasota

To St. Petersburg
To Tampa

TAMPA BAY

Passage Key

Rattlesnake Key

Exit 5

Exit 2 E. Exit 228

Terra Ceia

19

37TH ST E.

Anna Maria Pier

EMERSON POINT PARK

Snead Island

(MENDOZA RD.)

Prime Outlet Mall

Anna Maria Island

De Soto National Memorial

Gamble Plantation

Exit 224

Anna Maria

10TH ST W.

Palmetto

10TH ST E.

Holmes Beach

Perico Island

So. Florida Museum & Manatee Aquarium

Bradenton

Manatee River

MANATEE AV. E.

Exit 220

Palma Sola Bay

Village of the Arts

34TH AV.

Bradenton Beach

CORTEZ RD.

36TH AV. (ELWOOD PARK RD.)

MANATEE AV. W.

CORTEZ RD.

53RD AV.

53RD AV.

Exit 217

63RD AV. E. (SAUNDERS RD.)

Longboat Key

Sarasota Bay

WHITFIELD AV.

TALLEVAST RD.

UNIVERSITY PKWY.

Exit 213

GULF OF MEXICO

Sarasota/Bradenton Int'l. Airport

Ringling Museum of Art & Asolo Theater

Classic Car Museum

Sarasota Jungle Gardens

MARTIN LUTHER KING JR. WY.

Boulevard of the Arts & Van Wezel Hall

3RD ST.

Exit 210

QUICK POINT NAT. PRES.

KEN THOMPSON PARK

FRUITVILLE RD.

Sarasota Bay Walk, Pelican Man's Bird Sanctuary, & Mote Aquarium

Sarasota

St. Armands Circle

Selby Botanical Gardens

BAHIA VISTA ST.

WEBBER ST.

BEE RIDGE RD.

JOHN RINGLING CSWY.

SIESTA DR.

Exit 207

PROCTOR RD.

Siesta Key

Exit 205

CLARK RD.

Siesta Key Public Beach

✈ Airport
★ Point of Interest

Historic Spanish Point

To Ft. Myers

0   2   4
Miles

N

© The Countryman Press

By bus: The **Greyhound** (1-800-231-2222; www.greyhound.com) bus station is at Washington and Sixth, along US 301 and 2 blocks north of Fruitville Rd, Sarasota.

GETTING AROUND *By car:* **US 19** south from St. Petersburg ends in Bradenton; **US 301** south from Tampa ends in Sarasota at **US 41.** From the major north-south highways, use **FL 70 (Manatee Rd)** west to reach Bradenton Beach; **FL 780** (Fruitville Rd) east to **FL 789** to reach St. Armands and Longboat Key; **FL 72 (Clark Rd)** in Sarasota to reach Siesta Key; and **FL 681** from I-75 for the most efficient route to the Laurel/Nokomis/Venice area. **Albee Rd** and **Black Point Rd** connect Casey Key with the mainland, and **FL 776** takes you south from Venice to Englewood.

By bus: **NCAT** and **SCAT** (941-861-1234), 5303 Pinkney Ave, run all over Sarasota County between 5 AM and 8 PM. Bus fare is 50 cents, and unlimited monthly passports are $30. Pick up timetables at the visitors centers. Venice has its separate **SCAT About** route (941-863-1234).

By taxi: **Yellow Cab** (941-349-8885), 2011 Cornell St.

By trolley: **Trolley Systems of America** (941-346-3115; www.tsatrolley.com), 6840 Jarvis Rd, runs throughout downtown Sarasota. A single ride costs 50 cents.

PUBLIC REST ROOMS In Venice, you'll find them downtown in Centennial Park on Venice Ave. Beachfront parks include public rest rooms and changing areas.

PARKING The availability of parking varies tremendously throughout the region, but the good news is, most of it is free—including the natural-surface beach parking lots on **Anna Maria Island, Bradenton Beach,** and **Siesta Key,** as well as at the beachfront county parks in Venice. Downtown **Bradenton** and downtown **Sarasota** have metered spaces, but you can park along the bayfront in Sarasota for free (three-hour limit) and walk to the shopping district. **St. Armands** also has free three-hour street parking, and a large flat lot hidden behind the shops between Ringling Blvd and Blvd of the Presidents with free two-hour parking. In **Venice** there is a large free lot right off Venice Ave in the middle of downtown, and plenty of free street parking in the shopping district.

MEDICAL EMERGENCIES Call 911 for emergencies. There are many hospitals in the region with 24-hour emergency rooms, including **Sarasota Memorial Hospital** (941-917-9000), 1700 S Tamiami Trl; **Manatee Memorial Hospital** (941-746-5111), on US 41 in Bradenton; and **Bon Secours Hospital** (941-485-7711), on Business US 41 in Venice.

✳ To See

AQUARIUM ♿ 🐾 The world's first marine research center devoted to shark studies, **Mote Marine Aquarium** (941-388-2451; www.mote.org), 1600 Ken Thompson Pkwy, City Island, Sarasota, celebrated its 50th anniversary in 2005 by debuting a new multimedia presentation, *Shark Attack.* But don't wait for the

creatures of the deep to haunt you—
come and visit them yourself! Entering the main aquarium, you walk
through a darkened room filled with
tanks of saltwater creatures and
engaging exhibits. Pause and enjoy
the beauty of jellyfish with their trail-
ing tentacles glowing. The outdoor
tanks showcase mollusks and squid,
with a giant squid (pickled, not live)
for you to compare your size to. Then
it's on to tanks of Gulf sea life, including killifish and fiddler crabs and a
large touch tank with clams, sea urchins, and horseshoe crabs. Kids cluster
around Remarkable Rays, a touch tank with stingrays. In the Goldstein Marine
Mammal Visitor Center (follow the walk across the island), kids can climb
through a turtle excluder device and marvel at the many manatees (the permanent residents could not be returned to the wild after rehabilitation). Open daily
10–5, including holidays. Adults $15, children 4–12 $10, members free.

Sandra Friend

TOUCH TANK AT MOTE MARINE AQUARIUM

ARCHEOLOGICAL SITES

Bradenton
At **Shaw's Point,** now inside **De Soto National Memorial** (see *Historic Sites*),
archeologist S. T. Walker discovered a shell mound in 1879 that had been created
by an early culture along the shores of Tampa Bay, complete with fire pits. The
mound was nearly 600 feet long and 20 feet high at its highest. Despite the discovery of pottery shards within the mound, there was no government protection for
such important artifacts back then. By the 1930s, the mound had been pulled
apart and trucked away for road fill. Still, if you walk the trail to Shaw's Point,
you'll see the bleached oyster shells that were once a part of this large mound.

Osprey
At **Historic Spanish Point** (see *Historic Sites*), there are several sites of
significant archeological interest, most
notably the Archaic period midden
near the Guptill House, ca. 3000 B.C.,
and the Shell Ridge midden, which
juts out into Little Sarasota Bay and is
wonderfully presented inside "Window to the Past," an exhibit hall of
windows showing off one thousand
years of human history in the layers of
the midden as explored by archeologists as far back as 1871, when the
Smithsonian helped landowner John
Webb identify artifacts and bones.

CUTTLEFISH TANK AT MOTE MARINE
AQUARIUM

Sandra Friend

Snead Island

At **Emerson Point Preserve** (see *Parks*), stop at the Portavant Temple Mound to recapture a bit of prehistory. This flat-topped mound along the Manatee River is 150 feet long and 80 feet wide, and it once commanded a spectacular view, now obscured by centuries-old oaks. More than one thousand years ago, a village of the ancestors of the Timucua sat on this site. A smaller rounded subsidiary mound and several middens are scattered throughout the forest.

Terra Ceia

I circled the peninsula twice before finding **Madiera Bickel Mound Archeo-logical State Park** (941-723-4536), 57th St W, a prehistoric temple mound near Terra Ceia Bay. To find the site, do not turn at the Florida Heritage sign. Instead, turn west off US 19 at an abandoned gas station and follow Bayshore Dr for 1.3 miles to the parking area. A paved concrete path winds through the palm hammock to a set of stairs leading to the top of the 20-foot-tall temple mound, which was purchased and preserved by Mrs. Madiera Bickel in 1948, who turned it over to the state for caretaking. Paleoindian, Weedon Island, and Safety Harbor culture artifacts have been unearthed on the site. There are picnic tables along the path, but no interpretive information.

ART GALLERIES

Bradenton

An artist's colony just outside downtown, the **Village of the Arts** (941-747-8056; www.artistsguildofmanatee.org), between Ninth St W and 14th St W, south of Milk Ave, is a working artists' neighborhood of colorful historic bungalows, with a mix of studios, galleries, and housing. With an Artwalk on the first Fri and Sat of each month and regular "open shopping" hours of 11–4 Fri and Sat, it's a great place to shop for unique and whimsical art direct from the artists.

Englewood

Local artists such as Jeff Cornell, Colleen Henry, and Melissa Searle take center stage at the **Lemon Tree Gallery** (941-474-5700; www.lemontreegallery.com), 420 W Dearborn St, where delightful original paintings evoke the playfulness of life near the beach.

Longboat Key

Grab some fun at **KK's ARTique** (941-383-0883), 5360 Gulf of Mexico Dr, where appealing scenes of Sarasota mingle with classy art glass, mirror mosaics, fiber craft, and pottery.

St. Armands

You'll find galleries scattered throughout the shopping district on the Circle. **Maui Art** (941-388-5305), 321 John Ringling Blvd, features giclee paintings of ocean scenes. Artist David Miller often works in the front window. Art is fun at **Garden Argosy** (941-388-6402), 361 John Ringling Blvd, which features colorful metal pop sculptures perfect indoors or out, mermaid art, and vivid mirrors framed with inspirational art. At the **Giving Tree Gallery** (941-388-1353), Five Blvd of the Presidents, look for kinetic sculptures, carved wooden birds, and metal art.

Visit **Palm Avenue** for more than a dozen upscale fine-art galleries, including Butler & Butler Antiques & Fine Arts, Zeigenfuss, and the Medici Gallery. The street is best experienced during a First Friday walk, which starts at 6 PM. Just a few blocks away, at **Burns Court,** explore more galleries such as the **Blue House Gallery** (941-752-1513), with its fine jewelry, paintings, and sculpture.

Flanked by three-hundred-year-old oaks, the grand entrance to the **Gamble Plantation Historic State Park** (941-723-4536), 3708 Patten Ave (US 301), Ellenton, is reminiscent of a scene from *Gone With the Wind.* And like the mythical Tara, the last remaining antebellum plantation in South Florida played an important role in the last days of the War Between the States. As one of the first post-statehood settlers in southwest Florida, Maj. Robert Gamble established his 3,500-acre sugar plantation along the Manatee River in 1843, shipping his finished products downriver and out into the Gulf of Mexico to New Orleans. Built of tabby (a mix of oyster shells and lime) with walls 2 feet thick, his Greek Revival mansion was designed to trap cool air like a cave and to utilize rainwater cisterns for fresh water.

In 1865 the Confederacy fell. It was then the mansion played a crucial part in the end game of the war. Fleeing Richmond, Confederate Secretary of State Judah P. Benjamin disguised himself as a French journalist, "M. Bonfal," to travel to Florida. Reaching Brooksville in late spring, he enlisted the confidence of Capt. LeRoy Lesley. A $40,000 reward stood for Benjamin's capture, but Lesley was a loyal Confederate. He escorted Benjamin to the Gamble Plantation, where Capt. Archibald McNeil, the new owner of the plantation, hosted the "Brains of the Confederacy" in comfortable surroundings until arrangements could be made for a boat to Nassau. Union soldiers tracked the men down, and both Benjamin and McNeil had to flee to elude capture. The promised boat appeared, and Benjamin successfully emigrated to London, where he had a long and successful career in law.

As happened with many grand old plantations in Florida, the mansion was abandoned to the elements and left to deteriorate. In 1925 the United Daughters of the Confederacy purchased the land and donated it to the state with the proviso that it be designated the Judah P. Benjamin Confederate Memorial. Now restored to its original glory, the home features period furnishings and artwork, and is one of the few remaining examples of a Florida antebellum plantation. The UDC restored and maintains the Patten House (circa 1895) on the grounds of the state park, open by appointment and during special events. The state park has a nominal entrance fee, and there is an additional fee for a guided tour of the home.

Looking for working artists? You'll find them at the **Towles Court Artist Colony** (941-363-0087; www.towlescourt.com), 1943 Morrill St, located between US 301, Osprey Ave, Morrill St, and Adams Ln, downtown. In this neighborhood of 1920s bungalows, look for the **Katharine Butler Gallery** (941-955-4546), 1943 Morrill St, with rotating exhibits monthly in various media; **The Gallery** (941-730-6265), 252 S Links Ave, showcasing artists from around the world; **Celery Barn** (941-952-9889), 266 Links Ave, with painting, sculpture, and portraiture from local artists Jini Mount and Teresa D. Spinner; and bright and whimsical primitive and pop art at **Plum Door Gallery** (941-362-0960), 1950 Adams Ln. There are many other galleries as well, so park your car in one of the two large lots and wander through the community. Galleries and shops open 11–4 Tue–Sun, with Third Friday gallery walks at Towles Court 6–10 PM all year. See www.towlescourt.com/events.htm for the full schedule.

Venice

Bold acrylics drew me into **Artemisa** (941-484-9432), 219 W Venice Ave. Inside, I found beautiful Florida wildlife art and landscapes, including evocative scenes of the Big Cypress Swamp and Boca Grande by local artist James Crafford.

At **Clyde Butcher's Venice Gallery and Studio** (941-486-0811), 237 Warfield Ave, marvel at the massive black-and-white landscapes that capture the soul of wild Florida. This is where Clyde does his darkroom work, so if you'd like to see how these giant photos are printed, ask for a tour. Open weekdays.

BASEBALL Every spring, the **Pittsburgh Pirates** head to **McKechnie Field** (941-748-4610; http://pittsburgh.pirates.mlb.com/NASApp/mlb/pit/ballpark/pit_ballpark_springtrain.jsp), 1611 Ninth St W in Bradenton, their southern home, for spring training. Their nearby rivals, the **Cincinnati Reds,** hang out nearby at **Jeff Maultsby Field** (941-955-6501; www.cincinnatireds.com), 1090 N Euclid Ave, in Sarasota.

HISTORIC SITES

Anna Maria Island

Built in 1910, the **Anna Maria Pier** anchors the north end of the island and looks out over Tampa Bay. On a clear day, you can see Egmont Key, Fort De Soto, and the Sunshine Skyway Bridge in the distance. In addition to providing a place to fish, the pier has a restaurant where you can savor the view.

Bradenton

✍ Commemorating Spanish explorer Hernando De Soto's arrival at Tampa Bay in 1539, **De Soto National Memorial** (941-792-0458; www.nps.gov/desoto), end of 75th Ave W at Shaw's Point, was commissioned in 1940 as the probable landing site of the Spanish fleet. In addition to a replica Spanish camp with living-history interpreters and a visitor center with artifacts, exhibits, and a video on De Soto's expedition, the park has more than a mile of trails leading through the mangrove fringe to various points of historic interest. The peninsula served as a cattle shipping point during the 1800s and a lookout post for U.S. Navy blockaders during the Civil War. As you walk the path along the Manatee River, you'll encounter the

Holy Eucharist Monument, commissioned by the Diocese of St. Augustine in 1960 as a Catholic memorial in honor of De Soto. The nearby Memorial Cross remembers the 12 priests who accompanied De Soto on the expedition. Open 9–5 daily. Free.

Florida Heritage District signs on FL 64 at 27th St E direct you to **Braden Castle Park,** the site of the first **Tin Can Tourist Camp** in Florida and the former homestead of Dr. Joseph Braden. There isn't much left of his old tabby castle, but the view of the Manatee River is spectacular. The ruins are in the middle of a quaint village of tiny bungalows dating from 1924. It is still an active retirement community, so please be respectful when you visit, and don't block driveways or bother people.

Sandra Friend

BEACH STREET PIER, BRADENTON BEACH

At **Manatee Village Historical Park** (941-749-7165), 604 15th St E, explore historic landmarks brought here for preservation, such as the Bat Fogarty Boat Works, the Stephens' House, and the Wiggins Store. Open 9–4:30 Mon–Fri and 1:30–4:30 Sun (except Jul–Aug); closed Sat. Free. Behind the park (on an adjacent tract outside the fence) is the city's oldest cemetery, the **1815 Manatee Burying Ground,** where most of the county's earliest settlers are buried. The nearby business district at Ninth St E and FL 64 is the heart of **Old Manatee,** the first settlement in the county. Josiah Gates claimed his homestead here along the river in 1841.

Most of downtown **Bradenton** is a business district from the 1920s boom, but the city itself was founded as Braidenton in 1878. Watch for the Heritage District signs near 12th St W directing you to the Italianate **Post Office** and the **Bradenton Carnegie Library** (941-741-4070), 1405 Fourth Ave W, established in 1918 by Andrew Carnegie and an important repository of the early history of the region.

Bradenton Beach
Downtown Bradenton Beach is a quaint historic district with homes and businesses dating from the turn of the last century. At the end of Bridge Street, walk down the newly restored Bridge Street Pier, once part of the original plank bridge that was the only access to Anna Maria Island for nearly 40 years.

Longboat Key
Blue historic markers along the sidewalks paralleling Broadway Street denote key homes and businesses in the original **Village of Longbeach,** founded in 1885. There are still many quaint cottages on the side streets, but most of the historic village has been replaced by modern upscale homes.

Osprey

At **Historic Spanish Point** (941-966-5214; www.historicspanishpoint.org), 337 N Tamiami Trl, explore layers of history dating back thousands of years along the waterfront of Little Sarasota Bay, from Archaic period middens (see *Archeological Sites*) to mansions built over the past two hundred years by various inhabitants of the land—among them Mrs. (Bertha Honore) Potter Palmer, wife of a Chicago magnate and a savvy player in Florida's 1920s land boom. At one point, she owned more than a quarter of what is now Sarasota County. A museum on the property tells her story. Historic buildings of particular interest include Mary's Free Chapel, built with funds from friends of a young lady in the early 1900s who died of tuberculosis; the packing house, which shipped citrus fruit for many decades; the White Cottage, Jack Webb's home atop the Shell Ridge midden; and the Guptill Home, where in 1877, Frank Guptill built boats known as "sharpies," open flat-bottomed sailboats that could handle the shallow estuaries of Florida's coast. A replica of the boatwright's shop and of one of his boats, the *Lizzie G,* are on display. You are welcome to stroll the deeply forested grounds at your own pace. Take the side trails to explore secret gardens and eerie swamp forests. Four formal tours are offered daily for no additional charge, and volunteers present living history throughout the property on Sunday. The admission is well worth it: adults $9, Florida residents and seniors $8, ages 6–12 $3.

Palmetto

✐ At the **Palmetto Historical Park** (941-723-4991), 10th Ave and Sixth St W, experience a 1920 kindergarten schoolroom, peek into the town's first freestanding post office from 1880, and visit the military museum in the Cypress House. The 1914 Carnegie Library has an extensive amount of genealogical and historical information, as well as one of the few basements in the region—it was a requirement for the grant for the library to be built. Open 1–6 Tue, 8–noon and 1–5 Sat. Free.

Sarasota

At **Phillippi Estate Park** (941-316-1309), 5500 S Tamiami Trl, the historic Edson Keith Mansion is a beautifully restored two-story 1916 Italian Renaissance home designed by Otis and Clark that is used for civic functions. Walk the grounds, peek in the windows, and imagine what it was like to have this view all to yourself a century ago. It is occasionally open for viewing.

Terra Ceia

While there's little left of the original village save an enclave of rural homesteads, **Terra Ceia** (north of Palmetto off US 19) has two distinctive historic sites—the old Palmetto Elementary School and a post office (circa 1891) at the corner of Terra Ceia Dr and Center Rd.

Venice

The neighborhoods of Venice are architectural gems with a great deal of Mediterranean and Spanish Mission architecture from the 1920s. Make a point of driving through them after exploring the downtown area in the **Venezia Park** district, where there are more than 25 Mediterranean Revival homes; a tour brochure is available from the chamber of commerce. The **Old Venice Depot** (see *Railroadiana*) is also home to the Venice Historical Society.

Anna Maria City

✍ At the **Anna Maria Island Historical Museum** (941-778-0492), 402 Pine Ave, you can pose inside the Old City Jail (no prisoners, no windows!) with a jail-bird costume on, or go on a scavenger hunt with the kids for baby turtles, shark's teeth, and more. Open 10–12 Tue–Thu and Sat (May–Sep) and 10–3 (Oct–Apr). Free.

Bradenton

On the campus of Manatee Community College, the **Family Heritage House Museum** (941-752-5319; www.familyheritagehouse.com), 5840 26th St W, is a gallery and resource center for the study of African American achievements, as well as part of the National Underground Railroad "Network to Freedom" program, with extensive research materials. Open on Sat by appointment only.

✍ The **South Florida Museum** (941-746-4131; www.southfloridamuseum.org), 201 10th St W, is one of Florida's more intriguing collections of archeological and historic interest. While you'll hear a lot about Snooty, the museum's resident manatee, the real treasure here is the amazing **Tallant Collection** of Paleo-indian artifacts, including many excavated from mounds near Lake Okeechobee. In the Great Hall, a series of dioramas on Florida's long prehistory and history usher you back to the Tallant Gallery, where golden icons, pottery shards, and precious metal jewelry are on display. The 60,000-gallon **Parker Manatee Aquarium** is Snooty's home, where you'll learn about manatees and their part in Florida's ecosystems. In the **Spanish Plaza,** a replica home (to scale) shows off life as it was in Spain when Hernando De Soto came to these shores in the 1500s. The main floor also features a planetarium and Discovery Place, a hands-on workshop for kids. Upper-floor exhibits focus on regional history. Stop by the museum store on your way out to purchase replicas from the Tallant Collection, books, and great games and toys for the kids. Open 10–5 Tue–Sat, noon–5 Sun, and 10–5 Mon during the season (Jan–Apr, July) only. Adults $13.75, seniors $11.75, ages 4–12 $8.75.

Palmetto

✍ In the Palmetto Historical Park (see *Historic Sites*), the **Manatee County Agricultural Museum** (941-721-2034), 1015 Sixth St W, presents an excellent overview of the history of agriculture in this region, from citrus groves to commercial fishing. (Did you know, for instance, that the region was famous for gladiolas in the 1920s? And was the first place that pink grapefruit was bred?) Five galleries present artifacts, photos, tools, and exhibits explaining how farming built this county. Junior Agriculture activities provide fun stuff for the kids to do, such as mazes and puzzles. Open 10–noon and 1–4 Tue–Sat. Free.

Sarasota

At the **Museum of Asian Art** (941-954-7117; www.museumasianart.com), 640 S Washington Blvd, marvel at the intricacies of the Yangtze River Collection of Chinese jades, where flowing forms of mountains and trees come to life. Housed partially in a bank vault, the museum contains priceless treasures overseen by

Dr. Helga Wall-Apelt and is a must for serious collectors of Asian art. Open 11–5 Wed–Fri. Adults $5, children free. Photo ID required for entry.

Recognized worldwide for its Baroque masterpieces, the **Ringling Museum of Art** (941-358-3180; www.ringling.org), 5401 Bay Shore Blvd, is much more than a fine-art collection—it's a complex of museums that will satisfy everyone in the family. To start, a visit to **Ca' d'Zan** celebrates the life and times of John and Mable Ringling, who lived on the 66-acre grounds in this Venetian-style mansion, built in 1924 as Mable Ringling's dream home. Enter through the 24-carat gold-leaf doors into the solarium and tour this classic structure, which still contains 95 percent of the original items installed by the Ringlings. In its time, it was the largest home within Sarasota city limits, and it had a soundproof ballroom, central heating, and an Otis elevator. Of the four levels, two are shown on your tour. Afterward, walk the grounds to the **Circus Museum,** which contains an interactive "Magic Ring" ideal for kids to play out their circus fantasies, and it showcases circus wagon art, props and costumes, and the history of the "Greatest Show on Earth." Finally, explore the grand salons of the **Museum of Art,** each with its own color backdrop and tone presenting such masterpieces as Simon Vouet's *Time Discovering the Love of Venus and Mars,* and Peter Paul Rubens's *Triumph of the Eucharist.* This is one of Florida's top art destinations. Adults $15, seniors $13, students and Florida teachers $5, children under 5 free. Daily admissions to Ca' d'Zan (included in your general admission) are limited, so head there first—the first tour starts at 9:45 AM. Advance ticket purchase is recommended to guarantee a spot. The intimate "Private Places" tour of Ca' d'Zan is an additional $20 and is offered 12:30 and 2:30 Mon–Sat. Open 10–5:30 daily except Thanksgiving, Christmas, and New Year's Day.

Known as Bellm's when I was a kid, the **Sarasota Classic Car Museum** (941-355-6228; www.sarasotacarmuseum.org), 5500 N Tamiami Trl, still showcases the stuff Dad loves best—vintage autos, antique cameras, and antique phonographs. Open since 1953, the museum has more than one hundred automobiles in its collection and frequently refreshes the stock by trades and acquisitions. Adults $8.50, seniors $7.65, ages 13–17 $5.75, ages 6–12 $4.

JOHN AND MABLE RINGLING MUSEUM
OF ART

The John and Mable Ringling Museum of Art

PUBLIC ART That wasn't just a giant piggy bank—it's art. In **downtown Venice** you'll find artful pigs in interesting vignettes.

RAILROADIANA

Parrish
✍ At the **Florida Railroad Museum** (1-877-869-0800; www.frrm.org), 83rd St E off US 301, the museum *is* the train, run by volunteers, and it operates on weekends on a 6-mile stretch of original Florida Gulf Coast Railroad track from Parrish north to the town of

Willow near the Little Manatee River. Choose from air-conditioned coaches or open-air cars as the locomotive takes you on a smooth two-hour ride. Adults $10, children $6. A small gift shop is tucked away in rolling stock on a siding.

Venice

The Brotherhood of Locomotive Engineers (BLE) from Cleveland was instrumental in the growth of Venice. In 1925 the organization bought more than 50,000 acres and began developing around the waterways, with the city incorporated in 1927. Beneath the Venice Avenue Bridge, the **Old Venice Depot** stands from the Florida boomtown heyday, where the Seaboard Air Line provided passenger service until 1971, and the last circus train stopped here in 1992. A Seaboard Air Line caboose sits outside the station in a small park with picnic tables. The interior of the station has been restored and includes some exhibits and a gift shop. Open 10–4 Mon, Wed, and Fri—and sporadically, as it is staffed by volunteers. Fee.

ZOOLOGICAL PARKS & WILDLIFE REHAB

Sarasota

✍ Walk the trails at **Pelican Man's Bird Sanctuary** (941-388-4444; www.pelicanman.org), 1708 Ken Thompson Pkwy, to acquaint yourself with the dozens of permanent inhabitants of this long-standing wildlife rehab center, founded in 1980 by Dale Shields, the longtime "Pelican Man" who rescued birds wrapped in fishing line and nursed them back to health. Dale died in 2003, but his mission remains. "Peli the Pelican" provides fun facts and interpretive information at each exhibit. Learn bird calls in the various habitat areas and listen to the constant chirps and flurry of wings. Donation.

One of Florida's classics, **Sarasota Jungle Gardens** (941-355-5305; www.sarasotajunglegardens.com), 3701 Bay Shore Rd, celebrated its 60th anniversary in 2005 and is still as much fun as when I was a kid. Wander narrow, winding, natural footpaths through tropical plantings on 10 acres to explore themed areas such as the Tiki Gardens, the alligator and crocodile habitat, a fruit and nut garden, and Gardens of Christ. There are five animal-related shows throughout the day in various parts of the park. Of particular interest are the lakes where the flamingos hang out. The gardens participates in an active American flamingo breeding program, so the flamingos nest on an island in Mirror Lake. Open 9–5 daily; closed Christmas. Adults $12, seniors $11, children 3–12 $8.

A REHABILITATED PELICAN RETURNS TO VISIT PELICAN MAN'S SANCTUARY.

Sandra Friend

✳ To Do

BICYCLING ♿ On Siesta Key, rent bikes at **C.B.'s Saltwater Outfitters** (see *Boating*) to ride the island roads, or at **Siesta Sports Rentals** (941-346-1797), 6551 Midnight Pass Rd, where they also have all-terrain wheelchairs perfect for beach access.

BIRDING The secret sweet spot for birding on **Anna Maria Island** is well away from the crowd at the northern residential tip of the island, where the beach can be up to 300 feet wide, attracting flocks of colony birds such as terns, skimmers, and gulls. Park at Bayfront Beach Park and walk up Bay Street to the pathway leading to the beach. At **Myakka River State Park** (see *Parks*), the Birdwalk (elevated walkway) out into the river provides excellent opportunities for spotting all varieties of wading birds. Little-known **Red Bug Slough Preserve,** 5200 Beneva Rd, is listed as a "hot spot" by the local Audubon chapter for viewing bald eagles and wading birds. In search of Florida scrub jays? This elusive threatened species can be seen along the trails at **Oscar Scherer State Park** (see *Parks*)and a new colony is establishing itself at **Shamrock Park & Nature Center** (see *Nature Centers*). An urban gem in south Venice is the **Venice Area Audubon Rookery** (941-493-9476; www.veniceaudubon.org), accessed via US 41 to Annex Rd on the east side of the South Sarasota County Municipal Complex.

BOATING

Longboat Key

For a spin on Sarasota Bay, rent your own runabout, deck boat, or open skiff at **Cannons Marina** (941-383-1311; www.cannons.com), 6040 Gulf of Mexico Dr, with rates running from $65 for a half day to $350 for a full day. You are required to put down a $200 security deposit and are responsible for gas and oil. Open 8–5:30 daily.

Siesta Key

C.B.'s Saltwater Outfitters (941-349-4400; www.cbsoutfitters.com), 1249 Stickney Point Rd, offers rentals ranging from a 17-foot runabout to a deck boat, with rates starting at $95 for a half day. Captains and tours are available for inexperienced boaters. At the **Turtle Beach Marina** (941-349-9449; www.turtle beachmarina.com), 8865 Midnight Pass Rd, rent Wave Runners, kayaks, sport boats, and pontoon boats by the hour or day, or anchor for the weekend at the full-service marina.

ECOTOURS Departing from Mote Marine Aquarium (see *Aquarium*), **Sarasota Bay Explorers** (941-388-4200), 1600 Ken Thompson Pkwy, offers a variety of tours, including Sea Life Encounter Tours, Kayak Tours, and LeBarge Tropical Cruises. Choose from dolphin watching, sight-seeing, nature exploration, and sunset cruises. Rates start at $18 adult, $13 children 4–12 (under 4 free), and some tours can be arranged in tandem with aquarium tours.

Sarasota

At Myakka River State Park (see *Parks*), **Myakka Wildlife Tours** (941-365-0100), 3715 Jaffa Dr, offers cruises on the *Myakka Maiden* and the *Gator Gal*, the world's largest airboats that take you up into the shallow wetlands. Or opt for a **Tram Safari** on the park's back roads for wildlife viewing. Tours are $8 per person, $4 for children 12 and under.

FAMILY ACTIVITIES ✔ **G.WIZ—The Hands-On Science Museum** (941-309-4949; www.gwiz.org), 1001 Boulevard of the Arts, Sarasota, was designed with families in mind. Kids and adults interact in the various "zones" of the museum, including the WaveZone, where you experiment with light and sound, and the EcoZone, with critters and a butterfly garden. The KidsZone is for little ones 6 and under. Open 10–5 Tue–Sat, 1–5 Sun. Adults $9, ages 6–21 $6, ages 3–5 $2. Free parking.

✔ **Smugglers Cove Adventure Golf** (941-351-6620), 3815 N Tamiami Trl, Sarasota, is known for its pirate ships and live gators on the course—which the kids are allowed to feed!

FISHING Head for the flats of Sarasota County's bays with a guide from **C.B.'s Saltwater Outfitters** (see *Boating*) for tarpon, snook, and redfish on light tackle. All guides endorsed by Orvis. Bring your own tackle? Try dropping a line off the **Anna Maria Pier** or the **Bradenton Beach Pier.**

GAMING Bet on the greyhounds at the **Sarasota Kennel Club** (941-355-7444; www.sarasotakennelclub.com), 5400 Bradenton Rd, Sarasota, racing nightly except Sunday.

GENEOLOGICAL RESEARCH Settlers started pouring into Venice in the 1860s, eager to homestead free land offered by the U.S. government under the Homestead Act. The Webb family, settling near Osprey, were the first to settle in. Trace your local ancestry and study regional history at the **Venice Archives and Area Historical Collection** (941-486-2487), 351 S Nassau St, Venice, which is open 10–4 Mon and Wed.

GOLF Winding through lush woodlands and waterways, **Pelican Pointe Golf & Country Club** (941-496-GOLF), Center Rd off Jacaranda Blvd, Venice, offers 27 holes of play, lessons from PGA professionals, a dining room, and a full-service pro shop.

HIKING There are dozens of excellent places to hike in the region; virtually all listings under *Green Space* and *Wild Places* provide day hikes. For details on the 40-mile backpacking loop at **Myakka River State Park,** pick up a copy of *50 Hikes in South Florida.*

PADDLING There are four established Blueways trails in the "Paddle Manatee" (www.co.manatee.fl.us) program—the **Terra Ceia Paddling Trail, Manatee River Paddling Trail, Braden River Paddling Trail,** and **Sarasota Bay Paddling Trail.** Contact the county for a comprehensive guide, which includes access points, points of interest, and maps. To explore Sarasota Bay on your own, rent your craft at **Economy Tackle/Dolphin Dive Watersports** (941-922-9671;

www.floridakayak.com), 6018 S Tamiami Trl, Sarasota. If you're a newbie to sea kayaking, consider a guided tour or ACA-certified instruction in an "Introduction to Kayaking" course. Rent a kayak at **C.B.'s Saltwater Outfitters** (see *Boating*) to paddle up to Palmer Point, the remote south tip of Siesta Key.

SCENIC DRIVES Following coastal highways and byways from the Sunshine Skyway Bridge over Tampa Bay to the southern tip of Manasota Key, the **Gulf Coast Heritage Trail** leads you on some of the region's most scenic roads, including canopied Manasota Key Drive. More than one hundred points of interest are detailed on the brochure and map. For a copy contact any of the region's tourism centers (see *Guidance*).

SEGWAY TOURS I didn't believe it until I tried it—a Segway really does balance your weight, no matter how you lean! With the nation's first city Segway Tour, **Florida Ever-Glides** (941-363-9556; www.floridaever-glides.com), 200 S Washington Blvd, #11, Sarasota, offers guided trips around downtown Sarasota on their quiet little machines—after a training session so you feel comfortable maneuvering your craft. Tours run two and a half hours, including a brief how-to orientation, and cost $61 per person.

SWIMMING Beaches, beaches, beaches . . . that's what this coast is all about—so swim here! The Gulf of Mexico is shallow, clear, and warm (see *Beaches*). In addition, you can "take the waters" at **Warm Mineral Springs** (see *Springs*), Florida's only truly "hot" spring at 87°F.

TRAIL RIDING Across from **Lake Manatee State Park** (see *Parks*), **Lake Manatee Stables** (941-746-3697), FL 64, Rye, offers trail riding on the park's trail system. To get a taste of what the Cracker cowmen endured, bring your own horse to **Myakka State Forest** to ride the extensive trail system through the vast open scrub, or enjoy a shorter ride along the trails at **Myakkahatchee Creek Preserve** (See *Wild Places*).

WALKING TOURS The **Manatee Riverwalk** is a designated walking tour that covers historic sites in Palmetto, Bradenton, and Village of the Arts. Contact the chamber of commerce (see *Guidance*) for a brochure and map.

WATER SPORTS Siesta Key has them! Stop by **C.B.'s Saltwater Outfitters** (see *Boating*) for Wave Runner rentals ($80 per hour) from **Siesta Key Jet Ski** (941-313-7547), or hook up with **Aquarius Parasail** (941-346-3532; www.aquarius parasail.com) to dangle your toes in the surf as you skim behind 1,000 feet of line. On Anna Maria Island, visit **Native Rentals** (941-778-7757), 5342 N Gulf Dr, where they have ocean kayaks, snorkeling and fishing gear, and body boards.

✳ Green Space

BEACHES On **Anna Maria Island,** enjoy 7½ miles of aquamarine water, white sand, and dunes topped with sea oats along the Gulf of Mexico. **Manatee Beach**

tends to be the busiest, being near Bradenton, so head south of **Bradenton Beach** for the best stretches of sand. Free parking and rest rooms.

Since **Manasota Key** is primarily residential within Sarasota County, the beaches hidden along the canopied road are less crowded and more enjoyable. Stop at 14-acre **Manasota Beach,** 8570 Manasota Key Rd, or **Blind Pass Beach,** 6725 Manasota Key Rd, where you'll find a bayside nature trail.

Siesta Key is undisputedly tourist oriented, but with its unique soft sand—which rarely heats up underfoot—it's no wonder this beach is an international destination. The primary public beach access with the most parking is at **Siesta Beach,** 948 Beach Rd, where volunteers will help orient you to the beach ecosystems and the town. My favorite place is **Point O'Rocks Beach Access #13,** off Midnight Pass Rd south of Stickney Pt. Rd. There isn't a lot of parking here, but unless you're staying waterfront at Crescent Beach, it's the best way to get to the Point O'Rocks, a rocky reef formation with tidal pools, excellent for snorkeling and examining sea creatures up close in their natural habitat.

Venice Beach, 326 S Nokomis Ave, is best known for its shark's teeth. Fossil collectors from around the world come here in search of the Holy Grail—enormous teeth from *Carcharodon megalodon*, a prehistoric shark 52 feet in length. More commonly, you'll find small black fossil teeth from more average-size sharks. Along the Venice coastline, my favorite place is **Caspersen Beach,** 4100 Harbor Dr S, which has several miles of unspoiled natural waterfront to roam. If you're bringing Fido, stop instead at ☀ **Brohard Beach & Paw Park** (941-861-1602), 1600 Harbor Dr S, where dogs are welcome to frolic in the surf.

BOTANICAL GARDENS ⅖ ✍ For a relaxing afternoon, visit **Marie Selby Botanical Gardens** (941-366-5731; www.selby.org), 811 S Palm Ave, an oasis of formal gardens and natural habitats along Sarasota's waterfront. Start your tour by walking through the airlock of the Tropical Display House, where you'll marvel at a tunnel of tropical blooms. Stand still and take in the fragrance of hundreds of orchids before you head into the fernery as you exit. Following the pathway toward the bay, enjoy gardens of ferns, cycads, and bamboo, and take a side trip on the canopy walk en route to the succulent garden with its towering giant agave. Shaded by sea grapes, the path continues along Hudson Bayou to "The Point," where a bo tree shades the view. A boardwalk winds through the bayfront mangroves. Beneath the banyan trees, **Michael's in the Garden** is a café with self-serve gourmet sandwiches, ice cream, coffee, and tea. The classy building was once the Selby family's residence, and the dark pool in front of the home is a memorial to the family. Tropical plantings accent the native habitat along the waterfront on the way to **Paynes Mansion.** (Look up into the trees for a bromeliad garden!) The 1934 mansion houses exhibits of botanical art and a gift shop. At the Tree Lab, kids can play in the tree house canopy and peek in the frog nursery, where Harriet the Tarantula lives. Behind the buildings are herb, fruit, and container gardens. Open 10–5 daily; closed Christmas. Adults $12, ages 6–11 $6.

GREENWAYS Presently under development, the **Venetian Waterway Park** (941-488-2236) follows the Intracoastal Waterway from Nokomis to Venice, with trails on both side of the waterway. Bicyclists and walkers can enjoy the 5-mile section that is open to the public; another 5 miles are under construction.

NATURE CENTERS

Englewood
⌁ Enjoy the cool Gulf breezes at **Lemon Bay Park & Environmental Center** (941-474-3065), 570 Bay Park Blvd, where eagles nest amid the pines, and trails wind across 195 waterfront acres surrounding a nature center. Free.

Sarasota
Encompassing 190 acres along the Myakka River, **Crowley Museum & Nature Center** (941-322-1000; www.CrowleyMuseumNatureCtr.org), 16405 Myakka Rd, offers a variety of activities. Walk the boardwalk through Maple Branch Swamp and nature trails through the pine woods, visit the old Crowley pioneer homestead from the 1880s, watch living-history demonstrations at the blacksmith shop and sugarcane mill, and explore the museum filled with artifacts from Old Miakka. Open 10–4 Tue–Sun (Jan 1–Apr 30) and Thu–Sun (May 1–Dec 31). Fee.

Venice
⌁ At **Shamrock Park & Nature Center** (941-486-2706), 4100 W Shamrock Dr, scrub jays range across the 82 acres along the Intracoastal Waterway, but the real reason to come here is for the kids: The nature center is excellent, and the playground is a lot of fun, especially if they love dinosaurs. Free.

PARKS

Bradenton Beach
⌁ A unique gateway to the natural communities along the bay, **Leffis Key** (941-742-5923), Gulf Dr, protects 17 acres of waterfront. Access to the park is via gentle hiking trails and boardwalks through the mangrove forests and coastal berm, where you can peer out of overlooks across the bay and down into crystal-clear water to watch sea squirts and sponges on the rocks. Free.

Longboat Key
⌁ A 32-acre oasis on residential Longboat Key, **Joan M. Durante Community Park** (941-316-1988), 5550 Gulf of Mexico Dr, is a city park with extensive walkways through natural habitats and a man-made wetland, great views of Sarasota Bay, and picnic and playground facilities. Free.

Rye
With miles of equestrian trails and plenty of lakefront to keep anglers happy, **Lake Manatee State Park** (941-741-3028; www.floridastateparks.org/lake manatee/default.cfm), 20007 FL 64, is a popular recreation area on the remote eastern side of the county. Swimming is permitted in the lake, and there's a full-facility campground near the lake. Fee.

Sarasota
⌁ Established in 1934, **Myakka River State Park** (941-361-6511; www.florida stateparks.org), 13207 FL 72, provides endless opportunities for outdoor recre-

ation on more than 28,000 acres. Day-trippers can experience the only canopy walk in the United States—a swinging bridge more than 40 feet up in the live oak canopy, giving you a bird's eye view of bromeliads. Stop at the Myakka Outpost to board a modified airboat for a one-hour ecotour along the river, or rent bikes to ride dozens of miles of trails throughout the park. Birdwatchers will appreciate the Bird Walk, a long boardwalk out into the river with numerous opportunities for birding, while backpackers can enjoy the best multiday experience that southwest Florida has to offer—a 40-mile series of stacked loops passing through prairies, oak hammocks, and dozens of other habitats. Fee.

Whitaker Gateway Park (941-316-1172), 1455 N Tamiami Trl, marks the location of the original homestead of the Whitaker family, the first post-statehood settlers along Sarasota Bay. It offers fishing and picnicking along Yellow Bluff. Free.

Snead Island

Encompassing 360 acres, **Emerson Point Preserve** (941-748-4501), Tarpon Rd, protects the ancient Portavant Temple Mound (see *Archeological Sites*) as well as an interesting mix of habitats, including a rare look at the Tampa Bay estuary from its southern shore. Both a limestone path and a paved biking trail run around the park, and anglers can gain access to Tampa Bay down at the point. Snaking around the island, several hiking-only trails can be strung together with the limestone path for an easy and interesting 2.7-mile walk. Free.

Venice

Best known for its expanding Florida scrub jay population, **Oscar Scherer State Park** (941-483-5956), 1843 S Tamiami Trl, is a great place for a weekend getaway. Covering more than 1,300 acres of land, the park preserves a crucial chunk of scrub and scrubby flatwoods in the midst of burgeoning Gulf Coast development. Here you can bike and hike for dozens of miles, rent a canoe or kayak and paddle down South Creek, fish from the boardwalks or along Osprey Lake, or camp beneath the sand under live oaks. Fee.

SPRINGS

North Port

Dubbed "the Original Fountain of Youth," **Warm Mineral Springs** (941-426-1692; www.warmmineralsprings .com), 12200 San Servando Ave (along US 41), boasts Florida's only truly hot spring, with 87°F water year-round, and has the third highest concentration of minerals in a spring in the world. Privately owned, it has been a spa for many decades, with real mineral waters asserted to enhance your good health. General admission $16, 12 and under $7; massage therapy available for an hourly fee.

CANOPY WALK AT MYAKKA RIVER STATE PARK

Sandra Friend

Duette

Set aside as wilderness for the residents of Manatee County, **Duette Park** (941-776-2295), 2649 Rawls Rd, encompasses 22,000 acres of sandhills, prairie, river hammocks, and scrub, and it is the site of an active Florida scrub jay restoration program. It is the prime destination for the region's deer hunters in the winter and attracts anglers who enjoy fishing in a relaxed wilderness setting. Most of the park roads (designated "trails") are accessible only by four-wheel-drive vehicles, but they can be bicycled or hiked. Tent camping is $10/night for up to five people. Follow the signs off FL 64 to find the park. Fee.

North Port

Myakkahatchee Creek Preserve (941-486-2547), 6968 Reisterstown Rd, protects 160 acres along Big Slough, with scenic trails along this picturesque natural waterway sometimes perched on sand bluffs above the creek. Picnic area and canoe launch. Equestrians, bicyclists, and hikers welcome. Free.

With more than 8,500 acres of pine flatwoods, **Myakka State Forest** (941-255-7653), 4723 53rd Ave E, has miles of forest roads for off-road bicycling, horseback riding, and hiking. The tent campground costs $5 per tent for up to five people. Fee.

Parrish

Offering a smorgasbord of short hikes along and around the upper reaches of the Manatee River, **Rye Wilderness Park** (941-776-0900), 905 Rye Wilderness Trl, also features a tent campground open on weekends for $10 a night. Off FL 64 east; follow signs. Free.

Venice

Along the wild southern reaches of the Myakka River, **Jelks Preserve** (941-486-2547), along N River Rd (north of Center Rd), has a network of more than 3 miles of trails meandering through pine flatwoods, scrubby flatwoods, and oak hammocks on uplands above the Myakka River. Some trails lead to river views. Free.

West of I-75, the **T. Mabry Carlton, Jr. Memorial Reserve** (941-486-2547), 1800 Mabry Carlton Pkwy, encompasses 234 acres of pine flatwoods, scrubby flatwoods, oak hammocks, and open prairies. A 3-mile hiking trail touches on some of the habitats. Free.

✵ Lodging

BED & BREAKFASTS

Holmes Beach 34217

A grand 1925 coquina and cypress beach house surrounded by dunes, **Harrington House Beachfront** (1-888-828-5566; www.harringtonhouse .com), 5626 Gulf Dr, comes with all the comforts of home—and more. Borrow a bike or a kayak, or just lie on the beach and read. If it rains, you can watch movies in the living room. And don't miss breakfast—the food is top-notch, too. There are 8 well-appointed rooms in the Main House ($149–289) and 11 more rooms and suites ($149–329) in nearby historic beach houses owned by the family. Children 12 and over welcome.

Sarasota 34236

🦐 Capture the spirit of Old Sarasota at **The Cypress** (941-955-4683; www.cypressbb.com), 621 Gulf Stream Ave S. The inn is infused with a sense of artistry and style; jazz drifts through the corridors. Constructed by Jarvis Hardisty, a sailing instructor, this 1940 gem retains the elegant spirit of its past, especially as a lone hold-out against a line of condos along the waterfront. There are 12 mango trees shading the property, and the owner, Robert Belott, a retired photographer and gourmet chef, makes excellent use of them in breakfast and snack preparations. Each room ($150–260) is decorated with his brilliant photographs and filled with his family antiques. Kathyrn's Garden Room looks out into the mango trees, while the romantic and extremely popular Martha Rose Suite has a private balcony overlooking the bay and a sitting area with a Victorian sofa. Sitting out on the porch, cocktail in hand, with an assistant, George, offering you crêpes and cheese, you feel a sense of calm in this oasis in the city, knowing that numerous dining options lie within easy walking distance. It is a venue worthy of Hardisty's storied legacy— sophisticated and stylish, yet down-home Florida.

Venice 34285

One of the oldest homes in Venice, the **Banyan House Historic B&B** (941-484-1385; www.banyanhouse .com), 519 Harbor Dr, is shaded by an enormous banyan tree planted by Thomas Edison, a friend of the original owner, and boasts the first swim-ming pool built in Venice, carefully maintained with its original tile by the current owners. There are guest rooms ($119–159) in three buildings, including the main house, the carriage house, and the servant's quarters. The tropical courtyard is a great place to relax, and the breakfast room overlooks the Cherokee red patios. Three rooms have balconies and kitchenettes; a full breakfast is served to all guests. Closed Jul–Sep and Dec; apartments outside the main home are available during those periods on a monthly basis.

🦐 **Horse & Chaise** (941-488-2702 or 1-877-803-3515; www.horseandchaise inn.com), 317 Ponce de Leon Ave. In the family for more than 30 years, this 1926 Mediterranean Revival house (expanded years ago into a rest home) was converted by Lois and Jon Steketee into a relaxing inn show-casing the region's long and storied history in each of its eight rooms ($115–169). Stay in the Ringling Room to relive old circus memories, or settle back in the red, white, and blue Patriot Room, commemorating the old Venice Army Air Force Base. Guys can't help but play in the BLE Room—a Lionel train runs on an elevated track around the room. With a bottomless cookie jar in the kitchen, snacks and drinks always available in the dining room, and cold bottled water in your room, the inn will make you feel right at home. It's easy to mingle with fellow guests in the open, comfortable common areas, including the garden courtyards, but I especially appreciated being able to check my e-mail on the personal computer, with high-speed Internet access, provided for guests. Closed in June.

Cortez 34215

Tucked under a canopy of trees, **Holiday Cove RV Resort** (941-792-1111 or 1-800-346-9224; www.holiday coverv.com), 11900 Cortez Rd W, is an appealing destination minutes from the beach and seconds from an exploration of the estuary. Take advantage of their boat launch to putter or paddle out to the bay, or relax around the heated pool. Offering full hookups, $30–44 daily; boat slip $4 per day. Weekly, monthly, and seasonal rates available. Ask about summer specials.

COTTAGES

Longboat Key 34428

🖋 🌴 **Rolling Waves Cottages** (941-383-1323; www.rollingwaves.com), 6351 Gulf of Mexico Dr, is the kind of old-fashioned family beach getaway that I truly treasure. These eight 1940s cottages (one- and two-bedroom) are absolutely authentic, a slice of local history tucked under the palms and pines and overlooking the dunes. Each cottage ($145–325) has an updated kitchen, several beds, and large televisions with cable and VCR. Cribs and high chairs available on request. Borrow a bike to head up to St. Armands!

Siesta Key 34242

🐚 🌴 ▼ Fifteen years ago, Gail and David Rubinfeld found a tumble-down fish camp at the south end of Siesta Key and had a dream of turning it into a couples' getaway. And indeed, I've found few accommodations as romantic as the **Turtle Beach Resort** (941-349-4554; www .turtlebeachresort.com), 9049 Midnight Pass Rd, where you can lie in bed and look out over your own private bay view, or bask in your own private hot tub. Ten cottages ($250–435), with weekly rates available. Reserve early, as there are many repeat customers.

HOTELS, MOTELS, AND RESORTS

Anna Maria 34216

The **Rod & Reel Motel** (941-778-2780), 877 North Shore Dr, is your basic 1940s Florida motel, refurbished but with no real frills—and appealing as all get out because it's the kind of place that my family would stay at when I was a kid. Most of the kitchenettes ($74–149) have one double bed, some have two, and they're all on a nicely landscaped courtyard overlooking the bay. With the historic pier right here and an easy walk to the quiet north end beaches, it's a great location if you just want to get away and fish or read.

Bradenton Beach 34217

With an architectural style that enhances the old Bridge Street historic district, **Bridgewalk** (941-779-2545 or 1-866-779-2545; www.silver resorts.com/bridgewalk/bridgewalk_ home.htm), 100 Bridge St, offers luxurious modern studios, suites, and townhomes ($169–436) within an easy walk of beach and bay. The complex includes the Sun House Restaurant & Bar, a heated pool, and a day spa, and the quaint shops of historic Bradenton Beach are just footsteps away.

Families find a place in the sun at **Silver Surf Gulf Beach Resort** (941-778-6626 or 1-800-441-7873; www .silverresorts.com/surf/surf_home .htm), 1301 Gulf Dr N, where the beach is just across the street and the rooms are spacious enough to accommodate the entire brood. Choose from standard, studio, or suite ($91–200). With bead board–style walls, wicker furnishings, and touches of greenery, it feels like you're in the islands—and you are! On-site pool, free beach chairs, and rentals of Vespas, sea kayaks, and sailboards. If you're eligible, ask for Florida resident pricing.

☙ Settle into the **Tortuga Inn Beach Resort** (941-867-8842 or 1-877-867-8842; www.tortugainn.com), 1325 Gulf Dr N, and take advantage of a private dock on Sarasota Bay or the expansive beach across the street. The upscale rooms (hotel, studio, or suite, $149–299) center around a tropical courtyard and spacious heated pool. Weekly rates available.

Charming cottages tucked amid tropical vegetation await at **Tradewinds Resort** (941-779-0010 or 1-888-686-6716; www.tradewinds-resort.com), 1603 Gulf Dr N. Although they look like historic Old Florida seaside cottages, they are new and modern, with full amenities and daily housekeeping. Enjoy the beach across the street, or the pool just steps from your door. Choose from studios or one- or two-bedroom units ($145–329). Weekly rates available.

Casey Key 34275

Built in 1947, the **Gulf Shore Beach Resort Motel** (941-488-6210), 317 Casey Key Rd, features bungalows ($95–120 in season) with a classic Florida beachfront feel, each with terrazzo floors, wooden ceilings, and a tiled mural in the shower. The units include a bedroom and dining–full kitchen area, plus a front porch overlooking the common green with shuffleboard courts, and a walk over the rise to the dunes of the Gulf.

🐾 ☙ Add some retro *zing!* to your vacation with a stay at **Haley's Motel** (941-778-5405 or 1-800-367-7824; www.haleysmotel.com), 8102 Gulf Dr, where owners Tom Buehler and Sabine Musil-Buehler celebrated this classic resort's 50th anniversary in 2003. From the glass block corners and brightly painted doors to the tropical birds in their cages, this is a very eclectic and fun place. Tuck yourself into one of the updated-but-period 1950s rooms, or pick one of the neatly renovated rooms, studios, or apartments. Lounge at the pool, or read a book by the frog pond in the secret garden. Bikes and beach accoutrements free to guests. All pets welcome! The 14 units of varying configurations run $99–159.

An old-fashioned family seaside motel, the **White Sands Beach Resort** (941-778-2577; www.white sandsbeachresort.com), 6504 Gulf Dr, has rooms to fit every size group, with full kitchens, tiled floors, big bathrooms, and barbecue grills outside ($119–275; weekly rates available). The heated swimming pool overlooks the Gulf of Mexico, and it's an easy walk down to the beach.

Longboat Key 34228

Enjoy seaside serenity at **Riviera Beach Resort** (941-383-2552; www .rivierabeachresort.com), 5451 Gulf of Mexico Dr, an appealing little hideaway of apartments and studio rooms right on the Gulf. Sit out on your patio and listen to the waterfall in the tropical garden, or soak in the small heated pool after a dip in the sea. Large, tiled one- and two-bedroom suites with kitchens run $159–249. Weekly rates available, with discount for monthlong stays.

THE GULF COAST

Siesta Key 34242

🎣 🐾 Dangle a line (or your toes) off the deck on Heron Lagoon at the **Banana Bay Club Resort** (941-346-0113 or 1-888-622-6229; www.banana bayclub.com), 8254 Midnight Pass Rd, an appealing Superior Small Lodging surrounded by mangroves. This older motel has been completely converted to classy units in Caribbean tones, all very roomy, with full kitchens. Several waterfront rooms available, and all are nonsmoking and come with pillow-topped beds, free high-speed Internet, and one hundred minutes in free phone calls to anywhere. Rates run $115–249, depending on room size and season.

🦐 An intimate home away from home, the **Captiva Beach Resort** (941-349-4131 or 1-800-349-4131; www.captivabeachresort.com), 6772 Sara Sea Cir, is only moments from the beach. Since 1981 the Ispaso family has carefully updated and tended this 1940s motel nestled in a tropical forest, and it now boasts sparkling-clean rooms and suites in a variety of eight different configurations ($99–335), full kitchens, high-speed Internet access—and bottled water flowing out of every kitchen's tap! Visit their web site for a virtual tour of every room and a virtual walk to the beach.

🎣 Enjoy a touch of the circus at **The Ringling Beach House** (941-349-1236 or 1-888-897-9919; www.siesta keysuites.com), 523 Beach Rd, where suites in this 1920s Ringling home have playful names such as "Ringmaster" and "Seal," as well as roomy, fully updated interiors ($110–275). The adjoining **Siesta Key Suites** offers even more options on this steps-from-the-beach property.

🦐 ♿ 🎣 🐾 I directed my relatives to **Tropical Shores Beach Resort** (941-346-0025 or 1-800-235-3493; www.tropicalshores.com), 6717 Sara Sea Cir, a very family-friendly motel just a few minutes' walk from Point O' Rocks. There are 30 large, inviting units; tropical plantings throughout the property; and two heated pools. The staff is friendly and the rooms are spotless, with daily housekeeping (not a norm in these parts!). The family has owned the resort since 1955 and strives for 100 percent guest satisfaction. Their room rates range from $89 off-season for a deluxe efficiency to $495 in-season for a two-bedroom suite. Their adjacent budget property, the **Tropical Sun Beach Resort,** is a large 1950s motel just like I stayed in as a kid, with retro lime and black tiled showers, large rooms ($49–375) with futons, efficiency kitchens, and a guest laundry.

Venice 34285

A landmark of Old Florida, the historic **El Patio Hotel** (941-488-7702; www.venice-fla.com/elpatio), 229 W Venice Ave, dates from 1927 and has been operated since 1950 by the Miles family. It's right in the heart of the shopping district, above the shops—an excellent location if you're exploring by foot. An exterior walkway overlooks gardens, and an interior common space provides a comfortable place to read or have a cup of tea. The rooms and suites ($50–120) have older furnishings but are spacious and clean, and the baths are small, reflecting the era.

♿ 🎣 **Inn at the Beach Resort** (941-484-8471; www.innatthebeach.com), 725 W Venice Ave, is just steps from Venice Beach and the shopping district, offering large motel rooms with tiled floors and a mix of 13 different configurations among their 49 units. Rates start at $99 off-season and rise to $451 during high season for the two-bedroom garden suites. See their web site for virtual tours.

LONG-TERM RENTALS

Longboat Key 34228

With both Gulf and bay units, **McCall's Beach Castle** (941-383-3117), 5310 Gulf of Mexico Dr, offers spotless, quiet rentals with large one- and two-bedroom apartments, each with tropical decor, screened porch, a full kitchen, and an inviting pool and spa. Three-day minimum at weekly rates of $680–2,225, depending on size, location, and season; discounts for longer stays.

Siesta Key 34242

Settle into a spotless beachfront efficiency at **Sea Castle Beachfront Nelson** (941-349-2595 or 1-877-306-9177; www.sea-castle.com), 1003 Seaside Dr, where you can sit on the balcony and watch the sunset over Point O' Rocks or walk down through the soft sand to join the families on the beach enjoying this daily ritual. A motel since the 1950s, it's a fully renovated two-story complex where individual owners rent out various units, and it's extremely popular with families thanks to the pool, multiple beds, and beachfront view. Weekly rentals are $525–1,550 and include all facilities plus fully equipped kitchens. It's just a few minutes' walk to the shops and restaurants surrounding Old Stickney Point Road.

There are only seven units at **Siesta Sunset Beach House** (941-346-1215; www.siestasunset.com), 5322 Calle de la Siesta, which makes it an appealing home away from home with an easy walk to shops and restaurants in Siesta Village. I appreciated the oh-so-comfortable bed and bright, roomy interior, but each sparkling-clean unit also offers a fully equipped kitchen (dishes, linens, and all appliances), television and VCR (a 150-title library resides downstairs for your pleasure), and robes for the bath. Up to four bedrooms may be combined to accommodate large families. A crow's-nest sundeck on the top floor provides a perch to watch the sunset, and the courtyard contains a swimming pool and hot tub. You can borrow beach chairs from owner Murph Gordon as you head across the street to Siesta Beach Access #7, or grab a bike and head into the village. The weekly rental runs $550–1,250, with shorter stays possible during the off-season and package deals available.

✳ Where to Eat

DINING OUT

Longboat Key

Wine Spectator rates **Euphemia Haye** (941-383-3633; www.euphemiahaye.com), 5540 Gulf of Mexico Dr, as worthy of its Award of Excellence for its wine cellar, and the folks at *Florida Trend* give them the Golden Spoon for creative cuisine, intimate dining, and a dessert room—the Hayeloft. Tucked away in a tropical forest, this local gem offers a getaway for you and your sweetheart to savor a truly international menu, with gourmet creations such as Grecian lamb shank, shrimp Taj Mahal, roast duckling, and calves' sweetbreads grenoblois. Expect to drop $75 for dinner for two, and save room for delights at the Hayeloft, where you can choose from a dazzling display of desserts. Euphemia Haye has provided a consistent standard of excellence since 1975 and is a dining experience not to be missed.

Dine amid wine at **Mattison's Steakhouse & Wine Cellar** (941-387-2700; www.mattisons.com), 525 Bay Isles Pkwy, where a fine table awaits in the medieval-style wine cellar. A favorite with locals, Mattison's presents both traditional steakhouse offerings such as prime rib, New York strip, and surf and turf, as well as signature entrées such as their Steak Blue—a perfect rib eye dressed with Gorgonzola, apple-smoked bacon, port wine syrup, and truffle mashed potatoes. Entrées start at $18.95 for the chef's fresh vegetable platter and run to $60 for chateaubriand for two; sides, salad, and soup are extra. Their extensive dessert menu tempts with after-dinner wines, fine Scotch, and chocolate creations. Reservations recommended.

Sarasota

Almost completely hidden by a giant banyan tree, **5-One-6 Burns** (941-906-1884), 516 Burns Ln, is a sophisticated bistro with appealing offerings such as vanilla bean–glazed sea scallops, hummus, and grilled Brie. Lunch 11–5 and dinner after 5; entrées $15–21.

Overseen by Executive Chef Jean-Pierre Knaggs and his wife, Shay, since 1986, the **Bijou** (941-366-8111; www.bijoucafe.net), 1287 First St, is highly recommended as a superb downtown restaurant. Their wine list is extensive, and the classy entrées ($17–28) include veal Louisville, grilled salmon Verde, and grilled lavender honey-glazed quail, the recipes influenced by Jean-Pierre's South African and French heritage.

Dine in the middle of downtown at **Mattison's City Grill** (941-330-0440; www.mattisons.com), One Lemon Ave, where you can listen to live jazz as the sun sets while savoring a fresh pizza. A slice is $4. While the aroma of the brick oven tempts, you may prefer other Italian-influenced fare such as veggie panini, ripe tomatoes and *bocconcini* mozzarella, or *antipasta mista*. They serve burgers and grouper sandwiches too. Lunch $4–11, dinner $8–23.

The romantic ambiance of **Uva Rara** (941-362-9006), 440 S Pineapple Ave, makes it a perfect destination for a special night out. Enjoy Italian classics such as *linguni di mare*, or try *snapper meditteranes* (entrées $14–23). Dinner served Tue–Sun after 5:30.

My parents particularly enjoyed their evening at **Villa Francesco** (941-365-0000), 1603 N Tamiami Trl, where the trattoria ambiance brings the outdoors in—you'll feel you're dining in intimate elegance in an Italian garden. Enjoy *ravioli funghi porcini* (ravioli with porcini mushrooms), *saltimbocca borsellino, branzino in guazzetto,* and more (entrées $16 and up). Savor a selection from their wine list.

Siesta Key

Peruvian cuisine shines at **Javier's Restaurant and Wine Bar** (941-349-1792), 6621 Midnight Pass Rd, where ethnic specialties such as *picante de camarones* (large shrimp in spicy pepper sauce) and *lomo saltado* (beef tenderloin tips sautéed with Spanish onions, fresh tomato, garlic, and cumin) complement fine American favorites such as pepper steak, pasta jambalaya, and barbecue baby back ribs ($6–20). Open at 5 for dinner, Tue–Sat.

A lively new trattoria, **Mattison's Siesta Grill** (941-349-2800; www.mattisons.com), 1256 Old Stickney Point Rd, is a foodie fave featuring creative seafood and and Asian-Mediterranean fusion foods such as duck and mango spring rolls. The atmosphere is unique—the bar dominates the kitchen side of the bistro, with long tables encouraging guests to mingle; thin-screen televisions show the latest sports. Earth tones and palm trees accent the room. The large entrée ($20–28) portions are artfully presented. My grouper was buttery tender, the crust with a hint of basil, and I especially appreciated the olive tapenade that appears with your fresh bread.

🍴 For a romantic dinner on the bay, head to **Ophelia's** (941-349-3328; www.opheliasonthebay.com), 9105 Midnight Pass Rd, where large picture windows showcase the bayfront as you dine by candlelight. Savor a glass of wine as you experience a parade of sensory delights—my organic-greens salad was topped with pecans dipped in maple sugar, a crunchy sweet counterpoint to the greens and Gorgonzola cheese; my scampi had a garlicky zing; and the butternut squash was nutty sweet. The menu changes frequently, but one constant is the pleasant and attentive wait staff. Entrées run $23–35. There is an extensive wine list and a martini menu.

Terra Ceia

From the outside **Lee's Crab Trap** (941-722-6255), US 19 at the Terra Ceia Bridge, has that casual seafood house look, but let me assure you—it's not. This is a classy place with a 30-year history of pleasing locals with certified Angus steaks and seafood dishes with a gourmet touch. Lunch ($8–11), includes oyster and shrimp po'boys and Florida gator burgers. Crab is served 13 different ways at dinner, including imperial, supreme, and Norfolk; dinners $14 and up. Dress well (business casual or better); reservations suggested.

Venice

Seafood's the thing at **The Crow's Nest** (941-484-9551; www.crowsnest-venice.com), 1968 Tarpon Ctr Dr, a favorite at the Tarpon Center Marina since 1976. Grab some raw Apalachicola oysters and fresh Gulf shrimp, or savor the seafood bisque and steamed mussels. First courses ($4–10); fresh catches and entrées, ($15–24), include such delectables as walnut-crusted fillet of salmon and pesto baked striped bass, as well as an award-winning wine list.

Crabby mushrooms are an old family favorite, so it was great to find them at **Marker 4 Oyster Bar & Restaurant** (941-484-0344), 505 Tamiami Trl S, where the potato skins come as "Seafood Skins" and entrées ($8–17) range from rib-eye steak and traditional Captain's Platters (which include every type of seafood on the menu) to crunchy wasabi pea–crusted tuna.

Sharky's on the Pier (941-488-1456; www.sharkysonthepier.com), 1600 Harbor Dr S, has an on-the-beach atmosphere, but their culinary creativity is out of this world. Try the shrimp and blue crab au gratin (Florida blue crab, Gulf shrimp, and cheddar), Flounder San Juan (with artichoke hearts, spinach, and lobster sauce), or the intriguing Seafood Rainforest, where shrimp and scallops mix it up with veggies, mango, pineapple, and cashews. Entrées ($15–22). Pasta offerings, ($12–19), include a lobster Brie sauté.

Anna Maria

On the historic pier, **The City Pier Restaurant** (941-779-1667), 100 Bay Blvd, offers great views of Tampa Bay with your meal, which might include fish-and-chips, coconut shrimp, or a cherry snapper sandwich. Lunch and dinner, $6–7.

Rotten Ralph's (941-778-3953; www .rottenralphs.com), 902 S Bay Blvd, is the classic Florida waterfront restaurant that everyone sent me to—it's got that Cracker fish camp feel but is right in the heart of the marina at the end of the road. Cruise in, drive, or walk, and settle down for the basics ($11–17). All-you-can-eat British-style fish-and-chips ($8) are the specialty of the house.

Bradenton

With a loyal following, the **Anna Maria Oyster Bar** (941-792-0077; www.oysterbar.net), 6696 Cortez Rd W, moved landside a few years ago, still offering hot wings, frozen margaritas, their famous giant grouper sandwiches, and 25 cent oysters in a casual setting. Steamer pots (veggies, potatoes, and shellfish) run $20 and up, and dinners ($9–25) have every combination of seafood you can imagine. Two additional locations: 6906 US 41 and at 1525 51st Ave, Ellenton.

Grandma Yoders (941-739-2918), 5896 53rd Ave E, is a little strip-mall treasure that one of my girlfriends took me to for dinner. Enjoy good Amish cooking—especially heaping slices of pie—in a family atmosphere, where Manhattans (open-faced sandwiches on homemade bread) come with real mashed potatoes smothered in gravy. Open 11–8 Mon–Sat. Dinner entrées $7–9.

Founded in 1945 and overlooking the Braden River, **Linger Lodge** (941-755-2757; http://hometown.aol.com/ sgamsky), 7205 Linger Lodge Rd off Tara Blvd and FL 70, calls itself "Florida's Most Unusual Restaurant." Locals rave about the great food and real Florida atmosphere. All-you-can-eat fish fry daily for $9, prime rib on weekends for $15. Closed Mon.

A homestyle breakfast and lunch stop, **Peaches** (941-794-5140), 5702 Cortez Rd W, has eight omelet options, combo breakfasts, and plenty of pancakes to choose from, including peach almond. Breakfast $3–7. Open 6–2:30, this local chain has eight locations in the region.

French toast, pecan and banana pancakes, and Southern pancakes with grits—it's all part of the fare downtown at **Theresa's** (941-747-7066), 608 14th St W, where breakfast ($2–7) is served up friendly and fast. Open weekdays 7–2, weekends 8–2.

For a dainty spot of tea, go with the girlfriends to **Truffles & Treasures** (941-761-3335), 7445 Manatee Ave W. This Victorian tearoom is lace and frills and downright popular, especially for Mums bringing daughters out on the town. Formal teas include the Queens Tea ($13) and Lady Tiffany's Tea ($10), or you can opt for daily fare such as Truffles' signature spinach salad ($7). Open 11–3 Tue–Sat. Reservations recommended.

Bradenton Beach

Breakfast at the **Gulf Drive Café** (941-778-1919), 900 Gulf Dr, is a delightful way to start your day, enjoying a platter of hotcakes while watching the seagulls wheel over the Gulf. Breakfast ($4–6) is served anytime. Even at 8 AM there's a line for the seaside patio, where sea oats frame a panorama of blue, so arrive early! Their Belgium waffles are top-notch.

Cortez

Annie's Bait & Tackle (941-794-3580), 4334 127th St W, is a good old-fashioned fish camp befitting this historic fishing village, where you can grab a bucket of shiners and a fresh grouper sandwich or burger. Breakfast served weekends 6:30–11, lunch and dinner daily. Bait shop open daily, with fishing licenses and charters on the spot.

Holmes Beach

❧ There's heavy voodoo going down at **Mr. Jones BBQ** (941-778-6614), 3007 Gulf Dr, where New Orleans meets the Far East with burgers rubbed in secret spices ($6), five kinds of ribs (your choice of spare $13, baby back $17), and awesome exotics such as chicken shish kebob with rice biryani ($13) served up tikka masala style with a mass of my favorite sautéed veggies—peppers, onions, mushrooms, and tomatoes—and sides of raita, mango, and fresh coriander chutneys, as well as strips of French bread for dipping and a boatload of cold beer. Open for lunch and dinner daily.

Longboat Key

The busiest breakfast spot on the island is the **Blue Dolphin Café** (941-383-3787), 5370 Gulf of Mexico Dr, where the specialties include a breakfast wrap with homemade veggie chili, cheddar cheese, and scrambled eggs, or Belgium waffles with fresh fruit. Serving breakfast and lunch ($5–9).

Nokomis

It doesn't come fresher than **Pop's Sunset Grill** (941-488-3177), 112 Circuit Rd (off W Albee Rd at the bridge), where I watched for dolphins while waiting on a sampler skewer of shrimps and scallops and fresh green bean salad. Steamship pots, however, have been their stock in trade for more than 20 years and include corn on the cob, red potatoes, onions, carrots, celery, and your choice of fresh oysters, shrimp, snow crab, and middle neck clams ($26 full, $15 half). Feed a hungry appetite (or two) with one of these! Sunset Sandwiches and Beach Baskets of fried seafood run $7–10.

Osprey

Overlooking Little Sarasota Bay and Spanish Point with a killer view from its big picture windows, the **Flying Bridge Restaurant** (941-966-7431), 482 Blackburn Point Rd, is great for armchair birding. There are numerous options for sandwiches and salads at lunch, and dinners include seafood delights such as tequila-lime salmon, scallops Mornay, and snapper margarita ($14–16).

Palmetto

Model planes and historic photos of aviation set the tone at **Hot Rodd's Hanger** (941-729-2950), 120 Seventh St W, a busy restaurant with breakfast all day ($2–7), lunch sandwiches and salads ($3–7), and lots of dinner choices ($7–15)—roast pork and baked ham, alligator and coconut shrimp among them. But what'll really get you in the door are the milk shakes ($3)—choose from blueberry or peanut butter as well as the traditional flavors.

St. Armands Key

Hungry Fox Treetop Bistro (941-388-2222), 419A St. Armands Cir, offers a nice break from your day of shopping, serving "Floribbean cuisine with a flair" in dishes such as Caribbean French toast, Sarasota

club, Shrimp Islamorada, and jam-
balya. Open for breakfast, lunch, and
dinner, with entrées starting at $13.

Sarasota

They're not on the waterfront, but it
doesn't matter—fine fresh seafood is
what you'll get at **Barnacle Bill's**
(941-365-6800; www.barnaclebills
seafood.com), 1526 Main St, a local
favorite where the chef's suggestions
for dinner include seafood strudel,
shrimp and scallops Newburg, salmon
Peking, and potato-crusted grouper
($12–30). I appreciate the half portion
options *and* the fresh fish market on
the premises.

In the Gulf Gate neighborhood, en
route to Siesta Key, park and walk
around the block to select from an
interesting mix of restaurants, including a taste of New York's Little Italy at
the **Italian Village Deli** (941-927-
2428), 6606 Superior Ave; pasta and
Philly sandwiches at **Walt's Tuscany
Grill** (941-927-1113), 6584 Superior
Ave; fusion food at **Going Bistro**
(941-926-2994), 2164 Gulf Gate Dr;
and eclectic seafood entrées at
Greer's Grill (941-926-0606), 6566
Gateway Ave, a local favorite.

A waterfront restaurant with a classic
Florida fish camp feel—picnic tables
and all—the **Phillippi Creek Village
Restaurant & Oyster Bar** (941-925-
4444; www.creekseafood.com), 5353
South Tamiami Trl, is a local favorite
for fresh seafood. The extensive menu
includes steamer pots ($22 and up)
and combination platters ($10–16). I
enjoyed blue crab Norfolk, a buttery
preparation with a side of spicy parsley potatoes.

❦ Enjoy Pennsylvania Dutch treats at
Yoder's Restaurant (941-955-7771;
www.yodersrestaurant.com), 3434

Bahia Vista St, which opened in 1975
as the region's first Amish restaurant
(a cuisine that continues to spread,
thanks to a large Amish community
in rural Sarasota County). Patrons
come from afar to sample their 25 different varieties of homemade pies. At
breakfast ($3–7) it was busy; don't let
the lack of cars in the lot fool you.
The stuffed French toast stuffed me
but good, and the folks at the next
table looked puzzled by the heaps of
food that came with their breakfast.
Serving 6 AM–8 PM; closed Sun. Cash
only.

Siesta Key

❦ A local favorite, the **Broken Egg
Restaurant & Gallery** (941-346-
2750; www.thebrokenegg.com), 210
Avenida Madera, is where visitors rub
shoulders over a spectacular breakfast
and lunch menu, including crab cakes
Benedict, Jerry's Pancake (one massive buttermilk pancake with blueberries, bananas, and wheat germ),
and cheese blintzes. Dining at the
adjoining table, NBA announcer Dick
Vitale signed posters as my compan-
ions and I feasted on fresh fruit.
Check out the art gallery on your way
out—it's full of great little gifts!

At **The Deli @ Siesta Key** (941-349-
4696), 215 Avenida Madera, nosh on
classic stuffed specialty sandwiches
(with 20 options!), mega subs piled
high with Boar's Head or Hebrew
National meats, or grab a peanut butter and jelly sandwich if you choose.
Serving breakfast and lunch ($3–8).

Drop by for a daiquiri at the **Siesta
Key Oyster Bar** (941-346-5443;
www.skob.com), 5238 Ocean Blvd,
where fresh seafood and hot wings
are the hot stuff. Enjoy fresh oysters
and clams on the half shell, plus
award-winning wing sauce.

❧ Despite the bar as centerpiece of the dining room, **Turtles Restaurant** (941-346-2207), 8875 Midnight Pass Rd, is the family place on Siesta Key to take kids to dinner, with a $5 kids' menu and plenty of activity out on the marina to keep them curious. Colorful giclee murals by David Utz decorate the walls. The crab bisque hints of tomato, while the fresh snapper amandine is just superb. Serving lunch and dinner ($10 and up).

Venice

🦐 Chili dogs and root beer floats— staple foods from my childhood. And since 1957, **The Frosted Mug** (941-497-1611), 1856 Tamiami Trl, has been serving these and other old-time fast-food favorites daily. Dig into chili cheese fries, blue cheese bacon burgers, and 15 types of hot dogs, including New York, Polish, and Italian. Burgers $3–5, dogs $2–4, entrées $7–9.

A popular gourmet deli, **The Tomato Patch** (941-488-0828), 125 W Venice Ave, serves breakfast ($4–6) and lunch ($6–8) daily 10–3, with fruity French toast an appealing morning offering. For lunch, check out their full range of deli sandwiches and their specialty, the Tomato Patch tart.

BAKERIES, COFFEE SHOPS, AND SODA FOUNTAINS

Anna Maria

What's a beach without an ice cream parlor? **Mama Lo's By The Sea** (941-779-1288), 101 S Bay Blvd, serves up more than 40 different flavors of ice cream, frozen yogurt, and sorbet in every combination you can think of, and some of the choices are just awesome—coffee crunch, coconut, peppermint stick, and gator

tracks, to name a few. They serve lunch and fancy coffee drinks, too.

Bradenton

Everyone in town stops at the **Shake Pit** (941-748-4016), 3810 Manatee Ave W, between errands, a local favorite since 1959 with soft ice cream and great burgers. Just up the road, **Sweet Berries** (941-750-6771), 4500 Manatee Ave W, has frozen custard, sandwiches, and soups in a sit-down café.

St. Armands

Big Olaf Creamery (941-388-4108), 561 N Washington Dr, is a local favorite with great homemade ice cream.

A Michigan transplant, **Kilwins** (941-388-2000), 312 Blvd of the Presidents, is an old-fashioned candy and ice cream shop with excellent lemonade (especially on a hot day!), Mackinaw Island fudge, and ice cream flavors such as Traverse City cherry to choose from.

Step into the 1950s at **Scoop Daddy's** (941-388-1650), 373 John Ringling Blvd, where magnets and movie posters take you back in time while you slurp down that chocolate shake.

Sarasota

🦐 Enjoy delicious homemade ice cream at **Sarasota Scoops** (941-921-1003), 5353 S Tamiami Trl, handmade just up the road by mother-daughter team Janie and Becca McClain. And what flavors! Black raspberry with chocolate chips, Gator Tracks, Rasamataz (vanilla with chocolate chips and raspberry syrup), Key lime sorbet, and much more. Enjoy a scoop or a sundae in this snazzy little ice cream shop, where soft jazz complements the mosaic tables and bistro-style art. Open late.

Venice

In the historic Johnson-Schoolcraft building circa 1926, **The Island Gourmet** (941-488-8885), 305 Venice Ave W, has garnered the "Best in Venice" awards for many years for their coffee and wine bar and gourmet foods.

An old-fashioned ice cream parlor, **The Soda Fountain** (941-412-9860), 349 W Venice Ave, offers traditional favorites served up at their classic marble tables.

✳ Entertainment

Sarasota

Asolo Theatre Festival (941-351-8000 or 1-800-361-8388; www.asolo .org), FSU Center for the Performing Arts, 5555 N Tamiami Trl, offers professional actors in productions such as *The Crucible, Arms and the Man,* and *The Diary of Anne Frank* at the Mertz Theatre, a restored five-hundred-seat 1903 opera house transported here from Dunfermline, Scotland. Student productions from the MFA program at the Jane B. Cook Theatre offer a more intimate experience.

Performances are fun at the **Golden Apple Dinner Theatre** (941-366-5454 or 1-800-652-0920; www.the goldenapple.com), 25 N Pineapple Ave, a local landmark since 1971. Former Broadway thespians Roberta MacDonald and Robert Ennis Turoff, who established this venue as one of the nation's first dinner theaters, oversee a slate of Broadway musicals and theatrical productions accompanied by fine dining ($27–38). Closed Mon; Sat matinee offered at noon.

At the **Van Wezel Performing Arts Hall** (1-800-826-9303; www.vanwezel .org), 777 N Tamiami Trl, enjoy a smorgasbord of productions—top-quality dance, musicals, symphony orchestra, and comedy, including Broadway productions such as *STOMP* and *Beatlemania,* the magic of David Copperfield, and the music of Englebert Humperdinck. From October through May there's such an array of shows, you'd think you were in New York. Check their web site for this year's schedule and ticket prices.

✳ Selective Shopping

Anna Maria

You'd hardly believe that **Ginny's and Jane E's at the Old IGA** (941-778-3170), 9807 Gulf Dr, was once a supermarket, with its chic indoor "garden of antiques" feel. Local art mingles with antiques, a juice bar (featuring smoothies and coffee), and organic fruit and vegetables to make a comfy kick-back-and-relax atmosphere. Closed Mon.

Across from the Old City Pier, **Bayview Plaza,** at the corner of Bay and Pine, offers some great little shops, including **White Egret Boutique** (home decor and gifts), the **Paper Egret** (sundries and gourmet food), and **Two Sides of Nature,** with whimsical colorful toys and kitchen items, as well as a prolific stock of bright island T-shirts. But my favorite, **The Museum Shoppe** (941-779-0273; www.themuseumshoppe .com), 101 South Bay Blvd, is up on the second floor and takes a little effort to find, but it is well worth it if you love giving eclectic gifts. I found quill-and-ink sets for writers, sealing wax, heirloom toys, maps and globes, and local metal art depicting sea life.

Bradenton

A giant rooster tops **Bungalow Antiques** (941-750-6611), 1910 Manatee Ave E, making it easy to spot from the highway. This 1940s bungalow has rooms and rooms of great collectibles and decor items—lots of fun stuff! Open Wed, Sat, and Sun.

At **Carriage House Antiques** (941-747-9234), 3307 Manatee Ave W, I reveled in a room of Florida kitsch, picking up finds such as 1970s citrus trivets and 1940s playing cards. You'll also find fine furniture, vintage glassware, a book nook, and more from nearly 24 dealers within the maze of rooms in this cottage.

Break out those comfortable shoes! **The Red Barn Flea Market** (941-747-3794 or 1-800-274-FLEA; www.redbarnfleamarket.com), 1707 First St E, is one of the region's largest, with more than four hundred vendors indoors and two hundred more booths outside. Open 8–4 Fri–Sun; also open Wed during the winter months.

Bradenton Beach

The funky little downtown surrounding the Bridge Street Circle in Bradenton Beach has quite a few shops and restaurants, including **Two Sides of Nature** (941-779-2432), 119-B Bridge St; **Island Creperie** (941-778-1011), 127 Bridge St; the **Banana Cabana** (941-779-1930), 103 Gulf Dr N; and the **One Stop Shell Shop** (941-778-9195), 101 Gulf Dr, where the sign on the door says, WE WELCOME ICE CREAM CONES, BEACH ATTIRE, AND BARE FEET . . . AFTER ALL, THIS IS FLORIDA!

Cortez

Ahoy, mates! Stroll the salvage garden at **The Sea Hagg** (941-795-5756),

12304 Cortez Rd W, for a jumble of nautical goodies—some antique, some new, some indoors, some out. Open Mon–Sat.

Ellenton

There's no pretense at **Enterprise Auction Flea Market** (941-723-9424), 2408 US 301, just an overflowing collection of garage sale items, including stacks of books, furniture, clothing, and more. Open 9–5 daily.

The sprawling **Feed Store Antique Mall** (941-729-1379), 4407 US 301, is full of dealer booths inside an old-fashioned barn—a maze of bargains, just like an old-fashioned flea market. I found books, collectibles, a W. C. Fields lamp, and costume jewelry. Open daily.

Englewood

Once a fishing village, **Olde Englewood Village** (www.oldenglewood.com) dates from 1896 and now is the heart of a quaint shopping district. Wander Dearborn Street and pop in on the various galleries, restaurants, and boutiques, including **Blue Pagoda Florist & Gifts** (941-474-3255), 120 W Dearborn, with its huge oriental imports; **Day Lilies Gallery & Gifts** (941-473-1840), 477 Dearborn, enticing you in with wooden flowers, artsy palms and yuccas, metal birds, and mobiles; **Blueberry Muffin II Antiques & Collectibles** (941-473-7348), 447 Dearborn, with pottery, glassware, primitives, and home furnishings; and the **Amherst Depot** (941-475-2020), 349 Dearborn, a Lionel dealer with a Santa Fe symbol painted on the front door.

On the site of the historic Woodmere sawmill, the **Dome Flea Market** (941-493-6773; www.thedomeflea market.com), 5115 FL 776, has offered up bargains since 1974. Browse the many dealer booths for one-of-a-kind art and Florida gifts. Open 9–4 Fri–Sun.

Holmes Beach
At **Niki's Island Treasures & Antique Mall** (941-779-0729), 5351 N Gulf Dr in Dolphin Plaza, shop for stained-glass windows, retro chairs and tables, and all sorts of funky stuff.

Longboat Key
Creativity is in high swing at **KK's Artique** (941-383-0883), 5360 Gulf of Mexico Dr, with floral-patterned art glass, mosaic-framed mirrors, fiber craft, clay sculpture, and paintings of appealing Sarasota scenes.

Palmetto
With dozens of dealers under one roof, **Emiline's Antiques and Collectibles Mall** (941-729-5282), 1250 10th St E, offers plenty of possibilities, including everything from a 1916 cash register to Plasticville houses, pottery, salt shakers, fine china, and Fenton glass.

Harris & Company (941-722-9999), 501 Eighth Ave W, has an eclectic selection of antiques thanks to its many dealers. How about a fine-art photo of Tampa Bay, a Mills Brothers album, and a Tyco ore dump car?

St. Armands
Walk around the entire circle, and you'll be rewarded with a dizzying array of shops, far too many to mention here. Don't miss the side alleys, too, where more shops await. Here are some of the places that caught my eye:

Kids will love **The Alphabet Shop** (941-388-1505), 386 John Ringling Blvd, with its colorful clothing, books and wood puzzles, Curious George products, and Playmobil toys.

Artisans (941-388-0082), 301 John Ringling Blvd, has neon sculptures, glass art, and other fun and functional pieces. I found classic travel stickers for my antique steamer trunk and a great shawl here.

I loved it when I walked into **Circle Books** (941-388-2850), 478 John Ringling Blvd, and picked up one of my books—and the gal at the counter said it was selling briskly! This busy independent bookstore does a great job of promoting Florida authors, with frequent book signings by names big and small.

Grab your Florida souvenirs at **Destination Florida** (941-388-2119), 465B John Ringling Blvd, where you can choose from local art, bold T-shirts, and "Life is Good" products.

Exotic clothes and wood sculptures are a major part of **Ivory Coast** (941-388-1999), 15 Blvd of the Presidents, where you'll find many foreign objets d'art.

Leaping Lizards (941-388-2844), 372 John Ringling Blvd, has whimsical ceramics, fun cards, and great T-shirts.

At **People's Pottery** (941-388-2727), 362B John Ringling Blvd, look through boldly colored handbags and pottery, art glass, and jewelry.

Sage Spirit (941-388-2975 or 1-866-388-2975; www.sagespirit.net), 17 Fillmore Dr, has Native American jewelry, art, and collectibles.

From Dean Martin CDs to that perfect straw hat, **2 For Me, 1 For You** (941-388-9865), 319 John Ringling Blvd, has great goodies to choose from, including gourmet kitchen items and humorous handbags.

Sarasota—Downtown

A cluster of antiques shops and boutiques around **Historic Burns Square** makes **Pineapple Avenue** a great destination for browsers and buyers. Go for period home decor at **Jack Vinales** (941-957-0002; www .JackVinalesAntiques.com), 539 S Pineapple Ave, including Mission and art deco. At **Pineapple Bay Trading Company** (941-951-1965; www.pineapple-bay.com), 500 S Pineapple Ave, dig through gemstones and creative jewelry, antiques, and gifts. You won't go wrong with gifts from **The Wright Look** (941-330-1807; www.thewrightlookonline.com), 533 S Pineapple Ave, where I picked up a marine-themed mug for my dad's birthday. Stop in at the **Antique Emporium** (941-951-0477), 527 S Pineapple Ave, for a bevy of exotic items from the Far East.

Main Street is long and easy to walk, with street and lot parking nearby. Bibliophiles have several shops to choose from. Three stories tall, **Main Bookshop** (941-366-7653; www.main bookshop.com), 1962 Main St, fills the bottom floor with current books, the middle with overruns, and the top floor with used books. Open 9 AM– 11 PM daily, 365 days a year. **A. Parker's Books** (941-366-2898; www .aparkers.com), 1488 Main St, has well-arranged, packed narrow aisles filled with classic books, a special first-edition section, and many autographed books. **Helen's Books & Comics** (941-955-2989), 1531 Main St, is a used bookstore with more than fifty thousand paperbacks and comic books galore. **Sarasota News & Books** (941-365-3662; www.sara-sotanewsandbooks.com), 1341 Main St, anchors the bay end of the block with a great selection of magazines and current favorites. When you're done browsing the stacks, visit **The Toy Lab** (941-363-0064), 1529 Main St, for educational games, replica critters, and fun science toys.

Siesta Key

In Siesta Village, stop in and meet Ludwig Hagen, **The Potter** (941-346-1848), 5110 Ocean Blvd. Trained in Delft, Holland, he not only showcases fine functional pottery but also offers hands-on instruction right in the middle of the shop. **Lotions & Potions** (941-346-1546; www.lotions andpostions.com), 5212½ Ocean Blvd, has fine stuff for your hands and face. Browse the stacks at **Used Book Heaven** (941-349-0067), 5216 Ocean Blvd. **C.B.'s Saltwater Outfitters** (see *Boating*) is, according to the owner, "a smelly old bait shop turned into a boutique," and not only do they sell bait, they have high-end Orvis gear and sportswear.

Venice—Downtown

Downtown Venice has enough shops to satisfy even the hard-core shopper, with a variety ranging from fine art to absolute kitsch. Paralleling the busy face of the city, Venice Avenue, quiet Miami Avenue is where you'll find the antiques shops. Explore the cross streets for even more bargains. Here's a sample from downtown.

At **Backstretch Sweets** (941-485-4121; www.backstretchsweets.com), 276 Miami Ave W, they offer whimsical chocolate delights in the shapes of palm trees, alligators, horseshoes, high-heeled shoes, and the popular seashells. Stop in for a fresh treat!

With its eclectic mix of local- and world-interest titles, the **Bookstop** (941-488-1307), 241 W Venice Ave, is a must-browse. They carry a fine selection of new books, local authors, and a great kids' section.

Bringing the exotic to you, **Bula Imports** (941-486-1265; www.bula imports.com), 335A W Venice Ave, has the intricate *alebrijes* of the Zapotec Indians of southern Mexico—my favorite pieces of native art, creatures covered in tiny dots. You'll also find Balinese masks, aboriginal boomerangs, and onyx critters.

If antique glass is your weakness, stop in **Buttercup Cottage** (941-484-2222), 227 W Miami Ave, for ornate perfume bottles as well as cobalt, Fenton, jade, Vaseline, and ruby glass.

In the distinctly feminine **Cat's Meow** (941-486-1650), 235 W Miami Ave, linens and lace, hand-painted antique furniture, vintage wedding gowns, and crystal chandeliers let you re-create the past in your boudoir.

The **Green Butterfly** (941-485-6223), 209 W Miami Ave, is brimming with antiques for your dining room, including ruby glass, flatware, pottery, and fine china.

With numerous dealer booths, the massive **Merchant of Venice** (941-488-3830), 223 W Miami Ave, offers a great selection of gifts and antiques from every genre. Look for vintage toys and games, comics, Mexican pottery, fishing lures, and more.

Step into the past at **Nifty Nic Nacs** (941-488-8666; www.niftynicnacs .com), 219 Miami Ave W, my kind of antiques store. Dig through lots of cool kitsch from the 1950s, '60s, and '70s and check out all the harvest gold and avocado kitchenware, political buttons, and retro furniture.

The **Paper Pad** (941-488-8300), 213 W Venice Ave, isn't just a card and

stationary shop—they also have sushi sets, board games and puzzles, pottery, and gourmet gift items.

Much like the shell shops of my youth, **Sea Pleasures & Treasures** (941-488-3510), 255 W Venice Ave, is brimming with seashells from around the world, gifts made from seashells, and beach-related gifts and clothing. It's the place to pick up the specialized scoops for sifting for shark's teeth, and it has a museum display of fossilized shark's teeth found around the area.

Great gifts await at **The Tabletop** (941-485-0319), 205 W Venice Ave, such as Marilyn Monroe (Andy Warhol art) platters, classic clown cookie jars, and whimsical salt and pepper sets.

PRODUCE STANDS, FARMER'S MARKETS, SEAFOOD MARKETS, AND U-PICK

Bradenton
Since 1939, **Mixon Fruit Farms** (1-800-608-2525; www.mixon.com), 2712 26th Ave E, has served the region with farm-fresh citrus from their groves east of the city, which are open for guided tours Nov–Apr. Their store is open 9–5 Mon–Sat and features orange swirl ice cream, homemade cream and butter fudge, and many Florida gifts.

Sarasota
Founded in 1880 by a Civil War veteran, **Albritton Fruit Company** (941-923-2573; www.albrittonfruit .com), 5947 Clark Center Ave, can stake a claim as Florida's oldest family-owned business. In addition to citrus, they sell fresh-squeezed, nonpasteurized juices and gift items. They have four additional retail outlets in the

region, so don't be surprised to stumble across one in your travels.

Terra Ceia

At **Goodson Farms Produce** on US 41 just south of I-275, stop in for fresh fruit milk shakes and strawberry shortcakes during the growing season, Nov–May.

With 150 acres of groves in and around Palmetto, **The Citrus Ranch** (239-723-0504) has a stand on Buckeye Rd, 1½ miles east of US 41, where they sell packed citrus fruit gifts, loose fruit, and fresh-squeezed juices. Free samples!

✳ Special Events

January: **Sarasota County Art Day** (941-365-5118), held midmonth, is a community celebration of the arts in Sarasota on the streets of downtown.

Annual Sarasota Film Festival (941-364-6514), held the last week of the month, features more than 25 films, celebrity participants, and fun events, including an outdoor film screening, a gala party, and more.

March: **Sarasota Comedy Festival** (941-365-1277), held midmonth, is a week of fun and funny seminars, events, performances, and dinners benefiting the United Way of Sarasota County.

Annual Sarasota Jazz Festival (941-366-1552), end of the month,

features headline acts and jazz in public places.

April: **CSO Festival,** Gamble Plantation Historic State Park (see sidebar in *Historic Sites*), first Sat. Entertainment, food, antique autos, arts and crafts, and the Patton House open for tours.

Venice Shark's Tooth Festival (941-412-0402), first weekend, is a weekend of food, fossils, and fun at the beach near the Venice Pier, with more than one hundred artists showing off their work.

Spring Festival of Sarasota Ballet (941-351-8000), end of the month. A celebration of outstanding artistry and technique, held at the FSU Center for Performing Arts.

June: **Sarasota Music Festival** (941-953-4252), most of the month. Started in 1964, this annual celebration features more than 40 world-renowned guest artists and a hundred exceptional music students.

October: **St. Armands Art Festival** (941-388-1554), second weekend. More than 175 artists and craftspeople display their original artwork, including pottery, oils, watercolors, ceramic jewelry, and sculpture.

November: **Art Fest—Downtown Venice** (941-484-6722), first weekend. Juried show with 150 booths, food, and entertainment on Venice Avenue West.

CHARLOTTE HARBOR AND THE GULF ISLANDS

It is a quaint town of brick streets and Victorian gingerbread homes hidden by screens of tropical vegetation, the bright red blooms of hibiscus standing out against lush green foliage. It is a waterfront town, along a vast rippling current in which dolphins play and cormorants dive. Established in 1887, **Punta Gorda** is one of Florida's most charming cities, where historic cottages come in island colors such as mango, avocado, and lavender. As the heart of Charlotte County, it has a vibrant downtown with arts and dining. I fell in love with the historic district and thought about buying a house.

And then came Hurricane Charley, packing winds up to 145 miles per hour, roaring up the Peace River like a runaway train. Its cone of destruction was tight, but it hit hard and fast. Businesses I'd visited vanished. Century-old buildings crumbled. I watched the news reports and frantically e-mailed folks to make sure they were okay. Driving through town a short time later, I wept. It looked like a war zone.

However, Florida recovers quickly from natural events. Thanks to the resilient folks who live here, it's back to business as usual on Marion Avenue, where nightlife bustles again. Art is everywhere, especially murals—striking images on downtown historic buildings and even a sea turtle swimming across the side of the Dairy Queen at a prominent intersection at FL 776 and US 41. There aren't as many trees in the historic district, but proud owners have worked hard to save their treasures.

Punta Gorda is only one facet of this large county that surrounds Charlotte Harbor, where the Myakka and Peace Rivers meet. Imagine miles of mangrove-lined shoreline dense with the activity of egrets and herons, and vast sandy beaches where plovers and terns race along the sand. Or thousands of acres of pine flatwoods protected from development, where red-cockaded woodpeckers nest, eagles fly, and sandhill cranes gather in the open prairies. This is a birder's paradise, where every little park and preserve yields another find for your life list, from the vast Babcock-Webb Wildlife Management Area to the sandy tip of Stump Pass Beach State Park at **Englewood.** It's an angler's paradise, too, one of the world's top sportfishing destinations. You'll have a shot at tarpon, snook, redfish, barracuda, cobia, and grouper in the rich estuaries where the rivers meet the Gulf of Mexico. Cast off from the sleepy fishing village of **Placida,** or drop a line off the bridge at historic **El Jobean.**

Once the fishing grounds of the Calusa, the barrier islands have stories to tell, including those of pirate treasure. Among the most persistent is the legend of Jose Gasper, born of noble Spanish blood but turned pirate in the early 1800s, cruising the coast of Florida for his prey of Spanish and British ships. Local lore places **Gasparilla Island** as his longtime hideout, and the islands surrounding Boca Grande as the place where he and his brother buried multiple casks and chests of Spanish gold coins.

And then there are the modern-day pirates. In the early 1900s, developers with big dreams and land schemes moved into the wet prairies surrounding Charlotte Harbor, starting with John Milton Murdock, who obtained thousands of acres to resell to farmers and settlers. The new owners quickly discovered the seasonal flooding that is a natural part of southwest Florida ecosystems, and Murdock had to create drainage canals to make the farmland usable. Among the developers who kick-started growth at the turn of the last century was former governor Albert Gilchrist, president of the Boca Grande Land Company, who played a large role in the development of Gasparilla Island. The Charlotte Harbor and Northern Railroad was extended to the island to allow phosphate barges to offload their cargo to a shipping plant built in 1912, and phosphate was shipped out of the island until the 1970s. Simultaneously, wealthy Northeasterners discovered this island getaway, a hot spot in the 1920s when the Silver Star ran the rails from New York City direct to Boca Grande in 24 hours. Anglers came here for some of the best tarpon fishing in the world. Although much of Boca Grande lies in adjoining Lee County (see *Sanibel, Fort Myers, and the Islands*), its amenities are described in this chapter for sake of access—the only way to get there by car is across the Gasparilla Island Bridge at Placida.

GUIDANCE For brochures, maps, and reservations, either drop in at the **Southwest Florida Welcome Center** (941-639-0007; www.puntagordavisitor.info), 26610 S Jones Loop Rd, Punta Gorda, for information, or contact **Charlotte County Visitor's Bureau** (941-743-1900; www.pureflorida.com), 18501 Murdock Cir, Suite 502, Port Charlotte. Visiting Boca Grande? Stop at the **Boca Grande Area Chamber of Commerce** (941-964-0568; www.bocagrande chamber.com), next to Uncle Henry's Marina Resort (see *Lodging*).

GETTING THERE *By car:* **I-75** and **US 41** provide primary access to the region.

By air: The nearest airports include the **Sarasota International Airport** (see *The Cultural Coast*) and **Southwest Florida International Airport** (see *Sanibel, Fort Myers, and the Islands*).

By bus: **Greyhound** (1-800-231-2222; www.greyhound.com), 900 Kings Hwy, has a terminal in Port Charlotte.

By rail: **AMTRAK** (1-800-USA-RAIL), 909 Kings Hwy, connects from the nearest station to Port Charlotte via motor coach.

GETTING AROUND *By car:* **US 41** is the primary artery linking Punta Gorda, Charlotte Harbor, and Port Charlotte. **FL 771** connects Port Charlotte with Placida, where **FL 775** is the north–south route between Boca Grande, Cape Haze, and Englewood. **FL 776** is the direct route from Port Charlotte to Englewood. There is a toll of at least $5 to cross the bridge to Boca Grande.

By taxi: **Voyager Taxi** (941-629-2810) provides 24-hour taxi service throughout the area, while **Charlotte Shuttles & Airport Transportation, Inc.** (941-255-9117; www.charlotteshuttles.com), 2158 Gerard Ct, offers an airport shuttle service.

By water taxi: **Pirates Water Taxi** (941-697-5777), 6301 Boca Grande Causeway, provides water transportation to Little Gasparilla Island, Don Pedro State Park, the outer islands, and restaurants. Fares $7.50 per person, $15 minimum for a trip.

MEDICAL EMERGENCIES For major emergencies seek help at **Charlotte Regional Medical Center** (941-639-3131), Charlotte Harbor, or, if you're in the northeast part of the county, seek assistance over the county line in Venice at **Bon Secours Hospital** (941-485-7711) on Business US 41. In Boca Grande, call the **Boca Grande Health Clinic** (941-964-2276), and in Englewood, the **Englewood Community Hospital** (941-475-6571).

✳ To See

ART GALLERIES

Boca Grande
Both the **Hughes Gallery** (941-964-4273; www.hughesgallery.net), 333 Park Ave, and **Paradise! Fine Art** (941-964-0774), 340 Park Ave, present fine art by nationally renowned artists, as well as traditional interpretations of Florida landscapes. Nearby, the **Serendipity Gallery** (941-964-2166), Olde Theatre Mall, 321 Park Ave, is a quirkier place, filled with colorful art that appeals to those of us with flamingos on the bathroom wall and fish platters in the kitchen.

THE MARGARET ALBRITTON GALLERY IN PLACIDA
Sandra Friend

Placida
Whimsical fish and turtles decorate walls, ceiling, and windows at **Margaret Albritton Gallery** (941-698-0603), 13020 Fishery Rd, where it's tough to resist picking up at least one piece of her wildlife art, or a beach knickknack for the home.

Punta Gorda
The Punta Gorda Gallery Walk (941-743-1900) is held the third Thursday of every month from 5 to 8 PM. Among the galleries visited are the **Presseller Gallery & Delicatessen** (see *Eating Out*), where you

can dine among the creations of regional fine artists and digital media artists, and the **Sea Grape Artists Gallery** (941-575-1718; www.seagrapegallery.com), 113 W Marion Ave, a cooperative staffed by nearly 20 local artists. I particularly enjoyed Vicki Glynn's watercolors of the flora and fauna of Charlotte Harbor's coastlines.

At the **Visual Arts Center** (941-639-8810; www.visualartscenter.com), 210 Maud St, you can savor the art on display, browse through an extensive art library, take a workshop, or pick out an original gift from the gift shop. There are four main galleries with 12 shows per year, and more than 3,000 art books, tapes, and DVDs in the library. Classes are offered year-round, but the center does close on weekends during the summer months. In the courtyard you'll see a fountain preserved from Punta Gorda's first hotel. Free; donations appreciated.

HISTORIC SITES

Boca Grande

At Sandspur Park along Gulf Boulevard, the tall thin lighthouse you see is the **Rear Range Light,** an unmanned structure built in 1881 to be used in Delaware, and then moved to Boca Grande in 1927 for active duty. Built in 1890 to guide ships to Charlotte Harbor, the **Boca Grande Lighthouse** (see *Museums*) is one of the oldest structures in the region. It served as a working lighthouse for nearly 70 years and was fully restored in 1986 to serve as a museum. Nearby, the **Quarantine House** (to the left of the entrance to the state park where the lighthouse is located), circa 1895, housed sick crewmembers on ships visiting the city. It is privately owned.

El Jobean

Undergoing historic restoration, the circa 1922 **El Jobean Post Office & General Store** (941-627-3344), 4370 Garden Rd, when open, shows off artifacts from the early days of this planned community, which went bust in 1920. In 1931 the building served as a hotel and housed film crews from MGM. The original wooden railroad bridge over the Myakka River at the end of Garden Road is now the Myakka North Fishing Pier.

Placida

On the grounds of **Grande Tours** (see *Ecotours*), Capt. Marian Schneider preserved two interesting historic artifacts from the area: the original **bridge tender's cottage** from the first wooden railroad bridge (now a fishing pier) to Gasparilla Island, and a **homesteader's cistern** that once sat on her parents' property to accumulate much needed fresh water from rainwater.

Punta Gorda

Stroll the downtown and waterfront streets to see dozens of classic Victorian homes, cottages, and bungalows, all privately owned. **The Freeman House,** 639 E Hargreaves Ave, is a 1903 rural Victorian preserved by the Charlotte County Foundation; tours offered Dec–Apr, hourly 11–3 Fri–Sat (donation). At nearby **Punta Gorda History Park** (941-639-1887), 501 Shreve St, historic

158

THE GULF COAST

buildings were moved here to avoid demolition. The collection includes the original city jail, a Cuban cigar worker's home, and Trabue Cottage, the first land sales and post office in the city.

MUSEUMS

Boca Grande

An excellent introduction to regional history, the **Boca Grande Lighthouse Museum** (941-964-0060; www.barrierislandparkssociety.org/lighthouse.html) at Gasparilla Island State Park (see *Beaches*) explains how these barrier islands, once occupied by the Calusa, became Spanish settle-

Sandra Friend

BOCA GRANDE LIGHTHOUSE, CIRCA 1890

ments where fishermen created "ranchos," offshore fish farms that they tended. When the railroad came to Boca Grande to serve the growing phosphate industry along the Peace River, it brought Northern visitors who sought recreation with sportfishing and changed the nature of the town from a working maritime port to the exclusive enclave it remains today. The lighthouse is open Wed–Sun all year long, and Tue Feb–Apr. Donation.

Located south of channel marker 7 on Boca Bayou, the **Gasparilla Island Maritime Museum** at historic **Whidden's Marina,** Fifth Ave, revisits the grand era of commercial fishing in southwest Florida through artifacts and photographs displayed in the old Red Gill Fish House. Built in 1926, the marina is the oldest continuously operating business on the island and still serves its customers daily. Donation.

Charlotte Harbor

Overlooking Charlotte Harbor, the **Charlotte County Historical Center** (941-629-7278; www.charlottecountyfl.com/historical), 22959 Bayshore Rd, presents exhibits ranging from prehistory to today on local history topics as well as regular workshops. The Live Oak Emporium gift shop has educational toys, games, and books. Exhibits are open 10–5 Mon–Fri and 10–3 Sat. Donation.

Punta Gorda

The contributions of African Americans who helped to found Punta Gorda are memorialized at the **Blanchard House African American Heritage Museum** (941-637-0390), 406 Martin Luther King Blvd, which has a Black History Library and gift shop.

The **Florida Military Heritage Museum** (941-575-9002; www.mhaam.org), 1200 W Retta Esplanade B-4, displays a portion of its collection of more than twenty thousand military artifacts donated by veterans in order to interpret military history. Open 10–6 Mon–Sat, noon–6 Sun. Free.

Boca Grande

Once the terminus of the Charlotte Harbor and Northern Railway, which actively shipped phosphate brought to the wharf by barges until 1979, Boca Grande still has its **old railroad depot** downtown, built in 1911. It was one of three depots on the island and is now home to several shops and the Loose Caboose Restaurant (see *Eating Out*).

Punta Gorda

Built in 1928, the **Historic Train Depot** (941-639-6774; www.charlotte-florida .com/community/main2.htm), 1009 Taylor Rd, is one of only six Mediterranean-style railroad depots remaining in the United States. It now houses antiques shops. An excellent mural depicting the railroad era is across the street.

Although no structure remains from that era, you'll find a **historic marker for the Southwest Railroad Terminal** in front of the Isles Yacht Club on West Marion Drive, past Fishermen's Village.

✳ To Do

BICYCLING

Boca Grande

To get around Boca Grande's narrow tropical-canopied streets, consider picking up a bike at **Island Bike 'n Beach Rentals** (941-964-0711), 333 Park Ave. A bike path parallels the main highway from downtown Boca Grande along the old railroad line all the way to the causeway.

Cape Haze

A paved path connecting communities in the eastern part of the county, the **Cape Haze Pioneer Trail** (941-627-1628; www.charlottecountyfl.com/Parks/ capehaze.html), 1688 Placida Rd, starts at FL 771 near Rotunda and works its way through the massive circular-shaped planned community to the coast at Cape Haze along the route of the former Charlotte Harbor and Northern Railroad for 5 miles. Plans are to continue the route to Placida.

BIRDING Look for the elusive mangrove cuckoo among the tangled mangrove jungles of **Ponce de Leon Park** (see *Parks*), and seek sandhill cranes and red cockaded woodpeckers at **Babcock-Webb Wildlife Management Area** (see *Wild Places*). Eagles return to nest every winter at **Cedar Point Environmental Park** (see *Parks*). Virtually all of the public lands bordering Charlotte Harbor will help you add more species to your life list.

AVENUE OF PALMS TO THE BEACH IN BOCA GRANDE

Visit Florida

Boca Grande

Charter boats (with captain and crew) are available at **Uncle Henry's Marina Resort** (1-888-416-BOAT) to enjoy the barrier islands along Charlotte County's coastline. A half day runs $325 and up, full day $550 and up.

El Jobean

Holidaze Boat Rental (941-766-9900; www.holidazeboatrental.com), 4240 El Jobean Rd (FL 776), offers rentals of power boats, pontoon boats, fishing and sailing skiffs, and Jet Skis at this location near the mouth of the Myakka River. Rentals start at $125 per half day for a skiff.

Englewood

Explore Lemon Bay on a skiff from **Bay Breeze Boat Rental** (941-475-0733), 1450 Beach Rd, or **The Beach Place** (1-800-314-4838; www.capt-rockys -florida-deep-sea-fishing.com), 1450 Beach Rd, where skiffs are $70 for a half day in an 18-footer.

Placida

Gasparilla Marina (941-697-2280; www.gasparillamarina.com), 15001 Gasparilla Rd, is one of the largest in the area with 225 slips, overnight dockage with showers and a ship's store, large boat storage, and fuel. They rent boats, too.

Punta Gorda

Providing easy access to Charlotte Harbor and Pine Island Sound, **Burnt Store Marina** (941-637-0083; www.burntstoremarina.com), Burnt Store Rd, is a favorite for boaters headed to the south end of this region. Dockage runs $1.75 per foot per day.

Board a sunset cruise or ecotour at **Fishermen's Village** (see *Selective Shopping*) with the **King Fisher Fleet** (941-639-0969; www.kingfisherfleet.com), 1200 W Retta Esplanade; advance reservations suggested. The *Good Times II* is a roomy craft with a popular top deck. As you cruise out into the bay, dolphins frolic in the waves made by the boat's wake. If you're visiting at Christmastime, ask about their special Christmas Light Canal Tours that take you up into residential areas to see the lights from the water.

CRABBING From mid-October through May, it's perfectly legal for you to dive offshore of Charlotte County to **collect stone crab claws**—if you can stand the thought of removing them from their owners. The good news is, the crabs grow them back, so only take one from each critter. Limits set by the Florida Fish and Wildlife Conservation Commission (www.floridaconservation.org) are 1 gallon of claws per person (2 gallons per vessel), and all claws must be a minimum of 2¾ inches from elbow to tip. Divers must fly a diver-down flag.

ECOTOURS Enjoy a narrated voyage with **Grande Tours, Inc.** (941-697-8825; www.grandetours.com), 12575 Placida Rd, Placida, and pick your subject: shelling, dolphins, buried treasure—you name it! Take a cruise, rent a kayak, or book a guided fishing trip—these knowledgeable natives can do it all.

To see the Florida that Patrick Smith describes in *A Land Remembered,* take a trip back in time at the Babcock Ranch with **Babcock Wilderness Adventures** (1-800-500-5583; www.babcockwilderness.com), 8000 FL 31, Punta Gorda. On a 90-minute ride on a school bus converted into a swamp buggy, you'll tour a portion of the 91,000-acre Crescent B Ranch, a working operation where cowmen still ride the range for days after the herds of up to seven thousand head of cattle. Babies raised here are auctioned off to live on other ranches around the country. Along the route, you'll encounter herds of Cracker cattle, descendents of those brought to Florida by the Spanish in the 1500s, and historic Rouxville, a 1920s lumber town where nearly two hundred people once lived along the railroad in boxcars—the first "mobile home" park in Florida. Keep alert, as your driver will point out wildlife in the pine woods and through Telegraph Cypress Swamp, where herds of wild hogs roam and alligators sun on the banks of the creeks at the old railroad trestle. A stop in the swamp lets you experience the ancient cypresses along a boardwalk and meet resident Florida panthers in a large enclosure. When you return to the registration and gift shop area, walk through a cabin used in the movie *Just Cause* that now serves as a small museum recounting how R. V. Babcock came from Pittsburgh in 1914 and purchased hundreds of thousands of acres to expand their timber business. Tours (by reservation only) are held Nov–May between 9 and 3 daily, and Jun–Oct in the morning only. Call for specific times. Adults $17.95, ages 3–12 $10.95.

King Fisher Fleet (see *Boating*) offers dolphin watching cruises daily as well as sunset cruises every evening from Fishermen's Village.

FAMILY ACTIVITIES

Charlotte Harbor
Along the harbor, **Fish Cove Miniature Golf** (941-627-5393), 4949 Tamiami Trl, provides the kids some fun and adults an opportunity to unwind. Tropical plantings accent the mini-golf faux cliffs and water hazards.

Englewood
Pelican Pete's Playland (941-475-2008), 3101 S McCall Rd, has mini golf and go-carts, batting cages, and a miniature train. If the weather's yucky, you can play in the arcade.

Port Charlotte
Take the kids to **Sun Flea Market & Kidstar** (941-255-3532), 18505 Paulson Dr, with its slate of old-fashioned carnival rides, including a Ferris wheel. Of course, there's the flea market to browse, too.

FISHING If tarpon's your fish, you've found the holy land. For more than a century, anglers have descended on Charlotte Harbor as one of the world's top sport-fishing destinations. You'll have a shot at tarpon, snook, redfish, barracuda, cobia, and grouper in the rich waters where the rivers meet the Gulf. Numerous private guides are registered locally; your best bet is to check at one of the marinas (see *Boating*). One captain I know personally and will recommend for your outing is **Captain Van Hubbard/Let's Go Fishin', Inc.** (941-697-6944; www.captvan .com). Many fishing charters depart from Fishermen's Village (see *Selective Shopping*) in Punta Gorda, including those of the **King Fisher Fleet** (see *Boating*).

GOLF

Port Charlotte
Endless meandering waterways mark the course at **Deep Creek Golf Club** (941-625-6911; www.deepcreekgolf.com), 1260 San Cristoball Ave, a par 70 course designed by Mark McCumber. **Kings Gate Golf Club** (941-625-7615; www.kingsgategolf.com), 24000 Rampart Blvd, is a tough par 60 executive golf course. And a top pick by *Golf Digest*, the **Riverwood Golf Club** (941-764-6661; www.riverwoodgc.com), 4100 Riverwood Dr, offers true challenges created by its setting in a lush natural landscape of pines and oaks.

HIKING Cedar Point Environmental Park at Cape Haze and **Alligator Creek Preserve** at Punta Gorda (see *Parks*) are both managed by the Charlotte Harbor Environmental Center, which maintains an interpretive center at each park. Both have an excellent network of hiking trails on which you can spend several hours exploring coastal and uplands habitats. A 1-mile nature trail on the landside at **Don Pedro Island State Park** (see *Beaches*) loops through pine flatwoods and along the sometimes-wet mangrove fringe before leading you down to the ferryboat dock.

PADDLING Charlotte County Parks & Recreation (941-625-PLAY; www. charlottecountyfl.com), 2300 El Jobean Rd, Port Charlotte has aggressively set up a county Blueway to allow visitors to navigate the mangrove channels around

KAYAKING THE BLUEWAY AROUND CHARLOTTE COUNTY

Visit Florida

Charlotte Harbor. Contact the county for a complete guide to **Blueway Trails.**
Local kayakers have warned me that while much of the route can be explored as
day trips, some of it is not yet ready for use despite being included in the guide.
Check with local outfitters before setting out on a multiday trip. **Grande Tours,
Inc.** (see *Ecotours*) rents kayaks and leads guided kayaking trips, including
overnight trips with camping on some of the region's unspoiled barrier islands.

RACING At the **Charlotte County Speedway** (941-575-7223; www.charlotte
countyspeedway.net), 8655 Piper Rd, Punta Gorda, experience Saturday-night
racing on the ⅜-mile figure-eight asphalt track. Open Labor Day through June,
with numerous special events.

SAILING Learn to sail in the broad expanse of Charlotte Harbor with the **International Sailing School** (1-800-824-5040; www.intlsailsch.com), 1200 W Retta
Esplanade, Punta Gorda, or **B&D Sailing** (1-800-974-7325;
www.bdsailing.com), 19246 Palmdale Ct, Port Charlotte.

SCENIC DRIVES A slow drive—or, better yet, a bicycle ride—down **Banyan
Street in Boca Raton** will leave you marveling at the wonder of these fast-
growing tropical trees, members of the ficus family that so quickly knit a dense
canopy overhead while putting down roots from their branches. You'll feel like
you're in a tropical tunnel! And if you see a giant lizard cross the road, well, it's
not your imagination. A colony of iguanas lives on the island.

SCUBA Hit the depths with professional assistance from **DepthFinders Dive
Center** (941-766-7565; www.DepthFinders.com), 1225 Tamiami Trl, or **Fan-
tasea Scuba** (941-627-3888; www.fantaseascuba.com), 3781 Tamiami Trl, both
in Port Charlotte.

SHELLING Seashells along the sandy strands of the barrier islands can grow to
impressive sizes—but you'll have to be the early bird after high tide recedes
to claim your treasure. Look for the best shells where the tides sweep around
curved land at the tip of **Stump Pass Beach State Park** and **Boca Grande
Pass** within **Gasparilla Island State Park** (see *Beaches*).

WILDLIFE REHAB ♪ Volunteers look after injured birds and small mammals at the
Peace River Wildlife Center (941-637-3830; www.charlotte-florida.com/dining
andentertainment/peace/intro.htm), 3400 W Marion Ave, Punta Gorda, permanent
home to nearly one hundred raptors, herons, and songbirds. Animals brought here
go through triage in a "birds only" emergency room, stabilization in cages out of
public view, and then a flight cage or home care until they are able to be returned
to the wild. Many of the permanent residents are pelicans injured by discarded
monofilament fishing line, and they have their own big pool in the back, where
you can watch them gobble down fish at feeding time. Guided tours are given on a
regular basis, or you can walk through at your own pace. Donations greatly appreciated, as this has been a fully nonprofit labor of love for more than a decade, with
local veterinarians donating their time and equipment to care for injured wildlife.

BEACHES

Boca Grande

Gasparilla Island State Park (941-964-0375; www.flordiastateparks.org/gasparillaisland) is a string of five beaches along Gulf Boulevard, with the best (in my opinion) to be found at the mouth of Charlotte Harbor, in front of the historic Boca Grande lighthouse. Fee.

Cape Haze

Beachgoers seeking beachfront solitude in Charlotte County will find it at **Don Pedro Island State Park** (941-964-0375; www.floridastateparks.org/donpedro island/default.asp), a state-owned island accessible only by private boat or water taxi (see *Getting Around*) to Knight Island. The land base along FL 776 has a nice nature trail loop through a tall stand of pines.

Englewood

Where North Beach Road meets Gulf Boulevard, **Chadwick Park** (941-473-1018), 2100 N Beach Rd, is an enormous county beachfront park with ample parking, beach crossovers, and restaurants across the street. However, the best beach on the island is at its south end—**Stump Pass Beach State Park** (941-964-0375; www.floridastateparks.org/stumppass), 900 Gulf Blvd, where the highway ends. If you're lucky enough to find a parking spot, you'll enjoy several miles of a sliver of sand topped with maritime forest. A kayak launch lets you paddle up the bay side and view numerous osprey nests on the smaller surrounding keys. Fee.

ALONG PINE ISLAND SOUND AT PONCE DE LEON PARK
Sandra Friend

Punta Gorda

At **Ponce de Leon Park** (see *Parks*), **Rotary Beach** is the closest stretch of sand to town. It's a gathering place for locals to watch the sunset. Bring your lawn chair!

PARKS

Englewood

Protecting 115 pristine acres along an undeveloped coastline on Lemon Bay, **Cedar Point Environmental Park** (941-625-7529; www.checflorida.org/recreation/cedarpoint.htm), 2300 Placida Rd, is managed by the Charlotte Harbor Environmental Center and offers a quiet place to walk the trails and become familiar with natural habitats that have vanished due to development in the area. Start at the Visitor's Reception Center for a cinematic overview and information to take with you out in the field, then roam the seven marked trails to explore coastal pine flatwoods, coastal scrub, mangrove forests, and more. Enjoy the picnic area and playground near the front entrance, and launch your kayak into Oyster Creek for exploration of the preserve by water. Open sunrise–sunset, except when posted to protect eagle nesting; visitors center open 8:30–4:30 Mon–Fri.

Punta Gorda

Managed by the Charlotte Harbor Environmental Center (CHEC), **Alligator Creek Preserve** (941-575-5435; www.checflorida.org/recreation/ alligatorcreek .htm), 10941 Burnt Store Rd, encompasses more than 3,000 acres of Charlotte Harbor Preserve State Park, on which CHEC maintains their administrative office and classroom facilities. Several miles of trails and boardwalks run through a variety of ecosystems, from pine flatwoods to open prairies, needlerush marshes and mangrove-lined lakes. Visitors center open 9–3 Mon–Sat, 11–3 Sun.

Gilchrist Park (a City of Punta Gorda park), along the waterfront **Retta Esplanade,** is the closest to downtown in a string of parks along Charlotte Harbor at Old Punta Gorda Point. Follow the walkway toward Fishermen's Village through **Shreve Park** and **Pittman Park,** each protecting a slender slice of waterfront sea grapes and mangroves.

Deep in a mangrove forest, **Ponce de Leon Park** (941-575-3324), 4000 W Marion Ave, commemorates the Spanish explorer's reach to these shores with a small memorial and statuettes. De Leon died after he was wounded by Calusa warriors at nearby Pine Island Sound. The park offers a small beach, boat ramp, boardwalk, and rest rooms and is home to the Peace River Wildlife Center (see *Wildlife Rehab*). It's a popular spot to pull up a camp chair and watch the sunset. Open dawn–dark daily. Free.

WILD PLACES Adjacent to Babcock Ranch (see *Ecotours*), the **Babcock-Webb Wildlife Management Area** (941-575-5768; www.myfwc.com/recreation/ babcock_webb/default.asp), 29200 Tuckers Grade, covers more than 79,000 acres of pine flatwoods, prairie, wetlands, and oak hammocks to the east of Punta Gorda on Tuckers Grade. There are 37 miles of unimproved roads throughout the preserve, open to hiking, biking, and horseback riding, and a short hiking loop through a red-cockaded woodpecker colony. Fall brings in hunters from all over the region as they seek deer and wild hogs. But perhaps the most popular activity on the preserve is fishing at 395-acre Webb Lake,

FEEDING CRACKER CATTLE AT THE BABCOCK RANCH
Sandra Friend

which is stocked with largemouth bass, bluegill, freshwater snook, and many other species for catch-and-release. Fee.

Protecting large segments of coastline along the bay, **Charlotte Harbor Preserve State Park** (941-575-5861; www.dep.state.fl.us/coastal/sites/ charlotte), 12301 Burnt Store Rd, offers a place to wander off into the pine and palm flatwoods along the mangrove fringe and go birding. There are two primary access points: the Old Datsun Trail along Burnt Store Road, 1 mile south of Alligator Creek (see *Parks*), and along FL 771 between Rotunda and Placida. The Old Datsun Trail circles a large flatwoods pond and is easy to follow, and the FL 771 access is rugged and the trail not well marked, so a compass or GPS is suggested.

✳ Lodging

BED & BREAKFASTS

Port Charlotte 33948
& At **Tropical Paradise Bed & Breakfast** (941-624-4533; www .tropicalparadisebb.com), 19227 Moore Haven Ct, Joanne and Clift McMahon will treat you like part of the family. Choose from the Hibiscus Room ($75–95), a cheery Caribbean-themed bedroom with adjoining private bath, or the sumptuous Island Suite ($75–115), with hand-carved Honduran furnishings, en suite bath with whirpool tub, and a private exit to the pool area, which overlooks a scenic waterway. Kayak or fish or bring your own boat and dock it— with direct access to Charlotte Harbor, the McMahons enjoy the live-aboard cruiser life, and they offer discounts to MTOA (Marine Trade Owners Association) members.

Punta Gorda 33950
At the **Virginia House** (941-575-8841; www.vahouse.net), 233 Harvey St, Dr. Fred Fox is the proud caretaker of one of the city's oldest buildings, built in 1887 by Punta Gorda's founding father, Col. Isaac Trabue, as a community hall and church. The building was added on to in later years to convert it to a home, but the two rooms at this bed & breakfast—the Chancel Suite and the Sanctuary Suite—both reside in the original walls of the church. With its canopied bed and luxuriously large bathroom with claw-foot tub and shower (in what was once the choir's dressing room), the Chancel is the easy choice for a romantic getaway. Both rooms ($75–95) have outside entrances off their own private lanai. Discounts for longer stays.

CAMPGROUNDS

Port Charlotte 33953
A massive campground en route to the beach, **Encore SuperPark** (1-800-468-5022; www.rvonthego.com/ Harbor-Lakes-RV-Resort-CL25 -8.htm), 3737 El Jobean Rd, offers a vast array of activities and guest services—enough that most of the folks here each winter are here for the season. Overnight guests welcome ($32–40): 30 amp service on back-in sites, or tent sites with no hookups.

Punta Gorda 33955
❀ Tucked away in the woods off US 41 on the way to Fort Myers, **Sun-N-Shade Campground** (941-639-5388;

www.sunnshade.com), 14880 Tamiami Trl, provides a serene getaway for you and your RV with amenities such as a clubhouse, heated pool, shuffleboard, horseshoes, and a nature trail. Electric hookup and dump station; $23–29 per night, $145–175 per week.

HOTELS, MOTELS, AND RESORTS

Boca Grande 33921

Built in 1925, **The Anchor Inn** (941-964-5600; www.anchorinnbocagrande .com), 450 Fourth St, is the perfect getaway for aficionados of true Florida Cracker cottage style. Each room or suite ($147–278) comes with a full kitchen and your own courtesy golf cart for getting around the island. Multiday stays are expected, as there is an additional cleaning fee.

Touting "waterfront lodging on the bayou," **The Innlet** (941-964-2294; www.innletonthewaterfront.com), 11th St and East Ave, has a very pretty location with waterfront rooms ($115–175) on a mangrove-lined canal, ample parking for boat trailers, a restaurant on the premises, and boat slips and a boat ramp for visitors.

Uncle Henry's Marina Resort (941-964-2300; www.unclehenrysmarina .com), 5800 Gasparilla Rd, impressed me with their clean, spacious rooms ($110–167) and suites ($237–257), all with refrigerator, coffeemaker, and hair dryer. Dock your boat at the on-site marina, or rent a craft for quick access to the Gulf of Mexico.

Cape Haze 33946

You're whisked into another world at **Palm Island Resort** (941-697-4800 or 1-800-824-5412; www.palmisland .com), 7092 Placida Rd—namely, acres upon acres of an offshore island to explore. Bound to the mainland by a ferry service with prices high enough to discourage gawkers, Palm Island lies between Manasota Key and Little Gasparilla Island, and it was developed in the early 1980s while taking into careful account the natural habitats, especially the mangrove fringe and tidal flats. It's a great destination for families looking for a relaxing week on an unspoiled beach, with miles of tidal flats to walk. With the exception of the Harborside Villas, all units face the Gulf and sit behind the dune line. The fully equipped units range from one to three bedrooms (seasonal rates of $140–550 daily, $915–4,505 weekly) and include several free rides on the car ferry, depending on your length of stay. Once you park your car, transportation is limited to foot traffic and golf carts. The resort employs naturalist Al Squires (a native plant expert) to lead interpretive walks, provide narration on nature cruises, run a weekly series of nature talks at the clubhouse, and to keep an eye on the unique species found here, such as the least terns nesting along the beach. Amenities include four heated swimming pools and hot tubs, tennis courts and a tennis pro on staff, a

STUMP PASS AS SEEN FROM PALM ISLAND RESORT

Sandra Friend

nature center at the clubhouse, the "Island Kids" club, playgrounds, a recreation center, and rental of all types of water sports items. A full-service marina makes this a great stop for boaters, with 90 wet slips for dockage. To dine, guests can walk to the casual Rum Bay Restaurant and or take a free passenger ferry to Johnny Leverock's Seafood House on the other side of the channel.

Englewood 34223

Englewood Beach & Yacht Club (1-800-382-9757; www.vacationfla .com/ebyc.htm), 1815 Gulf Blvd, caught my eye as I drove down to the end of Manasota Key—lots of families frolicking around the pool, and a neatly kept common area. Units come in one, two, or three bedrooms and range from $600 to $910 per week; daily rates available in the off-season.

It's how a Florida beach vacation used to be—**Weston's Resort** (941-474-3431; www.westonsresort.com), 985 Gulf Blvd, is a family-friendly property at the south end of Manasota Key, adjacent to miles of unspoiled sand at Stump Pass Beach State Park (see *Beaches*), with pools, dockage, fishing guides, and plenty of waterfront views. They feature efficiency rooms ($55–80) and suites up to three bedrooms ($90–200). Weekly rates available.

Port Charlotte 33980

Cozy 1940s rooms await you at the **Banana Bay Waterfront Motel** (941-743-4441; www.bananabay motel.com), 23285 Bayshore Blvd, a perennial regional favorite. It's a Florida classic, with a little palm-lined sand beach on Charlotte Harbor, a pool overlooking the water, and tropi-cal plantings throughout. Enjoy standard motel rooms and efficiencies, some with waterfront views ($69–129).

Port Charlotte Motel (941-625-4177 or 1-800-559-5961; www.port charlottemotel.com), 3491 Tamiami Trl, a favorite with many travelers, is a very appealing family-operated mainstream motel with newly renovated rooms ($119–139) and a pleasant pool and hot tub area.

✳ Where to Eat
DINING OUT

Boca Grande
A local favorite since 1911, **The Pink Elephant** (941-964-0100), Fifth St (at the Gasparilla Inn), is best known for its fresh seafood, featuring locally caught grouper, pompano, and snapper served "Floribbean" style. An extensive wine list complements the menu, which also includes lamb, veal, and hand-cut Angus steaks. Lunch noon–2, dinner 6:30–9:30, Sunday brunch 11:30–2. Closed Mon.

In a historic downtown storefront, **The Temptation Restaurant** (941-964-2610), 350 Park Ave, has pleased its customers for more than 50 years with top-notch lunches and dinners featuring fresh local fish and seafood plus great steaks. Save room for dessert! Reservations recommended.

Punta Gorda
Food as art: that's **The Perfect Caper** (941-505-9009; www.the perfectcaper.com), 320 Sullivan St, where each appetizer, entrée, and dessert is its own perfect masterpiece. The kitchen is a stage, the restaurant a theater, the presentation creative. Borrowing heavily from Asian tradi-

tions, the fusion preparations are made with the freshest of ingredients, most flown in the same day. Wait staff slips out of the shadows to exchange dishes and freshen water. Served atop mashed potatoes surrounded by a sea of butter sauce and asparagus, my horseradish-crusted flounder had a perfect texture and just the right zing. Desserts are made fresh daily and include indulgences such as chocolate sorbet and Grand Marnier mousse. Perfection has its price: You will drop a bundle here. Dinner for one (sans alcohol) ran $54 plus tip. Reservations recommended.

Inside its hand-laid brick walls, **The Turtle Club** (941-637-9477; www .theturtleclubrestaurant.com), 139 W Marion Ave, is the happening place for relaxed fine dining downtown, where executive chef Tony Gonzales fires up creative selections such as Oysters Turtlefeller—a house special-ty topping fresh, plump Texas Hill-man's oysters with a Pernod-based mixture of fresh spinach, apple smoked bacon, shallots, garlic, and cream. Yum! Entrées ($13–38) change weekly, but when I dined they includ-ed Low County pot roast, honey and almond roasted salmon, aged center-cut New York strip, New Zealand rack of lamb, and an array of fish selec-tions seared on the flat-top grill, char-grilled, or blackened, served up with satisfying sides. Wine pair-ings from their five-hundred-bottle wine cellar are suggested on the menu. I savored the flaky, tender, crispy fried grouper and the subtle taste of Parmesan mashed potatoes, and I loved the chocolate turtle ice cream pie, one of several tempting desserts on the menu. Reservations suggested.

Boca Grande

Drop in for homemade ice cream or a sandwich at **Loose Caboose** (941-964-0440), 433 W Fourth St, in the old railroad depot, or take the time for Yankee pot roast or seafood pot-pie. Open for lunch daily; dinner served seasonally.

The only place to dine beachside in Boca Grande is the classic **South Beach Bar & Grille** (941-964-0765; www.southbeachgrille.com), 777 Gulf Blvd, a tropical-themed casual eatery with a screened room overlooking the placid waters of the Gulf framed by sea grapes. Lunch sandwiches and baskets ($5–13) include fried oysters, grouper Reuben, and grilled cheese. Entrées ($18–21) lean on the bounty of the sea, offering award-winning recipes such as Florida crab cakes and stuffed shrimp "South Beach"–style. Reservations suggested due to its popularity.

Englewood

For fresh seafood head to **Barnacle Bill's** (941-697-0711), 2901 Placida Rd, where they offer up broasted oys-ters (shuck 'em yourself!) in-season, grouper and shrimp prepared several different ways, and crab salad. Try their famous hamburgers, too. I'll avoid the liverwurst, but I can't say I've ever seen it on a menu before— my father will be pleased. Lunch and dinner, $5–14.

The name tempted me every time I passed, so I finally had to stop at **The Egg and I** (941-475-6252), 2555 Placida Rd, and you guessed it—worth the stop! Hearty breakfast offerings ($2–6) include eggs Bene-dict, creamed chipped beef, and *abel-skiver,* Danish pancake dumplings. Of course you can get eggs and grits, omelets, and dozens of interesting sides. Open for breakfast and lunch; closed Sun.

Placida

With its own fish market and a fleet of fishing boats docked outside, **The Fishery Restaurant** (941-697-2451; www.sunstate.com/fishery), 13000 Fishery Rd, puts on no frills—it's just plain good seafood. Open 11:30–9 daily; closed Mon.

Port Charlotte

Like a trattoria in Napoli, **Donato's Italian Restaurant** (941-764-1600), 1900 S Tamiami Trl, offers up the ambiance of the Old Country rather than the New York feel of most Italian places. Relax with the family and savor freshly made pasta, tasty soups, and soft, warm bread. I suggest the spicy Pasta Puttenesca, or delicious sausage Parmigiana; entrées run $10–15, with nightly specials. It's classy enough to qualify as fine dining, but no pretensions here—the wait staff will make you feel at home.

The parking lot is frequently full at **La Romana Café & Italian Grill** (941-629-0404), 3591 Tamiami Trl, recommended for their great pizza and a broad variety of Italian entrées, including shrimp scampi, chicken Piccata, and eggplant rollatini. Lunch and dinner, $6–16.

Olympia Restaurant (941-255-3440), 3245 Tamiami Trl, serves traditional Greek favorites such as gyros, souvlaki, leg of lamb, and moussaka ($7–8), as well as an eclectic variety of non-Greek food, from cheese omelets and beef liver to chicken à la king and crab cakes. Daily early-bird specials ($5.49) served 3–5.

Whiskey Creek Steakhouse (941-766-0045), 2746 Tamiami Trl, offers mouthwatering steak and burgers from prime beef raised in the Midwest, all seared over an aromatic open wood fire. Choose from entrées ($8–20) such as a fire-grilled kabob of sirloin, onion, and bell peppers; loaded chicken with hickory-cured bacon, sautéed mushrooms, and melted cheese; or their signature pulled pork barbecue.

Punta Gorda

For authentic Irish food and grog, visit **The Celtic Ray** (941-505-9219; www.celticray.com), 145 E Marion Ave, a happening place every evening. It's in the oldest continually operating building in Punta Gorda, built in 1910, and despite being buffeted mightily by Hurricane Charley, it's still hanging in there—with the threat of demolition overhead and a "Save the Celtic Ray" coalition under way. In addition to fine lagers, stouts, ales, and bitters on draught, they serve classic pub fare (all under $10) such as bangers, chicken curry, shepherd's pie, and Cornish pasty, all with sides of Irish soda bread. Open daily, food served until 10 PM, live music Wed night.

Choose from the masters at **Presseller Gallery & Delicatessen** (941-639-7776; www.pressellergallery.com), 213 W Olympia Ave, a unique and delightful meld of food and art. Dally with a Dalí (Sorrento and Spanish cheese on an appropriately crusty baguette) or savor a Renoir (Norwegian smoked salmon, goat cheese, onions, and tomatoes on a croissant); $4–11. Dine amid the creations of regional artists, or enjoy your meal outdoors.

Great for a hearty meal, the **River City Grill** (941-639-9080), 131 W Marion Ave, satisfies both meat and potato tastes and those desiring some-thing more—and living in one of those mixed marriages, I know what a find this is. Let your meat lover sali-vate over the aged New York strip or boneless center-cut pork chop while you dabble in chile-rubbed ahi or roti chicken potpie. Entrées $12–25.

BAKERIES, COFFEE SHOPS, AND SODA FOUNTAINS The **Boca Grande Baking Company** (941-964-5818), 384 E Railroad Ave, Boca Grande, features hearth-baked breads, fresh pastries, muffins, and scones, and a full-service coffee bar with your favorite coffee drinks. Open 7–7 Mon–Sat, 7–noon Sun.

✳ Selective Shopping

Boca Grande
Boca Grande Outfitters (941-964-2445; www.bocagrandeoutfitters.com), 375 Park Ave, carries "Life is Good" T-shirts and hats, a great selection of books on fishing, and sportswear. You can also pick up a pooper-scooper for your dog, a smart move if you're walk-ing him to tiny Sam Murphy Park along the block, a tropical oasis in the shade of coconut palms.

Featuring "art, antiques, and apparel," the **Galleria of Boca Grande** (941-964-1113; www.emwtrading.com), 410 Fourth St, has exotic home decor including hand-carved wooden flowers ($19) to a hand-carved rosewood altar ($1,000), or even a Balinese umbrella for under $200. It's an eclectic, appeal-ing collection for those who love the Far East. Open 11–5 Mon–Sat (closed Wed), noon–4 Sun.

Ruhama's Books in the Sand (941-964-0777), 5800 Gasparilla Rd, in the same plaza as Uncle Henry's Marina

Resort (see *Lodging*), is a great little independent bookstore with an emphasis on nautical books and local authors.

Englewood
Boutiques, antiques, and eateries define the shopping district dubbed **Olde Englewood Village** (941-473-8782; www.oldeenglewood.com) on Dearborn St, the heart of the old city on Lemon Bay. See *The Cultural Coast* for shopping details.

Placida
In addition to the **Margaret Albrit-ton Gallery** (see *Art Galleries*), Placida is home to a cute village of gaily painted beach bungalows that house a variety of artsy shops, includ-ing **Hatch Limited Artistry & Col-lectibles** and the **Placida Cove Gift Shop.** Most shops open at noon.

Punta Gorda
In downtown Punta Gorda, the shop-ping district includes Marion and Olympia Avenues west of US 41 and Sullivan Street, off Olympia. I walked the quaint downtown and visited the shops just two weeks before Hurri-cane Charley hit. Water and wind damage forced businesses to close, but by the end of 2005, some of the original shops were back in business. Among them are the **Artistic Gour-met** (941-575-6666), 117 W Marion Ave, which features upscale kitchen supplies, spices, and gourmet foods that delighted my brother-in-law the chef, and **The Purple House** (941-639-4040), 312 Sullivan St, a little boutique with gift items.

A massive complex of shops, restau-rants, and housing, **Fishermen's Vil-lage** (1-800-639-0020; www.fishville .com), 1200 W Retta Esplanade, is a destination in itself. There are dozens of shops to explore, but some simply drew me right in. At **Harbor Treasures,** they have minerals and jewelry, woodcarvings and wind chimes. **SS Rainbow** sells Florida products, from kitschy gifts to seashells and books. Give your kids a dollar and let them pick out some fun stuff. Upscale kitchenware is the focus of **Company's Coming,** where they have beautiful serving platters, dishes, and wine glasses. Buy your nautically themed Christmas ornaments at **Christmas by the Sea,** part of a larger gift shop, the **Sand Pebble.** I found great Christmas presents at **Laff Out Loud,** a nostalgia shop with games and toys appealing to my generation. **Pepper Berry Folk Art** features art pieces with gentle scenes of mermaids and seahorses, and dried flower arrangements. Find strings of tropical lights for your patio at the **Caged Parrot** and snazzy figurines and art glass at **Just Clowning Around.**

Bubble bath and fragrant soaps from **The Wash Basin** will set up a pampered evening for you.

PRODUCE STANDS, FARMER'S MARKETS, SEAFOOD MARKETS, AND U-PICK Charlotte County Citrus (941-639-4584), 28900 Bermont Rd (CR 74), is a working family citrus grove with a fruit stand, and they will ship your citrus home. And for more than 40 years, the folks at **Desoto Groves** (941-625-2737; www.desotogroves.com), 1750 Tamiami Trl, have been picking and packing citrus, and they won't let a little thing like hurricanes knock them down. Stop in and visit one of their local outlets for oranges, grapefruit, and more.

✳ Entertainment

FINE ARTS With performances by traveling troupes and local groups, the **Charlotte Performing Arts Center**

MURAL, DOWNTOWN PUNTA GORDA

Sandra Friend

(941-637-0459; www.cpac.cc), 701 Carmalita St, is the place where the play is just one of the things going on. In its 18th season in 2006, the **Charlotte Chorale** (941-204-0033) presents concerts Dec–Apr. A community tradition since 1955, the **Charlotte Players** (941-255-1022) present five plays during their season, Oct–May, and the **Charlotte Symphony Orchestra** (941-625-5996; www .charlottesymphony.com) performs Nov–Apr each season, with a holiday pops concert each Christmas. Check the web site for schedules and tickets.

✴ Special Events

January: Held annually since 2000, the **Charlotte Harbor Nature Festival** (239-995-1777; www.charlotte harborNEP.org), at the Charlotte County Sports Park, Port Charlotte, runs the last Saturday of the month and includes environmental displays, live music, children's activities, wagon rides, and guided walks into the adjacent Tippecanoe Environmental Park.

February: **Charlotte County Fair** (941-629-4252), 2333 El Jobean Rd, Port Charlotte. Held the last week of the month, this old-fashioned county fair has food, crafts, entertainment, rides, and a petting zoo and features daily shows and major musical entertainers.

Annual Florida Frontier Days (941-629-7278), Bay Shore Live Oaks Park, 22967 Bayshore Rd., Charlotte Harbor, held the second weekend of the month, celebrates regional history

with living-history demonstrations, artisans, old-fashioned games, storytelling, and classic Florida food.

March: Attracting seafood lovers from all over, the annual **Placida Rotary Seafood Festival** (941-697-2271; www.seafoodfestival.info) has fun events such as face painting, crab races, antique swap and sell, craftspeople—and, of course, lots of seafood!

For more than 25 years, the **Florida International Air Show** (941-575-9007; www.fl-airshow.com), Charlotte County Airport, Punta Gorda, has been a destination for aficionados of vintage and military aircraft. Enjoy exhibits, precision-flying teams, stunt pilots, and evening pyrotechnics.

April: **Punta Gorda Block Party** (941-639-3200; www.puntagorda blockparty.com), held midmonth, brings in top music acts on four stages, vendors and craftspeople with booths lining downtown streets, and festivities all evening.

August: Taking art to the streets, the **Plein Aire Art Festival** in downtown Punta Gorda encourages artists who paint in "open air" to capture city scenes and showcase their finished works at a gala cocktail reception.

December: Unique to this region and its many waterways are the **Lighted Boat Parades** that occur just before Christmas in **Englewood** (941-475-6882) and on the **Peace River** (941-639-3720). If you haven't seen one, it's quite a delight.

SANIBEL, FORT MYERS, AND THE ISLANDS

I t's tropical. It's enticing. Royal palms line the boulevards, sandal-clad Jimmy Buffet fans share the bars with yachtsmen and golfers, and the sea glimmers green against soft white sands. Hundreds of small islands dot the bays and sounds, awaiting exploration by a sea kayak, a fishing boat, or a quiet skiff. Layers of history lie beneath the shimmering sands and mangrove thickets of these Gulf Coast islands.

In A.D. 100, the Calusa established a city on Mound Key in Estero Bay. Spanish explorer Ponce de Leon met his match in 1521, receiving a mortal wound from a Calusa warrior in Pine Island Sound. Swashbuckling José Gaspar took over **Captiva Island,** raiding passing galleons on his way to Tampa Bay. From **Bokeelia** to **Bonita Springs,** Florida's pioneers plied the waters, setting up fishing camps, vegetable farms, and banana and coconut plantations. During the Seminole Wars, the small fortress of Fort Myers provided safe harbor to pioneers settling Florida's frontier. With millions of acres of open range along the Caloosahatchee River, ranchers such as Jacob Summerlin made fortunes by driving their cattle down to Punta Rassa, where the captains of Spanish galleons would pay them in gold. In 1861 Summerlin enlisted in the Confederate army as a Commissary Sergeant and was appointed to oversee northbound cattle drives to ensure a steady supply of beef to soldiers in Georgia. When the Union army occupied Fort Myers in 1865, two hundred Confederate soldiers marched south from Tampa in an attempt to take the fort back and stop raids on their cattle drives. The resulting four-hour skirmish was the southernmost engagement of the Civil War. The fort itself vanished as settlers poured into the area, eager to establish land grant claims during Reconstruction. Torn down piece by piece, the boards of the fort ended up in new downtown homes and shops.

Incorporated in 1886, the city of **Fort Myers** became a winter destination for tourists hopping steamships down the Gulf Coast. After a short visit in 1889, Thomas Edison built a grand estate on the Caloosahatchee River, where he could assemble a new laboratory devoted to the study of tropical plants. Edison transformed the little town as his industrialist and scientist friends became frequent visitors. Henry Ford bought an adjoining estate. His sophisticated circle of friends established the cultural core of Fort Myers, with its graceful historic downtown.

By overseeing the planting of hundreds of royal palms lining McGregor Boulevard, the old cattle-driving route, Edison ensured Fort Myers a lasting legacy as the City of Palms. Some of the original settlers were flower growers from Europe who made Fort Myers famous many decades ago as the "Gladiolus Capital of the World."

When the Tamiami Trail opened in the 1920s, the land boom started. As the population grew, the economy shifted away from agriculture. After receiving gunnery training at Page Field and Buckingham, thousands of World War II airmen returned to Fort Myers to live after the war. Tourists discovered the unparalleled shelling on **Sanibel Island,** the captivating beauty of Captiva Island, and the thousands of migratory birds that wintered on rookery islands in Pine Island Sound. The economy of the Fort Myers region now revolves around tourism and land development, with nearly a half million residents spilling down the coastline.

GUIDANCE Contact the **Lee County Visitor and Convention Bureau** (239-338-3500 or 1-800-237-6444; www.FortMyersSanibel.com), 2180 W First St, Suite 100, Fort Myers 33901, or visit their web site for extensive information. To pick up brochures, stop in the **Estero Chamber of Commerce Visitor Center** at Corkscrew Rd and US 41.

GETTING THERE *By car:* **I-75** provides direct access to Fort Myers, and **US 41,** the Tamiami Trail, shoots straight through its heart. Be especially cautious driving on I-75 between Fort Myers and Naples, as traffic is heavy and a lot of construction equipment clogs up the highway.

By air: **Southwest Florida International Airport** (239-768-1000), 16000 Chamberlin Pkwy, Suite 8671, Fort Myers, offers regular commuter service on more than a dozen different airlines, including Airtran, American, Continental, Frontier, and US Airways. International flights depart for Canada and Mexico daily.

By bus: **Greyhound** (239-334-1011; www.greyhound.com), 2275 Cleveland Ave, Fort Myers, provides transportation from the Jackson Street terminal, downtown.

GETTING AROUND *By car:* To reach **Pine Island,** use Pine Island Road. **Cape Coral** is best accessed by Colonial Boulevard and Del Prado Boulevard. During the winter "snowbird" season, traffic south of downtown Fort Myers increases in intensity as you head toward Bonita Springs and Fort Myers Beach. McGregor Boulevard provides a great scenic alternative to US 41. From I-75 use Daniels Parkway to access **Fort Myers Beach** and **Sanibel-Captiva,** and Bonita Beach Boulevard to reach **Bonita Springs** and **Estero Island.**

By ferry: **Key West Express** (239-463-5700 or 1-800-273-4496; www.seakey westexpress.com), 2200 Main St (Salty Sam's Marina), connects Fort Myers Beach and Key West. Passengers only; $73 one way, $129 round-trip.

PARKING Beach parking will cost you no matter where you go, and there are parking fees for most of the parks in Lee County, paid via a digital box for which you must have exact change. Save those quarters! In downtown Fort Myers, there is two-hour metered street parking and a parking garage.

MEDICAL EMERGENCIES **Lee Memorial Hospital** (239-332-1111), 2276 Cleveland Ave, serves the greater Fort Myers area. For Sanibel, Captiva, and Fort Myers Beach, the closest hospital is **Southwest Florida Regional Medical Center** (239-939-1147), 2727 Winkler Ave.

✳ To See

ARCHEOLOGICAL SITES

Cabbage Key

It's the only place I know of where you can explore ancient Calusa culture *and* order yourself a mouthwatering "Cheeseburger in Paradise"—**Cabbage Key** is a giant pile of oyster shells cast here by the Calusa thousands of years ago. They built canals, too, and you can explore the island via a nature trail that starts and ends at the inn and restaurant that was once mystery writer Mary Roberts Rinehart's home in 1938. To get here, take a water taxi (see *Boating*) or hook up with the folks at Tarpon Lodge (see *Lodging*) in Pineland, who own the place.

Estero

Launch your kayak from Koreshan Historic State Park (see *Historic Sites*) for a paddle into Estero Bay to see **Mound Key,** a man-made island of oyster shells rising 32 feet high, once the capital city of the Calusa, where King Carlos received the Spanish explorers who came to his shores in the 1500s.

Pineland

At the **Randell Research Center** (239-283-2062; www.flmnh.ufl.edu/rrc/), 13810 Waterfront Dr, explore the interpreted remains of an ancient Calusa city overlooking Captiva Pass and encompassing nearly 60 acres. Engineered thousands of years ago, this was the original city called "Tampa" by the Calusa, who were a seagoing culture with tools based on shells. They subsisted by fishing the vast estuaries between the Ten Thousand Island and Charlotte Harbor. Follow up to a ½ mile of interpretive trails to visit sites of interest, including several significant mounds on which temples and houses once perched, and a canal system that linked the village with the bay. An abrupt climatic change more than 1,500 years ago might have caused the inhabitants to abandon their waterfront property; the ridges show storm deposits from major hurricanes. A visitors center is under construction. Guided tours are offered weekly on Saturday at 10 AM (reservations a must), or you can walk the trails yourself. Open 10–4 daily. A donation ($7 adults, $4 children) is requested.

ART GALLERIES

Bokeelia

Under a bower of sea grapes, the **Crossed Palms Gallery** (239-283-2283; www.crossedpalmsgallery.com), 8315 Main St, showcases fine art and classy art glass, sculpture, and jewelry from local artists.

Cape Coral

A rotating slate of art shows fills the galleries at **Cape Coral Arts Studio** (239-574-0802), 4533 Coronado Pkwy. If you're staying in the region for an extended period, check into their ongoing workshops and fine-art classes. Open 9–5 Mon–Fri. Free.

Captiva Island

At **Jungle Drums** (239-395-2266), 11532 Andy Rosse Ln, nearly three hundred Florida artists are represented in all media, and the result is a store with dozens of pieces of naturally themed art that you'll want to take home. I found the copper mangrove "Captiva candelabra" tables especially appealing, as are the clay studio sushi platters, "Happy Glass" balls, and beach treasure boxes decorated with shells, beach glass, and copper. Owner Jim Mazzotta is best known for his vibrant island creatures and scenes that celebrate the margarita-and-sailing lifestyle.

Featuring oceanic art from local artists such as Nancy Wilson and Myra Robert, **Seaweed Gallery** (239-472-1167; www.seaweedgallery.com), 11513 Andy Rosse Ln, is a little niche of glass, ceramic, and paintings that evoke the magic of the sea.

Matlacha

Art galleries are tucked amid the shops lining the waterfront, including **Wild-Child Gallery** (239-283-6006), 4625 Pine Island Rd, with pottery, art glass, and vivid Florida landscape paintings; **Water's Edge Gallery** (239-283-7570), 4548 Pine Island Rd, with wildlife art; and the **Matlacha Art Gallery** (239-283-6453), 4637 Pine Island Rd, filled with delightful and unique pieces, from whimsical wire people to fish mosaics, wooden critters, and infrared photography. Step outside to the garden for even more art. Leona Lovegrove is the primary artist, but more than 40 other local artists are also represented at this gallery. From Nov–Apr enjoy **Art Night on Pine Island** 4–9 PM on the second Friday of each month as nine galleries on the island stay open late to showcase the artists and gourmet goodies, too.

Sanibel Island

Dubbed the "Island of the Arts," Sanibel has more than a dozen art galleries hidden in its byways and little malls. Start your exploration at **BIG (Barrier Island Group) Arts** (239-395-0900), 900 Dunlop Rd, the nonprofit cultural arts center downtown, where monthly displays are shown at the Phillips Gallery. Pick up a copy of the Sanibel Island art

SANIBEL LIGHTHOUSE

Sandra Friend

gallery guide here to discover the island's many other artists, among them Pam Rambo and her playful home accents at **Kirby Rambo Collections** (239-472-4944), 2340 Periwinkle Way, and Bryce McNamara's whimsical recycled art at the **Tin Can Art Gallery** (239-472-2902), 2480 Library Way.

BASEBALL Spring training is the hot topic in these parts, with the **Minnesota Twins** as the fifth team in more than 65 years to train in Lee County. They play at the William H. Hammond Stadium in south Fort Myers. Downtown, the **Boston Red Sox** play at the City of Palms Park (239-334-4700), 2201 Edison Ave. Call for tickets.

Few Florida historic sites see as many visitors as the **Edison and Ford Winter Estates** (239-334-3614; www.edison-ford-estate.com), 2350 McGregor Blvd, Fort Myers, managed by the City of Fort Myers. Encompassing 14 acres, this tropical paradise dates from 1886, when Thomas Edison established experimental gardens and a laboratory to determine the industrial uses of tropical plants. By the 1930s, he determined that 10 to 12 percent pure rubber could be extracted from a particular species of goldenrod. A tour through the estate is an immersion in a tropical forest, starting with what is claimed to be the third largest banyan tree in the

Rob Smith, Jr.

THOMAS EDISON'S FLORIDA LABORATORY AT THE EDISON AND FORD WINTER ESTATES

world, covering nearly an acre with its dense, glossy canopy supported by hundreds of tap roots as thick as tree trunks and providing a labyrinth of tree limbs to explore. The parade of botanical wonders continues along the tour route, beneath the dangling salami-like fruits of the sausage tree, past poisonous apple trees, blooming orchids, and forests of bamboo. Unfortunately, Hurricane Charley took out most of the dense tropical understory on the property, but most of the grand old trees are still standing. Knowledgeable guides lead each hour-long walking tour, which winds through the tropical plantings to stop at Edison's home office, swimming pool, and wharf before coming to Seminole Lodge, Edison's home. As befitting the inventor

Estero

Dr. Cyrus Teed founded a utopian settlement along the Imperial River in 1894. The well-preserved village is now part of **Koreshan Historic State Park** (239-992-0311; www.floridastateparks.org/koreshan/default.cfm), 8661 Corkscrew Rd. The Koreshans once numbered 250, and they believed in a hollow earth, the Golden Rule, communal property, and women's rights. Tours take you through the village, and you can enjoy the park's many other amenities—campground, picnic area, riverside nature trail, canoe launch, and fishing—on your own.

of the electric light, in 1887 Seminole Lodge was the first building in Florida to be illuminated. The novelty drew Edison's friends from around the world. This traditional Florida home uses breezeways and screened rooms to keep the rooms cool with the constant breezes across the Caloosahatchee River. Original furnishings grace each room. At the adjoining Mangoes, purchased by Edison's protégé, Henry Ford, the tour continues past a garage housing an original 1914 Model T, 1917 Ford Truck, and 1929 Model A before entering Ford's home for a look at life in the 1920s. Leaving the gardens, visitors explore Edison's original rubber laboratory—as intact as the day it shut down—and a museum containing Edison's many inventions, from the well-known light bulb and phonograph to the lesser-known movie projector and stock ticker. Open daily, except Thanksgiving and Christmas. Open 9–5:30 weekdays and Sat, noon–5:30 Sun. Adults $16, children ages 6–12 $8.50. Discounts for Florida residents and a special one-day family pass available.

PHONOGRAPHS AT THE EDISON AND FORD WINTER ESTATES

Visit Florida

Sandra Friend

THE KORESHAN COMMUNE, ESTERO

Sanibel Island

&. Find the original Sanibel at the **Sanibel Historic Village & Museum** (239-472-4648), 950 Dunlop Rd, where wooden walkways lead you through the village and gardens on the site of Bailey's landing, where the first general store stood. (Their family still has a store on Tarpon Bay Road.) Historic structures were moved here from around the island, including the Burnap Cottage (1898), Miss Charlotte's Tea Room (1926), the original post office (1926), and others. Open daily. The museum and houses are open limited hours.

MUSEUMS

Cape Coral

The small **Cape Coral Historical Society Museum** (941-772-7037), 544 Cultural Park Blvd, offers exhibits on the local burrowing owl population, a rose garden, a military museum, a Native American room, and a Florida Cracker homestead. Open 1–4 Wed, Thu, and Sun. Fee.

Fort Myers

&. ✐ Housed in the city's original Atlantic Coast Line depot circa 1924, the **Southwest Florida Museum of History** (239-332-5955; www.cityftmyers.com/museum/), 2300 Peck St, offers a broad perspective on the people and events that shaped this region. From the classy restored Pullman rail car Esperanza to vignettes on the fishing villages of Pine Island Sound, the museum provides a diverse collection of artifacts to explore. Researchers will find the Archival Research Center an invaluable resource for understanding the history of southwest Florida, and the museum store contains a good selection of Florida history books. Adults $9.50, seniors $8.50, children 3–12 $4. Open 10–5 Tue–Sat.

Kids will have a blast at the **Imaginarium Hands-on Museum** (239-337-3332; www.cityftmyers.com/attractions/imaginarium.aspx), 2000 Cranford St, where interactions with Florida's landscapes happen through standing in a thunderstorm, watching coral reef creatures in three 900-gallon aquariums, and getting blown away by a hurricane and reporting about it on the TV weather. Open 10–5 Mon–Sat, noon–5 Sun. Adults $8, seniors $7, ages 3–12 $5.

Pine Island Center

At the **Museum of the Islands** (239-283-1525; www.museumoftheislands.com), 5728 Sesame Dr, thousands of years of island culture are packed into the display cases. Marvel at Calusa figurines, including icons of sea turtles, alligators, and wolves, and look through photos and the family history of the earliest European settlers on the island. There is a well-labeled shell and fossil collection, and artifacts from early settlers, such as an 1800s antique doll buggy. Browse the gift shop for more books on regional history. Fee.

Sanibel Island

 ♿ ♪ You probably never knew that actor Raymond Burr of Perry Mason fame was an avid shell collector, and neither did I until I visited the **Bailey-Matthews Shell Museum** (941-395-2233; www.shellmuseum.org), 3075 Sanibel-Captiva Rd, a mecca for anyone who enjoys the beauty of seashells. Nearly two decades ago, Burr helped launch this museum, which prides itself on the most comprehensive collection in the world on the one island in the United States where shelling is world-class. A globe is the centerpiece of the Great Hall of Shells, showing where in the world you'll find specific species. Journey around the galleries to discover themed and regional exhibits, including shells as art: magnificent inlaid mother-of-pearl cabinetry and sailors' valentines. Natural bird and surf sounds add to the experience, and most of the exhibits put the shells in the context of where and how they live in offshore and inner bay habitats. The Children's Learning Lab has a touch tank and shell specimens, with hands-on games and puzzles. If you're planning to collect shells on this trip, don't miss the introductory movie, which gives important information on how to tell if your finds are alive or not before you remove them from their habitat. You're welcome to bring your own shells for identification. The gift shop has shell motif items, a great selection of guidebooks and serious scientific books on the subject, and children's toys and puzzles. Adults $7, ages 5–16 $4. Serious collectors will want to consider a membership to receive an information-packed newsletter.

RAILROADIANA Hop on board Florida's only dinner-train theater, the **Seminole Gulf Railway** (941-275-8487 or 1-800-SEM-GULF; www.semgulf.com), 4110 Centerpointe Dr at Colonial Station, Colonial Blvd and Metro Pkwy, Fort Myers, for a real treat as you figure out "whodunit" and feast on Black Angus steak, poached salmon, or chicken stuffed with walnut corn bread dressing. This diesel railway also offers scenic day trips of 20 and 30 miles up to and beyond the Caloosahatchee River trestle on Wed, Sat, and Sun, holi-days excepted. Day excursions cost $19.95 adults, $11.95 ages 3–12, with discounts for families.

WINERY The southernmost winery in the continental United States, **Eden Winery** (239-728-9463; www.eden winery.com), 19709 Little Ln off FL 80, Alva, is in the heart of the farming district and a popular stopoff for wine connoisseurs. Tastings run 30 to 40 minutes and include a discussion of the grapes and winemaking procedures. Fee.

INSIDE THE BAILEY-MATTHEWS SHELL MUSEUM

Sandra Friend

Bonita Springs

  A classic Florida roadside attraction, **Everglades Wonder Gardens** (239-992-2591), 27180 Old US 41, opened in 1936 as a wildlife rehab center by Lester and Bill Piper, and since my last visit was in the 1960s, I wasn't sure what to expect. I was delighted to see few changes: Although habitats are slowly undergoing replacement, the winding paths under a canopy of tropical trees remain the same. A tour guide takes you on an interpretive walk through and past the enclosures, where you'll see Florida native species up close. Kids love the bouncing swinging bridge over the alligator pit, and you can let the kids feed fish and turtles along the route. The resident Florida panther, born in 1978, is the oldest in captivity; several have been bred here and released into the wild. There is a sad irony to the many plaques that read A PROTECTED SPECIES DUE TO LOSS OF HABITAT, as natural habitats surrounding the park have vanished at an incredible rate over the past few years. Check out the natural-history museum in the gift shop, with pickled eggs, skulls, and photos from the founding of the park, once known as "Bonita Springs Reptile Gardens" and now in its third generation of family ownership. Before you head into the Everglades, this is a great place to see native creatures up close. Open daily 9–5. Adults $12, ages 3–12 $6, 2 and under free.

Sanibel Island

C.R.O.W. (239-472-3644; www.crowclinic.org), 3883 Sanibel–Captiva Rd, aka the Clinic for the Rehabilitation of Wildlife, features a wildlife video and lecture to explain the efforts of this nonprofit organization to treat, stabilize, and rehabilitate injured birds. Open Mon–Fri with presentation at 11 AM, Sunday at 1 PM. Fee.

✳ To Do

BICYCLING Everybody bikes on **Sanibel Island**—it beats sitting in long lines of traffic on Periwinkle Drive during tourist season. A canopied bike path paralleled Periwinkle prior to Hurricane Charley—the path is still there and heavily used, but a lot of it is in the sun. Side trails lead down to the Gulf, and the main trail continues the length of the island past Ding Darling National Wildlife Refuge toward Captiva Island.

AMERICAN CROCODILES AT EVERGLADES WONDER GARDENS
Sandra Friend

BIRDING It's a fact: More migratory birds pass through *this* part of Florida each winter than any other. And it's the thousands of birds that draw thousands of visitors eager for their first glimpse of a roseate spoonbill picking its way across the mud flats, or a mangrove cuckoo patiently sitting on a tree limb. **J. N. "Ding" Darling National Wildlife Refuge** (see *Wild Places*) is one of the country's top destinations for birding, best done along its trails and along Wildlife Drive. I have never made a visit to the refuge without spotting at least one roseate spoonbill. At the refuge's nearby **Bailey Tract** on Tarpon Bay Road, watch for osprey and red-tailed hawks fishing in the freshwater impoundments. Birdwatchers also flock to the trails at the **Sanibel-Captiva Conservation Foundation** (see *Wild Places*), where benches along the Sanibel River and the island's freshwater marshes provide quiet spots for viewing. From December through June, you'll see swallow-tailed kites nesting at **Six Mile Cypress Slough Preserve** (see *Preserves*) and all year long, families of Florida scrub jays flit through the scrub oaks at **Hickey's Creek Mitigation Park** (see *Wild Places*). On Pine Island, seek out the tough-to-find **St. Jude Nature Trail** of the Calusa Land Trust in St. James City, a narrow pathway that takes you out to a perfect birding spot in the midst of the mangroves.

BOATING

Fort Myers Beach
Most of the region's marinas will rent or charter boats for you to explore the wondrous backwaters of Pine Island Sound and Estero Bay, including **Fish Tale Marina** (239-463-3600; www.fishtalemarinagroup.cc), 7225 Estero Blvd, and **Salty Sam's Marina** (239-463-7333 or 1-888-796-6427; www.saltysamsmarina.com), 2500 Main St.

Pine Island
Out of Pineland Marina, **Island Charters** (239-283-1113), 13921 Waterfront Dr, offers 24-hour on-call water taxi service to the barrier islands of North Captiva, Cabbage Key, and Boca Grande, plus scheduled departures from 7 to 5 from Pineland on the island circuit daily. Charters available. Call in advance for reservations and cost. *Tropic Star* of **Pine Island** (239-283-0015; www.tropicstarcruises.com), also at Pineland Marina, is the cruise I took for a day on Cayo Costa to hike the trails and look for seashells. Reserve your seat in advance.

CRABBING From mid-October through May, it's perfectly legal for you to dive offshore to collect **stone crab claws**—if you can stand the thought of removing them from their owners. At least the crabs can grow them back. Prime sites include along the Sanibel Causeway; off Big Carlos Pass Bridge; and near the Boca Grande phosphate docks. Limits set by the Florida Fish and Wildlife Conservation Commission (www.floridaconservation.org) are 1 gallon of claws per person (2 gallons per vessel), and all claws must be a minimum of 2¾ inches from elbow to tip. Divers must fly a diver-down flag.

ECOTOURS ✐ With miles of unsullied coastline and vast estuaries to explore, ecotours are a popular method of getting out to see dolphin, manatee, rare birds, and more. **Captiva Kayak Company** (239-395-2925; www.captivakayak.com), 11401 Andy Rosse Ln, offers daily explorations to Buck Key. I've photographed dolphins frolicking in the wake of the *Lady Chadwick* on **Captiva Cruises** (239-472-5300; www.captivacruises.com), South Seas Resort Yacht Harbor, Captiva, which features shelling cruises and trips to the outer islands. The Sanibel-Captiva Conservation Foundation (see *Wild Places*) hosts a daily

90-minute **Dolphin and Wildlife Adventure Cruise.** At **Manatee World** (239-693-1434; www.manateeworld.com), Ft Myers, along the Caloosahatchee River at Coastal Marine Mart, FL 80, take a boat safari up the river in search of manatees. Advance reservations required.

FAMILY ACTIVITIES ✐ Take the kids out for some mini golf at **Golf Safari** (941-947-1377), 3775 Bonita Beach Rd, Bonita Beach, or **Smugglers Cove Adventure Golf** (941-466-5855), 17450 San Carlos Blvd, Fort Myers Beach, which is known for its pirate ships and live gators on the course. **Sun Splash Family Park** (941-574-0557; www.sunsplashwaterpark.com), 400 Santa Barbara Blvd, Cape Coral, offers giant waterslides and the "Main Stream River" inner tube ride, squirt playground for the kids, and acres of sunbathing. At **Mike Greenwell's Family Fun Park** (239-574-4386), Pine Island Rd, North Fort Myers, try out batting cages, four go-cart tracks, and the video arcade, or enjoy a hands-on learning experience at the **Children's Science Center** (941-997-0012), 2915 NE Pine Island Rd, North Fort Myers, where you can dig for fossils, walk the nature trail, check out a DNA strand, and more.

FISHING Known as the "fishingest bridge in Florida," the **Matlacha Bridge** on Pine Island Road, Matlacha, always hosts an assortment of characters every day. But if sportfishing is your bag, you've come to the right place. Virtually any marina on the coast (see *Boating*) can hook you up with a professional guide to chase after tarpon or spend a day on the flats. If you've always wanted to cast but never tried, sign up for the **Backwater Fishing School** (1-800-755-1099; www.genmarbackwaterfishingschool.com), hosted at Tarpon Lodge (see *Lodging*), a three-day course with hands-on experience to make you the expert you've always dreamed of being.

GAMING At **Naples–Fort Myers Greyhound Racing** (239-992-2411; www.naplesfortmyersdogs.com), 10601 Bonita Beach Rd, Bonita Springs, relax in the clubhouse or get involved in an unlimited-pot poker game during live races. Simulcasts are also offered.

HIKING Thanks to an aggressive public land-acquisition program, **Lee County** (www.leeparks.org) offers hikers dozens of spectacular choices for day hikes and a handful of places to take a backpacking trip. Many options are outlined in *50 Hikes in South Florida,* and most of the *Green Space* listings feature at least a nature trail for a short walk.

PADDLING The Great Calusa Blueway (239-461-7400; www.GreatCalusaBlueway.com) is one of Florida's most comprehensive saltwater paddling trails. Rent a kayak or bring your own and explore the sheltered waters of Estero Bay, or follow the trail along the island coastlines of Pine Island Sound. Launch points for Estero Bay include the Imperial River at US 41, Koreshan Historic State Park (see *Historic Sites*), Matanzas Pass Preserve (see *Preserves*), and Fish Tale Marina (see *Boating*), among many others. Check the web site or call for a comprehensive map of the paddling trail.

Kayak rentals are available at **Gulf Coast Kayak** (239-283-1125), 4530 Pine Island Rd, Matlacha, where they also offer guided tours. Learn more about the wonders of the mangrove forests of Ding Darling NWR by renting a kayak from **Tarpon Bay Explorers** (239-472-8900; www.tarponbayexplorers.com), 900 Tarpon Bay Rd, on Sanibel Island; guided tours available by reservation. Tours of Mound Key are available from **Estero River Outfitters** (239-992-4050; www.esteroriveroutfitters.com), as well as rentals to take a canoe out on Estero Bay on your own.

SAILING For more than 40 years, Steve and Doris Colgate's **Offshore Sailing School** (1-800-221-4326; www.offshore-sailing.com) has trained students how to raise a sail, catch the wind, and then tack back to port with a series of in-depth hands-on courses that turn landlubbers into live-aboards. Offered year-round out of the South Seas Resort marina on Captiva Island, Learn to Sail courses run from three to nine days. Check the web site for seasonal pricing.

SHELLING The parking fees are a small price to pay for access to **Sanibel Island** on the morning after a raging storm, as this barrier island is renowned as having the best shell-collecting beaches in North America. Beyond the typical jingle shells, quahogs, and cockles, you'll find such beauties as alphabet cone, sunray venus, thorny sea star, and apple murex. The secret? Sanibel is a barrier island with an east–west orientation, while Florida's barrier islands normally run north–south, protecting the coastline. Identify your finds with a visit to the Bailey-Matthews Shell Museum (see *Museums*). Peak season is May–Sep, off-season from the usual crowds, and local charter captains offer expeditions to islands and sandbars.

SWIMMING The beaches along Lee County's barrier islands are ideal for swimming—the Gulf waters are warm and clear. My favorite spot is **Bowman's Beach** on Sanibel Island, but you have dozens of places to choose from (see *Beaches*).

✴ Green Space

BEACHES

Estero Island

For a unique beach experience, visit **Lovers Key State Park** (239-463-4588), 8700 Estero Blvd (FL 865). A tram runs visitors through the mangrove swamps and out to the slim strip of beach, which is made up entirely of washed-up and eroded islands of seashells held together by cabbage palms, gumbo limbo, and mangroves. Shell collectors can have a blast just sifting through the bounty under their picnic table. Fee. The new bayside part of the park offers picnic tables, a playground, kayak launch, and rest rooms. Free. **Dog Beach** (941-463-2081), 160 Bahia Via, at Lovers Key just west of New Pass, is where you can let your canine friends romp in the surf. Free.

Fort Myers Beach

You won't go wrong with a visit to the beach, as the beaches around Fort Myers draw visitors from around the world. **Fort Myers Beach** provides easy access for visitors with small parking areas at the end of nearly every dead-end street along Estero Boulevard (FL 865), and a large parking area with facilities (showers, rest rooms) and picnic tables at **Lynn Hall Park** on northern Estero Boulevard. Or continue down the dead-end road to the north end of Fort Myers Beach for a quiet piece of sand all your own at **Bowditch Point Regional Preserve** (239-463-1116), 50 Estero Blvd, where you can meander bark-chip trails leading to great views of Matanzas Pass and Sanibel Island and find your own quiet slice of undeveloped beach tucked under the shade of mangroves. A wheelchair-accessible boardwalk leads from the central changing area and rest rooms to the beach. Open 8 AM until a half hour after sunset. Fee.

Pine Island

To feel like a castaway, take the *Tropic Star* (see *Boating*) from Pine Island to **Cayo Costa State Park** (941-964-0375; www.floridastateparks.org/cayocosta). No matter whether you spend a day or camp overnight at the primitive campground (cabins available by reservation), you'll enjoy the serenity of long walks along the beach of an unspoiled barrier island—great shelling guaranteed.

Sanibel-Captiva

Parking is more limited for the renowned beaches of **Sanibel and Captiva Islands,** and it'll cost you if you aren't staying on the island: In addition to the $6 toll for the Sanibel Causeway, you'll fork out $3 per hour at every beach parking lot on the islands. Each parking area provides rest rooms, a changing room with outdoor shower, and potable water. **Bowman's Beach** has a wilderness feel, while the **Sanibel Lighthouse Beach** is a popular sunning beach in the shadow of the historic lighthouse. **Gulfside Park** offers picnic tables and barbecue grills overlooking the ocean, as well as a nature trail. Anglers and sunset watchers head to **Turner Beach,** where Sanibel and Captiva Islands meet across the filled-in Blind Pass.

NATURE CENTERS Heaven and earth meet at the **Calusa Nature Center and Planetarium** (239-275-3183; www.calusanature.com), 3450 Ortiz Ave, Fort Myers, where a daily planetarium show (the only one in southwest Florida) complements the center's main mission of introducing you to the natural history of the Fort Myers area. Explore the reptile tanks to see the many species of turtles, snakes, lizards, and salamanders that inhabit the region, and learn the difference between the resident American alligator (pointed snout, dark body) and American crocodile (rounded snout, grayish body). A %0-mile wheelchair-accessible nature trail leads past an Audubon-maintained aviary of raptors and through a representative slough habitat, where volunteers battle to rid the swamp forest of invasive melaleuca. A rougher hiking trail starts at a replica Calusa village and loops around the center's 105 acres.

AT THE BEACH, SANIBEL ISLAND
Sandra Friend

Check the center's bulletin boards for information on ongoing environmental education programs open to the public. Open 9–5 Mon–Sat, 11–5 Sun. Adults $8, ages 3–12 $5.

PARKS

Alva
Several parks provide public access to the Caloosahatchee River, including the **W. P. Franklin Lock Recreation Area** off FL 80, with a picnic area and fishing. On the north side of the river, you can hike, camp, ride your bike, or bring a horse—the **Caloosahatchee Regional Park** (239-693-2690), 18500 N River Rd, has plenty of room for all sorts of activities. Walking trails lead out to riverside views, and wildlife encounters (especially with deer) are almost assured. Fee. **Manatee Park** (239-694-3537), 10901 Palm Beach Blvd, is a small park off the Caloosahatchee River providing seasonal access to view manatees near a power plant west of I-75. Free.

Fort Myers
Popular **Lakes Regional Park** (239-432-2004), 7330 Gladiolus Dr, provides 279 acres of outdoor recreation, from swimming and canoeing to bicycling and hiking. A 2½-mile paved trail system winds through the park, bridging numerous islands within the lakes. Wander the Fragrance Garden to take in the complex aromas. On weekends, you can rent paddleboats, kayaks, and canoes to explore the waterways. A water playground and a rock-climbing wall offer a place for kids to let off steam. Fee.

PRESERVES

Cape Coral
At **Four Mile Ecological Preserve** (239-574-0801), SE 23rd Ter, rent a canoe and explore secluded mangrove forests along the Caloosahatchee River, or take to the trail and enjoy a 1-mile stroll along a winding boardwalk. Walk softly, and you'll see yellow-crowned herons in the trees and little blue herons in the channels. Bring your fishing pole and relax along a pier with a broad view of the Fort Myers waterfront. This 365-acre saltwater marsh preserve provides a rare green space in the city of Cape Coral, next to the Midpoint Bridge. Free.

Fort Myers
With a network of boardwalks spanning this ecologically significant cypress slough, the trails of **Six Mile Cypress Slough Preserve** (239-432-2004), 7751 Penzance Blvd, enable you to enjoy lush bromeliads, primordial strap ferns, and flag ponds with resident alligators. Look closely in spring and summer for the delicate blooms of wild orchids in the cypress boughs. Free guided interpretive walks are offered Wed at 9:30 AM Jul–Oct. Fee.

Fort Myers Beach
Walk down the mangrove-lined trails of **Matanzas Pass Preserve** (239-461-7400), 199 Bay Rd, to experience the unique estuarine mangrove forest environment. Clad in red and black speckled shells, mangrove crabs scurry down the

gnarled roots of the red mangroves. The pathways lead you out to an unspoiled panorama of Matanzas Pass, where a canoe launch awaits your craft. Free.

WILD PLACES

Alva

With more than 1,100 acres protecting the realm of the Florida scrub jay and gopher tortoise, **Hickey's Creek Mitigation Park** (239-728-6240), 17980 FL 80, is a great getaway for long hikes, easy walks along the creek, and paddling on this winding cypress-lined blackwater creek. Fee.

Estero

Where the Estero River meets the bay, **Estero River Scrub Preserve** (941-463-3240; www.floridastateparks.org/esteroBay/default.cfm), end of Broadway west of US 41, has more than 5 miles of loop trails to walk and explore wet flatwoods and the tidal marsh on the edge of the estuary, where fiddler crabs scurry across the mud flats.

Fort Myers

A watery wilderness along the edge of Estero Bay, **Winkler Point** (941-463-3240; www.floridastateparks.org/esteroBay/default.cfm), end of Winkler Rd, offers a place just off the main highway to roam the wet flatwoods and estuarine fringe for up to 5 miles on trails where you are virtually guaranteed to get your feet wet. Free.

Sanibel Island

Encompassing more than half of Sanibel Island, **J. N. "Ding" Darling National Wildlife Refuge** (239-472-1100; http://dingdarling.fws.gov), One Wildlife Dr, hosts more than one hundred thousand visitors each year, the highest visitation in the entire National Wildlife Refuge system. Before taking to the trails or to **Wildlife Drive,** the popular one-way driving tour through the mangrove swamps, stop in at the visitors center for an excellent orientation on Sanibel's unique attraction to migratory birds. Closed Fri. Fee. Across the road, the **Sanibel-Captiva Conservation Foundation** (239-472-2329; www.sccf.org), 3333 Sanibel Captiva Rd, provides miles of hiking through tropical and coastal habitats, including a walk along the freshwater Sanibel River.

✳ Lodging

BED & BREAKFASTS

Bokeelia 33922

One of my most luxurious stays in Florida has been at the **Bokeelia Tarpon Inn** (239-283-8961 or 1-866-TARPON2; www.tarponinn.com), 8241 Main St, where there are no televisions in the great room, just a fine selection of music, board games, and books, and a pantry and fridge brimming with delights such as Dove ice cream bits, fresh tropical fruit, potpies, and cheese. Once a sea captain's home, this grand 1914 residence underwent $1 million in renovations to restore it to its natural beauty, with every heart pine and cypress board removed, refinished, and replaced. The simple, uncluttered furnishings of wood and white wicker make it easy to relax and enjoy the sea breezes off Boca Grande Pass. Each room ($159–295) has its own decorative flair, but you'll end up spending most of your time in the vast common areas, enjoying the views and the company. A gourmet breakfast is served for guests each morning.

Fort Myers 33901

& Dating from the days of Thomas Edison and built by timber magnate William H. Dowling in 1912 on the far shore of the Caloosahatchee River, the **Hibiscus House** (239-332-2651; www .thehibiscushouse.net), 2135 McGregor Blvd, was sawed in two in the 1940s and sent across the river on a barge to be set up in its present location along the Avenue of Palms. With tongue-and-groove pine walls and ceilings, original glass windows, and classy furnishings, the five-bedroom bed & breakfast provides an excellent venue for visitors who want to explore downtown and the historic district on foot. Decked out in light tropical decor, each of the five rooms has a special ambiance themed after local flora. The Palm includes a writing desk and television. Common spaces include a poinciana-shaded sitting room in the rear of the house, a small front parlor where guests can watch television or chat, and a massive dining area where a full gourmet breakfast is served. Innkeepers Leslie and Bill Seiden provide high-speed Internet access and keep the kitchen stocked with goodies for their guests. Rooms $119 and up, varying by season.

Matlacha 33993

✿ ❀ With its four spacious guest rooms, **Bayview Bed & Breakfast** (239-283-7510; www.webbwiz.com/ bayviewbb), 12251 Shoreview Dr, is a great little getaway just off the main thoroughfare. Balconies overlook Matlacha Pass, and a resident osprey hangs out around the docks. Grab a canoe, and paddle the estuary behind the house. Each room ($89–169) has a television and phone and a small fridge. Well-behaved children and small pets welcome.

CAMPGROUNDS

Pine Island 33956

If you're towing your rig and want to get away from it all, head for the quiet **KOA Pine Island** (239-283-2415; www.pineislandkoa.com), 5120 Stringfellow Rd, St. James City. In a secluded pine forest surrounded by mango groves, this campground offers a pool, spa, and exercise room, with rates starting at $38 for a tent site and $48 for an RV site. Kamping Kabins start at $60, and new park models at $134.

For a real deserted island getaway at an affordable price, pack your tent or reserve a cabin at **Cayo Costa State Park** (see *Beaches*), accessible only by boat. While marooned on this barrier island, explore more than 6 miles of hiking trails and walk miles of unspoiled beachfront, where shelling is some of the best in the United States. Primitive tent sites are $18; primitive cabins, $30. The park also manages the historic Jug Creek Cottages in Bokeelia, which start at $66 off-season and can be rented by the week.

North Fort Myers 33917

Along I-75 you'll see many camper manufacturers with large lots with RVs and trailers for sale off Luckett Rd; many are factory outlets. Scout the region around them for campgrounds and RV parks east of the city, such as **Upriver Campground Resort** (239-543-3330 or 1-800-848-1652; www.upriver.com), 17021 Upriver Dr, and **Sunburst North Fort Myers Resort** (239-543-3303 or 1-877-897-2757; www.rvonthego.com), 7974 Samville Rd.

COTTAGES

Fort Myers 33916
Coral-rock cottages around a circular lake define **Rock Lake Resort** (941-332-4080 or 1-800-325-7596; www.bestlodgingswflorida.com/rocklake/index.html), 2937 Palm Beach Blvd, a 1940s classic with nine efficiencies offering a charming slice of Old Florida. Kick back on the porch and read a book, or paddle along scenic Billy Creek, a tributary of the Caloosahatchee. Cottages run $74–105 and adjoin a new city park.

Sanibel Island 33957
For an intimate getaway with your sweetheart, try **Seahorse Cottages** (239-472-4262; www.seahorsecottages.com), 1223 Buttonwood Ln, an "adults-only" property in Old Town Sanibel. Lounge in the hammock, relax in the dip pool, take a bicycle and ride up to the shops, or grab beach umbrellas and towels and walk up the street to the Gulf. These housekeeping cottages include cable TV and VCR, CD and cassette players, and phones; guest laundry. Rates $75–230, depending on size and season.

HOTELS, MOTELS, AND RESORTS

Captiva Island 33924
& Stay in quaint, colorful 1940s beach cottages with gingerbread trim at **Captiva Island Inn** (1-800-454-9898; www.captivaislandinn.com), 11509 Andy Rosse Ln, where the hand-sponged walls lend an artsy touch in this very artsy downtown. Each building has its own name and theme (and, in some cases, story), be it the Orchid Cottage, where Anne Morrow Lindbergh stayed while writing her classic *Gift from the Sea;* or the Jasmine Cottage, which overlooks a secret garden. The inn also has a large house with upscale rooms centered around a massive common area, perfect for family reunions. Rates start at $99 per night.

& An enchanting mix of historic cottages and modern motel rooms, the **'Tween Waters Inn** (239-472-5161 or 1-800-223-5865; www.tween-waters.com), Captiva Rd, is an island getaway where authors, artists, and presidents have played since 1926. J. N. "Ding" Darling had his winter studio here, and you can now stay in it, or you can walk in the footsteps of Charles Lindbergh and Teddy Roosevelt by borrowing their getaway. The lovely Jasmine Cottage overlooks Pine Island Sound. The inn is a destination in itself—there are miles of uncrowded beaches, dockage, on-site fishing guides, guided kayaking tours, tennis courts, an Olympic-size pool, children's pool, and several on-site restaurants and shops. Rates ($165–490) vary by season and size of unit; weekly rates available.

Fort Myers 33916
Step back into classic road-trip tourism at the **Sea Chest Motel** (239-332-1545), 2571 E First St, a good old-time Florida motel with 30 spacious rooms and kitchenettes ($40–85), all with updated furnishings. There is a private pier for guests, and the swimming pool overlooks the Caloosahatchee River.

& On the waterfront south of town, **Winyah Hotel & Suites** (239-332-2048; www.winyah.com), 2038 W First St, is a modern two-story hotel with a massive riverside deck for guests to enjoy the view, a tiki bar, and a pool overlooking the Centennial Harbor Marina. The 28 comfortable rooms range from standard ($109) to suites ($149); continental breakfast is included. It's an easy walk to downtown and nearby restaurants. Boaters welcome!

Fort Myers Beach 33931

& ♥ ▼ Situated in the heart of downtown, the **Lighthouse Resort Inn and Suites** (239-463-9392 or 1-800-778-7748; www.lighthouseisland resort.com), 1051 Fifth Ave, provides a comfortable oasis of greenery where visitors can relax around the pools, make small talk at the tiki bar, and kick back on the balcony to watch the sunset. Easy access to the beach at Lynn Hall Park and the quaint shops and restaurants of downtown make this an ideal location for a multiday stay. This is a family-oriented facility, and pets are welcome for an additional charge. Most rooms contain either a kitchenette or full kitchen with full-size appliances, great for the needs of a family on the go. Each suite provides multiple bedrooms, a kitchen, and living/dining area. Although many of the units date back nearly 50 years, extensive renovations ensure up-to-date facilities. The newest section of the inn, added in 2000, features the largest suites and elevator access to the upper floors. Rooms $45–150, depending on season, size, and features.

& Hidden under the bridge, the **Matanzas Inn** (239-463-9258 or 1-800-462-9258; www.matanzasinn .com), 414 Crescent St, offers pleasant and spacious waterfront apartments on the bay and motel rooms shaded by mango trees, with 26 units of various sizes ($59–254) and a waterfront pool and spa. Daily housekeeping, guest laundry, an award-winning restaurant, and dockage round out the amenities. You're within a few minutes' walk of the bustling downtown and the beach.

North Fort Myers 33903

& Spacious waterfront rooms make the **Best Western Fort Myers Waterfront** (239-997-5511 or 1-800-274-5511; www.bestwesternwater front.com), 13021 N Cleveland Ave, stand out from the typical chain hotel; every room has a balcony overlooking the Caloosahatchee River, facing downtown on the far shore. The island-themed rooms ($89 and up) feature large closets, an oversize television, high-speed Internet access, and a huge tiled bathroom.

Pineland 33945

Be pampered in historic surroundings at **Tarpon Lodge** (239-283-3999; www.tarponlodge.com), 13771 Waterfront Dr, where the Wells family has greeted guests since 2000, building on a long history of hospitality. This genteel getaway attracted anglers back in 1926 as the Pine-Aire Lodge and continues to do so today. Of the 21 inviting guest rooms ($80–230) overlooking Pine Island Sound, choose from a room in the Island House annex or in the historic original lodge. The Useppa and Cabbage Key Rooms have fabulous sunset views. The landscaped grounds include a beautiful waterfront swimming pool and a pier where many visitors and locals amble out to watch the sun set over Useppa Island. The family also manages the rental cottages on offshore Cabbage Key, a quiet tropical getaway accessible only by private boat or local passenger ferry.

St. James City 33956

With free dockage right outside each front door, the **Water's Edge Motel and Apartments** (239-283-0515; www.thewatersedgemotel.com), 2938 Sanibel Blvd, is a gem of a family motel, now in the second generation of family ownership. Rooms range from standard motel ($59–69) through efficiency ($69–89) and one-bedroom apartment with hardwood built-ins ($99–179). It's a popular family-reunion destination, so book ahead!

Sanibel Island 33957

When I was a kid, my family stayed at the **Anchor Inn & Cottages** (239-395-9688 or 1-866-469-9543; www.sanibelanchorinn.com), 1245 Periwinkle Way, and every time I've visited Sanibel since, passing by the distinctive A-frame cottages reminds me of those childhood days. So I was delighted when I stopped in and discovered everything still has that "stopped in time" feel, sparkling new and clean and 1960s—solid construction with concrete walls and wooden ceilings, old-fashioned terrazzo floors and tiled showers, and verandas outside each of the 12 rooms ($139–199 for standard to two-bedroom efficiency, and $249 for the spacious A-frame cottages).

Within walking distance of the beach, **The Palm View** (239-472-1606 or 1-877-472-1606; www.palmviewsanibel.com), 706 Donax St, offers luxurious themed suites amid a tropical garden, where quiet outdoor courtyard alcoves and a Jacuzzi and barbecue grill await guests. Each newly reno-

vated unit offers a full kitchen, phone, and Internet access. Complimentary guest laundry and use of a kayak, bicycles, and beach toys are included with your stay. There are five units, including efficiencies and two-room suites ($85–185 depending on season and size).

The cozy, Caribbean-themed **Sandpiper Inn** (239-472-1529 or 1-877-227-4737; www.gosandpiper.com), 720 Donax St, has one-bedroom, one-bath suites with kitchen, sitting area, and a balcony or patio for you to catch the sea breeze. All housekeeping supplies are included, plus complimentary beach accessories, coolers, and bicycles. Adults only, $69–165.

Tucked away in a lush tropical garden, the intimate **Tarpon Tale Inn** (239-472-0939; www.tarpontale.com), 367 Periwinkle Way, has eight units along a private courtyard with hot tub and hammocks. Choose from partial or full kitchens. Each room has tiled floors and wicker furnishings, and guests can use the shelling table to clean their finds or borrow beach umbrellas and bicycles for an excursion. Rates $109–139 off-season, $189–220 in-season; includes a basket breakfast each morning.

❋ Where to Eat
DINING OUT

Captiva Island

❦ It's fun, funky, and 1940s—a pink palace of movie memorabilia, Christmas ornaments, and tin toys. One of Captiva's most distinctive dining experiences, **The Bubble Room** (239-472-5558; www.bubbleroomrestaurant.com), 15001 Captiva Dr, offers sinfully delightful desserts and mouthwatering fresh breads with some of the island's best seafood. Although the prices say fine dining, the atmosphere is casual—T-shirts and sandals are acceptable. Decked out in a unique scouting uniform, your "Bubble Scout" attends to your every request. Served from 11:30 to 2:30, lunch specialties include salads and sandwiches such as the Louis Armstrong, a piled-high New Orleans muffuletta, and the Famous Bubble Burger, a half pound of lean ground chuck cooked to order. For dinner try the Eddie Fisherman, a fillet of local grouper rolled in brown sugar and pecans and poached in a brown paper bag, or Some Like it Hot, tasty fresh Gulf shrimp in a garlic tequila butter sauce. Many patrons go for the Tiny Bubble, the least-expensive entrée option: a choice of appetizer, fresh breads, house salad, and a slab of one of the Bubble Room's tasty cakes. No matter how much room you leave for dessert, you'll be taking some of the generous portion home. Don't miss the fluffy White Christmas Cake, stuffed with slivered almonds and coconut, topped with whipped-cream frosting. With nearly a dozen dessert choices, you'll find a perfect match. Expect dinner for a couple to run at least $50.

In an elegant setting overlooking Pine Island Sound, **The Green Flash** (239-472-3337), 15183 Captiva Dr, offers tasty lunch ($7–10) and dinner ($14 and up) choices. I like the Fruit de Mer, with an assortment of sautéed seafood, and the grouper Café de Paris is the house specialty.

At 'Tween Waters Inn (see *Lodging*), the **Old Captiva House** serves up inspired variations on classic themes, including grilled jerk-rubbed grouper, oven-roasted snapper, seared New York strip au poivre ($21–34), and fusion appetizers such as lobster spring rolls with mango citrus coulis ($5–12).

Fort Myers

Since 1982, **The Prawnbroker** (239-489-2226), 13451 McGregor Blvd #16, has served up fresh fish in its fish market; check the daily "Fresh Fish Report" as you walk in. Enjoy your favorites fried, broiled, grilled, or blackened, or have your seafood in a classic pasta dish. Dinners $14–22. Your entrée comes with warm fresh bread, and the portions are nicely sized. I enjoyed a platter of light and tasty almond fried shrimp on my last visit.

Fort Myers—Downtown

Rich, dark wood and tasteful furnishings underscore the classy feel of **The Veranda** (239-332-2065), 2122 Second St, a fine restaurant in one of Fort Myers's most historic venues. Built in 1902 by Manuel Gonzales, son of one of the original settlers, the complex joins together two homes at the corner of Second and Broadway, downtown. Diners look out over a secluded courtyard of tropical plants, accented with a waterfall flowing down into the fishpond. First opened as a restaurant in the 1970s, The Veranda's lunch menu features tasty combinations such as Florida crab cakes with potato salad, or fried green tomato salad with tidbits of Virginia ham and blue cheese sprinkled across a bed of mixed greens. Lunches are served 11–2:30 and start at $8. The dinner menu ($15 and up) shifts the emphasis to seafood and meat, with chateaubriand, veal Piccata, grilled fresh Florida grouper, and the Southern Sampler of fresh fish, Gulf shrimp, and sea scallops in a lobster sherry cream sauce, delicious over a bed of fettuccine. Don't miss the tempting appetizers: oysters Rockefeller, escargot in puff pastry with Stilton blue cheese sauce, and Southern grit cakes with andouille sausage. Desserts include Bailey's cheesecake and a delectable chocolate pâté with raspberry coulis, an artful presentation of a slab of cold fudgelike chocolate with a ribbon of maple walnut on a platter of raspberry sauce. Doors open for dinner at 5:30, with meals served until 11.

Pineland

❦ A four-star culinary experience, the **Tarpon Lodge Restaurant** (239-283-2517), 13771 Waterfront Dr at Tarpon Lodge (see *Lodging*), overlooks Pine Island Sound. The slate of top-notch entrées ($17–30) includes preparations such as orange ginger–glazed chicken, veal Piccata, and aged filet mignon, and the tasty marinated portobello mushroom salad is a wonderful variant on traditional spinach salad. I appreciated the fresh-baked kalamata olive bread with olive oil for dipping, and my hearty New York strip came with compote of wild mushrooms; the rich and thick cream of mushroom soup was a delight. Meals are prepared using fresh herbs from the garden on-site. The friendly staff will gladly help you with recommendations to suit your palate. An added bonus is **Doc Ford's Lounge;** mystery lovers will appreciate that author and local resident Randy Wayne White hangs out here when in town. Reservations recommended.

Sanibel Island

As soon as it opened, eager fans showed up—**Doc Ford's Sanibel Rum Bar & Grille** (239-472-8311; www.docfordssanibel.com), 975 Rabbit Rd, is a big hit with the mystery

lovers' crowd as it's owned by author Randy Wayne White and set just a few minutes from the now-closed marina where Randy and fictional Doc Ford lived and worked. The exterior is painted with Florida forest scenes, the warm wooden interior evokes the sea, and the menu reflects the rural tropics in which Randy spent many years on assignment for *Outside* magazine. Choose from an extensive array of creative appetizers, inspired entrées such as Campeche fish tacos or banana leaf snapper, and unique salads and sandwiches. Lunch and dinner, $5–29; and don't forget to browse the Doc Ford books and souvenirs!

A top-notch seafood house, **Jacaranda** (239-472-1771), 1223 Periwinkle Way, consistently wins "Taste of the Islands" awards in all categories. Selections include Florida snapper en papillote, sesame-encrusted yellowfin tuna, roast duckling, Sanibel cowboy steak, and more. Dinner $19 and up. Enjoy fresh oysters at the raw bar on the patio.

EATING OUT

Bokeelia

The grits are great at **Auston's** (239-282-1161), 7373 Raymary St, a basic family diner with an extensive menu. Try a Gulf shrimp omelet, made with shrimp straight off a local shrimper's boat, or have mullet or grouper with your morning eggs. Open for breakfast, lunch, and dinner, with daily down-home specials—cash only!

❦ At the end of Stringfellow Road, the picture windows of **Capt'n Con's Seafood House** (239-283-4300) frame an idyllic Pine Island scene—fishing boats chug through the pass as brown pelicans dive in unison into schools of mullet shimmering beneath the waves. It's one of the oldest buildings in Bokeelia, the site of the original post office at the town's original steamer dock, circa 1904. Offering fresh fish, succulent steaks, and an ever-changing variety of down-home specials such as pot roast, meat loaf, and fried catfish, Capt'n Con's provides excellent value for your dollar, with daily all-you-can-eat seafood specials. Top your dinner off with a slice of homemade pie, and don't miss Fran's shrimp bisque, offered on Thursday. Entrées $8–16.

At Marker 8, the **Lazy Flamingo** (239-283-5959; www.lazyflamingo .com), 16501-B Stringfellow Rd, is a kick back and relax rustic Cracker shack with picnic tables and a bar— just the kind of place where you'll find the seafood you love. Grab shucked-to-order oysters, steamer pots, conch chowder, and grouper a few different ways, or go for the "Dead Parrot" wings and spicy french fries. It's a local favorite no matter the location (also found on Sanibel Island). Serving lunch and dinner, $5–18.

Bonita Springs
❦ Since 1929, the **Dixie Moon Café** (239-495-0023), 27755 Old US 41, has been a watering hole for travelers headed for the Everglades; the mileage to "Everglade" is even chiseled into the concrete. Serving "Southern food with an attitude," they whip up goodies such as nine different types of breakfast tacos, Dixie Benedict (grit cake, pan gravy, fried green tomatoes, hollandaise sauce, and potato casserole), and banana pancakes ($1–8). Lunch and dinner served, too.

Captiva Island
The lilac and green **Keylime Bistro** (239-395-0882; www.captivaisland inn.com), 11506 Andy Rosse Ln, will certainly catch your eye, and it's a blast to settle down to the Sunday jazz brunch with a bunch of friends. Try the chicken voodoo, with sautéed artichokes, tomatoes, kalamata olives, capers, basil, and garlic; or paella Valencia, including shrimp, scallops, calamari, mussels, chicken, and sausage. Yum! Lunch runs $5–9, dinner $10–23. Across the street, **R.C. Otters Island Eats** (239-395-1142), owned by the same folks, is a fun and colorful restaurant with an extensive vegetarian menu and a kid's menu. They serve steamer pots, cold strawberry bisque, and lobster rolls, so the menu is not one to miss. Open daily for all meals.

I've strolled down the beach more than once to **The Mucky Duck** (239-472-3434; www.muckyduck.com), 11546 Andy Rosse Ln, for fish-and-chips, and that's why this British pub is a favorite around here: It has great views of the Gulf and reliable grub. Chow down on oyster po'boy or duck fingers, or try Meat Loaf à la Jaybird, a specialty of the house. Lunch $4–14, dinner $17–33.

Fort Myers
❦ From the outside, the building is clearly a renovated Long John Silver's. But the inside sparkles with bright walls, piñatas, and colorful pastel Mexican festival flags strung from the rafters. Boasting "Authentic Mexican Cuisine," **La Casita** (239-415-1050), 15185 McGregor Blvd, delivers with a menu that is anything but Tex-Mex. The owners hail from the Guanajato region of Mexico, where sautéed onions and peppers accompany roasted

tomatoes and cilantro in freshly prepared enchiladas, chimichangas, tacos, and gorditas. Besides shredded beef or chicken, you can enjoy a mildly spicy potato filling. Platters come with soft, fresh Mexican rice and red beans. On weekends, house specialties include of genuine *menudo* (tripe soup) and *sopa de mariscos,* a seafood broth with grouper, octopus, and shellfish. Open 11–9; serves house margaritas and a wide variety of Mexican and domestic beers. Platters $8–13; thick homemade chips and a zesty cilantro salsa are provided as you peruse the menu.

Inside it's a Greek taverna; outside, smokers and Greek men (often one and the same) argue politics over coffee like they would along Syntagma Square in Athens. **Plaka II** (239-433-5404), 15271 McGregor Blvd, has all the Greek favorites, some with a local twist, such as tender Florida octopus with *skordalia* (a spicy potato-garlic dip), and golden fried marida smelts. Lunch and dinner, $4–14.

Fort Myers—Downtown

Under the distinctive downtown Arcade marquee, **April's Eatery** (239-337-4004), 2269 First St, serves breakfast and lunch Mon–Fri to downtown workers and visitors. Choose from hot sandwiches, 8-inch subs, or cold sandwiches such as crab, dill, and shrimp salad ($2–5). Morning choices include bagel sandwiches, toast, and muffins ($1–3).

Relax and sip a mango-cinnamon soda at the **Terra Cotta Café** (239-479-6264), 1418 Dean St, where meals come with a modern Italian flair—tasty creations include roast beef Wellington or cheddar-apple panini, spinach and cheddar crêpes, and grilled pineapple, walnut, and turkey salad ($4–8).

Fort Myers—East

I was very impressed by the ribs at the **Rib City Grill** (239-693-2223), 13908 Palm Beach Blvd, which is a regional chain but darn good. Combo dinners "from the pit" cost $9–13, and there are five types of salad on the menu, including crunchy grouper. I love the three-cheese fries, smothered in Monterey, cheddar, and pepper Jack with bacon. The coleslaw and baked beans are homemade, and desserts, such as the Chocolate Mousse Mania, just can't be passed up.

Matlacha

Always busy at dinnertime, the **Matlacha Oyster House** (239-283-2544), 3930 Pine Island Rd, has a 1970s nautical look about it and keeps the regulars coming back with fresh local shrimp and oysters, baked stuffed flounder, and other specialties ($9–15).

Enjoy Italian specialties along the mangrove-lined estuary at **Moretti's Seafood Restaurant** (239-283-5825), 4200 Pine Island Rd, a family-owned restaurant with classic seafood pastas, pizza, grilled beef, veal, and chicken. Open for lunch and dinner ($8–19).

A bustling breakfast stop, **Mulletville** (239-283-5151), 4597 Pine Island Rd, has good Southern classics on the menu, from grits to mullet, and features a mullet, shrimp, and Swiss omelet for $7.

Offering a great view of the islands, the **Sandy Hook Fish & Rib House** (239-283-0113), 4875 Pine Island Rd, serves up seafood classics in a comfortable family atmosphere. The "Sandy Hook Treasures" include more than a dozen seafood choices, from cracked conch to steamed crab legs and Florida lobster ($12–22).

North Fort Myers

For casual waterfront dining, **Pincher's Crab Shack** (239-652-1313; www.pincherscrabshack.com), 13021 N Cleveland Ave at the Best Western, is a fun and affordable choice with a great selection of seafood; the crab and corn chowder is spicy and downright addictive. If you order crab, you'll be pounding it with mallets on a brown paper–covered table; your fresh veggies and corn come served with real butter. Two other locations in town, with dinners starting at $10.

St. James City

Great aromas will pull you in to the **Double Nichol Pub** (239-283-5555), 3051 Stringfellow Rd, where the wooden bar is full of embedded nickels and you'll always catch a game on the TV. Try one of their popular sandwiches, such as the Steuben Ruby, a classic Reuben on rye, or the Holy Cow, with roast beef and Swiss cheese. Open at 11, with pizza, pub fare, burgers, and sandwiches ($5–8).

Sanibel Island

Gaily painted roosters and chickens set the tone at **Amy's Over Easy Café** (239-472-2625), 630 Tarpon Bay Rd, where your view is of the tropical forest outside, and the extensive breakfast menu includes Gulf shrimp omelets, Reuben Benedict, and stuffed French toast. Serving breakfast and lunch daily.

The fun place to eat on Sanibel is **The Island Cow** (239-472-0606; www.islandcow.com), 2163 Periwinkle Way, with a dining area that spills out of a historic home and onto the front porch, where you can dine perched on pastel chairs while watching the world walk by. Amazing home-cooked breakfasts (Crab cakes and grits! Stuffed French toast!), grilled goodies, greens, quesadillas, wraps, barbecue, steaks . . . the list goes on and on, and includes a kid's menu, too. They serve all meals daily and are well known for their ice cream floats (such as Purple Cows and egg creams), pies, and cakes.

The Lighthouse Café (239-472-0303), 362 Periwinkle Way, claims bragging rights for the "world's best breakfast," and the way folks were lined up for it, I'd believe it. Inside the brightly painted café, try exquisite specialties such as seafood Benedict—a grilled croissant topped with sautéed shrimp, crabmeat, and scallops with broccoli, mushrooms, two poached eggs, and fresh Alfredo sauce. Breakfast and lunch; lunch served 11–3.

BAKERIES, COFFEE SHOPS, AND SODA FOUNTAINS

Fort Myers Beach

I stopped in for ice cream at **Strawberrie Corner** (941-463-1155), 7205 Estero Blvd, and discovered they offer a pretty complete array of sandwiches for lunch ($4–7) in addition to sundaes, malts, cones, and, of course, strawberry shortcake.

Sanibel Island

Grab yourself a cold treat at **Pinocchio's** (239-472-6566), 362 Periwinkle Way, a popular family-owned shop with huge ice cream cones, sorbet sippers, Café Captiva frozen coffee drinks, and their own line of homemade candies, including sea foam, snow crabs, and dipped strawberries.

✳ Selective Shopping

Bonita Springs

Packed with a good mix of collectibles and decor items, **The Motherload** (239-948-1177), 27796 Old US 41 Rd, had everything from Gilbert & Sullivan LPs and an original Battleship game to an Esther Williams swimming instruction book.

Estero

There's plenty to explore at **Flamingo Island** (941-948-7799; www .flamingoisland.com), 200 yards west of I-75 on Bonita Springs Blvd, with more than six hundred dealer booths in a tropical setting. You can also pick up fresh fruits and veggies here.

Fort Myers—Downtown

Shaded by a giant banyan tree, the **Banyan Tree Books & Café** (239-332-0585), 1773 Fowler St, is a 1902 wood-frame bungalow where you can hang out and browse through recent tomes while sipping a cappuccino. Open 10–5 Tue–Fri.

Frog and the Fly (239-332-2510), 1525 Broadway, is filled with whimsical toys and antiques, from frog and alligator art to vintage jewelry and the puffy kitty pillow I had as a kid.

A store straight out of "chick lit," **Lady Bugs & Dragonflies** (239-332-3382), 2214 First St, has smarmy T-shirts, "Dirty Girl" products, and goofy toys such as "Instant Infant" and "Flat Cat."

In addition to the usual antiques store inventory, **Main Street Antiques & Collectibles** (239-689-6246), 2229 Main St, contains the contents of the old Flowers to 50s Vintage Department Store, which makes this a retro trip into your parent's 1970s basement—a delightful clutter of tree lamps, avocado easy chairs, and a paint-by-number-on-velvet Last Supper. Featuring goodies from the '50s, '60s, and '70s, the constantly changing inventory runs the gamut from psychedelic-patterned dresses and vintage Hawaiian shirts to Ronco appliances ("as seen on TV") still in the box since 1972. Poke through the shelves to find Viewmaster slides, 8 mm cartoon films, and other fun toys and books from your childhood. Note to album collectors—don't miss this selection!

Nora's Antiques (239-332-2778), 2229 Main St (upstairs), has a bit of everything spread out over a meandering warren of rooms presenting eclectic groupings, such as a lineoleum-floored kitchen with retro dishes and glassware, a closet with vintage clothing, a room with art glass, Hopalong Cassidy memorabilia, Hawaiian shirts, and more.

Fort Myers—East

Get lost amid hundreds of booths at **Flea Masters Giant Flea Market** (941-334-7001; www.fleamall.com), on FL 82, 1 mile west of I-75, where I stumbled across beautiful Balinese hand-carved cabinets for reasonable prices, fresh seafood and produce, and the usual booth after booth of cheap Asian goods.

Fort Myers—McGregor Boulevard

A giant golden Buddha is the don't-miss landmark for the McGregor Boulevard Antique District, where a handful of great shops are clustered near the College Parkway overpass. At the **McGregor Antique Mall** (239-433-0200), 12720 McGregor Blvd, browse collectibles such as political buttons and dolls, regional and national postcards, and salt cellars, as well as a fine collection of glassware and dishes. **The Old Village Square** (239-691-2211), 12710-4 McGregor Blvd, has antique pottery, teapots, Fenton glass, fine china, and hats and stoles.

Poke through vintage purses at **Judy's Antiques** (239-481-9600), 12710 Mcgregor Blvd, where you'll find fine silver and glassware. **George Brown Antiques** (239-482-5101), 12730 Mcgregor Blvd, features tableware, fine furnishings, and estate jewelry.

Matlacha
Island Shells & Gifts (239-283-8080), 4206 Pine Island Rd, is one of the largest gift shops in the area, and the prices are great. Pick up decor items with a nautical flair, select seashells, and browse through the books.

North Fort Myers
The Shell Factory (1-888-474-3557), 2787 N Tamiami Trl. Sure, it's kitschy, with row upon row of alligator heads, shark jaws, and coconut monkeys. But nowhere else on Earth will you find a finer collection of seashells under one roof. From its humble beginnings in 1942 as a shell shop, the Shell Factory has ballooned to a sprawling mega-complex, with family entertainment (the Octagon petting zoo, bumper boats, miniature golf), adult entertainment (karaoke at Captain Fishbones bar), and a virtual department store of gifts. In addition to Christmas ornaments, touristy T-shirts, and fudge, there are thousands of seashells and corals to look through, and the newest addition—the Glass Factory—adds a touch of class. Here, Bavarian glass-blowers and lampworkers from the Victor Alexander Studio create beautiful pieces of art glass, ranging from delicate flowers to massive bowls and plates. Take a tour through the glass museum, and watch the artists at work.

Sanibel Island
The **Islander Trading Post** (239-395-0888) is an antiques shop with well-organized collections of collections, from vintage drugstore items to ashtrays, Florida postcards and matchbooks, and even milk bottles.

The oldest bookstore on Sanibel Island is **MacIntosh Book Shop** (239-472-1447), 2365 Periwinkle Way, a historic beach cottage with a nice selection of new fiction, a local-interest section, a goodly number of nature and children's books, and a back room filled with used books.

Jazz drifts through the **Sanibel Island Bookshop** (239-472-5223), 1711 Periwinkle Way, where you can merge your right and left brain by browsing through both Sark's books and Ann Coulter. The store carries new books and has an extensive children's section, tasteful gifts and plush toys, and greeting cards.

PRODUCE STANDS, FARMER'S MARKETS, SEAFOOD MARKETS, AND U-PICK

Alva
Ritchey's Farm Fresh Produce (239-693-5092), 15500 FL 80, is a don't-miss family fruit stand with everything you can think of, from homemade jellies and jams to Hendry County citrus and Immokalee tomatoes. Farther west, **Dyess Groves** (239-728-2121), 17020 FL 80, offers fresh juice and fresh citrus.

Fort Myers
Since 1940, **Sun Harvest Citrus** (239-768-2686; www.sunharvestcitrus.com), 14810 Metro Pkwy, in the big green packinghouse, has been the place to get the pick of the citrus crop for this region. Enjoy free tours of the processing plant Nov–Apr. The store is open daily and offers soft-serve ice

cream (orange and vanilla swirl!), smoothies, Florida gifts, and gourmet food items in addition to their main crop.

Fort Myers—Downtown

Farmers bring their produce into town at the **Downtown Fort Myers Farmers Market** (239-332-6813), under the Caloosahatchee Bridge in Centennial Park, 9–2 Tue and 7–3 Thu.

Fort Myers Beach

Every Friday 7–noon Nov–Apr, peek under the Sky Bridge for the **Fort Myers Beach Farmer's Market** for booths and booths of fresh produce, seafood, cut flowers, houseplants, and baked goods. Parking is free during market hours.

Matlacha

The finest tropical produce from Pine Island's groves fills **Tropicaya Fruit & Gift** (239-283-0656; www.tropicaya.com), 3220 SW Pine Island Rd, where you can browse alligator brushes and hot sauces while waiting for your made-to-order soursop or mamey shake. Choose from more than a dozen tropical flavors, and nab a carambola (star fruit) or two to take home!

✳ Entertainment

FINE ARTS For an evening of fine music, check with the box office for the **Southwest Florida Symphony Orchestra** (239-418-1500), the only professional orchestra in the region. Playing both classical and popular music, they perform at both the **Barbara B. Mann Performing Arts Hall** (239-481-4849; www.bbmannpah.com), 8099 College Pkwy SW, Fort Myers, and at **BIG Arts** (239-395-0900), 900 Dunlop Rd, Sanibel Island.

In the 12,000-square-foot William R. Frizzel Cultural Center, the **Alliance for the Arts** (239-939-ARTS; www.artinlee.org), 11091 McGregor Blvd, Fort Myers, has public galleries with monthly exhibitions, theatrical productions, and art workshops.

THEATER ♿ At **Broadway Palm Dinner Theatre** (239-278-4422; www.broadwaypalm.com), 1380 Colonial Blvd, Fort Meyers, the buffet almost upstages the show at this regional theater—but not quite. Featuring professional performers, it hosts musicals and comedies year-round, with ticket prices starting at $25 for show only, $41 for matinee with buffet. Reserve in advance.

✳ Special Events

February: Brighten up at the **Edison Festival of Light** (239-334-2999; www.edisonfestival.org), midmonth, Fort Myers. Commemorating Thomas Edison's birthday, a lively lit-up parade kicks off this celebration of light and history, which includes a downtown block party, orchid show, huge arts and crafts fair, and the nation's largest after-dark parade.

March: **Sanibel Shell Fair** (239-472-2155; www.sanibelcommunityhouse.org), 2173 Periwinkle Way, Sanibel Island. More than four hundred species of shells wash up on Sanibel's shores, and collectors enjoy showing off their prizes at this annual gathering that started back in 1937, hosted by the Sanibel-Captiva Shell Club. Donation.

April: Film buffs will love the **Fort Myers Beach Film Festival** (239-765-0202; www.fmbfilmfest.com), last week of the month, with screenings, filmmaker panel discussions, and workshops as well as an elegant celebrity gala and screenings at the Fort Myers Beach Theatre. Free.

July: Mangos are a serious cash crop on Pine Island, so the **Pine Island Mango Mania Tropical Fruit Fair** (239-283-0888; www.mangomaniafl .com), midmonth, showcases these and other luscious tropical fruits during a weekend celebration. Fee.

November: **Fort Myers Beach Sandsculpting Festival** (239-454-7500), Fort Myers Beach. Try building the ultimate sand castle on the beach, where amateurs and pros compete for prize money while showing off their sand artistry. Free.

THE PARADISE COAST:
COLLIER COUNTY

From ribbons of white sand to the mangrove-dense maze of the Ten Thousand Islands, the haunting fog-shrouded cypress strands of the Big Cypress Swamp, and the vast sawgrass prairies that define the world's only Everglades, the southwesternmost outpost of Florida's Gulf Coast is undeniably its most majestic.

After the Civil War, settlers Roger Gordon and Joe Wiggins came to the region with their families to homestead. A small settlement emerged along the bay, which promoters described as "surpassing the bay in Naples, Italy." In 1887, the owner of the *Louisville Courier-Journal* and his business partners formed the Naples Company and purchased nearly the entire town. They built a long pier into the Gulf of Mexico for shipping. Social life centered around the Naples Hotel, where celebrities such as Greta Garbo and Gary Cooper stayed.

At the age of 26, Barron Gift Collier was a millionaire flush with cash from streetcar advertising. Coming to Useppa Island in 1911 on vacation from New York City, he decided to invest in the rugged coastline, buying huge tracts of land until he owned a full third of Lee County. In 1923 he promised the state of Florida he'd underwrite the struggling federal construction of the Tamiami Trail across the Everglades if his land could be broken off into a separate county, and the state approved. To provide an engineering headquarters for the project and a county seat for the new Collier County, the Barron River was dredged to create **Everglades City,** Collier's first planned community and the county seat. It took 13 years of backbreaking labor to construct the highway, and Collier sunk his business profits into turning swampland into real estate by digging drainage canals and building roads, further advancing development around Naples Bay.

In 1513, Ponce de Leon discovered the Calusa settlements in the **Ten Thousand Islands;** he would continue north to receive a mortal blow from a Calusa warrior in Pine Island Sound. As along the coast to the north, Cuban ranchos—netted fish farms in the shallow estuary—were a mainstay of the local economy until the Seminole War of 1836. Hardy settlers cleared some of the mangrove keys and established plantations growing corn and peas, pumpkins, tomatoes, citrus, and aromatic herbs. Settlers, traders, and Seminoles plied the waters to the

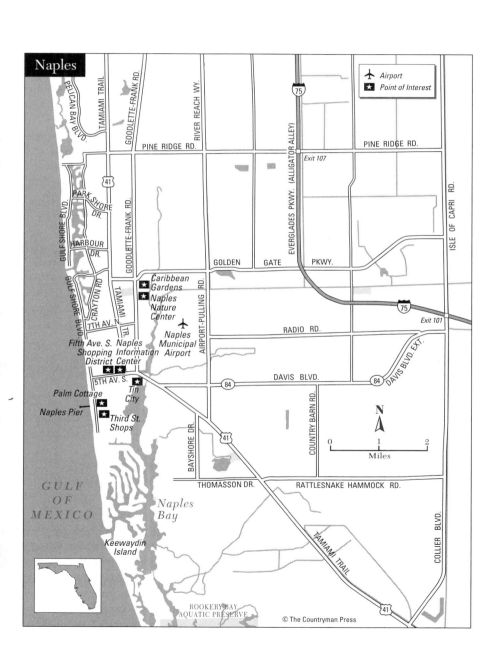

Naples

Smallwood Store (see *Historic Sites*) on **Chokoloskee Island** to exchange goods, and the Storter family homesteaded most of the surrounding islands. Chokoloskee wasn't connected to the mainland until 1954, when a causeway was built.

The post-statehood settlement of **Marco Island** happened in 1870, when William T. Collier and his family homesteaded at Key Marco, where the Calusa once lived, and incorporated the area as Collier City. With fishing villages established at Key Marco and **Caxambas** (the southern point), the region stayed quiet until the 1960s, when it was carved up for residential development and some of the first high-rise condos on the Gulf Coast appeared along the shoreline. **Goodland,** founded by squatter Johnny Roberts in the late 1800s, grew up on a 40-acre Calusa shell mound and is one of the few places you can see what the islands looked like before modern development.

GUIDANCE Preplan your visit with the **Greater Naples Marco Island Everglades Convention & Visitors Bureau** (1-800-688-3600; www.paradisecoast .com), 3050 N Horseshoe Dr, Suite 210, Naples. Once in the area, stop in at the **Naples Area Information Center** (239-262-6141; www.napleschamber.org), 895 Fifth Ave, to pick up brochures and maps and to make reservations.

GETTING THERE *By car:* **I-75** and **US 41** provide primary access.

By air: **Southwest Florida International Airport** (see *Sanibel, Fort Myers, and the Islands*) offers regular commuter service daily.

By bus: **Greyhound** (239-774-5660), 2669 Davis Blvd, Naples.

GETTING AROUND *By car:* Unless you're staying in downtown Naples and plan to spend your time there, a car is essential for exploring this vast region. **US 41** intersects all major side roads to outlying towns—take **FL 846** to Vanderbilt Beach and Immokalee, **FL 951** to Marco Island, **CR 92** to Goodland, and **FL 29** to Everglades City.

ALLIGATOR SCULPTURE, FIFTH AVENUE
Sandra Friend

MEDICAL EMERGENCIES For major emergencies visit **Naples Community Hospital** (239-436-5000), 350 Seventh St N, Naples. Marco Island has one clinic—the **Marco Healthcare Center** (239-394-8234), 40 S Heathwood Dr.

PARKING Downtown Naples provides free two-hour street parking, a large free parking garage just off Fifth Avenue, and a large, free, flat lot off Third Street. It does cost to park at most beachside parking areas, often a flat fee of $4—which is a great bargain for all day, but not for a quick sunset visit. Parking options are extremely limited on **Marco Island,** unless you are visiting a business or paying for beach parking.

✳ To See
ARCHEOLOGICAL SITES

Marco Island
Noted as a center of Calusa culture—which can now be seen only in the tiny Marco Island Historical Museum (see *Museums*)—the island yielded spectacular treasures in 1896, when archeologist Frank Cushing found an entire Calusa village preserved in muck at the site of what is now the Olde Marco Island Inn & Suites (see *Lodging*). Alas, Calusa shell mounds were long ago removed for roadfill or buried under construction sites; some remain hidden within the Ten Thousand Islands.

ART GALLERIES

Everglades City
The little **Glades Gallery** at Glades Realty (239-695-4299), 207 W Broadway, features the work of local artists, with fine-art paintings and sculpture side by side with craft items such as manatee pillows and painted hats.

Naples
It's claimed that Naples has more art galleries than any other city in Florida, and I have to concur—the sheer number of galleries is daunting even for a long weekend's worth of walkabout. I visited a handful, including the playful **Island House Gallery** (239-262-7455), 1154 Third St S, decorated with painted mirrors, fused glass, and twinkling lights; **Gallery Matisse** (239-649-7114), 1170 Third St S, featuring Impressionist art; and the **Dennison-Moran Gallery** (239-263-0590), 696 Fifth Ave S, a place of pure whimsy and ranked among the top one hundred fine-art galleries in Florida. At **Native Visions Gallery** (239-643-3735; www.callofAfrica .com), 737 Fifth Ave S, delight in wildlife and environmental art, featuring hot cast glass bowls and Judy Dy'Ans vivid renderings of Florida shorelines in oils. Broad Avenue is

NAPLES ART DISTRICT

Sandra Friend

Sandra Friend

GUESTS ON A SWAMP WALK AT CLYDE
BUTCHER'S OPEN HOUSE

"Gallery Row" just east of Third Street, where you can park and visit gallery after gallery. **Knox Galleries** (239-263-7994), 375 Broad Ave N, has massive outdoor sculptures of a pirate, manatee, and sea horse to lure you in, and the **Galerie du Soleil** (239-417-3450; www.galerie-du-soleil.com), 393 Broad Ave, is surrounded by beds of bright yellow blossoms.

Featuring the largest contemporary-art library in Naples, the **Von Liebig Art Center** (239-262-6517; www .naplesartcenter.org), 585 Park St, showcases more than a dozen rotating exhibits and permanent installations scattered throughout its two stories. Pieces are for sale in the Member's Gallery. Donation.

Ochopee

🌿 Way down deep in the Big Cypress Swamp, motorists encounter an unexpected sight—**Clyde Butcher's Big Cypress Gallery** (1-888-999-9113; www.clyde butcher.com), 52338 Tamiami Trl N, a roadside oasis where alligators cruise the pond out front, and outstanding natural art awaits inside. Often referred to as "the Ansel Adams of the Everglades," Clyde makes massive black-and-white images that capture the many moods of Florida's wild places; much of his work focuses on the Everglades and Big Cypress ecosystems. You'll also find the color photography work of Oscar Thompson and Jeff Ripple, creative cards by Clyde's wife, Niki, and books on wild Florida by their favorite authors. Every Labor Day weekend they host an open house on their property (a former orchid farm), featuring guided swamp walks (some led by your authors) to immerse you in the beauty and wonder of the swamp. Donations help nonprofit organizations that preserve the habitats.

HISTORIC SITES

Chokoloskee

🗡 A private family-owned attraction, the **Historic Smallwood Store** (239-695-2989; www.florida-everglades.com/chokol/smallw.htm) is the oldest general store in Florida, notorious as the site of frontier justice in 1910 when the men of Chokoloskee dispatched Ed Watson, a suspected murderer, with a volley of gunfire. The store sits at the end of Mamie Street on the waterfront just as it did in 1897, when Ted Smallwood set up a trading post to swap goods with the Seminoles. Ted died in 1951, but it remained a working store in the family until 1982, and it reopened as a museum under the guidance of Ted's granddaughter. The bottles behind the counter (check out "Wintersmith's Chill Tonic") and the boxes on the tables are all original; the counter itself is beveled to allow ladies in hoop skirts to stand closer.

Seminole artifacts fill some cases, as do many pieces of local history to sweep you back in time. A gift shop area has T-shirts, hats, and decor items. Open 10–5 Dec 26–May 1; 11–5 May 2–Dec 23 (closed Wed and Thu). Fee.

Naples

In Naples, **Third Street South** is a designated historic district, although its anchor—the **Old Naples Hotel**—has been replaced with a parking lot and upscale shopping mall. Numerous business buildings date from the 1920s, and many to the original settlement of the area. Walk just a block or two in any direction to find streets where little Cracker cottages still hide under a canopy of mango and ficus. If you take a walking tour of the surrounding neighborhood (see *Walking Tours*), you'll discover—if development remains at bay, which is never guaranteed—the **Haldemann-Price House,** 60 12th Ave S, Naples's oldest house (circa 1886), on the waterfront next to the pier, and **"Sea Villa,"** 40 13th Ave S, built in 1888 to overlook the ocean.

One of the last tabby cottages in Collier County, **Palm Cottage** (239-261-8164; www.cchistoricalsociety.com), 137 12th Ave S, built by Walter Haldemann in 1895, dominated the street when Naples was still a frontier outpost where Barron Collier's land office was a chickee with walls. The 3,500-square-foot cottage is made of insect-impervious Dade County pine and served many families over the years as well as for overflow accommodations for the Old Naples Hotel. Hedy Lamarr and other movie stars stayed inside these thick tabby walls, which help keep the rooms cool all year. Local spirit Alexandra Brown was the last owner prior to the cottage's purchase by the Naples Historical Society in 1978, and it's rumored she still keeps a kindly haunt over the place. A tour of the home showcases rooms with vintage details, including the 1906 kitchen with a GE icebox and antique stove. A gallery upstairs has fascinating scenes of Old Naples from the days when your address was "the house with green and white stripes" or "the house with diamonds."

Ochopee

The tiny **Ochopee Post Office** (239-261-8164), 3800 Tamiami Trl E, started its life as a tool shed but has housed the smallest post office in the United States since 1953 (it replaced the original 1932 post office, which burned down). Sitting all by itself along the roadside, it's an unmistakable landmark as you drive through the western Everglades.

MUSEUMS

Everglades City

Inside the 1927 Everglades Laundry building, the **Museum of the Everglades** (239-695-0008; www.florida-everglades.com/evercty/museum.htm), 105 Broadway Ave W, opened in 1998 to educate visitors about the long and storied history of this once-frontier outpost, a city created in the midst of the Everglades. There are exhibits on Prohibition, the Seminoles, and early schools, and a special focus on what made Everglades City (founded as "Everglade," by the way)—the construction of the Tamiami Trail. The city became host to railroad and highway construction workers, and Barron Collier had a land office in town. Vintage laundry and dry-cleaning equipment are on display, as well as movie memorabilia. The front foyer houses a gift shop and art gallery featuring the work of local artists. Free; donations appreciated.

Marco Island

It's a little confusing, but there are two versions of the **Marco Island Historical Museum** (239-389-6447; www.theMIHS.org); I visited **The Museum at Old Marco** adjoining the Olde Marco Inn, which takes up a couple of rooms in a motel-turned-shops. The small display focuses on Calusa culture (which is what Marco Island was famous for before the condos came along): The Key Marco Cat and Deer Head Mask were two spectacular finds in 1896, when archeologist Frank Cushing found an entire Calusa village preserved in muck. Alas, the items removed from the muck mostly disintegrated, but there are models and photos to show them off. Prior to the 1960s real estate boom, Old Marco Village was home to numerous clam canneries, including Doxsee and Burnham, and residents made their living off the sea. Free.

Naples

In the Collier County Government Center, the **Collier County Museum** (239-774-8476; www.colliermuseum.com), 3301 Tamiami Trl E, depicts ten thousand years of local history, from prehistoric mastodons and the people who hunted them through the grand Calusa empire, the rise of the Seminoles, and the pioneers who settled this rough frontier. Set on 5 acres, it includes historic swamp buggies, a logging locomotive, and two early Naples cottages. Open 9–5 Mon–Fri, 9–4 Sat. Free.

& "Art washes away from the soul the dust of everyday life" at the **Naples Museum of Art** (239-597-1111 or 1-800-597-1900; www.thephil.org), 5833 Pelican Bay Blvd, where a grand display of modern and classical art awaits. As you walk through the courtyard into the lobby, a massive Chihuly glass sculpture fills the space overhead, glinting in the sunlight. Rotating exhibits fill the first-floor Springborn Galleries; during my visit, modern Mexican masters. In the Von Liebig Galleries, I experienced innovative "correalism" with art suspended below eye level in a blue-curtained room, or popping out from curved paneled walls. Masters of Miniature in the Pistner Gallery showcased exquisite detail on miniature figurines and architectural models, including one of the Royal Opera, Versailles. A three-story glass sculpture is the centerpiece of the stairwell, and for an art glass aficionado like me, the Persian Ceiling corridor, another Chihuly creation, evokes a souk with glass as silk canopy, swirls of color and form punctuated by baubles and bowls. Exhibits spill into the adjacent Center for the Arts, where galleries showcased Winslow Homer's engravings and The Grand Tour in Miniature. Take a little piece of the museum home from the museum store, which offers colorful scarves, a great selection of art books, and objets d'art for the home. Open 10–4 Tue–Sat, noon–4 Sun. Adults $15, students $5.

Originally a classroom exhibit by local students, the **Southwest Florida Holocaust Museum** (239-263-9200; www.swflhm.org), 4760 Tamiami Trl N, Suite 7, in Sandalwood Square, provides a chronological look at the events that shaped the Nazi empire and its reprehensible genocides. Open 1–4 Tue–Fri and Sun. Free.

Everglades City

An operational passenger and freight depot for more than 30 years, the **Atlantic Coast Depot,** at the end of Collier Ave, is now the Everglades Seafood Depot (see *Dining Out*), but its starring role was in *Winds Across the Everglades,* filmed in 1960. The depot marks the end of the Atlantic Coast Line (ACL) on the southwestern coast of Florida.

Naples

✎ Enjoy railroad history *and* model trains at the **Naples Depot** (239-262-1776), corner of US 41 and 10th St S, where the historic Atlantic Coast Line depot houses a **Lionel Train Museum** with operational displays, exhibits on regional railroad history, an outdoor garden train to ride, and two significant pieces of rolling stock, the 1909 Soo Line Caboose and the 1947 Club Car. Take home railroad souvenirs and gifts from the Lionel Whistle Stop in the Southern RR baggage car. As this is a labor of love by local rail-fan volunteers, hours vary; call ahead. Adults $5, children $3.

SWAMP BUGGY RACES Invented in Naples in 1949 by Ed Frank to get through the rugged Big Cypress Swamp, the swamp buggy is a homegrown invention shown off on a regular basis at the **Florida Sports Park** (1-800-897-2701; www .swampbuggy.com), 8250 Collier Blvd, which features races between these enor-mous machines.

ZOOLOGICAL PARKS & WILDLIFE REHABILITATION ✎ At the **Aviary & Zoo of Naples** (239-353-2215; www.aviaryofnaples.com/park.htm), 9824 Immokalee Rd, Naples, visit with more than two hundred birds and see exotic creatures such as zebu and coatimundi, giant monitor lizards, and miniature barnyard animals. Open 10–4 Sat–Wed. Adults $8, ages 4–11 $4.

& ✎ Established in 1919, **Caribbean Gardens: The Zoo in Naples** (239-262-5409; www.napleszoo.com), 1590 Goodlette-Frank Rd, Naples, is an old family favorite of mine from the days of "Jungle Larry's Safari," a 1970s tourist attraction. An accredited zoo, it has large open-air enclosures with viewing platforms for most of its resi-dents, from the big cats to alligators. The air echoes with the whoops of howler monkeys; these and other primates live on islands in a lagoon, where you can visit them on the Pri-mate Expedition Cruise on a quiet electric boat, included free with your admission. There are several play-grounds scattered throughout the

GOPHER TORTOISE AT CARIBBEAN GARDENS

Sandra Friend

property, which still includes a bit of wild space and benches for quiet reflection amid the tropical landscaping, which dates back decades as a botanical garden. Renovations are still under way throughout the park. Regular "meet the keeper" and feeding events go on in the various enclosures all day; pick up a schedule as you enter the park. Before you leave, browse the gift shop, full of plush animals, nature-themed toys, and puzzles for the young ones. Adults $15.95, seniors $14.95, ages 4–15 $9.95; stroller rentals $5. Open 9:30–5:30 daily.

✍ Injured wildlife find a new lease on life at the **Naples Nature Center** (see *Nature Centers*), where birds regain their flight capability in large enclosures tucked away in the pine forest. A large wading pool is home to dozens of pelicans and herons. Up to 70 percent of the injured mammals and birds received here can be reintroduced to the wild.

✳ To Do

AIRBOAT RIDES It's almost a cliché along the Tamiami Trail, but airboat rides through the Everglades are the high-speed way to see the swamps up close and personal. Up at Lake Trafford, Ski Olesky will take you out on one of the most alligator-thick lakes in the state on **Airboats & Alligators, Inc.** (1-866-657-2214; www.laketrafford.com), 6001 Lake Trafford Rd, a ride you won't soon forget. Along the Tamiami Trail, you'll run across **Wooten's Everglades Airboat & Swamp Buggy Tours** (239-695-2781 or 1-800-282-2781; www.wootens airboats.com), US 41, in operation since 1953, with animal exhibits, alligator wrestling, a gift shop and snack bar, and tours every 30 minutes. In Everglades City, look for **Everglades Island Airboat Tours & Totch's Island Tours** (1-866-626-2833; www .airboateverglades.com or www.totchislandtours.com) along Collier Ave, or ride with a knowledgeable native on **Captain Doug House's Florida Boat Tours** (1-800-282-9194), departing from the Captain's Table Resort at Collier Ave and Broadway.

BICYCLING In downtown Naples, **The Bike Route** (239-262-8373), 655 Tamiami Trl N, offers rentals for in-town excursions; the historic district between Third St and the beach is especially suited for a bicycle tour. For a wilderness ride go to **Collier-Seminole State Park** (see *Parks*) for 3½ miles of off-road biking through pine forests and tropical hardwood hammock.

AIRBOAT TOUR OF EVERGLADES NATIONAL PARK

Greater Naples Marco Island Everglades CVB

BIRDING In Naples, driving along Airport-Pulling Road you'll see dozens of wood storks, herons, and other wading birds along the edges of the **Airport Road Canal.** At US 41 and Marco Island Road, **Eagle Lakes Community Park** (239-793-4414), 11565 Tamiami Trail E, is a top birding spot with more than 50 species spotted in an hour, including bald

eagles and every variety of heron in the state. **Caxambas Park,** at the end of
Marco Island, is a place to sit and watch thousands of birds fly in to their roosts
on the islands of Caxambas Pass at sunset. Around Marco Island and Everglades
City, the **Ten Thousand Islands** are home to large colonies of wading birds,
best seen on a boat trip.

BOATING

Marco Island

Board the **Marco Island Princess** (239-642-5415), 951 Bald Eagle Dr, for daily
sight-seeing cruises in the Ten Thousand Islands. For a day trip to Key West,
check into **Sea Key West Express** (1-888-539-2628; www.seakeywestexpress
.com), departing from Marco River Marina daily; the massive catamaran takes
three hours to get to its destination. Advance reservations required for all cruises. Rent your own craft at the **Cedar Bay Marina** (239-642-6717; www.cedar
baymarina.com), 705 E Elkham Cir.

Naples

Day Star Charters (239-417-FISH or 1-877-FLA-TOUR; www.daystarcharters
.org) runs trips of two to eight hours for fishing, shelling, and sight-seeing. Each
trip is chartered just for your party; call Capt. Kevin Bill for details. The **Naples
Princess** (239-649-2275), 550 Port-o-Call Way, offers sunset dinner buffet cruises and more. Learn the ropes at **Sailboats Unlimited** (239-649-1740; www
.sailboatsunlimited.com), Naples City Dock, or take a sail on **Sweet Liberty**
(239-793-3525; www.sweetliberty.com), 1484 Fifth Ave S, with your choice of
sight-seeing, dolphin watching, a shelling trip, or private charter. Advance reservations required for all cruises. **Brookside Marina** (239-774-9100), 2023 Davis
Blvd, rents powerboats and sells bait and tackle, and **Naples Bay Marina** (239-
774-0339), 1484 Fifth Ave S, has brand-new high-end boat rentals.

ECOTOURS

Everglades City

North American Canoe Tours (239-695-4666; www.evergladesadventures
.com) offers multiday guided paddling and camping trips into the islands with an
overnight at Ivey House (see *Lodging*); rates start at $600 for two days. Depart-
ing from the visitors center in Everglades City, **Everglades National Park
Boat Tours** (941-695-2591) offer narrated voyages through the Ten Thousand
Islands; buy your tickets (adults $21, ages 5–12 $11) inside the visitors center.
The trip runs one and a half hours.

Marco Island

Hang on for the ride of your life! A very different way to see the Ten Thousand
Islands is by **Everglades WaveRunner Guided Excursions** (239-394-2511,
ext. 2983), offered at the Marco Island Marriott Resort (see *Lodging*). I'd never
been on a WaveRunner before when I started this one-hour journey, and I have
to admit, I was terrified crossing the open ocean to Caxambas Pass and learning
to maneuver while sight-seeing at the same time. But once I became comfortable with the machine, the trip was a blast. It was great to see the coast of Cape

Romano and its crumbling "biosphere" home (which Hurricane Wilma subsequently washed away); even better to see hundreds of wading birds perched in the tangled mangrove forests and along the shores. If you're a WaveRunner newbie like me, I suggest you invest in an hour or two rental prior to your trip to get the hang of the machine before you follow your guide into the mangrove-lined wilderness. Cost $150 per person; riders can be solo or doubled up depending on your preference. Reservations essential.

Naples

Sign up with **Pelican Tours, Inc.** (239-267-0881; www.evergladesadventure .com) for a daylong whirlwind tour of the western Everglades and Big Cypress Swamp, with activities ranging from a historic walk through Everglades City to a jungle boat tour through the Ten Thousand Islands and a swamp walk in Big Cypress National Preserve. Reservations required; operators pick up participants in Fort Myers Beach, Bonita Springs, and Naples.

FAMILY ACTIVITIES Coral Cay Adventure Golf (239-793-4999; www.coral caygolf.com), 2205 E Tamiami Trl, is the king of regional miniature golf, with two 18-hole courses set amid faux reefs, caves, and waterfalls. At **King Richards Fun Park** (239-598-1666; www.kingrichardspark.org), 6780 N Airport Rd, ride the only permanent roller coaster in the area, splash around the water park, or take on the go-carts.

FISHING

Everglades City

For saltwater fishing, take a guided trip through the meandering maze of the Ten Thousand Islands with any of the great outfitters around here, including Captain Brock at **American Heritage Outdoor Adventures** (239-695-4150), or **Chokoloskee Charters** (239-695-9107; www.chokoloskeecharters.com).

Immokalee

For the best freshwater fishing in the region, visit **Lake Trafford Marina** (239-487-3794 or 1-866-657-2214; www.laketrafford.com), 6001 Lake Trafford Rd, for an outing on 1,500-acre Lake Trafford.

Naples

Head down to the **Naples Municipal Beach & Fishing Pier** (239-213-3062; www.craytoncove.com), 12th Ave S and Eighth St, to drop a line and see what bites, or for local guide services, consult with the folks at **Everglades Angler** (1-800-573-4749; www.evergladesangler.com), 810 12th Ave S, or **Mangrove Outfitters** (1-888-319-9848; www.mangroveoutfitters.com), 4111 Tamiami Trl E.

GAMING Play the slots or go for high-stakes poker and top-prize bingo at the **Seminole Casino Immokale**e (239-658-1313 or 1-800-218-0007; www .semtribe.com), 506 S First St, Immokalee. Open 24 hours with a full-service restaurant.

Marco Island

Designed to fit into its natural surroundings, **The Rookery at Marco** (239-793-6060; www.rookeryatmarco.com), 3433 Club Center Blvd, was recently redesigned by Robert Cupp Jr., with generous fairways and oversized greens. Semiprivate, it's open to guests of the Marco Island Marriott Resort (see *Lodging*).

Naples

High handicappers will delight in **Arrowhead Golf Club** (239-596-1000), 2205 Heritage Greens Dr, where the wide fairways and expansive greens make for a better-than-average day on the links.

HIKING This region is where I learned to get my feet really wet on a swamp tromp or two (or ten); the constant flow of clear, fresh rainwater in the Big Cypress Swamp and the Everglades means that if a trail isn't a boardwalk, you'll be slogging through a swamp. Not that it's a bad thing—it just getting used to walking where you can't see your feet. The southern terminus of the **Florida Trail** (1-877-HIKE-FLA; www.floridatrail.org) is at Loop Road in Big Cypress National Preserve. This National Scenic Trail continues north for nearly 45 miles before leaving Collier County. This particular section of the Florida Trail is the most rugged and remote in the state, best backpacked with a buddy. Stop by the **Kirby Storter Roadside** on the Tamiami Trail, Ochopee, for a pleasant 1-mile round-trip boardwalk through several Big Cypress habitats, courtesy of the Friends of the Big Cypress, or visit the **Florida Panther National Wildlife Refuge** for a wild walk through panther habitat. Virtually all the *Green Space* listings provide somewhere to hike; browse the Big Cypress chapter of *50 Hikes in South Florida* for details.

PADDLING

Big Cypress National Preserve

If you love wilderness paddling, the **Big Cypress National Preserve** (see *Wild Places*) is a place to lose yourself in a maze of mangrove tunnels and cypress-lined channels. Pick up *Day Paddling Florida's 10,000 Islands and Big Cypress Swamp* by my buddy Jeff Ripple, who's *the* expert on paddling the Big Cypress Swamp, for options such as the Turner River and Halfway Creek. Rent your craft in Everglades City, where ecotours operators (see *Ecotours*) rent gear and run guided paddling trips.

Everglades City

Explore the Gulf Coast of **Everglades National Park** (see *Wild Places*) by kayak. It takes two and a half hours to paddle to Sandfly Island, tides willing, where you'll find a 1-mile nature trail around this former stronghold of the Calusa. Nautical charts are recommended for all offshore paddling trips.

Naples

Paddle out into Wiggins Pass with a rental from **Cocohatchee Nature Center** (see *Nature Centers*) for some saltwater kayak exploration of the mangrove shoreline. Rates start at $12/hour for a canoe, $14/hour for a kayak.

NAPLES PIER AT SUNSET

Sandra Friend

SCENIC DRIVES For a tropical version of Beverly Hills, head south on Gordon Drive from the coconut palm–lined streets of **Old Naples** to gawk at the billionaires' seaside homes in **Port Royal.** Prefer a more natural setting? Head for the wilds east on the **Tamiami Trail** (850-410-5894), US 41 from Collier-Seminole State Park to the Big Cypress National Preserve, the first highway to slice through the Everglades. Grab a copy of the *Everglades Trail* (www.evergladestrail.com) brochure to make stops along the way at key places that affect the health and beauty of the Everglades habitats.

SHELLING In the afternoon at Vanderbilt Beach, I saw a motel guest cleaning up her collection of bright orange whelks, so the shelling is likely superb around **Delnor-Wiggins Pass State Park** (see *Beaches*).

SUNSET WATCHING Stay anywhere in **Naples,** and you'll find yourself drifting toward the Gulf of Mexico to watch the sunset with your neighbors each evening. Every numbered street ends at the Gulf, so you have plenty of palm-lined spots to choose from; the historic **Naples Pier,** however, tends to be a magnet for catching those final colorful rays. On **Marco Island,** enjoy a brilliant sunset at **Tigertail Beach** (fee), or watch the colors fade as the egrets flock home to roost at Caxambas Pass from **Caxambas Park** (free).

TOURS Before you go out on foot, get to know Naples by grabbing a **Naples Trolley Tour** (239-262-7300; www.naplestrolleytour.com), a narrated trip through the city with free reboarding privileges. Fee.

WALKING TOURS

Everglades City
Pick up a brochure at the Museum of the Everglades (see *Museums*) for a walking tour of **historic downtown Everglades City,** which was developed as a planned community by Barron Collier during the 1920s.

Naples
Check with the Third Street South Area Association (813-649-6707) or at Palm Cottage (see *Historic Sites*) for the detailed **Historic Walking Tour of Old Naples,** a self-guided tour that includes gems such as Martha's Cottage (circa 1922) at 205 11th Ave S and **"Pineapple Plantation"** at 1111 Gulfshore Dr, believed to have been designed in 1930 by Addison Mizner.

BEACHES

Marco Island
Tigertail Beach (239-353-0404), Tigertail Ct, offers a get-away-from-it-all strand well north of the line of tall condos that haunt **South Beach,** down at the end of the hotel strip on Collier Blvd. Both cost $4 for parking; follow signs to find them.

Naples
Walking down to the beach from the **Naples Pier** (239-213-3062), I was reminded of a pristine shoreline I once visited on the Arabian Sea—lined with coconut palms, with residences hidden far enough back in the vegetation so as not to spoil the view. And *that* is why they call this the Paradise Coast. North of the city, **Loudermilk Park,** Banyan Blvd and Gulf Shore Blvd N, is one of the more popular beachfront parks (fee).

Vanderbilt Beach
Vanderbilt Beach Road ends at the water's edge at **Vanderbilt Beach,** a county park with beach access adjoining the Ritz-Carlton, and **Delnor-Wiggins Pass State Park** (230-597-6196; www.floridastateparks.org/delnor-wiggins/default.cfm), 11100 N Gulfshore Dr, provides a sandy strand at the north end of the county.

BOTANICAL GARDENS

South Naples
Still under development but coming along in stages, the **Naples Botanical Garden** (239-643-7275; www.naplesgarden.org), 4820 Bayshore Dr, offers a quiet place to stroll pathways through a mix of formal gardens and wilderness habitats on 160 acres, including a new scenic trail through 30 acres of uplands and a butterfly house. The Tropical Mosaic Garden near the entrance evokes the sea. Open 10–4 Mon–Sat, noon–4 Sun. Adults $7, ages 6–12 $4, members free.

NATURE CENTERS The **Conservancy of Southwest Florida** (239-262-0304; www.conservancy.org), 1450 Merrihue Dr, manages two very different nature centers in Collier County: the Naples Nature Center and the Briggs Nature Center. Begun in 1964 to save a key bird nesting area, Rookery Bay, from development, this nonprofit organization focuses on southwest Florida's natural areas through science, public policy, wildlife rehabilitation, and education. Their efforts have preserved more than 300,000 acres of habitat in southwest Florida. Request their *Learning Adventures* booklet for a long list of very specialized ecotours, outdoor activities, and workshops that will keep you in tune with nature.

Marco Island
❧ ✿ Deep within in the mangrove forests of Rookery Bay near Marco Island, **The Conservancy's Briggs Nature Center** (239-775-8569), 401 Shell Island Rd, provides a boardwalk for wildlife viewing along Rookery Bay as well as tour boats, guided nature tours, and rentals of canoes and kayaks. Open 9–4:30 Mon–Sat. Fee.

&. ♪ For more than 25 years, **Rookery Bay National Estuarine Research Reserve** (239-417-6310; www.rookerybay.org), 300 Tower Rd, has showcased the efforts of marine scientists to document and understand the complexity of life in this unique 110,000-acre marine preserve. Start your introduction with a movie that gives the feel of this mysterious puzzle of ten thousand mangrove islands, and then explore with the senses. Surrounding the cinema is a natural art galley with images by local artists. Move on to the Aquaria Showcase to watch creatures in underwater habitats such as oyster beds and seagrass, walk past the working labs, and head upstairs for more exhibits and an observation deck. A bridge and boardwalk are planned to expand the experience. Ecotours depart from the back dock, and you can follow signs to a short nature trail. Fee.

Naples

&. ♪ Spread out over 14 acres, the **The Conservancy's Naples Nature Center** (239-262-0304), 1450 Merrihue Dr, adjacent to Caribbean Gardens, provides an afternoon's worth of experiences for visitors. Enjoy guided walks on the Arboretum and Hammock Trails at 11 and 2 daily, or wander the trails on your own. Naturalist Troy Frensley took me on a tour of the museum, where the "Florida: Coast to Coast" theme is reflected throughout the exhibits, from the nearshore touch tank to a walk through giant-size mangrove roots and a massive interactive exhibit on seashells. Check out the relief map: As water flows into South Florida, who relies on it when it gets there? Rotating exhibits showcase habitats in other regions. Wander through the well-stocked gift shop with its natural science books and toys to board a quiet electric boat for an interpretive tour up the Golden Gate Canal to the Gordon River, cruising down a winding passage through a tunnel of mangroves past palm hammocks with giant leather ferns. Yellow-crowned night herons nest on an island at the confluence of waterways. Visit the wildlife rehabilitation center (see *Zoological Parks & Wildlife Rehabilitation*) to meet some of the 2,500 creatures treated and released this year, and stop in the Wildlife Art Gallery near the parking area, where resident artist Chris Murray creates intricate wildlife sculptures in wood. More than seven hundred volunteers pull together to make this a very special place where you can touch nature while learning about it, too. Fee.

In North Naples, the **Cocohatchee Nature Center** (239-592-1200; www.coco hatchee.org), 12345 N Tamiami Trl, offers five daily one-and-a-half-hour narrated nature cruises down the Cocohatchee River and into the Gulf of Mexico at Wiggins Pass. Tours start at 10 AM and cost $24, half price for ages 12 and under.

PARKS A city park with a broad range of on-site activities, **Cambier Park** (239-213-3058), 735 Eighth St S, in the heart of downtown Naples, boasts an activity center, tennis courts, softball field, and massive "super playground" for the kids.

When Barron Collier died in March 1939, he was Florida's largest landowner. He wanted the federal government to create a national park that encompassed what was then the largest natural grove of royal palms in the United States, but the government wasn't interested. Instead, the state of Florida stepped in and created **Collier-Seminole State Park** (239-394-3397; www.floridastateparks .org/collier-seminole/default.cfm), 20200 E Tamiami Trl, Naples, which opened

Trail and a monument to Collier, the park offers several wilderness adventures.
Catch a guided pontoon boat tour into the mangrove waterways (additional fee),
launch your canoe or kayak for a paddling trip, experience miles of rugged bicycle
trails, camp out in a pleasant tropical campground, walk the nature trail, or go
for a hard-core 6½-mile hike-and-slog through the watery wilderness of Big
Cypress on a Florida Trail loop, with optional primitive camping. Fee.

PRESERVES

Immokalee

& ✐ With a world-class boardwalk through an old-growth cypress swamp,
Corkscrew Swamp Sanctuary (239-348-9151; www.audubon.com/local/
sanctuary/corkscrew) is an excellent place to first immerse yourself in the wilds
that are the Big Cypress Swamp. Protecting more than 11,000 acres, the preserve contains one of the last large virgin cypress stands in the United States
and, with it, a nesting colony of wood storks. You'll spot an endless array of birds
on the 2¼-mile loop trail. The site is a gateway for the Great Florida Birding
Trail's southern region, which will tip you off to dozens of additional places to
explore. Adults $10, students $6, Audubon members $5, ages 6–18 $4. Open
daily.

Naples

& **Naples Preserve,** at the corner of Fleischmann and US 41, is a little patch of
pine flatwoods in the middle of the city. It offers a visitors center and a boardwalk to explore the habitat.

WILD PLACES

Copeland

Best known for the elusive ghost orchid, **Fakahatchee Strand Preserve State
Park** (239-695-4593; www.floridastateparks.org/fakahatcheestrand/default.cfm),
137 Coastline Dr, comprises more than 85,000 acres, making it the biggest state
preserve in Florida. It is truly a watery wilderness, where the Fakahatchee
Strand runs 3 to 5 miles wide and 20 miles long, a swampy wilderness filled with
natural wonders. Forty-four species of orchids have been found here, giving the
park the nickname "Orchid Capital of the United States." Cruise Janes Scenic
Drive in search of Florida panthers, or walk the old cypress logging tramways to
explore the backcountry. The short Big Cypress Bend Boardwalk off US 41 provides a gentle introduction to this ancient swamp.

Protecting more than 26,000 acres of crucial habitat for Florida's most endangered species, the **Florida Panther National Wildlife Refuge** (239-353-8442;
www.fws.gov/floridapanther), FL 29 north of I-75, has an interpretive trail that
recently opened to the public. The same office manages the **Ten Thousand
Islands National Wildlife Refuge** (www.fws.gov/southeast/tenthousandisland),
which covers 35,000 acres where Fakahatchee and Picayune Strands spill their
fresh water into the Gulf of Mexico. Visit by boat (powered or paddled) from
Marco Island, Goodland, or Port of the Islands.

FLORIDA PANTHER

Visit Florida

Everglades City

The westernmost extent of **Everglades National Park** (1-800-365-CAMP; www.nps.gov/ever), FL 29, comprises Collier County's southeastern corner and can be accessed only by boat. Stop at the **Everglades National Park Gulf Coast Visitor Center** (239-695-3311), open 8–4:30 daily, which offers daily wheelchair-accessible boat tours (fee), "bike hikes" of Everglades City historic sites, "Full Moon" canoe trips once a month, nightly programs under the stars, and daily talks under the chickee outside as well as guided canoe trips. The bulk of Everglades National Park, including the 99-mile **Wilderness Waterway,** is discussed in the *South Miami-Dade: Food and Wine Country* chapter.

Naples

It stands as a monument to the ages-old Florida land scam: **Picayune Strand State Forest** (239-348-7557), accessed via Sabal Palm Rd, was once part of Golden Gate Estates, a 1960s planned community that just happened to seasonally flood when the salesmen weren't showing off the model homes. In the 1980s, the state started buying up the land for the state forest, but in order to do so, they had to track down and buy up acreage from more than seventeen thousand landowners—one of the most complex land acquisitions in Florida history. It's a watery wilderness enjoyed by swamp-buggy enthusiasts, daring hikers on the Sabal Palm Trail, as well as hunters during deer season.

Ochopee

Established by Congress in 1974 as the first National Preserve in the United States, **Big Cypress National Preserve** (239-695-1201; www.nps.gov/bicy), between Naples and Miami along the Tamiami Trail, protects more than 900 square miles of cypress and sawgrass habitats dependent on seasonal rains. Stop in at the Oasis Visitor Center, Ochopee, for an orientation to the preserve, and then immerse yourself into the environment via its trails, from the rugged **Florida Trail** (see *Hiking*) to the new **boardwalk at Kirby Storter Roadside** and the **Fire Prairie Trail** off Turner River Road. The preserve is open to hunting and includes miles of off-road-vehicle trails primarily used by swamp buggies, as well as a number of campgrounds (see *Campgrounds*) with varying facilities. The visitors center is open 8:30–4:30 daily year-round, except Christmas.

BED & BREAKFASTS

Everglades City 34139

On the National Register of Historic Places, the **Everglades Spa & Lodge** (239-695-3151; www.banks oftheeverglades.com), 201 W Broadway, plays off its past as the city bank (circa 1926) with six rooms ($110–135) with banking names. The "Dividends" is popular with anglers; the spacious room has a tiled shower and full kitchen. The original vault and fan are still a part of the building, which now also hosts a full-service day spa and salon.

There are two distinct faces to the **Ivey House** (239-695-3299; www .iveyhouse.com), 107 Camellia St, a popular launch point for adventures into the Everglades. The historic part of the complex includes 11 rooms built in 1928 as quarters for workers building the Tamiami Trail. It has small rooms ($50–75) with a dorm feel, and the original bathrooms are down the hall. Guests mingle in a large living area with television. The new part of the complex has 17 units ($75–140) centered on a tropical pool in a screened atrium, with shaded tables for guests to sit outside their spacious rooms. Each has a tiled floor, large bathroom, and a workspace, but Internet access isn't possible due to the remoteness of the area. You *are* in the Everglades, after all! A separate cottage houses up to four people ($125–140). Your room comes with a full breakfast served in the Ghost Orchid Grill (see *Eating Out*), and you can arrange ecotours and kayak or canoe rentals at the front desk. Call ahead—closed summer months.

CABINS AND COTTAGES

Everglades City 34139

Glades Haven Everglades Cozy Cabins (239-695-2746 or 1-888-956-6251; www.gladeshaven.com), 901 S Copeland Ave, make up a modern fish camp with nice park-model cabins (bedroom, sleeping loft, living-dining-kitchen area with cable TV) either on or near the waterfront. Ask about dockage with your rental ($70–110).

CAMPGROUNDS

Big Cypress Preserve

Big Cypress National Preserve Campgrounds (see *Wild Places*), along the Tamiami Trail, are rugged wilderness outposts. Facilities vary with location, and many are not open during the summer. Primitive campgrounds (minimal to no fee; no rest rooms) include the very remote **Bear Island** at the north end of Turner River Road; Burns Lake, along US 41; Pinecrest, off Loop Road; and Mitchell's Landing. I've camped at Monument Lake ($16, includes showers and flush toilets) and enjoyed it thoroughly; Midway (east of Oasis) recently reopened with new facilities.

Chokoloskee 34138

Along mangrove-lined waterways, **Outdoor Resorts of Chokoloskee Island** (239-695-3788), FL 29, provides waterfront RV camping with docks ($69), interior sites ($59), and motel efficiencies ($85). Boats, canoes, and kayaks can be rented on-site.

Marco Island 34145

Set in a lush tropical forest surrounded by Rookery Bay, the **Naples/ Marco Island KOA** (941-774-5455 or 1-800-562-7734; www.koakamp grounds.com/where/fl/09109), 1700 Barefoot Williams Rd, is just moments from nature centers and the beach for all sorts of outdoors fun; there's even an ecotour pickup at the park. Take your pick from RV and tent sites, Kamping Kabins, and a Kamping Lodge with kitchen and bath ($37–179).

Naples 34102

Shaded by tropical trees, the **Rock Creek RV Resort** (239-643-3100; www.rockcreekrv.com), 3100 North Rd, has 235 full hookup spaces ($40–50), a recreation room, shuffleboard, and a large heated pool. Slip your kayak in the creek and head down the Gordon River in a matter of minutes.

HOTELS, MOTELS, AND RESORTS

Everglades City 34139

There is no better place to settle into Collier County's past than the elegant **Everglades Rod & Gun Club** (239-695-2101; www.everglades chamber.com/rodandgunclub.com), 200 Riverside Dr, a hunting and fishing lodge with humble beginnings in 1864 that grew to a large complex on the Barron River around settler Allen Storter's home. Dark pecky cypress walls and mounted trophies emphasize the outdoorsy atmosphere of this former private club, which has hosted a bevy of presidents and celebrities over the years. Arrival used to be by boat into the spacious lobby, so the walk from the parking lot is through the narrow back entrance lined with historic clippings, past an intimate bar with local murals and a jukebox. There are 17 rooms with private baths ($85–125); cash only.

Goodland 34140

Since 1957, the little **Pink House Motel** (239-394-1313), 310 Pear Tree Ave, has had a fish-camp clientele and offers neat and clean paneled rooms ($49–59) overlooking the water. The one-bedroom unit has twin beds, perfect for fishing buddies, and the four-person penthouse runs $85–95. Located at Marker 7, with plenty of tie-up space on the wharf.

Marco Island 34145

At the **Marco Island Lakeside Inn** (239-394-1161 or 1-800-729-0216; www.marcoislandlakeside.com), 155 First Ave, I settled blissfully into one of the most comfortable beds I've encountered in my travels. Massive renovations have made this family-owned, family-managed inn a perfect spot to unwind. Each one- or two-bedroom suite ($86–275) boasts a full kitchen and living room/dining area separate from the romantic bedroom, tastefully decorated with original art. Choose from lakefront or poolside, and enjoy the new on-site bistro, **Sushi Blues & Steaks,** a classy urban restaurant with sushi bar and live piano.

A beachfront destination, the **Marco Island Marriott Resort & Spa** (239-394-2511 or 1-800-GET-HERE; www .marcoislandmarriott.com), 400 S Collier Blvd, has something for everyone, from on-site shopping and an elegant full-service spa to sight-seeing cruises, Faldo golf school, guided tours of the botanical wonders around the hotel, parasailing, and the only WaveRunner ecotour in the United States (see *Ecotours*). While the folks are at a convention, kids can join the Tiki Tribe to have daytime scavenger hunts and outdoor and arts activities. In the low season, rooms without views start at

$139; in high season, you'll pay up to $500 for a view of the Gulf.

In the **Olde Marco Island Inn & Suites** (239-394-3131 or 1-877-475-3466; www.oldmarco.com), 100 Palm St, the gorgeous lobby and main building date from 1883 and sit on a significant archeological site, part of an ancient city of the Calusa. The inn was built by Capt. Bill Collier and had 20 sleeping rooms and a two-story outhouse (as reported by *Ripley's Believe It Or Not*). Today, the original inn is only used for the lobby and restaurant. Guests are housed in modern condo rentals with Tommy Bahama room decor, covered parking, and an elevator to take you up, up, and away. Sunlight floods into each apartment unit, which has a full kitchen, large screened porch, and TV with VCR. Rates are based on size and season and start at $129.

Naples 34102

An all-suite hotel in Olde Naples, the **Edgewater Beach Hotel & Club** (1-800-821-0196; www.edgewater naples.com), 1901 Gulf Shore Blvd N, offers 125 beachfront suites with private balconies or patios, living room, dining room, kitchen, and separate bedroom and bath. Daily maid service includes dishwashing; complimentary valet parking. Choose your view and pick a decor—West Indies or beach house—then plunk down as little as $129 in the low season and up and c'mon down and relax. There are four on-site restaurants, a fitness center, water sports rentals, and children's activities.

& Step into old-world elegance at **The Inn on Fifth** (239-403-8777 or 1-888-403-8778; www.naplesinn.com/fifth), 699 Fifth Ave S, where the lobby is all marble and chandeliers—a new use for the historic First National Bank of Naples in the heart of the commercial district. This two-story hotel surrounds a courtyard pool and hot tub. The large contemporary rooms ($150 and up) feature sliding French doors to let in the sea breeze, plenty of natural light, 12-foot ceilings, wireless Internet, and comfy bathrobes. Inside the complex, relax at the Spa on Fifth, which opened in 2005 and offers a delightful array of body wraps, scrubs, facials, and massages.

& One of a rapidly disappearing breed—the 1940s Florida motor court—the **Lemon Tree Inn** (239-262-1414 or 1-888-800-5366; www .lemontreeinn.com), 250 Ninth St S, boasts luxuriously updated rooms around a courtyard with a Key West flair. Each room ($69–199, depending on season and size) speaks to an artist's sensibilities. I stayed in Casa Mara, #106, with the colorful fantasies of artist Mara Abboud adding vibrancy to a spacious room with a tiled kitchen area (bar sink, microwave, mini fridge, and coffeemaker); the furniture and linens evoked the tropics. On the patio, Adirondack chairs provide a place to read and relax. Continental breakfast is served poolside. It's an easy stroll to the shops on Fifth Avenue and about 8 blocks to the beach.

& With classic European styling, the **Trianon Hotel Old Naples** (239-435-9600 or 1-877-482-5228; www .trianon.com), 955 Seventh Ave S, is the posh place to stay downtown, and it's within easy walking distance to all of Fifth Avenue. Spacious and comfortable, the rooms and suites include a writing desk and marble-tiled bathrooms; "superior" rooms add a sofabed and small fridge, and suites have a wet bar. Enjoy a very private courtyard and pool, and relax with complimentary cocktails in the evening. Continental breakfast is served each morning. Less than a decade old, this hotel is owned by a long-standing local family with ties to Ritz-Carlton, but the prices here make elegance affordable—starting at $109 low season, $229 high season.

Vanderbilt Beach 34108

&. The coral pink **Inn at Pelican Bay** (239-597-8777 or 1-800-597-8770; www.innatpelicanbay.com), 800 Vanderbilt Beach Rd, towers over the surrounding pine forest. Inside, expect elegant surroundings; each spacious room ($89 and up) has a balcony or terrace, large desk, safe, and two phones.

In a place where condos line the oceanfront, the **Lighthouse Inn** (239-597-3345), 9140 Gulfshore Dr, stands out as a preserved piece of Old Florida, with its jalousie windows and 1940s exterior surrounding a coconut palm–shaded pool. The rooms ($50–125) are pleasant and bright; efficiencies have a full kitchen and tiled shower. Buzz and Judy have run this place since 1978, and I wish them many more years of success.

✳ Where to Eat

DINING OUT

Everglades City

A favorite of the celebrities who haunt this mangrove-lined frontier, the **Everglades Rod & Gun Club** (see *Lodging*) serves steaks and seafood with a focus on the native fish and shellfish that bring anglers here. Entrées include Swamp and Turf (frog's legs and a New York strip),

honey crispy fried chicken, and steamed shrimp in beer ($13–20). Serves lunch and dinner; appropriate dress (business casual or better) please. Cash only.

I celebrated New Year's Eve a couple of years ago at the **Everglades Seafood Depot** (239-695-3535), 102 Collier Ave, and that night, my life changed forever. Granted, it wasn't the seafood or the bubbly, but the company—but hey, you never know what'll work for you! Inside this 1928 railroad depot at the end of the line, you'll find great fresh shrimp, a large salad bar, and local signature entrées ($19–50) such as the Sunshine Special, a steamed seafood platter with snow crab, shrimp, mussels, and half a Florida lobster tail. Reservations suggested.

Oyster House Restaurant (239-695-2073; www.oysterhouserestaurant .com), 901 Copeland Ave, is where Chef Bobby shows off his expertise with the bounty of these local waters. Enjoy locally caught stone crab claws, fried gator, grouper "Oyster House style" and more ($17–24).

Marco Island

🍽 For Italian family-style dining, head to **Café Bubbalini** (239-642-1900; www.bubbalini.com), 1061 N Collier Blvd in Town Center, where creative entrées ($10–27) such as Ravioli Zooma-Zooma (made with basil, tomato, garlic, and cream) and M&M&M (mushrooms, *mosctaccioli*, and meat sauce) share the menu with seafood creations such as salmon *griglia*, grouper pasta, and shrimp Sinatra. I'm a sucker for Sinatra, so the crooner tunes drew me in from the sidewalk. Fresh bread comes with olive oil and herbs for dipping, the meat sauce has a garlicky zing, and one serving easily serves two ($5 sharing charge, though, so take it home if you can).

Naples

Downtown, **Fifth Avenue** is the place to see and be seen at dozens of trendy bistros with outdoor seating, including **Yabba Island Grill** (239-262-1221; www.yabbaislandgrill.com), 720 Fifth Ave S, laying claim to "Naples' Best Seafood"; **Café Lurcat** (239-213-3357), 494 Fifth Ave S, a fusion bistro with more than two hundred wine selections; and **Starplace, an Italian Osteria** (239-435-7701), 770 Fifth Ave S, where upmarket pizzas and antipasti platters shine.

A local standard for many years, **Andre's Steak House** (239-263-5851; www.andressteakhouse.com), 2800 Tamiami Trl N, offers four-star service, an award-winning wine list, and live entertainment as an adjunct to their succulent steaks. Reservations recommended.

A genial and popular trattoria, **Campiello Ristorante** (239-435-1166; www.campiello.damico.com), 11777 Third St S, features the best in Italian cuisine and seating that transports you to—well, Naples! True to its authentic roots, owners Richard and Larry D'Amico envisioned the restaurant as a lively center of neighborhood activity inspired by Florence and Sienna. Their extensive martini menu includes 28 choices (with The James Bond an option), and there is a page of fine wines to choose from. Lunch options include wood-oven pizzas ($11 and up), massive entrée salads, and muffuletta as one of many sandwiches. For dinner, consider osso buco or veal tagliatelle with spicy lamb sausage Bolognese ($16–38).

Vanderbilt Beach

BHA! BHA! (239-594-5557; www.bhabhapersianbistro.com), 847 Vanderbilt Beach Rd, brings the tastes of the Middle East to southwest Florida with classic Persian delights, belly dancers, and fortune tellers in a souk-like setting. Enjoy entrées ($15–19) such as salmon *zahedan* (sautéed with tomatoes, herbs, and olives) or duck *fesenjune* (succulent braised duck with orange, pomegranate, and walnut sauce).

EATING OUT

Chokoloskee

✦ A little café, a little boutique, and a lot of fun, **JT's Island Grill** (941-695-3633; www.chokoloskee-island.com), 238 Mamie St, is a great little eatery in the old McKinney store from 1890. Creative cuisine tops the menu, from Florida citrus salad (with candied walnuts, coconut, dried mango, and fresh organic oranges on organic greens) to an avocado BLT and mocha ice cream pie. The Key limeade is fabulous! Lunch daily; dinner and live music Thu–Sun. The store has a great selection of books on the region as well as local handcrafted gifts, navigational charts, Florida-related toys, and organic produce and foods; they also rent kayaks for exploring the Ten Thousand Islands.

Everglades City

Breakfast is served at the **Ghost Orchid Grill** inside the Ivey House (see *Lodging*); guests receive a complimentary meal, but you can stop in and order eggs and grits or pancakes off the menu, too ($2–6), during the winter season. Accented by orchids, this indoor garden comes alive with the photography of local artists Jeff Ripple and Connie Bransilver; you'll find their work and that of others, such as Peter Nolan, in the gift shop in the lobby.

It's a little bit historic site, a little bit art gallery, and a little bit museum. Unmistakable with the vintage cars and gas pumps out front, **Susie's Station Restaurant** (239-695-0704), 103 S Copeland Ave, has a pleasant country feel and serves up a variety of seafood baskets, fresh stone crab, and burgers ($6–15). Cash only, please.

Goodland

With a European feel, the **Little Bar Restaurant** (239-394-5663; www .littlebarrestaurant.com), 205 Harbor Pl, serves up fresh local avocados in their salads and a conch chowder worth stopping for. Open for lunch and dinner daily.

The quintessential Florida fish camp, **Stan's Idle Hour Seafood Restaurant** (239-394-3041; www.stansidle hour.net), 221 Goodland Dr W, is a destination every Sunday noon for live concerts on the water. No frills, no fuss—just fresh seafood ($8–11) at open-air picnic tables, and lots of appetizer choices.

Marco Island

Sit at picnic tables and eat your seafood off cafeteria trays at the it-can't-get-more-causal **Crazy Flamingo Raw Bar** (239-642-9600), 1035 N Collier Blvd at Town Center, where big steaming pots of oysters, mussels, and clams will tempt you with the aroma, and the smoked fish dip is fresh and good. The menu is mostly fish, little bull. Open 11 AM–2 AM daily.

The "Best Darn Barbecue" at **Porky's Last Stand** (239-394-8727), 701 Bald Eagle Dr, comes recommended from friends who grew up with the owner,

and it took one whiff of the smoke to convince me that this is an awesome place. Country family atmosphere, 1950s music, and great food—what more do you need? The meat is slow cooked over a wood fire, so enjoy spare ribs, smoked chicken, sliced pork or beef, and five different kinds of steak with choice of two sides ($9–24).

Right on the waterfront, the **Snook Inn** (239-394-3313; www.snookinn .com), 1215 Bald Eagle Dr, is a causal stop to drink margaritas and munch on shrimp; several folks suggested I have dinner here. The menu includes several preparations of grouper and shrimp, all the requisite shellfish, and a smattering of landlubber items, with entrées starting at $15. An extensive wine list complements your meal.

A shrine to the New York Yankees, **Susie's Diner** (239-642-6633), 1013 N Collier Blvd at Town Center, is a bustling breakfast nook where I appreciated that the host did not sit me, a single woman, at the counter stools but let me have my own little table despite the crowd. That morning's special was French toast topped with strawberries, blueberries, or banana, and you bet it was good for $7. Lightning-fast breakfast service and crumbly fresh biscuits with your order. Cash only.

Naples

Since 1959, **Aurelio's** (239-403-8882), 590 N Tamiami Trl, has been the king of regional pizzerias, offering both traditional and specialty toppings. Their secret trademarked dish, spinach calabrese, is a spicy vegetarian alternative to stuffed pizza. Sandwiches come hot off the grill, and the antipasto is heaping. Open 4–10; closed Monday. Dine in or carry out.

Florida's oldest authentic British pub is **The English Pub** (239-774-2408), 2408 Linwood Ave, where darts and pool are the order of the day, quiz night happens every Thursday evening, and traditional English breakfast (beans and toast, and even kippers!) is served every Sunday brunch, with roast beef and Yorkshire pudding Sunday evening.

❧ Since 1952, **Kelly's Fish House** (239-774-0494), 1302 Fifth Ave, has been *the* place in Naples for fresh seafood, but you gotta love fish to come here—that's what the menu is all about. Perched along the Gordon River, it's a truly unique piece of old Naples, the pillars and crossbeams plastered with seashells and every table a miniature beach of sand and seashells beneath plate glass. Picture windows provide a great view of the waterfront. But let's not forget the food! I was offered (and accepted) anchovies for my Caesar salad, which came with subtle garlic dressing. The hushpuppies are homemade. My shrimp scampi was as fresh as could be. The Key lime pie has a smooth, silky texture and subtle bite. There are dozens of options on the menu, from Everglades frog's legs to genuine Gulf snapper, pompano, and shrimp Creole, with entrées $14–22. If you arrive before nightfall, check out Kelly's Shell Shack in the parking lot—what an array of seashells to choose from!

With 50 varieties of gourmet burgers ($5–7) to choose from, **Lindburgers** (239-262-1127), 330 Tamiami Trl S, is a must for the serious burger buff. If you love aviation history, you'll love it here, too—it's like stepping into an airport hangar filled with memorabilia.

It's authentic—the interior of **McCabe's Irish Pub** (239-403-7170), 699 Fifth Ave, came straight from Dublin, and you can start off your day with bangers and mash or have an Irish stew for lunch. Open 7–11 daily, and on weekends until last call.

Savor "Mediterranean soul food" at **Pelagos Café** (239-263-2996), 4951 N Tamiami Trl #105, a chic Greek restaurant tucked in a strip mall. Recognizable Greek pop music drifted through the background while I made my selections from gyros and *keftedes,* veggie falfel, a *mezede* platter with calamari and *saganaki,* and more. I settled on moussaka, which had a hint of cinnamon and was presented with a perfect Greek salad. Pleasant wait staff, natural light, and the vivid paintings on the walls made for a great dining experience, with lunch around $10. Closed Sunday; reservations suggested.

Ochopee
❧ Perch yourself on the edge of the Everglades and watch the gators swim past at **Joanie's Blue Crab Café** (239-695-2682), 39395 Tamiami Trl, an unmistakable landmark on the Tamiami Trail famous for its fresh local seafood and "help yourself" service. Gator comes served with Indian fry bread, and you can try an Everglades Swamp Dinner, featuring gator nuggets and fritters and frog's legs for $15. Their crab cakes are famous, and the grouper sandwich is delicious. Open 10–5 daily.

BAKERIES, COFFEE SHOPS, AND SODA FOUNTAINS

Marco Island
In a strip mall at the corner of Bald Eagle and Collier, **Sweet Annie's Ice Cream Parlor** (239-642-7180),

692 Bald Eagle Dr, has that old-fashioned feel, with classic soda fountain tables, black-and-white–tiled floor, and lots of "penny candy," although it costs more these days! Open 11–11.

☀ Entertainment

FINE ARTS In addition to housing galleries associated with the adjacent Naples Museum of Art (see *Museums*), the **Naples Philharmonic Center for the Arts** (1-800-597-1900; www.thephil.org), 5833 Pelican Bay Blvd, hosts year-round performances from orchestras and chorale groups to headliner singers and more.

THEATER Enjoy a musical with your meal at the **Naples Dinner Theatre** (239-514-STAR or 1-877-519-7827; www.naplesdinnertheatre.com), 1025 Piper Blvd. Ticket prices start around $40 for adults; children are half price. Reservations required; resort casual dress a must.

For top-notch community theater, visit **The Naples Players** (239-263-7990; www.naplesplayers.org), 701 Fifth Ave S, at Sugden Community Theatre. Their season runs Oct–May and includes old standards such as *Annie Get Your Gun* as well as new critically acclaimed plays like *The House of Blue Leaves*.

☀ Selective Shopping

Marco Island
Adjacent to the Olde Marco Inn, **Everything Gourmet** (239-642-0212), 192 Royal Palm Dr, features gourmet goodies, Florida favorite foods, and tea sets.

Customers can sip tea while browsing magazines at **Sunshine Booksellers** (239-393-0353), 677 S Collier Blvd,

an independent bookstore with insightful new book selections and one of the most extensive children's book sections in the region.

Naples
In addition to being a mecca for art galleries, Naples offers more options for shopping in one compact area than any other Florida city I can think of—only St. Augustine and Key West come close. There are several distinct shopping districts in Naples, each with its own feel, including Central, Fifth Avenue South, and Third Street South.

Naples—Central
Across from Naples Community Hospital on US 41, there is a handful of narrow side streets with restaurants and shops—Central North, east to 10th—with a variety of options to explore. **Treasure Island Antique Mall** (239-434-7684), 950 Central Ave, is a rambling store with numerous dealer booths, including rare and antiquarian books from Wickham Books South, antiques and collectibles, classy armoires, 1970s retro decor items, antique clocks, and fine china.

Naples—Fifth Avenue South
Fifth Avenue South (239-435-3742; www.fifthavenuesouth.com) feels like a 1940s movie set with a modern flair, the street lined with dozens of fascinating shops and restaurants, a mix of classic buildings surrounded by re-creations of the past. A fanciful mural draws you to **The Wind in the Willows** (239-643-0663), 793 Fifth Ave S, a clothing store where textiles have textures. The tempting aroma of hot fudge spills out of **Kilwins** (239-261-9898), 743 Fifth Ave S; whimsical gifts await at the **Copper Cricket**

(239-213-0500), 555 Fifth Ave S; glass baubles dangle at the **People's Pottery** (239-435-0018; www.peoples pottery.com), 769 Fifth Ave S; and **Brambles** (239-262-7894), 340 Fifth Ave S, is an authentic English tearoom in a tropical garden. Brighten your night at **La Luce** (239-263-LUCE), 837 Fifth Ave S, where lamps are art—urban designs of fused glass create contemporary chic.

Separate from the downtown shopping district a little farther south, you'll find the popular, touristy **Tin City** (239-262-6100; www.tin-city .com), 1200 Fifth Ave S, with dozens of small shops featuring everything from home decor to fudge, T-shirts, and fine art. Across the street at the corner of Goodlette-Frank Rd and US 41, **Bayfront** (239-649-8700) is a large boutique shopping mall on Naples Bay with complimentary valet parking; the shops and restaurants remind me of the upscale choices found in the resorts of Las Vegas. Behind Tin City you'll find **Dockside Boardwalk** (www.dockside-board walk.com), 1100 Sixth Ave S, with a variety of shops.

Naples—Third Street South

Stop at the Concierge Kiosk (239-434-6533; www.thirdstreetsouth.com), Camargo Park, opposite Fleischmann Fountain, to get your bearings before hoofing it through this historic business district, where boutiques and art galleries nudge elbows with upscale restaurants. In the Olde Naples Building, circa 1921, **Fantozzi's** (239-262-4808; www.FantozzisGourmet .com), 1148 Third St S, sells cheese and wine and adds to the mix of Mediterranean aromas in the air. The Chumsky Building marks the original center of downtown Naples. Check

out the **Mole Hole** (239-262-5115), 1201 Third St S, for unusual gifts; **Attic Toys** (239-649-TOYS), 1307 Third St S, for heirloom dolls and nostalgic toys; and **Au Cashmere** (239-261-8887), 1300 Third St S, for luxurious clothing and accessories. **Tommy Bahama's** (239-643-7920), 1220 Third St S, started right here and has both a sportswear store and a themed restaurant.

Vanderbilt Beach

The Village on Venetian Bay (239-261-6100; www.venetianvillage.com), 4200 Gulf Shore Blvd N, is an upscale shopping mall with art galleries, boutique shops, European clothing stores, and waterfront restaurants.

PRODUCE STANDS, FARMER'S MARKETS, SEAFOOD MARKETS, AND U-PICK

Everglades City

Stop by **City Seafood** (239-695-4700), 702 Begonia St, to catch the catch right off the dock as early as 9 AM. Stone crab claws come fresh off their own boats.

Goodland

You won't find it fresher than right off the boat at **Kirk's Seafood Market** (239-394-8616), 417 Papaya St, where

ALONG FIFTH AVENUE

Sandra Friend

in-season you can pick up stone crab claws at rock-bottom prices, and shrimp and fish all year long.

Immokalee

Harvest Blueberry Store and U-Pick (239-657-4888; www.about harvest.org), 1312 W New Market Rd #1, is part of the "Harvest for Humanity" project, a 40-acre planned community for moderate- to low-income families. In the middle of the blueberry farm, the store offers fresh berries (in-season), or you may pick your own, as well as blueberry products such as syrup, preserves, T-shirts, and gifts. Open 7–2 Mon–Fri, 10–2 Sat–Sun.

✳ Special Events

February: Celebrating the life and work of the woman who made a difference to the survival of the Everglades, the **Marjory Stoneman Douglas Festival** (239-695-0008) happens the last week of the month in Everglades City, with lectures, art, slide shows, music, and living history.

June: Join in the mystical legends of the Big Cypress Swamp at the **Skunk Ape Festival** (239-695-2275; www .skunkape.info), held the second Saturday, Trail Lakes Campground, Ochopee, celebrating Florida's home-grown version of the yeti. Swamp buggy rides, live music. Fee.

Things get wild at **Spammy Jammy** (239-394-5663; www.LittleBar Restaurant.com), held the last Saturday, Goodland, at the Little Bar Restaurant. Join in the "Spam-a-Lot" spirit (this festival predates the Broadway play) by dressing in your "jimmies" and bringing your most artistic or tastiest Spam creation for judging.

August: **SummerJazz on the Gulf** (239-261-2222; www.naplesbeach hotel.com), held the last Saturday. Free beachside concerts at the Naples Beach Hotel & Golf Club, with food and beverages available.

October: **Swamp Buggy Races** (1-800-897-2701; www.swampbuggy .com), held the last weekend in Naples at Florida Sports Park. Time trials on Saturday, races on Sunday.

Florida's Freshwater Frontier

THE PEACE RIVER VALLEY:
HARDEE AND DESOTO COUNTIES

CENTRAL HIGHLANDS

LAKE OKEECHOBEE

Sandra Friend

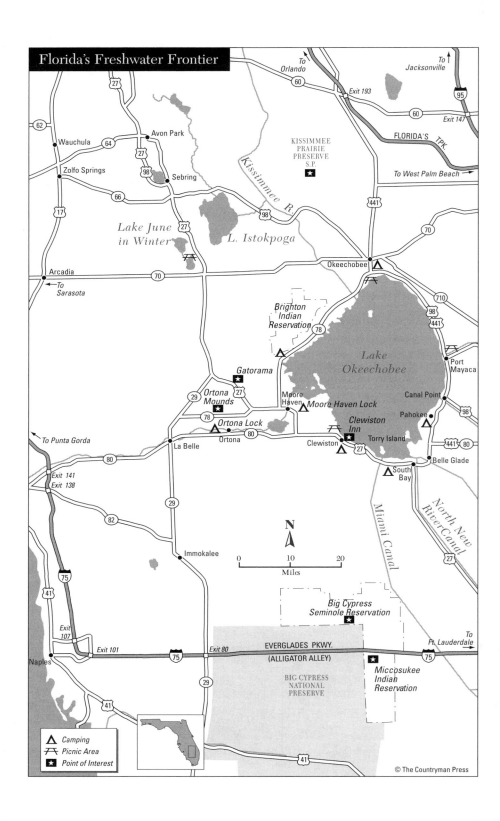

Florida's Freshwater Frontier

To Orlando
To Jacksonville
Exit 193
60
95
62
Exit 147
60
Wauchula
64
Avon Park
FLORIDA'S TPK
27
KISSIMMEE
PRAIRIE
PRESERVE
S.P.
Zolfo Springs
98
Sebring
To West Palm Beach
66
441
17
*Lake June
in Winter*
27
L. Istokpoga
70
Arcadia
70
Okeechobee
710
To
Sarasota
*Brighton
Indian
Reservation*
78
98
441
*Lake
Okeechobee*
Port
Mayaca
Gatorama
29
Ortona
Mounds
27
Moore
Haven *Moore Haven Lock*
Canal Point
Pahokee
78
Ortona Lock
*Clewiston
Inn*
To Punta Gorda
La Belle
80
Ortona
Clewiston Torry Island
441 80
80
Exit 141
Exit 138
South
Bay
Belle Glade
29
Miami Canal
*North New
River Canal*
82
27
75
41
Immokalee
0   10   20
N
Miles
Exit
107
*Big Cypress
Seminole Reservation*
Exit 101
EVERGLADES PKWY.
To
Ft. Lauderdale
75
Naples
75
Exit 80
(ALLIGATOR ALLEY)
29
BIG CYPRESS
NATIONAL
PRESERVE
*Miccosukee
Indian
Reservation*
41

▲ Camping
🕱 Picnic Area
★ Point of Interest

© The Countryman Press

THE PEACE RIVER VALLEY:
HARDEE AND DESOTO COUNTIES

A crucial chapter of Florida's frontier history played out along the Peace River. As the northernmost border of the Indian Territory, **Arcadia** earned a reputation in the 1800s as the rowdiest city in Florida, a frontier outpost where shootouts between cattle ranchers and cattle rustlers happened as a matter of course. The arrival of the Florida Southern Railroad through town created an economic boom that led to a thriving downtown through the 1920s. Lined with architectural marvels, the 58-block historic district has more than 370 buildings and homes on the National Register of Historic Places. Downtown is one of Florida's top destinations for antiques shoppers, where you can easily spend a day or two browsing the shops. While rustlers are no longer the problem they were, ranching and other agricultural interests remain the heart of DeSoto County's economy, with Ben Hill Griffin and more than a dozen other ranchers holding hundreds of thousands of acres in the region.

Farther north on the Peace River, **Wauchula,** Seminole for "cry of the sand-hill crane," is the county seat of Hardee County, and **Zolfo Springs** was an important crossroads for cattle drovers moving herds from interior ranchlands to the coast. **Bowling Green** started as a trading post that marked the northern extent of Seminole lands.

GUIDANCE The **DeSoto County Chamber of Commerce** (863-494-4033; www.desotochamber.net), 16 S Volusia Ave, Arcadia, and downtown merchants association have a small visitors center adjacent to a public park near the railroad depot. **Hardee County Chamber of Commerce** (863-773-6967; www.hardee cc.com), 225 E Main St, Wauchula, offers information on this rural county's attractions.

GETTING THERE *By car:* **US 17** links together the cities of this region, which sit 20 to 30 miles east of I-75. At least four exits along the interstate lead to Arcadia, so you won't miss it!

By air: **Sarasota Bradenton International Airport** (see *The Cultural Coast*) is the nearest major airport.

GETTING AROUND A car is essential for getting around this region, but 24-hour taxi service is available through **Peace River Cab** (863-491-7433).

MEDICAL EMERGENCIES For emergencies head to **DeSoto Memorial Hospital** (863-494-8401), 888 N Robert Ave, Arcadia.

PUBLIC REST ROOMS In Arcadia, you'll find them at the edge of the antiques district at the corner of DeSoto and Oak, behind the pavilion.

PUBLIC PARKING You'll find free street parking and surface lots in Arcadia, and some free and metered street parking in Wauchula near the restaurants.

✳ To See

ART GALLERIES

Arcadia
For evocative paintings of Florida landscapes and wildlife, visit **Debra Hollingsworth Galleries** (863-990-2800; www.debrahollingsworthgalleries .com), 4481 NE US 17. A fifth-generation Florida native, Debra reveals the soul of the land through her art.

Ona
You have to see it to believe it—**Solomon's Castle** (863-494-6077), 4533 Solomon Rd, isn't just a rambling medieval pastiche complete with a replica of a 17th-century Spanish galleon, it's a collection of galleries and the home of sculptor Howard Solomon. Well off the beaten path, this unique little kingdom sits along the splendor of Horse Creek. Stroll the castle and marvel at more than 80 interpretive stained-glass windows, or relax in the shadowy interior of the Boat in the Moat and enjoy some home-style cooking. Open 11–4 except Mon; closed Jul–Sep. Adults $10, children under 12 $4.

DOWNTOWN ARCADIA

Sandra Friend

HISTORIC SITES

Arcadia
With a 58-block historic district, there are many architectural marvels to explore on foot in downtown Arcadia, including the original **1883 Post Office** and the old **Opera House.** Stop in at Wheeler's Cafe (see *Eating Out*) to peruse photos and clippings that help interpret the town's long history.

At **Paynes Creek Historic State Park** (see *Parks*), a significant chapter in Florida history unfolded in 1849 when the federal government built a trading post on
the northern boundary of the Seminole Reservation on a creek that marked the
land boundary. Several months after the trading post opened, on July 17, 1849,
five Seminoles—one of whom was outlawed by his tribe—opened fire on the
trading post. Captain George S. Payne, Dempsey Whiddon, and William McCul-
lough were shot, and Payne and Whiddon died. Despite attempts by the tribes
to appease the U.S. Government, the incident sparked immediate conflict. With
ground broken in October 1849, **Fort Chokonikla** was the first fort built, and
the nearby creek was named for the captain killed at the trading post. Remains of
the fort and a memorial to the fallen soldiers are an integral part of this park.

Wauchula
Wauchula's historic downtown district is primarily made up of commercial buildings and the old **City Hall** across from The Quilter's Inn (see *Lodging*).

MUSEUMS At Pioneer Park (see *Parks*), the **Cracker Trail Museum** (863-735-
0119), 2822 Museum Dr, Zolfo Springs, showcases elements of the region's long
history, from prehistoric bones found in the Peace River to an adze used to kill a
Florida panther that attacked a pioneer's child back in the early 1800s. Artifacts
in the museum and adjacent barn bring to life pioneer hardships during the
post-statehood settlement of Florida—walk through an actual pioneer cabin and
poke around the blacksmith shop. Open 9–5:30 Tue–Sat. Donations appreciated.

RAILROADIANA Historic **railroad depots** sit in both downtown Arcadia and
Wauchula, and you'll find a **1914 Baldwin steam engine** (Engine #3) at the
front corner of Pioneer Park (see *Parks*) in front of the Cracker Trail Museum
(see *Museums*). It was used during the heyday of cypress logging along the Peace
River Valley.

RODEO The **All-Florida Championship Rodeo** (1-800-749-7633; www.arcadia
rodeo.com), Arcadia, dates from 1929 and is the state's oldest rodeo association
in the middle of cattle country. Where better to watch the cowmen at play?
Competitive events include bull rid-
ing, bareback riding, barrel racing,
saddle bronc, steer wrestling, and tie-
down roping. See a frontier shootout,
and watch the quadrille—best described as "square dancing on horseback." Performances begin 2 PM each
day of the event. Tickets are available
in advance or at the box office after
11 AM. The rodeo, a nonprofit event
that benefits the region, is presented
in May, July 4, and each fall.

THE CRACKER TRAIL MUSEUM
Sandra Friend

WILDLIFE REHAB A sanctuary for injured and orphaned wildlife, the **Hardee County Animal Refuge** (863-735-0330) can be found along the Peace River in the northwest corner of Pioneer Park (see *Parks*), Zolfo Springs. Visitors walk an elevated boardwalk to view the permanent refuge residents in a natural river hammock habitat. Open 10–4 daily except Wed. Fee.

Animals of a different stripe roam the enclosures at **Peace River Ranch & Refuge** (863-735-0804; www.peaceriverrefuge.org), 2545 Stoner Lane, Zolfo Springs. Here, abandoned exotics are cared for, from African servals to tigers and lynx; you'll find black bears and other large native mammals as well. The sanctuary is open to the public, but tours must be scheduled via appointment, either by phone or through their web site. Donations appreciated.

✳ To Do

BIRDING Watch for red-cockaded woodpeckers in the longleaf pine forests of **Deep Creek Preserve** (see *Wild Places*), and for wading birds along the shoreline of the Peace River and Paynes Creek at **Paynes Creek Historic State Park** (see *Parks*). I saw several osprey nests while walking along the river at **Pioneer Park** (see *Parks*).

BOATING **DeSoto Marina** is part of the complex at the Nav-A-Gator Grill (see *Eating Out*) in Lake Suzy, offering dockage ($4 per foot weekly, $8 per foot monthly, or $25/night) for cruisers coming up the Peace River; no live-aboards. Services include groceries, ice, bait, tackle, boat parts and supplies, the restaurant, cottages for rent, and kayak rentals. You can also charter a boat and captain; call for details.

DIVING **DeSoto Divers** (863-990-7425; www.desotodivers.cc), P.O. Box 1374, Arcadia 34265, offers courses from junior scuba through dive master as well as first aid and CPR.

ECOTOURS See the wild shorelines of the Peace River on **Nav-A-Gator Riverboat Tours** (1-800-308-7506; www.nav-a-gator.com), 9700 SW Riverview Cir, Lake Suzy, where you're virtually guaranteed to spot osprey, alligators, and wood storks. Pontoon boat trips ($20–23, including lunch) depart from the dock behind the Nav-A-Gator Grill; reservations required. Kayak and canoe tours offered, too.

FISHING Let Capt. Kirk guide you flats fishing on a 23-foot skiff (seats four) out in Charlotte Harbor. Book a trip through **DeSoto Marina** at the Nav-A-Gator Grill (see *Eating Out*), either $65 per person for half day, or a full boat charter for $250 half day, $450 full day.

FOSSIL HUNTING In the summer, the **Peace River** dries up, exposing countless fossils of prehistoric creatures buried in the creek beds. Bring a trowel or mattock to poke around for large shark's teeth, mammoth molars, and more. However, Florida archeological laws prohibit the removal of prehistoric bones or Indian artifacts, so be selective!

GOLF With 36 holes (18 championship, 9 regulation, 9 par 3), **Sunnybreeze Golf Course** (1-888-663-2420), 8135 SW Sunnybreeze Rd (off US 17), halfway between Zolfo Springs and Arcadia, provides a challenge for golfers of all experience levels. A fully covered driving range and pro shop round out the facility, which also offers greenside dining at the Veranda Grill, with lunch daily and dinner on Tue and Fri.

PADDLING Starting at the Fort Meade Outdoor Recreation Area in Polk County, north of Bowling Green, the 67-mile **Peace River Canoe Trail** provides a serene multiday journey down a slow-moving tannic river with sand bluffs, floodplain forests, and dense pine forests. Contact the Canoe Outpost for shuttles; the state Office of Greenways and Trails (850-245-2052 or 1-877-822-5208; www.dep.state .fl.us/gwt) can provide specific details and a map of the route. Check in with Becky at **Canoe Outpost–Peace River** (1-800-268-0083; www.canoeoutpost.com) to arrange a one- or two-day float down this majestic wilderness waterway, where towering cypresses and moss-draped live oaks line the shores. In addition to owning a large piece of riverfront property open to overnight camping, Canoe Outpost has two locations—upriver at Gardner, 855 River Rd, or downriver at Arcadia, 2816 NW CR 661. Now in their third generation of river rats, these are Floridians you can trust to show off one of the state's most beautiful rivers. Guided trips available, or simply rent and arrange a drop-off or pickup.

DeSoto Marina at the Nav-A-Gator Grill (see *Eating Out*) offers canoe and kayak rentals—$25 for up to four hours, $40 for a day. Head out on the river and explore, but return to dock by 4:30 PM. Guided trips available.

SCENIC DRIVES Follow the Peace River (and the route of Hurricane Charley) along **US 17,** a scenic highway that leads you up the entire Peace River Valley from Punta Gorda (its southern terminus) north through Arcadia, Zolfo Springs, Wauchula, and Bowling Green. Between the towns, you'll enjoy the pastoral cattle-ranch scenery.

TRAIL RIDING Hit the trails with **Ride-A-While Horseback Riding** (863-494-1946), CR 661A, Arcadia.

✳ Green Space
PARKS

Bowling Green
Protecting the confluence of the Peace River and Paynes Creek as well as an important historic site from the Second Seminole War, **Paynes Creek Historic State Park** (863-375-4717;

ALONG THE PEACE RIVER, ARCADIA
Sandra Friend

www.floridastateparks.org/paynescreek), 888 Lake Branch Rd, has several miles of pleasant hiking trails, a large picnic area with playground, and canoe launch to reach the Peace River. A visitors center (open 9–5 daily) interprets the significance of this site as it relates to the Seminole Wars. Fee.

Zolfo Springs

An expansive green space along the upper Peace River, **Pioneer Park** (863-735-0330), at the corner of US 17 and FL 64, has riverside picnic tables; a playground; a pleasant, shady campground (see *Campgrounds*); and a village of historic buildings surrounding the Cracker Trail Museum (see *Museums*). This is the regional venue for large outdoor events, and you can expect to find a flea market going on here most weekends. In March, crowds gather for Pioneer Park Days (see *Special Events*) to celebrate the region's past.

WILD PLACES A place for a quiet hike, **Deep Creek Preserve** (941-475-0769), just off King's Highway in Lake Suzy on the way to the Nav-A-Gator Grill (see *Eating Out*), protects more than 2,000 acres along the Peace River and its tributaries. Multiuse forest roads wind through the preserve to provide a network of trails.

Nearby, **R.V. Griffin Reserve** (1-800-423-1476), CR 769 N, was saved from becoming a "planned community" in the early 1990s. This wilderness area encompasses 374 acres of pine flatwoods, prairies, and marshes, with 22 miles of multiuse trails. A 303-acre reservoir on the property exists to hold water for regional use during the months when the Peace River dries up.

✳ Lodging

BED & BREAKFASTS

Arcadia 34266

Built in the late 1890s by one of Florida's first cattle barons, the **Historic Parker House** (863-494-1060 or 1-800-969-2499; www.historic parker-house.com), 427 W Hickory St, is a true Florida treasure. The Victorian rooms are immense, and owners Kay and Leonard Higley showcase the period with elegant furnishings. Enjoy a large screened veranda and the formal living room in addition to your own room or suite ($75–105).

Wauchula 33873

& If you're an obsessive quilter like some of my friends, then your next destination should be **The Quilter's Inn** (863-767-8989 or 1-877-664-8989; www.thequiltersinn.com), 106 S

Fourth Ave. Inside this 1925 bungalow, proprietor Pattie Detwiler (an avid quilter) displays her handiwork in all five guest rooms ($90–125). Each room features welcoming decor and is uniquely appointed with period antiques. The inn is also home to the Patchwork Café (see *Eating Out*).

CAMPGROUNDS

Arcadia 34266

Bluegrass reigns supreme at **Craig's RV Park** (863-494-1820; www .craigsrv.com), 7895 NE US 17, a gathering place for campers who like a little pickin' and grinnin'. Home of the Bluegrass Family Gathering, it's also a pleasant, sunny, family-owned campground with daily rates of $25, monthly $340. The back section of the park is where the music happens.

A favorite with snowbirds, **Little Willies RV Resort** (863-494-2717 or 1-800-222-7675), 5905 NE Old US 17, offers sunny grassy sites, full hookups, a clubhouse with scheduled activities, and a massive swimming pool. Open to RV and trailers only, $30/day or $180/week.

Families flock to the **Peace River Campground** (863-494-9693 or 1-800-559-4011; www.peacerivercampground.com), 2998 NW FL 70, which was set under a shady canopy of live oaks until Hurricane Charley came along. It'll take a while for the trees to recover, but they're still there—and so are the throngs who love this campground, especially tent campers. Primitive (no hookup) tent sites $28, water and electric $33, full hookup $37. Weekly and monthly rates available.

Lake Suzy 34266
✿ With frontage right on the Peace River, the **Riverside RV Resort & Campground** (863-993-2111 or 1-800-795-9733; www.riversidervresort.com), 9770 SW CR 769, is a very appealing destination for snowbirds and weekenders alike. Choose from shady or sunny sites, kick back at the pool and relax in the hot tub, or fish from the docks. There is boat trailer parking available and a boat ramp to slip your craft into the river. In-season daily rates for full hookup run $30–42; tent sites available Apr 1–Sep 30 for $26–30.

Zolfo Springs 33890
✿ Camp amid history at **Pioneer Park** (see *Parks*), where the cypresses and palms that shade your space watched as Seminoles camped here long ago. Most of the campsites overlook the wild beauty of the Peace

River. Rates $7 without electric, $11 with electric; includes bathhouse with showers. Pets permitted, but they must be leashed.

HOTELS, MOTELS, AND RESORTS

Arcadia 34266
♿ At the **Best Western Arcadia Inn** (863-494-4884 or 1-877-886-0797), 504 S Brevard Ave, enjoy newly remodeled rooms just a couple of blocks away from the antiques district. Each room ($59–189) comes with a mini fridge, microwave, and coffeemaker. You'll find me out back reading or swimming—the little oasis around the heated pool is a great getaway.

✳ Where to Eat
EATING OUT

Arcadia
Set in the pretty pink Koch Arcade from 1926, the **Arcadia Tea Room** (863-494-2424), 117 W Oak St, offers lunch daily (except Mon)—and not just little tea sandwiches, either. Try a one-third-pound sirloin burger, hot pastrami, Reuben, or a tasty vine-ripened tomato stuffed with seafood salad ($5–7). Top it off with a fresh-baked slice of apple pie.

🦞 Since 1929, **Wheeler's Cafe** (863-993-1555), 13 S Monroe Ave, has been the place where the locals eat, and when my friend Becky took me there, we sat right down with some folks we'd never met before—a first for me in an American restaurant! Great conservation ensued, and the food was pure Southern. When the café opened, a meal cost 35 cents, and dinner specials are still a bargain at under $6, including roast beef, ham steak, fried catfish, and more, with home-style sides. A hearty breakfast costs only a few bucks and is served up in minutes. Leave room for their "world-famous" peanut butter pie. Serves breakfast and lunch daily, dinner on weekends.

Lake Suzy

🐾 Now here's a place with real Florida character (*and* characters)—the **Nav-A-Gator Grill** (941-627-3474), 9700 SW Riverview Cir. It's a good old-fashioned fish camp that's a launch point for fishing, kayaking, ecotours, and more, but most folks come here for the food. Their grouper sandwiches are legendary, and local favorites such as sweet potato fries and swamp cabbage are not to be missed. Seafood baskets run $7–11, sandwiches $4–8, and dinners $12–25. Smokers (and those enjoying a beer) tend to gather 'round the fire ring out back, where you might catch someone strumming on a banjo or guitar. Walk back to the gift shop and the little museum—it's full of artifacts, from beads to pottery shards and bones, found on the bottom of the Peace River.

Nocatee

A beautiful mural of the Peace River covers one wall of **Allman's Plantation Restaurant** (863-494-9910), 4135 SW US 17, a family restaurant that offers wholesome family entertainment every weekend. Buffet $11, steaks and chops $8–21, early-bird dinners (served 11–4) $8–10.

Wauchula

An appealing choice along US 17, **The Bread Board Restaurant** (863-773-2337), 902 US 17 S, offers good comfort food like country fried steak and catfish, and tasty Southern treats like fried green tomatoes and fried eggplant sticks. Lunch and dinner, $4–13.

Housed in the old Florida Hotel, the **Main Street Pub** (863-773-6246), 222 W Main St, evokes the past with mirrors from the old hotel and interesting advertising art on the walls. The menu includes local specialties such as Paynes Creek Chicken (topped with grilled onions and mushrooms, bacon, and provolone) and the Main Street Sirloin. Lunch and dinner, $6–12.

Patchwork Café at the Quilter's Inn (863-773-5709), 106 S Fourth Ave. If you stay at The Quilter's Inn (see *Lodging*), enjoy a gourmet-style breakfast ($2–5)—featuring goodies such as Pattie's blueberry French toast and spicy hot pepper scrambled eggs—in this little corner of the inn. If you're just passing through, stop by anyway! There's plenty of room to relax on the patio and savor a chicken almond salad or a turkey Reuben ($4–6) for lunch.

Zolfo Springs

Stop for Southern basics such as catfish, steak, and shrimp at the **Pioneer Restaurant** (863-735-0726), 2902 US 17, just across from Pioneer Park. Sandwiches $2–3, dinners $4–10. Open daily for breakfast, lunch, and dinner; no credit cards.

A giant rooster tops **Rooster's** (863-735-2322), corner School House Rd and FL 66, so you won't miss it from the road. Good, filling country breakfasts (under $5), an ice cream counter, and Southern selections for dinner.

BAKERIES, COFFEE SHOPS, AND SODA FOUNTAINS

Arcadia

For cool treats downtown, head for the famous **Hot Fudge Shoppe** (863-494-6633), 13 S Polk Ave, where they make their own ice cream on the premises.

✳ Selected Shopping

Arcadia

A 1954 Coca-Cola sign dominates the wall at **Abigail's Antiques & Collectibles** (863-494-1434), 24 W Oak St, and it's for sale—along with a spectrum of vintage glassware, classic sheet music, costume jewelry, furniture, and much more.

Antiques & Books (863-491-0250), 23 W Oak St, offers browsers books, books, and more books, including a fine little cache of antiquarian titles and classic comics.

I saw some very appealing cedar chests at **Antiques on Oak** (863-494-2038), 132 W Oak St, where unique furnishings are just a part of the setting—look for Tiffany lamps, cookie jars, and fine glassware, too.

Appleberries Country Store (863-491-8884; www.appleberries.com), 207 Oak St, has a great mix of new and old, with primitive handcrafted furniture, country decor items, wreaths, and lotions.

British chintz floral plates are one of the unique items at **Barta & Herold Antiques & Design** (863-494-4477), 8 W Oak St, where you'll also en-counter Vaseline glass, radios, and upscale china cabinets.

Check out the cheery Christmas corner in the back of **Cherry Hill Antiques** (863-993-2344; www.CherryHillAntiques.com), 120 W Oak St, and a collection of beer steins in the front of the store. Many of their items can be viewed (and purchased!) online.

Housed in the historic Dozier's Department Store, **Isabelle's Fine Antiques** (863-491-1004), 104 W Oak St, has a little bit of everything, from postcards to printer's trays, wooden rolling pins, a root beer barrel, and a back room full of books.

One of the busiest mini malls in Arcadia, **Mary's Attic** (863-993-3538), 12 W Oak St, is chock-full of dealer booths showcasing collectibles, dishes, silver, primitives, and, in booth 33, a nice selection of antique rods and reels.

Collectors of albums and stereoscopes should pop into **Noah's Antiques** (863-491-7053), 6 W Oak St, where you'll find fine furniture and vintage glassware in the booths as well.

Oak Leaf Antiques & Collectibles (863-491-5044), 101 W Oak St, offers dealer booths with upscale items such as intarsia trays, a sterling silver tea server, classy quilts, and unforgettable Florida scenes by the Highwayman artists.

The upper floor of the landmark **Old Opera House,** circa 1920, is home to **Pyewackets** (863-494-3006), 106 W Oak St, a real treat—the old-time cinema is chock-full of antiques. Most are for sale, but some aren't, as many constitute a museum dedicated to the heyday of this film house. Browse through incredible collectibles, such as a Zoltan vintage fortune-teller machine (which *is* for sale), original movie posters (which aren't), and a whole room themed and maintained by the "phantom of the opera." The dealer booths and unique movie-history ephemera offer hours of browsing.

Duck inside **Treasure Alley** (863-993-1838), 122 W Oak St, to keep cool and browse their interesting mix of items, including military uniforms, mink stoles, and fishing rods.

A feminine display of Victoriana, **The Vintage Garden** (863-494-3555), 14 W Oak St, has classic cottage decor, plus vintage dresses and hats, purses, and costume jewelry.

PRODUCE STANDS, FARMER'S MARKETS, SEAFOOD MARKETS, AND U-PICK Along US 17, watch for roadside stands with fresh seafood and local produce. Among those I noted on my journey, the **Purple Pompano,** a fish market in Nocatee, seemed pretty busy, as did **Susie's Produce,** a roadside stand nearby. In Wauchula, it's hard to miss **Sandy's Big Tree Produce** (863-767-0868), 906 S Sixth Ave, for some of the region's freshest veggies and fruit.

✳ Special Events

February–March: One week, 120 miles, all on horseback: The **Florida Cracker Trail Ride** (www.cracker trail.org) harkens back to the day when Florida's cattle drovers moved their herds down the Peace River Valley to Punta Rassa. To draw attention to Florida's cattle heritage, members of the Florida Cracker Trail Association ride 15 to 20 miles each

day on "The Big Ride" from Bradenton to Fort Pierce. Catch the cowmen at Pioneer Park (see *Parks*) or at any of their stopping points on FL 64, US 98, or FL 68 along the route.

March: **Pioneer Park Days** (863-773-2161), at Pioneer Park, Zolfo Springs. Celebrate the region's rich history with pioneer craft demonstrations, country entertainment, good church food, and the fourth largest gathering of antique engines in the United States. Held the first weekend of the month; $2/day or $5 for a five-day pass.

Cracker Heritage Festival (863-767-0330), Wauchula, midmonth. Held on a Saturday by Main Street Wauchula, this festival focuses on regional heritage. Enjoy a pancake breakfast or barbecue lunch, Florida Cracker crafts, kids' activities, musical entertainment, and both silent and live auctions.

All-Florida Championship Rodeo, Arcadia (see *Rodeo*).

May: **Watermelon Festival,** Arcadia. Includes plenty of watermelon eating, seed spitting contests, and the crowning of the Watermelon Queen, as well as a Sugar Babes contest.

July: All-Florida Championship Rodeo, Arcadia (see *Rodeo*).

CENTRAL HIGHLANDS

Upon entering Highlands County you will know immediately that you are somewhere different, somewhere special. In a region full of down-home hospitality, you can enjoy art, culture, and history, along with vast natural areas. Drive along rolling hills and valleys, past orange groves, herds of cattle, life-size murals, and colorful caladium fields. Discover the county's 95 crystal-clear lakes—a favorite of anglers—bask on the sandy beaches, or take a hike through the many natural parklands. And for those seeking higher-adrenaline sports, there's even Le Mans racing.

Highlands County is located in the heart of the state, away from the coastal hustle and bustle, but within an easy two-hour commute to both coasts and the Orlando park attractions. This area has been long known to geologists as the southern portion of the Lake Wales Ridge, rising 200 feet above sea level. It is one of North America's oldest land forms and home to many of the oldest living lakes in North America. Highlands County separated from DeSoto County in 1921, adopting its name from the dominating topography. Long known as a retirement destination for seniors, the Norman Rockwell–type towns have recently seen an influx of young residents looking for affordable Florida housing. Three distinct communities divide the county: Avon Park, Lake Wales, and Sebring. The small township of **Lorida,** which means "flowery," is located just east of Sebring along Lake Istokpoga on FL 98.

At the north end of Highlands County sits **Avon Park.** Settled in 1884 by Oliver Martin Crosby, incorporated as a town in 1886, and incorporated as a city in 1926, the land reminded English settlers of Stratford-on-Avon, England. Known as the "City of Charm," the town is home to Lake Tulane, the oldest living lake in North America. From the 1940s through the 1980s, the board game checkers was a major-league sport, and you'll surely see some of the locals still playing today at the first "checker shelter," built during the 1940s and 1950s. Located in Veterans Square on the Mall on Main Street, the shelter honors veterans from World War I, World War II, and Vietnam. Avon Park is also home to South Florida Community College.

At the other end of the county, you'll find **Lake Placid,** the "Caladium Capital of the World." From July through October, there are acres of red and pink caladium fields exploding into color around town and off CR 621. The town is

BASS-FISHING MURAL, LAKE PLACID

also home to the largest collection of murals in Florida, with 40 murals depicting local history, flora, and fauna, which is why this town is also known as "The Town of Murals."

On a winter vacation, Dr. Melvil Dewey, creator of the Dewey Decimal System, visited the town of Lake Sterns and found it very similar to Lake Placid, New York. In 1927 he decided to settle here and had the town named Lake Placid. A mural depicting Dr. Dewey can be seen on Interlake Boulevard. (See *Murals.*)

In 1911, Ohio pottery magnate George E. Sebring went on a fishing trip and was captivated by the area around Lake Jackson (then known as Lake Hare). He soon bought 9,000 acres of palmetto-covered prairie as the location for his dream city. Naming the town **Sebring** after his hometown of Sebring, Ohio, he developed it to resemble a wheel, with the town center branching off in six spokelike streets from a small central park. A devout Christian, Mr. Sebring offered free land to any church that would establish itself, and by 1912 the town was officially founded. In keeping with his parklike vision, developers were instructed to plant a citrus tree in each residential lot. As the county seat, Sebring is said by some to be modeled after the ancient Syrian city of Heliopolis.

Sebring was also home to Hendricks Field, a military training base that housed B-17s gearing up for World War II. When sports-car enthusiast Alec Ulman flew into the airport in 1950, he thought it would make a great racetrack, and in 1952 the first sports-car endurance race, the 12 Hours of Sebring, was held. Today the Sebring Race Track is home to several American Le Mans endurance races.

GUIDANCE For more information about the area, contact **The Convention and Visitors Bureau of Highlands County, Inc.** (863-386-1316 or 1-800-255-1711; www.highlandscvb.com), P.O. Box 2001, Sebring 33871; or the **Greater Lake Placid Chamber of Commerce, Inc.** (863-465-4331 or 1-800-557-5224; www.lpfla.com), 18 N Oak St, Lake Placid.

GETTING THERE *By car:* **US 27** runs through the heart of the county. From Orlando or Tampa take US 4 to US 27 south; from Miami take US 95 north to Fort Lauderdale, then US 75 west to US 27 north; from West Palm Beach take FL 441 west to Belle Glade, CR 80 south to South Bay, and then US 27 north. Highlands County is a one- to two-hour drive from Central or South Florida.

By air: The major airports in the area are the **Greater Orlando International Airport** (407-825-2001; www.state.fl.us/goaa/ or www.orlandoairports.net), **Tampa International Airport** (see *Tampa and Hillsborough County*), and the **West Palm Beach Airport** (561-471-7420; www.pbia.org).

By rail: **AMTRAK** (1-800-872-7245; www.amtrak.com) provides regularly scheduled service to Sebring.

GETTING AROUND US 27 runs through the county from north to south, with several country roads branching off to the east and west.

MEDICAL EMERGENCIES For emergencies head to the **Florida Hospital Heartland Medical Center** (863-314-4466), 4200 Sun 'n Lake Blvd, Sebring, or **Florida Hospital Heartland Medical Center** (863-465-3777), 1200 US 27 N, Lake Placid.

PUBLIC PARKING Free parking can be found throughout the county.

✳ To See

CALADIUMS More than 90 percent of the world's caladium bulbs are grown in the Lake Placid area, and the annual Caladium Festival (see *Special Events*) in August draws more than one hundred thousand visitors each year. Throughout Lake Placid you will notice caladiums planted everywhere. Best viewed between July and October, fields of these large leafy plants can be seen on CR 621, as landscaping in residents' yards, on murals (see *Murals*), and even on trash cans! Bulbs can be purchased at the festival or through **Happiness Farms** (863-465-0044 or 1-866-892-0396; www.happinessfarms.com), 704 CR 621 E.

HISTORIC SITES

Avon Park
The **Union Congregational Church,** N Forest Ave, was built in 1892 on land donated by Avon Park founders Mr. and Mrs. O. M. Crosby. Previously founded as the Evangelical Church, the name was changed to Congregational in 1926.

The second oldest church in Avon Park is the **Episcopal Church of the Redeemer,** E Pleasant St, circa 1894. It was built with the assistance of the Diocese of Florida for communicants of the Church of England.

The **Bandstand** and a **Time Capsule** are located on Main St between Lake Ave and Forest Ave. The Bandstand was built in 1897 and previously stood in front of the Hotel Verona. The marble column Time Capsule was sealed in 1912 and is scheduled for opening in 2085.

Jacaranda Hotel opened during the roaring '20s in 1926. A place for high-class entertainment and good food, the hotel still serves up Southern hospitality (see *Dining Out*). The

HISTORIC TRAIN STATION, SEBRING

Kathy Wolf

Revivalist-style hotel is named after the Jacaranda tree that used to sit in its footprint.

Veterans Square on the Mall on Main Street honors veterans of World War I, World War II, and Vietnam. This is also where you will find the first "checker shelter."

The former **Seaboard Air Line Depot** is now home to the Avon Park Depot Museum (see *Museums*). The depot, built in 1926, was in service until 1978.

Lake Placid

On US 27 you'll find the **Lake Placid Tower.** When this local landmark was built in 1961, it was the world's tallest concrete block tower. Also known as the Tower of Peace and Happiness Tower, the tower reaches a height of 270 feet and can be seen from all over the county. Climb up to the "Eagle's Nest" to view a million acres of lakes, caladium fields, and citrus-covered hillsides.

Sebring

The Sebring City on the Circle 1920s town center houses many original buildings from the era. Currently being renovated for office and meeting space, the **E. L. Hainz Bloc Building,** circa 1923, housed the first county courtroom.

Edward L. Hainz house, located on 155 W Center Ave, is a fine example of an "airplane" or "camel back" bungalow.

The Mediterranean Revival–style **Tobin Building** (circa 1926), 101 S Circle Dr, was built as a commercial building during the great Florida land boom.

One of the oldest surviving commercial buildings can be seen at 113 S Circle. Built in 1913, it has been radically altered from the original, but it's still a significant historic structure.

Take particular note of the concave facades on the **J. B. Brown Building,** 201–207 S Circle Dr. Built in 1922, the structure housed a hardware store owned by one Jesse B. Brown.

The 1915 **Thomas Whitehouse Building,** 313 S Circle Dr, was built as a dry goods store, grocery, and hotel.

Just off the circle at 590 S Commerce Ave, you'll find the **Highlands County Courthouse.** The Classic Revival–style (circa 1927) building, designed by Fred Bishop, is Florida's oldest courthouse still being used as a courthouse today.

The **Nan-Ces-O-Wee Hotel** (circa 1923), 133 N Ridgewood Dr, the largest surviving commercial building in downtown Sebring, is said to be named after an Indian Princess. Sebring's first Jewish immigrants, Mike and Sadie Kahn, emigrated from Lithuania in 1921 and opened Kahn's Department Store on the ground floor of the hotel. In the 1960s the Kahn's created a Jewish cemetery by purchasing one hundred contiguous gravesites from the municipal cemetery. A time capsule in neighboring **Sadie Kahn Park** was sealed in 1923. Several Kahn descendants still reside in Sebring.

Not far from town center, on the corner of S Commerce and Eucalyptus, the 1930s **Stepping Stones Girl Scout Log Cabin** reminded me of the same structure I went to when I was in Girl Scouts back in Maine.

MURALS The **Town of Murals,** Lake Placid, has 40 murals represented on more than 27,000 painted square feet. More than 10 years ago, Bob and Harriet Porter brought together local artists to create the mural program, which is now copied by towns all over Florida. One of the finest examples is located on the side of Winn Dixie at US 27 and CR 621. The 175-foot-wide *Cracker Trail Cattle Drive* showcases the cattle drives of the area, both visually and with "ranch roundup" sound. Kids will enjoy the grunting of bears and buzzing of bees at *The Lost Bear Cub* mural on Inter-

Kathy Wolf

ON THE "MURALS OF LAKE PLACID" TOUR

lake Blvd. Each mural has secrets to discover. On the *Rare Resident–Florida Panther* mural on W Park Ave you'll want to look for the hidden kitten, owl, dragonfly, lizard, and tree frog. Down the street, next to the Lake Placid Histori-cal Museum, find the word *hello* on the *Train Depot* mural. At the Chamber of Commerce Welcome Center on N Oak St you can pick up a walking-tour guide ($3), which provides local history, artist biographies, and many tips on locating the hidden treasures on each mural. For more information about the murals, call the **Greater Lake Placid Mural Society** at 863-531-0211.

You can't help but notice the unique **trash containers** around town. Local artists again pooled their talents and created 15 receptacles as companion pieces to the murals. When you pull the handle on the *Clown* container, a clown pops up. Look for others, such as *Barn, Fishing Shack, Comic School Bus, 1927 Chrysler,* and the beautifully detailed *Caladium* container.

The town is always coming up with new creative projects. The newest venture are brightly colored **clowns** sitting on benches or leaning against fences at the RMCA Daycare Center on E Interlake Blvd and throughout Lake Placid. These full-size placards represent some of the clown graduates from Toby's clown school.

MUSEUMS

Avon Park
Avon Park Depot Museum (863-453-3525), 3 N Museum Ave. The pioneer spirit is beautifully displayed inside this former Seaboard Coastline railroad sta-tion (circa 1926). Walk through several rooms of history, including a colorful showcase of traditional Seminole dress. Prominently displayed is the novel *The Girl Who Loved Tom Gordon* by Steven King, loosely based on the New York Yankees' Tom (Flash) Gordon, a graduate of Avon Park High School. Make sure to pick up a copy of *Yesterday, A Family Album of Highlands County* by Elaine and Larry Levey. I was lucky enough to be accompanied by both of these knowl-edgeable authors for several days while they showed me the hot spots throughout

the county. You'll often find Elaine volunteering at the museum. Outside, the 1948 California Zephyr dining car is open for special functions. Open 10–2 Tue–Fri. Free; donations appreciated.

Museum of Florida Arts & Culture (863-453-6661; www.mofac.org), 600 W College Dr, on the SFCC campus. In the 1950s a small number of African American men painted Florida landscapes and sold them by the side of the road. The gorgeous renderings of the "Highwaymen" soon became highly collectible and now appear in many private collections and museums, including this one. In the concourse, you'll also find several striking murals and three-dimensional pieces by other talented Florida artists, and there is also an impressive display of Florida archeological artifacts. Free.

Lake Placid

Lake Placid Historical Museum (863-465-1771), 19 W Park Ave, is housed in the former ACL railroad depot, which is on the National Register of Historical Places. Here you'll see historic "sad" irons, Florida Indian artifacts, a linotype machine, a dress worn by Jacqueline Kennedy, and a unique collection of antique buttons artfully displayed. The history of the area is shown in photos and memorabilia. The museum is operated by the Historical Society of Lake Placid, which has been honoring their two eldest residents with the annual Pioneer Man and Pioneer Woman Award since 1982. Don't miss the museum's display of photographs of past recipients. Donation.

Toby the Clown College, Museum & Gift Shop (863-465-2920; www.tobythe clownfoundationinc.org), 112 W Interlake Blvd. "Toby" has been clowning around at local hospitals, day care centers, and birthday parties since 1980, and as a member of the World Clown Association, he will teach you all you need to know to become a clown through education and entertainment. You'll soon be worthy of performing at charitable functions and other events, or just for the fun of it. The gift shop has many clown-related items for sale. Call for hours. Donation.

Sebring

The **CCC Museum** (863-386-6094), the home of the State Civil Conservation Corps, is located at Highlands Hammock State Park (see *Parks*). In the early 1930s the Depression, a land boom bust, and two major hurricanes left Florida's economy deeply depressed. With one in four workers out of work, the CCC was created as part of President Roosevelt's New Deal during the Great Depression. Young men between 17 and 25 entering into a military lifestyle were provided an income of $30 a month, and of that $25 was sent home to their families. Days were spent planting trees, fighting fires, constructing public parks, and restoring historic structures. The "CCC Boys" also received vocational and academic instruction along with a variety of sports and recreational activities. Some of these young men later went on to become leaders in the community. The Sebring camp was the first of 86 camps established. In 1935 eight of these parks became the first Florida State Parks. All the camps were closed in 1942 due to World War II, with many enrollees joining the armed services. This building, built in the late 1930s, is now a museum housing an impressive collection of historical CCC artifacts and memorabilia. Donation.

✐ **Children's Museum of the Highlands** (863-385-5437; www.childrenmuse-umhighlands.com), 219 N Ridgewood. This nonprofit hands-on facility is one of the best children's museums I have come across. The attentive staff will help you expand your kid's creativity and exploration through the Amazing Maze, Water-works, Mini Grocery Store, Bubble Image, Doctor Scrubby's Office, WKID TV Station, Pedal Power, Note Nook, and Sebring Fire Tower. Open 10–5 Tues–Sat (until 8 on Thu). Fee.

At the **Highlands Art League & Museum** (863-385-5312; www.highlandsart league.com), 351 W Center Ave, local residents Elsa and Marvin Kahn have worked hard to make this "the village where art lives." This brightly colored artist colony, comprised of three historic homes overlooking Lake Jackson, is currently in the process of expanding. It offers many classes, contests, and shows throughout the year, including the Annual Highlands Art League Festival in November (see *Special Events*). Open 9–4 Mon–Fri. Donation.

You'll be greeted at the door by Howard Fleetwood, president of the **Military Sea Services Museum** (863-471-2386), 1402 Roseland Ave, where the Navy, Marine, and Coast Guard of the past and present are highlighted at this exten-sive military museum. Near the entrance there is an emotional exhibit that pays homage to MIAs and POWs. An empty place setting symbolizes the missing and captive who aren't home for dinner, while a wine glass is placed upside down to say, "I'm not here to toast with you."

ENTRANCE TO THE MUSEUM OF FLORIDA
ARTS & CULTURE (THE HIGHLANDS
MUSEUM OF ART)

Kathy Wolf

Then step through the watertight door, commonly found on naval ves-sels, and wander through 3,000 square feet of artifacts and memorabilia with a heavy emphasis on World War II. Mr. Fleetwood will be happy to show you items from the USS *Highlands* and discuss other historic ships and events. Named for Highlands County, this attack transport saw duty at both Iwo Jima and Okinawa. Other memorabilia include a "hook" from a Douglas A-4D used to catch the cable when landing on an air carrier, three types of shipboard bunks, and actual spikes made by Paul Revere in his foundry used to construct the USS *New Hampshire* (formerly the USS *Alabama*). Take note of a series of photographs of the USS *Ward DD-139*, the first U.S. ship to fire a shot just before Pearl Harbor. While guarding the entrance to the harbor on December 7, 1941, the *Ward* crewmen spotted a mini-submarine. The gun crew fired and sunk the sub just hours before the Japanese planes began their bombing campaign. The flag room houses a fine collection of military uniforms and flags from the three services and every state, including the rare 49-state American flag. Open 1–4 Sat. Fee.

Sebring Ridge Museum (863-402-1611), 121 N Ridgewood. Don't let the size of this small museum fool you. There is a wealth of Sebring memorabilia nestled in the ground floor of this 1920s historic building, including *Yesterday, A Family Album of Highlands County* by Elaine and Larry Levey and *The Last Great Ace: The Life of Major Thomas B. McGuire, Jr.,* a history of McGuire Air Force Base by Charles A. Martin. Intrestingly, both McGuire and Martin were raised in Sebring and attended the same high school. Another local gem that is displayed is *The Way Things Were: Short Stories of Past Experiences* by Reverend Robert J. Walker, which tells about growing up black, and *Ranch Boy* by H. Steven Robertson, a coming-of-age story told in great detail about ranch life in and around Sebring. A scale model of the town is also on display. Call for hours. Donation.

WINERY Head over to **Henscratch Farms** (863-699-2060; www.henscratch farms.com), 980 Henscratch Rd, Lake Placid, for a self-guided tour of this certi-fied "Florida Farm Winery." The 20-acre farm makes Southern-style wines from muscadine and scuppernong grapes, which are picked, crushed, fermented, and bottled right at this country winery. You can also pick up a fresh dozen of free-range eggs laid daily by their resident hens. Don't miss the annual Blueberry Festival (see *Selective Shopping* and *Special Events*). Open 9–5 Tue–Sat and noon–4 Sun.

✳ To Do

BICYCLING The sidewalk around **Lake Jackson** circles the lake for 11 miles, and there's plenty of room for bicyclists, hikers, and casual walkers. Another scenic ride is off US 27 heading west on SR 634, Hammock Rd, to **Highlands Hammock State Park.** Off-road cyclists will enjoy the loop at the **Preserve Highlands County Mountain Biking Park.** Great for beginner and experienced riders, the trails cover 1,600 acres of natural Florida wilderness. The multipurpose park is also a favorite of birders. The **Highlands County Pedalers Bicycling Club** does two 20-mile rides and two 40-100 mile-rides each week. Membership is not required to ride along. For more information call 863-382-6464.

BIRDING Keep your eyes peeled at **Avon Park Air Force Range & Wildlife Management Area,** home to the endangered red-cockaded woodpecker. To view the largest population of nesting osprey, head to **Lake Istokpoga.** Over at **Highlands Hammock State Park** (see *Parks*) and on the **Great Florida Bird-ing Trail,** you can see pileated woodpeckers, red-tailed hawks, wood storks, and little blue herons.

FISHING With 95 lakes in and around the county, there are numerous opportu-nities to fish. Contact Chuck T. Hendrix, a U.S. Coast Guard–licensed captain, at **Airboat Wildlife Adventures** (863-655-4737), Neibert's Fishing Resort,

4971 US 98, Sebring, for both fishing and wildlife viewing. Other reputable guides include Corbin Dyer at **Dyer Family Guide Service** (863-471-2656), 4811 Sturgeon Dr, Sebring; Mike and Leola Sobon at **Cypress Isle RV Park & Marina** (863-465-5241), 2 Cypress Isle Ln, Lake Placid; **Henderson's Istokpoga Fishing Resort** (863-465-2101), 35 Henderson Rd, Lake Placid; Dan Clark at **Fishy Fingers Guide Service** (863-465-8139), 210 Quail Run, Venus; and Gary Albin at **Trails End Fishing Resort** (863-655-0134), 4232 Trails End Rd, Lorida.

GOLF

Lake Placid
The former **Sun 'n Lake Country Club** has been taken over by new owners and renamed **Crystal Creek Country Club** (863-465-5303), 135 Sun 'n Lake Blvd. They welcome the general public on their 18-hole, par 64 course.

Sebring
The 18-hole, par 72, championship course at the semiprivate **Golf Hammock Country Club** (863-382-2151), 2222 Golf Hammock Dr, circles the clubhouse, allowing for frequent rest and snack stops on hot Florida days.

There are two challenging 18-hole courses at the **Sebring Spring Lake Golf & Tennis Resort** (863-655-1276), 100 Clubhouse Ln. Recent upgrades to their "old Osprey ninth hole" (a 1-acre piece known as the world's largest green) have converted it to the "World's Largest 18-Hole Putting Course," which includes sand and water hazards. It's a good courses for beginners, but there is also enough to challenge seasoned players.

Guests golf free at the **Sebring Lakeside Golf Resort,** 603 Lake Sebring Dr (see *Lodging*). The nine-hole, par 3 course is beautifully landscaped with ponds, streams, and waterfalls.

Sebring Municipal (863-314-5919) and **Harder Hall** (863-382-0500), both 18-hole, par 72 courses, are within a half mile of the Inn on the Lakes (see *Lodging*).

HIKING Several excellent hiking areas are located within Lake June-in-Winter Preserve State Park in Lake Placid (see *Parks*), Highlands Hammock State Park in Sebring (see *Parks*), and Avon Park Air Force Range & Wildlife Management Area in Avon Park (see *Wild Places*). Just east of Lorida, you can hike 9 miles of the Florida Trail in the Hickory Hammock Wildlife Management Area (see *Wild Places*).

RACING

Avon Park
Avon Park is home to the **Florida Lawnracing Association** (www.floridalawnracing.com, or call the Avon Park Chamber of Commerce at 863-453-3350), a national event that "turns a weekend chore into a competitive sport." Races with ride-on lawnmowers (blades removed) are scheduled throughout the year. The annual **NASGRASS Lawn Mower Race** is in March (see *Special Events*).

American Le Mans Series

AMERICAN LE MANS SERIES, SEBRING INTERNATIONAL RACEWAY

Sebring

Since 1952, the **Sebring International Raceway** (1-800-626-7223; www.sebringraceway.com), 113 Midway Dr, has provided fast action every March with their Twelve Hours of Sebring Endurance Race (see *Special Events*). The converted Hendricks Field, a World War II military training base, was also the site of the first Formula One race in North America in 1959. Since then, professional race car drivers, including Hollywood stars, have raced Cobras, Chapparels, Ferraris, Porches, and Ford GT40s on the 3.7-mile circuit. In 1970 Steve McQueen finished a close second to Mario Andretti. A multimillion-dollar renovation completed in 1999 added a new pit tower and media center. The Château Élan Hotel & Spa (see *Lodging*) is just off the hairpin turn.

Climb into the cockpit of a V-8–powered learning lab at the **Panoz Racing School** and **Audi Driving Experience** (1-888-282-4872; www.panozracing school.com) at Sebring International Raceway. Learn how to control understeer and oversteer skids, practice straight-line threshold braking and cornering techniques such as trail braking, and master the downshifting "heel and toe" technique. Then, take it to the track with the three-day racing program. You can even earn your SCCA license to race competitively.

SCENIC DRIVES The drive up **US 27** through rolling hills and countryside takes you through the heart of the county's three main communities of Avon Park, Lake Wales, and Sebring. You'll see acres of caladium fields in bloom during July and August all along **CR 621.**

SPAS Even if your favorite spa is near your home, the **Château Élan Spa** (863-655-6252; www.chateauelansebring.com), 150 Midway Dr, Sebring, is worth traveling the distance. And with spa packages (starting at $325) including overnight accommodations, you'll have no reason to hurry home. The Château Élan Spa uses Jurlique, a brand made from pure organic plant ingredients from Australia. These mild, natural products contain many herbs and botanicals with antioxidants to sooth and rejuvenate your skin. Try a Customized Aromatherapy Facial ($65) or Moor Mud Body Wrap ($80). The Unique Thalasso Wrapping ($75) recharges the mineral ions in the body, and this sea-based algae wrap can also be formulated for energy, balancing, or toning. Those wondering if the Hot Stone Massage ($70) really works or is just a gimmick will need to try it. First, smooth stones are heated and placed at different spots on your back and legs. Then, using the stones, aromatherapy oils are gently smoothed over your body, allowing the heat from each stone to penetrate deep into your muscles. This is good for those who need a deep massage, like those suffering from "computer shoulders," but don't want the pain of a traditional therapeutic massage. They made me a believer, and now that's my massage of choice. For exfoliations, try the Seaweed or Salt Glow ($50). Other services, such as the Spa Pedicure ($30) and Eyebrow Wax ($10) are a bargain. Treatments for men are also available. And don't forget to purchase some Jurlique rose or lavender hand cream, along with some of their other fine products. Bring your swimsuit and come early to warm up in the indoor whirlpool.

ULTRALIGHT AMPHIBIOUS AIRBOAT RIDES Have you ever wanted to fly off the water? Take to the sky in an **amphibious ultralight** with Jeff Hudson (863-382-3202) over Lake Istokpoga, where you'll soar only a few hundred feet off the water with unsurpassed views of local wildlife.

WALKING TOURS

Avon Park
The **Mile Long Mall** on Main Street extends from Lake Verona to US 27. The Mall is lined with many antiques shops shaded under a canopy of centuries-old trees. Once a single-lane road designed for the horse and buggy, the street was divided in 1920 into two parallel roads, leaving a park in the middle.

Lake Placid
Self-guided walking-tour booklets of the area's **40 colorful murals** (see *Murals*) and artistic trash cans are available throughout town. Make sure to stop at the Chamber of Commerce Welcome Center on N Oak St, where you can learn more about these murals from local guides and see original artist renderings. The booklet also provides clues to hidden objects included in the murals.

Sebring
Stroll around **Sebring Circle** and see historic buildings from the early 1900s. Center, Ridgewood, and Commerce Streets branch out from Circle Park and offer many shops to explore (see *Selective Shopping*).

✳ Green Space

NATURE CENTERS Learn more about the Lake Wales Ridge at **Archbold Biological Station** (863-465-2571), Old FL 8, Lake Placid, a working research center with a public outreach facility on-site. Stop in at the Main Building (open 8–5 Mon–Fr) to view a video and pick up interpretive information on the ½-mile nature trail that loops around the facility. Keep alert for Florida scrub jays, as they are often seen here. Free.

PARKS

Avon Park
Worth mentioning is the **Kapok Tree** located on the Main Street "Mall" in Avon Park. Normally grown in tropical climates, the 60-foot tree produces an impressive canopy in January and February. The pods on the lower part of the tree contain silklike material that was used in World War II to stuff life preservers.

Veterans Square in **Avon Park Mall** honors veterans of World War I, World War II, Korea, and Vietnam, and the names of 427 Avon Park–area men are inscribed on the monument. A star next to each name indicates those killed while in service to our country. The "checker shelter" houses a Veterans Honor Roll with nine Avon Park military veterans from World War I, World War II, and Vietnam.

Lake Placid

Preserving a large swath of the imperiled Lake Wales Ridge, **Lake June-in-Winter Preserve State Park** (863-386-6094), end of Daffodil St, lets you explore the unusual scrub habitat of the ridge on several miles of hiking trails and a short nature trail. Rare plants such as scrub plum, scrub hickory, spike moss, and scrub beargrass can be seen along the trails. Picnic table, rest room; day use only, self-pay fee.

Lorida

At **Istokpoga Park** (863-402-6812), US 98 west of Lorida, stroll the Bee Island boardwalk and cast for bass. This small park has a boat launch into Lake Istokpoga and picnic tables with grills. Free.

Sebring

Medal of Honor Park, south of Sebring off US 27 on George Blvd, showcases 18 heritage oaks and bronze plaques honoring the 18 recipients of the Congressional Medal of Honor.

CYPRESS SWAMP, HIGHLANDS HAMMOCK STATE PARK

Sandra Friend

Explore under a canopy of green in Florida's first state park, **Highlands Hammock State Park** (863-386-6094; www.floridastateparks.org), 5931 Hammock Rd. Five short interpretive trails lead you through ancient hardwood hammocks with centuries-old oak trees, along boardwalks following cypress-lined creeks and around marshy ponds, and through pine-flatwoods. Once home to the ivory-billed woodpecker, now more than half a dozen other woodpecker species can be seen throughout the park. (The ivory-billed, thought to be extinct, was recently sighted in 2004 in Cache River National Wildlife Refuge in Arkansas, giving new hope that this majestic bird may return to Florida as well. So birders, keep an eye out, and if you spot one contact the U.S. Fish and Wildlife Service.) From the Florida Parks web site you can print out a checklist of about two hundred birds that can be seen in the park, their status (abundant, common, rare), and what season you can expect to see them. The park has a large camp- ground and is especially popular for its on-site café (see *Eating Out*), which serves sour orange pie and other goodies made from fruits gathered in the forest. The **CCC Museum** (see *Museums*) relates the story of the Civilian Conservation Corps and their work in Florida, which in the 1930s helped build the backbone of what is now the Florida State Park system. Open daily 8–sundown. Fee.

WILD PLACES Encompassing more than 4,000 acres along the Kissimmee River, **Hickory Hammock Wildlife Management Area** (1-800-250-4200), along US 98 9 miles east of Lorida, is open to fishing, hunting, and hiking. A extremely scenic 9.2-mile segment of the Florida Trail passes through Hickory Hammock, with trailheads on US 98 and at the end of Bluff Hammock Road. At the south-ern end, enjoy dark hydric hammocks and a pleasant primitive campsite 3½ miles north of the trailhead. At the northern end, a lengthy boardwalk along the Kiss-immee River just south of the Bluff Hammock trailhead is well worth a visit for birding and photography.

Founded in 1941, **Avon Park Air Force Range & Wildlife Management Area** (863-452-4119; www.avonparkfr.com), in Avon Park, is comprised of 150,000 acres of mixed forests and rangeland, 32 nature trails that attract hikers and birders, and a nesting area for red-cockaded woodpeckers, Florida grass-hopper sparrows, and Florida scrub jays.

Just south of Avon Park is **Lake Tulane,** the oldest living lake in North America: It's estimated to be forty thousand years old, with the deepest layer of sediment around seventy thousand years old. Created by a sinkhole, the 70-foot-deep, crystal-clear lake covers 89 acres and has a clear, sandy bottom. Beneath that are layers of sediment reaching 60 more feet. Scientists are currently studying the lake, ideal for research, for information on what steers Earth's weather. The boat ramp for Lake Tulane is located on the west side of the lake. To get to the lake, take Anoka Avenue south from Main Street in Avon Park to Edgewood Street, and then turn left on Lakeview Boulevard and follow the road to the lake.

The 28,000-acre **Lake Istokpoga** has Florida's largest concentration of osprey nests and is world-renowned for its bass fishing. *Istokpoga* is a Native American word that means "waters of death." In the early 1900s Seminole Indians tried to cross the lake and were swallowed up by whirlpools, but today it is one of the best fishing lakes, with birds of many species and a large concentration of alliga-tors. With a shallow depth of only of 4 to 6 feet, Florida's fifth largest lake is located to the east of US 27 between Sebring and Lake Placid. Boat ramps are located just off US 98 at RV Park on Arbuckle Creek (small fee) and Istokpoga Park near Lorida.

I can't resist writing about **Lake Wolf.** The shallow, 122-acre, mucky-bottomed lake is only 2–6 feet deep, but it's a treasure as development has yet to encroach upon this little gem. To get to the boat ramp, take US 27 to Orange Blossom Boulevard, turn left, and follow the winding road to the boat ramp on the right, just off Lakeside Drive West.

✳ Lodging

CAMPGROUNDS, RV PARKS & FISH CAMPS

Lake Placid 33852

Located directly on Lake Istokpoga, **Cypress Isle RV Park & Marina** (863-465-5241; www.geocities.com/cypressislervl), 2 Cypress Isle Ln, offers tent sites (daily $15–25, weekly $90–150), and pop-ups and RV sites (daily $125–130, weekly $150–180). Each site has its own boat dock. Discounts are taken if you don't have a boat and for monthlong and full-season stays. Three fully equipped one-bedroom cabins are also available (daily $65–70, weekly $390–450). No pets.

There are no playgrounds or swimming pools at the rugged **Henderson's Istokpoga Fishing Resort** (863-465-2101), 35 Henderson Rd (off US 27 and CR 621), but serious anglers can pull in their RVs or bunk in one of the cabins for $79 a night.

Lorida 33857

Rent furnished waterfront cabins ($79–95 per day) complete with cable TV, heat and air-conditioning, full bath with linens, and well-equipped kitchen at **Trails End Fishing Resort** (863-655-0134; www.trailsendfishingresort.com), 4232 Trails End. The "wife-friendly" resort on Lake Istokpoga also offers sites for RVs ($25 per day) and doublewides $105–135 per day). Laundry room, public showers, bait and tackle store, fish cleaning room, and dockside gas are also on-site.

Sebring 33876

The casual **Neibert's Fishing Resort** (863-655-1416), 4971 US 98 on Lake Istokpoga, has sites for tents and RVs (both $20 per night), with discounts

for long-term residents. Also on-site are laundry facilities and a cocktail bar.

HOTELS, MOTELS, AND RESORTS

Avon Park 33825

In 2004 the **Jacaranda Hotel** (863-453-2211), 19 E Main St, saw its share of hurricanes, with Charley, Frances, and Jeanne crisscrossing over the county, but Avon Park is proud of its history and made sure that the 1926 Classical Revival–style hotel was completely restored. The quaint mini-suites have a separate bedroom and living area with French doors that open to the veranda ($75), and the maxi-suites have two double beds ($75). There are also cozy standard rooms with one double bed ($60). On the first floor, the lobby opens to the elegant formal dining room, where an all-you-can-eat buffet lunch (see *Dining Out*) is served, and where, from November through Mother's Day, pianist Jeff Klein plays tunes from yesteryear.

Sebring 33870

In the lobby sits a full size GTS, a specially designed car for the Panoz Racing School (see *Racing*). This should give you an indication of the high-energy atmosphere at the **Four Points by Sheraton Sebring, Château Élan Hotel & Spa** (863-655-6252; www.chateauelansebring.com), 150 Midway Dr, where the staff greet you like long-lost relatives. As the hotel is situated just off the legendary hairpin "Turn 7," you'll want to ask for a trackside room to experience all the sights and sounds of Le Mans racing without having to head over to the track. (I had to call my racing-fanatic son-in-law just to torture him.) The comfortable rooms include a heavy set of checkered drapes to block out early-morning sunshine, and the new Élan Elite rooms, on the top floor, offer a complimentary evening house cocktail, continental breakfast, extended checkout until 2 PM, refrigerators, comfy bathrobes, and 25-percent-off discounts for the gift shop, spa, and restaurant. All standard and elite rooms feature coffeemakers; satellite/cable TV featuring HBO, CNN, and ESPN; and wireless data ports. There's also a business center with quick Internet access for those who left their computers at home, and a fitness center, Jacuzzi, and outdoor pool. For a relaxing escape from fast-paced activities, check out the on-site **Château Élan Spa** (see *Spas*), and after the races, enjoy cocktails in the Hairpin Lounge or grab a bite at the **Esperante** restaurant (see *Dining Out*), located just off the lobby. Double and king rates are typically $79–169, but on race weeks rooms can go for upward to $500, depending on the event.

  Straddling Lake Jackson and Little Lake Jackson, the **Inn on the Lakes** (863-471-9400 or 1-800-531-5253; www.innonthelakessebring .com), 3100 Golfview Rd, is within walking distance to two golf courses (see *Golf*). Guest rooms ($74–99) offer double or king accommodations, most with panoramic views. The elegant suites ($99–150) have room to really stretch out, with a huge walk-in closet that would make even the fussiest diva excited. French doors open to a private balcony overlooking both lakes. When you are hungry, **Chicanes** (see *Dining Out*) serves up a fine selection of culinary delights. Relax at the beautifully landscaped lakeside pool, which has plenty of

lounge chairs to stretch out on. In the lobby, you'll find coffee ready to go each morning or when you have to leave this centrally located paradise. Pets are welcome in some rooms. I stayed here while trying to get home after a hurricane, which is not the ideal time to review a property. Still, the folks here were more than gracious, even with the hubbub of dozens of displaced families trying to do their laundry and grab a meal in the on-site restaurant. The room was just the tonic we needed for a day of rest— spacious, spotless, and classy, with a panoramic view of the pool and lake.

Listed on the National Register of Historic Places, **Kenilworth Lodge** (863-385-0111 or 1-800-423-5939; www.kenlodge.com), 836 SE Lakeview Dr, is a grand inn on a hill overlooking Lake Jackson. George Sebring, founder of this town, opened the lodge as a destination in 1916, and it's still a fascinating place to stay. The massive lobby has a grand staircase and 1950s television; one corner is taken up with a library from which you are free to borrow. The renovated-to-period elegant guest rooms in the main lodge ($70 and up) are a little small by today's standards, but they all have a premium TV and a mini fridge; the guest bathrooms are surprisingly large. There are suites (including a posh Presidential Suite) and apartments available as well, ranging from $95 to $160. Free wireless Internet, pool, deluxe continental breakfast, access to a local fitness center, and on-site activities.

Of all the places I have stayed at this year, the **Sebring Lakeside Golf Resort Inn & Tea Room** (863-385-7113 or 1-888-2SEBRING; www .2sebring.com), 500 Lake Sebring Dr, was one of the most relaxing and memorable. Built in 1926, the resort is located down a quiet road directly on Lake Sebring. I stayed in the honeymoon suite, which overlooks the lake on three sides. The garden entrance even has your very own mailbox. Owners Mark and Maria Baker have decorated the enormous suite with everything you'd need, including a fireplace open to both bedroom and living room areas. The king-size bed is dressed with sumptuous bedding, and the romantic bathroom has tiled arches to the private shower, scented candles in niches, and a large Jacuzzi overlooking a private garden. A full-size kitchen ensures you will never need to leave the room. But when you do, stroll down the white sandy beach and out on the dock stretching several yards over the lake. Take a swim in the oversize swimming pool, play a complimentary round of golf (see *Golf*), or pedal a bike down the quiet streets. Paddleboats are also available. Since not everyone will want to stay in the honeymoon suite, they have given the same attention to detail to their other suites and efficiencies. Three have Jacuzzis, most have lakefront views with screened porches, and all have access to the same amenities, including kitchens. Not just for couples, this is also a great place for families, and many family reunions are booked here each year. For those who don't want to cook, there's the inn's **Tea Room** (see *Dining Out*). The intimate resort has only 18 suites, including the honeymoon suite ($175–225) and other suites and efficiencies ($95–125). Reduced rates for extended stays; wireless DSL has recently been added.

✳ Where to Eat

DINING OUT

Avon Park

The all-you-can-eat buffet lunch at the **Jacaranda Hotel** (863-453-2211), 19 E Main St, has all the elegance of yesteryear. Each year residents and guests await the return of pianist Jeff Klein, who has regular engagements at several Hollywood celebrities' private parties (you'll have to ask him who). This talented musician tickles the ivories in grand style from November through Mother's Day. Lunch is served Sun ($10), Mon–Thu ($8), and Seafood Friday ($9); open for private parties only on Saturday. The Jacaranda Hotel also offers overnight accommodations (see *Lodging*).

Sebring

The cozy **Chicanes Restaurant & Bar** (863-314-0348) is located inside the Inn on the Lakes (see *Lodging*). For an appetizer, try the Tire Treads, deep-fried onions with Cajun dipping romelade ($4). For smaller appetites there is the cedar planked salmon with a hint of brown sugar and Dijon mustard ($10), or pork schnitzel, pan fried in German style ($10). Substantial entrées include chicken fusilli ($15), bourbon chicken ($15), and baby back ribs ($18). Save room for dessert, such as the bananas Foster ($6) or the Pile Up ($6), a chocolate concoction topped with vanilla ice cream, caramel, and hot fudge. For lunch there is an additional selection of salads ($6–10). The Chicanes name comes from the quick left-right zig-zag bends found on racetracks. The S turns, some with 90-degree angles, require a quick succession of braking, downshifting, and acceleration.

Look out on the legendary hairpin turn of the Sebring International Raceway (see *Racing*) while dining at **Esperante** at the Four Points by Sheraton Sebring, Château Élan Hotel & Spa (see *Lodging*). The restaurant serves breakfast, lunch, and dinner daily, with such delights as pan-seared baby rack of lamb crusted with herb goat cheese and drizzled with Indian-style curry ($23) or golden herb-infused Delmonico rib eye accompanied by a Marsala mushroom sauce ($20). Save lots of room for the Chocolate Uber Cake, a mountainous delight that will easily serve four. Or sip your dessert instead and order their new chocolate martini.

With a lakeside view, the **Tea Room at Lake Sebring** (863-385-7113 or 1-888-2SEBRING; www.2sebring.com), 500 Lake Sebring Dr, provides an elegant retreat. The $12 fixed-price lunch includes soup or salad, beverage, dessert, and a choice of entrée, such as chicken salad tossed with almonds, grapes, and apples; Asparagus Supreme, rolled in Virginia ham and aged Swiss cheese; medallions of pork tenderloin stuffed with ham and rosemary dressing; or Tea Tyme Finger Sandwiches, among the other chef's specialties. On Friday and Saturday, a five-course dinner ($40) offers two seatings with live entertainment and dancing. Jackets are required for dinner. Reservations strongly suggested.

EATING OUT

Lake Placid
You'll find hometown home-style cooking at **The Heron's Garden** (863-699-6550; www.heronsgarden.com), 501 US 27 N, a busy local restaurant where entrées run the gamut from frog's legs to ham steak, veal cutlet, and ravioli ($7–20). Locals also recommend **Main Street America** (863-465-7733), 22 S Main St, and **Schooni's Italian American** (863-465-5060), 210 N Main St.

Sebring
The **Hammock Inn** (863-385-7025), Three Picnic Area Rd, located at Highlands Hammock State Park across from the CCC Museum (see *Museums*), is a circa 1930s structure where chili dogs, chicken salad, burgers, and grilled cheese sandwiches are all served up for less than $5. For hungrier appetites, there's a smoked pork or smoked sausage with peppers and onions dinner for about $7. Don't leave without trying their wild orange pie, banana split cake, or one of their many cobblers. Desserts for less than $3? Why not order two? Make sure to check during the in season for weekend breakfasts, a fabulous Thanksgiving dinner ($11), and traditional Florida Cracker folk music events.

TEMPTING DELIGHTS AT THE HAMMOCK INN AT HIGHLANDS HAMMOCK STATE PARK
Kathy Wolf

Sherianne's Sweetie Pye's Restaurant (863-382-0441), 1320 US 27. For breakfast ($3–7) dig into omelets served with home fries or grits, French toast, pancakes, waffles, eggs, or biscuits with sausage gravy. For lunch there's a nice selection of freshly made sandwiches and juicy burgers ($4–6). Open Tues–Sun for breakfast and lunch.

Enjoy Greek favorites from the Old Country at **Takis Family Restaurant** (863-385-7323), 2710 Kenilworth Blvd, a small café where an Athenian family cooks up wonderful *dolmades,* moussaka, and gyros as well as American standards.

✳ Entertainment

DINNER SHOWS Who would have guessed that hidden in the town of Sebring is one of the best dinner shows around! Maintained and performed entirely by volunteers, the nonprofit **Highlands Little Theatre** (863-471-2522; www.highlandslittle theatre.org), 321 W Center Ave, is inside the Allen C. Atvater Cultural Center. Thanks to the dedication of patrons and residents, this little theater has been producing outstanding productions for more than 30 years. The two-hundred-seat theater has a professional backstage area with brightly lit dressing rooms and two full stories above the stage, allowing for a quick change of sets. I loved Ellen Lemus in the *Music Man* and hope to see her back on stage when I return. This versatile thespian recently received a Zenon award for Best Supporting Actress (2004). Tue and Wed evening performance $10 (no meal); Sun matinee $15 (dessert only), Fri or Sat evening $30 (full dinner). A cash bar is also available during dinner shows.

FOLK MUSIC Bring a lawn chair or blanket and listen to champion bluegrass music and traditional Florida Cracker folk songs at the **Hammock Inn** (see *Eating Out*). Events are scheduled around the country-style restaurant throughout the year, which also serves up traditional food. Depending on the time of day, the park admission fee of around $4 per carload may apply. Don't forget your bug spray!

✳ Selective Shopping

Avon Park
Walk outside along Florida's only **Mile Long Mall** in Avon Park. The mile-long walk extends from Lake Verona to US 27. Shaded by centuries-old trees, the mall is a great place for antiquing and touring historic buildings. The Avon Park Chamber of Commerce (863-453-3350) is located directly across from the tropical Kapok tree (see *Parks*). Stop by **Southern Exposure** (863-453-7477), 22 E Main St, next to the chamber office. It's the oldest structure on Main Street and houses original art and prints.

Lake Placid
Lake Placid has many places to browse for fine gifts, unique collectibles, art, and antiques. On Main Street you'll find 40 antiques dealers at **Poor Richards Antique Mall** (863-699-5480), 5 N Main St, including a nice selection of Florida history books. They have more antiques, shabby chic, and other neat stuff at **Old Friends** (863-465-4196), 213 N Main St. Nearby, discover wonderful accent furniture and garden gifts at **The Blueberry Patch** (863-465-5111), 214 N Main St. Along Interlake Boulevard is the **Garden of Alvyn**

(863-531-0100), 204 E Interlake Blvd, with more than 30 vendors showcasing many crafts, collectibles, and patented inventions. A few doors down there's **Suzanne's Antiques** (863-699-2744), 310 E Interlake Blvd. Don't miss stopping by the **Caladium Arts & Crafts Cooperative** (863-699-5940), 132 Interlake Blvd. This co-op, founded in 1993, houses a 120-member gallery under 10,000 square feet. All of the folk art, country crafts, and holiday decor are handcrafted by local artists and craftsmen. Classes are offered as well. At the **Lake Placid Mall & Museum** (863-465-1849 or 863-441-4959), 110 W Interlake Blvd, at the corner of West Interlake and the circle in Lake Placid, you can enjoy a walk down memory lane of 45,000 square feet showcasing antique cars and 1950s memorabilia. Search for a distinctive gift at **Goodness Gracious** (863-699-1711), 459 US 27 N, in the Tower Plaza, and say hi to owner Lorelei Dehne. For more antiques, gifts, and collectibles, go to **Park Avenue Antiques** (863-699-1949), 25 E Park Ave, and **The Avocado Plantation, Inc.** (863-465-1668), 212 CR 621 E.

Sebring

A few of the fun shops in Sebring are **Brenner Pottery & Craft Gallery** (863-471-2228), 104 Circle Park Dr, where you'll find handmade pottery in artistic surroundings; **Verdi** at Robbins Nursery (863-385-1145), 4801 US 27, for home and garden decor; and **Janet King, The Painting Studio** (863-314-0042), 215 N Ridgewood Dr, where you can select from a variety of original artwork and historical Sebring prints and note cards.

Depending on the season, you can pick your own strawberries (Dec–Mar), blueberries and blackberries (Apr–Jun), or grapes (Aug–Sept) at **Henscratch Farms** (863-699-2060; www.henscratch-farms.com), 980 Henscratch Rd, Lake Placid, where they also sell a great bottle of wine (see *Winery.* Open 9–5 Tue–Sat and noon–4 Sun.)

✳ Special Events

Second Saturday: Cars and motorcycles cruise in from 5:15 to 8 PM at the **Sebring Antique Car Cruise** (863-385-8448), Sebring Circle. Car-related collectibles are also for sale.

Check out the **Antique Fair** (863-465-4331) held 8–2 over at Stuart Park, Lake Placid.

First Thursday: Bring your chairs and blankets to **Sunset on the Circle** (863-382-7977) and listen to free music on Sebring Circle.

January: **Heritage Days** (863-465-4331), at the Edna Pierce Lockett Estate at US 98 and FL 721, Lake Placid. Spend a day on a 1900s working farm. Country cooking and live

POOR RICHARDS ANTIQUE MALL, LAKE PLACID

Kathy Wolf

entertainment of the period are featured.

February: **Lake Placid Country Fair** (863-465-4331), at DeVane Park. Crafts, food, and fun on the first full weekend of the month.

The **Highlands County Fair,** off US 27 down Highlands Ave, is always held the third week of the month. With food, music, and ribbons for "The Best," this county fair is a down-home tradition to be enjoyed by young and old. The orchid contest is one of the highlights.

March: **Twelve Hours of Sebring International Races** (1-800-262-7223). Car enthusiasts gather in Highlands County for the historic endurance race (see *Racing*). **Twelve Minutes of Sebring Endurance Race** (1-800-626-7223). Sod rebels from around the country compete on bladeless lawnmowers in this annual competition. Races run 12 minutes to mimic the Twelve Hours of Sebring Endurance Race (see *Racing*) and are held at the Avon Park Mower Plex on FL 64 west of Avon Park Airport, the nation's first dedicated lawnmower-racing facility.

NASGRASS Lawn Mower Race (863-453-3350). A national race with ride-on lawnmowers.

April: At **Ferrari Weekend,** held at Sebring International Raceway (1-800-626-7223), sleek Italian autos take to the tracks for high-speed thrills. You'll find parking lots all over town lined up with the colorful and expensive, including Dinos, Turismos, Testarossas, and more.

May: **Annual Blueberry Festival** at Henscratch Farms (863-699-2060; www.henscratchfarms.com), 980 Henscratch Rd, Lake Placid. Blueberry pie baking and eating contests, arts and crafts, and bluegrass music.

August: **Lake Placid Caladium Festival** (863-465-4331), Stuart Park, Interlake Blvd and Stuart St. After taking a bus ride ($8) to view the caladium fields and homes with caladium landscaping, you can purchase potted caladiums and pieces of art detailing these bright red and pink plants. Caladium history and growers' exhibits along with demonstrations on how to care for the plant are featured. The festival is held the last full weekend of the month.

October: **U.S. Sport Aviation Expo** (www.sport-aviation-expo.com), Sebring Regional Airport, Sebring. Exhibits highlight ultralight aircraft, fixed wings, trikes, powered parachutes, and gyroplanes.

November: **Annual Highlands Art League Festival** (863-385-5312; www.highlandsartleague.com) features "12 Hours of Art & Community for the Benefit of our Children." Enjoy special events for all ages, fine art, heritage crafts, music, food, and live entertainment.

Sebring Historic Fall Classic (863-655.1442 or 1-800-626-7223; www .sebringraceway.com). Legendary cars return for the Four Hours of Sebring endurance race with vintage, historic, GT, and prototype classes, the Rolex Endurance Challenge, and the American Muscle Car Challenge.

LAKE OKEECHOBEE

GLADES, HENDRY, OKEECHOBEE, WESTERN MARTIN & PALM BEACH COUNTIES

Covering 730 square miles, Lake Okeechobee is an inland sea. It's the second largest lake entirely within the United States, and it has a major girdle around it called the Herbert Hoover Dike, built for flood control after two devastating hurricanes in the 1920s killed thousands of residents by pushing the water right out of this shallow bowl and into the surrounding prairies. Only 15 feet deep in most places, the lake was once an integral part of water movement through the Kissimmee Valley and into the Everglades; now, the River of Grass relies on locks and canals to feed its need for fresh water. Thanks to the dike, the shoreline is managed by the Army Corps of Engineers, so there are no waterfront condos, no sprawling lakeside cities, and very few views—unless you climb atop the dike and take a walk.

Water has always been the lifeblood of the region. The Calusa found their way up from the southeastern coast and established villages along the lake they called "Mayami," the Big Water. In the 1800s settlers pushed their way up the Caloosahatchee River and founded **La Belle,** named for Laura and Belle, the daughters of Civil War hero Capt. Francis Asbury Hendry. Farming and ranching became the backbone of the economy around the lake as the town of **Moore Haven** was settled on the western shore. **Okeechobee** is the largest settlement on the eastern shore of the lake and the heart of South Florida's cattle country. Dating from the late 1800s, this frontier town saw its first explosive growth around 1915 as a port city for the fishing industry along the lake. The 1920s Florida land boom brought cattlemen to the area, and the town's livestock market—still going strong—opened in 1939. Planned by famed city planner John Nolan and established as a company town by the U.S. Sugar Company, **Clewiston,** the "Sweetest Town in America," also sprung to life during the land boom as the Atlantic Coast Line railroad pushed south into lands drained and "reclaimed" for farmland around the southern edge of the lake, leading to an influx of farm workers into **South Bay, Belle Glade,** and **Pahokee** by the 1920s. Sugarcane fields stretch to the horizon in what was once part of the Everglades "river of grass."

Refreshingly rural, this remains an agricultural region where cattle, sugar, oranges, and rice are the major crops. But that doesn't mean there's a lack of tourists. If you've ever wondered where all those RVs are headed down the interstates every winter, chances are they're staking out camp at one of the many, many campgrounds around Lake Okeechobee. Anglers arrive here from around the globe for legendary fishing. With fishing, hiking, birding, boating, and historic sites to visit, you'll find plenty to see and do. I know; I've spent three weeks of vacation here just for fun.

GUIDANCE For the cities of Clewiston and La Belle as well as greater Hendry County, stop in at the **Clewiston Chamber of Commerce** (863-983-7979), 544 W Sugarland Hwy, Clewiston, for brochures. In downtown Moore Haven, information from the **Glades County Chamber of Commerce** (863-946-0440), P.O. Box 490, Moore Haven 33471, can be picked up at the county courthouse. At the visitors center adjoining the police station downtown, the **Okeechobee County Tourist Development Council** (863-763-3959 or 1-800-871-4403; www.okeechobee-tdc.com), 499 NW Fifth Ave, Okeechobee, can load you up with maps and brochures. Contact the **Palm Beach County Convention and Visitors Bureau** (561-233-3000 or 1-800-833-5733; www.palmbeachfl.com), 1555 Palm Beach Lakes Blvd, Suite 800, West Palm Beach, in advance for a brochure on things to do and see in Pahokee, Belle Glade, and South Bay. For information about the lake, its water control structures (locks and dams), and campgrounds at those structures, contact the **U.S. Army Corps of Engineers South Florida Operations Office** (863-983-8101; www.saj.usace.army.mil), 525 Ridgelawn Rd, Clewiston.

GETTING THERE *By car:* **US 27** and **US 441** provide primary north–south access, with **FL 80** running east–west through La Belle, Clewiston, and Belle Glade. **FL 78** links Okeechobee to Moore Haven via Lakeport.

By air: The nearest major airport to the region is **Palm Beach International Airport (PBIA)** in West Palm Beach (see *North Palm Beach County*).

SMALL FARMS NEAR PAHOKEE

Sandra Friend

By bus: **Greyhound** (1-800-231-2222; www.greyhound.com) stops at 106 SW Third St, Okeechobee, and at the Clewiston 99 cent store, 125 S Dean Duff Rd, Clewiston.

By rail: **AMTRAK** (1-800-872-7245; www.amtrak.com) rolls through downtown Okeechobee.

By boat: The Okeechobee Waterway runs 152 miles from Port St. Lucie to Fort Myers utilizing the St. Lucie Canal, Lake Okeechobee, and the Caloosahatchee River. You can access Lake Okeechobee from either coast using your private boat.

GETTING AROUND *By car:* Unless you're boating, a car is necessary for exploring this region. To circle Lake Okeechobee clockwise starting at the city of Okeechobee, follow US 441 south to Canal Point, CR 715 south to Belle Glade, FL 80 west to Clewiston, US 27 north to Moore Haven, and FL 78 east back to Okeechobee. Mind the speed limits, especially around Clewiston, South Bay, and Belle Glade. An unfortunately high number of speeders on FL 80 led to strict enforcement of speed limits for safety's sake.

By boat: Open-water crossing of Lake Okeechobee is generally rough. A navigable route follows the shoreline of the lake, utilizing the deep-water Rim Canal in places and channel markers in dredged areas of the lake in other places. Consult navigational charts for details.

MEDICAL EMERGENCIES Medical facilities are limited around the lake. Your best bet for major emergencies is to get to **Hendry Regional Medical Center** (863-983-9121; www.hendryregional.org), 500 W Sugarland Hwy, Clewiston, or **Raulerson Hospital** (863-763-2151), 1796 US 441 N, Okeechobee.

✳ To See

ARCHEOLOGICAL SITES Hidden in the sugarcane fields along the Herbert Hoover Dike near Belle Glade lie the **Chosen Mounds,** a multilayered burial complex unearthed by Smithsonian researchers led by George Tallant in the 1930s. In addition to bones of the Calusa, a coastal people from Pine Island Sound, archeologists discovered pottery shards, conchs used as hoes, and porpoise teeth used for engraving. Some of the artifacts removed from this site and from a burial complex near **Nicodemus Slough** (FL 78 near Moore Haven) can be viewed at the South Florida Museum in Bradenton (see *The Cultural Coast*).

At the **Ortona Indian Mound Park** (863-946-0440), FL 78 west of US 27 and east of US 29, walk through part of a village complex from three thousand years ago and along canoe canals built by the Calusa not far from the Caloosahatchee River along Turkey Creek. A kiosk with interpretive information helps to orient you to the cultures that lived here and to follow trails around the site, which is heavily buried under vegetation. At 22 feet, the primary temple mound is the highest point in Glades County. Dispersed across 5 square miles, the overall complex is one of the largest prehistoric sites in Florida.

ATTRACTIONS

Big Cypress Seminole Reservation
At **Billie Swamp Safari** (1-800-949-6101; www.seminoletribe.com/safari), explore the Big Cypress Swamp with your guide on a massive swamp buggy or an airboat, stroll the grounds and admire native wildlife, stop in on the Herptarium to visit the snakes, or stay overnight in an authentic chickee (see *Campgrounds*), the South Florida version of a grass hut, and sit around a campfire listening to Seminole storytellers. It's a very different experience, one that will leave you with an appreciation of the Seminole and the habitats of the Big Cypress. Swamp buggy rides $25–30, airboat $15; discounts for children and seniors.

Sandra Friend

FEEDING THE OLD-TIMERS AT GATORAMA

Palmdale

A Florida classic since 1957, **Gatorama** (863-675-0623; www.gatorama .com), 6180 US 27, showcases an endangered Florida reptile that you won't see much of anywhere else— the American crocodile. Endemic to South Florida, these massive saltwater creatures breed from December through January; the colony here dates from the 1960s and now numbers 50. When you see owner Allen Register dangling food into the pond for the alligators to munch, you'll understand what a half century of growth means in gator terms: These creatures are huge! One large pond is divided in two by the walkway and fencing to keep the more aggressive alligators away from the American crocodile colony. Although the exhibits are old-style tiled pools, they showcase interesting creatures such as the mugger crocodile of India and the Nile crocodile. In 1987 the Register family began farming alligators for meat, and the demand outstrips their supply. Covered walkways lead you past the exhibits, but you'll spend most of your time marveling at the size of the reptiles cruising the big pond. Open daily. Adults $12, children $6.

CATTLE AUCTION Watch a live auction every week at the **Okeechobee Livestock Market** (863-763-3127), 1055 US 98 N, Okeechobee, where ranchers around the region round up their cattle for sale. It's free and fun. This is cattle country, where a 10,000-acre spread is not out of the ordinary. Florida has a long history of cattle ranching, dating from the Spanish explorers of the 1500s, and remains the third largest ranching state east of the Mississippi, with 1.1 million head of beef cattle and more than 150,000 head of dairy cattle.

HISTORIC SITES

Belle Glade
The **Torry Island Swing Bridge** on Torry Island Road is a unique handcranked swinging drawbridge connecting the largest island in Lake Okeechobee with the mainland, and it is the oldest remaining manually operated bridge in Florida.

Clewiston
You'll find dozens of historic sites clustered around downtown, starting with the **Bond Street Historic Business District** at Bond and Sugarland Hwy. Stop in at the chamber of commerce or The Clewiston Inn (see *Lodging*) for a walking-tour brochure (see *Walking Tours*) to explore the area, by foot or by car. Historic homes include the **B. G. Dahlberg Executive House,** 125 W Del Monte Ave; the **Captain Deane Duff House,** 151 W Del Monte Ave; and the

Percy Bishop House, 325 E Del Monte Ave, all built on the original lakeside bluff. **St. Margaret Catholic Church,** 208 N Deane Ave, is the oldest church in town, built in 1931. The quaint wooden **Army Corps of Engineers Settlement Homes** between Ponce de Leon and Royal Palm Ave, crossing the streets of Balboa, Arcade and Crescent, were built for the men working on the Herbert Hoover Dike in the 1930s after the hurricanes. The dedication marker for the dike is the **Hoover Dike Memorial,** which is above the boat ramp near the Clewiston lock. The dike took six years to build.

La Belle

On the National Register of Historic Places, the **Hendry County Courthouse,** FL 80 and FL 29, was built in 1926 in an Italian Renaissance Revival style. It features a four-story clock tower.

Moore Haven

Grecian columns flank the doorways to the **Glades County Courthouse** (863-946-6001), US 27 between Fifth and Sixth St, where you can walk inside and see the thick vault doors leading to the inner chambers, and huge historic maps on the wall.

By virtue of its age and location, the **Lone Cypress Tree,** Ave J and the Caloosahatchee River, qualifies as a piece of history—it served as a navigational marker for sailors on the river for more than a century.

Okeechobee

Stop and take a look at the massive **Okeechobee Freshman Campus Historical Mural** depicting the settlement of the area, painted on the side of the high school gymnasium at 610 SW Second Ave and Sixth St. It's almost criminal that the **Battle of Okeechobee Historic Marker** in front of the Old Habits Tavern, US 441 SE, is all that physically remains to commemorate one of the most significant battles of the Second Seminole War, the Battle of Okeechobee, which occurred on land near here that is now a housing development. An annual reenactment (see *Special Events*) brings this turning point in Florida's history to life.

Ortona

Cracker tales come alive, so to speak, at the **Ortona Cemetery,** FL 78 west of US 27 and east of US 29, in the middle of cattle country. Here, Seminole chief Billy Bowlegs III (who was 104 when he died) was interred in 1965, and saddles and cowboy boots decorate the resting places of the departed. A homemade headstone tells the story of a mother and children who died during the 1928 hurricane. This is the only interment site in Glades County.

MUSEUMS

Belle Glade

Commemorating the region's top folk historian, the **Lawrence Will Museum** (561-996-3453), 530 South Main St, in the Belle Glade branch library, offers a look into the research of the man who thoroughly studied the Okeechobee hurricanes, with artifacts and historical records. Free.

Big Cypress Seminole Reservation

Ah-Tah-Thi-Ki Museum (863-902-1113; www.seminoletribe.com/museum), corner of CR 833 and Government Rd, is the world's largest museum devoted to Seminole culture and heritage, with excellent interpretive displays teaching Seminole history. Inside the 5,000-square-foot exhibit hall are rarities "borrowed back" from the Smithsonian, such as medicine baskets and moccasins. The boardwalk behind the museum slips through a portion of the 60-acre swamp, leading to a living-history village. Open 9–5 Tue–Sat. Adults $6, students and seniors $4, children under 6 free.

Clewiston

When I first visited the **Clewiston Museum** (863-983-2870; www.clewiston.org/museum.htm), 112 South Commercial St, several years ago, I was pleasantly surprised that despite its small size, it was packed with bits of local history that I knew nothing about before, such as the No. 5 British Flying Training School housed in Clewiston during the 1940s, where British airmen came for fighter-

AGRICULTURAL TOURS

One of the most incomparable tours I've taken, **Sugarland Tours** (1-877-693-4372; www.clewiston.org/sugarlandtours.htm), 544 W Sugarland Hwy, offers a glimpse into both the history of Clewiston and of how sugar is processed, from the cane in the fields to the refined grains pouring into a bag. In this town, history and sugar are forever linked thanks to Charles Stewart Mott, who bought the bankrupt Southern Sugar Company in 1931 and reopened it as the U.S. Sugar Corporation, convincing investors that the Everglades muck was "black gold" for sugar growers. Most of the historic homes in

SUGARLAND TOUR

Sandra Friend

pilot training, and the history behind why the Hoover Dike was built, with dramatic photos of the destruction from the hurricanes of 1926 and 1928. I learned more about sugar processing than I'd ever known before, too, and it's Clewiston's biggest industry. The museum recently moved into larger accommodations with better exhibit space and multimedia presentations. Open 9–4 Mon–Fri. Fee.

La Belle

Housed in the historic home of the H. A. Rider family, the **La Belle Heritage Museum** (863-674-0034), 150 S Lee St, features exhibits on local and regional history. Open 2–5 Thu–Sat. Donation.

Okeechobee

Learn about life on Florida's frontier at the **Okeechobee Historical Society Museum & Schoolhouse** (863-763-4344); 1850 FL 70 N, the region's first one-room schoolhouse, built in 1907. Call to arrange a tour.

town are a part of that era of rebirth and expansion, and as we rode through the shaded residential streets, our tour guide explained who built which grand old home and why.

Once out in the fields, we drove through the Southern Gardens citrus processing plant and received a thorough explanation of how oranges become juice and concentrate, even though on that particular day, the plant wasn't in operation for us to get out and visit. We did disembark, however, along a string of railroad cars in a sugarcane field that was being harvested and watched the dinosaur-like harvester machines at work. Our guide pulled out a machete and chopped fresh cane for us to taste.

At the Clewiston Sugar Refinery, we watched from the safety of our bus as train cars offloaded their sugarcane into hoppers that carry the plant materials into the factory for processing. Donning shower caps and little plastic booties, we were allowed to watch processed sugar being bagged and stacked for shipment on the factory floor, with robotic arms spinning plastic webs around stacks of sacks and LP gas–driven loaders scurrying everywhere. After we returned to the bus for more exploration of historic sites in Clewiston, one unexpected stop was the Beneficial Insect Laboratory inside the U.S. Sugar research and development complex, where insects are being bred to naturally control pests such as citrus blackflies and sugarcane borers. The comfortable 24-passenger bus totes you from stop to stop, and you even get a buffet lunch at The Clewiston Inn as part of the trip. Tours are offered weekdays at 10 AM ($27.50 per person); reserve your spot at The Clewiston Inn front desk (see *Lodging*) or by calling the Clewiston Chamber of Commerce (see *Guidance*).

RAILROADIANA The **South Central Florida Express (SCFE) Depot** at W Aztec and W. C. Owen is home to the short line's rolling stock; stop here to take photos of the brightly painted locomotives. SCFE services the sugarcane fields to assist in the harvest.

SCENIC VIEWS The **Harney Pond Canal Overlook** near Lakeport, FL 78 at CR 721, extends nearly a half mile out into the lake, with an observation platform great for birding. At **John Stretch Park** (see *Parks*), US 27 between Clewiston and South Bay, climb up the dike for a view of the Rim Canal and the marshes beyond. Stop at **Moore Haven Recreation Area** or the **Parrott Avenue Wayside** along US 441 for views of the broad expanse of blue along the eastern shore of the lake. And for days and days of panoramic views, walk the **Florida Trail** (see *Hiking*) around Lake Okeechobee, which has my favorite scenic view—Indian Prairie.

✳ To Do

BICYCLING Atop the Herbert Hoover Dike, the **Lake Okeechobee Scenic Trail** (see *Greenways*) is now paved from Clewiston to the Pahokee Marina and Moore Haven to the Okee-tantie Recreation Area, providing nearly 50 miles for street bikes to roam.

BIRDING My personal experience is that birding is fabulous all around the lake—I haven't been disappointed yet. White pelicans soar over the open water, sandhill cranes gather in groups on the prairies near **Okeechobee,** bald eagles nest on **Torry Island,** and osprey creel from the melalecua snags all along the Rim Canal. For your best birding, hit the **Florida Trail** (see *Hiking*) around the lake and to the south through Hendry County, where you'll spot caracara along the edges of the sugarcane fields. The wayside at **Nicodemus Slough,** FL 78, is a good spot to sit and watch wading birds in the shallows of the marsh, and **Vance Whidden Park,** a low-lying area just up the road toward Lakeport, is purported to have great birding along the marshes.

BOATING Public boat ramps are available at all major recreation areas around the lake, including Clewiston Park, South Bay, Port Mayaca, and Alvin Ward Park in Moore Haven; there are numerous private ramps as well. Before heading out on the lake, boaters should pick up a navigational map at one of the marinas as this is one of the shallowest large lakes in the world. Among the many marinas servicing the lake are the **Belle Glade Marina** (561-996-6322), off FL 715 to FL 717, Belle Glade; **Buckhead Marina** (863-763-4716), 250 Buckhead Ridge Rd, west of Okeechobee off FL 78; and the **Pahokee Marina** (see *Campgrounds*). In Clewiston you can rent a pontoon or a fishing boat at **Angler's Marina** (see *Lodging*), $45–100 half day or $65–145 full day, gas included; or put in at adjacent **Roland Martin's Lakeside Resort** (see *Lodging*), a full-service marina. West of Moore Haven off FL 80, **The Glades** (see *Campgrounds*) has a deep-water marina along the Caloosahatchee River and can accommodate boats up to 60 feet, with dockage rates of 75 cents per foot per day (discounts for weeklong and monthlong stays).

Clewiston

⚓ Capt. Terry Garrels took me on one heck of a spin on **Big "O" Airboat Tours** (863-983-2037; www.bigofishing.com), 920 E Del Monte Ave, departing from Roland Martin's marina. Once through the lock and out into the lake, we followed the Rim Canal until the captain found a good break into the "grassy waters," the shallow marshes not far off the shoreline, and whizzed us through narrow passageways where alligators lounged, moorhens floated, and manatees surfaced. Unexpectedly, we came out into open water, which had enough bounce to it to make me feel like we were on the ocean. On our 10-mile route, Captain Terry made numerous stops to explain the habitats and wildlife we were seeing, including pointing out a lone pond apple tree growing in the shallows—according to historic accounts, a forest of these wizened trees once marched southwest from this lake's shores. $25 per person; reservations required.

Okeechobee

Although they don't go out into the lake, **Eagle Bay Airboat Rides** (863-824-0500; www.okeechobeeairboat.com), 900 FL 78 W, takes you on an hour-long tour (adults $25, ages 12 and under $15) of Eagle Bay Marsh and Limpkin Creek, once a part of Lake Okeechobee's shores. Watch for alligators, spot eagles and osprey, and bring your binoculars to spy the birds Captain Don points out. Ninety-minute tours out on Lake Okeechobee (adults $35, children $15) are also offered.

FAMILY ACTIVITIES ⚓ Enjoy a real old-fashioned movie theater experience at **Mann's Clewiston Theatre** (see *Entertainment*) in Clewiston, a restored beauty from 1941, or take the kids down to **Woodworks Park** on Osceola Ave in Clewiston, a gigantic wooden "super playground" from 1992, adjacent to the public library and pool complex.

FISHING If you like to fish, you've come to the right place! **Lake Okeechobee** is a mecca for anglers and has long been known for its great bass fishing—although water management of inflow and outflow via locks and dams has caused serious problems to the quality of the fishery in recent years. But the tiny village of Sand Cut (population eight) along US 441 lays claim to being the speckled perch capital of the world, and I've seen some serious catfish in anglers' boats as they waited in the locks. If you're a first-timer here, it's best to check in with one of the marinas (see *Boating*) or fish camps (see *Fish Camps*), or contact the Lake Okeechobee Guide Association (1-800-284-2446; www.fishokeechobee.com). One recommendation from my Ontario friend who comes down to fish every year: Stop in a bait-and-tackle shop such as **Garrard's Tackle Shop** (863-763-3416), 4259 US 441 S, Okeechobee,

FISHERMEN AT SAND CUT, "SPECK CAPITAL OF THE WORLD"

Sandra Friend

ask around, and you'll come up with a local who knows the waters like the back of his hand.

GAMING Who needs Vegas for slots? Here they are in the middle of cattle country at the **Seminole Casino Brighton** (1-866-2-CASINO), at the reservation west of Okeechobee off FL 70. Big-ticket bingo games, too. Closed Mon.

GOLF

Belle Glade
With its greens within sight of the Herbert Hoover Dike, the **Belle Glade Golf and Country Club** (561-996-6605), 110 SW E Martin Luther King Ave, is one busy place on weekends. This par 72 public course features 18 holes under tropical palms.

Moore Haven
At **The Glades** (see *Campgrounds*), the 3,178-yard, par 36 course makes use of natural landscaping along its nine holes. This public course is inexpensive, too, with greens fees starting at $12 to walk, $16 with cart for 9 holes, $25 for 18 holes. Call 863-983-8464 for tee times.

HIKING The granddaddy of hiking trails in this region is the **Florida Trail** (1-877-HIKE-FLA; www.floridatrail.org), which comes in from the south from Big Cypress Swamp and follows the water management canals through sugarcane fields and ranches for nearly 40 miles before reaching Lake Okeechobee, where it splits into two routes and encircles the lake for more than 110 miles. With numerous designated campsites (each with covered picnic bench and fire ring) on the lakeshore, this is a popular destination for backpackers, but it takes a special breed—you spend your time in the sun, and recently, nearly half of the trail has been paved by the state to accommodate other users. The rewards are the amazing views and astounding amount of wildlife you see from the Herbert Hoover Dike. Those wanting to walk around the entire lake on day hikes join up with the annual **Big O Hike** (see *Special Events*) each year, as both your authors have done. The linear Florida Trail continues north from Okee-tantie to follow the Kissimmee River north. A recent scenic side trail, the 5-mile **Raphael Sanchez Trail** at Okeechobee Ridge Park, accessed from the Port Mayaca Recreation Area, leads hikers on a shaded walk along the historic lakeshore. A new backpacking route to the Atlantic Ocean, the 72-mile **Ocean to Lake Trail** is a spur trail under development and leaves the Florida Trail near Port Mayaca to pass through DuPuis Management Area (see *Wild Places*).

A WEARY HIKER ON THE BIG O HIKE
Sandra Friend

North of Palmdale, **Platt Branch Mitigation Park** (863-648-3203), Detjens Dairy Rd, Venus, marks the southernmost extent of the Lake Wales Ridge, protecting more than 1,700 acres of scrub and scrubby flatwoods and the associated flora and fauna found in these rare habitats. Marked trails following Jeep roads create loop hikes of up to 5 miles; plans are for the trail system to be extended to allow backpacking along Fisheating Creek.

PADDLING Think of **Lake Okeechobee** like an inland ocean—it's big enough to get whitecaps and storm surges, and yet shallow enough to support a hefty alligator population. That said, not too many folks kayak out there, although following the shoreline looks like it would be nice. Instead, head to the **Fisheating Creek Canoe Trail** (863-675-5999), 7555 US 27 N, managed by the folks at Fisheating Creek Resort (see *Campgrounds*). Open year-round, the trail roughly parallels the route of US 27 and offers one- or two-day trips starting at either Venus or Burnt Bridge. On your float trip, you are welcome to camp in any dry, pleasant spot along this meandering cypress-lined creek, one of the most beautiful canoe runs in Florida. The livery provides shuttles ($15 one-day trip, $20 two-day trip) and canoe rentals ($17 half day, $25 full day); reservations required. If you can do only one paddling trip in South Florida, do this one.

SCENIC DRIVES Follow signs for the **Big Water Heritage Trail** all around Lake Okeechobee to discover points of scenic and historic interest. You can pick up a map and brochure at any of the visitors centers around the lake (see *Guidance*). Established in 2004 at the urging of Senator Bob Graham, the **Everglades Trail** (www.evergladestrail.com) is a driving tour that connects the dots of places linked to the natural heritage of the original Everglades. The entire region around Lake Okeechobee is a historic part of the Everglades drainage. Commemorating Florida's cattle ranching heritage, the **Florida Cracker Trail** passes through this region using US 98. Drive that route in the early morning, and you'll experience morning fog wrapping ranches in a dense mist and cows appearing like ghosts against silhouettes of cabbage palms.

SKYDIVING For a unique bird's-eye view of Lake Okeechobee, jump out of a perfectly good plane over sugarcane fields at **Air Adventures of Clewiston** (863-983-6151 or 1-800-533-6151), Air Glades Airport off US 27.

WALKING TOURS Pick up a **Clewiston Walking Tour** brochure at The Clewiston Inn (see *Lodging*) or chamber of commerce (see *Guidance*) and take a walk back into the 1920s by following the route down neighborhood streets to visit historic sites such as the original Clewiston School (circa 1927), St. Margaret's Catholic Church

FISHEATING CREEK, ONE OF THE BEST PADDLING STREAMS IN FLORIDA

Sandra Friend

(circa 1931), and 15 homes from the 1920s, including several on the National Register of Historic Places. Four different routes range from 1 to 2.9 miles, all starting at The Clewiston Inn.

✳ Green Space

GREENWAYS Managed by the Office of Greenways and Trails, the **Lake Okeechobee Scenic Trail** follows the Herbert Hoover Dike around the lake and is paved for street bikes and roller blading between Port Mayaca and Okee-tantie and Clewiston and Pahokee. Shaded benches provide resting spots; kiosks at major access points provide maps of the route.

PARKS Enjoy riverfront picnicking at shady **Barron Park** in La Belle along the Caloosahatchee River at FL 29, and fishing, boating (with on-site launch), and picnicking at **Clewiston Park** along the Herbert Hoover Dike, end of Francisco St. **John Stretch Park,** 47225 US Hwy 27, between Clewiston and South Bay, is a favorite picnic spot for motorists, who scramble up the dike to see the Rim Canal and lakeshore marshes. Between Belle Glade and Pahokee, **Rardin Park,** 4600 Bacom Point Rd, is set under the shade of massive ficus trees and has picnic tables and a playground; it's a steep but worthwhile walk up to the dike to see Torry Island and the sweep of the lake.

RECREATION AREAS/LAKE ACCESS POINTS Maintained by the Army Corps of Engineers, recreation areas around Lake Okeechobee provide a place for you to park and walk along the Herbert Hoover Dike; most of the recreation areas have boat ramps and picnic tables, and some have facilities. Key access points include **Port Mayaca,** at US 441 and FL 76; **Henry Creek** and **Nubbin Slough,** along US 441; and **Indian Prairie** and **Fisheating Creek,** along FL 78.

WILD PLACES

Canal Point
Open to equestrians, hikers, bicyclists, and hunters, the **DuPuis Management Area** (561-924-5314; www.sfwmd.gov/org/clm/lsd/dupindex.html), 23500 SW Kanner Hwy (FL 76), encompasses more than 21,000 acres of forests, prairies, and wetlands. Stop at the nature center at Gate 5 for an orientation to this magnificent preserve.

Devils Garden
Tough to get to, but worth the effort if you're an avid birder, both **Holey Land WMA** (http://myfwc.com/recreation/holey_land/default.asp) and **Rotenberger WMA** (http://myfwc.com/recreation/rotenberger/default.asp) protect thousands of acres of the original Everglades habitat of sawgrass marshes and host colonial nesting birds such as yellow-crowned night herons and cattle egrets. While hiking through Rotenberger, I've seen groups of roseate spoonbills winging their way across the marshes and crested caracara in the surrounding fields.

Lakeport
Along FL 78 between Nicodemus Slough and Fisheating Creek, **Vance Whidden Park** is an undeveloped park with a dirt road leading out to the prairies

along this single stretch of natural lakeshore on the northwest side of the lake, where there is a gap in the Herbert Hoover Dike for 3 miles to permit the Fisheating Creek floodplain to flow naturally into Lake Okeechobee.

Okeechobee

Protecting 75 square miles of open prairies dotted with palm and oak hammocks, **Kissimmee Prairie Preserve State Park** (863-462-5360), 33104 NW 192nd Ave, is Florida's second largest state preserve. You are welcome to bicycle or drive down miles of roads through the prairies; a system of hiking trails is in the works. There is a campground on-site.

✴ Lodging

CAMPGROUNDS

Big Cypress Seminole Reservation 33440

Get away from it all at the comfortable **Big Cypress RV Resort** (1-800-437-4102; www.seminoletribe.com/bcrv resort), CR 833, in the middle of the Big Cypress Seminole Reservation, just steps away from the Ah-Tah-Thi-Ki Museum (see *Museums*) and near the Billie Swamp Safari (see *Attractions*). RVs and tent campers welcome ($17–24), and well-appointed cabins are available ($65–75). The park has a clubhouse, aerobic trail, playground, miniature golf, heated swimming pool, and hot tub. Advance reservations suggested during the winter season.

Spend the night surrounded by the Big Cypress Swamp in an authentic Seminole chickee at **Billie Swamp Safari** (see *Attractions*). The small palm-thatched buildings sleep two for $35, or you can rent a chickee sleeping 8–12 people for $65. Linens, blankets, and bath towels included; all visitors share the bathhouse and have the opportunity to enjoy storytelling around the campfire (free) or joining a night swamp buggy tour (extra fee).

Clewiston 33440

Now under KOA management, the **Clewiston/Lake Okeechobee KOA** (863-983-7078 or 1-877-983-7078),

194 CR 720, is in a nicely shaded grove north of town. RV spaces start at $23 daily, and tent space (no hookups) for $20. There is one central bathhouse and a swimming pool. New to the property are rental cabins, including a honeymoon cabin with its own hot tub—ask about it.

Okeechobee Landings (863-983-4144; www.okeechobeelandings.com), 420 Holiday Blvd, caters to the RV crowd with sun-drenched spaces on concrete pads with 50 amp service and full hookups ($30 per day). Enjoy the heated swimming pool or hot tub, or arrange for a fishing guide. Tent camping, no hookups, runs $25, with a bathhouse available.

La Belle 33935

For a different type of outdoor experience, camp in the middle of an orange grove at **Grandma's Grove RV Park** (941-675-2567), 2250 W FL 80. You'll love it during the fragrant orange blossom season! $25 for full hookup; no tents.

The Army Corps of Engineers manages the **Ortona Lock Campground** (1-877-444-6777; www.reserveamerica .com), where groomed, grassy RV and tent sites ($20; water and electric) have a view of the Caloosahatchee River and access for fishing, off FL 80.

Lakeport 33471

❧ The **Aruba RV Resort** (863-946-1324; www.okeedirect.com/arubarv.htm), 1825 Old Lakeport Rd, is as appealing inside the park as it is from the road. Many sites are shaded with tropical vegetation, waterway access is a cinch, and the heated pool, café, and tiki bar out front are available to all guests. Full-hookup sites include slabs with picnic tables ($30 in the trees, $32 waterfront). Weekly, monthly, and quarterly rates, too.

Moore Haven 33471

At **The Glades** (863-983-8464; www.TheGladesResort.com), 4382 Indian Hills Dr off FL 80, relax in a cabin along the golf course (see *Golf*) or bring your RV and settle into a shaded lot not far from the Caloosahatchee River at the marina (see *Boating*). There are full hookups at your choice of three different campgrounds within this 480-acre complex ($20–30; weekly, monthly, and annual rates available). The cabins are brand new and run $65 a day.

Snuggled between the Herbert Hoover Dike and the Rim Canal, the **Marina RV Resort** (863-946-2255), 900 CR 720 NW, offers RV and tent camping right along the Florida Trail (see *Hiking*), with boating access to both the lake and the Caloosahatchee River. Shady sites are at a premium, but there is a nice central area with a pool, horseshoes, and shuffleboard, and the bathhouse is neat and clean. Full hookups $25, tents with electric $18, tents without $10. Rental boats available for $65 for eight hours.

Along US 27 north of town, **Robin's Nest RV Resort** (863-946-1298), 2365 US 27 N, is a large adult-oriented RV park with several small lakes on the property and a clubhouse with organ-ized activities. The full-hookup spaces ($21.40) are out in the sun, and amenities include a pool, golf course, shuffleboard, and horseshoes.

Okeechobee 34974

Bob's Big Bass RV Park (863-763-2638; www.bobsbigbassrvpark.com), 12766 US 441 SE, is set in the shade of grand old oaks on the Rim Canal and is a down-home place to settle back for some fishing. Full hookups run $20 a night; boat slip and sea-plane parking available.

❧ It's not just a campground—it's a vacation destination. At the **Okeechobee KOA Resort & Golf Course** (863-763-0231 or 1-800-562-7748; www.okeechobeekoa.com), 4276 US 441 S, you can play nine holes of golf, relax in the hot tub, grab a bike for a spin, or sip a cold one in the tiki bar. Their massive list of amenities makes this one of the country's top KOA destinations, and in winter you'll find most of their seven hundred spaces filled with Canadian snowbirds. Choose from paved 50 amp sites with full hookup ($56), cottages or cabins ($55–146), or your basic tent site ($32–50).

With a great location on the Kissimmee River at Lake Okeechobee, the **Okee-tantie Recreation Area** (941-763-2622), 10430 FL 78, is a county-run facility with 270 sunny RV spaces ($27.95) and tent sites ($24.50, no utilities) and a marina with boat rentals, bait and tackle, and ice and groceries.

Zachary Taylor RV Resort (863-763-3377 or 1-888-282-6523; www.campfloridarv.com), 2995 US 441 SE, is a pretty waterfront RV park on Taylor Creek that caters to the 55-and-over crowd with 240 full-hookup sites, screened-in heated swimming pool, and a recreation hall with many planned activities. Sites available nightly, weekly, monthly, or for the season, starting at $35 a night.

Pahokee 33476

Everglades Adventures RV & Sailing Resort (1-800-335-6560; www.evergladesadventuresresort.com), 190 N Lake Ave at the Pahokee Marina, is the only waterfront campground on Lake Okeechobee, where the waves lap right up to your campsite ($28–37) and outside your cabin ($75–190) porch—perfect for anglers to fish from their site!

Palmdale 33944

🦑 If you're looking for a getaway where the live oaks droop low and the Spanish moss waves in the breeze along a cypress-lined waterway, then head to **Fisheating Creek Resort** (863-675-5999; www.fisheatingcreekresort.com), 7555 US 27 N. This has been a favorite of my friends for years, but it's had a bad rap due to rowdy campers on the weekends. I'm assured the issue is under control, but weekdays are certainly the quiet days along this lazy creek. RV sites are clustered around a bathhouse/laundry area, with full hookups $15 a night. Primitive tent sites run $10 a night, and the best ones are along the creek, downstream from the camp store. The livery service runs shuttles and offers canoe rentals (see *Paddling*).

FISH CAMPS

Moore Haven 33471

A classic in these parts, **Uncle Joe's Fish Camp** (863-983-9421), 2005 Griffin Rd SE, opened in the 1940s and continues to serve serious anglers and their families with old-time cabins, tent space, and access straight into the lake via a boat ramp—no locks! Nothing fancy here, just serious fishing. Cabins have TV, air-conditioning, and heat and come fully equipped with dishes and linens. Cabins run $42.50 and up depending on size, tent space $12.50 a night, and reserved dock space $30 for guests. Laundry and shower room on premises. There is a $5 ramp fee for using their private ramp.

Okeechobee 34974

A quiet getaway for the fishing family, the **Angler's Villa Family Fishing Resort** (863-763-5060), 3203 SE 29th Ln, is just off the maze of waterways along Taylor Creek. Family owned and operated, this camp offers a delightful setting under the shady oaks. Rentals include fully equipped kitchens and cable TV (three-night minimum, $55). Heated, screened pool; gas and charcoal grills; and a fish-cleaning bench are on the premises, as well as a boat ramp and boat slips.

🦑 🐾 Evenings are always hopping at **J&S Fish Camp & Tavern** (772-597-4455), 9500 SW US 441 S, where the music spills out over the water and onto the highway. This is a fun, funky little Florida fish camp with island style, offering RV sites and tent sites ($18), boat slips, cottages ($45–65, depending on size), and one of the cutest bathhouses I've seen. Friendly pets welcome.

HOTELS, MOTELS, AND RESORTS

Clewiston 33440

Catering to sportfishermen with its quick access to the lake, **Angler's Marina** (863-983-BASS or 1-800-741-3141; www.anglersmarina.com),

910 Okeechobee Blvd, lets you pull your boat into covered dockage just steps from your room. Choose from cozy efficiencies or condos ($59–135); no pets.

❧ A true slice of Florida history, **The Clewiston Inn** (863-983-8151 or 1-800-749-4466; www.clewistoninn .com), 108 Royal Palm Ave, circa 1938, ushers you back in time. Step through the pillars to the elegant Southern lobby into a more genteel era, where it seems utterly appropriate to sip a mint julep in the Everglades Lounge while admiring J. Clinton Shepard's 1940s oil canvas mural of Everglades wildlife. There are 57 rooms ($99 and up), well kept and small but appropriate for the era in which they were constructed, and decorated in a style fitting the elegance of the hotel. Visit the Colonial Dining Room downstairs for a Southern-style fine-dining experience.

Pro bass fisherman Roland Martin parlays his fame at **Roland Martin's Lakeside Resort** (863-983-3151 or 1-800-473-6766; www.rolandmartin marina.com), 920 E Del Monte Ave, where spacious rooms ($68–88) provide a good night's sleep before you hit the lake. Tie up your boat at one of the 130 covered boat slips ($7 per night) or along the lengthy dock; visit the marina store for bait, tackle, or to arrange a fishing guide. RV sites run $30 per night for full hookup.

Lakeport 33471
The tiny **Aruba Motel** is part of the larger Aruba RV Resort (see *Campgrounds*), with four paneled motel rooms ($50) and three suites ($75–85), each with a small fridge, microwave, and TV. Sit out front

and watch the fish jump, or wander a few steps down to the tiki bar. Cash preferred; surcharge for credit card use.

The **Lakeport Lodge** (863-946-2020), FL 78 and CR 721, caters to anglers and is very busy on weekends. The 24 units include traditional motel rooms ($60) or suites ($70) offering a full kitchen, a living room/lounge area, and linoleum floors to minimize the impact of active outdoorspeople. Smoking is permitted, but not in the bedrooms. The newly reopened Lakeport Restaurant, featuring burgers and steaks, is just steps away.

Okeechobee 34974
At Buckhead Ridge, **Angler's Waterfront Motel** (863-763-4031; www .guideservice.com), One Sixth St (just off FL 78), has basic, clean efficiencies and waterfront apartments ($50–60) with parquet floors, showers, and a fridge—just what the busy angler is looking for. Guide service on-site.

Pier II Motel (863-763-8003 or 1-800-874-3744), 2200 US 441 SE, is a former chain motel renovated and now under local management. With enormous rooms, it's a comfortable place to stay ($60–80).

✳ Where to Eat
DINING OUT

Clewiston
One of my perennial favorites, the casual but elegant **Colonial Dining Room** at The Clewiston Inn (see *Hotels, Motels, and Resorts*) has undergone a full change of chef and staff since my visit. The prior menu focused on fresh local produce and fish and presented such classics as fried green tomatoes and Big O catfish cakes, with entrées $8–22.

La Belle

Don's Steak House (863-675-2074), 93 Hall St, is the place for steak in the region, what with all the cattle ranches to the north. Enjoy New York strip, Delmonico, top sirloin, porterhouse, prime rib, even filet mignon ($9–21), or grab a taste of seafood favorites such as grouper, fried catfish, or fresh Florida frog's legs ($13–19). Open for lunch and dinner; children's menu available.

Okeechobee

🐾 If it swims, crawls, or hops, they probably serve it up at **Lightsey's Seafood Restaurant** (863-763-4276), at Okee-tantie Recreation Area (see *Campgrounds*), where Florida's marine bounty takes center stage on the menu. Enjoy Florida lobster stuffed with crabmeat, fresh fried catfish and cooter, or a hefty plate of oysters ($11–20), and leave room for some delicious pumpkin fry bread.

EATING OUT

Belle Glade

Even though it's attached to a gas station, **Mrs. Georgia's Catfish House** (561-996-6464), 1400 S Main St, is still worth a stop for dinner if you like your catfish and cole slaw in great big heaps. Dinner with plenty in the doggie bag can be had for less than $10, and the family who runs the place now has Pakistani food on the menu, too.

Big Cypress Seminole Reservation

When I hiked into the **Swamp Water Café** at **Billie Swamp Safari** (see *Attractions*) one fine winter day, I was glad that the portions were huge, because they fit my appetite that day—the massive Indian Taco is made up on Indian fry bread (delightful and calorie-heavy) and loaded with beef, lettuce, tomato, and salsa. Serving lunch and dinner; $11 and up.

Clewiston

Scoopy Doo's Eatin Place (863-983-1116), 113 N Francisco St, recently opened up to cater to your sweet tooth with sundaes and fountain drinks, and to your overall hankering for some Italian food ($5–10) with cannoli, spaghetti, eggplant parmagiana, and pizzas. Traditional local favorites are on the menu, too. At press time it was possibly changing hands, so it's wise to call ahead.

Authentic Mexican shines at the **Sunrise Restaurant** (941-983-9080), 842 E Sugarland Hwy, where "special plates" of your favorite Mexican dishes run $6–7, and tacos, tamales, burritos, and more can be bought à la carte. I love their enchiladas, but you may opt for a seafood specialty, including shrimp tacos, frog's legs, or fried oysters. Open for lunch and dinner daily.

Fort Drum

North of Okeechobee, the **Fort Drum Diner** (863-763-8900), 32601 US 441, is an unassuming block building where you can sit and enjoy classic Clyde Butcher Florida landscape photography while the friendly staff serves up classic Cracker cooking such as quail, frog's legs, fried catfish, and pork chops ($6–13; nightly dinner specials $6).

La Belle

🐾 Since 1933, **Flora and Ella's Restaurant** (863-675-2891), 550 FL 80 W, now in roomy new digs, has brought in folks from afar with their excellent country cooking and famous to-die-for pies. Their fine Southern cooking includes such favorites as chicken and dumplings, Country Boy pot roast, catfish, and Hoppin' John. Yes, you can get okra, grits, and fried green tomatoes here! Dinners $6–10, slice of pie $2.50; mine was coconut cream and as heavenly fresh and fluffy as it gets.

Okeechobee

You won't go wrong with breakfast at **Mom's Kitchen** (863-763-7553), 909 S Parrott Ave—they serve it all day, they serve it up fast, and they serve it with grits if you like, all for less than $5 (unless you include a steak or pork chop with your eggs). Choose from more than a dozen types of omelets, or have homemade biscuits and gravy. Open for lunch and dinner, too.

Named for the first sheriff of this frontier region, **Pogey's Restaurant** (863-763-7222), 1759 S Parrott Ave, is a good family restaurant with breakfast worth stopping for; most choices are less than $5. I like the French toast, but their specialty is biscuits with sausage gravy.

🍽 Some of the best barbecue I've had in Florida comes from **Skip's Bar-B-Que** (863-763-8313), 104 SE Sixth St, but come prepared—I like mine salty, smoky, and succulent, and that's exactly how your chicken, pork, and ribs will turn out. Sandwiches $5–7 with sides, dinners $6–9. The cobbler is superb, too.

Pahokee

Jellyroll's Coffee Shop & Gift Boutique (561-924-0000), 129 Lake Ave, isn't just for java—it's the local hangout for scrumptious Mexican meals and general gossip and is named after a popular local character. Open 7–7, closed Sun.

Upthegrove Beach

🍽 If you want a great steak, don't look for a steakhouse—**Happy Hour** (863-467-6420), a tavern along US 441 at Upthegrove Beach, has the best steaks in the region. Honest. We took a tip from a local and discovered the best value for your money in an honest-to-goodness great steak. No frills, just basic sides and perfect beef for $8–15. Open 5–9 Mon–Sat.

BAKERIES, COFFEE SHOPS, AND SODA FOUNTAINS Kick back and relax at **Common Grounds** (863-902-9889), 104 Bond St, Clewiston, a downtown streetcorner café serving breakfast treats, soup and salad, and fresh tea and coffee.

✳ Entertainment

Restored by the Mann family, **Mann's Clewiston Theatre** (863-983-6494), 100 E Sugarland Hwy, Clewiston, dates from 1941 and still shows first-run films in a great historic setting with a classic old refreshment stand in the lobby. Open Thu–Sun; call for times. Adults $6, children $4.

✳ Selective Shopping

Clewiston

Bond Street downtown is the shopping district, with boutiques, a coffeehouse, and more. **Di's Country Primitives** (863-902-0949), 106 Bond St, has mugs and candles, gourmet goodies, and greeting cards. Get dressy at **Maggie Mae's Studio #71** (863-228-0508), 108 Bond St, with retro and vintage clothing, jewelry, feather boas, and snazzy purses. I've found plenty of goodies at **Second Chance Boutique and Gifts** (863-983-8865), 113 Bond St, where they have great prices on antique glassware and newer decor items.

At **Roland Martin's Lakeside Resort** (see *Hotels, Motels, and Resorts*), the marina store is one of the best places in town to shop. Sure, you can buy bait, but why not a tie-dyed T-shirt for the kids? They carry sportswear from Columbia and Fresh Produce, Guy Harvey T-shirts, Hawaiian shirts, and even hula dancer and tiki salt and pepper shakers.

La Belle

You'll find a bevy of unique items at **Country Peddler Antiques** (863-675-3822), 265 N Bridge St—when I poked around, I came up with a traveling pulpit for circuit preachers, Noritake china, and an elaborately gilded clock amid primitives and glassware.

I know of no other honey outlet in Florida, so make a beeline to **Harold P. Curtis Honey Co.** (863-675-2187 or 1-888-531-9097; http://curtishoney .hypermart.net), Bridge St, in the historic downtown district. It's a storefront for a family business that dates from 1921. You've heard of orange blossom honey, but how about palmetto and mangrove? In addition to honey and honey products, they have beautiful beeswax candles for sale, too.

Moore Haven

Anne-Tiques (863-946-9100), corner of 100 J and First St, is the one and only antiques shop in town, and it's crammed to the gills with lots of stuff.

Stop in and say hi to local legend Sam Griffin at **Fisherman's Haven Handmade Lures** (863-983-3441 or 1-800-541-4530), where Sam has been hand-tying these little pieces of art for decades. If you ask, he'll tell you all about when Uncle Joe's Fish Camp got started. Fine tackle and more.

Okeechobee

Park Avenue is the historic downtown district just steps away from the chamber of commerce, where you'll find a handful of antiques shops and boutiques. Among them are **The Dust Collector,** 118 Park Ave, with a heavy emphasis on Asian items and collectibles; **The Outpost** (863-763-7255), 330 Park Ave, a sportswear shop with Columbia, Quicksilver, and Roxy, as well as surf-related hats and sandals; and **Silver Spoon Antique Mall** (863-763-0609), 401 Park Ave, where the dealer booths have a fine selection of quilts, vintage furnishings, china, glassware, and home decor items.

Co-op Antiques, 2303 S Parrott Ave, features craft items and gift baskets, vintage dresses, and glass salt cellars.

The oldest flea market in the region, **Cypress Hut Flea Market,** 4701 US 441 N, is a giant garage sale with everything including the kitchen sink—even fine antiques, sterling jewelry, and fine leather.

Antique lures are a big lure at **Ironbelly Antiques & Collectibles** (863-357-2366), 238 US 441 N, which also has lace and lamps, glass prisms, vintage clothing, and costume jewelry.

Along US 441, the massive **Trading Post Flea Market** (863-763-4114) is a popular draw on weekends (8–3), with both new cheapie items and vintage treasures on display.

PRODUCE STANDS, FARMER'S MARKETS, SEAFOOD MARKETS, AND U-PICK Hazellief Groves (863-763-3767), 1600 SE 32nd Ave, Okeechobee, has a storefront on US 441 right across from the Wal-Mart, selling fresh citrus from their family groves.

January: Birds of a feather flock to the **Big O Birding Festival** (863-946-0300; www.bigobirdingfestival.com), held the last weekend, for workshops, field trips, and rare birds best seen in this region, such as the Everglades snail kite and Audubon's caracara. Fee.

February: **Cane Grinding Festival** (863-946-0440), Ortona, first weekend. An old-fashioned sugarcane grind and boil held at Ortona Indian Mound Park (see *Archeological Sites*), with music and food, too.

Battle of Okeechobee Reenactment, Okeechobee, last weekend, near Kings Bay along US 441 SE. On Christmas Day 1837, the Seminoles, led by their medicine man Abiaka, ambushed a unit of U.S. Army soldiers led by Col. Zachary Taylor. The fighting raged for three hours, and more than a hundred men fell. This battle was a turning point that dubbed Taylor "Old Rough and Ready" and drove the Seminoles deep into the Everglades for nearly a century. The reenactment captures both sides of the story.

Swamp Cabbage Festival (863-675-0125), La Belle, last weekend. Celebrate "hearts of palm" at riverfront Barron Park with food, music, and crafts.

March: **Chalo Nitka Festival** (863-946-0440), Moore Haven, first weekend. "Day of the Bass" in Seminole,

this festival celebrates fishing on Lake Okeechobee at Chalo Nitka Park on 10th St, with Seminole crafts and food as well as local entertainers.

April: **Belle Glade Black Gold Festival** (561-996-2745), Belle Glade, third weekend, brings in artists, musicians, and a crafts fair to celebrate the rich, dark earth that gives sugarcane and vegetables grown here their sweet flavor.

Clewiston Sugar Festival (863-983-7979), Clewiston, third Saturday, is a celebration of the end of the sugarcane harvest with entertainment, food, and crafts.

September: **Okeechobee Cattlemen's Rodeo** (863-763-6464), at the Cattlemen's Rodeo Arena, US 441 N. Held annually on Labor Day weekend, the rodeo brings in the cowmen from the ranches surrounding Okeechobee to showcase their riding and roping skills.

November: **Big O Hike** (1-877-HIKE-FLA; www.floridatrail.org), Thanksgiving week. Since 1992, a group of hikers from the Florida Trail Association have walked around the lake on a 109-mile series of nine-day hikes each year, with designated group camping and social activities along the way.

Grassy Waters Festival, Pahokee, third weekend. A delightful cross between a church picnic and a county fair, this lakeside festival mixes gospel music with amusement rides, a petting zoo, food vendors, and tricycle races.

The Treasure Coast

INDIAN RIVER COUNTY

ST. LUCIE COUNTY

MARTIN COUNTY

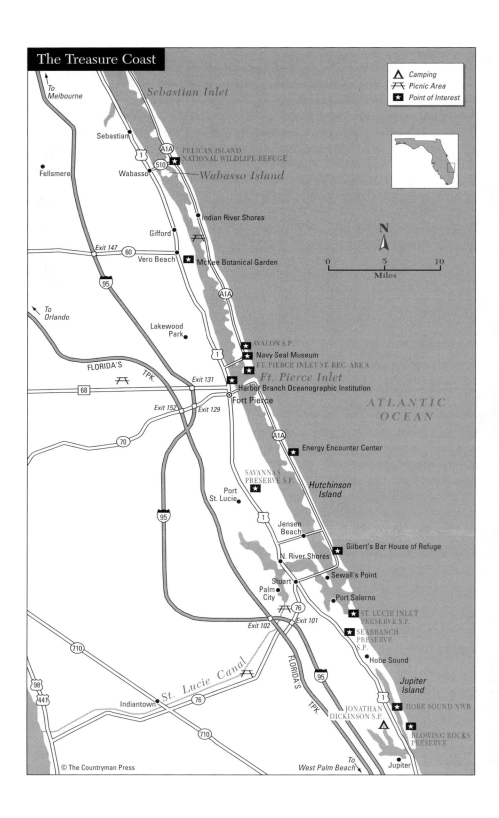

The Treasure Coast

Camping
Picnic Area
Point of Interest

To Melbourne

Sebastian Inlet

Sebastian

PELICAN ISLAND
NATIONAL WILDLIFE REFUGE

Wabasso

Wabasso Island

Fellsmere

Indian River Shores

Gifford

Exit 147

Vero Beach

McKee Botanical Garden

To Orlando

Lakewood Park

AVALON S.P.

Navy Seal Museum

FT. PIERCE INLET ST. REC. AREA

FLORIDA'S TPK.

Exit 131

Ft. Pierce Inlet

Harbor Branch Oceanographic Institution

Fort Pierce

Exit 152

Exit 129

ATLANTIC
OCEAN

Energy Encounter Center

SAVANNAS
PRESERVE S.P.

Hutchinson
Island

Port
St. Lucie

Jensen
Beach

Gilbert's Bar House of Refuge

N. River Shores

Sewall's Point

Stuart

Palm
City

Port Salerno

ST. LUCIE INLET
PRESERVE S.P.

Exit 102

Exit 101

SEABRANCH
PRESERVE
S.P.

Hobe Sound

St. Lucie Canal

Jupiter
Island

Indiantown

FLORIDA'S TPK.

JONATHAN
DICKINSON S.P.

HOBE SOUND NWR

BLOWING ROCKS
PRESERVE

To
West Palm Beach

Jupiter

N

0   5   10
Miles

© The Countryman Press

INDIAN RIVER COUNTY

When you hear the name Indian River, it's synonymous with citrus—and indeed, thousands of acres in the western half of the county are devoted to immaculate rows of grapefruit, orange, and other succulent fruits. But the earliest pioneers to this region found it to be a jungle, hard to pull a wagon through and mostly underwater. In 1887 Henry T. Gifford and his family came to the bluffs of the Indian River Narrows to build their homestead. Within a few years, enough settlers joined them to petition for a post office, and Henry's wife, Sara, submitted the name "Vero," the Latin adverb for "truth." By November 1891, not only was there a post office, but Indian River County was carved out of neighboring Brevard and St. Lucie Counties. Mr. Gifford was behind the effort to build a road between Sebastian and Fort Pierce, which was dubbed the Dixie Highway. The Florida East Coast Railroad, Henry Flagler's rail line, began service through the county in 1893, providing citrus growers and fishermen fast shipping to northern markets.

When Waldo Sexton came to Vero in the early 1920s, he—like many other speculators in Florida's land boom—saw opportunity. He created the first dairy in the county and shipped out products in his refrigerator trucks, involved himself in citrus growing and packing, and established a real estate firm to draw northern investors south. He built the Driftwood Inn, a rambling two-story hotel in Vero Beach. And with Arthur McKee, he opened the McKee Jungle Gardens, a tourist draw even today. As marshlands were drained for agriculture and housing, residents poured in, with the population increasing from 793 to 2,226 in 1930.

Today, this lightly populated county continues to hum along on a base of agriculture and light industry, its visitors most interested in the outdoors. They are attracted to the coast for the gentle beaches and great fishing and birding along the Indian River Lagoon, and to the marshy beginnings of the St. Johns River by the beauty of dense forests, cypress strands, and wide-open marshes. As you drive down US 1 toward Sebastian, notice the banana trees growing wild along the Indian River Lagoon—a reminder of an agricultural past that continues to be a strong anchor for this community today.

GUIDANCE For more information on the area, get in touch with the **Indian River Chamber of Commerce** (772-567-3491; www.indianriverchamber.com), 1216 21st St, Vero Beach 32960.

GETTING THERE *By car:* Use I-95 or US 1 to reach Fellsmere, Sebastian, Vero Beach, and Oslo. FL 60 connects Florida's Turnpike with Vero Beach.

By air: **Melbourne International Airport** (321-723-6227; www.mlbair.com), One Air Terminal Parkway, is the closest airport to the region, offering commuter flights daily on Delta. The region is also within range of Palm Beach International Airport (see *North Palm Beach County*).

GETTING AROUND *By car:* A car is necessary for visiting the county unless your destination is Vero Beach, where there is a lot to see and do within walking distance of hotels and B&Bs. Most services are along US 1 and FL A1A, and along FL 60 in Vero Beach.

MEDICAL EMERGENCIES For emergencies head to **Indian River Memorial Hospital** (561-567-4311), 1000 36th St, Vero Beach.

✷ To See

BASEBALL In 1948 the Brooklyn Dodgers decided to settle in Vero Beach for spring training—and although the team has moved, their spring training ritual remains the same. The **Los Angeles Dodgers** still hit the field at **Bud Holman Stadium** (772-569-6858), 4101 26th St, in **Dodgertown** (see *Lodging*) Feb– Apr, followed by their farm team the Vero Beach Dodgers, Apr–Sep 1.

HISTORIC SITES

Fellsmere
Fellsmere was the vision of E. Nelson Fell, who in 1910 bought 118,000 acres from the railroad land company to create several cities. Fellsmere is the only one that has survived and thrived, in part due to having its own railroad that ensured shipment of citrus from surrounding farms to the Florida East Coast Railroad in Sebastian. Downtown Fellsmere is small and walkable, and its many historic sites include the **1913 City Hall, 1916 Fellsmere School,** several churches, the **1915 Fellsmere Inn,** and the **1920s land office,** now home of the Marsh Landing restaurant (see *Eating Out*).

Grant
Stop in at the **1916 Grant Historical House & Fisherman's Park** (321-723-8543), 5795 US 1, to see a restored pioneer Cracker home that is the centerpiece of this wayside park along the Indian River Lagoon. The home is open for tours 10–4 Tue–Fri; the park is open daily sunrise–sunset and has a walking trail, riverfront boardwalk, and fishing dock.

A hurricane in July 1715 sunk an entire flotilla of Spanish galleons loaded with gold and silver just off the coast of Sebastian Inlet. Nearly 1,500 men made it to shore and made camp at the inlet until they were rescued. Years later, the Spanish returned to the camp to attempt to raise some of their treasure and return it to Spain. The **Spanish Fleet Survivors and Salvors Camp** is on the National Register of Historic Places and is located inside Sebastian Inlet State Park (see *Beaches*).

MUSEUMS

Sebastian

Renowned for the treasures he recovered from the 1622 wreck of the *Atocha* off Key West, Mel Fisher is considered a giant in the field of treasure hunting. Stop in at **Mel Fisher's Treasure Museum** (772-589-9875), 1322 US 1, to see artifacts from the *Atocha* and from the 1715 Spanish fleet that sank off the coast between Sebastian Inlet and Fort Pierce. Open 10–5 Mon–Sat, noon–5 Sun. Fee.

Sebastian Inlet

At **Sebastian Inlet State Park** (see *Beaches*), the **McLarty Treasure Museum** (772-589-2147), 13180 FL A1A, focuses on artifacts recovered from the shipwrecked Spanish fleet of 1715, found along the Treasure Coast. The movie *Treasure: What Dreams Are Made Of* explains modern-day salvage efforts. Open 10–4:30 daily; small fee. ✍ Also inside the park, the **Sebastian Fishing Museum** (772-589-9659), south side of the Sebastian Inlet Bridge, covers the long history of the region's fishing industry, with replicas of a fish house and dock, and a 24-minute video on the Indian River Lagoon. Open 10–4; free with park admission.

Vero Beach

Inside the historic 1935 Vero Beach Community Building, dedicated in 1935, the **Indian River Citrus Museum** (772-770-2263), 2140 14th Ave, explores the history of citrus growing in the region, from the Spanish explorers who first brought orange trees to Florida to today's high-tech processing and packing. Archives, artifacts, and guided citrus tours are all part of the experience. Open 10–4 Tue–Fri. Fee.

Considered the largest facility of its kind on the Treasure Coast, the **Vero Beach Museum of Art** (772-231-0707; www.vbmuseum.org), 3001 Riverside Park Dr, offers five art

CRUISING THE INDIAN RIVER

Visit Florida

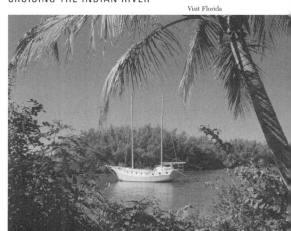

galleries, a sculpture garden, an art library, museum store, and numerous spaces for seminars and classes, including an outdoor foundry. Objects from the museum's permanent collection are rotated through several of the galleries; the Schumann Florida Gallery showcases Florida art. Classes are offered to the public on a regular basis. Open 10–4:30 Tue–Sat, 1–4:30 Sun. Fee.

RAILROADIANA ✒ Built in 1903, the former Florida East Coast Railroad Station is now the **Vero Beach Railroad Station Exhibit Center** (772-778-3435), 2336 14th Ave. Stop in and see their permanent model-railroad display showcasing a journey through Indian River County. Open 10–1 Mon, Wed, and Fri. Free.

✳ To Do

BIRDING Don't-miss birding sites in the county include **Pelican Island National Wildlife Refuge** (see *Preserves*), with its nesting colony of brown pelicans; **Fort Drum Marsh Conservation Area** (see *Wild Places*), where sandhill cranes and caracara are commonly sighted; and **Blue Cypress Conservation Area** (see *Wild Places*), with foraging and nesting habitat for the snail kite. Many of the islands of the Indian River Lagoon are rookeries or roosts for colonial nesting birds such as herons, pelicans, and ibis, so a cruise along the waterway at dusk or dawn will yield spectacular sightings.

BOATING Cruising the Indian River Lagoon is a favorite pastime of locals. If you've brought your own, you can anchor in deep-water slips at the **Sebastian River Marina & Boatyard** (772-664-3029), 8525 N US 1, Sebastian, a full-service marina, or pull in at the **City Marina at Marker 139** (772-978-4960) in Vero Beach; make reservations 48 hours in advance.

FISHING Saltwater or freshwater—your choice! **Sebastian Inlet** is a popular location where king mackerel, snapper, and grouper hang out around the jetties. If you hook up with a local captain for a deep-sea trip, expect to find wahoo, tuna, and marlin well offshore. Check in at Captain Hiram's (see *Eating Out*) to book an excursion with **Voyager Party Fishing** (772-388-0011). Inland, **Blue Cypress Lake** (see *Wild Places*) is known for its largemouth bass and black crappie, and **Stick Marsh,** a reservoir in the northwest corner of the county, has been named one of the Top 10 black bass lakes by the Florida Fish & Wildlife Conservation Commission.

HIKING While many of the county's trails are multiuse, there are several gems that are "hiking only" and well worth a morning's walk. Start with **Oslo River-front Conservation Area** (see *Preserves*) for a meander through the "jungle" that the early pioneers encountered. For more adventure head out to **Fort Drum Marsh Conservation Area** (see *Wild Places*), which has a beautiful boardwalk through a cypress dome and an often-challenging walk around Hog Island, a somewhat dry spot otherwise surrounded by the marshes from which the St. Johns River rises. And even if you're traveling without children, don't miss the **Environmental Learning Center** (see *Nature Centers*) at Wabasso Island, with its many boardwalks and short trails.

PADDLING Ply salt water or fresh water with **Tropical Kayak Tours** (772-778-3044; www.tropicalkayaktours.com), where avid kayaker Ronda Good leads you on an adventure into the tropical heart of Indian River County. Her broad slate of tours includes numerous local destinations such as Blue Cypress Lake and the Sebastian River; tours of the Indian River start at $40. Call or e-mail to arrange reservations; lunch is provided.

✳ Green Space

BEACHES

Sebastian Inlet

Spanning two counties across one of the Indian River Lagoon's major inlets, **Sebastian Inlet State Park** (321-984-4852; www.floridastateparks.org/sebastian inlet/default.cfm), 9700 S FL A1A, is a popular destination for surfers and anglers. A1A runs right through the park, which includes the beach and fishing pier, an on-site outfitter, a full-service campground, a nature trail, and the McLarty Treasure Museum (see *Museums*). Open 8–sunset daily. Fee.

Vero Beach

There are five oceanfront public parks along this golden strand, stretching from **Golden Sands Beach Park** (772-388-5483), 1.4 miles north of CR 510, to **Round Island Beach Park** (772-231-2604), south of Beachland Blvd. All provide rest rooms and showers, picnic tables and grills, and a playground. Free.

BOTANICAL GARDENS When I was a kid, it was a natural attraction called McKee Jungle Gardens that had been around since 1929. A victim of the Disney era, it closed its doors in 1976, and most of the land was sold to developers. But 18 acres of the original garden remained, and local enthusiasts rallied to save it. Reopened in 2001 as the **McKee Botanical Garden** (772-794-0601; www.mckeegarden.org), 350 US 1, Vero Beach, this beautiful subtropical hammock bursts with brilliant natural color in every season. A botanical reference library is on-site. Open 10–5 Tue–Sat, noon–5 Sun. Fee.

NATURE CENTERS ♿ ✐ Kids will love all there is to see and do at the 51-acre **Environmental Learning Center** (772-589-5050; www.elcweb.org), 255 Live Oak Dr, Wabasso Island, with its hands-on interpretive stations along nature trails snaking through a variety of near-shore habitats, from coastal hammock to mangrove fringe. The Welcome Center has exhibits and a gift shop; pick up a

CAMPING OUT AT SEBASTIAN INLET STATE PARK

Visit Florida

Visit Florida

SUNRISE ON VERO BEACH

map here to begin your exploration of the campus, which hides such goodies as a Wet Lab with touch tanks, the Waterside Pavilion to picnic in, a tiki hut, a Dry Lab with computers, a butterfly garden, a greenhouse, a native plant garden, and much more. Three-hour canoe trips on the Indian River Lagoon are offered every Sat morning (call for reservations). To reach the nature center, exit from CR 510 from the causeway onto Wabasso Island and drive north. Open 10–4 Tue–Fri, 9–noon Sat (until 4 in winter), 1–4 Sun. Free; donations appreciated.

PRESERVES

Orchid Island

In bits and pieces over 20 miles of coastline along FL A1A from Melbourne

LOGGERHEAD WITH TRACKING DEVICE, ARCHIE CARR NATIONAL WILDLIFE REFUGE
U. S. Fish & Wildlife Service

Beach to Wabasso Beach, **Archie Carr National Wildlife Refuge** (561-562-3909; www.fws.gov/archie carr) protects the most significant sea turtle nesting ground in the United States. More than 25 percent of all loggerhead sea turtles and 35 percent of all green sea turtles return to this shoreline to nest. Named for University of Florida zoologist and conservationist Archie Carr, the refuge seeks to protect a total of 900 acres of coastal scrub and untrammeled beachfront for sea turtle nesting. Visitors are welcome to enter at adjacent beachfront park access points and walk the shoreline; turtle nests are marked. Free guided sea turtle walks are offered in June and July, 9–midnight; advance reservations required (recommended up to a month in advance; call 321-984-4852).

   In 1903 President Theodore Roosevelt dedicated **Pelican Island National Wildlife Refuge** (561-562-3909; www.fws.gov/pelicanisland), FL A1A, 3.5 miles north of CR 510, as a preserve for a breeding colony of endangered brown pelicans, creating the nation's first National Wildlife Refuge. The preserve now encompasses 500 acres of impoundments along the Indian River Lagoon as well as 2.2-acre Pelican Island, which can be seen from an observation tower at the end of the Centennial Trail. The trail was the first of new visitor improvements added for the preserve's centennial. (Previously, birders had to visit by boat.) Two multiuse trails loop 2.5 miles each around the impoundments, perfect for a bike ride or a long walk, where, on my very first visit, I saw roseate spoonbills in the trees. The Centennial Trail is wheelchair-accessible and another great birding spot. Open 7:30–sunset daily. Free.

Oslo

Protecting 336 acres along the Indian River Lagoon, **Oslo Riverfront Conservation Area** (904-529-2380), Oslo Rd just east of US 1, is a haven for botanical diversity, with some of the tallest wild coffee you'll ever see; the "Awesome Pine," a National Champion slash pine; and more than 20 rare species of plants, including Simpson's stopper, coral-root orchid, and whisk fern. Bromeliads grow densely on every tree in the hammock. Three miles' worth of nature trails wind through the preserve, leading you to surprises such as an overlook on a mangrove-lined lagoon and to a historic coquina quarry. Open sunrise–sunset daily; free. Informative guided walks are offered Wed and Sun at 9 AM; meet at the park entrance.

WILD PLACES

Fellsmere

With nearly 22,000 acres straddling the C-54 canal and waterfront along the St. Sebastian River, **St. Sebastian River Buffer Preserve State Park** (321-953-5004; www.floridastate parks.org/stsebastian/default.cfm), 1000 Buffer Preserve Dr, spills across Brevard and Indian River Counties and offers outdoor activities that include nearly 50 miles of equestrian trails with primitive campsites, overlooks on the canal for manatee watching, a shooting range, and nature trails. A visitors center (open 8–5 Mon–Fri) is located off CR 507 north of Fellsmere.

TRAIL AT ST. SEBASTIAN RIVER BUFFER PRESERVE

Sandra Friend

South Indian River County

Protecting 54,000 acres along the chain of lakes that is the lower St. Johns River, **Blue Cypress Conservation Area** (321-676-6614) has access points off Blue Cypress Lake Rd and CR 507 north of FL 60. Most folks come here for the fishing, but you can launch a canoe or kayak and experience what Florida looked like centuries ago along these cypress-lined waterways. Access to miles of levees for birding is best from Blue Cypress Recreation Area off CR 507, where there are also several primitive campsites.

An excellent place for birding, **Fort Drum Marsh Conservation Area** (321-676-6614), 9.2 miles east of Florida's Turnpike Yeehaw Junction exit along FL 60, is a 21,000-acre wilderness that encompasses the headwaters of the St. Johns River. I've seen caracara and sandhill cranes along the entry road. The preserve offers a day's worth of walking along the levees as well as two developed hiking trails with primitive campsites; the Hog Island Trail has a gorgeous boardwalk bridging the "mainland" with Hog Island through a mysterious cypress swamp. The preserve also offers fishing, canoeing, bicycling, and seasonal hunting. Free.

✴ Lodging

CAMPGROUNDS If you have a boat or canoe, bring a tent and sufficient fresh water and claim one of the hundreds of **uninhabited islands in the Indian River Lagoon** as your own for the night; leave-no-trace rules apply. For details contact the St. Sebastian River Preserve (321-953-5004), 1000 Buffer Preserve Dr, Fellsmere. Landlubbers can head to one of the sites at **Sebastian Inlet State Park** (see *Beaches*).

HOTELS, MOTELS, AND RESORTS

Sebastian 32958

Settle into the island mood at **Captain Hiram's Key West Inn** (772-388-8588), part of a tropical resort complex along the Indian River Lagoon at Marker 66. Adding to the relaxed atmosphere, there's a room to please everyone—from motel rooms to Jacuzzi suites to mini suites with wet bars, and even suites with bunk beds for the kids ($89–159).

A quiet, old-fashioned place, the **Sandrift Motel** (772-589-4546 or 1-800-226-4546), 14415 US 1, has basic motel rooms, efficiencies, and suites at reasonable rates ($55–75). I've stayed here and had a good night's sleep while exploring the region. You'll appreciate the sparkling pool and the Marker I Restaurant just a few steps away.

ALONG THE BOARDWALK AT FORT DRUM MARSH

Sandra Friend

Vero Beach 32963

Baseball fans—here's an opportunity for you. Set right in the middle of the Los Angeles Dodgers's spring-training camp, **Dodgertown Sports & Conference Center** (772-569-4900), 3901 26th St, lets you settle into baseball heaven, just steps from the action. Each of the 89 rooms and suites ($89–109) includes high-speed Internet, coffeemakers, and hair dryers, and the grounds offer an Olympic-size swimming pool, volleyball, basketball, tennis, jogging trails, and a fitness center.

A slice of the Keys along the Atlantic, the **Islander Inn** (1-800-952-5886; www. theislanderinn.com), 3101 Ocean Dr, is a delightful romantic escape with Caribbean charm. Each of the 16 uniquely decorated rooms ($99–135) has that island flair and includes a mini fridge for late-night noshing; efficiencies include full kitchens and private patios.

With a tropical setting and wrought-iron balcony railings, the **Sea Turtle Inn** (772-234-0788 or 1-877-998-8785; www.seaturtleinn.net), 835 Azalea Ln, offers a comfortable home away from home, just steps from the Ocean Drive shopping district and the beach. Accommodations include efficiencies and poolside apartments ($99–215).

✳ Where to Eat

DINING OUT

Vero Beach

Excellent food and an oceanfront view—what more can you ask for? My experiences at the **Ocean Grill** (772-231-5409; www.ocean-grill.com), 1050 Sexton Plaza, have been relaxed and satisfying. Dating from 1949, the restaurant sports unique decor with pioneer Waldo Sexton's imprint. Each

evening, several fresh catches are offered, broiled, Cajun, grilled, or fried. Roast duckling is a house specialty, but I opted for the coquilles St. Jacques, which came out creamy and succulent, brimming with mushrooms and crab. Dinner with a glass of wine from their extensive list will set you back $30–50 a person, but the experience is well worth it.

EATING OUT

Fellsmere

Worth driving out of your way for, **Marsh Landing** (772-571-8622), 44 N Broadway St, is a classic Florida Cracker restaurant serving up swamp cabbage, fried green tomatoes, and "swamp critters" such as gator, frog's legs, and catfish. You can't miss this historic building in downtown—it was the land office during the 1920s boom. Open for breakfast, lunch, and dinner daily; entrées $10 and up.

Sebastian

When on the sea, eat more seafood! **Captain Hiram's Restaurant** (772-589-4345), 1606 N Indian River Dr, offers a delectable selection of the finest around, from fresh oysters to half-pound broiled lobster tail to "angry" Dungeness crab and crab-stuffed baked shrimp. You won't go away hungry! Landlubbers can enjoy char-grilled rib eye and jerked chicken breast; there's a kid's menu, too. Serving lunch and dinner; entrées $13–25.

Vero Beach

From its humble beginning as an ice cream parlor in 1945, the **Patio Restaurant** (772-567-7215; www .veropatio.com), 1103 21st St, has become one of the best-loved landmarks in Vero Beach. The stunning wrought iron and tile throughout the restaurant is centuries old and was imported from Europe by Addison Mizner, the architect renowned for his work throughout Palm Beach. And what's the connection? Credit Waldo Sexton, the restaurant's founder and 1920s boom developer, for piling up "old discards" such as tiles and chandeliers from various ritzy buildings in "the patio." These pieces were incorporated into the restaurant's decor in 1959. Light and color play through the stained-glass panels above the French doors. It is a place to savor dinner, to enjoy the experience. The menu focuses on fresh local seafood and prime cuts of steak, but there are also daily early-bird specials such as coconut shrimp and chicken Piccata.

✳ Selective Shopping

Vero Beach
Find chic home decor at **California Dreamin'** (772-299-0131), 2007 Indian River Blvd, including funky art glass, African imports, and original art.

If you're looking for that perfect kayak, look no further than **Indian River Kayak & Canoe** (772-569-5757 or 1-800-881-7403; www.paddle florida.com/irkc.html), 3435 Aviation Blvd, one of the largest paddle-sports outfitters on the Atlantic Coast, with "demo days" the first Sunday of each month.

With undoubtedly the most extensive selection of children's books in Florida, the **Vero Beach Book Center** (772-569-2050; www.theverobeach bookcenter.com), 2145 Indian River Blvd, is one of the larger independent bookstores in the state and stocks an excellent array of new books for the grown-ups, too. Author events are frequent and feature top Florida authors. If you're a bibliophile like I am, don't miss this store!

ST. LUCIE COUNTY

I n the late 1800s, more than 20 small settlements existed along the Treasure Coast, and it's along those same barrier islands and the Indian River Lagoon that you'll find the beauty of St. Lucie County. Named by Spanish explorers in the 1560s, the region was once populated by the Ais and Jeaga, indigenous hunters and gatherers whose people eventually died off after exposure to European illnesses. During the Second Seminole War in the 1830s, the First Artillery chose a high bluff about 4 miles south of the inlet to build a blockhouse they called Fort Pierce, in honor of their commander. The city of **Fort Pierce** is one of the oldest on Florida's South Atlantic coast, incorporated in 1901. Once known for its fisheries and pineapple farms, Fort Pierce evolved into one of Florida's 1920s boomtowns, which its architecture showcases today after successful downtown redevelopment efforts.

Once an outpost of unspoiled beaches and quiet villages, St. Lucie County has exploded in population growth over the past decade, changing the face that visitors see—especially along Florida's Turnpike and I-95 around **Port St. Lucie.** Where citrus groves and pine forests once stretched to the horizon, now there are residential communities. The western part of the county is still citrus and ranching country. Called the "Grapefruit Capital of the World," the county still leads all others in Florida in citrus production.

GUIDANCE **St. Lucie County Tourism** (1-800-344-TGIF; www.visitstluciefla .com), 2300 Virginia Ave, Fort Pierce 34982, and the **St. Lucie Chamber of Commerce** (772-468-9152; www.StLucieChamber.org), 482 Indian River Dr, Fort Pierce 34950, and 1626 SE Port St. Lucie Blvd, Port St. Lucie 34952, can provide more information about the area.

GETTING THERE *By car:* Use **I-95** or **US 1** to reach Fort Pierce, St. Lucie, Port St. Lucie, and Jensen Beach. **FL 70** connects Florida's Turnpike with Fort Pierce.

By air: **Palm Beach International Airport** (see *North Palm Beach County*) is the closest major airport.

GETTING AROUND *By car:* A car is necessary for visiting the county. Most services are along US 1 and FL A1A, and along FL 70 in Fort Pierce.

MEDICAL EMERGENCIES In Fort Pierce head for **Lawnwood Regional Medical Center** (772-220-6866; www.lawnwoodmed.com), 1700 S 23rd St. In Port St. Lucie your nearest emergency room is at **St. Lucie Medical Center** (772-335-1405; www.stluciemed.com), 1800 SE Tiffany Ave.

✷ To See

ARCHEOLOGICAL SITES At **Spruce Bluff Preserve** (772-462-2526; www.stlucie co.gov/erd/spruce-bluff/ais.htm), Peru St and Dar Ln, Port St. Lucie, follow the **Ais Mound Trail** to discover a midden from the ancient Ais culture of southeast Florida. The mound is 20 feet high and nearly 180 feet in diameter and is now topped with large trees.

ART GALLERIES Founded in 1961, **The A. E. "Bean" Backus Gallery** (772-465-0630; www.backusgallery.com), 500 N Indian River Dr, Fort Pierce, focuses on the work of Backus, whose lush impressionist Florida landscapes (1940s–1960s) captured the wild nature of the state's rugged beauty. Backus had many students over the years, and Alfred Hair, a talented African American protégé, brought Backus's inspiration to a group of fellow landscape painters now honored as the Highwaymen, who sold their impressionist landscapes out of the backs of their cars. Perched on the banks of the Indian River Lagoon, the 4,000-square-foot gallery showcases a portion of their permanent collection of Backus's work, plus several galleries displaying the works of other Florida artists. The gallery is open 10–4 Tue–Sat, noon–4 Sun, except during the summer months, when visits are by appointment. Free.

BASEBALL Spring training heats up in late February when the **New York Mets** arrive at Tradition Field Stadium (772-871-2115), 525 NW Peacock Blvd, Port St. Lucie, their 100-acre facility with a 7,300-seat stadium. The minor-league St. Lucie Mets take the field in early April. Call ahead for tickets.

HISTORIC SITES **Downtown Fort Pierce** boasts a broad range of classic Florida architecture, from Cracker homes to late-19th-century revival businesses and Spanish Mission buildings from the 1920s. Stop at the visitors center located in the **1910 Seven Gable House,** 482 Indian River Dr, to pick up walking-tour information. In 1875 the **P. P. Cobb Building,** 408 N Indian River Dr, served as one of the first trading posts along the Cracker Trail. This cypress-sided building is still used for retail businesses today. Built in 1925, the **historic City Hall,** 315 Ave A, was in use until 1972; preservationists saved it from the wrecking ball, and it is now used for banquet rentals and office space. Visited by stars of the silver screen such as Sally Rand and Tom Mix, the **1923 Sunrise Theatre** (772-461-4775; www.sunrisetheatre.com), 210 S Depot Dr, was once the largest vaudeville theater on Florida's east coast. After extensive renovations, it recently reopened as the Theatre for the Performing Arts with regularly scheduled shows. The city itself was named after Fort Pierce, built by the U.S. Army during the Second Seminole War on the high bluff overlooking the Indian River Lagoon; a historic plaque at the site is all that remains to commemorate the spot.

Fort Pierce

Explore the region's maritime past at the **St. Lucie County Historical Museum** (772-462-1795; www.stluceico.gov), 414 Seaway Dr, where the wreck of the 1715 Spanish fleet comes alive in the Galleon Room, brimming with replicas of gold and silver coins, pottery, and household items. In addition to the important Harry Hill photographic collection, which documents St. Lucie County between the 1880s and 1920s, the museum has a fire house with antique engines, a Seminole encampment, artifacts from the original Fort Pierce, and a 1907 settler's home. The museum's **Pineapple Patch Gift Shop** is an excellent source for regional and Florida history books. Open 10–4 Tue–Sat, noon–4 Sun. Fee.

North Hutchinson Island

In the birthplace of the navy demolition teams, where better a museum to honor them? The **Navy UDT-Seal Museum** (772-595-5845; www.navysealmuseum .com), 3300 N FL A1A, recounts the courage and history of navy frogmen, Seals, and underwater demolition teams through well-interpreted artifacts and time-line-based exhibits. Open 10–4 Tue–Sat, noon–4 Sun, 10–4 Mon (Jan–Apr only). Fee.

✳ To Do

BOATING Located downtown, the **Fort Pierce City Marina** (772-464-1245 or 1-800-619-1780; www.fortpiercecitymarina.com), One Ave A, offers 284 slips on the Indian River Lagoon, with fishing and sailing charters available dockside.

DIVING **Dixie Divers Southeast Diving Institute** (561-468-4809), 1717 S US 1, Fort Pierce, offers a full range of dive classes, including dive master. Certified scuba divers will want to head for **Fort Pierce Inlet State Park** (see *Beaches*) to check out a reef just 100 yards from the beach; diver-down flag required. Check in at **Dive Odyssea** (772-460-1771), 621 N Second St, Fort Pierce, for fresh air and instructions on where best to charter a boat and head to the off-shore reefs and wrecks.

DRIVING TOURS Celebrating the life of one of Florida's most important folk-lorists, the new **Zora Neale Hurston "Dust Tracks" Heritage Trail** (www .st-lucie.lib.fl.us/zora) starts at the Zora Neale Hurston Branch Library, 3008 Ave D, Fort Pierce, and leads you on a journey through the novelist's many connections to Fort Pierce. There are eight stops along the way, with detailed interpretive information.

ECOTOURS

Fort Pierce

Departing from the South Bridge Marina, **Dolphin Watch & Wildlife Eco Tours** (772-466-4660; www.floridadolphinwatch.com) takes you on a narrated journey through the Indian River Lagoon, where dolphin sightings are frequent and the birding is superb. You'll tour both the fringe of Fort Pierce Inlet State

Park and Jack Island Preserve. Reservations required; call for cruise schedule and current pricing.

Port St. Lucie

The seasonal **River Lilly River Cruise** (772-489-8344), departing from Rivergate Park, explores the North Fork of the St. Lucie River, a beautiful backwater lined with palms and dense natural foliage. Watch manatees and dolphins, and spot alligators and river otters. Call for schedule and current pricing.

FAMILY ACTIVITIES ✆ At their St. Lucie Nuclear Power Plant, South Hutchinson Island, Florida Power & Light presents the **Energy Encounter Center** (772-468-4111 or 1-877-FPL4FUN; www.FPL.com/encounter), an interactive introduction to how energy powers the world, with more than 30 interactive displays. Operate the controls of a miniature nuclear reaction, walk a treadmill to power home electronics, or go on the popular Energy Treasure Hunt. At the College of Turtle Knowledge, an exhibit ties into the importance of their waterfront as a sea turtle nesting ground. Ask for an "eco-detective backpack" for the kids before heading out to Turtle Beach (see *Preserves*) just up the street, and inquire into their turtle walks during June and July nesting. Open 10–4 Sun–Fri. Free.

GAMING If you've not experienced the high-speed game of jai-alai, a Basque sport where the ball whizzes past at speeds of up to 175 miles per hour, stop in at **Fort Pierce Jai-Alai** (1-800-JAI-ALAI), Kings Hwy near Florida's Turnpike and I-95, Fort Pierce, to watch the mesmerizing action and, if you're so inclined, to bet on it. The complex includes elegant dining and inter-track wagering as well. Call for schedules; seasonal, running Nov–Apr.

GOLF Since 1938, the **Indian Hills Golf Course** (772-465-8110), 1600 S Third St, Fort Pierce, has been an important part of the community, challenging golfers with a par 72 course designed by Herbert Strong.

HIKING For solitude amid the pines and ponds, head to the **Indrio Savannas** (see *Wild Places*) to stretch your legs; on **Jack Island** (see *Preserves*) work your way through a mangrove puzzle for 5 or more miles. With several miles of trails to choose from, the **Oxbow Eco-Center** in Port St. Lucie (see *Nature Centers*) is a sure bet for an enjoyable morning hike with or without the kids. There are many other public lands in St. Lucie County with shorter nature trails; see *Green Space* for more ideas.

HORSEBACK RIDING Enjoy the exhilaration of riding a horse down the beach along **South Hutchinson Island.** St. Lucie Parks & Recreation (772-489-4386) sponsors this unique experience, and reservations are essential for the 90-minute rides. Rides are typically arranged each Sunday, departing from Frederick Douglass Memorial Park (see *Beaches*), and riders must be at least 10 years old.

PADDLING By kayak, the **Indian River Lagoon** is a marvel of wildlife—there is no better way to see manatees and sea turtles up close. Check in at **Dolphin Watch** (see *Ecotours*) for rentals. If you've brought your own, consider a lazy paddle up the **North Fork of the St. Lucie River,** launching from either the Halpa-tiokee unit of the **St. Lucie Inlet Preserve State Park** (see *Wild Places* in *Martin County*,) off US 1 in Port St. Lucie (where a hand cart is a must to get down the 0.5-mile, often soggy nature trail to the dock) or from the more easily accessible **White City Park** (561-462-1521), 1801 W Midway Rd, Fort Pierce, where a paddle south lets you admire the moss-draped live oaks along the shoreline and explore the cul-de-sacs and oxbows where manatees hide in the wintertime.

SURFING For surfers in the know, **Fort Pierce Inlet State Park** (see *Beaches*) is a primo destination on the Treasure Coast. On the north side of the inlet, the North Jetty receives swells from the south and east, and no matter the time of year, the waves appear—best caught at high tide. The downside? The crowds. Hit the surf early on weekdays for the prime peaks.

WILDLIFE & MARINELIFE VIEWING

Fort Pierce

The world-renowned **Harbor Branch Oceanographic Institution** (772-465-2400; www.hboi.edu), 5600 N US 1, is the home port of Johnson-Sea-Link submersibles and offers lectures, trips, and tours, many open to the public. Exhibits are throughout the campus; call ahead for lecture and tour information.

☞ At the **Manatee Observation & Education Center** (772-466-1600; www .manateecenter.com), see manatees up close along Moore's Creek, a favored gathering spot. An observation tower provides a view from above, and the exhibition hall, complete with movies, will further your knowledge of these gentle giants. Open 10–5 Tue–Sat, noon–4 Sun (Oct–Jun); 10–5 Thu–Sat (Jul–Sep). Fee.

☞ Adjacent to the St. Lucie County Historical Museum (see *Museums*), the **Smithsonian Marine Ecosystems Exhibit at the St. Lucie County Marine Center** (772-462-FISH; www.sms.si.edu/SMEE/smeehome.htm), 420 Seaway Dr, shows off a 3,300-gallon living coral reef and other living exhibits of Florida's coastal habitats, including mangrove forests and seagrass communities. These are not your typical aquarium exhibits—they are working models of the habitats, with interaction between all organisms living in each community. Open 10–4 Tue–Sat, noon–4 Sun. Fee. Free on Tuesday.

✱ Green Space

BEACHES

North Hutchinson Island

Surf's up at **Fort Pierce Inlet State Park** (772-468-3985), 905 Shorewinds Dr, one of the best places to hang 10 along this stretch of coastline. The 0.5-mile beach is popular for swimming, snorkeling, and sunbathing, and Dynamite Point was a training site for navy frogmen during World War II. Add picnic tables and nature trails, and it's a great family destination. Open 8–sunset daily; fee. Nearby **Pepper Park,** north on FL A1A, provides a launch point north of the inlet for snorkelers and scuba divers to explore Spanish galleons wrecked in the 1700s, just yards offshore; free.

Sandra Friend

TRAILS AT OXBOW ECO-CENTER

South Hutchinson Island

Driving south from Fort Pierce down FL A1A, you'll find many beach access points provided by **St. Lucie Parks & Recreation** (561-462-1521). Just 4 miles south is **Frederick Douglass Memorial Park,** 3500 S FL A1A, with picnic pavilions, bathrooms and showers, lifeguards, and a wheelchair-accessible beach crossover. Enjoy more of a wilderness feel at **Blind Creek Beach,** 5500 S FL A1A, just north of the nuclear power plant. South of the plant is **Walton Rocks Beach,** 6501 S FL A1A, with rest rooms and picnic tables and a rocky reef exposed at low tide. **Herman's Bay,** 7800 S FL A1A, has paved parking and dune crossovers.

Finally, **Waveland Beach,** 10350 S FL A1A, offers another large oceanfront park with lifeguards, rest rooms and showers, a concession stand, and a boardwalk.

BOTANICAL GARDENS Wander the garden rooms at **Heathcote Botanical Gardens** (772-464-4672; www.HeathcoteBotanicalGardens.org), 210 Savannah Rd, Fort Pierce, a collection of formal specialty gardens including an Herb Garden, a Reflection Garden, a Palm and Cycad Walk, and more. Their gift shop offers local art, Florida gardening and plant books, and children's toys and trinkets. The gardens and shop are open 9–5 Tue–Sat year-round and 1–5 Sun Nov–Apr. Fee; guided tours available.

NATURE CENTERS & ♪ The **Oxbow Eco-Center** (772-785-5833; www.stlucie co.gov/erd/oxbow), 5400 NE St. James Dr, Port St. Lucie, is a 220-acre preserve along the North Fork of the St. Lucie River with trails radiating out from the nature center. Some of the trails are wheelchair-accessible boardwalks, but most take you out into the wilds of pine flatwoods, scrub, hardwood hammocks, and tall bluffs and swamps along the river. Wildlife is abundant; bring your camera! Guided walks available. Open dawn–dusk daily. Free.

PARKS

Fort Pierce

Offering a large campground with a view of the massive freshwater savannas along St. Lucie's coast, **Savannas Recreation Area** (1-800-789-5776), 1400 E Midway Rd, has freshwater fishing, nature trails, canoe rentals, and boat ramps. Fee.

Port St. Lucie

♪ In a forest along the C-24 Canal, **Oak Hammock Park** (772-878-2277), 1982 Villanova Rd, has two pleasant nature trails, with the Oak Trail meandering

Sandra Friend

MANGROVE-LINED BOARDWALK AT TURTLE BEACH

through a grove of ancient live oaks. There is a fishing boardwalk, picnic tables, and a playground as well. Free.

PRESERVES

North Hutchinson Island
Just 1.5 miles north on FL A1A from Fort Pierce Inlet, **Jack Island Preserve State Park** (772-468-3985) offers a place for solitude and the opportunity to watch ospreys in graceful flight above the Indian River Lagoon. A narrow bridge connects the parking area with 5 miles of trails through mangrove-lined impoundments; an observation tower provides a bird's-eye view of surrounding islands. Open 8–sunset daily. Free.

South Hutchinson Island
🦅 An interpretive trail introduces you to the coastal dune habitat at **Ocean Bay Natural Area** (772-462-2526), FL A1A, 4.5 miles north of Jensen Beach Blvd, where you'll tunnel through dense sea grapes, gumbo limbo, and strangler fig on a 15-minute walk. Free.

🦅 **Turtle Beach,** just north of FP&L Gate 2, is on the grounds of Florida Power & Light's nuclear power plant and offers a 1-mile interpretive boardwalk through a mangrove forest as well as access to the beach. Stop in at the Energy Encounter Center (see *Family Activities*), 10–4 Sun–Fri, to sign in and pick up "eco-detective backpacks" for the kids to make exploring the trail and its habitats more fun. Gates locked at 8 PM. Free.

WILD PLACES

Indrio
Some of the area's best bird-watching can be found at **Indrio Savannas Natural Area** (772-462-2526), Tozour Rd and US 1, where marsh impoundments attract a variety of wading birds in this 423-acre preserve. More than 5 miles of hiking

MORENA CAMERON SLIPS THROUGH A SEA GRAPE TUNNEL AT OCEAN BAY NATURAL AREA.

Sandra Friend

trails meander through pine flatwoods, open prairies, and along the impound-ments. Open sunrise–sunset daily. Free.

Port St. Lucie

⚓ Stretching more than 10 miles from Fort Pierce to Jensen Beach, **Savannas Preserve State Park** (772-398-2779; www.floridastateparks.org/savannas/default .cfm), 9551 Gumbo Limbo Ln, protects the longest remaining freshwater savan-na on Florida's east coast. Teeming with wildlife, these marshes are less than 3 miles from the sea. In St. Lucie County, access the park east of US 1 off Walton Rd on Scenic Park Dr, where the Environmental Education Center is your best place to start for an overview of the habitats; it's also the gateway to nearly 8 miles of multiuse trails. Canoe and kayak rentals are available each Sat, Oct–May. Free.

✷ Lodging

CAMPGROUNDS

Fort Pierce 34982

Hang out on the wild side at **Savan-nas Recreation Area** (772-464-7855; www.stlucieco.gov/leisure/savanna .htm), 1400 Midway Rd, a county park on the western shore of Savan-nas Preserve State Park, where tent camping is available on unimproved sites, and there are improved sites for RVs and campers. Launch a kayak into the savannas, or walk along their edge on a nature trail to an observa-tion tower.

Port St. Lucie 34952

The **Port St. Lucie RV Resort** (772-337-3340 or 1-877-405-2333; www.portstluciervresort.com), 3703 SE Jennings Rd, offers RV and camping spaces for $36 nightly. Most visitors are in for the season. Enjoy an air-condi-tioned clubhouse with big-screen TV, fax, and pool table, or lounge around the heated pool.

HOTELS, MOTELS, AND RESORTS

Fort Pierce 34946

& ☙ Kick back and relax in a pleasant island-themed room at the **Fountain Resort** (772-466-7041; www.fountain resort.net), 4889 N US 1, an intimate accommodation with a heated pool and spa as the centerpiece of the grounds. Each room, suite, or effi-ciency ($79–109 May 1–Dec 15 and $119–159 Dec 16–Apr 30) offers wire-less Internet, satellite TV, and DVD players. Guests also enjoy a compli-mentary continental breakfast.

SEA GRAPE LEAVES

Sandra Friend

Port St. Lucie 34986

♿ A true golfer's destination, **Kolter Resorts at PGA Village** (772-466-6766 or 1-877-519-6766; www.pga villagehomes.com/accommodations .php), 9700 Reserve Blvd, offers three spectacular courses designed by Pete Dye and Tom Fazio, all within an easy walk of your spotless guest room or villa in the center of a premier golfing community. Rooms start at $94, villas at $146.

South Hutchinson Island 34950

Just 2 blocks from the beach at Fort Pierce Inlet, the **Dockside Harbor Light Inn** (772-468-3555 or 1-800-286-1745; www.docksideinn.com), 1160 Seaway Dr, offers a variety of well-kept rooms in a lush tropical setting. Guests have access to two heated pools and a whirlpool as well as fishing piers and dockage. Rates range from $70 off-season, $79 in-season for a standard room to $255 for the Presidential Waterfront Suite.

✱ Where to Eat

DINING OUT

Fort Pierce

For the freshest seafood head to **Ian's Tropical Grill** (772-595-5950), 927 US 1, where the day's catch of pompano or red snapper may be served up with coconut rice (complete with bits of real coconut), steamed veggies, or mango chutney. Known for their creativity, they'll tickle your taste buds, and they offer an extensive wine list. Featuring early-bird specials 3–6 for $15; dinner entrées to $35.

Port St. Lucie

Proud of their fine homemade Italian cuisine, **Ottavios Italian Cuisine** (772-871-9239), 7125 S US 1, will "make any dish you want," and for

that I'd drive several hours just to dine on olive puttanesca at this popular destination. Reservations recommended.

EATING OUT

Fort Pierce

It's a 1950s neighborhood roadhouse, so you gotta stop here. **Pineapple Joe's Grill & Raw Bar** (561-465-6930), 6297 N US 1, serves up no-frills, made-right-here American standards such as burgers, fish and chicken sandwiches, spicy wings (including Jamaican jerk style) and Florida fun stuff—gator bites, fried shrimp, and fresh oysters ($4–10). Don't miss the stuffed mushrooms!

Kick back along the Indian River at the original **Tiki Bar & Restaurant** (772-461-0880), two Ave A, an open-air chickee where the music draws a crowd, and despite the Jimmy Buffet casual atmosphere, the food is top-notch, from Florida lobster tail to Black Angus steaks. Dinner entrées $15 and up.

Port St. Lucie

For a taste of the Caribbean, try **The Calypso Pot** (772-878-5044), 354 S Port St. Lucie Blvd, an authentic island restaurant serving curries and roti, with Trinidad specialties such as calypso rice, soursop, peanut punch, and homemade ginger beer. Entrées $3–12. Open for breakfast, lunch, and dinner; closed Sun.

The parking lot was packed at **Norris' Famous Place for Ribs** (772-464-7000), 6598 S US 1, and from the aroma inside, it was no surprise, since they serve award-winning baby back ribs, prime rib, and more to satisfy every meat lover, with entrées starting at $7. Open daily for lunch and dinner.

✳ Selective Shopping

Most folks don't know about historic White City (now unincorporated) in the middle of the county, but if you stop in the **White City Historical Antique Mercantile** (772-461-9003), 1000 W Midway Rd, Fort Pierce, in a building dating from 1901, you can browse through dealer booths for fabulous treasures.

✳ Special Events

First Friday: Held the first Friday of every month. **Friday Fest** (772-466-3880; www.MainStreetFortPierce .org), held in downtown Fort Pierce from 5:30 to 8:30 PM, is the biggest street festival along the Treasure Coast, attracting more than five thousand people each month for live music, food and drinks, and the arts. Free.

December: **Sights and Sounds on Second** (772-466-3880; www.Main StreetFortPierce.org), downtown Fort Pierce, is the region's annual Christmas celebration, with Santa making his way through the city, a Christmas parade, a petting zoo, and lots of activities for the kids. The daylong event (1–6 PM) ends with the lighting of the City of Fort Pierce Christmas tree at the Indian River Drive roundabout. Free.

MARTIN COUNTY

Stretching from the Atlantic Ocean to Lake Okeechobee, the southernmost county of the Treasure Coast encompasses a mix of millionaires' mansions and orange groves, historic towns and burgeoning subdivisions, pine forests and beautiful beaches.

The region's communities have a long and storied history. Long before the first Europeans reached Florida's shores, the Ais, Jeaga, and Tequesta peoples lived along the region's waterways. Around 1565, Spanish explorers sailed down the Indian River looking for shipwreck survivors and setting up missions to convert the natives. They built a fort at the mouth of a large river and called it St. Lucie.

In 1696 the British ship *Reformation* sank along **Jupiter Island,** and its Quaker survivors, including Jonathan Dickinson and his wife, were found by the natives and spent six weeks working their way up the coast to St. Augustine. His diary serves as the only English-language record of interactions with these peoples. Today, Jupiter Island is most notable for its famous residents and their grand homes along the Indian River Lagoon—hometown boy Burt Reynolds among them.

James Hutchinson received a land grant from the Spanish governor of Florida in 1811. After losing crops and cattle to Seminole raiders, he petitioned for and received the barrier island that now bears his name, **Hutchinson Island,** and moved there, where pirates eventually attacked his plantation. In the 1860s Union gunboats and Confederate blockade runners played a game of cat and mouse around the islands and lagoons along the coast as the Confederates attempted to bring in supplies from the Bahamas.

By 1815 the government of Spain handed out land grants in the **Hobe Sound** area, where homesteaders started farms in the piney woods. A century later, the Olympia Improvement Corporation moved in and planned to turn the settlement into a Greek-themed village where movies could be made. Like most of the 1920s boom projects, this one collapsed after the 1928 hurricane. In the 1940s the army opened Camp Murphy as a training station for soldiers to learn a new technology—radar. The pine hills where Camp Murphy sat along US 1 were turned over to the state after the base was decommissioned and became Jonathan Dickinson State Park.

A Danish immigrant, John Laurence Jensen, arrived along the Indian River in 1881 and established a pineapple plantation around which the town of **Jensen Beach** grew. With the arrival of Henry Flagler's Florida East Coast Railroad in 1894, the ready markets for pineapples and citrus drove the economy. By 1895 Jensen was the "Pineapple Capital of the World," shipping more than a million boxes of pineapples each June and July. Fish houses opened along the Indian River for packing the sea's bounty.

The settlement that sprung up around the railroad in the 1880s was first dubbed Potsdam by a Dutch settler and was later renamed **Stuart** after Homer Hine Stuart Jr., a pineapple grower. In the early 1900s the Ashley Gang, a family of outlaws who lived in the south part of the county, terrorized Stuart with frequent robberies until a sheriff gunned them down in Sebastian in 1925. During the 1920s, the boom brought many new residents to the city and a great deal of new construction, shown in the architecture of the fine historic downtown.

With the railroad came tourists, and competition for them. In the early 1920s S. Davies Warfield, a Baltimore banker, bought up large tracts of land in the mostly uninhabited western reaches of the region and planned **Indiantown,** with its centerpiece his fine hotel, the Seminole Inn. His niece Wallis Warfield Simpson attended the grand opening; later in life, she became the Duchess of Windsor.

By 1925 residents became fed up with high taxes and lobbied Governor John Martin to allow them to secede from Palm Beach County. The governor showed as the guest of honor for the May 29, 1925, celebration that named the county in his honor. Stuart became the county seat. Today's Stuart is a mecca for sport-fishing, and this gem of the Treasure Coast remains an undiscovered jewel that you'll enjoy exploring.

GUIDANCE The **Martin County Tourism Development Council** (772-288-5901; www.martincountyfla.com), 2401 SE Monterey Rd, Stuart 34996, can provide you with more information about the area.

GETTING THERE *By car:* Use **Florida's Turnpike** to reach Stuart, and **I-95** for Jensen Beach, Palm City, Stuart, and Hobe Sound.

WATERFRONT IN STUART
Visit Florida

By air: **Palm Beach International Airport** (see *North Palm Beach County*) is the closest major airport.

GETTING AROUND *By car:* A car is necessary for visiting the county. Most services are along **US 1** and **FL A1A.** US 1 passes through all of the county's coastal towns. Cove Rd and Bridge Rd connect I-95 with US 1, Bridge Rd leads from Hobe Sound to FL A1A on Jupiter Island, and **FL 76** heads west from Stuart to Indiantown.

✳ To See

ARCHEOLOGICAL SITES At **Indian Riverside Park** (561-221-1418), Palmer Ave and Indian River Dr, Jensen Beach, most visitors are there for the pier, the riverside walkway, and the beautiful pavilion where you can sit and watch the sunrise. But this park also contains a large midden known as Mount Elizabeth and was the site of a village during the Late Archaic and early St. Johns periods, circa 1000 B.C. to A.D. 1. Open sunrise–sunset daily. Free.

ART GALLERIES

Hobe Sound

Make an appointment to visit the **Midtown Payson Galleries** (772-546-6600), 11870 SE Dixie Hwy, to view the varied work of artists such as Cynthia Knott, Richard Mayhew, and William Thon.

Stuart

Open to a wide range of artists, the **Courthouse Cultural Center** (772-288-2542; www.martinarts.org), 80 SE Ocean Blvd, features installations overseen by the Martin Arts Council. Many of these are juried shows of local art, and exhibits change every six weeks or so.

At the **Geoffrey Smith Gallery** (772-221-8031; www.geoffreysmith.com), 47 W Osceola St, marvel at the bronze-cast sculptures of one of Florida's top sculptors, Geoffrey C. Smith. His work captures the beauty of South Florida's wildlife.

Explore Florida landscapes through the work of Stuart native Kevin Hutchinson at **Hutchinson's Gallery of Great Things** (772-287-1447; www.Hutchinson ArtGallery.com), 300 Colorado Ave, Suite 204, where his original oils bring alive the lush scenery of the region.

For more than 30 years, they've been throwing clay at the **Rare Earth Gallery** (772-287-7744; www.rareearthgallery.com), 41 SW Flagler Ave. Under new ownership, it remains a busy pottery offering unique handcrafted art.

With more than a thousand original oils on display, the **Stuart Gallery** (772-283-9978), 55 SW Flagler Ave, is bound to have something that fits your home decor.

HISTORIC SITES

South Hutchinson Island

At the St. Lucie Rocks, shipwrecked sailors swam to shore and safety at a place known to all on the sea—a House of Refuge. A system of these seaside houses ran up and down the Florida coast in the late 1800s, stocked with fresh water and provisions and manned by a lightkeeper. **Gilbert's Bar House of Refuge,** 301 SE MacArthur Blvd, is the last remaining of this maritime safety net. Built in 1875, it is the oldest standing structure in the county and contains a museum devoted to the maritime heritage of the region. Open 11–4 Tue–Sun. Fee.

Stuart

What is now the **Courthouse Cultural Center** (see *Art Galleries*) has a long and storied history. Built in 1908 as the first schoolhouse in Stuart, the building became the Martin County Courthouse. The staff outgrew the building by 1936, but rather than move, the county applied to the WPA for an addition. Designed by famed architect L. Phillip Clarke, the approved addition incorporates post-Depression art deco elements, including idealistic symbols and inscriptions, cast friezes, and cornices. Nearly demolished in 1989, the building was saved by a group of concerned citizens. Inside the building, the judges vault, marble staircase, and terrazzo floors were restored, and some of the court's artifacts remain.

MUSEUMS

South Hutchinson Island

Opened by Harmon P. Elliot to honor his father, Sterling, an inventor, the **Elliot Museum** (772-225-1961), 825 NE Ocean Blvd, celebrates American ingenuity and creativity and boasts a collection of local and Florida history. Open 10–4 Mon–Sat, 1–4 Sun. Fee. Gilbert's Bar House of Refuge (see *Historic Sites*) sits adjacent.

Stuart

Love boating? Then don't miss the **Maritime & Yachting Museum** (772-692-1234; www.mymflorida.org), 3250 S Kanner Hwy, where volunteers bestow loving care on the restoration of a growing fleet of classic wooden boats, including the *Vintage Rose,* a 1934 Chris-Craft triple-cockpit motorboat; *Caretaker,* a 1950 Century Seamaid with its original engine; and *Annie,* a Bahamas dinghy from the 1950s. Their extensive collection covers not just antique boats but also ship models, maritime artifacts, traditional boatbuilding tools, marine engines, maritime art, and a maritime library. Open 11–4 Thu–Sat, 1–5 Sun.

History buffs will enjoy the **Stuart Heritage Museum** (772-220-4600), 161 SW Flagler Ave, for a look back into the county's past, with artifacts, exhibits, and architecture dating from the 1890s. Donation.

WILDLIFE & MARINELIFE VIEWING Explore 40 acres of coastal habitats at the **Florida Oceanographic Conservation Center** (772-225-0505; www.florida oceanographic.org), 890 NE Ocean Blvd, South Hutchinson Island, where mangrove-lined nature trails lead to the Indian River Lagoon and you can tour the lagoon by pontoon boat on daily ecotours (advanced reservations required). An ideal place to introduce children to marine science, the complex includes a children's activity center and stingray pavilion; plans are under way to add a sea turtle pavilion, coastal exhibit hall, and the Treasure Coast Fishing Center, focusing on game fish. Open 10–5 Mon–Sat, noon–4 Sun. Adults $8, children 3–12 $4.

✳ To Do

BOAT TOURS Set sail on *Island Princess* **Cruises** (772-225-2100; www.island princesscruises.com), 555 NE Ocean Blvd, Stuart, to explore the county by water on any of their regularly scheduled cruises, including holiday dinner cruises; the

Jupiter Island Luncheon Cruise, which showcases celebrity homes on the Indian River Lagoon; an afternoon cruise on the St. Lucie River; or the Nature Cruise through St. Lucie Inlet Preserve State Park (see *Wild Places*), accessible only by boat. Call for reservations and current schedule, since most cruises are seasonal. Adults $17 and up, children $14 and up.

HIKING With more than 20 miles of trails, **Jonathan Dickinson State Park** (see *Parks*) is one of Southeast Florida's top destinations for hikers. But the rest of the county offers some nice trails, too. The delicate coastal scrub at **Seabranch Preserve State Park** (see *Parks*) can only be explored via its hiking trails. **Hawks Bluff** at Jensen Beach in the south end of Savannas Preserve State Park (see *St. Lucie County*) showcases six habitats in less than a mile. For more possibilities see *Green Space*.

HORSEBACK RIDING For an excursion on the beach or a guided trail ride in one of the region's parks, check in at the **Palm City Equestrian Center** (772-223-8448), 6780 SW Martin Hwy, Palm City. They offer lessons and day camps as well.

PADDLING At **Hosford Park** (561-288-5690), 7474 SE Gaines Ave, put in at the canoe launch for a journey down the South Fork of the St. Lucie River. **Jonathan Dickinson State Park** (see sidebar opposite *Parks*) is especially popular with paddlers for its access to the wild and scenic Loxahatchee River. For sea kayakers launching from the beaches, call the Florida Oceanographic Society at 772-225-2300 for daily weather information. At Port Salerno, **St. Lucie Inlet Preserve State Park** (see *Wild Places*) can be reached only by boat.

SNORKELING If you've brought your snorkel and fins, don't miss **Bathtub Reef** at Bathtub Reef Park (see *Beaches*), a perfect "starter" snorkel for the young ones because of its shallow, clear, waveless water. The reef is made up of tubes created by millions of tiny worms called *Sabellariid*.

✳ Green Space
BEACHES

Hobe Sound
At the end of Bridge Rd, **Hobe Sound Beach** is the easiest-to-access beach in the region, popular for snorkeling and sailboarding. It has lifeguards, a concession stand, a picnic area, and rest rooms. At the north end of Jupiter Island is a more remote beach popular with anglers, part of **Hobe Sound National Wildlife Refuge** (see *Wild Places*).

Jupiter Island
For a taste of the unexpected, visit **Blowing Rocks Preserve** (772-744-6668), 574 S Beach Rd, where you'll find Florida's only sea caves. A rocky outcropping of Anastasia limestone defines portions of the shoreline from Jupiter Island north to Fort Pierce, and here the rocky shelf is tall enough to have wave-sculpted caves inside. At times of high tide and high waves, water spurts out natural

chimneys in the tops of the caves, hence the name. The caves can be explored only at low tide. A nature center on the Intracoastal side is the focal point of a natural habitat restoration area with trails. Swimming not permitted. Open 9–5 daily. Fee.

South Hutchinson Island

Cross FL 732 (Jensen Beach Blvd) to Hutchinson Island to explore Martin County's northerly beaches. At the junction of FL 732 and FL A1A, **Jensen Beach Park** (772-334-3444) is a popular destination with picnic tables and volleyball courts. Head south to encounter a string of varied public beaches. A perfect beach for young children, **Bathtub Reef Park** (772-288-5690), 1585 SE MacArthur Blvd, stretches nearly a quarter mile and is protected by a shallow offshore reef, forming a shallow basin where the surf is gentler. At low tide, poke around the tide pools to see starfish, seagrass, and more, or snorkel along the offshore reef. The park includes a nature center and boat dock, rest rooms and showers, an on-duty lifeguard, and a boardwalk along the river. Leashed pets permitted. As you head south, you'll encounter **Chastain Beach** (772-221-1418), guarded only during the season, and the beaches at the tip of the island: **Stuart Beach,** with amenities including a playground and a 250-foot boardwalk, and **Gilbert's Bar House of Refuge** (see *Historic Sites*). Beach access is free at all parks.

NATURE CENTERS ✍ The former Jensen Beach Elementary School, built by the WPA in the 1930s, is now the regional **Environmental Studies Center** (772-219-1887; www.esc.sbmc.org), 2900 NE Indian River Dr, Jensen Beach. Used for on-site education for more than 30 years, the facility has a marine life museum and saltwater aquariums. Ideal for family visits, the center is open to the public 9–3 Mon–Fri during the school year. Free.

PARKS Along the North Fork of the St. Lucie River, **Halpatiokee Regional Park** (772-221-1418), 7645 SE Lost River Rd, Stuart, offers more than just the ballfields you see from the entrance. A paved bike path circles the park, and nature trails meander off into the woods to lead you through thickets of saw palmetto to the river. A canoe launch associated with the park is close to FL 76. Free.

Explore coastal scrub habitat at **Seabranch Preserve State Park** (772-219-1880; www.floridastateparks.org/seabranch/default.cfm), FL A1A, 1 mile south of Cove Rd, Stuart, where on my first visit I encountered both Florida scrub jays and a gopher tortoise while walking the 4.5 miles of hiking trails. Free.

In the middle of downtown Stuart, **Shepards Park** is the place to watch the sunset over the St. Lucie River along the river walk, or to have a picnic on the river's edge.

WILD PLACES

Hobe Sound

Nearly 1,000 acres of coastal habitats, including dunes and sand pine scrub, comprise **Hobe Sound National Wildlife Refuge** (772-546-6141; www.fws .gov/hobesound), with the visitors center located 2 miles south of Bridge Rd on

A vacation destination in itself, massive **Jonathan Dickinson State Park** (772-546-2771; www.floridastateparks.org/jonathandickinson/default.cfm), 16450 SE Federal Hwy, Hobe Sound, has something for everyone. Hikers enjoy nearly 20 miles of trails, including two backpacking loops (with a lengthier trail currently under construction); bicyclists have the Camp Murphy Off-Road Bicycle Trail to explore; and paddlers can launch into the Loxahatchee River for a pleasant trip up one of Florida's designated Wild and Scenic Rivers. When the tide is up, a concessionaire runs a nature cruise up the river to the homestead of Trapper Nelson, a legendary figure in Loxahatchee history. Nelson established an encampment with cottages, picnic shelters, and a zoo, a popular getaway in the 1930s and 1940s. If the tides are right, the boat tour will drop you off at Trapper Nelson's, where a ranger leads an interesting interpretive walk around the encampment. If you do nothing else on your visit, don't miss the climb up to the top of Hobe Mountain Tower, from which you can see most of Jupiter Island and the Atlantic Ocean. This 11,000-acre park was formerly a military installation, and you'll see remnants of old buildings along many of the trails. There are two large campgrounds and cabins for rent (see *Campgrounds*), canoe rentals, picnic areas, short nature trails, a playground, and so much to do you'll visit again and again. Open 8–sunset daily. Fee.

HOBE MOUNTAIN TOWER, JONATHAN DICKINSON STATE PARK

Sandra Friend

US 1. A short nature trail loops through the scrub habitat at the visitors center; a separate unit of the refuge protects sea turtle nesting habitat at the north end of Jupiter Island. Summer sea turtle walks are offered Jun–Jul; call ahead for reservations. Free.

Jensen Beach

Stretching more than 10 miles from Fort Pierce to Jensen Beach, **Savannas Preserve State Park** (772-398-2779; www.floridastateparks.org/savannas/default.cfm), 9551 Gumbo Limbo Ln, protects the longest remaining freshwater savanna on Florida's east coast. Teeming with wildlife, these marshes are less than 3 miles from the sea. On the south end, access the park off Jensen Beach Rd, where entrance is through a picnic and wildlife-watching area. For a short hike encompassing most of the region's ecosystems, stop at the Hawks Bluff entrance off Savannah Rd; the 1.1-mile loop trail drops off the dunelike bluffs to follow the water's edge. Free.

Port Salerno

Accessible only by boat, **St. Lucie Inlet Preserve State Park** (772-219-1880; www.floridastateparks.org/stlucieinlet/default.cfm) encompasses a remote barrier island with mangrove forests, tropical hammocks, and a pristine beach favored by sea turtles for nesting in the summer months. Fee.

HOBE SOUND NATIONAL WILDLIFE REFUGE
Sandra Friend

✳ Lodging

BED & BREAKFASTS

Indiantown 34956

Dating from 1927, the **Seminole Country Inn** (772-597-3777; www.seminoleinn.com), 15885 SW Warfield Blvd, is an important historic landmark from the 1920s land boom that still welcomes guests with the grace befitting Southern tradition. The inn boasts the original pecky cypress ceilings, polished hardwood floors, and brass fixtures enjoyed by those who attended the gala grand opening, including the owner's niece, Wallis Warfield Simpson, the future Duchess of Windsor. The romantic rooms ($65–125) let you step back in time; snuggle under a quilt beneath a drape of mosquito netting. An in-house café offers lunch for guests and dinners in the grand Windsor Dining Room certain days of the week (see *Eating Out*).

Stuart 34994

Romantic old Key West–style rooms await at **Inn Shepards Park Bed & Breakfast** (772-781-4244; www.inn shepard.com), 601 SW Ocean Blvd, complete with the swirl of mosquito netting billowing around your comfortable bed. Each of the four well-appointed rooms ($85–185) come with cable TV, DVD players, and soft-as-silk linens and robes. Located right in the downtown historic district, it's a relaxing home away from home with kayaks, bicycles, beach gear, and coolers available for guests.

CAMPGROUNDS

Hobe Sound 33455

Providing the full range of camping amenities, **Jonathan Dickinson State Park** (see sidebar opposite *Parks*) has everything, from 12 riverside cabin rentals to primitive backpacker campsites. The popular River Camp is near the Loxahatchee River and provides shady sites, while Pine Grove Campground, closest to US 1, provides easy access to the front gate if you're using the park as your home base during a vacation week. Pine Grove accepts leashed pets, but River Camp does not.

HOTELS, MOTELS, AND RESORTS

Jensen Beach 34957

Colorful and whimsical, the intimate **Four Fish Inn** (772-334-2152 or 1-866-401-7898; www.4fishinn.com), 2100 NE Indian River Dr, offers your choice of motel rooms, sparkling efficiencies, or single-bedroom apartments with modern kitchens and beautiful waterway views ($75 and up).

  Amid an 8-acre tropical paradise in the historic district, **River Palm Cottages & Fish Camp** (772-334-0401 or 1-800-305-0511; www.river palmcottages.com), 2325 NE Indian River Dr, provides an Old Florida–style getaway that's become hard to find along the Atlantic Coast. The old-style bungalows have sparkling modern interiors with bold island decor, tiled floors, and full kitchens. Rates vary according to cottage size and season, starting as low as $79 for a bungalow that sleeps two. The grounds include a pool, putting green, hammocks between the palms, and a private beach on the Indian River Lagoon. Pets are welcome!

✳ Where to Eat

DINING OUT

Stuart

The Ashley Gang, notorious Florida outlaws, knocked off the Bank of Stuart numerous times between 1915 and their demise at the hands of the law nearly a decade later. In a unique nod to this period of Florida history, the **Ashley Restaurant & Bar** (772-221-9476), 61 SW Osceola St, in the historic Bank of Stuart building, offers an elegant place to dine. Tempting appetizers ($8–11) such as crunchy corn oysters and crispy Brie sticks are the warm-up for entrées ($13–25) that include pan-seared salmon, tuna, and chicken breast, and a delightful steamed and grilled vegetable platter for vegetarians. Open for lunch and dinner; entertainment offered most nights until last call.

Renowned for its extensive wine list (more than one hundred selections) and its uniquely Florida cuisine, **The**

Flagler Grill (772-221-9517; www .flaglergrill.com), 47 SW Flagler Ave, is a "casual upscale" dining experience, thanks to restaurateurs Paul and Linda Daly, whose background with private clubs and fine wine bring the best to their guests. Savor escargot baked in blue cheese crème fraîche for starters, and move on to a signature entrée such as herb-crusted red snapper or pan-seared, macadamia-crusted mahimahi with a coconut rum beurre blanc sauce. Open for dinner only, daily during the winter season; reservations suggested.

Start your day early at the **Osceola Street Café** (772-283-6116; www .osceolastreet.com), 26 SW Osceola St, which opens 6 AM for breakfast with fresh baked bagels, egg sandwiches, and a hot cup of joe. Lunch is served 11–3, including sandwiches and salads ($5–10). Dinner, Wed–Sat, tempts with tapas and entrées ($16–30) prepared with the finest of fresh vegetables and meats, with an ever-changing menu.

EATING OUT

Hobe Sound

You can't miss **Harry & The Natives** (772-546-3061; www.harryandthe natives.com), 11910 US 1, with its old-fashioned cabins decorated with nautical bits and bobs, a plane crashing through one building, and signs, signs, signs—read 'em all. Opened as the Cypress Cabins and Restaurant on December 7, 1941, it's *the* local hangout, with great seafood and burgers for lunch and dinner, big drinks, and live music most nights. Serving breakfast ($4 and up) 7–11 Tue–Sun, with funky fun stuff such as bananas Foster French toast, coconut pancakes, and gator hash. The menus are a

hoot, and as for payment, they'll accept "cash, dishwashing, honey dipping, oceanfront homes, table dancing, our gift certificates, Visa, and MasterCard."

Indiantown

The **Seminole Country Inn** (see *Bed & Breakfasts*) offers two delightful dining experiences. For lunch stop by the **Foxgrape Café** (11–3 Tue–Sat) for grilled meats, good country sandwiches such as slow-roasted roast beef and oven-roasted turkey, and local favorites such as alligator bites, fried okra, and fried green tomato sandwiches ($4–8). In the evenings, step back in time into the **Windsor Dining Room** (5–8:30 PM Tue–Sat), as elegant in its cypress walls and palladium windows as it was 70 years ago, for fine meals prepared "farm fresh," including Grandma Mimi's fried chicken (that good buttermilk style), country roast pork loin, and fresh catfish ($7–14). A traditional Southern Country Brunch is served every Sunday 9:30–2.

Stuart

For delicious California-style Mexican food, visit **Baja Cafe** (772-286-2546; www.bajacafe.com), 300 S US 1, where you can dine on a Tequila Sunrise burrito filled with shrimp marinated in tequila, orange juice, and lime; or enjoy pollo asada, dressed with burgundy butter. Entrées $9–16; lunch portions are just as delicious but are much lighter on the wallet.

I heard it in a hurricane—**Wahoo's on the Waterfront** (772-692-2333; www .wahoosstuart.com), 400 NW Alice Ave, is a don't-miss stop for fabulous local seafood, with a killer view of the Intracoastal. The fresh catch comes in daily, including swordfish, cobia, dolphin, and the namesake wahoo, and you can have it fixed up char-grilled, Cajun blackened, sautéed, poached, or Wahoo style with roasted peppers, onions, and garlic. Or choose off the menu with entrées starting at $14. Open for lunch and dinner, with a special Sunday brunch; live music nightly.

BAKERIES, COFFEE SHOPS, AND SODA FOUNTAINS

Stuart

Stop in at **Aunt D's General Store** (772-781-9959), 5 SW Flagler Ave, for a taste of old New England—authentic Italian ice, coffee and cookies, and penny candy.

✳ Entertainment

Stuart

Built as a silent-movie theater in 1926, the **Lyric Theatre** (772-286-7827; www.lyrictheatre.com), 59 SW Flagler Ave, has been beautifully restored to its former glory and is *the* local venue for top-notch concerts, shows, and cultural events.

✳ Selective Shopping

Jensen Beach

She sells seashells at **Nettles Nest Shells and Gifts From the Sea** (772-229-8953), 11035 S Ocean Dr, where you'll find spectacular corals and fine specimens from around the globe.

Stuart

For classy collectibles stop in **Always & Forever** (772-287-8883; www.always-forever.com), 37 SW Osceola St, where you'll find top names such as Waterford, Swarovski, Lladro, and Moorcraft.

At **Bella Jewelry and Gifts** (772-219-8648; www.bellajewelryandgifts.com), 39 SW Osceola St, the selection isn't just jewelery, but includes home decor and New Age items—crystals, fossils, feng shui supplies, and aromatherapy, too.

Like a little museum, **Glass N Treasures** (772-220-1018), 53 SW Flagler Ave, is packed with collectibles, including Civil War items and travel brochures.

Victoriana awaits at the quaint **Humble Heart** (772-223-5505), 313 Colorado Ave, including a year-round Christmas room, garden accessories, and home furnishings.

Gardeners will love **The Love Garden** (772-287-5276; www.LoveGarden.us), 19 SW Flagler Ave, with its garden-themed decor for the home, splendid fountains, silk plants, and exotic pottery.

🐾 Pups are welcome at **Puppuccino** (772-781-4203; www.puppuccino.com), Three SW Flagler Ave, a unique boutique for your favorite pet. Purchase accessories, canine fashions, and doggie treats!

Palm Beach

NORTH PALM BEACH COUNTY

CENTRAL PALM BEACH COUNTY

SOUTH PALM BEACH COUNTY

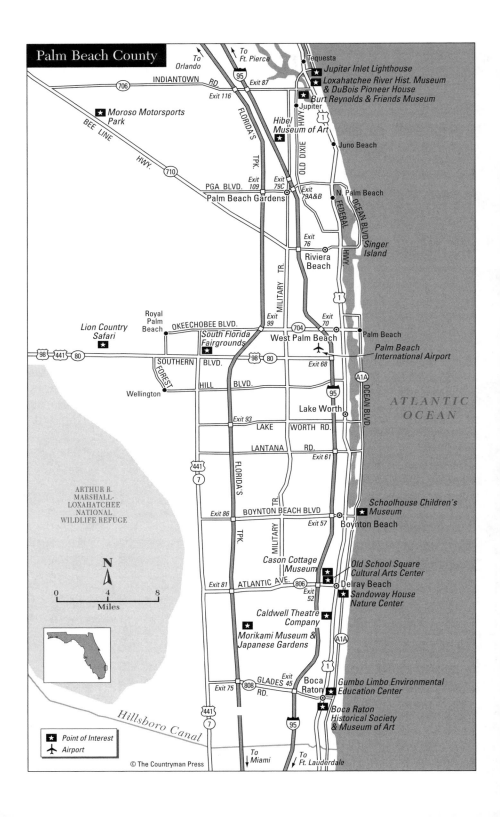

NORTH PALM BEACH COUNTY

New World explorers and today's adventurers consider **Jupiter** an important navigational point when planning trips around Florida's coastline and points as far south as Latin America. Jupiter, the easternmost point in Florida, was named **Jupiter Inlet** in its early records. The legend goes that local Jega Indians called themselves Jobe. When English settlers heard the name, it sounded to them like "Jove," which was also the name for the god Jupiter, so they began calling the region Jupiter, and it remains so to this day. The area became widely known after Jonathan Dickinson and his party were captured and held hostage by local Indians on the site where the DuBois pioneer home (see *Historic Sites*) now sits. The most identifiable landmark in the area is the Jupiter Inlet Lighthouse. Erected in 1860, it remains an important navigational beacon. **Juno Beach** was once Dade County's link to northern Florida by way of the Celestial Railroad. The name Celestial Railroad came from the stops that were made: Juno, Venus, Mars, and Jupiter. In 1890 the village of Juno was named the county seat, covering the region of the railroad from just north of Jupiter and south to Biscayne Bay in Miami-Dade County. The Celestial Railway was sold in 1896, and the county seat reverted to Miami four years later. To the north of Jupiter is the small village of **Tequesta,** named after the Tequesta Indians.

GUIDANCE For information about Jupiter, Tequesta, and Juno Beach, contact the **JTJB Chamber of Commerce** (561-746-7111; www.jupiterfl.org), 800 N US 1, Jupiter 33477. Another area resource is the **Palm Beach County Convention and Visitors Bureau** (561-233-3000), 1555 Palm Beach Lakes, Suite 800, West Palm Beach 33401.

GETTING THERE *By car:* From **I-95** take exit 79 for Palm Beach Gardens (PGA Blvd) and exit 87 for Jupiter (Indiantown Rd). From **Florida's Turnpike** take exit 109 for Palm Beach Gardens and exit 116 for Jupiter.

By air: **Palm Beach International Airport (PBIA)** (561-471-7420), 1000 Turnage Blvd, West Palm Beach, is situated adjacent to I-95.

By rail: **AMTRAK** (561-832-6169 or 1-800-USA-RAIL; www.amtrak.com) serves the area; the nearest station is at 201 Tamarind Ave, West Palm Beach.

Tri-Rail (1-800-TRI-RAIL; www.tri-rail.com) service connects Palm Beach, Broward, and Miami-Dade Counties, and it also connects to several stations in central and south Palm Beach County. The nearest connection is at the Gardens of Palm Beaches Mall, 3101 PGA Blvd, Palm Beaches (561-775-7750), where it connects with Palm Tran (see *Getting Around*).

By bus: **Greyhound** (561-833-8534 or 1-800-231-2222; www.greyhound.com), 205 S Tamarind Ave, West Palm Beach.

GETTING AROUND *By bus:* The **Palm Tran** (561-841-4287; www.co.palm-beach .fl.us/palmtran) service area covers malls and tourist spots throughout Palm Beach County and south Palm Beach Gardens.

By water taxi: **Water Taxi of the Palm Beaches** (561-775-2628; www.water -taxi.com), 11511 Ellison Wilson Rd (at Panama Hattie's).

PARKING Public parking is readily available at no cost in the cities in the northern part of the county.

MEDICAL EMERGENCIES Area hospitals include **Columbia Hospital** (561-842-6141), 2201 45th St, West Palm Beach, and **Palm Beach Gardens Hospital** (561-622-1411), 3360 Burns Rd, Palm Beach Gardens.

PUBLIC REST ROOMS The beach areas and most city parks all have rest rooms available to the public at no cost.

✳ To See

ART GALLERIES

Jupiter

The nonprofit **Hibel Museum of Art** (561-622-5560; www.hibelmuseum.org), 5353 Parkside Dr, is where you can go to appreciate the beauty and peace brought to life in Edna Hibel's works of art. The museum also offers concerts, lectures, and art festivals throughout the year. Open noon–5 Tue–Thur, 10–9 Fri adn Sat, 1–5 Sun. Free.

For those who want to purchase an original Hibel, head over to the **Edna Hibel Museum Gallery** (561-622-1380), 661 Maplewood Dr, Unit #12, which supports the museum. As one of South Florida's finest artists, Edna Hibel has received numerous prestigious awards, and her works are exhibited in museums and galleries in more than 20 countries on four continents. More selections of her original paintings, lithographs, porcelains, drawings, and sculpture are also on display in Palm Beach and Lake Worth.

Stuart

Beautiful marine and aquatic paintings can be admired and purchased at **Profile International Art Gallery** (561-220-3370; www.apbico.com/websites/others/

progallery), 3746–48 E Ocean Blvd, Harbour Bay Plaza. You can almost feel
yourself swimming underwater surrounded by tropical fish and manatees! The
gallery is also an official framemaker to the President of the United States.
There is another location at 50 S US 1, Jupiter (561-747-7094).

Tequesta
The **Lighthouse Center for the Arts** (561-746-3101; www.lighthousearts.org),
373 Tequesta Dr, was founded by Christopher Norton, son of the founders of
the Norton Museum of Art, (see *Central Palm Beach County*) in 1963. The center features a variety of exhibits and educational programs and is dedicated to
bringing art to all ages. The nonprofit museum also has an excellent gallery
store. Open 9:30–4:30 Mon–Sat. Free.

HISTORIC SITES Built in 1898, the **DuBois Home** (561-747-6639; www.jupiter
lighthouse.org and www.lrhs.org), 19075 Dubois Rd, Jupiter, sits on a midden (a
Native American shell mound). The site where Jonathan Dickinson and his party
were held captive in 1696, the home is also listed on the National Register of
Historic Places. Harry and Susan DuBois used Florida pine and cypress when
designing the home to resemble homes built in the late 19th century in New
Jersey, where Harry grew up. The home is decorated with antiques and memorabilia of the era, providing a glimpse of the way life used to be for well-to-do pioneers. Open 1–4 Wed and Sun. $2 donation appreciated.

A landmark for the region, the **Jupiter Inlet Lighthouse** (561-747-6639), 805
N US 1, Jupiter, built in 1860, survived the Civil War (when its Fresnel lens was
hidden by local Confederates in Lake Worth) and continues to be a navigational
beacon today. It's quite a view from the top, and worth the dizzying spiral climb
to get there. Tours start at the visitors center. Open 10–4 Sun–Wed. Fee.

MUSEUMS Burt Reynolds has made Jupiter his home for most of his movie and
television career, so it is no wonder that he has assembled a fine collection of
artifacts and memorabilia not only on his life, but also from his wide circle of
friends. At the **Burt Reynolds & Friends Museum** (561-743-9955; www.burt
reynoldsmuseum.org), 100 N US 1, Jupiter, sports fans and film buffs will enjoy
seeing such items as Muhammad Ali's boxing gloves; Gene Autry's and Roy
Rogers's boots; Trigger's original sales
receipt; letters from Cary Grant,
Carol Burnett, and Jack Lemmon;
and movie props such as the canoe
from *Deliverance* and the *Smokey
and the Bandit* car. Open 10–4
Wed–Sun. Fee.

Call for an appointment to view
archeological artifacts being
processed right before your eyes from
The Last Galleon (561-747-7700),
603 Commerce Way, Jupiter, the oldest Spanish galleon found in Florida

JUPITER INLET LIGHTHOUSE
Palm Beach County Convention & Visitors Bureau

waters. This is the only facility in the United States that allows the public to watch while history is being uncovered.

✐ Learn about the ancient Tequesta, the shipwreck of Jonathan Dickinson, and the hardy pioneers who settled this region at the **Loxahatchee River Historical Museum** (561-747-6639; www.lrhs.org), 805 N US 1, adjacent to the Jupiter Inlet Lighthouse (see *Historic Sites*) in Jupiter. In addition to the artifacts and exhibits inside the museum, you can explore a replica Seminole village and the Tindall House, recently moved on-site. Open 10–5 Tue–Fri, noon–5 Sat and Sun. Fee.

BASEBALL Catch a home run at **Roger Dean Stadium** (561-775-1818, www .rogerdeanstadium.com), 4751 Main St, Jupiter, where the Jupiter Hammer-heads, Palm Beach Cardinals, Florida Marlins, and St. Louis Cardinals are up to bat. Tickets $7–22.

ZOOLOGICAL PARKS & ANIMAL REHAB

Juno Beach
✐ Located inside **Loggerhead Park** (see *Parks*), the **Marinelife Center of Juno Beach** (561-627-8280), 14200 US 1, specializes in the rescue and rehabilitation of sea turtles. The facility includes an interpretive center with aquariums showcasing native sea life, a library, and the large turtle tanks outside. Open 10–4 Tue–Sat, noon–3 Sun. Free; donations appreciated.

Jupiter
✐ More than three thousand wild animals receive care at the **Bush Wildlife Sanctuary** (561-575-3399), 2500 Jupiter Park Dr. The nonprofit facility provides an educational environment where you can learn about some of Florida's flora and fauna up close and personal. Open to visitors 10–4 Tue–Sat. Free; donations appreciated.

✳ To Do

BIRDING Most of the region's natural areas offer excellent bird-watching, particularly for wading birds and shorebirds. **Florida scrub jays** may be seen at **Jupiter Ridge Natural Area** (see *Preserves*), and herons and egrets along Lake Worth Creek at **Frenchman's Forest Natural Area** (see *Preserves*).

BOAT TOURS Tour the Intracoastal Waterway or Loxahatchee River on the *Manatee Queen* **Pontoon Boat** (561-744-2191; www.members.aol.com/manateequeen), at the Crab House, 1065 FL A1A, Jupiter. The Jupiter Island tour showcases multimillion-dollar homes; the Loxahatchee River tour features wild and natural areas. Adults $24, children $15.

NATURE TOURS At **John D. MacArthur Beach State Park** (561-624-6952), North Palm Beach, you can take guided nature tours (free) Wed–Sun and kayak tours ($20 single kayak, $35 double kayak) daily at high tide. Local guides will take you snorkeling (bring your own gear) through the reefs Jun–Aug. Fee per carload for park admission.

PADDLING Canoe down Florida rivers with **Canoe Outfitters of Florida** (561-746-7053 or 1-888-272-1257; www.canoes-kayaks-florida.com), in Riverbend Park, 900 W Indiantown Rd, Jupiter, about 1¼ miles west of I-95. Located at the headwaters of the Loxahatchee River, Canoe Outfitters takes you on a six-hour journey from Jupiter all the way to Jonathan Dickinson State Park. Discover a peaceful, quiet environment as you pass through a forested area where eagles and osprey perch while alligators sun themselves on the banks. $40 per person in two-person canoe; includes guide.

The **Jupiter Outdoor Center** (561-747-9666; www.jupiteroutdoorcenter.com), 1000 FL A1A, Jupiter, offers stargazing adventures throughout the year. Guides take you around Pelican and Adventure Islands, and afterward you can toast marshmallows by the campfire.

WALKING TOURS The town of Jupiter's **Riverwalk** (561-746-5134) follows a 2.5-mile course along the Intracoastal Waterway from Jupiter Inlet past shops, restaurants, and natural areas, all the way to Jupiter Ridge.

WATER PARKS At **Rapids Water Park** (561-842-8756; www.rapidswaterpark .com), 6566 N Military Trl, West Palm Beach, the main event is the Big Thunder, a giant funnel 60 feet in diameter and 55 feet long. Float down the 9-foot tunnel through dark twists and curves as your speed increases, then drop 45 degrees through the funnel, slide around and around, and exit into the landing pool. Other high-speed thrills are also available, but for those who want to relax, there's the Lazy River. $28 for all, with children under 2 free.

✳ Green Space
BEACHES
Juno Beach
Juno Beach is a fine family beach for snorkeling and swimming in the emerald green waters. Several parks provide access, including popular **Loggerhead Park** (see *Parks*). **Juno Beach Park** (561-626-5166), 14775 FL A1A, is one of the area's more popular beaches, with lifeguards on duty; a pedestrian pier (561-799-0185) offers access for fishing. Free.

Jupiter
Carlin Park, 400 S FL A1A, has nature trails, lifeguards on duty, and picnic facilities, and it's a good snorkeling beach. Free.

Jupiter Beach Park (561-624-0065), 1375 Jupiter Beach Rd, and **Ocean**

CORAL COVE, JUPITER ISLAND
Sandra Friend

Cay Park, 2188 Marcinski Rd, are two of the more popular lifeguard-attended beaches in Jupiter.

Tequesta

Off the beaten path a little, north of Jupiter along FL A1A, **Coral Cove** (561-966-6600), 19450 Beach Rd, offers an unusual look at the Atlantic Ocean, thanks to the picturesque rocky shoreline and its many tidal pools and unusual formations. When the water is calm and clear, this is a great snorkeling spot, especially as there are 2 acres of natural rock reef for tropical fish to play in. Free.

PARKS

Juno Beach

Sandwiched between US 1 and FL A1A, **Loggerhead Park** (561-626-5166), 1111 Ocean Dr, has a great children's playground, an observation tower overlooking the Atlantic from a tall dune, and access beneath FL A1A to the beach. It's also the gateway to two other natural attractions: the **Marinelife Center of Juno Beach** (see *Zoological Parks & Animal Rehab*) and **Juno Dunes Natural Area** (see *Preserves*). Open 8 AM–11 PM daily. Free.

Jupiter Farms

&. With 800 acres in cabbage palm hammocks and restored marshes along the Loxahatchee River, **Riverbend County Park** (561-966-6660), Indiantown Rd, just west of the river, offers river access for paddlers (with an on-site livery) and several miles of hard-packed hiking trails, suitable for wheelchairs with assistance. Free.

PRESERVES

Juno Beach

&. ♂ Protecting a ribbon of saw palmetto–topped dunes along US 1, **Juno Dunes Natural Area** (561-233-2400) is accessed from **Loggerhead Park** (see *Parks*), with the nature trail starting across from the children's playground area. A paved wheelchair-accessible trail crosses ancient dunes to a high point with an observation shelter overlooking the Atlantic Ocean. A natural-surface trail loops downhill and through the dense coastal scrub vegetation. Open sunrise–sunset daily. Free.

HIKERS AT RIVERBEND COUNTY PARK
Sandra Friend

Jupiter

&. ♂ To explore a scrub habitat where the dunes gleam like snow, visit **Jupiter Ridge Natural Area** (561-233-2400), 1 mile south of Indiantown Rd on US 1. This beautiful 267-acre preserve along the Intracoastal Waterway almost ended up as a Wal-Mart two decades ago; now, as you walk the trails, notice the delicate scrub plants

JUPITER RIDGE NATURAL AREA

Sandra Friend

and colony of Florida scrub jays. A small portion of the trail is paved, with an overlook on the waterway. Open sunrise–sunset daily. Free.

Jupiter Island

For a taste of the unexpected, visit **Blowing Rocks Preserve** (772-744-6668), 574 S Beach Rd, where you'll find Florida's only sea caves. A rocky outcropping of Anastasia limestone defines portions of the shoreline from Jupiter Island north to Fort Pierce, and here the rocky shelf is tall enough to have wave-sculpted caves inside. At times of high tide and high waves, water spurts out natural chimneys in the tops of the caves, hence the name. The caves can only be explored at low tide. A nature center on the Intracoastal side is the focal point of a natural habitat restoration area with trails. No swimming permitted. Open 9–5 daily. Fee.

Palm Beach Gardens

& ✑ Explore natural habitats at **Frenchman's Forest Natural Area** (561-233-2400), Prosperity Farms Rd, where three trails wind through the forest along Lake Worth Creek; the red-blazed Cypress Trail leads you across a boardwalk through a cypress swamp. Open sunrise–sunset daily. Free.

✳ Lodging

CAMPGROUNDS

Riviera Beach 33404

Peanut Island Campground (561-845-4445), 6500 Peanut Island Rd, is run by the Palm Beach Parks and Recreation Department (www.pbc gov.com) and is only accessible by boat. The island park has 20 tropical campsites, each with tent pad, grill, and picnic table. Rest rooms on-site with showers. A park supervisor is always on-site for your assistance. Reservations are recommended.

Jupiter 33477

The only oceanfront hotel in Jupiter is the **Jupiter Beach Resort** (561-746-2511), Five N FL A1A, where the extensively remodeled rooms ($187 and up) have appealing tropical decor, marble floors and shower stalls in each bathroom, furnished balconies, and high-speed Internet access. Guests have direct access to the beach or can enjoy the hotel pool; poolside café and fine dining on-site. Valet parking available.

✳ Where to Eat

DINING OUT

Jupiter

For fine dining, **BarryMore's Prime Steaks & Chops** (561-625-3757), 4050 S US 1, should be high on your local list. Their steaks are aged a month before serving, and their lamb chops are range-fed from Colorado; South African lobster tail is flown in daily. All entrées ($17–29, with a unique selection each evening) are satisfying, and the relaxed atmosphere encourages you to enjoy a cognac at the hand-tooled mahogany bar after dinner. Reservations recommended.

Dinner comes with a most excellent view at **Jetty's** (561-743-8166), 1075 N FL A1A, where the Jupiter Lighthouse is the centerpiece of the panorama. The menu is upscale seafood and steak and includes interesting combinations such as coconut shrimp with filet mignon tenderloin tips, and filet mignon with lump crabmeat in béarnaise sauce. Entrées $17 and up.

Palm Beach Gardens

Palm Beach Gardens has a real four-leaf clover, and as I recently visited

Ireland, I can't resist stopping at **Paddy Mac's** (561-691-4366; www.paddymacspub.com), 10971 N Military Trl, for traditional Gaelic fare. European Master Chef Kenneth Wade, Irish born and raised, previously worked at Ashford Castle, and his head chefs are also from the Emerald Isle. Chef Wade's culinary delights far surpass the usual pub fare, with reasonably priced entrées $14–25. Lunch and dinner; traditional Irish music and dancing.

EATING OUT

Jupiter

A hometown family burger joint, **Blondie's Bar & Grill** (561-743-3300), 10160 W Indiantown Rd, has deli sandwiches and salads, wings and dogs, and their special "Phyl-u-Up" Maryland crab soup. Serving lunch and dinner ($6–12).

A local favorite, the **Crab House Restaurant** (561-744-1300), 1065 N Ocean Blvd (FL A1A), offers fresh seafood, along with snow crab and Maryland blue crab, in a casual dockside atmosphere. Menu items run $12–26, but they are famous for their all-you-can-eat fresh seafood and salad bar ($19 at lunch $26 at dinner). The *Manatee Queen* Pontoon Boat tour (see *Boat Tours*) departs from their dock.

A birch beer float and a junkyard dog—that's lunch for me at **The Dune Dog Drive In** (561-744-6667), 775 Alt FL A1A, my favorite stop after a long hike at nearby Jonathan Dickinson State Park. The place is a funky beach shack set in a parking lot along Old Dixie Hwy, with Jimmy Buffet blasting and food ($4 and up) served at picnic tables. The family atmosphere at lunchtime makes way for barroom trolling after dark (margaritas are a specialty here).

🦪 Good food at bargain prices—that's the **Lighthouse Restaurant** (561-746-4811), 1510 N US 1, a local fixture where patrons Burt Reynolds and Tom Poston smile down from autographed photos on the walls. Breakfast is hearty—I could hardly finish an omelet—and even the dinners pack a lot of food. I highly recommend the grilled crab cakes, a house specialty. They're open for breakfast, lunch, and dinner, but busiest at breakfast. Entrées $9–15.

When you have enough money, you can move anything—and such is the case with **Rooney's Public House Abacoa** (561-694-6610), 1153 Town Center Dr, where the entire pub was imported from Ireland. Good Irish cuisine, a properly stocked bar, succulent steak and seafood, and live music every weekend. What more can a redheaded lad or lass ask for?

Setti's Italian (561-745-7525), 10136 W Indiantown Rd, features tempting appetizers such as clams casino, mozzarella caprese, and mussels marinara, and traditional Italian entrées such as lasagna, pasta with clam sauce, and homemade gnocchi. Entrées $10–13, with basics like pizza, calzones, and hot wings on the menu, too!

Tequesta
Pour me something tall and strong at the **Square Grouper** at Castaways Marina (561-575-0252), 1111 Love St, on the Intracoastal near Alan Jackson's house; the video for the Jackson-Buffet duet "5 O'Clock Somewhere" was partially filmed here. The menu is limited to your basic bar fare, but this is a great place to sit and sip a tall one while watching sailboats drift past. Live music Tue and Fri–Sun.

✳ Entertainment
PERFORMING ARTS

Jupiter
The 225-seat **Atlantic Theater** (561-575-3271; www.theatlantictheater .com), 6743 W Indiantown Rd #34, brings fresh, new drama and comedy to the area with insightful productions. Live music featuring local talent is also performed.

The historic **Maltz Jupiter Theatre** (561-743-2666; www.jupitertheatre .org), 1001 E Indiantown Rd, once the Burt Reynolds dinner theater, was renovated in 2004. Open since the 1980s, the theater has been transformed into a six-hundred-seat playhouse featuring professional productions of musicals, dramas, comedies, and classics, often with world-renowned celebrities.

Contemporary and classical productions are professionally presented at the **Shakespeare Festival** (561-575-7336), Carlin Park Amphitheater, 400 S FL A1A (just south of Indiantown Rd).

✳ Selective Shopping
ANTIQUES AND COLLECTIBLES

Jupiter
There's a nice selection of antiques and collectible treasures at **Hunt Treasure Antiques** (561-748-0608), 1532 N US 1; **Pottinger & Reed Art & Antiques** (561-744-0373), 112 Seminole Ave; **Sims Creek Antique Mall** (561-747-6785), 1695 W Indiantown Rd; and **Trifles Treasures & Antiques** (561-747-7225), 220 S Old Dixie Hwy.

Jupiter

Pick up a good read for yourself at **Angels Dream** (561-748-0283), 601 W Indiantown Rd, or for your kids at **Sunshine Kids Books** (561-575-6400), 5500 Military Trl, Suite 22.

BOUTIQUES AND SPECIALTY SHOPS

Jupiter

Harbor Clothing Boutique (561-747-5330), 2127 US 1, offers an extensive line of Brighton purses and jewelry.

SPORTING CENTERS

North Palm Beach

Once you've experienced the area's rivers and inlets, you'll want your own kayak, so head over to **Adventure Times Kayaks** (561-881-7218), 521 Northlake Blvd.

MALLS AND OUTLETS

Palm Beach Gardens

Serious shoppers head to **The Gardens Mall** (561-622-2115), 3101 PGA Blvd, where you can find all the trendy fashions to make your style sizzle.

✳ Special Events

February: The annual **ArtiGras Fine Arts Festival** (561-694-2300; www.artigras.org), Central Blvd, Jupiter, just north of Donald Ross Rd. Music, entertainment, ArtiKids, food, wine tasting, and lots of art. Fee.

March: Artists from all over the United States and Canada present their original paintings, crafts, photography, copper and wood sculptures, and jewelry at **Artfest by the Sea** (561-746-7111; www.jupiterfl.org), Juno Beach. Musicians playing everything from flutes to guitars walk around and serenade.

CENTRAL PALM BEACH COUNTY

The focal point of Central Palm Beach County is, of course, **Palm Beach.** The Intracoastal Waterway is all that separates the 16-mile-long barrier island from the mainland cities of Lake Worth and West Palm Beach. Land of the social elite, the "Island" is the winter home to many celebrities, international business magnates, and, of course, seasonal residents from social hot spots in New England, such as the Hamptons and Martha's Vineyard. The town's money-eyed inhabitants spend a great deal of time fund-raising for both humanitarian and artistic causes—the Kravis Center was built totally on donations. Created by Henry Morrison Flagler in 1894, after his opening of the Royal Poinciana Hotel, the island with small-town character displays spectacular Mediterranean architecture throughout. Flagler's "Whitehall" (see *Historic Sites*), built in 1901 for his wife, Mary Lily Kenan, can be seen on the right as you cross over the bridge on Okeechobee Blvd (FL 704). Back on the mainland, West Palm Beach provided homes to those who worked for the upper-class residents, or for many nouveau riche who couldn't quite afford the exclusivity of the "Island." However, the **City of West Palm Beach** has its own piece of paradise, with its scenic waterfront views of the Intracoastal Waterway, sunny palm-lined streets, quaint shopping districts, and active downtown district.

At the southwest side of Palm Beach on the mainland sits **Lake Worth.** A polished gem, Lake Worth's original landowners, Samuel and Fannie James, actually first named the town Jewel. In 1911 the Jameses sold the town to Palm Beach Farms Company, and plans were formulated for a city along the water. In 1912 the town name was changed to the Townsite of Lucerne, but its name was changed yet again when it opened its first post office, as there was already a town in Florida named Lucerne. The city was incorporated in 1913 as the City of Lake Worth after Gen. William Jenkins Worth, who was instrumental in ending hostilities with indigenous Indians in 1842. Finnish immigrants are an integral part of the town's population and culture, and they constitute nearly half of the town's residents. They began migrating to the area as early as 1906 and bring one of the biggest events out for all to enjoy in the annual Finnish-American heritage celebration, Finlandia Festival (see *Special Events*).

Many affluent businessmen wintering in South Florida soon began acquiring land to the west of Palm Beach for spacious estates and future investment

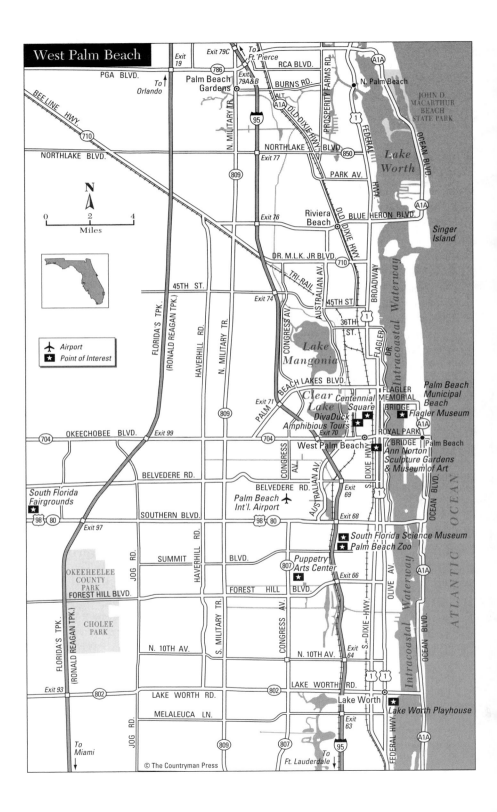

opportunities. New York businessman C. Oliver Wellington was one of them, purchasing a large plot of land and calling it the Flying C.O.W. Ranch after his initials. The parcel spanned thousands of acres and remained private property until his death in 1959. As estate taxes grew, his heirs began developing some of the property as exclusive upscale plots, and the community of **Wellington** was born. By the 1970s, the first phase of the well-planned community was well under way. In the mid-1980s the Wellington Club was built for a central point for social gatherings. In 1993, Glenn Straub, a mining and asphalt tycoon, bought the club, and it became the Palm Beach Club. Home to the Winter Equestrian Festival, the PBPC features past and future Olympians in jumping and dressage events, along with several "Sport of Kings" polo matches. The Village of Wellington wasn't incorporated until 1995 and is now known as the winter equestrian capital of the world. As it's a true equestrian community, you'll find tack shops, show centers, miles of trail riding, and riding lessons for both novices and professionals.

Nearby **Royal Palm Beach** is the only land-locked Palm Beach County municipality with *beach* in its name. Purchased in 1959 by Philadelphia supermarket magnates Sam and Hattie Friedland, the former 65,000-acre Seminole Tribe hunting ground was later sold to Miami developer Arthur Desser, and it has grown into a thriving suburban community.

Trying hard to stave off the onslaught of development, **Loxahatchee Groves,** founded in 1917, is the oldest of the western communities. An estimated four thousand residents live on just under 8,000 acres. It was founded in 1917 by Southern States Land sales manager George Bensil, who remained a resident until his death in 1961.

GUIDANCE For information about the area, get in touch with the **Palm Beach County Convention and Visitors Bureau** (561-233-3000), 1555 Palm Beach Lakes, Suite 800, West Palm Beach 33401.

GETTING THERE *By car:* From **I-95,** exits 66 to 76 take you Palm Beach and West Palm Beach. Exit 70 (Okeechobee Blvd) takes you to most of the cultural areas.

From **Florida's Turnpike** use exits 97, 98, or 99 for Palm Beach or West Palm Beach and exit 93 for Lake Worth.

By air: **Palm Beach International Airport (PBIA)** (561-471-7420), 1000 Turnage Blvd, West Palm Beach, is situated adjacent to I-95.

By rail: **AMTRAK** (561-832-6169 or 1-800-USA-RAIL; www.amtrak.com). Take the Silver Service/Palmetto route to 201 S Tamarind Ave, West Palm Beach.

WEST PALM BEACH SKYLINE
Palm Beach County Convention & Visitors Bureau

Tri-Rail (1-800-TRI-RAIL; www.tri-rail.com). Service area includes Palm Beach, Broward, and Miami-Dade Counties. Connects to Palm Tran routes at Mangonia Park Station, 1415 45th St; West Palm Beach Station, 203 S Tamarind Ave; and Lake Worth Station, 1703 Lake Worth Rd. Use Palm Tran Route 40 or 44 for West Palm Beach Airport access.

By bus: **Greyhound** (561-833-8534 or 1-800-231-2222; www.greyhound.com) has service to 205 S Tamarind Ave, West Palm Beach.

GETTING AROUND *By car:* To get the heart of Palm Beach Island, from I-95 take exit 70, Okeechobee Blvd (FL 704), and head east toward the downtown area, then cross over the bridge and you're there. Pay particular attention when you cross over the bridge, as Henry Flagler's home Whitehall (see *Historic Sites*) is to the right overlooking the water.

To get to Lake Worth from I-95, exit at either Sixth or 10th Ave and head east about 1 mile to US 1/FL 805/Dixie Hwy. Lake Ave/FL 802 E is between Sixth and 10th. Go north on US 1 from Sixth Ave and south on US 1 from 10th Ave. There are several one-way streets in the Lake Worth downtown area: Lake Ave runs west to east from US 1 to the beach; Lucerne Ave runs east to west from the downtown area to US 1.

By bus: The **Palm Tran** (561-841-4287; www.co.palm-beach.fl.us/palmtran) service area covers malls and tourist spots throughout Palm Beach County. Tri-Rail connects to several Palm Tran routes at Lake Worth, Mangonia Park, and West Palm Beach stations.

By trolley: **Lolly the Trolley** (561-586-1720), Lake Worth's community transit, covers all of Lake Worth every day 9–5. Fee.

By water taxi: **Palm Beach Water Taxi** (561-683-TAXI or 1-800-446-4577; www.palmbeachwatertaxi.com), Sailfish Marina, 98 Lake Dr, Palm Beach Shores (Singer Island). Pick up the water taxi at Sailfish Marina, or at Phil Foster Park, 900 E Blue Heron Blvd; downtown West Palm Beach's Clematis Street District; Palm Harbor Marina, 400 N Flager Dr; Riviera Beach Marina, 200 E 13th St. You can also catch a water taxi to Peanut Island from Panama Hattie's or the West Palm Beach Marina.

PALM BEACH TROLLY
Palm Beach County Convention & Visitors Bureau

PUBLIC REST ROOMS The beach areas and most city parks all have rest rooms available to the public at no cost.

PARKING City garages and parking lots offer the first hour for free.

Garages are located at Banyan Blvd and Olive Ave, Evernia St and Dixie Hwy, and the Police Garage at 600 Clematis St. Fees are $1 per hour 24 hours a day Mon–Sat; free Sun. All lots and garages charge a flat fee of $7 for overnight parking 10 PM–6 AM.

Parking lots are located at the corner of Datura St and Dixie Hwy, the 500 block of Clematis St, and the City Hall lot at Banyan Blvd and N Narcissus. Fees are $1 per hour, and lots are open 6 AM–10 PM.

Several **meters** are also located throughout West Palm Beach, Palm Beach, and the beach areas. Those also run about a $1 per hour.

Public parking in the cities in the western part of the county is readily available at no cost.

MEDICAL EMERGENCIES Several fine hospitals are located near Lake Worth, the closest being the **JFK Medical Center** (561-965-7300), 5301 S Congress Ave, Atlantis. Other area hospitals include **Columbia Hospital** (561-842-6141), 2201 45th St, West Palm Beach; **Palm Beach Gardens Hospital** (561-622-1411), 3360 Burns Rd, Palm Beach Gardens; and **Wellington Regional Medical Center** (561-798-8500), 10101 Forest Hill Blvd, Wellington.

VALET Most restaurants and luxury hotels in the beach area, and especially on the "Island," offer valet services. Some restaurants and hotels have only mandatory valet parking. Inquire when making reservations.

✳ To See

ART GALLERIES **Bruce Webber Gallery** (561-582-1045), 705 Lucerne Ave, Lake Worth. Nineteenth-century to contemporary original works of art in oil, acrylic, and watercolor along with fine-art photography. Next door, at 709 Lucerne Ave, **MaryAnne Webber's Gallery** showcases fine crafts, gifts, and jewelry from South Florida artists and around the United States. A trompe l'oeil mural along the side of the gallery complements the two structures.

The **Edna Hibel Museum and Gallery** (561-533-6872), 701 Lake Ave, Lake Worth, exhibits the fine art of South Florida artist Edna Hibel. She is the recipient of numerous prestigious awards, and her works have been exhibited in museums and galleries in more than 20 countries on four continents. Selections of her original paintings, lithographs, porcelains, drawings, and sculpture are also on display in Jupiter and Palm Beach.

HISTORIC SITES For information on many historical places throughout Palm Beach County, visit the **Historical Society of Palm Beach County** (561-832-4164; www.historicalsocietypbc.org), 1398 N Country Rd, Suite 25, in the Paramount Building.

Lake Worth

During the 1920s Florida land boom, Pittsburgh socialite John Phipps developed the pineapple fields around the intersection of Pershing and Flagler drives in Lake Worth into the **El Cid Neighborhood,** comprised of expensive Mediterranean Revival and Mission-style homes. The neighborhood was named after medieval Spanish hero Rodrigo Diaz de Vivar—*Cid* is a translation from Arabic, meaning "lord."

Lake Worth Pier (561-533-7367) has long been known as the site of some of the world's best ocean fishing. The 960-foot-long pier is as close to the Gulf Stream as you can get without a boat. You can fish for bluefish, snapper, and sand perch 24 hours a day or simply watch the sunrise over the crystal-clear ocean. Bait and rental poles are available.

Explore nearby **Peanut Island** (561-845-4445), located in the Lake Worth Lagoon. This 79-acre island of lush mangroves and Australian pines is home to the Palm Beach Maritime Museum (see *Museums*), the historic former Coast Guard Station, and the nuclear fallout shelter built to protect President Kennedy in case of war during the Cuban Missile Crisis. Access is by boat or ferry from Phil Foster Park and Riviera Beach Marina (call Seafare Water Taxi at 561-339-2504 for transportation). Dock spaces are open to the public, and there are 20 tent sites for camping.

Palm Beach

Bethesda-By-The-Sea Episcopal Church (561-655-4554; www.bbts.org), Barton Ave and N County Rd, is one of the more beautiful churches in all of Florida and the first Protestant church built in southeast Florida (in 1889). The church now serves all races, nations, and creeds, and many well-to-do socialites and celebrities have been married at the church, including Donald Trump, who exchanged vows here with Melania Knauss in January 2005. (You must be a member of the church, however, should you want to hold your own wedding here.)

The glamorous, European-style **Chesterfield Hotel,** 363 Cocoanut Row, is listed on the National Register of Historic Places. Built in 1926 as The Lido-Venice bed & breakfast, the hotel was renamed in 1928 as The Vineta. The three-story Mediterranean Revival–style structure is a good representation of resort hotels built during the Florida land boom of the 1920s. The name changed again in 1985 to The Chesterfield (see *Lodging*), and the boutique hotel is now a member of the Red Carnation Hotel Collection and Small Luxury Hotels of the World.

Mar-A-Lago, meaning "from lake to sea," was purchased by Donald Trump in 1985 from the Post Foundation as a winter home. The grand estate, originally built in 1927 by legendary cereal heiress Marjorie Merriweather Post (then Mrs. Edward F. Hutton), required extensive restoration, and Mr. Trump spent the better part of 18 years ensuring careful and accurate historic restoration of the "Jewel of Palm Beach." The 110,000-square-foot Mediterranean Revival mansion has 118 rooms, including 58 bedrooms, 33 bathrooms, and 3 bomb shelters. The lush 20-acre estate is now home to the members-only Mar-A-Lago Club. It can be seen from the water or Ocean Dr.

The second church erected in southeast Florida (after Bethesda-By-The-Sea Episcopal Church, above), **Old Bethesda-by-the-Sea Episcopal Church,** located in the Clematis Street Commercial Historic District west of Dixie Hwy, is now a private residence.

Henry Flagler constructed the **Royal Poinciana Chapel,** 60 Cocoanut Row, in 1898 to serve winter guests. The earliest organized church in Palm Beach, the chapel originally sat on Whitehall Way and was moved to its present location in 1973.

Palm Beach's oldest house and the first winter residence of Henry Flagler, the circa 1886 **Sea Gull Cottage,** 58 Cocoanut Row, is now the parish house of Royal Poinciana Chapel (see above). It was moved in 1984 from its original site next to the Royal Poinciana Hotel and restored in 1984. Please view from the exterior only.

Henry Morrison Flagler built his grand estate, **Whitehall** (561-655-2833), One Whitehall Way, in 1902 as a wedding present for his wife, Mary Lily Kenan Flagler. The 55-room, 60,000-square-foot Gilded Age mansion was grander than any other mansion at the time. The marble entrance hall, double staircase, colossal marble columns, and red barrel tile roof are just some of the exquisite details. Now a museum, the mansion's period rooms are decorated in such styles as Louis XIV, Louis XV, Louis XVI, Italian Renaissance, and Francis I. My favorite section is the china, of which there is a plate for every occasion. Located across from the Okeechobee Blvd (FL 704) bridge, the home can partially be seen when you cross the bridge. Henry Flagler's private Railcar #91 is part of the museum's collection (see *Museums*).

West Palm Beach

In 1893 the town of West Palm Beach was laid out in a grid pattern, leaving a triangular space, known as **Flagler Park,** on the east end of Clematis to be used as a public area. In 1923 the Memorial Library was built on the site, rebuilt in 1962, and remodeled in 1994. The plaza is still the center of downtown activities. Note the small, triangular, in-ground fountain resembling the original plot. A marker is at the corner of Clematis St and Flagler Dr.

Built in 1920s and '30s on the highest coast ridge between downtown West Palm Beach and Miami, the **Flamingo Park** subdivision was home to some of the area's most prominent residents. Homes were built in several architectural styles, such as Mission, Mediterranean Revival, Frame Vernacular, Masonry Vernacular, Art Moderne, American Foursquare, Colonial Revival, and Craftsman/Bungalow. One notable home, the Alfred Comeau House (circa 1924), is located at 701 Flamingo Dr. The neighborhood's historical marker is located at Park Place and Dixie Hwy.

HENRY FLAGLER'S WHITEHALL

Kathy Wolf

A unique example of early-20th-century railroad architecture in the Mediterranean Revival style, the **Seaboard Airline Station,** 203 S Tamarind Ave, opened in 1925 and was the flagship station of the Seaboard line. AMTRAK and the Tri-Rail are both serviced from this station. See the historical marker in the station courtyard.

Lake Worth

The 2,600-year-old "Sport of Kings" is heralded at the **Museum of Polo & Hall of Fame** (561-969-3210; www.polomuseum.com), 9011 Lake Worth Rd. The permanent exhibit displays more than two thousand years of polo history throughout the world and American polo history from 1904. Special exhibits change annually. Look for A Day in the Life of a Polo Pony in 2006. Open 10–4 Mon–Fri and 10–2 Sat (during the season). Donation.

The history and culture of Lake Worth's Polish, Finnish, and Lithuanian immigrants come alive at the **Museum of the City of Lake Worth** (561-586-1700; www.lakeworth.org), 414 Lake Ave, City Hall Annex. Seven rooms full of artifacts, books, photos, memorabilia, and antiques display "days gone by." Open 9:30–12:30 and 1:30–4:30 Mon and Wed–Fri.

Palm Beach

Henry Morrison Flagler Museum (561-655-2826 or 561-655-2833; www.flagler.org), One Whitehall Way, is home to one of "America's Castles." Whitehall, built in 1901 by Henry M. Flagler, was a wedding present to his third wife, Mary Lily Kenan Flagler (see *Historic Sites*). The grand mansion is decorated in many European styles reminiscent of the Gilded Age. Flagler, cofounder of Standard Oil Co., was instrumental in bringing the railroad to the southeast region of Florida and down through the Keys. His private railroad car is on display in the new Beaux-Arts-style building next to the main house. The 8,000-square-foot building, built specifically to hold the car, is the first building of its kind constructed in the United States in the past 60 years. Whitehall is listed on the National Register of Historic Places and can be viewed 10–5 Tue–Sat and noon–5 Sun. Adults $10, children 6–12 $3. Admission is free to members of the museum.

Opened in 1999, the **Palm Beach Maritime Museum** (561-540-5147; www.pbmm.org), in Currie Park, 2400 N Flagler Dr, has four facilities: the former U.S. Coast Guard Station, boathouse, and President John F. Kennedy command post and bomb shelter on Peanut Island (see *Historic Sites*); the marine science field office and dock on the Intracoastal Waterway; an educational center, preview building, and ferry dock at Currie Park in West Palm Beach; and the Palm Beach Maritime Academy K–8 Charter School. Access is by boat or ferry from Phil Foster Park and Riviera Beach Marina. Open 10–2 Mon–Wed and Fri, noon–4 Thu. Closed Sat and Sun. Cost for Peanut Island Tour: Adults $7, seniors $6, students 5–17 $5, under 4 free. Ferryboat is an extra charge. Call 561-832-7428 for more information.

West Palm Beach

Sitting on just under 2 acres, the **Ann Norton Sculpture Gardens** (561-832-5328; www.ansg.org), 253 Barcelona Rd, features monolithic sculptures set amongst three hundred species of tropical palms. The historic home, listed on the National Register of Historic Places, displays more than one hundred various sized sculptures created by Ann Weaver Norton. Open 11–4 Wed–Sun (Oct–May) and Fri–Sat (Jun–Aug). Closed Sep. Fee.

If you haven't been to the **Norton Museum of Art** (561-832-5196; www .norton.org), 1451 S Olive Ave, then this is a must-see. Florida's largest and most impressive art museum was recently expanded. Permanent collections feature many of the grand masters, such as Chagale, Gauguin, Klee, Matisse, Miró, Monet, Picasso, and an impressive collection of Jackson Pollock, along with other great American and international artists. The glass ceiling by Dale Chihuly, known for his expertise in glassblowing, feels like an undersea odyssey. Industrialist Ralph Hubbard Norton, who headed the Acme Steel Company in Chicago, and his wife, Elizabeth Calhoun Norton, founded the museum in 1941. Permanent collection: Adults $8, ages 13–21 $3, under age 13 free. Free admission to West Palm Beach residents on Sat. Palm Beach County residents can view the museum at no charge on the first Sat of the month. There is an extra charge for all on special exhibitions. Call for more information.

Open since 1980, the **Ragtops Motorcars Museum** (561-655-2837 or 1-877-RAGTOPS; www.ragtopsmotorcars.com), 2119 S Dixie Hwy, is housed in three buildings covering 2 entire city blocks. You'll experience yesteryear with vintage automobiles, memorabilia, a soda bar, and a 1954 vintage silver dining car. "The Station" features vintage station wagons and a unique gift boutique. Open 10–5 Mon–Sat. Fee. Classic cars from the collection are available for purchase.

The **South Florida Science Museum** (561-832-1988; www.sfsm.org), 4801 Dreher Trail N, is not your typical science museum. This facility houses Florida's only science-themed mini golf, along with a natural-history display of Florida ice age fossils. There are also lots of hands-on and interactive experiments. You'll also find dozens of fresh- and saltwater tanks up to 900 gallons at the **McGinty Aquarium.** Their pair of white spotted bamboo sharks actually mated during Hurricane Wilma and produced one viable semitransparent egg. Over at the **Aldrin Planetarium** you'll embark on a galactic odyssey seeking out nebulas and constellations while sitting in comfy inclined chairs. Open 10–5 Mon–Fri, 10–6 Sat, and noon–6 Sun. Museum admission: adults $8, seniors 62 and up $7.50, children 3–12 $6, under 3 free. Planetarium $2 additional.

Go way back in time to experience one hundred years of Florida's rich history from the 1850s to the 1950s. Sitting on 10 acres, **Yesteryear Village** (561-795-6402 or 561-795-3110; www.southfloridafair.com/yesteryearvillage.html), South Florida Fairgrounds, 9067 Southern Blvd, displays a large collection of original and replicated buildings, fully furnished with period items from a simpler time. You'll walk through edifices such as an old school, a blacksmith shop, and a general store. **The Bink Glisson Historical Museum** is located inside a replica of an 1858 Haile plantation house. Bink Glisson, a self-taught wildlife and landscape artist, settled in Florida in the early 1920s and was instrumental in the development of Wellington. Many of his paintings are on display in the home. The original classic Cracker house still stands in Alachua County, Florida. The village is also home to the **Sally Bennett Big Band Hall of Fame Museum,** which displays memorabilia by such musicians as Tommy Dorsey, Buddy Rich, Glenn Miller, and Duke Ellington. Open noon–5 Tue–Fri. Hours may change according to special events, so please call ahead. Fee for guided tours.

Wellington

Tournament play is at its best Jan–Apr at the **Palm Beach Polo & Country Club** (561-798-7000; www.palmbeachpolo.com), 11199 Polo Club. High-goal polo games are played on 11 world-class polo fields. The PBPC also presents the National Horse Show and Winter Equestrian Festival (see *Special Events*).

Equestrians gather from all over the world at **Stadium Jumping, Inc.** (561-793-5867; www.stadiumjumping.com), 14440 Pierson Rd, where the famed Winter Equestrian Festival (see *Special Events*) is held from late January to mid-March. Hunter, jumper, equitation, and dressage events are scheduled over an eight-week period. The USEF National Grand Prix Freestyle is also held here in March. Many past, present, and future Olympic champions compete in both events.

West Palm Beach

Learn how to play croquet the English way at the **National Croquet Center** (561-478-2300; www.croquetnational.com), 700 Florida Mango Rd. The 19,000-square-foot clubhouse presents tournaments and schedules classes throughout the year. Every Saturday morning the center offers free two-hour Golf Croquet starting promptly at 10. You must be at least 12 years old, and all instruction and equipment is provided. Reservations are recommended if there are more than four in your group. Flat-sole shoes are a must. For those who want to learn more, half-day clinics are held 8:30–12:30 by Archie Peck, the center's Director of Croquet and four-time national champion. There is a fee for the clinic, and reservations are required. Open 9–5:30 Mon–Sat and 10:30–4:30 Sun, depending on events and tournaments.

ZOOLOGICAL PARKS & WILDLIFE REHAB Situated on more than 23 lush, tropical acres, the **Palm Beach Zoo at Dreher Park** (561-533-0887; www.palm beachzoo.com), 1301 Summit Blvd, West Palm Beach, is home to more than nine hundred animals from Florida, Central and South America, Asia, and Australia. The new "Tropic of the Americas" features Mayan pyramids where you find bush dogs and jaguars, including cubs Caipora and Izel, who were born at the zoo on December 9, 2005. These cubs are extra special, as they were the first born to the zoo and arrived only a few weeks after Hurricane Wilma. Paddocks house a variety of free-roaming animals, from the majestic Bengal tiger to the rabbit-size Malayan mouse deer. Bring your bathing suit on hot days to cool off in the Interactive Fountain (changing cabanas available). Open daily 9–5. Adults $13, seniors 60+ $10, children 3–12 $9, under 3 free.

✳ To Do

CRUISES Take a trip over to Freeport, Bahamas, on the majestic *Palm Beach Princess* or the new contemporary *Cloud X* ("Cloud Ten") ferry. The 420-foot, 1,300-passenger ***Palm Beach Princess*** cruise ship (1-800-841-7447; www .palmbeachprincess.com) sails twice daily from the Port of Palm Beach for five-hour lunch or dinner cruises that include casino gambling, live entertainment, a pool, skeet shooting, and lavish buffets. The stylish 122-foot, 367-passenger

Cloud X ferry (1-866-GO-FERRY; www.cloudx.com) speeds you to the island in about three hours. The catamaran-style SWATH ferry offers casino gambling and three lounges.

FAMILY ACTIVITIES **Adventure Mini Golf** (561-968-1111 or 1-877-580-3117), 6585 S Military Trl, Lake Worth. Two 18-hole courses feature cascading waterfalls, rapids, and hours of delight in the game room with snack bar.

The world's largest croquet complex, **National Croquet Center** (561-478-2300; www.croquetnational.com), 700 Florida Mango Rd, Lake Worth (see *Sports*), features its own "golf croquet" and is open year-round for sport and entertainment.

GOLF **Lake Worth Municipal Golf Course** (561-533-7365), One Seventh Ave N, Lake Worth. Of the 145 golf courses in Palm Beach County, Lake Worth just happens to have one of the finest and most affordable. Designed by William Langford and Theodore J. Moreau, the municipally owned 18-hole, par 70 course has been open since 1924. Overlooking the scenic Intracoastal Waterway, the public golf course is one of the few on a waterfront venue. The **Lake Worth Country Club** is also open to the public and features leisurely lunches, elegant dinners, and a classic Sunday brunch.

HIKING One of the best places to go hiking is in the **Corbett Wildlife Management Area** (561-625-5122), off Seminole-Pratt-Whitney Blvd, with more than 60,000 acres of wild and watery wilderness. A 17-mile section of the Ocean-to-Lake Trail passes through the preserve. (See *Wild Places.*)

RACE CAR DRIVING More than seven hundred sports cars and motorcycle events are held each year at **Moroso Motorsports Park** (561-622-1400; www .morosomotorsportspark.com), 17047 Beeline Hwy, Palm Beach Gardens. Driver-development programs and open test days for both sports cars and motorcycles are held on the 2¼-mile road course and ¼-mile drag strip. Kids older than 8 will want their turn at the wheel on the competition-grade ⁹⁄₁₀-mile Kart Track.

SCUBA & SNORKELING **Lake Worth Lagoon** is recognized as one of the most important warm-water manatee refuges on the east coast of Florida. These "sea cows" are often observed resting or feeding near submerged sea grass beds during winter months. An artificial reef, completed in 1995, plunges to depths of 440 feet. Created using tons of rock, barges, freighters, and even a Rolls Royce (!), this living reef system is home to many fish and other marine life.

SPA THERAPY Select one of the flavor-of-the-month body scrubs at **The Breakers** (561-655-6611 or 1-800-833-3141; www.thebreakers.com), One S Country Rd, Palm Beach, such as decadent chocolate, coffee, tropical mango, and Key lime, and seasonal offerings such as pumpkin spice.

TOURS It's a quacking good time! Part boat, part bus, the amphibious *Diva-Duck* (561-844-4188; www.divaduck.com), 501 Clematis St, West Palm Beach,

A few miles west of Palm Beach you'll find a treasure at **Lion Country Safari** (561-793-1084; www.lioncountrysafari.com), 2003 Lion Country Safari Rd, Loxahatchee. I can't believe I've lived here for almost 20 years and just recently visited this reserve. Now we make the drive out west at least twice a year. If you can't go to Africa, then we'll bring Africa to you. That was the thought in 1967 when a group of South African and British entrepreneurs opened the first "cageless" park in America. Drive through the 350-acre preserve where a thousand animals roam freely. The park is divided into seven sections: Las Pampas, grasslands where llamas, rhea, fallow deer, and Brazilian tapirs graze; Ruaha National Park, where you'll see greater kudu, impala, and aoudad; the dry Kalahari Bushveldt, where Gemsbok and Lechwe antelope leap past you; the Gir Forest, where you can look closely to see the impressive Asiatic water buffalo; The Gorongosa, where African lions dominate; the famed Serengeti Plains, home to the African elephant, eland, ostrich, wildebeast, and more; and the Hwange National Park, where you'll see herds of zebras running along with white rhinos while chimpanzees play and giraffes tower above you. You will be driving at a snail's pace through the park so as not to injure any animals, so allow about one to two hours for the 5-mile safari. And please, no matter how tempting, keep your windows rolled up just like they tell you, and never, ever get out of your car. These animals are wild and can be very inquisitive: The ostrich and

LION AT LION COUNTRY SAFARI

Kathy Wolf

giraffes especially love to surprise you. My favorite sections were the Hwange National Park, where a herd of zebras took off ahead of me, racing along the plain, and The Gorongosa, where the "King of Beasts" rules. One female lion let me know for certain that I was in her territory when she ran to the front of my car and greeted me with a deafening roar. I was so glad I didn't take the Mazda Miata! She was about the same size. The parks, which work as part of the Species Survival Plan (SSP) and are members of the American Zoo and Aquarium Association (AZA), have been instrumental in the continued survival of the white rhinoceros. And as a licensed rehabilitation facility, the park often takes in Flori-da rescues, such as the brown peli-can. With the new Safari World

Lion Country Safari

BABY UKUBWA AT LION COUNTRY SAFARI

expansion, the park adds an additional 53 acres to include a children's Safari Splash Interactive Spray Ground, a 55-foot Ferris wheel and other cool kiddie park rides, an Aldabra tortoise exhibit, a giraffe feeding exhibit, and a Safari Hedge Maze. A picnic area is also available, so plan to make a day of it. The park also has a KOA campground. To traverse the park, you may use your own approved vehicle (convertibles are not allowed, and open-bed trucks must be empty), or park your car ($3.50) and rent a car ($10) or van ($15). This is worth the extra price—remember, these are wild animals, and while most stay clear of your vehicle, I found some to be quite interested in my window washers and side mirrors. Rental cars and vans are first come, first served. No pets are allowed in the park, but they do offer free kennels while you visit. Open 9:30–4:30 (with the park closing promptly at 5:30) daily. Admission: Ages 10–64 $21, seniors 65+ $19, children 3–9 $17, ages 2 and under free. Check the web site and local grocery stores and flyers for dis-count admission coupons.

will take you over land and sea on a 75-minute, fully narrated musical tour of downtown CityPlace, historic Palm Beach neighborhoods, Lake Worth Lagoon, Peanut Island, and down the Intracoastal Waterway past magnificent mansions. All tours depart from Hibiscus St in CityPlace, just west of the railroad tracks, except on Wed, when they depart from Singer Island. Adult and children older 10 $23, children 4–10 $15, children under 4 $5.

WATER PARKS

Royal Palm Beach

Calypso Bay Waterpark (561-790-6160; www.pbcgov.com), 151 Lamstein Ln, is located in Seminole Palms Park, one of Palm Beach County's parks. It features an 870-foot river ride, two four-story-high water slides, and a lily pad walk, along with full-service concessions. Adults and children over 12 $10, children 3–11 $7, children 1–2 $3, infants under 1 free.

West Palm Beach

You'll find 22 acres of action-packed thrills at **Rapids Water Park** (561-842-8756; www.rapidswaterpark.com), 6566 N Military Trl. At Big Thunder, one of the largest water rides in Florida, you ride on a four-person tube through a 9-foot dark tunnel and then round and round through a funnel at speeds of up to 20 miles an hour before dropping to a landing pool below. You won't need tubes or rafts on Body Blasters as you slide your way through 1,000 feet of darkness, and at Pirate's Plunge you zip down two speed slides before dropping seven stories. Tubin' Tornadoes will have you twisting and turning, you'll spin and swirl through mist on one of two Superbowls, or you can ride a whitewater adventure over three waterfalls at Riptide Raftin. Over at Big Surf, you can catch a 6-foot wave in the 25,000-square-foot wave pool. Milder rides such as the Lazy River, Splish Splash Lagoon, and the toddler Tadpool ensure a fun day for everyone in your family. Open daily mid-Mar to late Aug, and weekends Sep to mid-Oct. Admission $30; children under 2 free.

✳ Green Space

BEACHES

Lake Worth

At **Lake Worth Beach** (561-533-7367), FL A1A, there is 1,300 feet of guarded beach perfect for sunning, surfing, and volleyball, and you can rent cabanas, boogie boards, rafts, chairs, and umbrellas. The 962-foot fishing pier is sure to please anglers, and there are rental poles and bait available. Other amenities include restaurants and stores, showers, and picnic facilities. Lifeguards on beach 9–5; handicapped assistance if requested. Open daily. Free.

Singer Island

& ♫ Popular for sunning and snorkeling, **John D. MacArthur Beach State Park** (561-624-6950), 10900 FL 703, is a beautiful natural area between the Lake Worth Lagoon and the Atlantic Ocean. The park maintains an excellent nature center with interpretive information on the creatures of the lagoon and rocky reef. The main portion of the park connects with the beach via a broad boardwalk over the flats, a great spot for birding. There are two nature trails in the park, one through the tropical forest behind the dunes and the other, the Satinleaf Trail, a short interpretive trail that starts at the parking area and makes a loop through the native tropical hammock. At the beach, MacArthur's rocky reefs and tidal pools are ideal for snorkeling. Park rangers run guided kayaking tours of the lagoon; call for details and times. Open 8–sunset daily. Fee.

Kathy Wolf

ENJOYING THE BEACH AT PALM BEACH

BOTANICAL GARDENS Sitting on just less than 2 acres, the **Ann Norton Sculpture Gardens** (561-832-5328; www.ansg.org), 253 Barcelona Rd, West Palm Beach, features monolithic sculptures set among three hundred species of tropical palms. The historic home, listed on the National Register of Historic Places, displays more than one hundred various size sculptures created by Ann Weaver Norton. Open 11–4 Wed–Sun Oct–May and Fri–Sat Jun–Aug. Closed Sep. Fee.

An oasis of beauty near the West Palm Beach International Airport, **Mounts Botanical Garden** (561-233-1749; www.mounts.org), 531 N Military Trl, West Palm Beach, packs plants from around the globe into a 14-acre park. Themed sections break up your stroll through the gardens, from Florida natives to tropical fruits to Australian eucalyptus and African baobab trees. The gardens took a major hit from the 2005 hurricane season, but you can expect the tropical plantings to fill in quickly. The Garden Shop stocks an excellent selection of books, including hard-to-find tomes on gardening and natural habitats in Florida. Open 8:30–4:30 Mon–Sat and 1–5 Sun. Donation.

MOUNTS BOTANICAL GARDENS, WEST PALM BEACH

Sandra Friend

NATURE CENTERS &. ❧ Perched on the edge of the Loxahatchee Slough, the water supply for West Palm Beach, **Grassy Waters Preserve** (561-627-8831), 8264 Northlake Blvd, West Palm Beach, surrounds you with the Everglades as they always were, before cities along Florida's east coast drained them. The preserve features a nature center for orientation, the Rain-catcher Boardwalk for an immersion into the cypress slough habitat, and a set of rugged hiking trails just up the road behind the Fish & Wildlife Commission headquarters building. Regular guided tours are offered, including off-trail swamp tromps and paddling trips. Fee.

&. ♂ Hidden at the back of vast Okeeheelee Park (see *Parks*), **Okeeheelee Nature Center** (561-966-6660), 7715 Forest Hill Blvd, West Palm Beach, provides interpretation of the habitats and their inhabitants found along a network of hard-packed lime rock trails that fan out behind the center for a couple of miles of walking. One path leads to a permanent deer exhibit. Free.

♂ **Pine Jog Environmental Education Center** (561-686-6600), 6301 Summit Blvd, West Palm Beach, preserves a patch of pine flatwoods amid suburban sprawl. Park near the exhibit center and stop in for an interpretive brochure and overview of local habitats, then walk the ½-mile Wetland Hammock Trail around a flatwoods pond teeming with birds. Open 9–5 Mon–Sat and 2–5 Sun. Free.

PARKS

Lake Worth

Bryant Park (561-533-7359), corner of Golfview and Lake Ave, right on the Intracoastal Waterway. Regular concerts are held at the Bandshell, with seating for five hundred, or bring your own chairs and blankets. There are rest rooms and a boat ramp on-site. Across the bridge, also on the water is **Barton Park,** by the Lake Worth Beach lower parking lot. It has picnic tables and pavilion, rest rooms, and a playground.

John Prince Park (561-966-6660), 2700 Sixth Ave S, stretches from Lake Worth Rd to Lantana Rd along Congress Blvd, facing Lake Worth. Tucked in the back of the park off Prince Dr, there's a delightful campground (265 sites for RV or tent camping—some on waterfront) and adjoining nature trail system. Other activities include a 3-mile paved bike/walking trail, fishing, canoeing, golfing, and birding. Pets welcome on a 6-foot leash.

West Palm Beach

One of the county's largest recreational parks, **Okeeheelee Park** (561-966-6660), 7715 Forest Hill Blvd, has a wide range of activities to choose from— dozens of picnic pavilions, ball fields, tennis courts, rental paddleboats, a water-ski course, paved bike trails, municipal golf course, and natural area with nature center and several miles of hiking trails winding through the pine flat-woods.

WILD PLACES At the western edge of "civilization" along Northlake Blvd, **Corbett Wildlife Management Area** (561-625-5122), off Seminole-Pratt-Whitney Blvd, West Palm Beach, encompasses more than 60,000 acres of wild and watery wilderness, brimming with blossoms in summer. A 17-mile section of the Ocean-to-Lake Trail passes through the preserve, accessed at Everglades Youth Camp along with the 1-mile interpretive Hungryland Boardwalk through a cypress slough. This is a popular winter destination for the county's deer hunters, who use large-tired swamp buggies to prowl off-road. Primitive camping is available to hunters and backpackers; day-use fee applies.

✳ Lodging

BED & BREAKFASTS

Lake Worth 33460

The first thing you notice when you drive up to the **Mango Inn** (561-533-6900; www.mangoinn.com), 128 N Lakeside Dr, is the immaculately groomed gardens surrounding the two-story building bathed in sunshine. Yes, you can't miss the eye-stopping yellow-painted inn nestled next to a delightful cottage. Tucked away on a quiet side street 2 blocks from the Intracoastal, the Mango Inn is within easy walking distance to the beach and the funky downtown area. Built in 1915, this local treasure was rescued and restored by Erin and Bo Allen, originally from Michigan. As you step through the front door you are greeted with the clean aroma of fresh cut flowers grown in the carefully tended garden. Cozy up to the coral fireplace or stretch out and grab some rays next to the heated swimming pool and circular waterfall. When you are ready to rest your head, retire to your own immaculate room or suite, complete with private bath. Fall into the lush down pillows and curl up under the monogrammed designer bed linens. For longer stays, request the cozy 1925 Pineapple Cottage, with fireplace and full kitchen; or the 1925 Mango Little House, complete with kitchen facilities. Mornings bring a new sensation with fresh baked blueberry gingerbread pancakes, cashew-mango muffins, and cinnamon-raisin scones with clotted cream and blackberry butter. Dine with other guests in the welcoming dining room or on the intimate veranda overlooking the pool. Before you head to the beach, have Erin pack you a picnic basket of light snacks and beverages. Rates $140–275 in-season, $110–175 off-season.

Innkeepers Mike and Lori Breece have taken great care in maintaining the architectural beauty of **Sabal Palm House** (561-582-1090; www.sabal palmhouse.com), 109 N Golf-view Rd. Built in 1936, the two-story house is located at the foot of the Intracoastal Waterway bridge and is a short walk or trolley ride to the beach, quaint shops, and cafés. Each room is named and decorated in the style of a master artist. Request the luxurious Renoir Suite, with its king-size canopy bed and private Jacuzzi bath for two. Watch the sun go down through the double French doors or relax on your own private balcony. Each of the guest rooms includes a private bath and French doors overlooking either the tropical courtyard or Intracoastal Waterway. Romance is in the air—from the sunny Chagall, warmth of the Rockwell, or French Country flair of the Lautrec, you are sure to find a room that will fit your mood. Rates $140–265 in-season, $125–210 off-season.

Palm Beach 33480

One of the few bed & breakfasts on the "Island," the **Palm Beach Historic Inn** (561-832-4009 or 1-800-918-9773; www.palmbeachhistoricinn .com), 365 S County Rd, is only a few steps from Worth Ave and the beach.

Complimentary continental breakfast is served in your room. Eight guest rooms and four suites, with king or queen beds, are all located on the second floor. Rates $200–405 in-season and $110–225 off-season, depending on room size.

West Palm Beach 33401

In the heart of the downtown shopping district near CityPlace is **Grandview Gardens Bed & Breakfast** (561-833-9023; www.grandview-gardens.net), 1608 Lake Ave. The intimate 1923 Mediterranean Revival villa has only five guest suites. Decorated in Spanish Mediterranean style, each suite has its own private entrance and is set around the 30-foot swimming pool and tropical gardens. Innkeepers speak a variety of languages: English, German, Spanish, and French. Rates $125–199, depending on season, and include a breakfast buffet.

West Palm Beach 33407

Innkeepers Elaine and Frank Calendrillo are your hosts in the Tuscany-style villa (circa 1926) **Casa de Rosa Bed & Breakfast** (561-833-1920 or 1-888-665-8666; www.casaderosa .com), 520 27th St, in Historic Old Northwood. Beautifully landscaped gardens surround the heated pool. With just four rooms, this is the perfect romantic getaway or an alternative from hotels for the executive business-person. The Italian architecture, painted in marigold yellow, features upper- and lower-story verandas with 22 arches. The luxurious 20-by-30-foot White Rose Room has a king-size bed and a bathroom with two vanities—unique in bed & breakfasts, the room opens to the veranda through three French doors. The Beach Rose Cottage has a fun beachy theme complete with kitchen, the

charming Tuscany Rose Room Suite features a queen-size poster bed and French doors, and the the comfortable Tropicana Rose Room ensures you a peaceful night's sleep. Rates $145–225 in season, $130–200 off-season.

Built during the Florida land boom in 1922 by Mayor David Dunkle, the **Hibiscus House Bed & Breakfast** (561-863-5633 or 1-800-203-4927; www.hibiscushouse.com), 501 30th St, is on the National Register of Historic Places. Rooms have romantic queen-size beds, such as the four-poster rice bed in the Green Room, and the Peach Room has a wood ceiling canopy. The two-room Burgundy Suite has a sitting room, fireplace, and a queen-size cherry four-poster bed. A full breakfast is served on china, silver, and Waterford crystal in the formal dining room or in the tropical gardens surrounding the pool. Rates $125–210 in season, $95–150 off-season.

CAMPGROUNDS

Lake Worth 33461
John Prince Park Campground (561-582-7992 or 1-877-992-9925), 4759 S Congress Ave, offers 265 rustic campsites with water and electric hookups for tents or RVs. Sites, especially the coveted waterfront sites, fill up fast, so reservations are recommended. The campground is operated by the Palm Beach Park and Recreation Department (www.pbcgov.com), and a manager resides on-site for your convenience.

HOTELS, MOTELS, AND RESORTS

Lake Worth 33460
GulfStream Hotel (1-888-540-0669; www.thegulfstreamhotel.com), One Lake Ave, recently restored to its

original grandeur, is member of the prestigious Historic Hotels of America. Whether you're on a romantic getaway or a business trip, the full-service hotel will attend to your every need in a grand and tropical setting. Overlooking the Intracoastal Waterway, the GulfStream offers guests a full range of amenities, from the poolside café to the richly appointed dining room. Call or log on to web site for rates.

Palm Beach 33480

The 1907 **Bradley House** (561-832-7020 or 1-800-822-4116; www.bradley housepalmbeach.com), 280 Sunset Ave, houses 31 suites in a gracious Mediterranean-style mansion. Rates (depending on season): deluxe studio $85–259, one-bedroom suite $105–379, two-bedroom suite $149–549, penthouse suite (with two bedrooms, patio, and gazebo) $295–875.

Built in 1926 during the Florida land boom, the European-style **Brazilian Court** (561-655-7740 or 561-838-4445; www.thebraziliancourt.com), 301 Australian Ave, offers 108 rooms and condo suites in sunny yellows and floral fabrics. Concierges speak a variety of languages. The famed Frédéric Fekkai Spa is on-site. Call for rates.

A legendary grand dame, **The Breakers** (561-655-6611 or 1-888-THEBREAKERS; www.thebreakers .com), One S Country Rd, exudes everything luxurious about Palm Beach. The luxury 560-room hotel was founded by Henry Flagler in 1896 and built in the Italian Renaissance style. The oceanfront property covers 140 acres and is listed on the National Register of Historic Places. Some of the features are two 18-hole golf courses, 10 tennis courts, and a 20,000-square-foot luxury spa. Rooms

and suites are spacious and luxuriously appointed. The Breakers is also a great destination for families. The 6,160-square-foot Family Entertainment Center includes an oceanfront heated pool, more than 20 arcade games, a toddler's playroom and craft area, a children's movie room, and computers with Xbox. Rooms are childproofed: Electrical outlets and table corners are protected, and plastic bags are removed from trash cans. And if your family really wants to spread out, you can link up to five adjoining rooms. For nights out, the staff has selected experienced and fully screened babysitters. Worth a peek around even if you don't stay there. Rates $219 and up.

The Chesterfield Hotel (561-659-5800 or 1-800-243-7871, www.chester fieldpb.com), 363 Cocoanut Row, was built in 1926 and is on the National Register of Historic Places (See *Historic Sites*). The Mediterranean Revival–style boutique hotel is only 2 blocks north of world-famous Worth Ave. Guest rooms and deluxe suites are decorated with gorgeous fabrics, fine furnishings, and tasteful antiques. Amenities such as jellybeans for you and treats for your pet are just some of the attention to detail that the Chesterfield provides. Pets are allowed with prior notice, and the hotel provides a range of pet beds, menus, and pet-related treats and amenities. Each afternoon, traditional English tea is served in the wood-paneled library. The legendary on-site Leopard Lounge remains one of the trendiest hot spots on the "Island." Call for rates.

Opulent British Colonial style is evident at the **The Colony Hotel Palm Beach** (561-655-5430 or 1-800-521-

5525; www.thecolonypalmbeach.com), 155 Hammon Ave. Only a few steps from famous Worth Ave and 100 yards from the beach, the 90 newly renovated rooms, suites, and villas ensure ample accommodations for the discriminating vacationer. The unique Florida-shaped pool is just off the famed Bimini Bar. Rooms $300–440 in-season (call for off-season rates); villas $1,200 and up per week and $18,000–25,000 per month in-season, $575–850 per night off-season.

The Euro contemporary–style **Heart of Palm Beach Hotel** (561-655-5600 or 1-800-523-5377; www.heartofpalm beach.com), 160 Royal Palm Way, is nestled in a quiet neighborhood just a block from the beach, restaurants, and nightlife. It has spacious rooms and luxurious suites and a full-service spa that surround a heated pool. Reasonable rates start at $159.

✳ Where to Eat

DINING OUT

Lake Worth

At **Bizarre Avenue Cafe** (561-588-4488), 921 Lake Ave, Granny's attic meets Bizarro World in a creatively decorated, offbeat café. Settle into the overstuffed chairs and sofas, and if you like one, you can take it home! All of the furnishings and bric-a-brac are for sale. The carefully selected, ever-changing decor is arranged in intimate groupings and surrounded by rich redbrick walls. The eclectic menu echoes the atmosphere with such scrumptious delights as chicken–artichoke heart crêpes and an assortment of tapas, sandwiches, pasta, and salads. Desserts are made fresh locally and complement the season—we had the Pumpkin Crunch when we visited

in the fall. The wraparound bar serves wine and beer. Plan to stay late, as this place is open until 11 PM weekdays and midnight Fri and Sat.

Dave's Last Resort and Raw Bar (561-588-5208), 632 Lake Ave. Looking for a place to relax with friends? The open, airy dining room/bar boasts a plethora of TVs, with a variety of broadcast sports. The booths and tabletops are laden with copper and outlined with etched maple leaves. Light knotty pine, lots of it, completes the rustic feel. This is the place to go when you have a "manly" appetite. Start with the Raw Bar Sampler, which includes oysters, clams, snow crab, white and rock shrimp, and even crawdads. Still hungry? Then order up the house favorite—a 20-ounce porterhouse with garlic mashed potatoes. Open daily for lunch, dinner, and—as all good last resorts—late into the night.

Palm Beach

Muer Seafood restaurants (www.muer .com) began as a family of restaurants in 1964, and while Landry now owns the chain, the culinary control is still in the hands of the Muer chefs. Along the water, **Charley's Crab** (561-659-1500), 456 S Ocean Blvd, offers the best in seafood dishes, from classics such as bouillabaisse ($19) to imaginative dishes such as the Szechuan-style Dungeness crab clusters ($23). At 207 Royal Poinciana Way, **Chuck & Harold's** (561-659-1440) caters to the well-heeled locals. Favorites are Chuck & Harold's Fishwich ($9) and the Muer classic Maryland crab cakes ($22). A great place to sip Bloody Marys is outside in the garden café. Both locations are celebrated for their Sunday brunch. Lunch and dinner served Mon–Sat. (See also

Oceanside: Eastern Broward County for Pal's Charley's Crab, on the Intracoastal Waterway in Deerfield Beach.)

A Palm Beach classic, the **Leopard Lounge and Restaurant** (561-659-8500 or 1-800-243-7871; www.red carnationhotels.com), 363 Cocoanut Row, serves breakfast, brunch, lunch, afternoon tea, and dinner. The jungle-themed lounge, British Colonial furnishings, and black and red laquer trim evoke a private-club atmosphere, and it offers a variety of live music, entertainment, and dancing.

EATING OUT

Lake Worth

Every town has one or two culinary treasures, and **John G's** (561-585-9860), 10 S Ocean Blvd, is *the* local favorite. Start your day in this nautical setting, watching the sunrise while feasting on Canadian peameal bacon flanked with scrambled eggs, or try the cinnamon nut French toast or blueberry pancakes. This place is always rated at the top of the "Best" lists, so get there early, as it's known for its long lines. On Sunday, the owner, Mr. John G himself, serves chocolate-dipped strawberries to those patiently waiting. It's conveniently located across from the beach, so you'll want to come back and grab lunch as well. Try the some of the deep-sea favorites, such as fried clams and crab cakes or fresh fish fillets. And don't forget to save room for dessert! Open daily 7–3.

Key West Crossing (561-588-9900), 617 Lake Ave. Stop into this funky ice cream parlor for a piece of Key lime pie and coconut ice cream. Play checkers on one of the colorful tables, or shop for eclectic gifts and treats such as Key lime syrup. Open daily 11–11.

The hub of the Finnish community since 1955, the fabulous **Scandia Bakery and Coffee Shop** (561-582-1600), 16 S Dixie Hwy, is also the headquarters for the annual Finlandia Festival (see *Special Events*). Read the bulletin board, some of which is in English, while having your Cardimom cake and coffee. Make sure to take home a fresh hot loaf of Finnish or Russian rye bread. Open for breakfast and light lunches 8–4 Mon–Sat and 8–2 Sun.

✳ Entertainment

NIGHTCLUBS What better way to unwind after a day of shopping and beach cruising than at the **Bamboo Room** (561-585-BLUE; www .bamboorm.com), 25 South J St, Lake Worth? Touted as having the best blues artists on the touring circuit, this casual club presents the real deal—blues from the Mississippi Delta, along with local and national jazz and folk artists. As you pass the antique ticket booth in the lobby, take note of the club's signature bamboo walls, original artwork, and blues memorabilia. Order a drink from the 1920s and '30s, a house specialty, while sitting at the copper-topped bar. An impressive backdrop displays hundreds of pieces of art deco–style barware and vintage cocktail shakers. There are two shows nightly, but get there early—seating is limited to an intimate 150.

PERFORMING ARTS

Lake Worth

Since 1987, the nationally renowned **Demetrius Klein Dance Company** (561-586-1889), 811 Lake Ave, has swept away critics across the country with their unique choreography and physical modern dance form. The company's active performance schedule produces a dozen full concerts a year.

The fully restored **Lake Worth Play-house** (561-586-6410), 713 Lake Ave, is comprised of two theaters. The three-hundred-seat main theater presents Broadway-style plays and musicals to appreciative audiences. Built in 1924, the interior is a spectacular example of period design. The 70-seat **Stonzek Studio Theater,** at 709 Lake Ave, showcases experimental works and is reminiscent of New York's intimate off-Broadway scene.

Manalapan

Dedicated to introducing new and developing work, the 258-seat **Florida Stage Professional Theatre** (561-585-3433 or 1-800-514-3837; www.floridastage.org), 262 S Ocean Blvd, produces contemporary works by both established and emerging playwrights. Located in the Plaza del Mar between the Atlantic Ocean and the Intracoastal Waterway. Summer and season tickets $35–45; opening night $75.

West Palm Beach

Classical and contemporary dance is presented at **Ballet Florida** (561-659-1212 or 1-800-540-0172; www.balletflorida.com), 500 Fern St, at locations around the tri-county area. Under the direction of founder Marie Hale, celebrated choreographers from around the world direct 22 professional dancers in such works as Twyla Tharp's *Baker's Dozen;* Ben Stevenson's *Five Poems,* with costume and scenery designed by actress Jane Seymour; and, of course, the holiday favorite *The Nutcracker.*

The four-hundred-seat **Cuillo Centre for the Arts** (561-835-9226), 201 Clematis St, features live theater such as pre-Broadway shows, concerts, and play readings.

Conveniently located just east of I-95, **The Kravis Center for the Performing Arts** (561-833-8300 or 1-800-KRAVIS-1; www.kravis.org), 701 Okeechobee Blvd, was built totally on donations from local residents. The center is named for its main benefactor, Raymond F. Kravis, a geologist from Oklahoma and winter resident of Palm Beach for more than 35 years. As such it has had the funding to produce some of the region's best ballet, theater, and musical performances. Three venues, the 2,200-seat Dreyfoos Hall, the 1,400-seat Gosman Amphitheater, and the 300-seat Rinker Playhouse, offer performances from intimate lecture series to large-scale Broadway productions.

Palm Beach Opera (561-833-7888 or 1-888-88-OPERA; www.pbopera.org), 415 S Olive Ave, holds performances at the Kravis Center. The opera company has a half dozen operas and symphonic concerts during the season and an outreach program to assist both children and aspiring opera singers. One of their educational programs, The Family Opera Series, is hosted by canine tenor The Great Poochini, a costumed character in tails.

✳ Selective Shopping

Lake Worth

Even if you don't own a dog, you'll want to stop at the delightful **Paws on the Avenue** (561-588-6533), 409 Lake Ave. Top dog Caroline Clore has created a doggone oasis for your furry friend. You'll want to adorn your canine or feline with an attractive bandanna or choose from the vast collection of clothing specifically created "fur" style and function. Your hungry canines will drool with delight at the gourmet pet treats at Café le Paws. And don't forget to pamper your little dah-ling at the Day Spa with an herbal bath, paw soak, and therapeutic massage.

West Palm Beach
The best boot fitter around, professional outfitter Glen Kinsey will fit you with all the necessary backpacking gear for your hiking adventure at **Backpacker's General Store** (561-439-6500), 4376 Forest Hill Blvd. A nice selection of quality tents, packs, climbing, and mountaineering gear is available. Open 10:30–6 Tue–Sat.

SHOPPING AREAS

Lake Worth
I counted 43 antiques shops in the Lake Worth downtown area on and around Lake Ave and Lucerne Ave, the virtual hub of the antiques community, so you'll be sure to find what you're looking for, whether it is collectibles, fine art, estate jewelry, Oriental carpets, or classic heirlooms. At **Carousel Antiques** (561-533-0678), 815 Lake Ave, you have two full floors to browse through; fine linens are found at **RoundAbout Antiques** (561-845-1985), 824 Lake Ave; and the **Lake Avenue Antiques Mall** (561-586-1131), 704 Lake Ave, has something for everyone.

Palm Beach
Worth Avenue (561-659-6909; www .worth-avenue.com) is the pinnacle of luxury shopping. All the big names are here, along with some new ones. You'll find old favorites such as **Cartier** (561-655-5913), 214 Worth Ave; **Chanel** (561-655-1550), 301 Worth Ave; and **Hermès** (561-655-6655),

255 Worth Ave; along with some of the finest antiques shops in the world. The **Lilly Pulitzer** line (www.lilly pulitzer.com), the epitome of the preppy lifestyle, with pink and green floral prints, can be found at **C. Orrico** (561-659-1284; www.corrico.com), 336 S County Rd.

West Palm Beach
If Worth Ave gives you sticker shock, there is still excellent shopping to be had on the mainland at **City Place** (561-366-1000; www.cityplace.com), 701 S Rosemary Ave, where you find regulars such as **Banana Republic** (561-833-9841) and **Williams-Sonoma** (561-833-0659). Local favorite **Sandy Paws** (561-802-4397; www.sandypawswpb.com), 632 Hibiscus St, has munchies and doggie duds with Palm Beach style. To get to S Rosemary Ave, take I-95 exit 70 to Okeechobee Blvd, and go east less than a mile. Shops are open 10–9 Mon–Thu, 10–10 Fri and Sat, and noon–6 Sun. Valet parking available at some locations.

FARMER'S MARKETS West Palm Beach Greenmarket (561-659-8003; www.cityofwpb.com), Second St between Olive Ave and Flagler Dr and Narcissus St between Clematis St and Flagler Dr. Every Sat Oct 18–Apr 25.

✳ Special Events
Weekly/Monthly: **Evening on the Avenues** (561-582-4401), Cultural Plaza near "M" St, Lake Worth. Held 6–10 PM the first and third Fri of every month. Enjoy live music, arts and crafts, food, and lots of shopping at specialty stores along Lake Ave and Lucerne Ave, as well as an array of classic cars lining "J" St.

Bonfire on the Beach (561-533-7359), Lake Worth Beach. Held 7–9 PM the second and fourth Fri Nov–Feb. Stroll along the white-sand beach and let the balmy breezes blow through your hair. Then, cozy up with a loved one until the last embers wane. You'll want to toast marshmallows.

Motown favorites come alive every Fri night at **The Colony Hotel** (see *Lodging*), Palm Beach, with music from the 1960s to the '80s, such as the Temptations, the Supremes, and Marvin Gaye.

A one-hour **Historic Walking Tour of Worth Avenue** (561-659-6909; www.worth-avenue.com) starts at 11 AM at the Gucci Courtyard, 256 Worth Ave, West Palm Beach, the second Wed of the month Oct–May and the first Sat of the month Jun–Aug. Call for reservations. Free.

On the first weekend of every month, hundreds of antiques and collectibles dealers feature items from knick-knacks and fine collectibles to books and furniture at the **West Palm Beach Antique & Collectibles Show** (1-800-640-FAIR), 9067 Southern Blvd, South Florida Fairgrounds, West Palm Beach.

Clematis by Night, in Centennial Square at the top of Clematis St, West Palm Beach, features a fountainside concert from 5:30 to 9 every Thursday night. Listen to rock, rhythm and blues, swing, blues, reggae, and soul while browsing through the international crafts bazaar. The free event is hosted by the City of West Palm Beach.

Pack up the family and bring a picnic basket to the **Meyer Amphitheater** (561-659-8007), West Palm Beach, to listen to local bands at sunset on the water every Sunday. Free.

January: The South Florida Fairgrounds, West Palm Beach, is home to the **South Florida Fair** (561-793-0333; www.southfloridafair.com).

Winter Equestrian Festival (561-793-5867; www.stadiumjumping.com) is held late Jan to mid-Mar at the Palm Beach Polo & Country Club at 11199 Polo Club and Stadium Jumping at 14440 Pierson Rd, Wellington. The largest equestrian event in the world is where the best of the best hunters and jumpers compete, along with dressage and equitation events on more than four thousand horses.

February: **Finlandia Festival** (561-582-1600), Lake Worth. Since 1985, Bryant Park has been transformed into the "Tori," a Finnish-style marketplace. Celebrate with this cultural community—the second-largest Finnish community in the world outside of Finland—and enjoy vibrant music, dancing, Finnish foods, and handicrafts.

The **Street Painting Festival** (561-582-4401; www.streetpainting.com) is held each year in downtown Lake Worth. The tradition of street painting originated in Italy in the 16th century, but it has been the main event in Lake Worth only in the past decade. Watch the streets come alive as the artists use chalk to transform the pavement into works of fine art. Strolling minstrels, jazz, classical music, dance, theater, improvisation, and an array of streetside cafés complete the old-world atmosphere. Children of all ages will love the Children's Meadow, where they can create their own street paintings.

Spring is in the air at the **Palm Beach Tropical Flower & Garden Show** (561-655-5522), between Evernia and Banyan St along Flagler Dr, West Palm Beach.

March: The **Worth Avenue Association Pet Parade and Contest,** Palm Beach, puts even Westminster on notice. The "Island" society's best groomed dogs, cats, birds, and even bunnies strut their stuff at this annual event.

The **Annual Palm Beach Boat Show** (1-800-940-7642), along the West Palm Beach waterfront, displays more than a thousand boats and yachts.

The Palm Beach Zoo at Dreher Park (see *Zoological Parks & Wildlife Rehab*), West Palm Beach, is home to the annual **Mardi Gras—New Orleans Jazz Carnival** (561-533-0887).

April: You won't want to miss the **Caribbean Carnivale,** Bryant Park, Lake Worth, a lively tropical celebration of island life and culture featuring live reggae music, arts and crafts, and a variety of Caribbean foods and activities.

May: The annual waterfront **Sunfest** (561-659-5980 or 1-800-SUNFEST; www.sunfest.com), downtown West Palm Beach, offers name-brand entertainment and the best of food and art. Sometimes it is held earlier in the year, so call ahead or check the web site.

The Puppetry Arts Center and Gold Coast Storyteller performs at the **Annual Story Telling Festival** (561-967-3231), West Palm Beach.

December: A holiday favorite, the annual **Holiday Boat Parade of the Palm Beaches** (561-832-8444; www.pbboatparade.com) floats boats and yachts along the Intracoastal Waterway, north from Peanut Island to Jupiter.

SOUTH PALM BEACH COUNTY

I n 1894, settlers began to push into southeast Florida. Nathan S. Boynton, a former Civil War major from Michigan, settled in **Boynton Beach,** naming it after himself. Major Boynton built the Boynton Beach Hotel as his family's winter residence, and around the turn of the century the hotel became a social destination for northerners escaping the cold winter months. Another group of Michiganders, led by William Linton and David Swinton, settled in **Delray Beach,** so named after the Spanish word for "the king." The town is a leader in the preservation of local history, with many buildings around town restored to their original glory. The area, rich for planting fruits and vegetables, brought a number of Japanese farmers around the turn of the 20th century. These farmers formed the Yamato Colony, growing pineapples on the land now just east of I-95 in **Boca Raton.** The Morikami Museum and Japanese Gardens is all that is left of the colony. The Spanish name Boca Raton is often translated into the "Mouth of the Rat" or "Rat's Mouth," but "Raton" was a term that was once used to mean a cowardly thief. So the true translation of the town's name is thought mean "Thieves Inlet." In the 1960s South Florida experienced a huge land boom, and many technical companies, such as IBM, moved to the region. In 1981 the first IBM personal computer was developed here.

GUIDANCE **Palm Beach County Convention and Visitors Bureau** (561-233-3000), 1555 Palm Beach Lakes, Suite 800, West Palm Beach 33401.

GETTING THERE *By car:* From I-95 take exits 56 to 59 for Boynton Beach, exits 51 and 52 for Delray Beach, and exits 44 to 50 for Boca Raton.

From Florida's Turnpike use exit 85 for Boynton Beach (Boynton Beach Blvd), exit 81 for Delray (Atlantic Ave), and exit 75 for Boca Raton (Glades Rd).

By air: **Palm Beach International Airport (PBIA)** (561-471-7420), 1000 Turnage Blvd, West Palm Beach, is situated adjacent to I-95.

By rail: **AMTRAK** (561-832-6169 or 1-800-USA-RAIL; www.amtrak.com). Take the Silver Service/Palmetto route to 345 Congress Ave, Delray Beach.

Tri-Rail (1-800-TRI-RAIL; www.tri-rail.com). Service area includes Palm Beach, Broward, and Miami-Dade Counties. It connects to Palm Tran routes at

THE BAREFOOT MAILMAN

By the mid-1800s, before there were roads or railways, people were beginning to make their way south, settling up and down the coast of South Florida. With mail delivery only as far south as Palm Beach, the U.S. Postal Service soon needed a way to deliver mail to the pioneers along the stretch of coastline between Lake Worth and Biscayne Bay. So in 1885 they enlisted a few young men to carry the mail along the only solid path—the beach. Since it was steaming hot and impossible to travel through the sand with any speed, the mail carriers soon went barefoot and walked along the edge in the surf, and the legendary "Barefoot Mailman" was born. Starting by boat in Palm City (now Palm Beach), mailmen were brought as far as the Boynton Beach Inlet and then ventured forth on foot along the 80 miles of coastline to Miami, which was then known as Lemon City. The entire 136-mile round-trip took six days to complete by trudging along the beach by foot and an additional 56 miles by small boats, which they had secretly stashed along the shores. With only one day to rest, the carrier started his exhausting expedition all over again by Monday morning. As for the wages, carriers were paid $175 every three months. Seven years later, in 1892, a road was extended from Lantana to Miami, thus ending the need for the Barefoot Mailman.

Boynton Beach Station, 2800 High Ridge Rd; Delray Beach Station, 345 Congress Ave; and Boca Raton Station, 601 NW 53rd St.

By bus: **Greyhound** (561-272-6447 or 1-800-231-2222; www.greyhound.com) has service to 402 SE Sixth Ave, Delray Beach.

GETTING AROUND *By car:* I can't tell you how many people heading south along I-95 mistake Atlantic Ave (in Palm Beach County) and Atlantic Blvd (in Broward County). Yes, it's true—I've been one of them! Both roads exit from I-95 east to the beach and west to the far reaches of the counties. If your destination is Delray Beach, then take Atlantic Ave. If you want to visit Pompano Beach, Fort Lauderdale, or the western suburbs in Broward County, such as Tamarac and Coral Springs, then keep driving and exit on Atlantic Blvd.

By bus: The **Palm Tran** (561-841-4287; www.co.palm-beach.fl.us/palmtran) service area covers malls and tourist spots throughout Palm Beach County. Tri-Rail connects to several Palm Tran routes at Boynton Beach, Delray Beach, and Boca Raton stations.

By trolley: Tri-Rail connects with the **Boynton Beach Trolley** (561-572-0550; www.boyntonbeachtrolley.com). The Congress Ave route runs 7:15–6:15 Mon–Fri; the Ocean Ave route runs 11–10 Thu–Sun. Free for both residents and visitors.

PARKING Public parking in the cities in the south part of the county is readily available at no cost. Some garages and lots near the beach charge a small fee. In some of the trendy spots, parking meters along beachfronts and shopping areas will run you a good $1 per hour.

MEDICAL EMERGENCIES Area hospitals include **Bethesda Hospital** (561-737-7733), S Seacrest Blvd, Boynton Beach, and **Columbia Hospital** (561-842-6141), 2201 45th St, West Palm Beach.

PUBLIC REST ROOMS The beach areas and most city parks all have rest rooms available to the public at no cost.

VALET Most restaurants and luxury hotels around Boca Raton and in the beach area offer valet services. Some restaurants and hotels have only mandatory valet parking. Always inquire when making reservations.

✳ To See

HISTORIC SITES Throughout the region, many markers have been erected to further detail certain historical moments and places.

Boca Raton

The marker located along the west side of FL A1A in Spanish River Park in Boca Raton memorializes the **Barefoot Mailman** (see box on p. 353). Between the 1880s and early 1890s, U.S. mailmen walked along this beach, delivering mail from Palm Beach to Miami. The round-trip was made in six days.

The **Boca Raton Town Hall,** 71 North Federal Hwy, houses the Boca Raton Historical Society. Architect Addison C. Mizner is mainly responsible for the Mediterranean Revival style found here and throughout the town of Boca Raton. Completed in 1927, the Town Hall also housed both the fire station and police department. The gilded dome on the bell tower is its shining jewel. Listed on the National Register of Historic Places in 1980, the building is now used by the Boca Raton Historical Society as a local history museum (see *Museums*).

A marker for the **Florida East Coast Railway Depot** is at 747 S Dixie Hwy. In 1895 Henry Flagler's railroad reached Boca Raton, and in 1930 a railway depot for passengers was built. The station operated until 1968. The station was restored in 1989 by the Boca Raton Historical Society and is listed on the National Register of Historic Places. The beautifully designed building is in the Mediterranean Revival style. Take particular note of the arched loggia, pitched gable roof, and delicate spiral columns.

Boynton Beach

If you follow Ocean Ave to FL A1A, you'll come to a private residence sitting on the land where the **Boynton Beach Hotel** once stood. The winter home of the town's founder, Maj. Nathan S. Boynton, became victim to the 1926 hurricane and was never rebuilt. The only remaining structures are two small cottages. Surviving historical records are located at the Boynton Beach Library.

The circa 1925 **Boynton Beach Women's Club,** 1010 S Federal Hwy, was designed by Addison Mizner in the Mediterranean Revival style. The two-story structure has a loggia on three sides. It was the town's social hub until the 1930s and is now privately owned.

One of Palm Beach County's sweetest landmarks is the **Little Red Schoolhouse** (561-832-0731), 2145 S Ocean Blvd, in Phipps Ocean Park. The 1886 schoolhouse was the first built in what was then Dade County. Educational tours are given on weekday mornings. Free.

Delray Beach

The 1915 **Cason Cottage** (561-243-0223 or 561-274-9578; www.delraybeach historicalsociety.com) is built in the Old Florida Vernacular style with Dade County pine. Restored in 1988, it was the former retirement home of the Rev. and Mrs. John R. Cason Sr., community leaders. Many relatives of the Methodist minister still reside in the area. The Delray Beach Historical Society office is located in a historic bungalow on the property. Open for tours Tue–Fri.

The oldest hotel in Delray and a member of Historic Hotels of America is the **Colony Hotel and Cabana Club,** 525 E Atlantic Ave (see *Lodging*). The 1926 Old Florida–style hotel is lovingly restored and sits in the heart of the downtown cultural area amid fine restaurants and art galleries.

Along the city's municipal beach along FL A1A, you'll find a marker commemorating the **Delray Wreck.** About 150 yards offshore, at the bottom of the ocean in 25 feet of water, rests the SS *Inchulva,* grounded during a hurricane in 1903. The ship, also known as the "Delray Wreck," is a popular diving spot.

At 200 NE First St you'll find a marker for the **Florida East Coast Railway.** Only a 40-foot freight section remains of the old 1896 railroad station. In 1994 the only surviving section of the station was bought by the Delray Beach Historical Society and moved to its present location.

One of the greatest historical preservation projects is the **Old School Square** (561-243-7922; www.oldschool.org), 51 North Swinton Ave, at the corner of Atlantic Ave and Swinton Ave. Comprised of three buildings—the Delray Beach elementary school (circa 1913), high school (circa 1925), and gymnasium (circa 1926)—it is now home to the Cornell Museum of Art & History (see *Museums*), the Crest Theatre (see *Performing Arts*), the restored gym, and several vintage classrooms.

A marker for **Orange Grove House of Refuge No. 3, 1876–1927** is found along FL A1A, north of Atlantic. One of several homes built by the Treasury Department for shipwrecked refugees, this site is named for the nearby wild sour orange grove.

Stop into the **Sundy House,** 106 S Swinton Ave, for lunch or dinner, or stay overnight in the quaint bed & breakfast (see *Lodging*). The circa 1902 Victorian house is the oldest home in Delray Beach and home to the town's first mayor. The wide-open verandas are perfect for sipping an afternoon tea.

Boca Raton

The **Boca Raton Historical Society** (561-395-6766; www.bocahistory.org), 71 N Federal Hwy, provides guided tours of the Boca Express Train Museum, the Boca Raton Resort & Club, and other places of historical significance throughout the City of Boca Raton.

Delray Beach

On the fourth Saturday of the month you can take a narrated trolley tour of historic Delray Beach offered by the **Museum of Lifestyle & Fashion History of Delray Beach** (561-243-2662; www.mlfhmuseum.org). The one hour and 45-minute tour explains the history of Delray Beach and the diversity of its multicultural settlers, along with stops at some of the town's historic churches, hotels, and homes. The trolley picks up you up at 11 AM at the 1904 historic German chapel at Trinity Lutheran Church, located at the corner of Lake Ida Rd and North Swinton Ave. Call ahead or register the same day at 10 AM at the 1904 chapel. The $10 fee also covers admission to the museum (see *Museums*).

MUSEUMS

Boca Raton

Many historical exhibits are on display at the **Boca Raton Historical Society** (561-395-6766; www.bocahistory.org), 71 N Federal Hwy, where you will also see the Boca Express Train Museum (see *Railroadiana*). Historical tours available.

The 44,000-square-foot **Boca Raton Museum of Art** (561-392-2500; www.bocamuseum.org), 501 Plaza Rd, Mizner Park, features a fine collection of American and European art, along with an outdoor sculpture garden of contemporary pieces of monumental size. Open 10–5 Tue–Fri (until 9 on Wed) and noon–5 Sat and Sun. Adults $15, seniors $12, students $8. Prices reduce to about half during the off-season when special exhibitions are not shown.

✑ At the **Children's Museum** (561-368-6875), 498 Crawford Blvd, kids can use large magnetic pieces to create their own "Picasso," step back in time and shop for groceries in a replica of Boca Raton's first grocery store, make handmade postcards at Oscar's Post Office, and learn how to care for pets at the Audubon & Friends naturalist exhibition. Open noon–4 Tue–Sat. Fee.

Boynton Beach

✑ Walk into the **Children's Museum** (561-742-6780; www.schoolhousemuseum.org), 129 E Ocean Ave, and you'll be greeted by a replica of the Jupiter Inlet Lighthouse (see *North Palm Beach County*), then step back in time to the 1800s and dress up like a Florida pioneer and experience how life used to be. Different historic themes are presented throughout the year. Open 10–5 Tue–Sat and 1–4 Sun. Fee.

Delray Beach

Housed in the historic Delray Elementary School (circa 1913), the **Cornell Museum of Art & History** at Old School Square (561-243-7922; www.oldschool.org), 51 N Swinton Ave, features four galleries, a two-story atrium, a tearoom, and a gift shop. The town's historical archives, which contain photographs, books, and maps, are located on the second floor. (See *Historic Sites*.)

Japanese immigrant and pineapple farmer George Morikami donated 200 acres to use for a museum showcasing Japanese culture. The **Morikami Museum** (561-495-0233; www.morikami.org), 4000 Morikami Park Rd (off Jog Rd between Linton Blvd and Clint Moore Rd), is the only museum of Japanese culture in the United States. Surround yourself with serenity as you walk past a cascading waterfall and through pine tree–lined nature trails that wind around the lake while experiencing different

Morikami Museum & Gardens

MORIKAMI FLAT GARDEN

types of gardens. The 9th- to 12th-century Shinden Garden is modeled after those found on estates of Japanese nobility. The Zen-inspired 14th- and 15th-century rock gardens display a contrasting stark simplicity. There's even a bonsai garden. Inside, discover more than five thousand pieces of art and objects in the museum, and take off your shoes and walk through a traditional Japanese home. A library, gift shop, and teahouse are also on-site, and each Saturday you can take part in a traditional sado tea ceremony. The Morikami also offers classes, along with several educational events and cultural festivals throughout the year (see *Special Events*). Open 10–5 Tue–Sun. Adults $10, seniors $9, children $6.

The **Museum of Lifestyle & Fashion History** (561-243-2662; www.mlfh museum.org), Delray Beach, offers exhibits showcasing fashion trends in architecture, furnishings, toys, and vintage fashions. Past exhibits have included 40 Years of the Barbie Doll, with more than 80 vintage dolls on loan from Mattel; Teddy: The Bear Beginnings, on the history of the teddy bear; "The Lunch Box Exhibit," which showcased the history of the lunch box and Thermos from 1902; and Hats, Handbags & Gloves, which displayed accessories from vintage couture to modern designers. The 8,000-square-foot facility has also been home to traveling exhibits from the Smithsonian Institution. A permanent Southeast Florida Style exhibit and a Tanzania Art & Culture Gallery are planned, along with special exhibitions. Guided tours, lectures, and children's arts and crafts programs are held on the third Sunday of each month starting at 2:30. The guided one-hour tour takes you through the current exhibit. The children's program features hands-on activities relating to the current exhibit and is geared toward children ages 4–12. (See also *Historic Tours*.) NOTE: As of press time, the museum is displaying its exhibits at different locations in town—due to the recent hurricanes—until it can find a new permanent home. Call ahead for locations, hours, and admission fees.

POLO The **Royal Palm Polo Club** (561-994-1876; www.boca-polo.com), 18000 Jog Rd, Boca Raton, sits on 160 acres and encompasses seven polo fields, 320 stalls, and a polo stadium. Two games are played at 1 and 3 every Sunday Jan–April, with the pinnacle of events, the Monty Waterbury Cup Final, in late March. Adults $10, children under 12 free.

RAILROADIANA The **Boca Express Train Museum** (561-395-6766; www .bocahistory.org), 747 S Dixie Hwy, offers guided tours of not one, but two 1947 streamliner railcars (both on the National Register of Historic Places), a 1940s Seaboard caboose, and a Baldwin steam engine, all housed in a 1930 FEC train depot that contains additional memorabilia relating to train travel in the 1940s. Open 1–4 Fri during the season (Nov–Apr). Fee.

✳ To Do

BOAT TOURS Loxahatchee Everglades Tours, Inc. (561-482-6107 or 1-800-683-5873; www.evergladesairboattours.com), 15490 Loxahatchee Rd, Boca Raton. Glide over the river of grass while seated on elevated airboats, from which you can see alligators, great blue herons, red shoulder hawks, turtles, and the occasional cottonmouth moccasin. Pass through sloughs and hammocks on airboats just right for your party, from the 8-person *Eagle* to the 20-person *Gator* and *Osprey*. Knowledgeable guides introduce you to the vast Everglades ecosystem and explain the history, biology, and geology of what you'll see on the tour. Open daily 9:30–4; closed Thanksgiving, Christmas, and New Year's Day. Three types of tours: 30-, 60-, and 90-minute. Reservations recommended.

DAY SPAS

Boynton Beach
Gianna Christine Salon, Spa, and Wellness Center (561-742-8858; www.gcspa .com), 395 N Congress Ave. The Aveda lifestyle spa offers a variety of relaxing and rejuvenating treatments in an earth-friendly environment. Try the two-hour Himalayan Rejuvenation Treatment ($150), which involves a series of exfoliation and massage techniques, steam purification, and other water treatments with plant-based products designed to integrate body, mind, and soul. The Ocean Rain Paraffin Cocoon ($145) starts with an exfoliating treatment and antistress oil and continues with a warm blue ocean rain paraffin with aloe vera and peppermint for extra hydration. Their excellent hair salon makes sure you are in top shape from head to toe. Try the Deep Conditioning Steam Treatment and Shampoo ($55) or the Anti-Stress Scalp and Neck Treatment ($55)—both include blow-dry and styling. And all hair and scalp treatments include a complimentary Rosemary Mint Awakening Body Treatment with soothing scalp, neck, and shoulder massage. Open 9–5 Mon–Tue, 9–9 Wed–Thu, 9–7 Sat, and 11–5 Sun. Reservations are recommended, but walk-ins are accommodated if an attendant is available.

Delray Beach
Treat yourself to a massage inside the crisp treatment rooms or outdoors in your own private cabana overlooking the sunning pool at **Spa Eleven** (561-278-1100;

www.spaeleven.com), 14140 N Federal Hwy. Relaxation, sport, and pregnancy massages run $80–105 for 55 minutes and $155–195 for 110 minutes. Or treat yourself to one of the Eleven Journeys, such as the Rose Indulgence ($290), which includes a Rose Essence scrub, manicure, and pedicure, along with a reflexology treatment. Open 10–8 Tue–Thu, 9–7 Fri and Sat, and 11–6 Sun. Reservations are suggested, but they'll take walk-ins if there's an opening.

FAMILY FUN Drive go-carts and bumper cars at **Boomers! Boca Raton** (561-347-1888; www.boomersparks.com), 3100 Airport Rd, Boca Raton. Bumper boats, go-carts, mini golf, rock wall, arcade games, and laser tag. Open noon–10 Mon–Thu, noon–midnight Fri, 10 AM–midnight Sat, and 10–10 Sun.

HIKING You can get lost for miles on the dikes of **Loxahatchee National Wildlife Refuge** (see *Wild Places*), but most of the hiking opportunities in this part of the county run more toward the mild side. Enjoy birding along boardwalks at Green Cay Wetlands and Wakodahatchee Wetlands; wander the nature trails at Serenoa Glade and Delray Oaks. See *Green Space* for more ideas.

PADDLING Loxahatchee Canoeing Inc. (561-733-0192; www.canoetheever glades.com), 12440 FL 7, Boynton Beach. Paddle a canoe or kayak on a 5½-mile trail through the Loxahatchee National Wildlife Refuge (see *Wild Places*). You can easily guide yourself, as interpretive signs are posted along the trail; or a knowledgeable guide is available to point out indigenous wildlife, such as rare birds, butterflies, and, of course, alligators. Rates are $25–30 for a half day, plus a $5 park fee. Reduced rates in the summer months.

TENNIS Home of the International Tennis Championship, the **Delray Beach Tennis Center** (561-243-7360; www.delraytennis.com), 201 W Atlantic Ave, Delray Beach, is where you'll see pro tennis tournaments with celebrities such as Venus and Serena Williams and Boca native Corina Morariu. Both kids and adults can play or take lessons on 14 clay courts and 7 hard courts.

CYPRESS BOARDWALK, LOXAHATCHEE NATIONAL WILDLIFE REFUGE   Sandra Friend

WATER PARKS You'll have a splashing good time at **Coconut Cove Waterpark & Recreation Center** (561-274-1140 or 561-790-6160; www.co .palm-beach.fl.us/parks), 1200 Park Access Rd, South County Regional Park, Boca Raton. The park's features include a 986-foot river ride, two 220-foot water slides, and a children's water playground. Open late spring to early fall. Adults 12 and up $10, children 3–11 $8, children 1–2 $3, infants are free. Reduced rates after 3 PM.

✳ Green Space

BEACHES

Boca Raton

Hitting the beach in Boca Raton is a pricey proposition—up to $18 per day for a parking pass (nonresident) to take advantage of **South Beach Park, Red Reef Park,** and **Spanish River Park** along Ocean Blvd. A cheaper alternative is the county-managed **South Inlet Park** (561-276-3990), 1298 S Ocean Blvd, an 11-acre facility with lifeguards, picnic area and pavilions, and a saltwater fishing pier. Fee.

Delray Beach

Delray Municipal Beach (561-243-7250) dates from 1922 and has public access through several parks along Ocean Blvd. Heading north from downtown, they are **Sarah Gleason Park, Sandoway Park, Anchor Park,** and **Atlantic Dunes Park.** Of these, Atlantic Dunes has the most natural feel and has surf chairs available for guests with limited mobility. Each of the beach-access parks has metered parking.

BOTANICAL GARDENS & Walk among some of the world's most colorful orchids at the headquarters to the **American Orchid Society (AOS) Visitors Center and Botanical Garden** (561-404-2000 or 1-877-ORCHIDS; www.aos.org), 16700 AOS Lane, Delray Beach, located next to the Morikami Museum (see *Museums*). View thousands of tropical flora as you wind through 3½ acres of themed gardens, water features, and cypress-pond boardwalk, then relax and take in a peaceful moment inside the 4,000-square-foot atrium greenhouses. The large collection of orchids throughout the property is clearly labeled, and there are also other exotic species such as phais, palms, cycads, and a rare African baobab tree. The Orchid Emporium gift shop is full of books, gardening items, a selection of orchids (like the one that smells like chocolate!), and several fine orchid-related souvenirs and collectibles. Open 10–4:30 Tue–Sun. Adults $8; children under 12 free. Throughout the year classes are offered for only $35 for beginning and advanced orchidteers, which includes a free copy of *Orchid* magazine and an orchid plant for you to take home and nurture.

DELRAY BEACH

Sandra Friend

NATURE CENTERS

Boca Raton

& 🐾 In South County Regional Park, the **Daggerwing Nature Center** (561-488-9953), 11200 Park Access Rd, offers interpretive habitat displays and a ⁵⁄₁₀-mile boardwalk into a lush, tangled jungle of strangler fig and pond apple trees. The nature center is open 1–4:30 Tue–Fri and 9–4:30 Sat; boardwalk open during daylight hours. Free.

Kathy Wolf

ORCHIDS AT THE AMERICAN ORCHID
SOCIETY VISITOR CENTER AND BOTANICAL
GARDEN

 ♿ ∅ With touch tanks, hands-on activities, and boardwalks and an observation tower to explore, the **Gumbo Limbo Environmental Education Center** (561-338-1473), 1801 N Ocean Blvd, is a great family destination along the mangrove-lined shores of the Spanish River. Trails lead through bowers of mangroves and out to the edge of the clear waterway, where manatees and mangrove pufferfish may be seen. The center is open 9–4 Mon–Sat and noon–4 Sun. Donation.

Boynton Beach

♿ ∅ Just a few years ago, **Green Cay Wetlands and Nature Center** (561-966-7000), 12800 Hagen Ranch Rd, was a pepper farm managed by my friends Ted and Trudy Winsberg. Rather than sell their land to developers as many farmers around them did, they wanted a lasting legacy for the community and worked with the county to create a wetlands water-reclamation park. While the plantings are relatively new, herons and ibis have already taken up residence in the impoundments. A 1½-mile boardwalk circles the park for optimal birding. The park is open sunrise to sunset daily; the beautiful new nature center, with indoor turtle and alligator ponds, a wetland diorama, movies and exhibits, and a gift shop, is open 1–4:30 Tue–Fri and Sun, and 8:15–4:30 Sat. Free; donations appreciated.

Delray Beach

Located in a 1936 beachfront home is the **Sandoway House Nature Center** (561-274-7263; www.sandowayhouse.com), 142 S Ocean Blvd. Restored to its original condition, it provides a living history to the area with educational exhibits and events about natural ecosystems. Learn about ocean reef fish, the Florida spiny lobster, and nurse sharks during their Coral Reef Pool Shark Feedings held at scheduled times throughout the week; take in the night sky on the monthly astronomy nights; or discover the diversity of Florida's native plants and animals during the Nature Walk, held the last Saturday of the month (see *Special Events*). Open 10–4 Tue–Sat and noon–4 Sun. Fee.

BOCA RATON AS SEEN FROM GUMBO
LIMBO ENVIRONMENTAL EDUCATION
CENTER

Sandra Friend

PARKS

Boca Raton

♿ ∅ Enter a tangled jungle of mangroves along the scenic Spanish River boardwalk at **James A. Rutherford**

Park (561-393-7700), NE 24th St, off US 1. The park is also a launch point for kayakers, with an on-site livery, and it features a playground, picnic area, and fitness trail. Open dawn–dusk daily. Free.

Red Reef Park (561-393-7810), FL A1A (North Ocean Blvd). Snorkel the unique rock and reef outcroppings or take a nature walk through the 67-acre park. The oceanfront park is also home to the 20-acre Gumbo Limbo Environmental Education Center (see *Nature Centers*).

& ✍ Kids will love the Children's Science Explorium at **Sugar Sand Park** (561-347-3913), 300 S Military Trl, featuring hands-on science experiments and oversize artifacts for play. Set in a sand pine scrub, the 132-acre park includes paved and natural surface nature trails, ball fields, and a large playground. Open 8–sunset daily. Free.

Delray Beach
Head to **Lake Ida Park** (561-966-6600), 2929 Lake Ida Rd, for waterskiing and boating fun. The 209-acre park also has a fishing pier, observation platform, picnic areas, and a 2½-acre dog park complete with Fido Fountain and separate sections for small and large dogs.

PRESERVES

Boca Raton
& ✍ Accessed through George Snow Park, **Serenoa Glade Preserve** (561-393-7700), NW 15th St, protects a sliver of the original Atlantic Coastal Ridge in Boca Raton, topped with a pine forest. A ½-mile trail leads through the forest; the entrance is hidden back by the tennis courts. Open 8–sunset daily. Free.

Boynton Beach
& ✍ **Seacrest Scrub Natural Area** (561-233-2400), south of Boynton Beach Blvd on Seacrest Blvd, protects a 58-acre patch of sand pine scrub habitat that is home to gopher tortoises. Several nature trails, including a paved trail, wind through the forest. Make sure you close the gate behind you to keep the tortoises in! Open sunrise–sunset daily. Free.

& ✍ For fabulous birding, visit **Wakodatahatchee Wetlands** (561-641-3429), 13026 Jog Rd, early in the morning, when wading birds and migratory visitors are most active. Built as a natural water reclamation facility, the preserve features an ⁹⁄₁₀-mile boardwalk where I've seen purple gallinules roosting on every visit. Open sunrise–sunset daily. Free.

Delray Beach
& ✍ A short walk takes you back to nature at the **Delray Oaks Natural Area** (561-233-2400), Congress Ave at 29th St, where a 1-mile loop trail leads through 25 acres of picturesque oak hammock along what was once the Yamato Marsh. Open sunrise–sunset daily. Free.

WILD PLACES Covering 221 square miles of sawgrass, cypress, and tree islands, **Arthur R. Marshall Loxahatchee National Wildlife Refuge** (561-734-8303; http://loxahatchee.fws.gov), 10216 Lee Rd, off US 441 south of Boynton Beach

Blvd, Boynton Beach, defines the eastern edge of the Everglades. Stop at the visitors center for interpretive information, exhibits, and a movie; walk the Cypress Boardwalk to immerse yourself in a forest primeval. Endless miles of dike-top walking or bicycling are available; most visitors complete the Marsh Trail, with an observation tower providing a bird's-eye view of the impoundments, or take to the canals via canoe. Birding here is superb, with sightings of Everglades snail kites possible. Day use only. Open dawn–dusk daily. Fee.

✳ Lodging

BEACH HOUSES AND INNS

Delray Beach 33483

🐾 Tropical paradise surrounds the secluded **Crane's Beach House** (561-278-1700 or 1-866-372-7263; www.cranesbeachhouse.com), 82 Gleason St, yet it is only a short walk from Delray Beach's trendy downtown area. Rooms and suites, decorated in beachy Key West style, range from $136 to $485, depending on season and room. Pet-friendly rooms are also available. Gated security entrance, two pools, sandy beach, Internet.

Former home of Delray Beach's first mayor, the intimate 1902 **Sundy House Inn** (561-272-5678 or 1-877-439-9601; www.sundyhouse.com), 106 S Swinton Ave, offers a glimpse down memory lane. Relax in Victorian splendor on the wraparound veranda, sit in the lush tropical Taru Gardens, or take a dip in their unique fresh water swimming pool, with African cyclids swimming next to you while the *Plecostomus* keeps things tidy. Stay in the new equestrian-themed Stables guest rooms, the quaint luxurious cottage with its own Jacuzzi and fireplace, or one of the richly appointed one- or two-bedroom studios complete with their own kitchens. You won't have to go far for drinks or dinner; **De La Tierra** (see *Dining Out*) is one of the finest restaurants in South Florida and is right on-site. Rates $310–650.

Spacious suites with fully equipped kitchens right on the beach make **Wright by the Sea** (561-278-3355 or 1-877-234-3355; www.wbtsea.com), 1901 S Ocean Blvd, a favorite for family reunions and business travelers. There's plenty of space to spread out, whether you want to lie by the pool, barbecue at the chickee hut, or walk along the private beach. Complimentary beach cabanas and wireless high-speed Internet. Studio and one- and two-bedroom suites $109–339.

HOTELS

Boca Raton 33432
The Boca Raton Bridge Hotel (561-368-9500 or 1-866-909-2622; www.bocaratonbridgehotel.com), 999 E Camino Real. This boutique-style hotel is a little-known secret, even to locals. Located directly on the Intracoastal Waterway and a short stroll to the beach, it offers in-room Internet access, with WiFi in the lobby and Internet Cafe. Check out their Sunday champagne brunch at Carmen's At The Top of the Bridge. Low- to high-season rates $159–269; junior suites $199–309; VIP suites $279–409.

Delray Beach 33483
The **Colony Hotel and Cabana Club** (561-276-4123 or 1-800-552-5363; www.thecolonyhotel.com), 525 E Atlantic Ave. The lobby, with wood-burning fireplaces and white wicker

furniture, beckons you to a more romantic time. Relax in the rooms decorated with Old Florida appeal in vintage tropical fabrics and many original pieces of furniture. As Delray Beach's oldest hotel (circa 1926), The Colony is a member of the Historic Hotels of America and founding member of Green Hotels (www .greenhotels.com). Sensitive to environmental concern, the hotel is active in recycling and water conservation and provides guests with educational information on environmental awareness. It's located near the trendy downtown area, where you'll find lots of shopping, entertainment, and eateries. Rates in-season $215–310; off-season $180–245.

RESORTS

Boca Raton 33432
Built in 1926, the **Boca Raton Resort & Club** (561-447-3000 or 1-800-327-0101; www.bocaresort.com), 501 E Camino Real, is the pinnacle of luxury resorts on the Gold Coast. Elegant rooms, suites, and bungalows with inspiring views make this a sought-after destination for both tourists and locals. Accommodations feature Spanish-Mediterranean, Moorish, and Gothic antiques and architecture and cosmopolitan or nautical themes. Throughout the 356-acre resort you'll find six pools, a ½-mile private beach, par 71 golf course, golf practice range and putting green, 18 Har-Tru clay tennis courts, oceanfront and lakefront restaurants, on-site shops and boutiques, a new children's playground with water park and tricycle track, Spa Palazzo, and an enhanced fitness center. Rates $230–775, depending on style and season.

✳ Where to Eat
DINING OUT

Boca Raton
Undoubtedly one of the more beautiful restaurants in South Florida, **The Addison** (561-395-9335; www.the addison.com), Two E Camino Real, is a great place for that romantic dinner. American, steak, and continental entrées $22–35. Dinner nightly.

Always on the Top 10 lists, **Kathy's Gazebo Café** (561-395-6033; www .kathysgazebo.com), 4199 N Federal Hwy, is an elegant night out. The decadently rich food, extensive wine list, and top-of-the-line service are what you'd expect from a fine restaurant. The house favorites are the fresh Dover sole (flown from Holland) amandine or meunière ($37) and classic bouillabaisse with lobster, shrimp, clams, and mussels in a hearty broth flavored with garlic, saffron, and tomatoes ($38). Reservations strongly recommended. Gentlemen will need a jacket. Lunch Mon–Fri; dinner Mon–Sat.

Delray Beach
New chef and general manager Kevin Graham brings **De La Tierra at Sundy House** (561-272-5678 or 1-877-439-9601; www.sundyhouse.com), 106 S Swinton Ave, to a new level after celebrity chef Johnny Vinczencz departed to open his own restaurant the next county over (see *Oceanside: Eastern Broward County*). Eat inside in one of the elegant or funky rooms (the Warhol Room is decorated in pop art) or outside in the lush botanical Taru Garden. Their off-site farm supplies fresh produce for exquisite food with continental and Florribean flair. Entrées such as coconut and wasabi encrusted mahimahi or chateaubriand

with foie gras run $27–38. Save room for dessert—their exceptional pastry chef, Jerry Valvano, whips up a killer plantain dulce de leche crème brûlée with cinnamon cream ($12). Lunch, dinner, and quite possibly one of the best places for a romantic brunch.

Pineapple Grille (561-265-1368; www.pineapplegrille.com), 800 Palm Trl, is just a few blocks away from the main downtown area, and it is by far worth the extra effort to find it. One of my family's favorites for years, the tropical-themed restaurant is the place go for fine Caribbean-inspired cuisine. Brightly colored fish hang from the ceiling or watch you through the windows from the garden area. The eclectic furnishings make it easy to relax, but the food is supercharged. Chef Donna has a wild creative streak that comes out in her nightly specials, so menu items change often. Start with jerk shrimp, mango, and avocado cocktail ($10) as an appetizer, then select a salad such as pecan crusted goat cheese and spinach ($9), made with local Loxahatchee farm-raised goat cheese and served with spinach and jalapeño plum vinaigrette; or poached pear salad endive with pistachios, served with Cabrales blue cheese and beet vinaigrette. Favorite entrées include Lorelei yellowtail with lime pepper sauce ($21) and pan-seared New Zealand lamb chops with Harissa-garlic sherry, molasses, and anise mint sauce ($25). The one item that we always order here is the macadamia nut crusted crab cakes as either an appetizer ($9), an entrée ($18), or to take home for later. You'll want to wash it all down with their special Paradise Tropical Iced Tea ($2). The meals are so fabulous that I never seem to save room for dessert,

but they have some fabulous treats made daily. Lunch only Mon, lunch and dinner Tues–Fri, dinner Sat and Sun. They also serve a magnificent brunch on Sunday.

EATING OUT

Boca Raton
Anyone who works in or around Boca Raton is familiar with **Byblos Restaurant** (561-338-0300), 158 NW 20th St. Tucked at the end of a strip mall, the tiny eight-seat restaurant is more famous for its take-out than eat-in. But many business locals make it a quick stop for lunch, with lines out the door, so stop by early or later in the day. The authentic Middle Eastern foods are reasonably priced at around $6. The sampler platter includes your choice of Kebbe nuggets; spanakopita (spinach and feta pie); stuffed grape leaves (with or without lamb); *fatouch* or tabbouleh salad; cucumber, hummus, or baba ghanoush dips; and pita bread. If you still have room, they also have baklava. Open 11–6 Mon–Sat.

Open since 1979, **Tom's Place** (561-997-0920), 7251 N Federal Hwy, is a must-visit. The legendary rib shack used to be an army barracks, and now the bustling eatery offers pulled pork, ribs, and chicken on family-style platters, served with corn bread and greens. Hands down the best barbecue sauce, with many trying to figure out the recipe. Menu items are $8–15, with an early-bird special for $8.

Delray Beach
Peel some shrimp, then grab a burger and a beer at **Boston's on the Beach** (561-278-3364; www.bostonsonthe beach.com), 40 S Ocean Blvd. The

Key West Basket with fried shrimp, grouper fingers, catfish fingers, conch fritters, and french fries is a favorite of both tourists and locals. Breakfast, lunch, and dinner $5–25. Open daily 7 AM–2 AM, with nightly entertainment. **The Upper Deck** is a little less casual, with lunch $7–20 and dinner $15–30. Sit out on the open-air patio for the best view of the beach.

ICE CREAM AND CHOCOLATES **Cold Stone Creamery** (561-278-4900), 110 E Atlantic Ave, Delray Beach. In 1988, Arizonians Donald and Susan Sutherland made their own version of smooth and creamy ice cream, custom blending each serving on a frozen granite stone (the "Cold Stone"), then serving it up in a fresh-baked waffle cone. You'll find such blendings as Cookie Doughn't You Want Some, Fruit Stand Rendezvous, and Nights in White Chocolate, but don't even look at the fat grams. Yum!

Chocoholics unite and meet at **Kilwin's** (561-278-0808; www.kilwins .com), 402 E Atlantic Ave, Delray Beach, where you'll find everything from barks, bonbons, and brittles to truffles, turtles, and taffy.

✳ Entertainment
PERFORMING ARTS

Boca Raton
Student and professional performances are presented at **Boca Ballet** (561-995-0709; www.bocaballet.org), at Florida Atlantic University, University Theater (Griswold), 777 Glades Rd.

The 305-seat **Caldwell Theatre Company** (1-877-245-7432; www .caldwelltheatre.com), 7873 N Federal Hwy, is the setting for professional theater musicals and Broadway and

off-Broadway shows, and it is one of Florida's four state theaters.

Talented students from around the world, along with artist faculty, present orchestral performances throughout the year at **Lynn University Conservatory of Music** (561-237-9000; www.lynn.edu/music), 3601 N Military Trl.

Delray Beach
The historic Delray High School (circa 1925) at Old School Square (see *Historic Sites*) is the home to **Crest Theatre** (561-243-7922; www .oldschool.org), 51 N Swinton Ave. The 323-seat theater presents a variety of professional productions, such as Broadway, cabaret, music, and dance, throughout the year. Special guest artists are often featured in the six restored classrooms and two art studios. Performances are on Fri–Sun evenings ($38), and Sat and Sun matinees ($40).

The 238-seat **Delray Beach Playhouse** (561-272-1281; www.delray beachplayhouse.com), 950 NW Ninth St, overlooking scenic Lake Ida, is one of the nation's oldest community theaters, presenting theatrical and musical productions for nearly 50 years.

✳ Selective Shopping

Boca Raton
Stroll through the palms at trendy **Mizner Park** (561-447-8108; www .miznerpark.org), 433 Plaza Real, where you'll be surrounded by boutiques, restaurants, a movie theater, art galleries, and lots of schmoozing. On the north end, the **Amphitheater** has special musical events, and in the central park, art festivals and vintage automobile events are often scheduled.

Boutique shops and trendy restaurants are set in old-world elegance at **Royal Palm Place** (561-362-8340; www.royalpalmplace.com), 302 S Federal Hwy.

Anchored by such biggies as Neiman Marcus, Macy's, Bloomingdales, Saks Fifth Avenue, and even Sears, the **Town Center at Boca Raton** (561-368-6000; www.towncenteratboca raton.com), 6000 Glades Rd, also has your basic mall stores in between and then some. Check out the new Nordstrom wing for specialty shops such as Coach, Cole Haan, Williams-Sonoma, Kate Spade, and Crane & Co., which has an extensive stationery selection for those who still write by hand.

Boynton Beach
For the serious bibliophile, **Past Perfect Florida History** (561-742-7822 or 1-888-828-7822; www.past-perfect -florida-history-books.com), 640 E Ocean Ave, #3 Ocean Plaza, is a bookstore run by two folks who have a deep background in Florida history and are delighted to point you in the right direction for your research. Featuring not just nonfiction but an extensive selection of Florida fiction, it's a place to bring your wish list.

Delray Beach
Stroll down quaint brick sidewalks in the charming **Atlantic Avenue District** (561-278-0424), where you'll find traditional downtown shopping, gourmet restaurants, a cozy bistro, and more than 150 different boutiques, art galleries, and antiques shops along Atlantic Ave and Swinton Ave.

Serious readers will love the **Levenger Outlet** (561-274-0904 or 1-888-592-7461; www.levenger.com), 420 S Congress Ave, where fine reading accessories are sold, including pens, briefcases, lamps, leather goods, reading tools, and furniture.

In the Pineapple Grove historic district, you'll find great shopping at the **Ocean City Lumber Company** (561-276-2323). Browse through the trendy boutiques, art galleries, and restaurants in the former lumberyard and areas between NE Second Ave and Pineapple Grove Way.

GREEN MARKETS

Boca Raton
Every Saturday from October to May, fresh fruits and vegetables, along with fresh cut flowers and arts and crafts, can be found at the **Boca Raton Greenmarket** (561-393-7827), Royal Palm Plaza south parking lot (intersection of South Mizner Blvd and Federal Hwy). The nonprofit market also features a continental breakfast and live music 10–noon.

Delray Beach
Delray Beach Greenmarket in the Park (561-279-7511), in downtown Delray Beach, Worthington Park at SE Second Ave, is the place to go for fresh produce each Saturday Oct–Apr.

BOCA RATON SHOPPING DISTRICT
Visit Florida

✳ Special Events

Third Sunday of the month: ♪ Guided tours, lectures, and children's arts and crafts programs are held at the **Museum of Lifestyle & Fashion History** (561-243-2662; www.mlfh museum.org), starting at 2:30. Arts and crafts program is free for the kids but requires preregistration. All others: $5 for adults and children over 12. (See *Museums.*)

Fourth Saturday of the month: A one hour and 45-minute narrated trolley tour of historic Delray Beach is offered by the **Museum of Lifestyle & Fashion History** (561-243-2662; www.mlfhmuseum.org) and includes such sites as the 1904 Historic Chapel of Trinity Lutheran Church, the 1926 Colony Hotel, the 1896 Mt. Olive Baptist Church, and the 1936 Sandoway House Nature Center (See *Historic Sites.*) Adults $10, children under 18 free.

Last Saturday of the month: Take a 30- to 60-minute **Nature Walk** through sand dunes and gardens at the Sandoway House Nature Center (561-274-7263; www.sandoway house.com), 142 S Ocean Blvd, Delray Beach, while discovering the beautiful flora and fauna of Florida. The $3 fee also includes admission to the nature center (see *Nature Centers*).

January: The first-class **Annual Downtown Delray Festival of the Arts** (561-279-1380), on Pineapple Grove Way between the Intracoastal and the beach, Delray Beach, offers works of art for everyone's taste and budget, from $50 to more than $20,000.

When the sun goes down in January and the temperature begins to dip into the 60s, Floridians call that a cold night, so there's no better way to warm up than with the sizzling **Art & Jazz on the Ave** (561-279-1380, ext. 17; www.downtown delray beach.com), Delray Beach. Restaurants, art galleries, and shops along Atlantic Ave and Pineapple Grove Way open their doors in the evening from 6 to 10, Oct–Jun. Call for dates.

February: For more than 20 years, the **Annual Outdoor Juried Art Festival** (561-392-2500) at the Boca Raton Museum of Art (561-392-2500; www.bocamuseum.org), 501 Plaza Rd, Mizner Park, Boca Raton, has been showcasing works of art from more than 250 artists from around the world. (See *Museums.*)

You'll discover flora, fauna, and fun at the annual **Everglades Day Festival** (561-734-8303), Loxahatchee National Wildlife Refuge, Boynton Beach. Educational activities and live animal presentations are featured.

The **Hatsume Fair** at the Morikami Museum (561-495-0233; www .morikami.org), 4000 Morikami Park Rd, Delray Beach, celebrates the first bud of spring. The festival features three entertainment stages and has demonstrations ranging from martial arts to bonsai care. Artisans and food vendors are also present at the Morikami's largest event. (See *Museums.*)

Start the year with the **Oshogatsu-Japanese New Year Celebration** at the Morikami Museum (561-495-0233; www.morikami.org), 4000 Morikami Park Rd, Delray Beach. The annual event features a sado tea ceremony, hands-on calligraphy and New Year's card making, and games. (See *Museums.*)

March: The two-day **Annual Boca Bacchanal—A Celebration of Wine** (561-395-6766) is presented by the Boca Raton Historical Society, Boca Raton. The festival, a benefit for local children's charities, features a gala auction.

March–April: Learn about the galaxy at the Sandoway House Nature Center (561-274-7263; www.sandoway house.com), 142 S Ocean Blvd, Delray Beach, through telescopes and lectures at the monthly **Astronomy Night,** usually held on Wed. The $3 fee also includes admission to the nature center (see *Nature Centers*).

April: ✐ The annual **Kidsfest** (561-368-6875) is one day of continuous entertainment and activites held at the Children's Museum on 498 Crawford Blvd, Boca Raton (see *Museums*).

✐ Hands-on activities take center stage at the **Morikami Museum's Children's Day Celebration** (561-495-0233; www.morikami.org), 4000 Morikami Park Rd, where you'll learn the fine art of Japanese toy making, origami, and fish painting or make a giant carp streamer. Several stages feature Japanese and American performances. $5 for all ages. (See *Museums*.)

May: The **Annual Hot-Air Balloon Race and Festival** (561-279-1380) is located on Atlantic Ave between FL A1A and the Intracoastal, Delray Beach. The daylong event features music, crafts, food, children's activities, and a chance to meet the pilots and ask questions like "What is an envelope?" and "Why do I have to get up so early to take a ride?"

June: Baby, it's hot outside, so there's no better way to cool off than with

Art & Jazz on the Ave (561-279-1380, ext. 17; www.downtowndelray beach.com), Delray Beach. Restaurants, art galleries, and shops along Atlantic Ave and Pineapple Grove Way open their doors from 6 to 10 so you can wander through the downtown area in the cool of the night. Call for dates.

August: **Bon Festival,** inspired by Obon, a three-day holiday honoring ancestors, is celebrated at the Morikami Museum (561-495-0233; www .morikami.org), 4000 Morikami Park Rd, Delray Beach. Highlights include taiko drumming and traditional Japanese folk dancing, followed by an evening ceremony where lanterns are lit and placed on the Morikami Pond to guide the ancestors' souls home. The evening culminates with a fireworks display. Adults $10, children $5, under 3 free. (See *Museums.*)

October: Don't miss the annual **Delray Beach Orchid Society Show & Sale** held at the Old School Square, 51 Swinton Ave, Delray Beach, where you'll see the best of elegant and colorful orchids, along with a variety of supplies and classes on "how to" care. (See *Historic Sites.*)

October–April: Free **outdoor movies** are shown on one Friday night each month at the Old School Square Entertainment Pavilion (561-243-7922), Delray Beach. If you don't have your own lawn chair, you can rent one. From 6 PM on.

October–June: Downtown Delray Beach sizzles with **Art & Jazz on the Ave** (561-279-1380, ext. 17; www .downtowndelraybeach.com). Restaurants, art galleries, and shops along Atlantic Ave and Pineapple Grove Way open their doors on select evenings from 6 to 10. Call for dates.

November: Pack your breath mints and head to the **Annual Garlic Fest** (561-279-7511), Old School Square Grounds, in downtown Delray Beach.

The **Southern Handcraft Holiday Show & Sale** showcases beautiful decorations, ornaments, and more to decorate your home with Southern flair. Located at the Old School Square, 51 Swinton Ave (see *Historic Sites*), Delray Beach. The annual three-day event is Thu–Sat.

December: The **Annual Boca Raton Holiday Boat Parade** (561-845-9010) lights up the holiday night as colorful boats sail up the Intracoastal Waterway from Boca Raton toward Delray Beach.

The family-friendly, nonalcoholic **First Night** New Year's Eve Celebration (561-279-1380; www.downtown delraybeach.com) is held each year all through the downtown Delray Beach area.

Greater Fort Lauderdale

OCEANSIDE:
EASTERN BROWARD COUNTY

INLAND:
WESTERN BROWARD COUNTY

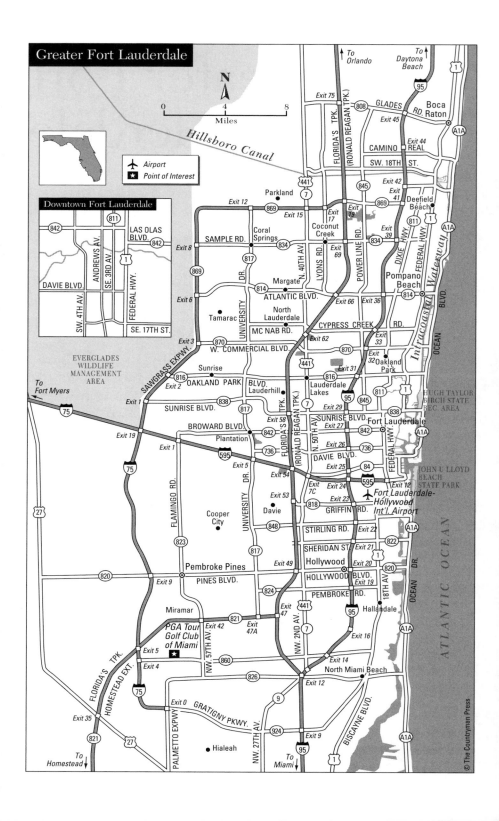

OCEANSIDE:
EASTERN BROWARD COUNTY

In the late 1800s South Florida was virtually an untapped frontier, with only a few dozen Seminole families inhabiting the region. **Dania** (now Dania Beach) is the oldest incorporated city (circa 1904). **Pompano,** at the northern end of the county, became the second town to incorporate in 1908. **Fort Lauderdale,** once a small pioneer village of 250 residents, became the central hub in 1915. With the arrival of Henry Flagler's railroad, several other beachfront cities emerged, such as **Hollywood** and **Deerfield Beach.** The western reaches of the county weren't developed for another 50 years, with Sunrise and Davie being the first to push west. When the Corps of Engineers drained the Everglades in 1906, developers soon began planning family-oriented communities, such as Coral Springs and Weston. Broward County is one of three counties that constitute the South Florida "Gold Coast," so named due to the arrival of northerners looking to buy vacation land. The Gold Coast reaches from Palm Beach County all the way to Miami-Dade County. The centrally located Broward County was incorporated in 1915 and was named for governor Napoleon Bonaparte Broward. It includes popular beachside towns such as Dania Beach, Deerfield Beach, Hollywood, Fort Lauderdale, **Lauderdale-by-the-Sea,** and the island community of **Wilton Manors.** Urban sprawl reaches to the west with suburban neighborhoods and parks (see *Inland: Western Broward County*)

GUIDANCE Contact the **Greater Fort Lauderdale Convention and Visitors Bureau** (954-765-4466 or 1-800-22SUNNY; www.sunny.org), 100 E Broward Blvd, Suite 200, Fort Lauderdale 33301, for more information on the area.

For information about Hollywood contact the **Hollywood Office of Tourism** (954-923-4000 or 1-800-231-5562; www.visithollywood.org), 330 N Federal Hwy, Hollywood 33020.

GETTING THERE *By air:* **Fort Lauderdale–Hollywood International Airport** (954-359-6100; www.fll.net) has easy access to I-95, US 595, I-75, and FL 1, as well as Port Everglades.

By car: **I-95** runs north and south and is a good route to take for the areas in the east section of the county. **Florida's Turnpike** runs north and south more toward the center of the county and is good to access the western regions.

By rail: **AMTRAK** (1-800-872-7245; www.amtrak.com) provides regularly scheduled service to Fort Lauderdale.

GETTING AROUND *By car:* When I first moved to greater Fort Lauderdale, I had a hard time finding my way around. So I used the acronym COSBY to determine where I was at any given time along I-95: When traveling from north to south, "C," for Commercial Blvd, will bring you to the northern sections of Fort Lauderdale, such as Pompano Beach to the east and Coral Springs to the west; "O," Oakland Blvd, and "S," Sunrise Blvd, will bring you all the way from the Fort Lauderdale beaches to western Broward cities such as Sunrise and Plantation; and "B," Broward Blvd, will bring you to the heart of Fort Lauderdale and the Arts and Science District. Finally, I use "Y" as a marker for US 595, which runs past the airport from Port Everglades to I-75 North (Alligator Alley), taking you west to Naples. The city of Hollywood can be reached off I-95 south of the airport from Griffin, Stirling, or Sheridan. Scenic FL A1A runs along the beaches.

By streetcar: The complimentary **Downtown A&E Trolley Line** operates throughout Fort Lauderdale's Riverwalk Arts & Entertainment District on Fri 5–11 PM and Sat noon–11 PM. The route travels from the Arts & Entertainment Garage (opposite the Broward Center for the Performing Arts) through Old Fort Lauderdale Village, Las Olas Blvd, the Museum of Art, and Stranahan House, with stops along the way.

Holly Trolley (954-445-6841) operates throughout Hollywood's dining, shopping, and beach areas and also provides transportation to Seminole Hard Rock Hotel & Casino. Regular fare $1; round-trip to casino $15. Call for schedule.

FORT LAUDERDALE WATER TAXI

Visit Florida

By water taxi: A great way to see luxurious homes along the Intracoastal Waterway is on the Water Taxi (954-467-6677; www.watertaxi.com). The route runs from Oakland Park Blvd to the Riverwalk Arts & Entertainment District. Adults $5 one way, children and seniors $2.50; all-day fare $7. Multiday tickets available at reduced prices. The Water Taxi also offers day trips on Tue and Sat to Miami's South Beach Art Deco District for only $18.

PARKING Fort Lauderdale city parking garages are located at the Arts & Science District, 101 SW Fifth Ave; Bridgeside Place, 3020 NE 32nd Ave (near Oakland Park Blvd); City Park, 150 SE Second St; and City Hall. Rates differ from coin by the hour to flat rates per entry. Some garages have attendants and some have meters. See www.fortlauderdale.gov for more information.

You'll find metered parking throughout Fort Lauderdale, Hollywood, and the beach areas.

PUBLIC REST ROOMS The beach areas and most city parks all have rest rooms available to the public at no cost.

VALET Most restaurants and luxury hotels in the beach area offer valet services. Some restaurants and hotels have only mandatory valet parking. Inquire when making reservations.

MEDICAL EMERGENCIES Several hospitals are located throughout Broward County. **Broward General Medical Center** (954-355-4400), 1600 S Andrews Ave, Fort Lauderdale, is just one of them. Contact **North Broward Hospital District** (954-759-7400; www.browardhealth.org) for a hospital near your vacation destination.

✳ To See

ART GALLERIES

Fort Lauderdale
The 10,000-square-foot **Las Olas Art Center** (954-763-8982; www.lasolasart center.com), 600 SE Second Ct, is a place where you'll see more than two dozen resident artists creating new works. Wander through their galleries for shopping or inspiration. The center offers classes, lectures, shows, and exhibitions throughout the year.

Hollywood
The Art & Culture Center of Hollywood (954-921-3275; www.artandculture center.org), 1650 Harrison St, was founded in 1975 to promote contemporary and innovative artists. Housed in a 1924 Spanish mansion in the heart of downtown Hollywood, it has become the center of this city's art district and offers theater performances, gallery exhibitions, and classes for children and adults.

Owner Robyn Crosfield's gorgeous award-winning mosaics are just one of the reasons to stop at **Mosaica** (954-923-7006; www.emosaica.com), 2020 Hollywood Blvd. I love art glass and found the starfish and showy bowls intriguing. Select from large objets d'art such as Robyn's mirrors and mosaic-trimmed furniture to small gifts such as the metal art lizards and enameled boxes. Open daily.

HISTORIC HOMES In the heart of Fort Lauderdale sits the **Bonnet House Museum & Gardens** (954-563-5393; www.bonnethouse.org), 900 N Birch Rd, named after the yellow water lily that once grew in the property's marshland. Once home to Frederic Clay and Evelyn Fortune Bartlett, both avid art collectors, the plantation-style home now houses a historical museum and art gallery. Tours are available, with the last tour starting at 2:30. Open year-round 10–4

Bonnet House

BONNET HOUSE CHICKEE BRIDGE

Wed–Sat, noon–4 Sun. As you tour the grounds, you'll walk under mangrove trees and through fruit groves of avocado, mango, and guava, while Brazilian squirrel monkeys watch you with great interest. Admission to the grounds: $9; admission to the grounds and plantation home: adults $15, seniors 60+ $11, students 6–16 $10, children under six free. Call ahead for tour schedules, as the plantation home may be closed for wedding parties.

The turn-of-the-20th-century (circa 1913) Florida Vernacular-style **Stranahan House** (954-524-4736; www.stranahanhouse.org), 335 SE Sixth Street (corner of Las Olas Blvd), Fort Lauderdale, is the oldest structure in Broward County. Ohioan Frank Stranahan was Fort Lauderdale's first Postmaster. He married Ivy Julia Cromartie, the area's first teacher, and soon their house was the center of social events. It remained their personal residence until her death in 1971. Furnished with antiques and memorabilia from their life, the house is open 10–3 Wed–Sat, 1–3 Sun. Adults $5, children under 12 $2.

HISTORIC PLACES Since 1938, **The Elbo Room** (954-463-4615; www.elbo room.com), 241 S Fort Lauderdale Beach Blvd, Fort Lauderdale, has been the area's number-one watering hole. World War II sailors came here in the 1940s, and then spring breakers dominated the scene during the later part of the century when the movie *Where the Boys Are,* with Connie Frances and George Hamilton, made Fort Lauderdale Beach spring break central. Today people 21 and older stop by for a drink and to check out tiny bikinis and a bit of history.

HISTORIC STRANAHAN HOUSE

Visit Florida

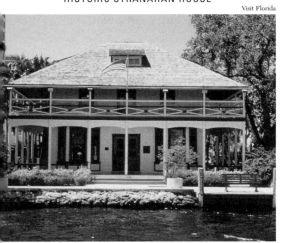

MUSEUMS

Dania

A fishload of fun awaits at the **International Game Fish Association (IGFA) Fishing Hall of Fame & Museum** (954-922-4212; www.igfa.org), 300 Gulf Stream Way, with an art gallery, fish gallery, tackle gallery, historical displays, and exciting interactive experiences, including simulated fishing. My brother, an avid angler, took the deep-sea fishing challenge and landed a big virtual marlin! Open 10–6 daily. Adults $6, children 3–16 and seniors 62+ $5. Parking is

Fort Lauderdale

The **Fort Lauderdale Antique Car Museum** (954-779-7300; www.antique
carmuseum.org), 1527 SW First Ave (Packard Ave), is dedicated to the preservation and history of the Packard Motor Co. The extensive collection includes 22
Packard automobiles dating from 1909 to 1940, such as the 1922 Packard Model
1-16 Sport Phaeton and the 1929 Packard Model 645 Dual Cowl Phaeton previously owned by the Schmidt family of Schmidt Brewing Company. The museum
also contains the FDR gallery and library dedicated to the late Franklin D. Roosevelt, and many related automobile memorabilia, including hood ornaments
and vintage tools. Open 10–4 Mon–Fri; call for hours Sat and Sun. Donation.

Host to national and international aquatic competitions, the **International
Swimming Hall of Fame Museum & Aquatic Complex** (954-462-6536; www
.ishof.org), One Hall of Fame Dr, features a 10,000-square-foot museum full of
Olympic memorabilia from more than one hundred nations. Families $5; adults
$3; students, seniors, and military $1; children under 12 free.

In 1986 the **Museum of Art** (954-525-5500; www.moafl.org), One E Las Olas
Blvd, opened its 65,000-square-foot building designed by renowned American
architect Edward Larabee Barnes, after growing from a small storefront space on
Las Olas Blvd (which is now Johnny V's; see *Dining Out*) from 1958. Today it has
an additional 10,000 square feet and draws crowds from around the world for its
permanent art collections and large-scale exhibitions such as Princess Diana, St.
Peter and the Vatican, and King Tut. In 2006 look for Platonic Solids, a show
focusing on light art by local artist Matthew Schrieber, along with paintings from
Alfred Hair and Harold Newton of The Highwaymen. Fall 2006 through spring
2007 brings Chicano Visions, which features works from Cheech Marin's private
collection. I can't wait to see what they schedule in the years to come! The permanent collection features more than 6,200 various artworks from American impressionist William Glackens, Picasso ceramics, contemporary Cuban art, and CoBrA,
one of the country's largest collections of works by the Northern European artists
(Copenhagen, Brussels, and Amsterdam). Adults $6, seniors and students $5, children $3. Ticket prices vary for special exhibits, such as King Tut ($20–30).

One of the area's best-kept secrets, the 256-seat **Norma & William Horvitz
Auditorium,** at the Museum of Art, is home to the **Inside Out Theatre Company** (www.insideouttheatre.org), which offers diverse and intelligent productions
such as *Whose Life Is It, Anyway?* and *A Year with Frog & Toad,* based on the
children's book. (See *Performing Arts.*)

✒ Plan to spend an entire day at the **Museum of Discovery & Science** and the
five-story **Blockbuster 3D IMAX Theater** (954-467-6637; www.mods.org),
401 SW Second St. The 52-foot-high Great Gravity Clock greets you as you
enter the atrium, and then you can explore living plants and animals at Florida's
Ecoscapes and try several interactive adventures in Gizmo City. The Discovery
Center is specifically geared toward little ones younger than 6. Theater: Open
10–5 Mon–Sat and noon–6 Sun, with extended hours for the IMAX theater on

the weekend. Tickets can be purchased separately for the museum or IMAX theater. Single ticket: adults $9, seniors $8, children 2–12 $7. Combo ticket: adults $14, seniors $13, children 2–12 $12, children under 2 free.

The Old Fort Lauderdale Village & Museum (954-463-4431; www.oldfort lauderdale.org), 231 SW Second Ave, depicts the development of Fort Lauderdale from 1870 to 1930. Guided tour of the King-Cromartie House must be reserved in advance. Open noon–5 Tue–Sun. Adults $8, children 6–16 $3, children under 6 free.

Hollywood

See native wildlife, such as alligators and the Florida panther, up close at the **Seminole Okalee Indian Village & Museum** (954-797-5570; www.seminole tribe.com), Seminole Hard Rock Hotel & Casino, 5710 Seminole Way. Education shows include alligator wrestling, and also on display is an excellent collection of Seminole cultural and historical artifacts. Open 9–5 Tue–Sat, 10–5 Sun. Fee.

WILDLIFE VIEWING Thousands upon thousands of live butterflies surround you at **Butterfly World** (954-977-4400; www.butterflyworld.com), 3600 W Sample Rd, Coconut Creek, an 8,000-square-foot conservatory. The beautiful 10-acre tropical gardens are also home to hummingbirds, lorikeets, and an insectarium. Walk among waterfalls, orchids, and peaceful ponds while you learn about these graceful winged creatures. Open 9–5 Mon–Sat, 1–5 Sun. Adults $18, children 4–12 $13, children under 4 free.

✳ To Do

BICYCLING Take a bike tour of Fort Lauderdale (954-588-9565) along the beach, through historical neighborhoods, and through trendy Las Olas Blvd. Tours depart from the **Tour Hut,** 101 S FL A1A (1 block south of Las Olas Blvd). Small groups ride for about two hours. $30; includes bike rental.

BOAT TOURS

Deerfield Beach

Rockmore Cruises (954-426-4006; www.rockmore.us), 1755 SE Third Ct, operates from the docks at Pal's Charley's Crab (see *Dining Out*). The 90-minute narrative sight-seeing cruises take you along the Intracoastal Waterway. Morning sight-seeing cruise: adults $15, children $9; luncheon cruise: $40; evening cocktail cruise: $20. Reservations recommended.

Fort Lauderdale

Sail along Millionaire's Row and the Venice of America on ***Carrie B.* Harbor Tours** (954-768-9920; www.carriebcruises.com), 1402 E Las Olas Blvd #1029, along the Riverwalk. The one-and-a-half-hour, fully narrated tours go out at 11 AM, 1 PM, and 3 PM. Evening tours, at 7 and 9 PM, are partially narrated and last two hours. Adults $15, children $9. Check the web site for coupons.

For more than 60 years, the ***Jungle Queen* Riverboat** (954-462-5596; www .junglequeen.com), 801 Fort Lauderdale Beach Blvd (FL A1A), has cruised along Fort Lauderdale's Intracoastal Waterway for sight-seeing and dinner cruises. Choose from three narrated tours: the three-hour sight-seeing cruise (adults $14, children $10); the all-you-can-eat barbecue and shrimp dinner cruise (adults $32, children $18); or the cruise to Miami's Bayside Marketplace (adults $18, children $13).

The *Sea Experience* (954-394-8732; www.seaxp.com), Bahia Mar Resort, 801 Seabreeze Blvd, offers glass-bottom boat tours for those who want to stay dry. Adults $23, children $12. Snorkeling is also available (see *Snorkeling*).

Tropical Sailing Catamaran Charters (954-579-8181; www.tropicalsailing .com), 801 Seabreeze Blvd, offers full-moon, stargazing, sight-seeing, wine-tasting, and sunset cruises on the *Spirit of Lauderdale* catamaran. Three trips daily; rates start at $29.

CARRIAGE TOURS Whether you want a quick tour, or if romance is in the air, a great way to see Las Olas is in a **Royal Horse Drawn Carriage** (954-971-9820; www.royalcarriagesfl.com). Percheron or Clydesdale horses carry you though Las Olas and the Arts District and along the Fort Lauderdale beach. Rides depart Wed–Sun from SE Eighth Ave and E Las Olas Blvd.

ECOTOURS A full day of ecoadventure awaits at **Everglades Day Safari** (239-472-1559 or 1-800-472-3069; www.ecosafari.com), Fort Lauderdale, where you'll be taken on a boat ride through mangroves, a nature walk deep into a cypress swamp, a wildlife drive through the backcountry, and an airboat ride through the Everglades "River of Grass" with Miccosukee Indians. Safaris depart Fort Lauderdale at 7:45 AM and return about 5:30 PM. Adults $135, children under 12 $99. Lunch is included.

FAMILY ACTIVITIES Drive go-carts and bumper cars at **Boomers** (954-921-2416; www.boomersparks.com), 1801 NW First St, Dania. They also have mini golf, arcade games, laser tag, and batting cages. Open 10 AM–11 PM Sun–Thu, 10 AM–2 AM Fri and Sat.

Over at **Dania Beach Hurricane** (954-921-RIDE; www.xcoaster.com), 1760 NW First St (next to Boomers), Dania, you can ride a real wooden roller coaster reaching speeds up to 55 miles per hour. Open 10 AM–11 PM Mon–Fri, with extended hours until 2 AM on weekends.

GAMING

Dania

You can see the world's fastest sport, jai alai, at **Dania Jai Alai** (954-920-1511 or 954-426-4330; www.dania-jai-alai.com), 301 E Dania Beach Blvd, Dania. Originating in the Basque region of Spain, the sport found its way into many cultures and is common in Latin America. A wicker basket is attached to a player's arm, who then uses it to hurl a rubber ball against a three-walled court. The game is much faster than racquetball, with balls reaching speeds of 150 miles per hour. Bets can be placed on players.

My cousin convinced me to play the slots with her one evening at the **Seminole Hard Rock Hotel & Casino** (954-327-7625; www.seminolehardrockhollywood .com), One Seminole Way, just off US 441. After following her lead on a "hot" machine, I hit a payoff of $159 on a dollar played. Of course, I was already down $25 by then, so not being much of a gambler, I cashed out and walked out with a smile. Compared to Vegas, the gaming area is much more open and the noise level is higher, but you'll still find the throngs playing slots (no quarters, how- ever—it's all done with bills and tickets) or gathering at the poker tables. Open 24 hours, 7 days a week, and you can never tell exactly what time it is inside. The complex has a separate high-stakes bingo hall as well.

GHOST TOURS Maybe because its in my own backyard, but I just love the **Fort Lauderdale Ghost Tour** (954-290-9328; www.fortlauderdaleghosttour.com). The 60- to 90-minute walking tour meets at SE Sixth Ave and E Las Olas Blvd and takes you along trendy Las Olas Blvd and the historical New River. The tour covers a lot of area, so wear comfortable shoes. Adults $15, children 5–10 $10, children under 5 free. Reservations required. No credit cards.

GONDOLA TOURS Your own personal gondolier will take you through Fort Lauderdale's "Venice of America" as you glide along in authentic hand-carved wooden boats at **Gondola Servizio** (1-866-737-8494; www.gondolaservizio .com), 1109 E Las Olas Blvd, Fort Lauderdale. Music and romance fill the air as you pass by Venetian-style architecture, stately homes, and quaint shops on a truly romantic experience. As a partner with Stork's Las Olas (see *Eating Out*), they will also prepare a gourmet food and wine package to your specifications. Then nuzzle up in the *puparino,* or for larger groups, their two gondolas will seat up to six. Gondola rides are $50 for the first couple for a half-hour tour, with $10 for each additional person, or $120 for the first couple for the one-hour tour per couple, with $10 for each additional person. Reservations are recommended, but they will also take walk-ups when available. The private tours board between Stork's and Rino's Tuscan Grill. For a same-day reservation, you must call Stork's at 954-522-4670. Open night and day year-round.

PADDLING

Fort Lauderdale
Paddle past unique architecture, historical sites, and unique wildlife with **Full Moon Kayak Co.** (954- 328-5231; www.fullmoonkayak.com). The fully guided and narrated tours operate in both urban and natural settings.

SEMINOLE HARD ROCK CASINO, HOLLYWOOD   Seminole Hard Rock Hotel & Casino

Hollywood

Rent kayaks or canoes at **Anne Kolb Nature Center** (see *Nature Centers*) and explore on your own through tidal wetlands, mangrove forests, and out onto the lake.

SNORKELING If you can't get to the Keys for snorkeling, hop on the *Sea Experience* (954-394-8732; www.seaxp.com), Bahia Mar Resort, 801 Seabreeze Blvd, Fort Lauderdale, for a snorkeling tour. Adults $30, children $18, including all gear. Glass-bottom boat tours are also available (see *Boat Tours*).

SURFING Hang 10 at Deerfield Beach (see *Beaches*), where surfing is allowed in select locations. The folks over at Island Water Sports Surf Superstore (see *Selective Shopping*) offer free surf lessons every Sat morning at the Deerfield Beach Pier.

WALKING TOURS The arts and culture center of Broward County is in the **Riverwalk Arts & Entertainment District** (954-468-2540), between SW Seventh Ave and SW Second Ave, Fort Lauderdale, where you can stroll along the river from the Broward Center for the Performing Arts to the shops Las Olas Blvd. The **Riverwalk/Espanade Park** (954-561-7362; www.goriverwalk.com), 1350 W Broward Blvd, Fort Lauderdale, is in the heart of the upbeat and thriving area.

✻ Green Space

BEACHES

Dania Beach

✐ Sea turtles nest along the shore at **John U. Lloyd Beach State Park** (954-923-2833; www.floridastateparks.org/lloydbeach/default.cfm), 6503 N Ocean Dr, and when the hatchlings emerge each fall, there can be up to ten thousand of them headed for the surf! Located just south of Port Everglades, the park is a crucial natural habitat on a shoreline crowded with development. Enjoy the beaches, walk the nature trail, or bring a kayak and ply the mangrove-lined channels. Open 8–sunset daily. Fee.

Deerfield Beach

The **City of Deerfield Beach** (www.deerfield-beach.com) has one of the prettiest, family-friendly beaches in the county. The award-winning "Blue Wave" beach earned this distinction for their clean water and beach conditions, safety, and their conservative efforts. The 1-mile stretch of beach has nine lifeguard towers with lifeguards present every day from 9 to 5. Take your short or long board, as surfing is permitted on the north side of the pier and south of tower #9. Check the web site for beach conditions and surf cam. Sorry, no dogs.

Fort Lauderdale

Fort Lauderdale's main beach area along FL A1A was once the hot spot for spring break. When the Tonga swimsuit was banned in the 1980s in an attempt to quiet the area, the spring breakers went elsewhere. The beach now beckons a

LAUNCHING A SAILBOAT AT DEERFIELD
BEACH

more open-minded audience geared toward an alternative lifestyle. Note the very cool, wavy neon wall that runs along edge of FL A1A. On the other side of the street, numerous beachfront shops, restaurants, and nightclubs look out on one of the prettiest beaches in Fort Lauderdale.

NATURE CENTERS

Coconut Creek

&. ♂ An oasis in this densely populated area, **Fern Forest Nature Center** (954-970-0150), 201 Lyons Rd S, has more than 2 miles of nature trails to wander, including the Cypress Creek boardwalk, which follows the rocky edge of now-dry Cypress Creek, a sad comment on the canalization of the county's natural waterways. More than 34 species of ferns grow throughout this verdant park. Stop at the nature center first for an overview of the habitats before hitting the trails. Open 8–6 daily. Free.

Dania

&. ♂ Broward County's first nature center, **Secret Woods Nature Center** (954-791-1030), 2701 W FL 84, is hidden in a tangled jungle of mangroves along the New River. The center features interpretive displays and an active beehive; visitors come to enjoy the extensive boardwalk through the mangrove forest, where you can always spot ibises along the waterway. Open 8–6 daily. Free.

Hollywood

At West Lake Park, **Anne Kolb Nature Center** (954-926-2410), 1200 Sheridan St, sits above the south side of an extensive mangrove-lined lagoon, West Lake. Two interpretive trails radiate from the center, which features interpretive displays, rotating art exhibits, and a tall observation tower accessed by elevator. The park features extensive paved biking trails, ecotour operators from a dock next to the nature center, and kayak rentals for you to explore this ecosystem on your own. Open 9–5 daily. Fee.

FORT LAUDERDALE BEACH

PARKS

Coconut Creek

Tradewinds Park (954-968-3880), 3600 Sample Rd, is so packed with activities that you can spend a full day there. Sample Rd breaks the park into two sections, North and South. Beyond the traditional pursuits of walking and biking, ballfields and picnicking, there are some very different things to do. At North Tradewinds Park, kids and rail fans will get a blast from the one-eighth life-size live steam engines running out of Godwin Station, pulling train cars that you can sit on and ride. See the **Tradewinds & Atlantic Railroad** (www.livesteamers.org/schedule.htm) schedule for operating times and dates. The 600-plus-acre park also has **Tradewinds Stables** (954-968-3875), offering guided trail rides ($23) and a farm with barnyard animals. **Batting cages** are also available ($15 for 30 minutes). In South Tradewinds Park, visit **Butterfly World** (see *Wildlife Viewing*), said to be the largest butterfly conservatory in the world. You can also rent canoes and kayaks to ply the chain of lakes, bring your Frisbee to tackle the disc golf course, or slip back along the trails at the southernmost end of the park to find a boardwalk through a primeval pond apple swamp.

Deerfield Beach
Deerfield Island Park (954-360-1320), 1720 Deerfield Island Park Rd, provides an opportunity to "get away from it all" on an island in the Intracoastal Waterway, with 1⅘ miles of trails and boardwalks to explore. This day-use park can be accessed only by boat. Free shuttle boats leave at prescheduled times; call ahead for schedule.

Fort Lauderdale Beach
❦ Right across the street from the beach, **Hugh Taylor Birch State Park** (954-564-4521; www.floridastateparks.org/hughtaylorbirch/default.cfm), 3109 E Sunrise Blvd, is the former estate of Chicago attorney Hugh Taylor Birch and protects a coastal hammock in this urban area. Built in 1940, Birch's home, TerraMar, displays both Mediterranean and art deco styles and serves as the park's visitors center (open 10–4 daily). The quiet park is nestled between the beach and the downtown area, providing a serene escape from the hustle and bustle of city life. The park also has two nature trails, canoe rentals for plying the waters of a coastal dune lake, and plenty of picnic spots. You can walk over to the beach or picnic along the Intracoastal Waterway. This is one of the best places for in-line skating, with a road that passes under a peaceful canopy of trees and then along the water. Open 8–sunset daily. Fee.

Hollywood
Broward County Parks and Recreation (954-357-8100; www.broward.org/parks) lists several natural areas throughout the county. One of my favorites is 1,500-acre **West Lake Park** (954-926-2410; www.broward.org/parks), 750 Sheridan St, which offers hiking, biking, and paddling opportunities. Canoeists and kayakers can rent or bring their own, and then paddle through mangrove trails and out onto wide-open lakes. Don't miss the nature exhibit in the main building, where you'll learn about tidal marshes and local wildlife. The **Anne Kolb Nature Center** (see *Nature Centers*) also has a fishing pier and five-story observation tower. Fee.

Oakland Park
❦ Despite the road noise from nearby I-95, **Easterlin Park** (954-938-0610), 1000 NW 38th St, is a pretty little place with camping along a pond and a "designated urban wilderness" where a nature trail winds through the tropical forest,

and ancient cypresses rise from the edge of a swamp. Playgrounds, picnic areas, and fishing round out the experience. Call for camping reservations. Open daily. Fee on weekends and holidays.

✳ Lodging
COTTAGES

Pompano Beach 33062
Cottages By The Ocean (954-956-8999; www.4rentbythebeach.com), 3309 SE Third St, offers six 1940s Key West–style studio cottages only 2 blocks from the beach and is a member of Superior Small Lodging. The cottages were renovated only a few years ago and include king beds, a barbecue area, and cable television. Nonsmoking; small dogs welcome. Rates $550–1,000 weekly; $1,650–3,500 monthly.

HOTELS, MOTELS, AND RESORTS

Fort Lauderdale
▼ **The Flamingo** (954-561-4658; www.theflamingoresort.com), 2727 Terramar St, Fort Lauderdale 33304, a luxury gay hotel, is in the heart of the gay district only a few blocks from the beach. British West Indies decor includes such details as four-poster beds and crisp clean white-on-white linens. Many of the spacious rooms and suites open through French doors directly into the courtyard, where you'll find fountains, gardens, and a heated swimming pool. Other amenities include continental breakfast and full concierge service. Rooms and suites $130–330.

Hidden from the hustle and bustle of the main roadways, **Lago Mar Hotel Resort and Club** (954-523-6511 or 1-800-LAGOMAR; www.lagomar .com), 1700 S Ocean Ln, Fort Lauderdale 33316, is located directly on one of the best beaches in the area.

Spacious rooms and luxury suites are decorated in tropical splendor. Beds are oh so soft, from the pillow-top mattresses to the sumptuous duvet covers. Amenities include an Olympic-size pool, a 9,000-square-foot lagoon-style pool set in a tropical paradise, a 500-foot beach with private beach cabanas, an on-site full-service spa, a fitness center, beachfront volleyball, tennis courts, a children's play area, a giant outdoor chessboard, shuffleboard, putting course, private oceanfront balconies, and other services found at major resorts. Guest rooms, executive suites, and a penthouse with beachfront views $150–755 depending on season. Valet parking is available if you need it, but self-parking is close at hand.

Shhh, **Pillars at New River Sound** (954-252-3416; www.pillarshotel .com), 111 N Birch Rd, Fort Lauderdale 33304, is a secret! This low-key luxury boutique hotel has 23 rooms and suites located in a tropical paradise right on the Intracoastal Waterway. The fully restored 1938 property was previously a private residence. Tastefully appointed rooms feature 14-foot ceilings with British Colonial and island plantation themes. The cozy library features hundreds of books and videos and even a baby grand piano. There is a heated freshwater pool and a waterfront courtyard with a lush tropical garden, and the beach is nearby. Queen or king beds in superior rooms and suites $199–500.

▼ Located in Victoria Park, **Pine-apple Point Guest House** (954-527-0094 or 1-888-844-7295; www.pineapplepoint.com), 315 NE 16th Ter, Fort Lauderdale 33304, is within walking distance to the trendy Las Olas district and nearby Wilton Manors. The 1930s guest house is comprised of seven Old Florida buildings housing 27 luxury rooms and suites within a tropical garden setting. The resort caters to gay men only, and clothing is optional around the heated pool. Several types of accommodations are available: double and king beds in rooms, bungalows, suites, cottages, one- to four-bedroom villas ($189–399), and a three-story villa with four bedrooms and an elevator ($750–900 depending on season). Suites offer separate living rooms and dining areas along with full kitchens. Amenities include high-speed wireless Internet, refrigerators, cable TV, and VCRs, and there is a swimming pool, a lap pool, and two whirlpools.

Old-world charm and elegance will captivate you at **Riverside Hotel** (954-467-0671 or 1-800-325-3280; www.riversidehotel.com), 620 E Las Olas Blvd, Fort Lauderdale 33304. Located in the vibrant Las Olas Blvd district, the city's oldest hotel (circa 1936) was a favorite of the Du Pont family and later, former President Ronald Reagan and other well-known celebrities. Guest rooms and suites ($125–295) are spread between the original six-story landmark building and a 12-story tower, which caters to executives. Modern amenities include a swimming pool, cable television, data ports, and refrigerators. Over in the Executive Tower you'll find two-room suites ($600) with oversize Jacuzzi tubs.

▼ Plush towels, designer linens, and spa amenities are just a few details that are offered at **The Royal Palms Resort** (954-564-6444 or 1-800-237-7256; www.royalpalms.com), 2901 Terramar St, Fort Lauderdale 33304. The clothing-optional resort caters exclusively to gay men. Amenities include a tropical heated pool, Wi-Fi, cable TV, and refrigerators. Queen or king beds in pool or garden rooms or suites $189–340.

✳ Where to Eat
DINING OUT

Deerfield Beach
You remember the pier that got all the press during the numerous hurricanes? The one that received continuous pounding surf and hurricane-force winds, and despite all that still didn't blow down? Well now is your chance to see it just outside the windows at **JB's Restaurant & Bar** (954-571-5220; www.jpbsonthebeach.com), 300 N Ocean Blvd. One of the few right-on-the-beach restaurants with a truly spectacular view, JB's has an extensive menu with an assortment of Florida-style appetizers ($8–15), salads ($6–18), seafood and char-broiled entrées ($13–19), sandwiches ($9–14), and a variety of desserts. Try the Carribean Chicken ($15), cooked on their wood-fired char-broiler, marinated and grilled with mango jicama sauce and served with rice; the Beachside Blackened Fish Tacos ($13), with marinated greens, tomatoes, cheddar cheese, and mango sauce; or the wood-grilled barbecue baby back ribs ($22), with coffee/bourbon barbecue sauce, corn on the cob, and sweet potato fries.

Fort Lauderdale

Hard to find, but worth the search is **By Word of Mouth** (954-564-3663; www.bywordofmouthfoods.com), 3200 NE 12th Ave. The restaurant built its reputation completely by word of mouth more than two decades ago and continues to be one of the best gastronomic delights, always rating high on reviewers' "best of" lists. Start off your meal with portobello mushrooms with lump crabmeat ($14) or escargots with Pernod crème in pastry shell ($13), and then select an entrée such as shrimp with sweet curry basil ($16), roasted vegetable lasagna with béchamel sauce ($14), or pan-seared grouper with spinach Chardonnay reduction ($17). Finish with one of their specialty cakes, such as Chocolate Orgasm, or our favorite, Carrot Praline ($8). Menu and bakery selections change daily, but if you call a few days in advance, they may make one of their 50 gourmet desserts specifically for your visit. They will also make full-size cakes for you to take home. (We bring home the Carrot Praline cake too often to mention.) Lunch is served Mon–Fri starting at 11 AM; dinner is served Wed–Sat starting at 5 PM.

Café Matarano (954-561-2554), 3343 E Oakland Blvd, at the corner of FL A1A, is a fantastic restaurant, but please leave the kids at home. This *Sopranos*-type restaurant feels like you might be in Little Italy instead of a few steps from Fort Lauderdale Beach. During dinner, gangster movies play overhead on flat screens, while disco lights and '80s music keeps things lively. Be forewarned that your waiter will explain the menu in descriptive detail, but without the benefit of pricing (if you have to ask, then you shouldn't be here—for those who have to ask, most entrées are $25–65). Our family loves this place for the meatball appetizers (two enormous meatballs with a small salad for $14 are just how our in-laws make them back home). Fresh, authentic ingredients are imported from places such as Tuscany, Salerno, Calabria, Sicily, and Modena. If you want a unique dining experience with a very good chance of seeing celebrities (such as James Gandolfini, Liza Minelli, and Dan Marino), then this is the place. Reservations are not accepted, so expect lines on the weekends and in-season of at least an hour.

The 1920s **Casablanca Cafe** (954-764-3500), 3049 Alhambra St on Fort Lauderdale Beach, offers a fabulous ocean view in an historic Moroccan-style villa. Menu items from tropical to North African are served nightly (about $20–30). You often find waiters, and sometimes guests, singing along at the downstairs piano bar in the casual atmosphere. Cozy corners can be found upstairs, with the outside deck offering a view of the beach. Valet parking recommended, as street parking is hard to find. And they don't take reservations, so get there early. Open daily until 1 AM; dinner served until 11 PM.

Charley's Crab (954-561-4800; www.muer.com), 3000 NE 32nd Ave, is a must for locals and tourists alike. The restaurant overlooks the Intracoastal, so you'll often see a nice-size yacht moored at the dock. Eat inside with modern elegance or on the outside terrace. Lunch and dinner are served daily. Their sister restaurant, **Pal's Charley's Crab** (954-427-4000), is located on the Intracoastal Waterway at 1755 SE Third Ct, Deerfield Beach.

A longtime favorite is the **15th Street Fisheries** (954-763-2777; www.15 streetfisheries.com), 1900 SE 15th St, a casual seafood restaurant overlooking the Intracoastal. They serving more than 12 fresh fish items for lunch and dinner daily.

Local celebrity chef Johnny Vinczencz recently opened his own restaurant, **Johnny V** (954-761-7920; www .johnnyvlasolas.com), 625 E Las Olas Blvd, after working as a sous chef for Dennis Max, a pioneer in South Florida cuisine in the 1980s and '90s, and then as executive chef for Astor Place in Miami Beach and De La Tierra in Delray Beach (see *South Palm Beach County*). Gourmets take note: Johnny V creates such appetizers as Jamaican jerk seared fresh tuna; Callaloo Stew; Bammy, aka coconut yucca cakes ($13); roasted garlic clams sautéed with Jamon Serrano red chile corn broth; and JV BBQ "Stix" ($12). Entrées may include fresh corn crusted yellowtail snapper, lemon Boniato mash, roasted corn sauce, and smoked pepper relish ($27); red chile venison chop, venison sausage, a trio of baby baked potatoes, wilted spinach, and blackberry demiglaze ($32); or the famous wild mushroom pancake "short stack" with roasted portobello, balsamic syrup, and sun-dried tomato butter ($11). An extensive selection of more than 40 cheeses is available paired with intricate salads and fresh fruits. Desserts are equally impressive. Open for lunch and dinner daily (except Super Bowl Sunday). Reservations recommended.

Reservations are a must at the **Left Bank** (954-462-5376), 214 S Federal Hwy, a great place for romance. The small, intimate restaurant serves classic French and nouvelle American cuisine for dinner nightly.

A Broward institution, **Lester's Diner** (954-525-5641), 250 FL 84, is open 24/7, offers an extensive menu, and serves breakfast all day. Another location is out west in Sunrise (see *Inland: Western Broward County*).

A longtime favorite of tourists and locals alike, the **Mai-Kai Polynesian Restaurant and Dinner Show** (954-563-3272; www.maikai.com), 3599 N Federal Hwy, brings the South Seas to life within their Polynesian garden restaurant. Hostesses dressed in sarongs serve exotic tropical drinks, and the Polynesian floor show (adults $10, children under 12 free) makes for a fun evening with family or friends. Dinner served nightly. Expect valet parking as street parking is limited.

For fine Italian cooking, family-owned **Regalo** (954-566-6661), 4215 N Federal Hwy, is one of those hidden finds, offering fresh, original dishes and an extensive wine menu. Lunch served Mon–Thu; dinner served Mon–Sat from 5 PM.

You'll love cracking your own crabs at the casual, waterfront **Rustic Inn Crabhouse** (954-584-1637), 4331 Ravenswood Rd. The steamed garlic blue crabs are served on newspaper-covered tables. Lunch and dinner served daily.

Casual dockside dining along the New River is at **Shirttail Charlie's** (954-463-3474; www.shirttailcharlies.com), 400 SW Third Ave. Pull up your boat and dig into local fresh seafood, alligator, and conch. The waterfront restaurant offers a free after-dinner river cruise, or you can take the boat to and from a performance at the Broward Center for the Performing Arts (see *Performing Arts*). Lunch and dinner served daily.

Once a spring break favorite, **Shooter's Waterfront Cafe** (954-566-2855; www.shooterscafe.com), 3033 NE 32nd Ave, still attracts a lively crowd. Cigarette boats and luxury yachts line the dock along the Intracoastal Waterway. You can eat in or out, or just hang out at the bar. Open daily until late.

Tucked just off of US 1 and Oakland Park Blvd, **Tea at Lily's** (954-565-1144), 3020 N Federal Hwy, provides an elegant escape from shopping the nearby boutiques. Sisters-in-law Maureen and Dolly Van Hengel offer soup ($5), salads ($10), quiche ($9–11), and light sandwiches ($7–10) with a European flair. Light classical music plays in the background while you dine on such delicacies as pâté and French Brie, strawberry chicken salad, and tortellini salad with sun-dried tomato pesto. For afternoon tea select the Cream Tea ($9), which includes a pot of imported tea and scones with preserves and Devonshire cream, or High Tea ($16), which includes a pot of imported tea and a selection of finger sandwiches, mini scones, and pastries. During winter season, the Chamber Music Recital High Tea ($38) is available, and a Mother's Day fashion show is often scheduled. Desserts include such confections as forest fruit tart with Chantilly cream, cappuccino mousse cake, and a very moist carrot cake. Beverages include wine by the glass, European coffee, and cappuccino, and of course a large assortment of tea. Reservations recommended, especially for High Teas. Open 11–5 Mon–Sat.

Hollywood

Revitalized downtown Hollywood has an amazing array of international restaurants. For the best Spanish food, there's **La Barraca Tapa Bar & Cafe** (954-925-0050), 115 S 20th Ave; for Irish food and entertainment, there's **O'Hara's Jazz Cafe & Swing Street Bistro** (954-925-2555), 1903 Hollywood Blvd; Romanian food is served at **Transylvania** (954-929-0777), 113 S 20th Ave; and you'll find good Mediterranean cuisine at **Zaraka Restaurant & Lounge** (954-966-6669), 715 S 21st Ave.

Lauderdale-By-The-Sea

The beachfront **Aruba Beach Cafe** (954-776-0001), right on the beach at Commercial Blvd and FL A1A, offers Caribbean and West Indian favorites. Lunch, dinner, and a Sunday breakfast buffet are served.

The trendy art deco–inspired **Blue Moon Fish Company** (954-267-9888), 4405 W Tradewinds Ave, is located directly on the Intracoastal Waterway and is known for its Sunday gospel brunch. Lunch and dinner served daily.

EATING OUT

Dania Beach

✐ Celebrating 50 years of goodness in 2006, **Jaxson's** old-fashioned ice cream parlor (954-923-4445; www.jaxsonsicecream.com), 128 S Federal Hwy, is a must for any tourist or local. Ice cream and toppings are prepared daily right on the premises. The huge sundaes ($9–10) are almost impossible to finish, but we keep trying. Other cool creations are the old-fashioned banana split ($8), colossal parfaits ($9), and, for parties of four or more, there's the Kitchen Sink ($9 per person). This amazing sundae is served in an actual kitchen sink and is a creation that you make with the guidance of Jaxson's own professional soda jerks. For a truly special event, get a dozen of your close friends together and order the Punch Bowl Sundae ($80). Oh, and Jaxson's also serves excellent salads ($9), burgers ($8), sandwiches ($7–9), wraps ($8), and junior meals ($6). Just make sure to save room for the ice cream!

Fort Lauderdale
At **Stork's Las Olas** (954-522-4670; www.storkscafe.com), 1109 E Las Olas Blvd, Jim Stork offers 13 different varieties of coffee beans, breakfast pastries, garden salads and sandwiches, mousses, and cakes, tortes, and pies—by the slice, or take home a whole one. All bakery items are made fresh daily, from scratch, using top-notch ingredients. There's another location in Wilton Manors near Five Points on 2505 NE 15th Ave (954-567-3220).

Hollywood
On a stroll through downtown, my friends and I found the **Universe Café** (954-920-3774), 1925 Hollywood Blvd, open on a Sunday, and we popped inside for a delightful lunch. It was tough to choose between the various salads ($6 and up) and sandwiches, but I went with the crab cakes and enjoyed them immensely. Open daily for breakfast and lunch.

Wilton Manors
▼ Fresh gourmet coffee, cappuccinos, iced lattes, macchiato, chai tea, fruit smoothies, and an assortment of desserts can be found at **Java Boys** (954-564-8828; www. javaboys.net), 2230 Wilton Dr. Not for everyone, the mostly male hangout bears the rainbow flag and has buff nude pho-

tos on the walls. Bring your laptop to make use of their Wi-Fi hookup.

✳ Entertainment
Fine or casual dining, shopping, art galleries, and all sorts of entertainment from dancing to movies can be found along the **Las Olas Riverfront** (954-522-6556; www.riverfrontfl.com), 300 SW First Ave, Fort Lauderdale. The Sunday Jazz Brunch is held the first Sunday each month. To get there, follow Broward Blvd to Brickell Ave (SW First Ave) and turn right (south). A parking garage is on SW First Ave, and valet parking is available as well.

DINNER SHOWS Mai-Kai Polynesian Restaurant and Dinner Show (see *Dining Out*), Fort Lauderdale, authentically re-creates a Polynesian village, complete with tiki torches, thatch roof, and wooden plank entrance.

JAXSON'S KITCHEN SINK SUNDAE
Kathy Wolf

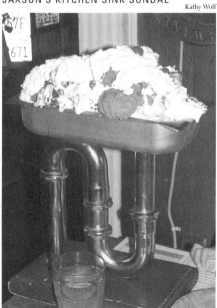

Fort Lauderdale

See a show at the **Broward Center for the Performing Arts** (954-462-0222; www.browardcenter.org), 201 SW Fifth Ave. Overlooking the New River and Riverwalk Arts District, the state-of-the-art complex showcases Broadway productions and the **Florida Grand Opera** (954-728-9700; www.fgo.org).

All the productions at the **Fort Lauderdale Children's Theatre** (954-763-6882; www.flct.org), 640 N Andrews Ave, are performed by children ranging in age from 6 to 18, and the technicians and backstage crew are also younger than 18. Come see what these talented youngsters can do at shows such as *Aladdin's Lamp* and *Grease*. Drama classes and camps are also available. Adults $15, children under 12 $12.

Socially relevant and thought-provoking theater is presented at the **Inside Out Theatre Company** at the **Museum of Art Fort Lauderdale** (see *Museums*). Tickets $30, with discounts for students and museum members.

Hollywood

The Art & Culture Center of Hollywood (see *Art Galleries*), in the heart of downtown Hollywood, has professional dance and theatrical performances, gallery exhibitions, and classes for children and adults. The Art & Culture Center also manages the programs at **The Hollywood Central Performing Arts Center** (954-924-8175; www.artandculture center.org), 1770 Monroe St, where dance performances are presented. Adults $25, seniors $23, members and students $20.

✳ Selective Shopping
ANTIQUES AND COLLECTIBLES

Fort Lauderdale

Great vintage, antique, and consignment furniture and accessories can be found at **Beachcomber Consignments** (954-630-0911), 3042 N Federal Hwy; **Decades Design Group** (954-564-0454), N Federal Hwy; and **June Sharp Antiques and New Trends** (954-565-8165), 3000 N Federal Hwy.

Flagler Antiques (954-463-0994; www.flaglerantiques.com), 720 N Flagler Dr, specializes in art nouveau and art deco French antiques.

For the best in midcentury and atomic modern, check out **Space Modern** (954-564-6100), 2335 NE 26th St, or **Art Modern** (954-567-9502), 2673 N Federal Hwy (which has a second location in trendy Wilton Manors).

Wilton Manors

You'll find lots of fun and funky items at **50's, 60's, 70's Living** (954-565-5316), 2207 Wilton Dr; **Modern Rage** (954-328-6834), 2205 N Dixie Hwy; and **Nostagia Modern** (954-537-5533), 2097 Wilton Dr.

For those looking for country decor, make sure to stop into nearby **Shabby Cottage Chic** (954-564-2740), 2415 N Dixie Hwy.

BOUTIQUES AND SPECIALTY SHOPS

Fort Lauderdale

❀ Open since 1999, **The Bone Appetite Bakery** (954-565-3343; www.azboneappetit.com), 3045 N Federal Hwy, offers healthy treats for both dogs and cats. Bring your pets along so they can pick out their own treats, or have a gift basket made up to bring home. Pet-related gifts are also available.

Groovy and funky things can be found at **Jezebel** (954-761-7881; www.no newstuff.com), 1980 E Sunrise Blvd, which also offers excellent vintage clothing.

Along **Las Olas Blvd** (www.lasolas boulevard.com) you'll want to stop by several shops. In 1917 the charming area was just a dirt road that brought visitors to the famous Fort Lauderdale Beach. Now it is lined with quaint boutiques, art galleries, bistros, and cafés. Some of my favorites are **Joe Picasso's Interactive Studio & Cafe** (954-462-2551), 888 E Las Olas Blvd, where you can create your own mosaic or throw your own pot on the potter's wheel. At **Bijou and Color** (954-600-7349), 701-B E Las Olas Blvd, you can select one of their signature pieces of jewelry crafted from natural gemstones found all over the world, or design one yourself with the assistance of their talented in-house design team. **Needlepoint Originals** (954-463-1955), 702 E Las Olas Blvd, features hand-painted needlepoint canvases designed by the very talented Joan Bancel, along with adaptations inspired by the works of modern masters. **Atlantic Yard** (954-779-1191), 2424 E Las Olas Blvd, has unique and unusual gardening goods and stylish teak furniture. Romantic decorative items for your table, along with fine gifts and antiques, can be found at **Casa Chameleon** (954-763-2543), 619 E Las Olas Blvd. **Call of Africa** (954-767-9714), 807 E Las Olas Blvd, features original art by premier nature artists, such as my personal favorites, painters John Seerey-Lester, Claire Naylor, and Kim Donaldson, and master bronze sculptor Loet Vanderveen.

Sometimes you find the unexpected in unusual places—that's the fun in exploring. While having a geological survey of England framed, I found such a place at **Outrageous Framing** (954-537-9320), 3020 N Federal Hwy. The small gallery is one of the best in the area for quality custom picture framing, including museum-quality work. While framing is their forte, this shop is also an excellent place for unique gifts and accessories. Check out the showcase with exquisite handmade purses and hair accessories fashioned by local artisans.

Step inside **Special Editions** (954-561-0423), 3000 N Federal Hwy, and experience a unique gift shop filled with exquisite gifts and elegant decor for the home. This is where you'll find just the right gift or home accessory not found in malls or department stores. I love my new candlesticks, by Two's Company, with a little frog covered in Austrian crystals looking up toward an enameled turquoise tulip. Similar items sold here are usually available only to professional decorators and impossible to find anywhere else. The store also carries an excellent line of Arthur Court.

Whole Foods Market (954-565-5655), 2000 N Federal Hwy, is the place to go for all your natural grocery needs. The full hot and cold salad bar, juice bar, and café make this a great place for lunch or a quick and easy dinner. Two other stores are located inland: 810 University Dr, Coral Springs (954-753-8000), and 7720 Peters Rd, Plantation (954-236-0600).

Hollywood

Intricate masks, musical instruments, and large pieces of hand-carved furniture from the Far East take center stage at **Chantik Imports** (954-920-6009), 1911 Hollywood Blvd.

Spend a day in downtown Hollywood browsing the many shops in the **Downtown Hollywood Art and Design District** (www.downtown hollywood.com), encompassing the blocks from 20th Ave to Young Circle on Hollywood Blvd and Harrison St, where the streets are packed with boutiques, galleries, bistros, and sideway cafés.

While my daughter was pregnant with my new grandson, I was constantly searching for attractive maternity wear so she wouldn't have to wear the clownlike outfits that were my only options back when I was carrying her. My search was over when I met Velicia Hill, former runway model and fashionista. One of the nicest and classiest women I know, Ms. Hill owns **Hollywood Mama** (954-929-8886), 2037 Tyler St, designing a great deal of her hip and happening inventory. From trendy T-shirts to elegant evening dresses, you'll be sure to find a unique and glamorous wardrobe to celebrate the diva in you.

With art directly imported from Africa, **Indaba Gallery** (954-920-2029; www.indaba.com), 2029 Harrison St, offers a unique selection of stone and wood sculptures, handwoven baskets and beadwork, and beautiful batiks. Open daily.

Step into the mystic at **The Jeweled Castle** (954-920-2424), 1920 Hollywood Blvd, an otherworldly realm of crystals, gargoyles, Egyptian art, New Age books and music, and an on-site tarot reader. Open daily.

🐾 If your little one is a pint-size canine, then head over to **Teacups Puppies & Boutique** (954-985-8848), 3180 Stirling Rd, which specializes in canine couture and luxury items for your teeny-weenie pooch. Here you'll find designer dog carriers, bows and collars studded with Swarovski crystals, and sumptuous dog beds.

If you love rummaging through books like I do, don't miss **Trader John's Book & Record Exchange** (954-922-2466), 1907 Hollywood Blvd, a densely packed bookstore selling used titles covering every subject you can think of; antiquarian books area sold as well. Open daily 10–10.

Oakland Park

🐾 If your dog is really your child, take him over to **Central Bark Doggy Day Care and Boutique** (954-568-DOGS; www.centralbarkusa.com), 3699 N Dixie Hwy, where your canine is treated like one of the family. For only $23 you can drop off your pooch for an entire day, so you can enjoy local attractions or do some shopping. For an extra fee the Doggie Salon will have your best friend groomed and gorgeous upon your return. This haven for dogs also offers doggie birthday parties! Make sure to check out their extensive boutique shop. Updated shots and behavior assessment required. The advance application can be downloaded from the Internet.

MALLS AND OUTLETS The **Festival Marketplace** (954-979-4555; www .festivalfleamarket.com), 2900 W Sample Rd, Pompano, is a welcome retreat from the South Florida heat. The indoor, air-conditioned flea market is home to more than six hundred vendors that feature new merchandise at reduced prices. Open daily. Valet parking available.

FARMER'S MARKETS For more than 70 years, **Mack's Groves** (1-800-327-3525; www.macksgroves.com), 1180 N Federal Hwy, Pompano Beach, has been a local favorite for Florida-grown naval oranges, pink seedless grapefruit, tangerines, honey bells, and even beefsteak tomatoes. In 1954 Ed and Frankie Vrana purchased the roadside business, and rather than change the name, they decided to keep Mack's Groves in honor of Mr. Mack, who had already operated the successful business for 20 years. And you don't mess with success! Now run by the fourth generation of Vranas, the business still offers fresh Indian River fruits and gift baskets with fruit, nuts, jams, and candy. Shipping is available within the United States and to most areas of Europe.

SPORTS CENTERS

Dania

Outdoors enthusiasts should head to **Outdoor World Bass Pro Shops** (954-929-7710; www.basspro.com), 200 Gulf Stream Way, where they'll find fishing, boating, and camping supplies in a 160,000-square-foot showroom. Make sure to check out the International Game Fish Association (IGFA) Fishing Hall of Fame & Museum next door (see *Museums*).

Deerfield Beach

Surf's up at **Island Water Sports Surf Superstore** (954-427-4929 or 1-800-873-0375; www.islandwatersports .com), 1985 NE Second St, where you can get all you need in surf or skate products. Free surf lessons are given every Sat morning at the Deerfield Beach Pier. All equipment is provided; just bring your towel. Call the store to sign up. Open 9–8 Mon–Sat and 9–6 Sun. Check out the surf on

the web cam or call the Surf Report line at 954-421-4102.

Fort Lauderdale

Head to **Peter Glenn** (www.peter glenn.com) for fine sporting attire, wake boards, kayaks, and camping gear. But don't be surprised to see lots of ski wear and mountaineering equipment: South Florida has one of the largest ski clubs in the nation. Since 1958 the Vermont-based store has offered excellence in outdoors wear and equipment. There are two Fort Lauderdale locations: 2901 W Oakland Park Blvd (954-484-3606) and 1771 E Sunrise Blvd (954-467-7872).

✳ Special Events

Second and Fourth Friday of the month: **Broadwalk Friday Fest** (954-924-2980), Hollywood Beach. Listen to live jazz along Hollywood's signature 2½-mile "Broadwalk" from 7 to 10 PM.

January: The **Country Chili Cookoff** (954-764-7642), held at C. B. Smith Park, Pembroke Pines, features country music with celebrity singers along with a competitive chili cook-off.

The **Deerfield Beach Festival of the Arts** (954-480-4433), NE Second Street and Pioneer Park, Deerfield Beach, has been going strong for nearly three decades and features more than one hundred juried artists.

One of the top art festivals in the nation, the **Las Olas Art Fair** (954-472-3755), Fort Lauderdale, features the best in art, music, and food.

February: The best jazz acts in the country converge at the **Annual Riverwalk Blues & Music Festival** (954-523-1004), Riverwalk Park, downtown Fort Lauderdale.

More than three hundred tribes celebrate American Indian culture at the **Annual Seminole Tribal Fair** (954-797-5551), One Seminole Way, Hollywood, at the Seminole Hard Rock Hotel & Casino. The cultural event has been running for more than 35 years.

All ye lords and ladies head over to the **Florida Renaissance Festival** (954-776-1642) for jousting knights, fanciful fairies, and maids spreading merriment. Located at Quiet Waters Park, Deerfield Beach, for six weekends from February to mid-March.

March: **Las Olas Art Fair II** (954-472-3755), Fort Lauderdale. A second dose of the January show, where you'll find national and local artists, such as the wildlife color photography of South Florida native Mark J. Thomas (www.blueiceberg.com).

April: ▼ The **Florida Gay Rodeo Association's (FGRA) Inaugural Sunshine Stampede** (954-680-3555), Bergeron Rodeo Grounds, 4271 Davie Rd, Davie, hosts the first ever IGRA-sanctioned rodeo in Florida.

May: Continuous live Cajun zydeco music, creole food, and lots of crawfish can be found at the **Cajun Zydeco Festival** (954-771-7117), Quiet Waters Park, 401 S Powerline Rd, Deerfield Beach.

The annual **Fort Lauderdale International Boat Show** (954-764-7642) is always a busy event. The largest boat show in the world covers six sites around Fort Lauderdale, with more than 1,600 vessels and 60 super yachts.

November: Pompano Park Racing in Pompano Beach is home to the annual **Broward County Fair** (954-922-2224), where you'll find lots of midway rides and exhibits.

December: You have to see the **Fort Lauderdale Winterfest Boat Parade** (954-767-0686) at least once in your lifetime. The quality event is often televised, but seeing it in person is a unique and unforgettable experience. The boat parade travels from the Port Everglades to Lake Santa Barbara, and many hotels offer packages so you can view the show from your room.

INLAND:
WESTERN BROWARD COUNTY

The western reaches of Broward County remained virtually untouched until the 1950s and '60s, with **Sunrise** and **Davie** as the first to be incorporated. **Plantation** was originally developed with 1-acre "long lots" where produce and fruit trees could be grown to support the rapidly expanding beachside areas. Then, several family-oriented communities, such as **Coral Springs** and **Weston,** stretched west to the very edge of the Everglades as developers created "planned neighborhoods." The expansion continued as recently as the 1990s, when environmental efforts prevented any further expansion.

GUIDANCE For more information on the area, contact the **Greater Fort Lauderdale Convention and Visitors Bureau** (954-765-4466 or 1-800-22-SUNNY; www.sunny.org), 100 E Broward Blvd, Suite 200, Fort Lauderdale 33301.

GETTING THERE *By car:* **Florida's Turnpike** runs north and south, more toward the center of the county, and is good to access the western regions. Take the **Sawgrass Expressway** exit 10 for faster access to western cities such as Coral Springs, Sunrise, Plantation, Davie, and Everglades's attractions.

By air: **Fort Lauderdale–Hollywood International Airport** (954-359-6100; www.fll.net) has easy access to I-95, US 595, I-75, and FL 1, as well as Port Everglades.

By rail: **AMTRAK** (1-800-872-7245; www.amtrak.com) provides regularly scheduled service to Fort Lauderdale.

GETTING AROUND *By car:* **University Drive** is the main north–south route. Use the COSBY crossroads acronym (see *Getting Around* in the *Oceanside: Eastern Broward County* chapter). FL 869, more commonly known as the **Sawgrass Expressway,** wraps around the western cities from Coral Springs to Sunrise. (Note that Broward Blvd does not extend to the Sawgrass Expressway.)

PARKING Public parking in the cities in the western part of the county are readily available at no cost.

PUBLIC REST ROOMS Public rest rooms are limited to malls and some city parks.

VALET Most restaurants and attractions in the county's western cities are self-parking. Some malls and the occasional restaurant or hotels may offer valet services during their busy time or for special events.

MEDICAL EMERGENCIES Area hospitals include **Coral Springs Medical Center** (954-344-3000; www.browardhealth.org), 3000 Coral Hills Dr, Coral Springs; **Northwest Medical Center** (954-974-0400; www.northwestmed.com), 2801 N FL 7, Margate; and **Westside Regional Medical Center** (954-473-6600; www.westsideregional.com), 8201 W Broward Blvd, Plantation.

✳ To See

ART GALLERIES The Coral Springs Center for the Arts (954-344-5999), 2855 Coral Springs Dr, Coral Springs, is a performing-arts facility and a museum of fine art. Private meeting rooms and catering are available.

AUTOMOBILES Local car clubs converge at a local shopping mall parking lot for one of the largest collection of vintage hot rods and late-model suped-up cars and tricked-out rides each Friday night at the **Tower Shops** on University Dr, Davie, just south of US 595.

HOCKEY The Florida Panthers take to the ice at the **BankAtlantic Center** (954-835-8000; www.bankatlanticcenter.com), 2555 Panther Pkwy, Sunrise, which is also a main venue for concerts and family shows.

MUSEUMS

Davie
✧ The hands-on **Young at Art Children's Museum** (954-424-0085; www.youngatartmuseum.org), 11584 FL 84, provides a variety of activities to expand your child's mind and release some of that expressive energy. At Global Village you'll dig for artifacts, visit an African village, and learn about origami. In Earth-Works you'll climb aboard a giant recycling truck and learn about resource management. Kenny's Closet takes you through the psychedelic world of international artist Kenny Scharf, where works of art are lit by black lights and your child can create her own pop art masterpiece. A special gallery, Playspace for Toddlers allows the little ones to explore movement and hands-on activities specific to their age level. Open year-round 10–5 Mon–Sat, noon–5 Sun. Closed Thanksgiving, Christmas, and New Year's Day. Adults and children $6, children under 2 free.

Plantation
✧ The hands-on, interactive **My Jewish Discovery Place Children's Museum** (954-792-6700; www.sorefjcc.org), 6501 W Sunrise Blvd, is full of Jewish culture and history. You'll discover how to cook a festive holiday meal in Home for the Holidays; blast off in Discovery Station, complete with NASA jumpsuits; dress up as a doctor or ambulance driver at Hadassah Hospital; and write your wishes

and prayers on the stone replica of Jerusalem's Western Wall. Open 10–5 Tue–Fri, noon–4 Sun. Fee.

RODEO Since 1986 the **Five Star Davie Rodeo** (954-384-7075; www.fivestar rodeo.com), Davie Arena, Davie, has featured championship barrel racing, bronc riding, team roping, steer wrestling, and bull riding.

STARGAZING Learn about the sky at **Buehler Planetarium and Observatory** (954-201-6681; www.iloveplanets.com), Broward Community College, Central Campus, 3501 SW Davie Rd, Davie. The state-of-the-art planetarium provides interesting shows about legends of Native Americans, New World explorers, galaxies, Egyptian lore, and and even a solar experience through a magic rocket. The observatory houses 20 telescopes for celestial viewing, including the 16-inch LX200 telescope. Call for schedule. Fee.

✳ To Do

ECOTOURS For a quick eco trip, the **Everglades Holiday Park** (954-434-8111 or 1-800-226-2244; www.evergladesholidaypark.com), 21940 Griffin Rd, Fort Lauderdale, offers one-hour guided tours on airboats, or rent a fishing boat and explore a bit of the Everglades on your own. Adults $20, kids $10; includes one-hour airboat ride followed by a 15-minute alligator show. Fishing guides and gear are also available. A Florida fishing license (required) can be bought on-site. Check the web site for coupons.

Sawgrass Recreation Park (954-389-0202 or 1-800-457-0788; www.everglades tours.com), US 27 (2 miles north of I-75), Fort Lauderdale, features an 18th-century Indian village, alligator wrestling, birds of prey, and airboat rides. Open daily, with guided airboat tours 9–5. Adults $20, children $11.

FAMILY ACTIVITIES 🖉 "Kids can do what they wanndo do" at **Wannado City** (954-838-7100 or 1-888-926-6236; www.wannadocity.com), Sawgrass Mills Mall, 12801 W Sunrise Blvd, Sunrise. The indoor theme park takes children's museums and super-sizes them with America's first indoor role-playing venue, which allows kids to participate in tons of different careers. Open daily. Adults $16, children $35, children under 3 free.

SKATE AND BIKE PARKS 🖉 The 333.3-meter concrete track at the **Brian Piccolo Velodrome** (954-437-2600 or 954-437-2626; www.broward.org/parks), 9501 Sheridan St, Cooper City, has a maximum banking of 28 degrees. It is open for public use for $3–4, depending on time of day. Bikes are available for rent for an additional fee. The free criterium course adjacent to the velodrome is used by cyclists and in-line speed skaters.

TRAIL RIDING **The Bar-B-Ranch** (954-424-1060; www.bar-b-ranch.com), 1300 Peaceful Ridge Rd, Davie, is Broward County's oldest and largest public riding stable. Equestrians of all ages and experience levels can ride ponies or horses on scenic trails. Lessons are also available. Open 9–5 daily.

WATER PARK Splash around at **Paradise Cove** (954-357-8115), C. B. Smith Park, 900 N Flamingo Rd, Pembroke Pines, where you'll find two interactive water playgrounds, water slides, and a tube ride. Open daily 9:30–5 May–Labor Day; weekends only Apr, Sept, and Oct. Admission $7.

❋ Green Space

BOTANICAL GARDENS The 60-acre **Flamingo Gardens & Wray Botanical Collection** (954-473-2955; www.flamingogardens.org), 3750 S Flamingo Rd, Fort Lauderdale, is a unique wildlife sanctuary. Take a tour through a citrus grove and a two-hundred-year-old hammock, check out the bird of prey center and free flight aviary, and see alligators and pink flamingos. Open 9:30–5 daily; closed Mon during the hot summer months. Adults $15, children 4–11 $8, children under 4 free. Discounts available for seniors, students, AAA members, and armed service personnel.

DOG PARKS

Coral Springs
🐾 Coral Springs was recently listed as one of the top 10 cities to be dog. I don't even own a dog, but I like to go with my friends to **Dr. Paul's Pet Care Center Dog Park** (954-752-1879; www.toppetcare.com), 2915 Sportsplex, just to watch the merriment. The spacious 2-acre dog park allows enough room for all breeds to run, play, and socialize unleashed. Agility equipment, a wading pool, and a track that wraps around the perimeter of the park offer even more opportunities for exercise. Sit on a bench and observe your pooch from under a canopy of trees or at one of the shaded picnic tables. A separate play area for small dogs and puppies ensures a safe area where the little ones won't get run over by the larger breeds. The nonprofit organization holds the annual Dog Day Run & Kids Dog Show along with a Gala Auction each March (see *Special Events*).

Plantation
🐾 **Happy Tails Dog Park** (954-452-2510), 6600 SW 16th St at Seminole Park, is the place for the annual Doggie-Palooza Dog Expo (see *Special Events*). Dog-related events, vendors, and demonstrations by Police K-9s. Dogs of all sizes are welcome to mix and mingle, but they must have current inoculations.

NATURE CENTERS Go bird-watching and look for wildlife as you walk along boardwalks at **Fern Forest Nature Center** (954-970-0150), 201 Lyons Rd S, Coconut Creek. Broward County Parks and Recreation (954-357-8100; www .broward.org/parks) offers several natural and family recreational areas through-out the county.

PARKS

Davie
&. ✔ At **Tree Tops Park** (954-370-3750), 3900 SW 100th Ave, off Nob Hill Rd, you can rent a canoe and paddle the ponds, fish in the ponds and wetlands, have a picnic, or take the kids to the playground and Safety Town. It's a great site for

wildlife watching, with several miles of paved and unpaved paths winding through beautiful live oak hammocks, along open flatwoods ponds, and out into adjoining Pine Island Ridge Natural Area, an archeological site where the Miccosukee had a large village prior to the Second Seminole War. Open 8–sunset daily. Fee on weekends and holidays.

PURPLE GALLINULE

Kathy Wolf

Plantation

🦮 A former University of Florida agricultural experimentation farm, **Plantation Heritage Park** (954-791-1025), 1100 S Fig Tree Ln, offers picnicking under the trees, fishing in its ponds, a large playground, and the Anne Kolb Memorial Trail, a ¼-mile loop through representative native plant communities. Open 8–7:30 daily. Fee on weekends and holidays.

Sunrise

🦮 🐾 Covering more than 650 acres along the edge of the Everglades, **Markham Park** (954-389-2000), 16001 W FL 84, offers a variety of pursuits, including a mountain bike trail, model airplane field, biking and jogging path, swimming pool complex with misters, target range, picnic shelters, rental canoes to ply the lakes, and nature and equestrian trails. The park also has an 86-site campground for RVs and tents, and a 3-acre **dog park** for your favorite canine. Open daily; hours vary by season. Free.

PRESERVES

Coral Springs

♿ 🦮 A wonderland of oversize ferns surrounds you on the ½-mile boardwalk through **Tall Cypress Natural Area** (954-357-8100), Turtle Run Blvd, north of Sample Rd. Birders, bring binoculars to watch for downy woodpeckers.

Parkland

♿ 🦮 The 20-acre **Doris Davis Foreman Wilderness Area** (954-357-8100), Parkside Dr, south of Loxahatchee Rd, has a beautiful ½-mile nature trail through a tropical forest and cypress swamp, with a long boardwalk a major feature. Open 8–6 daily. Free.

FERN FOREST NATURE CENTER

Sandra Friend

EVERGLADES AIRBOATS

Kathy Wolf

Tamarac

 ✦ 🐾 Tiny **Woodmont Natural Area** (954-357-8100), NW 80th Ave, ³⁄₁₀ mile north of McNab Rd, is a 22-acre patch of pine flatwoods, the last undeveloped land in Tamarac, with a ⁴⁄₁₀-mile walking trail great for birding. Open 8–6 daily. Free.

WILD PLACES Visible from the Sawgrass Expressway and I-75 North, the **Everglades Conservation Area** consists of natural sawgrass marshes broken into three impoundment areas that provide water for the people of Broward and Miami-Dade Counties. Public access is off ramps along the Sawgrass Expressway and through the Francis S. Taylor WMA, with boat launches off I-75, and public use is primarily for fishing along canal banks or from small craft.

✷ Lodging

HOTELS, MOTELS, AND RESORTS

Plantation 33322

🐾 **Plantation Holiday Inn Express Hotel & Suites** (954-472-5600; www .fll-plantation.holiday-inn.com), 1701 N University Dr, is ideally situated for the business traveler, but it makes for a great central location for vacation travelers as well. Deluxe accommodations or suites have complimentary Wi-Fi hookups, on-site guest laundry, and a fitness center—those are just a few of the perks. A complimentary shuttle service is provided to local attractions and shopping areas. This hotel is especially friendly to pets, with complimentary pet treats, a welcome letter from the General Manager's dog or cat, and information on local pet-friendly restaurants, specialty shops, dog parks, and boarding. Litter boxes, pet pads, and walking services can also be arranged. And when the maid comes to turn down your bed, a small treat will be left for your pet as well. Rooms $109–189; suites about $40 more.

✷ Where to Eat

EATING OUT

Coral Springs

🐾 Well-behaved dogs are welcome outside at **Gold Coast Grill** (954-255-3474; www.goldcoastseafoodgrill.com), 2752 N University Dr, in The Walk. Seafood is their specialty, with dishes such as blue cheese–pecan crusted swordfish ($18), Dijon tomato horseradish crusted salmon ($18), and orange-honey glazed Chilean sea bass ($22). For landlubbers there's the 8-ounce center cut filet ($19), mustard crumb stuffed chicken ($17), and Missouri smoked baby back ribs ($18). Lunch is served Mon–Fri; dinner nightly.

Since 1986, **Larry's Ice Cream Parlor** (954-752-0497), 749 University Dr, has been the local favorite of middle school kids and their parents. We moved to South Florida in 1987, and it took no time at all for my kids to find it, often caught sneaking across the street to spend their allowance.

Lunch sandwiches are available, but let's face it—we are all going there for the ice cream. Even though larger stores have been built up around it, the friendly-family shop is still the same after all these years. Shakes, malts, sundaes, and such are under $5. Open daily until 6 PM.

Plantation

I don't usually mention major chain establishments, but the unique grouping of several coffee shops within walking distance to each other makes this destination worth checking out, especially if you have varied coffee aficionados in your family, as I do. The **Viscaya Plaza,** at the corner of Nob Hill Rd and Cleary Blvd, was a regular stop for me during my daily commute. After parking in the middle of the lot, my son sleepily sauntered over to **Dunkin' Donuts** (954-452-0391), while my daughter scurried to **Einstein Brothers** (954-423-3030). I headed to **Starbucks** (954-382-0559), which, in my opinion, has the best quad venti cappuccino, vital to keeping my brain functioning when working on tight deadlines.

Sunrise

Lester's Diner (954-525-5641), 1399 NW 136th Ave, is your best bet for a great meal near the Sawgrass Mills Mall. Open 24/7, they offer an extensive menu at reasonable prices that will make everyone happy, with breakfast served all day. A huge selection of pies, cakes, and pastries are baked on the premises daily and are displayed in a case just as you walk in the door. Yum! There is another location east toward the airport (see *Oceanside: Eastern Broward County*).

Poppy's Pizza South (954-474-0671), 8373 W Sunrise Blvd, is known more for their take-out pizza than anything else. For more than 25 years, the family-owned business has offered local patrons the best pizza ($6–15) and Italian dinners ($6–15) I've found anywhere in the county. The owner was even consulted on a pizza shop in Galway, Ireland! I don't know what they put in their meatballs, but they keep me coming back time and time again. Their spaghetti sauce is like my in-laws', and the fresh, hot garlic rolls are smothered with fresh garlic. Open daily for lunch and dinner.

You won't find a better sandwich shop anywhere in Sunrise than **Sharpie's Hoagies** (954-845-0999), 13101 W Sunrise Blvd, in the Sawgrass Commons Shopping Plaza. Sandwiches and salad platters are made fast to your specifications in this sports-themed eatery. Locals line up during the lunch hour, yet they still manage to get everyone back to work on time. The 8-inch cold or hot hoagie ($5–6) is more than enough to satisfy even a linebacker's appetite. You'll want to take half of the 12-inch hoagie ($7–9) home for dinner. Salads ($4–6) and deli sandwiches ($5–6) are great for light eaters. Open daily for lunch until early dinner.

Tamarac

I've been going to the **Beverly Hills Café** (954-722-8211), 7041 W Commercial Blvd, since 1987 and always seem to return at least twice a month. My favorite bartender, Dave, always has a seat ready for me whether I take out or eat in. The menu is so large and varied that I still haven't sampled everything. My favorite is the Beverly Hills Cobb Salad ($11), which is so large I have enough left over for lunch the next day, and the Signature Toll House Pie ($5), rich with chocolate and topped with vanilla ice cream. For something different try the Fruit Salad Fantasy ($7), with an assortment of fresh fruit, cottage cheese, and yogurt honey dressing, just to get the pumpkin bread. All entrées and salads served with amazing dinner rolls that are slightly crunchy on the outside and soft and warm on the inside. This location is a favorite of the senior crowd, who come for the specials that include entrée, beverage, and house dessert all for under $12. The quieter section is the front room next to the bar, where you can sit in a booth and look out the windows at passing traffic.

✳ Entertainment

FINE ARTS

Coral Springs

The **Coral Springs Center for the Arts** (954-344-5999; www.coral springscenterforthearts.com), 855 Coral Springs Dr, features several national touring theatrical and musical performances for the western county's residents, along with an excellent fine-arts museum.

Plantation

Dedicated to contemporary and original works, the **Mosaic Theatre** (954-577-8243; www.mosaictheatre.com), 12200 W Broward Blvd, is a welcome addition to the western county's cultural experience. Professional shows Thu–Sat evenings, with matinees on the weekends. Adults $27, seniors $21, students $15.

✳ Selective Shopping

ANTIQUES AND COLLECTIBLES

Davie

J.C.'s Collectibles (954-648-5611), 6870 Stirling Rd (enter from inside the Birdcage Bar & Restaurant) and 6761 W Sunrise Blvd, Bay 2, Planta-

tion. While the shop focuses mostly on NASCAR collectibles, owner John Marino was instrumental in locating a vintage collection of Matchbox Superfast cars from the early 1980s so I could replace the set my son had when he was a little boy.

BOUTIQUES AND SPECIALTY SHOPS

Coral Springs

Accent on Country (954-755-3939), 11530 W Sample Rd, a cute country-themed store, has a huge display of Dept 56 villages. The ever-changing displays and lovely ladies have kept me coming back for nearly two decades. If you can't find it here, you don't need it. Watch for guest appearances of collectibles artisans, such as Jim Shore.

A Nose for Clothes (954-753-0202), 1315 University Dr, sets the trend with the newest, latest, and greatest fashion finds. The owner travels the world (and the New York garment district) looking for unique contemporary designer fashions that are fun, chic, and wearable for women of all ages. Boutique wear is in both the original designer look as well as the less-expensive version. You'll find items here that you won't find anywhere else. I still have a zebra scarf that I purchased here years ago, and I recently bought a hot pink purse for a mere $55 at the Plantation store (835 N Nob Hill Rd; 954-382-1080).

If you long for turquoise, terra-cotta, and the other earthy colors of the Southwest and Mexico, then head into **Southwest Sensations** (954-341-8111; www.southwestsensations .com), 7467 W Sample Rd. This piece of heaven stands out with an extensive array of pottery, accessories, and furniture. Owner Ben Fritti or any of his staff will be happy to assist you while you browse through the well-laid-out studio.

Pembroke Pines
If you are ready to furnish that vacation home, stop by **North Carolina Furniture Showrooms** (954-453-4750), 10151 Pines Blvd, and speak with Marty or Jerry. Marty has single-handedly helped me furnish my entire house at prices that no one else in South Florida could touch. He saved me several hundred dollars on a fabulous credenza that I had spotted at another store, got me a replacement piece that I had purchased from a manufacturer in Maine decades ago, and will definitely be my source for my new grandson's bedroom suite. If they don't have it on the floor, ask to see the catalogs. They carry most of the major brands and some not so well known, but with great quality and value.

Plantation
Footprints (954-475-1520), 252 S University Dr (across from the Broward Mall). As a huge Brighton fan since the early 1990s, I love stopping in here just to see what's new. The savvy ladies will be more than happy to show you the vast collection of Brighton purses, shoes, jewelry, and other Brighton accessories. Watch for seasonal sales.

🐾 Take Fluffy or Spot to **Three Dog Bakery** (954-424-3223), 236 S University Dr (across from the Broward Mall), for the world's best all-natural dog treats. The large pastry case displays more than one hundred fresh baked treats. The shop also has a neat collection of doggie boutique wear. Leashed dogs are welcome. Open daily.

For a quick bite, organic produce, gourmet cheeses, natural groceries, or vitamins, **Whole Foods Market** (954-236-0600), 7720 Peters Rd, is

the place to go, with other locations in Coral Springs (810 University Dr; 954-753-8000) and Fort Lauderdale (2000 N Federal Hwy; 954-565-5655).

MALLS AND OUTLETS The king, queen, and kingdom of shopping is out west at the **Sawgrass Mills Mall** (954-846-2300; www.sawgrassmills mall.com), 12801 W Sunrise Blvd, Sunrise. The mile-long mall has more than three hundred name-brand stores, outlets, and restaurants. Open daily. The newest addition to the mall, the Colonnade, on the south side of the mall, offers high-end clothing and decor as well as trendy gourmet restaurants. In The Oasis, **Ron Jon Surf Shop** (954-846-1880; www.ronjons.com) is where you'll find a the latest in surf gear and apparel, along with a 1935 Rolls-Royce Phantom II Woodie.

✳ Special Events

January and February: **A Walk On The Wild Side At Flamingo Gardens** (954-473-2955), 3750 S Flamingo Rd, Davie, offers a behind-the-scenes tour of their bird- and animal-care area. See birds of prey and learn how to identify native birds. Adults $8, children 4–11 $6.

March: The annual **Coral Springs Dog Day Run & Kids Dog Show** (954-752-1879; www.toppetcare.com), Sportsplex Park, is held to raise funds for Dr. Paul's Pet Care Center Dog Park (see *Dog Parks*), along with other pet-related charities. The Gala Auction is always on the night before.

Doggie-Palooza Dog Expo (954-452-2510), Happy Tails Dog Park, 6600 SW 16th St, at Seminole Park. Dog contests, adoptions, vendors, and working dog demonstrations.

Miami Metro 7

THE GABLES, THE GROVE,
AND MIAMI CITYSIDE

SOUTH BEACH AND
MIAMI OCEANSIDE

SOUTH MIAMI–DADE:
FOOD AND WINE COUNTRY

Visit Florida

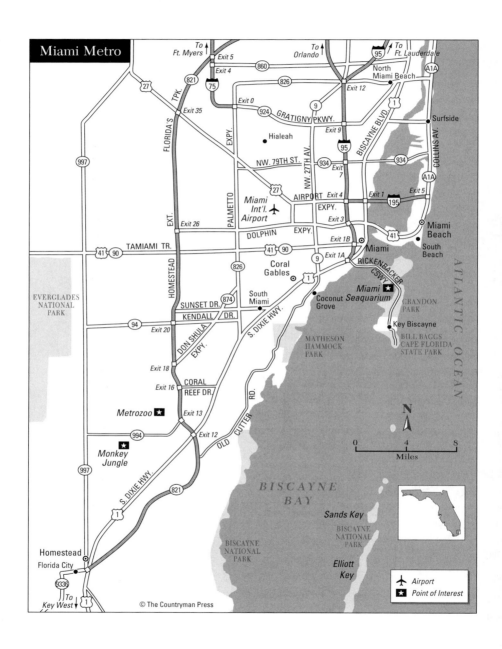

Miami Metro

MIAMI METRO

Miami was incorporated in 1896, with its first towns being Coconut Grove and Lemon City (now Overtown), and is thought to have been inhabited some 2000 years ago, based on the discovery of the Miami Circle (a Native American version of Stonehenge). The first known inhabitants, the Tequesta Indians, were visited in 1566 by Spaniards and were soon decimated by European diseases and conflict. By the 1800s, the first permanent settlers arrived, attracted to the region by government offers of 160 free acres to those who would homestead. As land became scarce, developers dredged canals to open up more land in the pristine Everglades. Soon swampland was converted to citrus groves, and the area south of Miami continues to produce a large selection of tropical fruits to this day. The post-boom era brought a new art deco style to the region, seen most prominently along the Miami beaches between 6th and 23rd Streets; the Art Deco Historic District, the region between Ocean and Alton Roads, was listed in 1979 on the National Register of Historic Places. Following World War II, Miami gave birth to the cruise ship industry, with more than a dozen gargantuan vessels lined up along "Cruise Ship Row" off downtown Miami. Its home port of call is "Cruise Capital of the World." Since the 1960s, thousands of Cuban immigrants have come to this area to escape Castro's Cuba, making today's Miami a bilingual community with trendy restaurants, boutiques, vivacious music, and historical and cultural centers.

PARROT AT PARROT JUNGLE ON WATSON ISLAND

Sandra Friend

THE GABLES, THE GROVE, AND MIAMI CITYSIDE

T he cityside of Miami is teeming with so much to do, you'll forget about the beautiful beaches. In Coral Gables, home to the University of Miami and formerly the National Hurricane Center, you'll enjoy the 1920s Mediterranean architecture of George Merrick found throughout the town. With the Biltmore Hotel as its centerpiece, the area is known for its affluent citizens, who create a rich cultural oasis of theaters and fine boutiques. In Coconut Grove (locally known as "the Grove") you can browse the many galleries in the thriving bohemian community or sit along a number of dining spots overlooking Biscayne Bay. Downtown Miami is home to the American Airlines Arena, where you can see the Miami Heat along with several featured concerts.

GUIDANCE The **Greater Miami Convention and Visitors Bureau** (305-539-3000; www.miamiandbeaches.com) is the main connection for tourist information. For a vacation guide call 1-888-76-MIAMI or 305-447-7777.

GETTING THERE *By air:* **Miami International Airport** (305-876-7000; www.miami-airport.com) is centrally located in the county. **Fort Lauderdale–Hollywood International Airport** (954-359-6100; www.fll.net) is also within easy access to the region.

By bus: **Greyhound** (1-800-231-2222; www.greyhound.com). Several locations will take you to the main areas of Miami-Dade County: **Miami North** (305-688-7277), 16000 NW 7th Ave; **Miami Central** (305-871-1810), 4111 NW 27th St; **Miami Downtown** (305-374-6160), 36 NE 10th St; and for the south end of the county, **Miami Cutler Ridge** (305-296-9072), 10801 Caribbean Blvd, at the American Service Station.

By rail: **AMTRAK** (1-800-872-7245; www.amtrak.com) provides regularly scheduled service to Miami. The **Miami Station** (305-835-1221) is at 8303 NW 37th Ave.

GETTING AROUND *By bus:* **Metrobus,** Miami-Dade Transit, Customer Services (305-770-3131; www.miamidade.gov/transit). With more than 300 routes covering Miami-Dade County, you can easily get to your destination. Bus 57 goes to

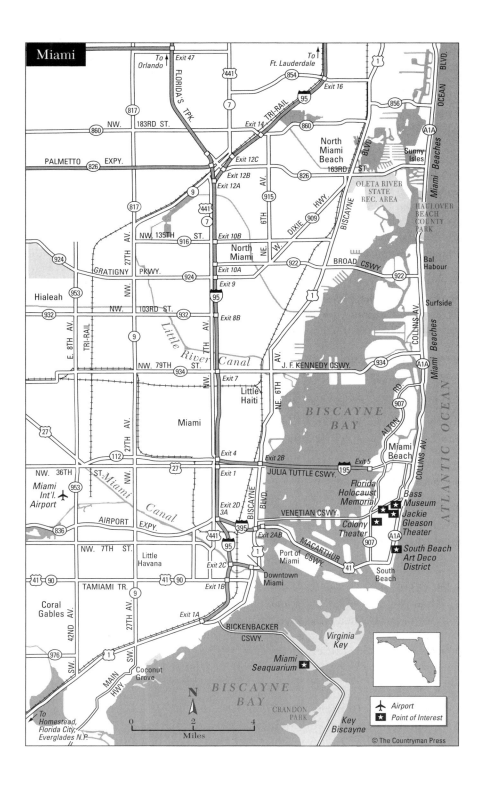

Miami International Airport and also connects with the Tri-Rail Station. You can pick up printed Metrobus route maps and schedules at the airport's information center in Concourse E. Bus 34, the Busway Flyer, will bring you south to Florida City and Homestead. You can also transfer from several routes to the Metrorail and Metromover (see *By rail*, below).

By trolley: The eco-sensitive hybrid-electric **Coral Gables Trolley** (305-460-5070; www.citybeautiful.net) takes you throughout the Gables. The trolley has two routes along Miracle Mile and Ponce de Leon Boulevard. The free service also has stops at the Venetian Pool and the Biltmore Hotel.

By rail: **Tri-Rail** (305-836-0986; www.tri-rail.com) is a convenient way to travel from Miami to West Palm Beach. Tickets are not sold on the train. You must purchase a ticket at the station on the day of use. The train runs in six sections, and tickets are purchased according to the number of sections. A ticket from West Palm Beach to Miami costs around $5.50. On weekends and holidays, the full fare for the entire system is a flat rate of $4. The Tri-Rail ticket allows you to transfer to Metrorail at no additional cost. The electric-powered **Metrorail** covers 22 miles of the city on an elevated track, from Kendall to Medley. Full fare: $1.50. The **Metromover,** an elevated people mover covering nearly 4½ miles of the Miami business district, including Brickell Avenue, is free to ride. Metrorail, Metrobus, and Metromover are part of Miami-Dade Transit, Customer Services (305-770-3131; www.miamidade.gov/transit).

PARKING Make sure to have some change on hand, as most districts have metered parking. Some parking areas have maximums, so check the meter for restrictions. Solar-powered Pay and Display (P&D) machines require payment at a central location, usually within four cars. These meters take not only coins and dollar bills but also VISA and MasterCard. Private and government parking lots and garages are conveniently located around town. Fees range from $1 to $1.25 per hour to flat rates of $4–15.

VALET You'll be hard-pressed to find a restaurant, hotel, or shopping district that doesn't offer valet services; sometimes you'll have no choice, as some establishments don't allow self-parking. You'll find most of the area's valet parking managed by private companies. All reputable establishments will have one that carries a liability policy. In most situations, however, you won't be able to add the valet parking fee to your hotel or dining bill. In South Florida it is customary to tip when you drop off your car, *and* when you pick it up. Most valets are happy with $1–2, but if you are driving a luxury vehicle or fancy sports car and want them to keep a close eye on it, expect to tip them $5–10. Inquire about valet policies when making reservations.

MEDICAL EMERGENCIES You'll find the best of the medical profession at several medical centers around the Miami metro area. For general emergencies, head to **Cedars Medical Center** (305-325-5511; www.cedarsmedicalcenter.com), 1400 NW 12th Ave, or to **Jackson Memorial Hospital** (305-585-1111; www.um-jmh.org), 1611 NW 12th Ave. **Bascom Palmer Eye Institute** (305-326-6000 or 1-800-329-7000; www.bascompalmer.org), 900 NW 17th St, is known the

world over for the best care in ocular diseases and surgery. At the north end of
Miami, seek out **North Shore Medical Center** (305-835-6000; www.north
shoremedical.com), 1100 NW 95th St, Miami, or **Parkway Regional Medical
Center** (305-651-1100; www.parkwaymedctr.com), 160 NW 170th St, N Miami
Beach, for general emergencies. **Mount Sinai Medical Center** (305-674-2121;
www.msmc.com), 4300 Alton Rd, specializes in cardiovascular and cancer services.
In South Miami–Dade you'll find **South Miami Hospital** (786-662-4000;
www.baptisthealth.net), 6200 SW 73rd St, just one of many hospitals in the Baptist Health network. The medical center located the farthest south is **Homestead Hospital** (786-243-8000; www.baptisthealth.net), 160 NW 13th St, and is
the only emergency center for 18 miles in all directions of the city. In late 2006,
a new Baptist Health facility will be located just east of Florida's Turnpike on the
north side of Campbell Drive at SW 312th St. For diver emergencies, the **Key
Largo Recompression Chamber** (911 if emergency, 1-800-NO-BENDS for
information) is located in Key Largo.

✳ To See

ARCHEOLOGICAL SITES While clearing a site for new development in 1998,
workers uncovered the ancient **Miami Circle,** 401 Brickell Ave. Archeologists
and the people of Miami Beach went to great lengths, which included heated
debate, to preserve the site. Still under excavation, the Circle is believed to be a
Tequesta Indian site dating back 1,800 to 2,000 years. Further research is being
conducted to assess similarities between Mayan sites and the Miami Circle. Con-
sisting of 24 holes cut into limestone bedrock, the Circle has been speculated to
be a central ceremonial site or possibly a celestial calendar. Located at the mouth
of the Miami River, the 38-foot-wide circle can be viewed only by private tour
(see *Tours*). Many artifacts found at the site, such as shell-tools, stone axe-heads,
and human teeth, are on display at the **Historical Museum of Southern Florida** (305-373-0011; www.historical-museum.org), 101 W Flagler St, Miami (see
Museums), where you'll also see a scaled-down replica of the Miami Circle.

ART GALLERIES

North Miami
With more than four hundred works in its permanent collection, the **Museum
of Contemporary Art (MOCA)** (305-893-6211), 770 NE 125th St, N Miami,
displays cutting-edge contemporary pieces in a wide variety of media. You'll see
pieces from abstract impressionist Louise Nevelson, photographic images from
Zoe Leonard, and works relating to music by visual artist Christian Marclay.
Open 11–5 Tue–Sat, noon–5 Sun, and 7–10 the last Friday evening of every
month. Adults $5, seniors and students with ID $3. Free for MOCA members,
North Miami residents, and children under 12.

The **MOCA at Goldman Warehouse** (305-893-6211; www.mocanomi.org), 404
NW 26th St, is a satellite branch of the Museum of Contemporary Art, exhibiting
emerging artists. Open 12–5 Thu–Sun. Admission $2 (applicable toward $5
admission to MOCA). Free for MOCA members, North Miami residents, and
children under 12.

Sandra Friend

BIRD SHOW AT PARROT JUNGLE ISLAND

ATTRACTIONS The new **Parrot Jungle Island** (305-400-7000; www
.parrotjungle.com), 111 Parrot Jungle Trail, Miami, is located on Watson Island, just off the MacArthur Causeway. It was previously located farther south, where Pinecrest Gardens now stands (see *South Miami–Dade: Food and Wine Country*). You'll find the same colorful macaws (there are thousands of them), but the park has other creatures as well. Marvel at Crocosauras, a 2,000-pound saltwater crocodile; Hercules, the Liger (part lion, part tiger); and Peanut Butter and Pumpkin Pie, twin female orangutans. Guests will enjoy the spectacular animal shows in the Parrot Bowl and Winged Wonder, or a relaxing walk through the Ichimura Miami Japan Garden and beautiful tropical landscape. Open daily 10–6. Adults $26, children 3–10 $21, under 3 free. Senior, military, and student courtesy discounts are a few dollars less. Parking $6 per vehicle.

HISTORIC SITES

Coconut Grove
The oldest home in Miami-Dade County, in its original location, is situated on the shore of Biscayne Bay at the **Barnacle State Historic Site** (305-448-9445; www.floridastate
parks.org), 3485 Main Hwy. Built in the 1800s as the home of one of Coconut Grove's prominent pioneers, Ralph Middleton Munroe, it is surrounded by a hardwood hammock, the last of its kind in the area. In the home you'll see unique architecture, sweeping verandas, and furnishings of the era. Open 9–4 Fri–Mon. Guided tours are offered at 10, 11:30, 1, and 2:30.

An incredible display of grandeur and one of the more beautiful pieces of architecture in South Florida is the **Vizcaya Museum and Gardens** (305-250-9133; www.vizcayamuseum
.org), 3251 S Miami Ave. It was built as a winter home (1916–1925) during

FORMAL GARDENS, VIZCAYA

Sandra Friend

the Gilded Age for James Deering, vice president of International Harvester and brother to Charles Deering (see Deering Estate in *South Miami–Dade: Food and Wine Country*). The home features 34 rooms, decorated with art and furnishings from the 15th to the 19th centuries, where several important documents have been signed, such as the first Free Trade Agreement between the United States and a South American country (Chile). Outside, exotic orchids can be seen in the David A. Klein Orchidarium, and fountains grace 10 tropically landscaped gardens. Open 9:30–4:30 daily. Adults $12, Miami-Dade residents $9, children 6–12 $5, under 6 free.

Coral Gables

Coral Gables Merrick House (305-460-5095; www.coralgables.com), 907 Coral Way (circa 1899–1907), is the boyhood home of George E. Merrick, founder of Coral Gables. The home features the Merrick family's art, furniture, and memorabilia of the 1920s. Guided tours are presented Wed and Sun at 1, 2, and 3. Adults $5, seniors and students $3, children 6–12 $1, under 6 free.

Miami

Built in 1825 and rebuilt in 1846, the **Cape Florida Lighthouse** at Bill Baggs Cape Florida State Park (see *Beaches*) is the oldest standing structure in Miami-Dade County. Park staff and volunteers offer free tours of the lighthouse at 10 AM and 1 PM Thu–Mon; show up a half hour before departure to reserve a space. It's a spiral climb of 109 steps to the top, with a bird's-eye view of downtown Miami and Biscayne Bay as your reward. The Light Keeper's Quarters are included on the tour.

Completed in 1925, the 255-foot **Freedom Tower** (305-375-1492), 600 Biscayne Blvd, was built as a memorial to Cuban immigrants and is often referred to as Miami's "Ellis Island." A striking centerpiece in downtown Miami, the Mediterranean Revival building houses a museum, with displays on the boat lifts of Cuban refugees and the history of Cuba, a library, a meeting hall, and the Cuban American National Foundation.

MUSEUMS

Miami

At the **Historical Museum of Southern Florida** (305-375-1492; www.historical -museum.org), 101 W Flagler St, you'll see artifacts from the Miami Circle (see *Archeological Sites*) while learning about South Florida history dating back 10,000 years. Walk down into a small-scale replica of the Miami Circle, about 12 feet in diameter, and see some of the artifacts found at the site. Marvel at the workmanship on the *Miami Centennial Quilt*, which has blocks representing the Barefoot Mailman (see *South Palm Beach County*), the Biltmore (see *Lodging*), and Julia Tuttle's Orange Blossoms, which were sent to Henry Flagler (see *Central Palm Beach County*) to inform him that Miami was a great paradise to which he should consider extending his railroad. Exhibits, such as the History of Miami Beach, change throughout the year. Tours available in English and Spanish by appointment. Call for prices. Open 10–5 Mon–Sat, 10–9 Thu, 12–5 Sun. Adults $5, children 6–12 $2, under 6 free.

✐ Kids will have fun in 14 galleries at the **Miami Children's Museum** (305-373-5437; www.miamichildrensmuseum.org), 980 MacArthur Causeway. The museum offers many interactive exhibits. At the Castle of Dreams, climb through a two-story castle and see sands from around the world; learn how to be a vet at Pet Central; or become a camera operator at Television Studio. Open 10–6 daily. Adults and children $10, babies under 12 months are free. Parking is $1 per hour.

The **Miami Museum of Science and Space Transit Planetarium** (305-646-4200; www.miamisci.org), 3280 S Miami Ave, is notyour ordinary science museum. At the **Falcon Batchelor Bird of Prey Center** (305-646-4244), you'll see rare birds of prey, from the tiny burrowing owl to the majestic bald eagle. Throughout the museum experience live science demonstrations and theater shows. At the planetarium you can view the galaxy on the 65-foot-diameter domed projection screen, or take in a laser show to the sounds of Pink Floyd, Nine Inch Nails, and the Grateful Dead on the first Friday of every month. Make sure to browse through the excellent museum store before leaving. Open 10–6 daily; last ticket sold at 5. Adults $20, seniors 62+ and students with ID $18, children 3–12 $13, under 3 free.

SPORTING EVENTS Florida loves its sports teams, and we think we have the best teams in the nation. In Miami, the **Miami Dolphins** football team (www.miamidolphins.com) and the **Florida Marlins** baseball team (www.marlins.mlb.com) both play at Pro Player Stadium (305-623-6100), 2269 NW 199th St. The **Miami Heat** basketball team (www.nba.com/heat) plays at the American Airlines Arena (786-777-1000), 601 Biscayne Blvd. And you'll find the **Florida Panthers** hockey team (www.floridapanthers.com) up in Broward County at the BankAtlantic Center (954-835-8000), One Panther Pkwy, Sunrise.

TOURS Dragonfly Expeditions (305-774-9019 or 1-888-992-6337; www.dragonflyexpeditions.com), 1825 Ponce de Leon Blvd, Coral Gables, believes in true "green" travel, immersing travelers in unique destinations, with minimal impact on the environment. Their tours incorporate flora and fauna, along with history and culture. You'll enjoy Miami Magic City Bus and Walking Tour, which explores the area's colorful heritage. On the Ghosts and Gravestones tour you'll uncover the mystery of the Miami Circle (see *Archeological Sites*) with an expert archeologist, and then visit the Miami Cemetery to learn about Miami's pioneers and settlers. On the Havana Nights tour you'll be transported to another world, where you'll enjoy a dinner on Little Havana's lively main street, Calle Ocho, then watch the art of cigar rolling and later learn Latin dances at a Cuban nightclub. Tours $30–100.

✳ To Do

FAMILY ACTIVITIES Have a blast at the **Crandon Park Family Amusement Center** (305-361-7385), Key Biscayne, at Crandon Park (see *Beaches*), which includes a 1949 carousel, an old-fashioned outdoor roller rink, a dolphin-shaped splash fountain, and a beachside playground as well as a Tropical Jungle Hayride. Open 10–7; fees for carousel and hayride.

Aventura

Two 18-hole courses designed by Robert Trent Jones Sr. are located at **Turnberry Isle Resort & Club** (305-932-6200; golf concierge, 786-279-6580; www.fairmont.com/turnberryisle), 19999 W Country Club Dr. The tropically landscaped par 70 **North Course** plays around Lake Boros, while the watery par 72 **South Course** tests your driving skills. More than forty thousand balls are retrieved from the water each year at the last hole, the famous "Island Green."

Coral Gables

Play on an 18-hole, par 17 course with the grandeur of the **Biltmore Hotel** (305-460-5366 or 305-445-8066; www.biltmorehotel.com), 1210 Anastasia Ave, as a backdrop. The hotel was built in 1925 by architect Donald Ross. Also run by the Biltmore is the inexpensive and easy to play 9-hole **Granada Golf Course** (305-460-5367), 2001 Granada Blvd. Three dogleg fairways provide a good challenge for both novice and experienced golfers, and the small course has no water hazards.

Doral

The famed **Doral Golf Resort and Spa** (305-592-2000, 305-592-2030, or 1-800-71-DORAL; www.doralresort.com), 4400 NW 87th Ave, offers 90 holes on the Blue, Great White, Silver, Gold and Red Courses. Opening in the 1960s, the courses have been host to many of golf's greatest champions. You'll enjoy driving where legends played on the Blue Monster with its famous fountain at the18th hole, or the palm-tree-lined Great White Course, redesigned by Greg Norman in 2000, with coquina sand and 222 Scottish-style bunkers.

Key Biscayne

The 18-hole par 72 championship **Crandon Park Golf Course** (305-361-9129; www.miamidade.gov/parks/parks/crandon_golf.asp), 6700 Crandon Blvd, is a nature lover's delight. Mangroves and lush tropical foliage surround you at the secluded setting overlooking Biscayne Bay. At one beautiful and challenging hole you'll find water on both sides of the fairway.

HIKING At Crandon Park, **Bear Cut Nature Preserve** (see *Nature Centers*), Key Biscayne, provides a place to stretch your legs. The 1.3-mile Osprey Beach Trail is a broad path along the coastal dunes with beach crossovers. It ends at a paved path; follow that to walk a boardwalk through the mangrove forest to an overlook of a 6,000-year-old fossil reef on Biscayne Bay. Near the nature center are two loop trails to introduce you to the tropical hardwood hammock: the Bear Cut Nature Trail and the Tequesta Hammock Trail, each 0.3 mile.

SWIMMING Spend a day in paradise: Nestled in the heart of Coral Gables is a unique swimming hole, the **Venetian Pool** (305-460-5357; www.venetianpool.com), 2701 DeSoto Blvd. You'll enjoy swimming in and out of caves carved out of coral rock, and under stone bridges and waterfalls. Then lie on the sandy beach, or lounge on the lawn. Surrounded by a lush tropical landscape and exquisite architecture, the historic landmark is designed to resemble a Venetian-style lagoon. Open all year, with reduced hours in winter. Apr–Oct open seven days: adults $10, children 3–12 $6. Nov–Mar open Tue–Sun, closed Mon: adults $7, children 3–12 $4. No babies or toddlers; children must be 38 inches tall and show proof that they are 3 years old.

✳ Green Space

BEACHES

Key Biscayne

The sparkling waters of Biscayne Bay invite at **Bill Baggs Cape Florida State Park** (305-361-5811; www.floridastateparks.org/capeflorida/default.cfm), 1200 S Crandon Blvd, which is rated as one of the Top 10 beaches in the United States. Bask in the sun in the shadow of the historic Cape Florida Lighthouse (see *Historic Sites*); rent bicycles or surreys to enjoy the bayside bicycle path with its view of Stiltsville, a collection of old fishing shacks in the shallows offshore; walk the 1.5-mile nature trail through coastal habitats; or rent sea kayaks at the marina to ply the bay waters. The embers were still smoldering from a fire at the Lighthouse Café the day I arrived, but the park promises to have this popular restaurant up and running by late 2006. Open 8–sunset daily. Fee.

With 2 miles of beach to choose from, **Crandon Park** (305-361-5421), 4000 Crandon Blvd, is a popular choice for sun worshippers. Opened in 1947, the park spans from Biscayne Bay to the Atlantic Ocean, and an offshore sandbar protects the famed white-sand beach, making it an ideal swimming and shelling spot. Lifeguards are always on duty, and coconut palms and sea grapes frame the view. In addition to the beach, the park offers solitude at **Bear Cut Nature Preserve** (see *Nature Centers*) or laughs at the **Crandon Park Family Amusement Center** (see *Family Activities*). **Crandon Park Golf Course,** an 18-hole championship golf course, is also on the grounds. Open 9–5 daily. Fee.

LIGHTHOUSE AT BILL BAGGS CAPE FLORIDA STATE PARK

Sandra Friend

BOTANICAL GARDENS

Coconut Grove

Listed on the National Register of Historic Places, the 8-acre **Kampong** (305-442-7169; www.ntbg.org/gardens/kampong.html), 4013 Douglas Rd, is part of the National Tropical Botanical Garden. Noted plant expert David Fairchild selected plants from around the world that he thought would add aesthetic value to the nation, bringing them here to cultivate. You'll walk

through a wide variety of colorful flowering and tropical fruit trees. Open
Mon–Fri, by appointment only. Guided tours available.

Coral Gables

The expansive **Fairchild Tropical Gardens** (305-667-1651; www.ftg.org),
10901 Old Cutler Rd, established in 1938, is a peaceful tropical paradise. Walk
through the 83-acre botanical garden, where you'll enjoy seven regions, including Windows to the Tropics, a 16,428-square-foot conservatory featuring rare
orchids, aroids, bromeliads, and fruit trees; the McLamore Arboretum, which
displays more than 740 species of tropical flowering trees on 8 acres; and the
world-renowned Montgomery Palmetum, with an impressive selection of palms
from all parts of the globe. The newest section, the William F. Whitman Tropical
Fruit Pavilion, features a 38-foot-high pavilion where you can view exotic tropical fruit species from areas such as Borneo and the Amazon. The Keys Coastal
Habitat, a local favorite, attracts migratory birds and Florida fauna with plants
native to South Florida and the Florida Keys. Narrated open-air tram tours, and
guided walking tours. Gift shop sells a nice selection of tropical gardening books.
Open 9:30–4:30 every day except Christmas. Adults $20, seniors 65+ $15, children 6–17 $10, children 5 and under and Fairchild members free.

NATURE CENTERS ♿ Offering art exhibits, interactive displays, aquariums, and a
beautiful little gift shop, the **Marjory Stoneman Douglas Nature Center** is
the gateway to **Bear Cut Nature Preserve** (305-361-6767), 6767 Crandon
Blvd, Key Biscayne. This little-known preserve lies at the far northern end of the
Crandon Park (see *Beaches*) parking lots. Protecting 280 acres of natural habitats on Biscayne Bay, the preserve has several nature trails that introduce you to
tropical forest, coastal dunes, and the mangrove forest, as well as a paved pathway for bicycles and wheelchairs. Not to be missed is the boardwalk to the fossil
reef overlook on Biscayne Bay. Open 9–5 daily. Fee.

PARKS

Miami

Natural pine flatwoods and a spot of rare pine rocklands habitat are the focal
points of the 65-acre **A. D. Barnes Park** (305-666-5883), 3401 SW 72nd Ave,
where paved trails radiate from the **Sense of Wonder Nature Center** (9–6
Mon–Fri, 10–6 Sat and Sun) into the surrounding tropical hardwood hammock
and pines. When the nature center is closed, use the **Leisure Center** entrance,
which has some interesting outdoor art. Open sunrise–sunset. Free.

North Miami

Featuring a natural limestone arch that was the original "Gateway to Miami" and
a bridge on the Military Trail of the 1800s, **Arch Creek Park** (305-944-6111),
1855 NE 135th St, protects a sliver of tropical hammock that is a known archeological site, a village of the Tequesta between 500 B.C. and A.D. 1300. Nature
trails wind through the lush landscape, scant steps from Biscayne Boulevard.
The arch itself collapsed in the 1980s but has been reestablished in place with a
little human help. A small museum on-site explains the historical and archeological significance of this small but important park. Open 9–5. Free.

The site of a turn-of-the-20th-century rock quarry, **Greynolds Park** (305-945-3425), 17530 W Dixie Hwy, protects 249 acres nestled along the Oleta River, including the mangrove-lined riverbanks and old quarries filled with water and surrounded by tropical hardwood hammocks. The tower, built of leftover stone, is a prominent manufactured feature. The park offers a popular municipal golf course, canoe and paddleboat rentals, hundreds of picnic tables, and two nature trails. The Lakeside Nature Trail circles the old quarries, while the Oleta River Nature Trail is a boardwalk through a dense mangrove forest. Open sunrise–sunset. Fee on weekends.

✳ Lodging

HOTELS, MOTELS, AND RESORTS

Coconut Grove, 33133

At **Grove Isle Hotel & Spa** (305-858-8300; www.groveisle.com), Four Grove Isle Dr, you'll be greeted with exotic jungle murals and towering gold columns topped with green palm fronds in the main lobby. After check-in, curl up on one of the hammocks overlooking the bay, play life-size chess with 3-foot pieces on the pool deck, and on cool nights cozy up at the outdoor fire pit. You'll find luxury accommodations ($279–529) in a variety of choices. The five Grand Luxury Bayfront Suites are situated on the corners of the hotel, providing the best water views. They include such plush amenities as a flat-screen plasma TV and a four-poster king bed. For romance, the spacious Bay Suite Studios feature an elevated bedroom with king canopy beds and butterfly netting. Elegant Colonial decor is found in the Luxury Bayfront Rooms, with either king or two queen beds. And overlooking the marina, you'll watch sailboats glide by from one of the Luxury Bay Suites with king and queen beds.

Coral Gables, 33134

Old-world elegance greets you at the **Biltmore Hotel** (305-445-1926; www.biltmorehotel.com), 1200 Anastasia Ave. Built in 1926, the grand hotel has seen its fair share of presidents, royalty, and celebrities, so you'd expect it to be expensive. However, I found it very affordable during the summer months. Stepping back in time, you'll find white-glove service greeting you upon your arrival and throughout your stay. When we asked where the ladies' room was, the maid dropped her broom, escorted us to the nearest lounge, and opened the door. The European ambiance is evident, from the gargoyles on the staircases to the tiny finches in the grand-lobby birdcage. Once in your room you'll be treated to feather beds, Egyptian-cotton duvet covers, and signature robes and slippers. You won't miss your high-tech toys—high-speed Internet (Ethernet connection), cable TV, digital on-demand movies, and Sony PlayStation are in each room ($279–589). The hotel features the lush tropical landscaping of Canary palms, bougainvillea, and hibiscus; romantic balconies; complimentary carriage rides throughout Coral Gables, an on-site spa, a championship golf course (see *Golf*), fine dining (see *Dining Out*), and the largest pool in the continental United States. The 700,000-gallon pool once hosted water ballets and water polo. For that special night, the 1,830-square-foot two-story Everglades "Al Capone" Suite features hand-painted ceiling scenes of the Everglades, a private elevator, and a baby grand piano ($1,250–1,995 per night).

Checking into **Hotel St. Michel** (305-444-1666 or 1-800-848-HOTEL; www.hotelstmichel.com), 162 Alcazar Ave, I felt as if I was in Europe again. Built in 1926, the charming inn has 27 rooms ($175–325), all with different personalities. Weary travelers will appreciate the attentive service, which starts at check-in and continues throughout your stay. In my room, I found fresh fruit and fresh ice that hadn't even begun to melt! Rich imported chocolates and an assortment of fine toiletries, including a mending kit, were also waiting. The room was decorated in elegant antiques, buttery walls, and—true to European style—the windows opened so that I could bring in the balmy night air. After dining downstairs (see *Dining Out*), I fell off to sleep in the king-size bed, snuggling under fine linens. Each morning you'll enjoy continental breakfast (the croissants are the largest I've ever seen), fresh-squeezed orange juice, and coffee or a variety of European teas. The hotel is conveniently located only a block from the famed Miracle Mile shopping district (see *Selective Shopping*).

Miami, 33131
🐾 Guests with pets will enjoy the **Mandarin Oriental** (305-913-8288; www.mandarinoriental.com), 500 Brickell Key Dr, where they can walk their dog on the beautiful South Lawn overlooking Biscayne Bay. Your pet will also be provided with a plush pet bed, food bowls, and a fun treat. Rates are $233–1,283. The luxurious Biscayne Suite goes for $2,283 during low season, $3,566 during high season.

DINING OUT

Coconut Grove
With tiny monkeys hanging off chandeliers, you'll know you're in for a unique treat at the bohemian-style **Baleen,** located in the Grove Isle Club and Resort (305-860-4305; www.groveisle.com), Four Grove Isle Dr. You'll find plump oversized crab cakes and Asian bouillabaisse. Breakfast 7–11, lunch 12–3, dinner 6:30–10, staying open until 11 on Fri and Sat nights. Dinner entrées $28–48.

A visit to Miami isn't complete without a stop into **Monty's Stone Crab Raw Bar** (305-856-399; www.montysstonecrab.com), 2550 S Bayshore Dr. With live calypso and reggae music playing, you'll feel like you're on a Caribbean island as you dine while looking out over Biscayne Bay. Start with their famous she-crab soup, loaded with crab, for only $6. Then savor such dishes as mango barbecue salmon ($24), island-style red snapper ($24), or Florida bouillabaisse ($25). Entrées $15–39; crab and lobster dishes at market price. Open 11:30 PM–1 AM daily, sometimes later on the weekends.

Go up, up on the rooftop and you'll be rewarded with a stunning view while dining at **Panorama Restaurant** (305-529-2828; www.sonesta.com/coconutgrove), 2889 McFarlane Rd. The contemporary restaurant is on the eighth floor of the Sonesta Hotel. And you'll keep your waistline intact, as they feature a complete South Beach Diet menu. Open daily for breakfast, lunch, and dinner. Entrées $18–27.

Coral Gables, 33134
While visiting the Biltmore Hotel (305-445-1926; www.biltmorehotel

.com), 1200 Anastasia Ave, you'll want to experience their world-class cuisine. Featuring the finest in French food, the chic **Palm d'Or** is a favorite of both locals and celebrity guests. Entrées include duck confit, pan-seared wild striped bass, and seared baby lamb chop ($39–70). Open for dinner only. At **1200 Courtyard Grill,** you'll dine in the open courtyard on Mediterranean and South Floribbean fare. Entrées $14–35. Open for breakfast, lunch, and dinner. Poolside at **La Cascade,** you'll find light Caribbean specialties such as chilled Andalusian gazpacho and Don Quixote Salad. Entrées 7–15. Open for lunch and dinner.

Since 1975, the **Canton Chinese Restaurant** (305-448-3736; www .cantonrestaurants.com), 2614 Ponce de Leon Blvd, has been a local favorite. Maybe it's the huge portions, or honey chicken and canton steak served family-style, or simply the friendliness of the staff that keeps everyone coming back year after year. Open for lunch and dinner. This place is busy, so reservations are a good idea.

New American and Latino flavors blend with the Caribbean at **Carmen the Restaurant** (305-913-1944; www .carmentherestaurant.com), 700 Biltmore Way, located in the David William Hotel. Chef Carmen Gonzalez serves up her passion in an elegant cozy boutique. Seating only 100, this makes a great place for intimate conversation. Exciting entrées, from yucca *mofongo* stuffed spiny lobster and island *mojito,* to *culebran cobia* with white bean stew and *calabaza* fritters ($26), to domestic lamb chops with *malanga* mash ($48). Open for lunch 12–2 Tue–Fri, dinner 6–10 Tue–Thu, 6–11 Fri and Sat, and 6–9 Sun.

You'll experience Hispanic cuisine at its finest at the lively **Chispa** (305-648-2600; www.chisparestaurant .com), 225 Altara Ave, in the Collection Building. Sample such signature dishes as roasted sweet peppers and goat cheese ($7), salmon ($9) or shrimp ceviche ($10), roasted mahi *relleno* ($21), and shrimp and *lechon asado* risotto with *sofrito* sauce ($26). Open for breakfast, lunch, and dinner.

A Miami landmark, **Christy's Restaurant** (305-446-1400; www.christys restaurant.com), 3101 Ponce de Leon Blvd, is famous for midwestern beef, such as the 16- to 18-ounce prime rib of beef ($35), and fresh Florida seafood, such as the fresh filet of snapper amandine ($24). Save room for the impressive baked Alaska for two ($11). Reservations required. Open for lunch 11:30–4 Mon–Fri, dinner 4–10 Sun–Thu and 4–11 Fri and Sat.

The neighborhood **Jake's Bar and Grill** (305-662-8632; www.jakesbar .net), 6901 Red Rd, offers excellent New American fare. Start with a selection of tapas ($10) or pan-roasted jumbo lump crab cake with smoke-house almond tartar ($9), then move on to roasted Caribbean seafood stew with coconut shellfish broth ($17) and *churrasco* grilled skirt steak with chimichurri, tomato-poblano relish, and beans and rice ($15). Open for dinner.

One of the chefs who put New World cuisine on the map and made South Florida a top culinary destination is Chef Norman Van Aken. He is considered one of the best of South Florida's celebrity chefs, and his signature meals are, in my opinion, without equal. **Norman's** (305-446-6767; www.normans.com), 21 Almeria Ave, features wood-burning ovens in a lively setting. Your taste buds will enjoy crab stuffed *sui mei* dumplings with ginger butter ($13) as an appetizer; for the main entrée, try corn bread and pistachio stuffed quail surrounded by thin slices of marinated duck breast pomegranate with moonshine chutney reduction ($38) Open for dinner only, 6–10, with cocktails beginning at 5.

Another culinary celebrity, Chef Douglas Rodriguez, brings his Latin influence to a traditional steakhouse. At **Ola Steak** (305-461-4442; www.ola steak.com), Suite 1320, 320 San Lorenzo Ave, in the Village of Merrick Park, you'll feast on 100 percent certified organic Uruguayan wet-aged beef and Black Angus dry-aged beef.

Dine outside overlooking Matheson Hammock at **The Red Fish Grill** (305-668-8788; www.redfishgrill.net), 9610 Old Cutler Rd. Start with a nice tropical tricolor salad ($7), and then spice things up with a *churrasco* steak with Argentinean chimichurri and Spanish rice ($25). Entrées $19–33. Open for dinner only.

Whether for breakfast before shopping, or a nice treat for dinner or brunch, by far my favorite place to dine is **Restaurant St. Michel** (305-446-6572; www.hotelstmichel.com), 162 Alcazar Ave. Set in a European-style hotel, the intimate restaurant serves fresh seafood, aged prime meats, and "to die for" desserts. I'm still reeling over the chocolate Grand Marnier soufflé ($9) served with rich chocolate sauce (as if it needed more), and fresh whipped cream, all perfectly paired with a tawny port. Before getting to dessert, try the Lobster 4 Ways (roasted tail, empanada, risotto tempura, and bisque) or the grilled salmon with fried oysters and green horseradish sauce. Vegetarians will love the

polenta cannelloni filled with mascarpone and wild mushrooms, served with an herbed tomato fondue. Restaurant St. Michel is also a great place for breakfast weekdays before work or before shopping on Miracle Mile (see *Selective Shopping*). Enjoy steaming-hot coffee or teas, fresh-squeezed orange juice, and an enormous croissant with imported jams. Dinner entrées $16–34. Open for breakfast 7–9 Mon–Fri; for Sunday brunch 11–2:30; for lunch and dinner 11 AM–10:30 PM Sun–Thu, 11 AM–11:30 PM Fri and Sat. Live entertainment on Friday and Saturday nights.

Downtown Miami
At the Mandarin Oriental (305-913 8358; www.mandarinoriental.com), 500 Brickell Key Dr, you'll have a choice between **Azul** (305-913-8254) and **Café Sambal** (305-913-8251). Azul offers Mediterranean flavors with Asian influences. Your taste buds will want to start with an appetizer of seared scallops and foie gras, celery root hoecake, and Granny Smith apples. Azul is open for lunch 12–3 Mon–Fri, and dinner 6:30–11 Mon–Sat. Over at Café Sambal, shrimp *hargau* with garlic froth, chervil, and squid ink vinaigrette is

COCONUTS

Sandra Friend

just one of the entrées on the Asian-inspired menu. You can also order from their sushi and sake menu. Café Sambal is open daily for breakfast, lunch, and dinner 6:30 AM–11 PM.

Gloria and Emilio Estefan Jr.'s **Bongos Cuban Café** (786-777-2100; www.bongoscubancafe.com), 601 Biscayne Blvd, features Cuban cuisine in a tropical art deco–style café where you can gaze at the cruise ships, at the Port of Miami, Biscayne Bay, and the Downtown Miami skyline. The lively restaurant is a great place to go before or after a game or concert at the American Airlines Arena. You'll find Cuban menu items such as *ropa vieja* and *bistec la Milanesa*. Kids have their own menu with *bistec de Palomilla* (a Cuban-style grilled steak), and *chicharrones de pollo* (lightly floured boneless chicken nuggets). Open for lunch 11:30–5 Fri–Sun, dinner 5–11 Wed–Sun.

The power lunch is king at **The Capital Grille** (305-374-4500; www.thecapitalgrille.com), 444 Brickell Ave. Located next to the Miami Convention Center, it is know for its dry-aged steaks and outstanding wine list. You'll find dry-aged steak au poivre with Courvoisier cream sauce, and the Grille's signature veal chop, to be some of the juiciest. Your toughest executive decision will be selecting from the more than five thousand bottles of wine on the wall. When celebrating landing the big deal, you'll want to order a wine from the Captain's List, which features rare wines and champagnes.

Miami's newest restaurant, **Karu & Y** (305-710-1835; www.karu-y.com), 59 NW 14th St, opening in July 2006, is the place where art and culinary cuisine meet. Sit back and enjoy the strik-ing architecture and artistic pieces on the wall and on your plate. The menu features flavors of *Alta Cocina* ("Cuisine of the Americas"). Open for dinner; stay late in the "Y" Ultra Lounge.

Set in the richness of deep mahogany walls, the award-winning **Morton's the Steakhouse** (305-400-9990; www.mortons.com), 1200 Brickell Ave, features the best in steaks and wines. Whether you select Oskar or filet Diane, end with Morton's legendary hot chocolate cake. You'll want to dress up a bit at this restaurant and, depending on beverage choices, expect dinner for two to be about $170. Open for lunch and dinner.

EATING OUT

Coconut Grove

Watching your weight is easy at **Café Tu Tu Tango** (305-529-2222; www.cafetututango.com), 3015 Grand Ave. The all-appetizer-size menu offers creative dishes inspired by fine-art pieces. Located in trendy CocoWalk, the artistic restaurant has a relaxed atmosphere with prices from $4 to $11. Open for lunch and dinner daily 11:30 AM–midnight Sun–Wed; until 1 AM Thu; until 2 AM Fri and Sat.

Mix and mingle with local residents at the **Greenstreet Outdoor Lounge & Restaurant** (305-444-0244; www.greenstreetcafe.net), 3110 Commodore Plaza. The popular spot with red velvet sofas on the sidewalk offers something for everyone, from tabbouleh salad (47), jalapeño poppers ($7), or conch fritters ($8) as appetizers to veggie wrap ($9), pesto ravioli ($12), margarita pizza ($10), or Orange Duck ($12) for an entrée. You'll want to be early in line for Sunday breakfast, to get one of their famous muffins. Open for breakfast, lunch, and dinner daily 7:30 AM–10:45 PM, and till 11:45 PM on Fri and Sat.

The Nicaraguan steakhouse, **Los Ranchos Steak & Seafood Cantina** (305-461-8222; www.losranchossteak house.com), 3015 Grand Ave, is known for its *churrasco* ($16–18) served with *gallo pinto* (rice and plantains). You'll also want to try their *tres leches* ("Three Milks") dessert. Entrées $11–19. Open for lunch and dinner noon–10 Sun, 11:30–10 Mon–Fri, noon–11 Sat.

✎ Family-friendly **Señor Frog's Bar & Grill** (305-448-0999; www.senor frogsfla.com), 3480 Main Hwy, features great Mexican cuisine. You can order one of their famous sombrero dishes, the fresh green tomatillo enchiladas ($15) or *pollo en mole verde* ($16). Open for lunch and dinner 11:30 AM–midnight. There's another location over in South Beach.

Downtown Miami

You might think you have to purchase an admission ticket to get into **Lake-side Café** (305-400-7000; www .parrotjungle.com), 1111 Parrot Jungle Trail at Parrot Jungle Island (see *Attractions*), but you don't. You'll dine in tropical surroundings on the outdoor terrace while gazing over Flamingo Lake at a flush of pink flamingos. It won't be long before you want to step inside the park to view the other colorful birds, along with the beautifully landscaped Miami Japan Garden. Imaginative wraps, sandwiches, and burgers $5–8.

✳ Selective Shopping

BOOKSTORES

Coral Gables

At **Agartha Secret City** bookstore (305-441-1618; www.agarthasecret

city.com), at their new location on 133 Giralda Ave, spiritual seekers will find a wide selection of New Age and metaphysical materials. Along with books, they also carry a nice line of incense, music, and furnishings. Seminars such as Candle Magic and About Buddhism, and events with reading and energy therapies, are scheduled throughout the year. Stop by or call for a current schedule. Open 12 PM–10 PM Tue–Sat; 7 PM–10 PM Sun.

You'll always find something new at the independent **Books & Books** (305-442-4408; 1-888-626-6576; www .booksandbooks.com), 265 Aragon Ave. Inspiring readers and writers with its architectural beauty, the 9,000-square-foot Mediterranean-style building (circa 1927) is on the Coral Gables Register of Historic Places. Note the original tile floors, fireplace, beamed ceilings, and floor-to-ceiling dark-wood shelves. The locally owned bookstore also has locations in Miami Beach and Bal Harbour (see *South Beach and Miami Oceanside*). And at their Levenger Outlet in Delray Beach (see *South Palm Beach County*), you'll find book accessories and reading tools. Open 9 AM–11 PM every day.

Enjoy browsing rare and antique books at the quaint **Fifteenth Street Books** (305-534-6758; www.fifteenth streetbooks.com), 296 Aragon Ave. The bookstore has a nice collection of Cuban and rare 15th-century books, and a comfy reading room. Open 11–7.

FARMER'S MARKETS The **Coconut Grove Farmers Market** (305-794-1464), Grand Ave and Margaret St, is open 11–7 Sat, year-round. You'll find everything from tropical produce to exotic plants here.

✹ MIRACLE MILE SHOPS IN CORAL GABLES

My favorite shopping area is the **Miracle Mile** (305-569-0311; www.shop coralgables.com) in Coral Gables. Its spacious streets, great eateries, and friendly people are worthwhile reasons to take a drive away from the beach and explore inland. Service seems to be tops at every shop. Before her wedding, my daughter and I visited a dozen bridal boutiques throughout South Florida, but only **Chic Parisien** (305-448-5756; www.chicparisienbridal.com), 118 Miracle Mile, treated her like a queen. When the dress she finally chose was no longer being carried, the lovely ladies at Chic Parisien put me in touch with the designer and we were able to purchase the dress. Years later, when she was pregnant, we found **M & M Maternity** (305-448-7386), 136 Miracle Mile, only a few doors down the street. These folks know how to treat a pregnant mama. A personal dresser greets you and helps you select just one piece or an entire wardrobe. There's no pressure, though; you can browse on your own if you like. The staff want you to feel comfortable and are willing to wait on you hand and foot—a nice treat when you're tired and puffy. In

MALLS AND OUTLETS

Coral Gables

Anchored by Neiman Marcus and Nordstrom, the exclusive shopping destination **Merrick Park** (305-529-0200; www.villageofmerrickpark.com), 358 San Lorenzo Ave, is known for firsts. Designers such as CH Carolina Herrera (305-448-3333; www.carolina herrera.com), Donald J Pliner (305-774-5880; www.donaldjpliner.com), and Jimmy Choo (305-443-6124; www.jimmychoo.com) are among the first boutiques to grace South Florida at Merrick Park. Trendy moms will also want to bring the kids to Janie and Jack (305-447-0810; www.janieand jack.com), and Pottery Barn Kids (305-446-6511; www.potterybarn kids.com). Not your average mall; the upscale village atmosphere is features tropical foliage, elegant fountains, and unique architecture. You'll also have a wide selection of fine eateries from

which to choose. Shops are open 10–9 Mon–Sat, 12–7 Sun.

Miami

You'll be in the heart of downtown Miami, but you'll feel like you are at a Caribbean market at **Bayside Marketplace** (305-577-3344; www.bay sidemarketplace.com), 401 Biscayne Blvd. Located near the American Airlines Arena, the lively open-air mall features calypso and reggae music in the central entertainment area.

✳ Entertainment

MUSIC

Coral Gables

You'll find several world-class jazz and classical artists performing at **Coral Gables Congregational Church** (305-448-7421, ext. 20; www.coral gablescongregational.org), 3010 De Soto Blvd, Coral Gables. The beautiful her eighth month of pregnancy, my daughter cringed at the thought of trying on even one more frock; they let me take an assortment of outfits on consignment so she could try them on in the comfort of her home. If I had lived closer to the shop, they would have had the clothes delivered. Now that's service! And the prices are low ($8–30 for tops; $12–60 for bottoms), too. While the shopping district of Miracle Mile is flush with bridal boutiques (more than 30 shops), you'll also find specialty shops such as **The Dog Bar** (305-441-8979; www.dogbar.com), 259 Miracle Mile, where you can dress up your dog or cat in the finest apparel, then spoil your pet further with a unique toy or healthy treat. Open 11–7 Mon–Wed, 11–9 Thu and Fri, 10–7 Sat, 12–5 Sun. Also on Jefferson behind Lincoln Rd in South Beach (see *South Beach and Miami Oceanside*). To get that cool Miami look, head to **Guayaberas Etc** (305-441-9891; www.guayaberashirt.com), 270 Miracle Mile, for chic tropical wear. Open 10–7 Mon–Sat. And along with **Graziano's Gourmet** shop (305-460-0001; www.grazianosgroup.com), 2301 Galiano St, you'll also find more than 40 places to eat. When your feet get tired, hop on the free **Coral Gables Trolley** for a view of the city (see *Getting Around*).

church (circa 1923–1925), built in the Mediterranean Revival style of that era, features a bell tower and grand Baroque entranceway—a favorite of brides. The church presents several renowned artists and musical programs, such as their Summer Concert Series, throughout the year.

Miami

For more than six decades the **Florida Grand Opera** (1-800-741-1010; www.fgo.org), 1200 Coral Way, has been thrilling audiences throughout South Florida with performances of favorites such as *The Barber of Seville* and *Carmen*. In fall 2006, performances will move from the Miami-Dade County Auditorium, their home for more than 50 years, to the Ziff Opera House at the Miami Performing Arts Center (www.miami pac.org). The center is on both sides of Biscayne Boulevard, between NE 13th and 14th Streets.

THEATER

Coconut Grove

The former 1926 movie house, **Coconut Grove Playhouse** (305-442-4000; www.cgplayhouse.org), 3500 Main Hwy, has been presenting innovative and original productions since 1956. The theater has been known to bring in acclaimed actors such as Jack Klugman and the late Tony Randall in Neil Simon's *Sunshine Boys*, and Hal Holbrook in *Death of a Salesman*. You many also see fine musicals, such as *Finian's Rainbow*. Performances: Tue–Sat evenings, and Sat and Sun matinees ($35–55).

Coral Gables

✑ The 600-seat **Actors' Playhouse at The Miracle Theatre** (305-444-9293; www.actorsplayhouse.org), 280 Miracle Mile, presents professional award-winning theatrical productions for all ages. The balcony of the main stage has been transformed into the 300-seat Children's Theatre. In the intimate 100-seat black box, you'll experience innovative new work and cutting-edge experimental theater. In 2007, expect performances such as *Tomfoolery* by Tom Lehrer, and the world premiere of *The Boy from Russia* by Florida playwright Susan Westfall. Mainstage performances: Wed–Sat evenings, and Sun matinee. $45 Fri and Sat; $38 all other times. At the Children's Theatre, all seats are $12.

GableStage (305-445-1119; www .gablestage.org), 1200 Anastasia Ave, presents innovative and thought-provoking productions, including premieres of award-winning plays in South Florida. Performances Thu, Fri, and Sat at 8; Sun at 2 and 7. Tickets: $40 Sat, $35 all other times.

Miami Design District
Contemporary performances are presented at the **Miami Light Project** (305-576-4350; www.miamilight project.com), 3000 Biscayne Blvd, where you'll see cutting-edge productions along with performances by the world-renowned Mad Cap Theatre Company.

✳ Special Events
February: The annual **Coconut Grove Art Festival** (www.coconutgroveartsfest.com) is the number one arts festival in the nation. More than three hundred artisans are selected by jury, with only the best showcasing their arts and crafts. Usually held over the President's

Day holiday weekend, 9–6 Fri, 10–6 Sun and Mon. Admission $5 per day or $12 for all three days.

Early June: The annual weeklong **Goombay Festival** (305-372-9966), 3802 Oak Ave, Coconut Grove, celebrates the Grove's heritage. First settled by Bahamian immigrants in the 1890s, today the Grove transforms Grand Avenue into Nassau's Bay Street. You'll see bright and colorful Junkanoo costumes, eat Bahamian foods, and shop a wide variety of crafts while listening to the lively Caribbean beat.

July: Taste something different at the **International Mango Festival** (305-667-1651; www.fairchildgarden.org), Fairchild Tropical Botanic Garden, 10901 Old Cutler Rd, Coral Gables, where you can learn more about how to cook with this tropical fruit. Enjoy the Mango Brunch and Mango Auction, while kids enjoy special activities.

🖉 *October:* The **Miami Carnival** (305-538-7882; www.miamicarnival .net), Bicentennial Park, 1075 Biscayne Blvd, has been an annual event since 1984. Miami sizzles with traditional celebrations of the West Indies. Come for the Main Parade and Jr. Kiddies Parade to see the colorful costumes (NE 36th St and NE Second Ave), and then stay for the food and live music, which goes on until 11 PM.

December: The **Orange Bowl Festival** (305-341-4700; www.orangebowl .org) features the annual football game surrounded by the always sold out Coaches Luncheon and Kick Off Party.

SOUTH BEACH AND MIAMI OCEANSIDE

Trendy South Miami Beach has been a mecca for the "beautiful people" for decades. All along Ocean (Deco) Drive you'll find celebrities, partygoers, models, and moguls, but don't let that turn you away. I found South Beach (SoBe) to be very family friendly as well. Rich with art and architecture, the Art Deco Historic District is between Ocean Drive and Alton Road. Here pink, turquoise, and yellow boutique hotels and neon eateries dominate the skyline. All along Collins Avenue and Lincoln Road you'll find high-fashion shops and eateries. Partygoers will want to take an afternoon siesta. While most clubs open at 10 PM, they typically don't get moving until after midnight. Even if you aren't into club hopping, you'll want to experience at least one club, as this area is like no other in the United States. For those who remember the TV show *Miami Vice,* Española Way is where most of the outside shots were filmed.

North Miami Beach becomes more residential, reaching north to Bal Harbour, Surfside, and Sunny Isles. In the late 1800s, settlers were granted 160 acres by the government. In 1890, Capt. William H. Fulford homesteaded the section of North Miami Beach, selling the entire plot, and then some, in 1917, to Ohio newspaper owner Lefe Allen and Joshua Flaynold. The wide-open streets are a testament to Mr. Allen's plan for a perfect city. In 1927, North Miami Beach was incorporated as the City of Fulford, after the original homesteader. The name was changed to its current moniker in 1931. Locals call the area north of 41st Street "Condo Canyon": From the 1950s through the '70s, unrestricted zoning codes led to this stretch of tall cubical-like structures.

GUIDANCE The **Greater Miami Convention and Visitors Bureau** (305-539-3000; www.miamiandbeaches.com) is the main connection for tourist information. For a vacation guide call 1-888-76-MIAMI or 305-447-7777.

GETTING THERE *By air:* **Miami International Airport** (305-876-7000; www.miami-airport.com) is centrally located in the county. **Fort Lauderdale–Hollywood International Airport** (954-359-6100; www.fll.net) is also within easy access to the region.

By bus: **Greyhound** (1-800-231-2222; www.greyhound.com). Several locations will take you to the main areas of Miami-Dade County: **Miami North** (305-688-7277), 16000 NW 7th Ave; **Miami Central** (305-871-1810), 4111 NW 27th St; **Miami Downtown** (305-374-6160), 36 NE 10th St; and for the south end of the county, **Miami Cutler Ridge** (305-296-9072), 10801 Caribbean Blvd, at the American Service Station.

By rail: **AMTRAK** (1-800-872-7245; www.amtrak.com) provides regularly scheduled service to Miami.

GETTING AROUND *By bus:* **Metrobus,** Miami-Dade Transit, Customer Services (305-770-3131; www.miamidade.gov/transit).

By rail: **Tri-Rail** (305-836-0986; www.tri-rail.com) is a convenient way to travel from Miami to West Palm Beach. Tickets are not sold on the train. You must purchase a ticket at the station on the day of use. The train runs in six sections, and tickets are purchased according to the number of sections. A ticket from West Palm Beach to Miami costs around $5.50. On weekends and holidays, the full fare for the entire system is a flat rate of $4. The Tri-Rail ticket allows you to transfer to Metrorail at no additional cost. The electric-powered **Metrorail** covers 22 miles of the city on an elevated track, from Kendall to Medley. Full fare: $1.50. The **Metromover,** an elevated people mover covering nearly 4½ miles of the Miami business district, including Brickell Avenue, is free to ride. Metrorail, Metrobus, and Metromover are part of Miami-Dade Transit, Customer Services (305-770-3131; www.miamidade.gov/transit).

PARKING Make sure to have some change on hand, as most districts have metered parking. Some parking areas have maximums, so check the meter for restrictions. Solar-powered Pay & Display (P&D) machines require payment at a central location, usually within four cars. These meters take not only coins and dollar bills but also VISA and MasterCard. Private and government parking lots and garages are conveniently located around town. Fees are $1–1.25 per hour, with flat rates of $4–15.

OCEAN DRIVE

Kathy Wolf

VALET You'll be hard-pressed to find a restaurant, hotel, or shopping district that doesn't offer valet services; sometimes you'll have no choice, as some establishment don't allow self-parking. You'll find most of the area's valet parking managed by private companies. All reputable establishments will have one that carries a liability policy. However, in most situations, you won't be able to add the valet parking fee to your hotel or dining bill. In South Florida it is customary to tip when you drop off your car, *and* when you pick it up. Most valets are happy with

$1–2, but if you are driving a luxury vehicle or fancy sports car and want them to keep a close eye on it, expect to tip them $5–10. Inquire about valet policies when making reservations.

MEDICAL EMERGENCIES Miami is home to some of the finest hospitals in the world (See *The Gables, the Grove, and Miami Cityside*). For general emergencies, head to **Cedars Medical Center** (305-325-5511; www.cedarsmedical center.com), 1400 NW 12th Ave, or **Jackson Memorial Hospital** (305-585-1111; www.um-jmh.org), 1611 NW 12th Ave. At the north end of Miami, seek out **North Shore Medical Center** (305-835-6000; www.northshoremedical .com), 1100 NW 95th St, or **Parkway Regional Medical Center** (305-651-1100; www.parkwaymedctr.com), 160 NW 170th St, North Miami Beach.

✳ To See

MONASTERY The oldest building in the Western Hemisphere, the **Ancient Spanish Monastery** (305-945-1461; www.spanishmonastery.com), 16711 West Dixie Hwy, North Miami Beach, was built in Segovia, Spain, in 1141. Brought to America by William Randolph Hearst, the monastery was reassembled in 1952 on its current site. Open 9–5 Mon–Sat, 1:30–5 Sun. Adults $5, seniors 55+ $2.50, students $3, children under 12 $2.

ART GALLERIES Located in the Art Deco Historic District, **The Wolfsonian** (305-531-1001; www.wolfsonian.org), 1001 Washington Ave, South Beach, displays fine arts produced between 1885 and 1945. You'll see European and American exhibits, such as a poster from the World's Fair and many from the age of machinery. My favorite piece, in the Celtic Revival style, is by acclaimed Irish illustrator and stained-glass artist Harry Clarke. The stained-glass window panel was commissioned in 1926 for the International Labor Building, League of Nations, Geneva, but it was never installed. The 71½-by-40-inch window features, in exquisite detail, 12 vignettes of Irish poets' and writers' works, such as *The Weaver's Grave* by Seumas O'Kelly. Open 12–6 Sat–Tue, 12–9 Thu and Fri. Adults $7; seniors, students, and children 6–12 $5; under 6 free.

STAINED-GLASS DETAIL AT THE WOLF-SONIAN

Kathy Wolf

HISTORIC PLACES

North Miami Beach
You'll find a two-sided marker at **Haulover Beach,** originally known as Lighthouse Dock. Legend has it that a man named Baker "hauled over" fishing boats from the bay to the ocean around 1810. The dock was built in 1926, by Capt. Henry Jones,

with the first dock permit from the War Department. International sport-fishermen docked here in the early 1900s, using charter boats to fish the waters for such big game as marlin and sailfish. The dock was replaced in 1952 by the marina.

South Beach

The marker on Española Way indicates the **Art Deco Historic District,** a 1-square-mile area in South Beach. With its Spanish and nautical influence, this popular district includes some of the finest architectural examples of the Bohemian period. Note the cobalt blue neon on the 1939 Breakwater Hotel, the window eyebrows on the 1954 Shelborne, and the porthole windows and smoke-stack-like neon tower of the 1938 Essex House Hotel. Art deco buildings were initially painted white, off-white, or beige with a contrasting color on just the trim. It was not until the 1980s that vibrant colors covered the main sections of the buildings, when Leonard Horowitz of the Miami Design Preservation League (MDPL) designed the color schemes for more than 150 buildings. The late 1930s and early '40s brought the "streamline" period, with the sleek nautical design of luxury cruise ships. You'll see this design incorporated into many boutique hotels. The mid-1950s brought larger buildings with a minimalist mid-century modern style of architecture that signaled the end of the art deco period.

Walking along Ocean Drive, you'll be surprised to find yourself suddenly standing in front of the **Versace House.** While you would expect the home to sit farther from the road, the home is only a few feet from the sidewalk, providing an excellent view of its architecture. **Casa Casuarina,** at 1116 Ocean Dr and known to most people as the **Versace House,** was built in 1930. It was modeled after the Alcazar de Colon in Santo Domingo (built by Christopher Columbus's son circa 1510), reputed to be the oldest home in the Western Hemisphere. In 1992, famed fashion designer Gianni Versace purchased the home as a beach house. Designer of the 1980s series *Miami Vice* look—a pastel T-shirt and white jacket often seen on Don Johnson's "Sonny Crockett"—Versace was influential in creating the new South Miami Beach scene. Soon after his arrival it became the "place to be seen," and many posh eateries and boutiques popped up along Ocean Drive, making SoBe a destination for the rich and famous. Madonna, Sly Stalone, and Elton John were frequent guests at the mansion. Unfortunately the life of the much-loved Versace was cut short in 1997 when he was murdered at the steps of the home. Casa Casuarina has since been sold to a private owner. The home is now a members-only club and can be rented out for functions if you have the dough—rentals start at $10,000 and are creatively catered by Barton G (see *Dining Out*).

CASA CASUARINA, VERSACE'S FORMER HOME

Kathy Wolf

& **The Holocaust Memorial** (305-538-1663; www.holocaustmmb .org), 1933–1945 Meridian Ave, Miami Beach. Emotional and moving, the bronze sculptures of tormented men, women, and children cling to a giant arm tattooed with a number from Auschwitz, the arm reaching to the sky in search of hope and life. The central sculpture is accessed from a tunnel where haunting voices of Israeli children sing songs of the Holocaust over an audio speaker. The granite Memorial Wall details the chilling period during which more than 6 million Jews were murdered. The memorial is outdoors and free to all. Open 9–9 daily.

MUSEUMS

Miami

The **Miami Art Museum** (305-375-3000; www.miamiartmuseum.org), 101 W Flagler St, presents international art of the 20th and 21st centuries. The permanent collection, Miami Currents: Linking Community and Collection, showcases Miami artists. You'll also view several U.S. and international artists' works, such as Nairobi-born Wangechi Mutu's new piece, *You tried so hard to make us away*, created of ink, acrylic, glitter, fur, contact paper, and collage, or George Segal's painted plaster sculpture, *Abraham's Farewell to Ishmael.* Open 10–5 Tue–Fri, noon–5 Sat and Sun. Adults $5, seniors $2.50, children under 12 and students free. Entrance to the museum is free on the second Saturday of each month and every Sunday.

Miami Beach

& The **Bass Museum of Art** (305-673-7530; www.bassmuseum.org), 2121 Park Ave, located in the heart of the historic Art Deco Historic District, offers a fine display of European paintings and exhibitions of contemporary art. The 1930 art deco building houses five galleries, a café, and an extensive gift shop. On the grand ramp is a monumental tapestry, an altarpiece by Botticelli and Ghirlandaio. Open 10–5 Tue–Sat, 11–5 Sun. Free docent tours every Saturday at 2. Adults $8, seniors and students $6, children under 6 free. The second Thursday of each month is free from 6 to 9.

The **Jewish Museum of Florida** (305-672-5044; www.jewishmuseum.com), 301 Washington Ave, is housed in a 1936 synagogue. The art deco building features 80 stained-glass windows, a marble bimah, and a copper dome. The museum displays traveling exhibits reflecting Florida Jewish history from 1763. Open 10–5 Tue–Sun. Adults $6, seniors 65+ and students $5, children under 6 free. On Saturday the public enjoys free admission.

North Miami

Seeking a fresh approach, the **Museum of Contemporary Art** (305-893-6211; www.mocanomi.org), 770 NE 125th St, offers provocative and mind-bending exhibitions. I believe that art should make you feel something, and at this creative art house you will have feelings you didn't know existed. Here art is constructed of unusual materials and presented in a spacious gallery. Open 11–5 Tue–Sat, 12–5 Sun, last Fri of each month 7–10. Adults $5, seniors and students $3, children under 12 free. Open Tuesday all day by donation.

TOURS **Dragonfly Expeditions** (305-774-9019 or 1-888-992-6337; www.dragonflyexpeditions.com), 1825 Ponce de Leon Blvd, Coral Gables, believes in true "green" travel, immersing travelers in unique destinations, with minimal impact on the environment. Their tours incorporate flora and fauna, along with history and culture. The tours accommodate several levels of ability, from city walks and bicycle rides to paddling and hiking over varied terrain. These educational and fun tours range from $30 to $100. (See also *The Gables, the Grove, and Miami Cityside,* and *South Miami–Dade: Food and Wine Country.*)

✳ To Do

GLIDING TOURS If you don't want to walk to tour the lovely architecture in South Beach, you can glide on a Segway Human Transporter with **Florida Ever-Glides** (305-695-4245; www .floridaever-glides.com), 233 11th St, Suite 104, Miami Beach. Expertly guided 2½-hour journeys depart daily at 8:30, 1, and 5:30. You'll be given instructions on how to operate your Segway HT before taking off to view the Art Deco Historic District (see *Historic Places*), South Beach, Southpointe Park, Cruise Ship Row, and other interesting spots along the way. To help you stay hydrated and refreshed in the Miami heat, drinks and snacks are provided on this tour. With only 15 people in the group, you'll be assured to hear your guide detail all the features of this architectural delight. Meet at Washington and 11th behind Miami Subs in the peach building. Adults and children over 12 $65. You must weigh between 100 and 290 pounds to ride.

WALKING TOURS A trip to South Florida wouldn't be complete without a tour of the nation's largest 20th-Century National Register Historic District (see *Historic Places*). Starting at the Miami Design Preservation League (MDPL) Art Deco Welcome Center, you'll be guided past some of the eight hundred historical buildings created in the 1920s and '30s. The 90-minute tour of the **Art Deco Historic District** (305-531-3484 or 305-672-2014; www.mdpl.org), 1001 Ocean Dr, Miami Beach, features three dominant architectural styles: art deco, Mediterranean Revival, and MiMo (Miami Modernism). Tours begin at 10:30 AM Wed, Fri, Sat, and Sun, and at 6:30 PM Thu. Adults $20, seniors and students $15, children under 12 free.

If you want to view the area on your own the Art Deco Welcome Center offers **self-guided audio tours** of the Art Deco Historic District in English, Spanish, Portuguese, German, or French. Offered 10–4 daily. Adults $15, seniors and children $10.

✳ Green Space

BEACHES You'll always see kites fluttering over **Haulover Park Beach** (305-947-3525 or 305-944-3040; www.miamidade.gov/parks), 10800 Collins Ave, Miami Beach, a 1.5-mile stretch of coconut palm–lined beach just north of Bal Harbor. With lifeguards and concession stands handy, it's one of the more popular public beaches in the region, especially for surfers. A large portion at the north end of the beach is officially "clothing optional." Gawkers and improper behavior are not tolerated; once on the beach, you'll want to check in at the information flag to receive a flyer on beach etiquette, rules, and a brief orientation. While everyone gets along quite nicely, there are distinct sections for gays and straights. On the Intracoastal side, the beach has a full-service marina and restaurant, a nine-hole golf course, and a kite shop. Open sunrise–sunset. Fee.

PARKS A mecca for mountain bikers, **Oleta River State Park** (305-919-1846; www.floridastateparks.org/oletariver/default.cfm), 3400 NE 163rd St, North Miami, offers more than 10 miles of challenging mountain bike trails—amazing for such an urban area! There are shorter trails for novices, including a paved trail. The park spans from the mangrove forests of the Oleta River to the Atlantic Ocean, enabling visitors to enjoy the beach or kayak through a maze of mangroves. On-site outfitter **Blue Moon Outdoor Center** rents kayaks, canoes, and bikes. Open 8–sunset. Fee.

✳ Lodging

HOTELS, MOTELS, AND RESORTS

Bal Harbour, 33154

The luxurious rooms and suites at the European-style **Sea View Hotel** (305-866-4441 or 1-800-447-1010; www.seaview-hotel.com), 9909 Collins Ave, will treat you to the finest in service and luxurious accommodations. Although it's located on the beach, you'll also want to lounge around the heated swimming pools. The poolside cabanas are reminiscent of a time gone by. Well worth the extra price, the Key West–style cabanas have refrigerators, a walk-in closet, bathroom with showers, and their own private patio. On rainy days, you'll be glad you're only a block from the elite Bal Harbour Shops (see *Eating Out* and *Selective Shopping*). Rooms feature rich furnishings, and all have refrigerators. For those with allergies, hypoallergenic bedding can be requested. $153–500.

Miami Beach/South Beach

The 1956 **Eden Roc Renaissance Resort & Spa** (305-531-0000 or 1-800-327-8337; www.edenrocresort .com), 4525 Collins Ave, 33140, offers deluxe accommodations with spacious rooms ($149–529) and sumptuous linens. Guests come for the world-renowned spa, and large pool and deck, just off the beach. As of February 2006, they no longer accept pets.

Art deco design is everywhere at the **Essex House Hotel and Suites** (305-534-2700; www.essexhotel.com), 1001 Collins Ave, 33139. Built in 1938, it features lines from luxury cruise ships—in the lobby as well as the 61 rooms and 19 spacious suites, where beige and russet linens accent rich mahogany furnishings. The bathrooms will make any diva squeal with delight. They're so enormous, you can spread out when getting ready for a night of clubbing. They also have several mirrors, including a lighted make-up mirror. After a night on the town, you'll be glad the spacious Jacuzzi is large enough so that your entire party can sit around it soaking their feet. Between beach time and clubbing, you'll enjoy sitting in the tropical courtyard with cascading bougainvilleas and a burbling fountain, or lounging in the lobby where you'll be sure to meet new people. Service is excellent and the concierge will be more

ESSEX HOUSE

Kathy Wolf

than happy make dinner reservations for your or put you on your favorite nightclub's list (see *Nightclubs*). You'll find phenomenal deals in low season with rates from $89 to $139. High-season rates run $179–249.

The Hotel (305-531-3222; www .thehotelofsouthbeach.com), 801 Collins Ave, 33139, designed by Todd Oldman, offers four floors of 48 rooms and four suites ($225–405) in eye-popping greens, yellows, and blues. Bathrooms feature hand-brushed tiles, tie-dyed robes and rain-head showers. You'll also enjoy the views from the rooftop lap pool. Browse through the gift shop, where you can purchase some of Todd's orig-inal tie-dyed robes and bags.

Only a block from the beach, in the heart of South Beach, the **Hotel Astor** (305-531-8081 or 1-800-270-4981; www.hotelastor.com), 956 Washington Ave, 33139, is by far my favorite place to stay. You'll know you are in for a new experience as you approach the breathtaking cut coral stone façade of this 1936 art deco hotel. In the lobby, the original Vitro-lite wall panels surround stark white modern furniture, and a dramatic staircase leads you down to the Metro Kitchen and Bar. Outside you can

relax in the garden by the vertical water sculpture, and a new pool is coming in 2007. The quaint boutique hotel offers 40 rooms and suites ($150–400) decorated in crisp whites, soft taupes, chocolates, and brushed chrome. Impressively clean for a bou-tique hotel in South Beach; the housekeeping attendants are restrict-ed to a minimal number of rooms to ensure every attention to detail. The 1,100-square-foot Astor Suite books for upward of $1,000.

Surfside, 33154
One of the last small family motels along the strip, the **Best Western Oceanfront Resort** (305-864-2232; www.bwoceanfront.com), 9365 Collins Ave, sits oceanfront with bal-conies overlooking the swimming pool, tropical atrium, or the sea. Although some of the rooms do show their age (the challenge of seaside accommodations), most are recently renovated and include mini kitchens with fridge, microwave, coffeemaker, and toaster. Junior and one-bedroom suites ($159 and up) include an oceanfront continental breakfast with tropical fruit and juice.

Each of the suites at the **Lilypad Suite Hotel** (305-866-9266; www .lilypadhotel.com), 9400 Collins Ave, offers a full kitchen, nice-size bath-room, and tasteful decor; standard rooms have two double beds and a writing desk. Rooms $75, suites $95 and up.

✳ Where to Eat
DINING OUT

Aventura
I first met Allen Susser at a fund-raiser. One of the nicest celebrity chefs in an industry where ego is

dominant, Chef Allen is a leader in charitable work, devoting great personal involvement to the homeless and elderly. **Chef Allen's** (305-935-2900; www.chefallens.com), 19088 NE 29th Ave, offers a comfortable atmosphere, and his warm personality has infected his staff. Start with a number of ceviches ($14), such as the shrimp and avocado ceviche with Kaffir lime, coconut milk, scallions, and pappadam, or the diver scallop ceviche on rice paper nest, smoked pineapple, and jalapeño foam. You'll enjoy creatively prepared entrées such as pistachio-crusted black grouper with fricassee of rock shrimp, mango, leeks, and coconut rum ($29), tangerine and toasted-cumin seared rare tuna with wasabi mashed potato, green papaya slaw, and pineapple ginger nage ($30), or the kumquat-glazed seared Muscovy duckling breast with smoked shallot mashed potato, duck leg confit, bok choy, and apricot pan sauce ($30). The lemon-scented Earl Grey tea crème brûlée is an unusual treat for dessert ($9), served with a white chocolate macadamia nut biscotti cookie and fresh berries. Order early if you want the Valrhona chocolate truffle soufflé with Chantilly cream and velvet chocolate sauce ($20 for two). Bring your camera; each menu item is a unique piece of art, and you'll want to remember the experience. Open for dinner nightly starting at 6.

Bal Harbour

While shopping at the elite Bal Harbour Shops, you'll want to take lunch at **Carpaccio** (305-867-777). At this elegant indoor, and casual outdoor, restaurant, power lunchers reign. You'll find a variety of fresh salads, pastas, and of course thinly sliced carpaccio. A great place for people-watching and celebrity spotting; but keep your camera at home, as cameras aren't allowed anywhere in the mall. Open for lunch 11:30–4:30, dinner 4:30–11. Entrées $8–19. Valet parking at the mall is $12.

Miami Beach/South Beach

A favorite of my family for birthday celebrations, I keep thinking of excuses to return to **Barton G, The Restaurant** (305-672-8881; www .bartong.com), 1427 West Ave. This restaurant takes all the stuffiness out of fine dining with fun drinks, yummy entrées, and wildly creative desserts. Start with their signature drink, the Sabrinatini, made with Absolut Mandarin, Watermelon Pucker & Champagne, with a tiny chocolate monkey that hangs on the edge of the glass ($12, but worth it). For an appetizer ($8–21) try the trio of crab tacos with cilantro, red pepper kimchee, and yellow pepper ginger, or Lobster Pop-Tarts (lobster and Gruyère in a flaky crust), with a trio of sauces. You'll enjoy such entrées as the Bar-G-Cola salmon with Coca-Cola sauce, sunflower seed crusted grouper with saffron mash, or the pear and walnut brioche crusted lamb chops ($16–64). Save room for dessert ($13–34). The Big Top Cotton Candy will have everyone sharing, and the Chocolate Grand Canyon with fudgey chocolate cake in a canyon of chocolate, rivers of raspberry fudge, and Butterfinger rocks will send you over the edge. Reservations are recommended, and dining is inside or in the garden.

At **Doraku** (305-695-8383; www. sushidoraku.com), 1104 Lincoln Rd, Japanese-trained executive chef Hiro Terada serves two styles of Japanese cuisine: Kansai, a traditional style, and

Tokyo, a contemporary style. Appetizers ($6–14) include the Maine lobster sushi roll. Sushi and sashimi ($2–6 apiece) have unique delicacies such as sea urchin and octopus. The extensive selection of sake is imported from various regions of Japan, along with their signature fruit sake infused with pineapple, cherry, and mango. Lunch noon–3:30 PM Mon–Fri; dinner 5 PM–midnight Mon–Thu, 5 PM–1 AM Fri, 3 PM–1 AM Sat, 3 PM–11:30 PM Sun. A fabulous Happy Hour is held Monday through Friday from 5 to 8, with a complimentary buffet on Friday.

The glamorous **Forge Restaurant** (305-538-8533; www.theforge.com), 432 41st St, has been a Miami Beach landmark for decades. The award-winning American steakhouse offers white-tie service in an antique setting and features more than three hundred thousand wines in their eight-room wine cellar. You'll have a hard time choosing between lamb osso buco with seafood saffron risotto, Forge Duck with black currant sauce, or the veal chop with sun-dried tomatoes, encrusted with fresh mozzarella. Broiled steaks feature four complimentary house sauces: Classic Java, Forge A.1., Four Mustard Horse-

GRILLFISH RESTAURANT

Kathy Wolf

radish Lime, and Béarnaise. You'll want to choose made-to-order Belgium chocolate or Grand Marnier citrus soufflé with your entrée, as they take 30 minutes to prepare. The Forge Blacksmith Pie has been a classic for more than two decades. Open 4–midnight Mon–Thu; 5 PM–3 AM Fri and Sat, noon–midnight Sun. Expect prices $51 and higher.

At the moderately priced **Grillfish** (305-538-9908; www.grillfish.com), 1444 Collins Ave, you'll first take note of the floor-to-ceiling erotic mural behind the large stone bar. Ornate columns, massive mirrors, and candlelight continue the ambiance of sensuality. Chalkboard menus, situated around the room, feature such freshly caught fish as mahimahi ($18), whole yellowtail snapper ($20), and wahoo ($17). Each fish dish is served with a choice of sweet onion or creamy garlic tomato sauce and is accompanied by pasta or salad. The menu also offers a selection of meats, such as filet mignon with horseradish cream ($24) and veal Marsala ($17). Save room for one of their desserts, such as black Russian banana split ($6) or mango Key lime pie ($7). Open daily, 5:30 till late.

For fresh crab, **Joe's Stone Crab Restaurant** (305-673-0365; www.joesstonecrab.com), 11 Washington Ave, can't be beat. Growing from a little lunch counter to the present-day homage to the crab, the restaurant founded by Joe Weiss in 1913 is as much of Miami Beach's history as Flagler's Railroad (see *Palm Beach County*). The restaurant operates on a seasonal schedule, dependent on the crabs (typically Oct 15–May 15). You can't make reservations, so you'll want to get there early, or expect to wait.

Entrées $7–49, with market prices dictating. Open for lunch 11:30–2 Tue–Sat, dinner 5–10 Mon–Thu, 5–11 Fri and Sat, 4–10 Sun.

Family-friendly **Señor Frog's Mexican Grill** (305-673-5262; www.senor frogsfla.com), 616 Collins Ave, features great Mexican cuisine, where you can order the Moo Flute, a rolled and crisp hard tortilla filled with marinated steak, chicken, or cheese, topped with guacamole and sour cream ($15), or one of their famous sombrero dishes. Open for lunch and dinner. Open daily 11:30 AM–midnight, later on weekends—as the crowd dictates. There is another location in Coconut Grove.

EATING OUT

Bal Harbour
On the second floor of the Bal Harbour Shops, you'll enjoy imported teas and French pastries at **Lea's Tea Room & Bistro** (305-868-0901). The European-style café serves a delightful selection of baked goods and ice creams. At lunch you can order salads and sandwiches. Open 9:30–8:30. Breakfast dishes $6–8; lunch and dinner $7–14. Valet parking $12.

Miami Beach/South Beach
A classic **kosher** deli, **Arnie & Richie's** (305-531-7691), 525 41st St, is a busy breakfast nosh, with bagels and lox, pickled green tomatoes, and eggs several ways.

The neon sign beckons you to **Jerry's Famous Deli** (305-532-8030; www .jerrysfamousdeli.com), 1450 Collins Ave. The lively deli, where you'll often spot a host of celebrities, is open 24 hours every day. Hefty portions and friendly service dominate with such varied entrées as white spaghetti ($10), corned beef and cabbage ($15), fajita plate ($13), and chicken breast schnitzel ($16). You'll find more than six hundred traditional deli favorites, along with enormous sandwiches, salads, and pizzas. Plan to stop by often for dessert, as their bakery features such delights as Hungarian walnut cake for only $3.

Also open 24 hours (see Jerry's, above) is the **News Café** (305-538-6397; www.newscafe.com), 800 Ocean Dr. A great place to celebrity-watch, the café is a central meeting point for top models. Start your day with breakfast. For only $7 you can order

JERRY'S FAMOUS DELI

Kathy Wolf

the Continental Special with assorted pastries, hot coffee, and juice. For heartier appetites they have Benedicts, omelets, quiche, French toast, and pancakes ($6–11). Later in the day, you'll enjoy entrées such as seafood paella ($23); the vegetarian favorite, portobello mushroom with spinach and tomato over rice ($9); and a variety of pasta, pizza, and Mediterranean dishes.

Surfside

There's a delectable selection at **Kastners Pastry Shop** (305-535-2255), 9465 Harding Ave, a **kosher** bakery and grocery store.

Enter the souk at **Moroccan Nights** (305-865-5333), 9555 Harding Ave, for a Middle-eastern experience you won't forget. Dining is along benches lined with pillows, and the food is strictly **kosher.**

One of my aunt's favorite **kosher** eateries, the **Surfside Café** (305-867-3151), 9490 Harding Ave, offers a tasty variety of panini sandwiches (including Greek, Italian, smoked salmon, and three cheese), salads, and pasta, including penne *arrabiata.*

Hot with *Miami New Times* readers, **Sushi Republic** (305-867-8036), 9583 Harding Ave, has all the sushi favorites, including rolls, special rolls, and sashimi ($3–11) and combo dinners ($12–19). Open daily.

✴ Selective Shopping

ANTIQUES AND COLLECTIBLES

Miami Beach/South Beach

At **Antique Collectable Market** (www.antiquecollectiblemarket.com), you'll find 80 or more dealers lined up in the open-air mall on Lincoln Road. The market is open only on

Sunday from 8 to 5. Located just a couple of blocks from the Lincoln Road Farmers Market held the same day (see *Farmer's Markets*).

BOOKSTORES

Miami Beach

Staving off the major bookstores, the independent **Books & Books** (1-888-626-6576; www.booksandbooks.com) at Miami Beach (305-532-3222), 933 Lincoln Rd, and Bal Harbour (305-864-4241), 9700 Collins Ave, is the main bookstore to head to for a wide selection of reading and fun. It's not unusual to see a best-selling author browsing the isles or signing books. The large magazine collection and newsstands contain publications and papers from around the world. The locally owned bookstore also has locations in Coral Gables (see *The Gables, the Grove, and Miami Cityside*), and at Levenger Outlet in Delray Beach (see *South Palm Beach County*), where you'll find book accessories and reading tools. Open 10–11 Sun–Thu, 10–midnight Fri and Sat.

BOUTIQUES AND SHOPS

Miami Beach/South Beach

The 1950s-style mall on Lincoln Rd at 16th St (305-531-3442) is a perfect place to shop, dine, or just have fun with the family, even the dog. Closed to traffic, the pedestrian-only mall covers 8 city blocks. When looking for a night-out ensemble, seek out **Chroma** (305-695-8808), tucked in an alcove at 920 Lincoln Rd. A favorite of mine is **White House/Black Market** (305-672-8006; www.whiteandblack.com), 1106 Lincoln Rd. No big-name brands here; the shop features private labels made in a timeless style. And the reasonably priced quality clothes and accessories can be worn day or night. Don't forget your pet. ❖ **The Dog Bar** (305-532-5654; www.dogbar.com), 1684 Jefferson Ave, has duds, toys, and treats for both dogs and cats in the SoBe style. Open daily; most shops open by 11 AM. City parking for Lincoln Road Mall is available between Lincoln Rd and 17th St.

Surfside
Surfside's business district offers interesting shops to explore. An urban chic boutique, **Tangerine** (305-868-6090), 9457 Harding Ave, has fabric art, pottery, and crocheted shawls in the windows. **Absolut Flowers** (305-866-5288), 9481 Harding Ave, is jam-packed with trendy home decor and tall glass vases. Reminding me of the marketplace in Goa, West Indies, **Lace Star Designer Fabrics** (305-868-5550), 9593 Harding Ave, has a stunning display of beaded fabrics and boasts the "most variety of one-of-a-kind beaded French lace in the world." Look for classy handbags and painted tote bags at **Moon Over Miami** (305-865-0735), 9455 Harding Ave.

FARMER'S MARKETS

Miami Beach/South Beach
The special event company, **The Market Company** (305-531-0038; www.themarketcompany.org), runs a cool version of the farmer's and festival markets. Locals know that the **Lincoln Road Farmers Market,** 600 Block of Lincoln Rd (between Lenox Ave and Washington Ave), is the freshest market around. Featuring local fruits, vegetables, fresh cut flowers, baked breads, and jams and honey. Open year-round on Sunday: 9–7, Apr–Oct; 9–6, Nov–Mar. **Española Way Weekend Festival**

features multicultural gifts, clothing, and jewelry in the South Beach Historic Spanish Village. You'll find the market on 428 Española Way (between 14th St and 15th St, and Drexel Ave and Washington Ave), 10–6 Sat, 11–9 Sun; and **FestivArt,** Fri and Sat 7–midnight. The **Market Company store** is at 428 Española Way.

MALLS

Bal Harbour
Bal Harbour Shops (www.bal harbourshops.com) is the shopping center of the rich and famous. You'll be shopping elbow to elbow with the world's elite. While $600 shoes and $2,000 blouses are available, you can also find nice bargains and excellent sales. Hey, the rich like to save money too. Built in 1965 by owner-developer Stanley Whitman on an old World War II army barracks, the alfresco mall creates a relaxing environment. Take your cue from the turtles in the lush tropical koi pond—slow down and relax; this is a mall of grace and calm. Start your day at **Lea's Tea Room & Bistro** (see *Eating Out*) for a cup of tea and French baked goods; spend the day exploring the shops; and then grab lunch or dinner at **Carpaccio** (see *Dining Out*). The mall is anchored by Neiman Marcus (305-865-6161; www.neimanmarcus .com), and you'll find many "firsts" here. **Giuseppe Zanotti** (305-868-0133; www.giuseppe-zanotti-design .com) offers a unique collection of bejeweled shoes and purses. The fine craftsman dictates that every woman own at least one pair. You'll want to stop in at the **House of Harry Winston** (786-206-6657; www.harry winston.com) just to see the unique

jewels. The connoisseur of gems, Winston created an entirely new way to cut stones, and their brilliance is evidence of his mastery. Winston's most famous piece, the Hope Diamond, resides at the Smithsonian Institution. While the ladies shop, men will enjoy **The Art of Shaving** (305-865-0408; www.theartofshaving .com), where they can get the Royal Shave or an aromatherapy treatment. Part old-fashioned barbershop and part day spa, the shop features shaves the old-fashioned way. Starting with a hot face towel and facial massage to open and cleanse the pores, the barber then applies warm shaving cream with a badger brush, and with an authentic straight razor skillfully shaves your whiskers, not once, but twice—first down, then up. Afterward a mask is applied to rejuvenate the skin. The finishing touch is a splash of rosewater and lavender oil. You'll feel like a new man. My son begs for this treatment each birthday. You can purchase their line here as well. The Straight Razor Shave is $35, the Royal Shave $55. So that superstars can shop like normal people, Bal Harbour

Shops has a strict paparazzi policy— no cameras. If caught using a camera, you may be escorted out of the mall; so leave yours in your car or purse. Open 10–9 Mon–Sat; mall stores 12–6 Sun. Parking $12.

✳ Entertainment

DANCING We are so lucky to have **The Miami City Ballet** (1-877-929-7010; www.miamicityballet.org), 2200 Liberty Ave, Miami Beach/South Beach, and luckier to have artistic director Edward Villella leading it. With an operating budget of more than 10 million, the company of 50 dancers is one of the largest ballet corps in the United States. The founder of the company, Villella, in 1997 received the prestigious National Medal of Arts from President Clinton, and was also named a Kennedy Center Honoree. Marrying the classical techniques of choreographer George Balanchine with his own style, Villella brings a fresh approach to dance. His four-act ballet, *The Neighborhood Ballroom,* premiered in 2003. The company's repertoire

KOI POND TURTLES AT BAL HARBOUR SHOPS

ART DECO ON SOUTH BEACH

includes 82 ballets, with masterworks from George Balanchine, Twyla Tharp, and Paul Taylor, along with original works from Villella and other gifted choreographers. Call for show times, location, and pricing.

NIGHTCLUBS

Miami Beach/South Beach

Clubs open and close like swinging doors in South Beach. The hottest clubs continually reinvent themselves. My daughter and I enjoy the following, which, as of this writing, have managed to stay the test of time. Often just the street address is enough to direct you to the newest hip and happening club.

Amika (305-534-1499; www.amika miami.com), 1532 Washington Ave. If it weren't for the line at the door, you probably wouldn't know Amika was there. The former synagogue has seen its fair share of clubs, but Amika has hung in there, possibly due to owner and former model Tony Guerra. So expect to see lots of beautiful people

gyrating on the lively open dance floor, cuddling in the rear lounge, or schmoozing in the VIP Loft.

At **Crobar** (305-672-8084; www .crobar.com), 1445 Washington Ave, a glassed-enclosed VIP room overlooks the main dance floor, where serious dancers strut their stuff. The state-of-the-art sound system is one of the best on the beach, with international DJs regularly spinning the latest tunes. I can't wait to see what they'll do at their new location on 50 NE 11th, where they'll reopen in November 2006. And I'm not sure what will pop up in their old space, but it will be worth watching.

My personal favorite is **Mansion** (305-532-1525), 235 Washington Ave, part of the Opium Group (www. opiummiami.com). This large cavernous club is housed in a 1936 French casino, with six bars on two levels—each bar playing a different beat. The main room is like something out of a movie. You'll be in awe of the ornate fireplaces, Venetian glass

NAVIGATING NIGHTCLUBS

You don't have to be a millionaire, celebrity, or a 20-something size 2 to gain entrance to the famous clubs of South Beach. The trendy dance-club atmosphere of SoBe is like no other, with architectural details and energy reminiscent of the 1980s *Miami Vice* television series. Even if you never go to clubs, plan to experience at least one. So, here are the rules: First, dress accordingly. Clubs don't allow jeans, no matter how much they cost. A simple black outfit is all you need. Or take time to shop Lincoln Road (see *Selective Shopping*) to get the latest "in" outfit. Ladies will want to throw on some makeup and style their hair. Men should be well groomed. Next, arrive early—around 10–11 PM. Even then, expect to wait. Clubs don't typically get hopping until well after midnight, and waits of an hour are not uncommon. If you're aware of this, you'll be patient. Everyone eventually gets in. The clubs also like to show a lengthy line to create an atmosphere of "this must be the place to be tonight," and a full club is much more entertaining. Getting in is easier if you cluster in small groups of women, or with an even number of men and women. Groups of men should break up or attach themselves to a group of women. I don't know why, but men will stand in line forever if they are grouped together. When approaching the doorman, don't say anything—just smile. If you have bought a table or know your name is on The List, then give your name and wait patiently. And don't bother to grease doormen's palms.

mirrors, towering arches, dramatic crystal chandeliers, and twin sweeping staircases, which lead to VIP rooms. The club also plays host to fashion shows, boxing matches, and concerts. Mansion's sister club is over on Collins Avenue. **The Opium Garden** (305-531-5535), 136 Collins Ave, is a Zen-like oasis. Dance under the stars in the roofless open-air courtyard, with lush Asian-style gardens, complete with Buddha statues. Balmy breezes surround you in this exotic, surreal world. Upstairs at **Privé** you'll need a VIP pass to hang with the hip people. The ultrachic design, a favorite of celebrities, features organic oak, natural hide sofas, and a dramatic waterfall.

Hip-hop rules at **State** (305-531-2800), 320 Lincoln Rd. It's dark and sexy, and ladies get in free all night long on Friday.

THEATER

Miami Beach/South Beach
Opening in 1934 as a movie house for Paramount Pictures, the **Colony Theatre** (305-674-1040), 1040 Lincoln Rd, is a fine example of the art deco style and is listed on the National Register of Historic Places. Redesigned with new acoustics, but retaining the historical architecture, the theater is host to a variety of performing arts such as dance, concerts, comedy, and film festivals.

They'll think even $50 is cheap, and you won't get in any faster. If you plan on frequenting the same club for several nights, however, you might slip them a $20 or more *after* they move you past the velvet rope, just on the off chance that they might remember you each night. Be forewarned: Tipping may not get you in any faster. The easiest way to ensure entrance is to put your name on a list, which can be done in a number of ways. The first is to have your hotel concierge call and put your name on The List. Although this is a free service, $10 is a nice gesture to give the concierge when the reservation is made. The second, and more expensive, way to gain entrance is to buy a table. You'll have to cough up several hundreds of dollars to reserve one, but a reserved table includes a bottle or bottles of your choice of liquor ($225 per bottle and up). All mixers are provided, and you'll be assured table service. If you haven't reserved a table, don't even think of sitting down unless invited. Unlike the days of "get there early to get the best seat," all tables are available by reservation only. Even if you don't reserve a table, plan to spend a bundle. Admission to clubs varies but typically runs around $20. Once inside you'll spend about $7 for beer and wine, and $12 and up for mixed drinks, so a table reservation may be the best bargain for a group. If you haven't been clubbing in a long time, or ever, you may want to book a club tour. The tour host can gain immediate entrance to numerous clubs, and the tour often includes some drinks. Call the Greater Miami Convention and Visitors Bureau (see *Guidance*) for a selection of approved club-tour operators. Most clubs are open 10 PM–5 AM.

Under the direction of Jude Parry "the mistress of pantomime," the **Gold Coast Theatre Co.** (305-538-5500) specializes in mime and physical theater with strolling characters, improvised fun, and at times audience participation. The company often plays to homeless shelters and at safe houses for victims of domestic abuse. Public performances are often held at the Colony Theatre on Lincoln Road (see above). Call for locations and current schedule.

✳ Special Events

January: **Miami Beach Art Deco Weekend Festival** (305-672-2014; www.mdpl.org), along Ocean Dr, between 5th St and 15th St. You'll love the big bands and artistic antiques as you step back to the art deco period (circa 1925–1945). Presented by the Miami Design Preservation League.

February: A celebration of food and fun awaits you at **Fab Fest: Taste of the Beach** (305-754-5886), Ocean Dr between 7th St and 8th St. The festival features a wide selection of wine and food from around the world. You'll also enjoy live entertainment while selecting a unique gift crafted by local artisans.

The **Miami International Boat Show and Sailboat Show** (www .miamiboatshow.com) takes over the

Miami Beach Convention Center and many marinas around the city. More than 2,300 marine manufacturers showcase vessels of your dreams, along with accessories such as nautical clothing, teak deck chairs, and the all-important sunglasses.

October: Experience the excitement and colors of a 2000-year-old traditional sporting event. Sponsored by the United Chinese Association of Florida, the **South Florida Dragon Boat Festival** (305-345-8489; www.miamidragonboat.com) is held at Haulover Park and Marina (see *Beaches*). More than two-dozen slim canoe-like boats are decorated with brilliant colors and a hand-painted dragon's head. Teams of up to 20 rowers each race against each other, many for local charities. You'll enjoy a weekend of fun with martial arts demonstrations, an egg roll eating contest, a kid's kite contest, and authentic Asian food booths.

SOUTH MIAMI–DADE:
FOOD AND WINE COUNTRY

At the tip of Miami-Dade County lies an area teaming with tropical agriculture. It was first opened to settlers in 1898, and for decades the only access to the county was via the Homesteaders Trail. It wasn't until Henry Flagler's railroad accessed this remote county, bordered by the Atlantic Ocean to the east and the Everglades to the west, that the area began to develop. Severe hurricanes have hit here twice—in 1926, and again in 1992 when Hurricane Andrew struck. True to the pioneer spirit, however, residents have consciously rebuilt and restored many historic buildings, including the Mediterranean Revival buildings in the quaint business district on Krome Avenue. Expansion has been rapid in Miami-Dade County, one of the last areas in South Florida still open for development. The Homestead Miami Speedway is just one of many attractions added to this tropical location. Florida City, considered the gateway to the Everglades and offering many eco-friendly activities, has seen an increase in tourism. Once thought of as a place to pass through on the way to the Keys, the southern cities of Miami-Dade County have blossomed into an area rich with gourmet delights while preserving their agricultural heritage—nearly half of the country's winter vegetables in the United States are grown here. U-pick and roadside fruit and vegetable stands are abundant. You'll find avocados, guava, mangos, mamey, and papaya picked fresh from the fields. And because this region is so close to the harvest, it has seen a growth in tasty eateries and innovative wines such as Lychee and Carambola.

GUIDANCE The **Greater Miami Convention and Visitors Bureau** (305-539-3000; www.miamiandbeaches.com) provides a wide array of information. For a vacation guide call 1-888-76-MIAMI or 305-447-7777. For information on the immediate area, the **Tropical Everglades Visitor Center (T.E.V.A.)** (305-245-9180 or 1-800-388-9669; www.tropicaleverglades.com), 160 US 1, Florida City, can direct you to the little out-of-the-way places.

GETTING THERE *By car:* Head south on the **US 1** or, to avoid traffic jams, take the Homestead Extension of **Florida's Turnpike,** which dumps you out onto US 1 in Florida City.

By air: The closest airport is **Miami International Airport** (305-876-7000; www.miami-airport.com), 34 miles from Florida City and Homestead.

By bus: **Greyhound** (1-800-231-2222; www.greyhound.com) has a station in Homestead and will also take you into the Keys. **Metrobus,** part of Miami-Dade Transit, Customer Services (305-770-3131; www.miamidade.gov/transit), runs along US 1A from Miami to Florida City and Homestead.

GETTING AROUND *By car:* **US 1** will take you straight into the Keys. The main business section is a few blocks west on Krome Avenue (Old US 27).

PARKING Public parking in the southern part of the county is readily available at no cost.

MEDICAL EMERGENCIES While some of the best hospitals in the world are located in metro Miami, you'll find excellent health care in the south end of the county as well. **Homestead Hospital** (786-243-8000; www.baptisthealth.net), 160 NW 13 St, is the only emergency center for 18 miles in all directions of the city. In late 2006, a new facility will be located just east of the Florida Turnpike on the north side of Campbell Drive, at SW 312 St. **South Miami Hospital** (786-662-4000; www.baptisthealth.net), 6200 SW 73 St, also part of the Baptist Health network, is located farther north, near Kendall. For diver emergencies, call the **Key Largo Recompression Chamber** (911 if emergency; 1-800-NO-BENDS for information) in Key Largo.

✳ To See

ARCHEOLOGICAL SITES At the **Deering Estate at Cutler Ridge** (see *Historic Sites*) join a walking tour (included in admission) for a glimpse into prehistory, meandering through the tropical forest, through the site of the 1800s village of Cutler, and across a stone bridge, and culminating in a walk to a Tequesta burial mound from the 1600s.

ART GALLERIES The not-for-profit artist community at **ArtSouth** (305-247-9406; www.artsouthhomestead.org), 240 N Krome Ave, Homestead, is spread over 3½ acres. You'll find the studios of 35 fine artists on the campus. In the two-story Fine Arts Building, you'll feel strong emotions when viewing the works of Joe Parker, and an organic connection with Carol Jaime's soulful woodcarvings. You'll also experience the human condition with the rich tropical flora of Vanessa Bryson's oil, watercolor, and pastel paintings. The new Fine Crafts & Sculpture Building features pottery, ceramics, and works in metal. Over at the historic Sanctuary, various performing arts are presented throughout the year. An Open House, with all studios open and live entertainment, is held each month on the second Saturday.

The garden paths will draw you in to several quaint shops and galleries in **Cauley Square Historic Village** (305-258-3543; www.cauleysquareshops.com), 22400 Old Dixie Hwy (US 1), Miami. Open 10–5 Tue–Sat, 12–5 Sun. You'll often find an artist at work at **The Art Place. O'Sew Crafty** features handmade items from local artisans. And **Atabey** has unique crafts from the Dominican Republic and Latin America.

CORAL CASTLE

Kathy Wolf

ATTRACTIONS Romance knows no limits at **Coral Castle** (305-248-6344 or 1-800-366-0264; www.coralcastle .com), 28655 S Dixie Hwy, Homestead. From 1923 to 1951, Latvian immigrant Edward Leedskalnin built a stunning architectural structure to recapture the unrequited love of Agnes Scuffs. After the young lady canceled the wedding just one day before the event, the 26-year-old jilted groom began a lifelong quest to win her back. Working alone, Leedskalnin carved more than 1,100 tons of coral rock by hand, placing each section on 10 acres, all without the use of machinery. Originally called Rock Gate Park, Coral Castle features the Heart Table, Moon Garden, Polaris Telescope, and even the AC-Generator. To protect his privacy, he surrounded the castle with 8-foot walls that are 3 feet thick. Thirty-minute audio tours provide details of the castle in four languages, explaining the many interesting facts of Ed Leedskalnin's life ("Sweet Sixteen" by Billy Joel was written about Leedskalnin's lost love). The young runaway bride eventually married someone else. Ed's remains are buried in Miami Memorial Park Cemetery. Open 9–8 Mon–Thu, 9–9 Fri–Sun. Adults $9.75, seniors 62+ $6.50, children 7–12 $5, under 7 free.

AVIATION A wide selection of classic and military aircraft is on display at the **Wings Over Miami Museum** (305-233-5197; www.wingsovermiami.com), Kendall-Tamiami Executive Airport, 114710 SW 128th St, Miami. Aircraft is displayed in the hangar, outside, and at times in the air. Open 10–5 Thu–Sun. Adults $10, seniors $7, children $6.

HISTORIC SITES

Cutler Ridge
Step into South Florida's past at **The Deering Estate at Cutler Ridge** (305-235-1668; www.deeringestate .org), 16701 SW 72 Ave, where pioneer families settled the village of Cutler, one of the first in the region, and the Richmond family built a grand home in 1896 overlooking Biscayne Bay. In 1900, they opened the Richmond Cottage, the first hotel

MANGROVES, DEERING ESTATE

Sandra Friend

DEERING ESTATE

Sandra Friend

between Coconut Grove and Key West. These two buildings are among the last examples of early Frame Vernacular architecture in South Florida. Purchased by industrialist Charles Deering in 1913, the estate expanded with additional buildings, including his grand Mediterranean Revival "Stone House" and a boat basin, where today manatees frolic. Now a county park, the estate encompasses nearly 450 acres, a large portion of it left as natural tropical forest and accessible on guided tours only, where you'll see the remains of the original village and a burial mound from the 1600s. Adults $7, children $5; includes guided tour of the Stone House and the trails at set times throughout the day. Open 10–5 daily, except Christmas and Thanksgiving.

Redland

In the **Redland Historic Agricultural District** north of Homestead, the cultivation of tropical fruits, flowers, and palm trees is big business, with nearly three hundred ornamental growers, vegetable farms, bonsai, and water lily nurseries. According to some of its residents, Redland is Brigadoon, a fabled land that no one else can see. Only one home is allowed on every 5 acres, and the dark, rich soil is perfect for tropical flora grown nowhere else in the United States.

Several **historic coral rock houses** built by the region's early pioneers can be seen in the vicinity of the original Orchid Jungle, SW 157th Ave at Newton Rd, Homestead, now **Hattie Bauer Hammock Park.** At 15730 SW 272nd St, **"Windwood"** is a beautiful example of a coral rock home; the **Cooper Residence,** 14201 SW 248th St, built in 1933, has wrought-iron gates; the home and carriage house are mortared coral rock. The **Redland Farm Life School** on SW 162nd Ave is the region's original schoolhouse.

MUSEUMS

Florida City/Homestead

The 1904 Frame Vernacular **Florida Pioneer Museum** (305-246-9531; www.flamuseums.org), 826 N Krome Ave, Florida City, was built as a residence for an agent of the Florida East Coast Railroad. The 1½-story home, listed on the National Register of Historic Places, features turn-of-the-20th-century memorabilia. Open only Wednesday and Saturday afternoons from 1 to 5.

At the **Historic Homestead Townhall Museum** (305-242-4463; www.fla museums.org), 41 N Krome Ave, Homestead, you'll discover artifacts and memorabilia of the area, including more than four hundred historical pictures. Open 11–5 Tue–Sat. Free.

NATIVE AMERICAN PLACES Originally members of the Creek Nation, the Miccosukee Indians have adapted to several changes in their history. From the struggle with early settlers to the draining of their land during the Land Boom, they have kept with their traditions while adapting to the modern world. At the **Miccosukee Indian Village** (305-223-8380; www.miccosukee.com), Mile Marker 70, US 41, Tamiami Trail, you'll be guided on a tour that explores their history, culture, and lifestyle. **Miccosukee Resort & Gaming** (305-242-6464), 500 SW 177th Ave, Miami, offers exciting hours of video pull-tab machines, Lighting Lotto, and 58 poker tables. Many locals head to High Stakes Bingo, where you can win thousands of dollars. Village open 9–5 daily. Gaming open 24 hours.

ORCHID GROWERS The county is one of the largest orchid-growing regions, the Redland, and you can visit a number of local nurseries. Stop in and inhale the sweet fragrance at **Soroa Orchids** (305-247-2566; www.soroa.com), 25750 SW 117th Ave, on Krome Ave, or venture a few streets back to fabled **R.F. Orchids** (305-245-4570; www.rforchids.com), 28100 SW 182nd Ave. In its third generation of growers, this family operation is the most-awarded grower in the United States, and the owner is a top speaker on the subject of orchids. We were greeted with cherry limeade, and encountered a profusion of colors and aromas of the finest orchids, as written about in *The Orchid Thief.* I know little about orchids, but the array of varieties was simply dazzling; this is a must-stop for orchid collectors. Open 9–5 Tue–Sun.

Baldan Orchids (305-232-8694), 20075 SW 180th Ave, are open 9:30–5 Sat and Sun, and feature blooming-size *Phalaenopsis.* **Redland Orchids** (305-246-2473), 26620 SW 203rd Ave, specialize in *Cattleas, Oncidiums,* and *Encyclias* and are open 8–4 Mon–Fri. You'll find a wide variety of orchids and tropical exotics at **Impact Orchids & Exotics** (305-257-5771), 14400 SW 248th St. **Motes Orchids** (305-247-4398; www.motesorchids.com), 25000 SW 162nd Ave, knows all about *Vandas.* **Carib Plants** (305-245-5565; www.caribplants.com) are open 8–5 Mon–Fri and 8–1 Sat. They feature *Phalaenopsis, Cattleyas, Broughtonias, Oncidiinae,* and *Psychopis.* The folks at **Whimsy Orchids** (305-242-1333), 18755 SW 248th St, are open 9–4 Tue–Sat, with *Equitant oncidiums (Tolumnia)* as their specialty. Call for appointment. Pick up an *Orchid Guide to South Florida* at the Tropical Everglades Visitor Center, for a wider listing of these growers.

MICCOSUKEE MUSEUM, TAMIAMI TRAIL
Visit Florida

RAILROADIANA Ride the rails at **The Gold Coast Railroad Museum** (305-253-0063; www.goldcoast-railroad.org), 12450 SW 152nd St (Miami Metrozoo Entrance), Miami. The museum features the history of trains, along with real—yes, you can ride them—trains. Starting in 1956, Richmond Naval Air Station, a former World War II airship base, was transformed into a living museum with more than 3 miles of tracks and an assortment of working historic trains. Inside the enormous airship hangar, you'll explore the armor-plated Ferdinand Magellan, which served Presidents Roosevelt, Truman, and Eisenhower; the Silver Crescent, a California Zephyr with visa-dome observation deck; a 1922 steam locomotive, a Seaboard wooden caboose, and many more trains. Sit in the passenger coach and enjoy a 20-minute ride on a diesel-electric standard-gauge train, or ride up front with the engineer in the cab. Kids will love the Edwin Link Children's Railroad, which runs on 2-foot track. The beautifully landscaped tracks over in the Floyd McEachern Model Train Exhibit provide inspiration to collect your own railroadiana. Open 11–3 Mon–Fri, 11–4 Sat and Sun. Adults $5, children under 12 $3. Train rides available on weekends for an additional $2.25–11.

WILDLIFE VIEWING You'll spot a variety of wildlife all along any of the roads in this region. In particular, head out on Palm Drive and along US 192 at dusk or dawn; you'll be sure to spot ibis, egrets, and the occasional opossum. Head south on US 192 to reach Everglades Outpost and Everglades Alligator Farm (see *Wildlife Rehabilitation & Zoological Parks*).

WINERY ❧ A garden paradise awaits you at **Schnebly Redland's Winery** (305-242-1224 or 1-888-717-WINE; www.schneblywinery.com), 30205 SW 217th Ave, Homestead, where from the visitors center you can sit and taste wine as twin waterfalls drop 18 feet into a cool tropical pond. Denisse and Peter Schnebly began as tropical packers. Realizing that the slightly blemished fruit not suited for the marketplace could be turned into unique wines, they sought out a vintner, Doug Knapp, and over several years developed distinguished wines made from such tropical fruits as carambola, passion fruit, guava, mangos, and Asian lychees. The Schneblys' entrepreneurial spirit has created a mecca for a new agricultural business in southern Miami-Dade County. Agri-tours, wine festivals, and walks through the orchards are just part of the new Food and Wine Country. Try the Carambola, made from star fruit, which is reminiscent of Pinot Grigio. The Mango, resembling a White Zinfandel, is great with pasta. For a wine that's good with just about everything, try the unique taste of Rose Guava. The light and crisp Lychee has become a must-have on my holiday table. And you'll love Passion Fruit with any dessert. Wines

STEAM ENGINE, GOLD COAST RAILROAD MUSEUM

Kathy Wolf

YOUNG ALLIGATORS AT EVERGLADES ALLI-
GATOR FARM

Kathy Wolf

are reasonably priced at $14–20 per bottle. The wine-tasting room is open 10–5 Mon–Fri; 10–6 Sat; 12–5 Sun.

WILDLIFE REHABILITATION & ZOOLOGICAL PARKS

Homestead

✿ You'll see thousands of gators at **Everglades Alligator Farm** (305-247-2628; www.everglades.com), 40351 SW 192nd Ave. At this real working alligator farm, hundreds of tiny alligators live in "grow out" pens, while the larger reptiles lounge along a vast tropical lake. Make sure to check out the Sebastopol geese. These snowy-white fowl have unique curled feathers, preventing flight. The clean grounds have a rustic feel, providing you with a natural experience. The farm is home to a wide assortment of nonreleasable wildlife and carries the best collection of animal educational books around. Airboat rides take you along the "river of grass," where you'll see an abundance of wildlife, including gators, in their natural habit. Admission includes the airboat ride. Open 9–6 daily except Christmas. Adults $17, children 4–11 $10, under 4 free. Check their web site for a coupon.

✿ The **Everglades Outpost** (305-247-8000; www.evergladesoutpost.org), 35601 SW 192nd Ave, is primarily a rehabilitation and release facility of wild and exotic animals. The sanctuary provides a safe and nurturing atmosphere for nonreleasable wildlife and exotic species, such as those confiscated by authorities. Founders Bob Freer and Barbara Tansey welcome you to the facility to view the various animals and to learn more about these injured or abused creatures and their plight. Among some of the "guests" you might encounter are Florida panthers; albino and orange tigers; a grizzly bear and a cinnamon phased black bear; mandrill, macaque, and capuchin monkeys; fallow deer; a pair of sloths; a lesser anteater; and wolves, including Tasha, a female timber wolf, and Yukon, the alpha male artic wolf. One-day membership: adults $7, children under 12 $5; annual membership: $50; family membership (up to five people): $100. Their adopt-an-animal program allows you to sponsor an animal for a year.

WOLF AT EVERGLADES OUTPOST

Kathy Wolf

Miami

✒ One of the best zoos in the nation, **Miami Metrozoo** (305-251-0400; www
.miamimetrozoo.com), 12400 SW 152nd St, features more than 1,300 animals and
is cageless. After passing through the entrance, you'll soon come upon the Bengal
tigers, including a rare white Bengal in the Pride of Asia habitat. I've sat for hours
watching these majestic beasts as they played in and out of their swimming pool,
with Asian ruins as the backdrop. Another favorite are the Cape hunting dogs with
their beautiful tan, white, and black markings. You'll often see them frolicking with
pups. You'll smell the eucalyptus as you get near the peaceful koala exhibit, where
the first koala on the East Coast was born. Throughout, animals are grouped
according to geographic territories that cover most areas of the world. The park is
huge, so expect a lot of walking. Tired feet will be happy to take the free monorail,
which runs throughout the property, hop on a guided tram tour, or rent one of the
covered bicycle carriages. Open daily 9:30–5:30; ticket booth closes at 4. Adults
13+ $12, seniors $11, children 3–12 $7, under 3 free. Bicycle carriages are rented
out for two-hour periods. The smaller carriage carries three adults and two children ($21); the larger carriage carries six adults and two children ($42). The new
Wild Earth Jeep Simulator, which will take you on virtual African safari, is $5.

Since 1935, **Monkey Jungle** (305-235-1611; www.monkeyjungle.com), 14805 SW
216th St, has been the place where "the humans are caged and the monkeys run
free." Experience mammals close to our hearts and genetic makeup while enjoying
the 30-acre tropical rain forest. You'll see monkeys swinging freely overhead or
playing in the swimming pool. Presentations on primates are offered throughout
the day to enrich your adventure. Home to more than four hundred primates, representing 30 species, the Monkey Jungle is a protected habit for endangered primates, and one of few in the nation. Gibbons, guenons, spider monkeys, colobus,
and the tiny endangered Golden Lion Tamarin are just some of the primates you'll
encounter. The park also houses more than five thousand specimens of fossil
deposits. Open 9:30–5 daily. Adults $21, seniors 65+ $18, children 3–9 $15.

Village of Pinecrest

✒ The lovely oasis at **Pinecrest Gardens** (305-669-6942; www.pinecrest
gardens.com), 11000 SW 57th Ave, also has a Petting Zoo (see *Botanical
Gardens*). Open 8–sunset daily. The Petting Zoo is open periodically throughout the day, in short sessions, at 11,
1, 3, and 5. Free for everyone.

TIGERS, MIAMI METROZOO

Kathy Wolf

✴ To Do

FAMILY ACTIVITIES ✒ Rev your
engines on two high-quality go-cart
tracks at **Speed Demons of Florida
City** (305-246-0086; www.speed-
demonskarting.com), 453 N Krome
Ave, Florida City. Whether you're
young or old, experienced or novice,
the European-designed carts are
sure to satisfy your need for speed.

The challenging ¼-mile main track is a favorite of seasoned drivers, ages 15 and up. The rooftop junior track is for younger or less experienced racers. Adult carts are available on the junior track for those who wish to race with their kids. PRO Track and Game Room open 1–10 Mon–Thu, 1–midnight Fri, 11–midnight Sat, 11–9 Sun. Rookie track opens a few hours later and closes earlier. Member and nonmember admission fees. PRO (15 years and up): single race $17–20, five races $75. ROOKIE (8–14 years): single race $12–15, five races $50.

HIKING

Everglades National Park

Most of the region's hiking is concentrated in the vast wilds of Everglades National Park. At **Shark Valley** (see *Wild Places*), the Bobcat Boardwalk is an enjoyable 0.5-mile stroll through a tropical hammock and out through the saw-grass prairie. The 1-mile rugged **Otter Cave Hammock Trail** follows a rough limestone trail through a dense tropical hammock and is prone to flooding.

Along the Main Park Road in Everglades National Park, numerous short trails, most a half mile long or less, enable you to explore specific habitats. All trail-heads are signposted and most have parking areas. The popular **Anhinga** and **Gumbo Limbo Trails** at Royal Palm Hammock provide excellent wildlife-watching and take only an hour or so of gentle meandering to complete. The **Pinelands Trail** is a 0.5-mile paved trail through a rare pine rocklands area. **Pay-hay-okee** showcases the vast sawgrass prairie with its cypress domes. **Mahogany Hammock** is a loop through a dense tropical hammock. **West Lake** has a boardwalk loop through the mangrove forest out to the lake. **Eco Pond,** at Flamingo, is a gentle stroll around a roosting area for herons and roseate spoonbills.

Hikers willing to pack on a few miles should head for the **Snake Bight Trail,** which leads 1.6 miles straight out to an overlook on Florida Bay; the **Rowdy Bend Trail,** a 2.6-mile narrow track through fields of salt hay and buttonwoods; the **Bear Lake Trail,** a 3.2-mile round-trip through dense mangroves to the shores of Bear Lake; and the **Christian Point Trail,** a 3.6-mile round-trip that takes you through the mangrove forest close to Florida Bay. At the back of the campground in Flamingo, the **Bayshore Loop** leads you 2 miles along Florida Bay and through the remains of the old village of Flamingo.

MAHOGANY HAMMOCK BOARDWALK
Sandra Friend

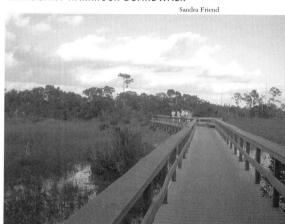

MOTOR SPORTS Homestead Miami Speedway (305-230-7223), One Speedway Blvd, Homestead, is where you'll find NASCAR stock cars racing up to 190 mph on 20-degree turns. The track is also a venue for motorcy-cle races.

PADDLING The granddaddy of long paddling trips in Florida is the 99-mile **Wilderness Waterway,** stretching from Flamingo to Everglades City. Snaking through a maze of mangrove islands where the freshwater sheet flow of the Everglades and Big Cypress meet Florida Bay, the Wilderness Waterway is a true challenge for paddlers. Nautical charts show marked campsites on islands, and on chickee platforms built where there is no dry land. The route takes nine days to paddle, and solid logistical planning for safety and enjoyment of the trip. A backcountry permit is required from Everglades National Park to use the campsites. Check in at either the Flamingo or Gulf Coast Visitor Centers prior to your departure.

If you're bringing your canoe or kayak to Everglades National Park, you'll find many launch points along the southern portion of the Main Park Road. Canoe trails near Flamingo include the 5.2-mile **Nine Mile Pond Loop;** the 2-mile **Noble Hammock Trail;** the 11-mile **Hells Bay Trail,** winding through a maze of mangroves; the **Bear Lake Canal Trail,** which you can follow for up to 22 miles round-trip; the 6.8-mile **Mud Lake Loop;** and up to 15.4 miles round-trip on the **West Lake Trail,** through heavy alligator and crocodile habitat. Check in at any of the park's visitor centers for information and maps for these trails.

SCENIC DRIVES At Everglades National Park, the 38-mile **Main Park Road** provides one of South Florida's most scenic drives, starting at the park entrance gate near the Ernest Coe Visitor Center and ending at Flamingo Visitor Center, the jumping-off point for excursions into Florida Bay.

SKYDIVING Take your bravery to new heights at **Skydive Miami** (305-759-3483), 28730 SW 217th Ave, at Homestead General Airport, Homestead. How high can you go? Tandem jumps start at 8,000 feet, but you'll want to experience the jump from 13,500 feet to enjoy a full one minute of free fall. Open six days a week, closed Tue. Basic Tandem (8,000 feet) $169, Deluxe Tandem (10,000 feet) $199, Extreme Tandem (13,500 feet) $219. To prove your daring, make sure to get a video, photo package, or DVD: $69 each, or all three for $99.

SNORKELING Take a short drive to **Keys Diver, Inc**. (305-451-1177), 99696 Overseas Hwy, Key Largo, for some of the finest snorkeling in the region. (See also *Upper and Middle Keys.*)

TOURS Dragonfly Expeditions (305-774-9019 or 1-888-992-6337; www .dragonflyexpeditions.com), 1825 Ponce de Leon Blvd, Coral Gables, believes in true "green" travel, immersing travelers in unique destinations, with minimal impact on the environment. Their tours incorporate flora and fauna, along with history and culture. You'll enjoy Hidden Gardens of South Florida, which tours botanical treasures; the Florida Everglades Backwater tour, where you'll travel into the "river of grass" with experienced field biologists and naturalist guides ($75); or the inexpensive Everglades Experience, where you'll meander through an ancient cypress dome. Make sure to sign up early for the exceptional Photography Expedition with award-winning "Wild Florida" photographer Jeff Ripple. Tours are priced from $30 to $100.

You'll enjoy canoeing, wet walks in a cypress dome, stargazing, and sight-seeing at **Everglades Hostel Guided Tours.** On each tour a wilderness expert will guide you through a variety of habitats. Full-day tour runs $50 for registered guests, $75 for walk-ins. Half-day tours also available.

Experience the diversity of the Redland Historic Agricultural District on the **Redland Tropical Gardens Tours** (305-247-2016), 22540 SW 177th Ave, Redland, which showcase the growers of this unique region. Tours run 9 AM–1 PM. Prices vary.

Rob's Redland Riot Tour (305-443-7973; www.redlandriot.com) is by far the best way to see the rural farming and historic areas of southern Miami-Dade County. Rob's informative tours provide interesting information, visit historical sites, and stop at several tropical roadside stands. You'll visit such places as Cauley Square, Redland Fruit and Spice Park, R.F. Orchids, Schnebly Redland's Winery, Robert is Here, Florida Pioneer Museum, Redland Hotel, Historic Homestead, and a number of designated Historic Homes. Prices vary. You can also walk or drive the tour yourself: A free self-guided map is on the web site.

&. Explore the "river of grass" on **Shark Valley Tram Tours** (305-221-8455), Shark Valley Visitor Center, Everglades National Park. The two-hour tram ride follows a 14-mile paved loop (shared with bicyclists) through the open sawgrass prairie to a large observation tower, where you disembark and spend 15 minutes or so enjoying the view; you can see for miles. Your guide points out wildlife and indigenous flora along the way, and explains how the Everglades formed and are nourished by a steady flow of water. Tours run 9–4 daily, Dec–Apr (reservations a must), and 9:30–3, May–Nov. Adults $15, children $8. Mosquito head nets and full insect protection recommended on summer tours.

✳ Green Space

BEACHES One of the region's little-known secrets is **Homestead Bayfront Park** (305-230-3033; www.miamidade.gov), 9698 SW 328th St, Homestead. A great family beach, the salt-water lagoon fluctuates with the tide. A playground, picnic areas, barbecue grills, and a sandy beach are surrounded by beautiful palm trees. Open sunrise–sunset. Admission $4 per vehicle.

THE EVERGLADES "RIVER OF GRASS" AT PAY-HAY-OKEE

Sandra Friend

BOTANICAL GARDENS

Village of Pinecrest

✐ Once the location of Parrot Jungle, **Pinecrest Gardens** (305-669-6942; www.pinecrestgardens.com), 11000 SW 57th Ave, has continued nurturing the decades-old natural areas. The original Parrot Jungle opened in 1936 and is now in Miami (see *The Gables*,

Continued on page 458

Sandra Friend

ALONG THE ANHINGA TRAIL, EVERGLADES NATIONAL PARK

EVERGLADES NATIONAL PARK

"There are no other Everglades in the world." So began *River of Grass,* the 1947 classic by Marjory Stoneman Douglas. Dedicated on December 6, 1947, by President Harry S Truman, **Everglades National Park** (305-242-7700), 40001 FL 9936, Homestead, was the culmination of decades' worth of effort to preserve and protect the uniqueness of South Florida, with visionaries like Ernest Coe, David Fairchild, John Pennekamp, and Ms. Douglas leading the charge. Within the 2,358 square miles of Everglades National Park, the park boundaries protect the largest sawgrass prairie in North America, the largest mangrove forest in the Western Hemisphere, and dozens of intriguing and rare habitats like tree islands and pine rocklands. Landscapes are majestic here, sweeping panoramas of marsh and cypress.

What many visitors don't realize, however, is that the Everglades extend far beyond the protected boundaries of Everglades National Park, that the "river of grass" was once fed directly by Lake Okeechobee, and flowed both south and east toward the sea. Land reclamation efforts in the early 1900s uncovered rich black muck beneath the Everglades, kicking off an agricultural boom around the lake as the swamp was drained. When the population exploded along Florida's east coast, more Everglades were drained to provide land: first for farms, and more recently for subdivisions and shopping malls pushing as far west as are legally permitted, built on ancient swampland now disguised with ornamental plantings and sod. Despite the vastness of Everglades National Park, its boundaries cannot prevent the life-sustaining sheet flow of water into the park from carrying harmful agricultural and residential runoff generated by surrounding regions through the Everglades and into Florida Bay. The boundaries cannot prevent the wind from spreading the seeds of invasive exotic shrubs and trees, nor can they prevent thoughtless people from releasing tropical pets into the wild, creatures like anacondas and iguanas and parrots that compete with indigenous wildlife for resources.

Everglades National Park provides a place to contemplate a wilderness dependent on water, where the wildest of Florida's creatures still roam. Despite the issues that threaten its future, it is still a place of grandeur, where thunderheads form above vast prairies, and panthers slink through tree islands. To learn more, explore!

An important note about visiting Everglades National Park: Mosquitoes are an ever-present force, even in winter. They are at their peak in midsummer (tent campers, beware) and wane in January; but they never, ever leave. Carry mosquito head nets, bring your favorite repellant (it probably won't help), and use full-body coverage (long-sleeved shirt, long pants) when hiking, especially after a rainfall.

If you plan to wander off-trail, consult a park ranger before doing so, for safety's sake. Everglades National Park has unique natural hazards to consider, including jagged deep holes in the limestone karst, extremely poisonous plants, and plenty of wildlife. A ranger can help guide you away from any known trouble spots.

EVERGLADES VISITORS CENTERS

Shark Valley Visitor Center (305-221-8776), Tamiami Trl, open 8:30–5 daily, has two-hour narrated tram rides (see *Tours*) along a 14-mile paved loop through the "river of grass," with a stop at an observation tower. Visitors are also welcome to bike or hike the loop, but there is no shade. Off-trail "slough slogs" get you up close and personal (adults 13+ $15, children12 and under $7). To reach Shark Valley, follow US 41 (Tamiami Trail) west from Miami. The park's entrance is within the Miccosukee Reservation. The main portion of the park is reached via US 1 or Krome Avenue in Florida City to FL 9993. Unless you visit the park with a local tour operator, a car is essential for getting around.

At the beginning of the Main Park Road to Flamingo, the **Ernest Coe Visitor Center** (305-242-7700) is the snazziest of the visitors centers in the park, with detailed exhibits on ecosystems, history, and the flora and fauna of this vast preserve, as well as a large-screen movie theater to introduce you to the world's only Everglades. Purchase tickets here for guided activities, which include the two-and-half-hour Everglades Wet Walk (adult $15, children $7), which takes you out into the rugged "river of grass," and the Three-in-One Bike Hike ($20, bike included; $15 if you bring your own bike and helmet) through pine rocklands and sawgrass prairies on a system of rugged old limestone roads. Freebie interpretive walks are also still offered on a regular basis on the Anhinga Trail and at Mahogany Hammock.

The **Royal Palm Visitor Center**, 4 miles west of the main entrance station, is a relic of Royal Palm State Park (circa 1916) and the starting point for two of the park's most popular walks, the Anhinga Trail and the Gumbo Limbo Trail. Open 8–4:15 daily. Free ranger-guided walks include the Anhinga Amble at 10:30 AM and the 'Glades Glimpse at 1:30 PM.

The **Flamingo Visitor Center,** at the end of Main Park Road, offers exhibits, information, and backcountry permits. Staff are on hand 9–5 daily, late November–May 1. The Flamingo complex includes the visitors center, marina, gift shop, and restaurants, and the Flamingo Lodge and Campground. The visitor center and marina have reopened, but no other facilities have been available since the destruction caused by hurricanes Katrina and Wilma.

the Grove, and Miami Cityside). In 2002, the Village of Pinecrest purchased the 22-acre site and created an oasis for all to enjoy. Walk under towering banyan trees; stroll through the botanical garden, searching for rare plants; sit and gaze at the graceful waterfowl at Swan Lake; or just enjoy the tropical landscape and natural streams. Kids 3–12 can get wet and silly at Splash 'N Play and will also enjoy the petting zoo, butterfly exhibit, and playground. Open 8–sunset daily. Splash 'N Play and the Butterfly Exhibit are open from 9 to one hour before park closing. The Petting Zone is open in four short sessions throughout the day, so as not to tire the animals. Free for everyone.

Redland
& From its humble beginnings—cultivars donated by local growers—**Redland Fruit and Spice Park** (305-247-5727; www.fruitandspicepark.org), 24801 SW 187th Ave, has blossomed into a showcase of tropical fruits, flowers, and spices grown commercially in this region. As you walk the pathways through themed gardens, it's okay to sample fruits that have fallen to the ground— just avoid them in the poisonous plants area. A network of trails fans out throughout the park to enable you to explore at your own pace, or you can join a guided tour on a tram that stops at points of interest. Browse the gift shop on your way out for cookbooks, scholarly books on fruit, and fruit products. Open 10–5. Fee.

PARKS

Cutler Ridge

✔ At **Bill Sadowski Park & Nature Center** (305-255-4767), 17555 SW 79th Ave, walk the Old Cutler Ridge Nature Trail to immerse in an ancient hardwood hammock, a primeval forest of Old Florida surrounded by today's suburbia. The park also features a nature center with live animals, native tree arboretum, butterfly garden, playground, canoe launch, and picnic area. A public observatory is open Saturday nights 8–10 PM. Free.

Kendall

✔ Just a few blocks from Florida's Turnpike, **Kendall Indian Hammocks Park** (305-596-9324), 11345 SW 79th St, protects a stand of natural forest known as the Snapper Creek Glade. Trails meander through the tropical hammock, and a picnic area and playground adjoin. Free.

Redland

✔ At **Castellow Hammock Park** (305-242-7688), 22301 SW 162nd Ave, explore a remnant of the original habitat of the Redland, a tropical jungle with a rocky limestone floor and deep solution holes. The nature center has a great overview of the region, as well as a butterfly garden popular with photographers. Behind it, you'll find an 0.5-mile nature trail, well worth a visit to understand just how radically the land in South Florida has been changed. Open sunrise–sunset. Free.

WILD PLACES **Biscayne National Park** (305-250-PARK; www.nps.gov/bisc/), 9700 SW 328th St, Homestead. One of Florida's offshore parks, Biscayne protects the mangrove coastline of South Dade, living coral reefs, and islands that managed to escape development. Recreational opportunities include snorkeling and scuba diving, canoeing and kayaking, and hiking and camping on the islands of the park, but access to the park is only by boat. For an overview of the park's habitats and resources, stop at the Dante Fascell Visitor Center, exit 6 off Florida's Turnpike (follow the signs). Open 9–5 daily. A park concessionaire (305-230-1100) provides snorkeling, scuba diving, and glass-bottom boat tours of the reefs; call for reservations and cost.

✳ Lodging

BED & BREAKFAST

Redland 33170

🐾 ▼ Fruit trees from every continent create a oasis in the farming district at the **Grove Inn Country Guesthouse** (305-247-6572; www.groveinn.com), 22540 SW 177th Ave, a delightful getaway. The 14 rooms are named for tropical fruits, and you can walk around the garden and sample their name sakes in-season. It has the feel of an updated 1940s motel with shabby chic decor; each cozy room includes a kitchenette with a mini fridge and a microwave. Paul Mulhern and Craig Bulger coaxed this phoenix from the ashes of a rundown motel, and the transformation is simply amazing. Add your name to the auto-graph tree, and then relax in the hot tub or under the arbor as the Christmas lights and candles flicker; plans are for a swimming pool to be added out back in the near future. A gourmet breakfast is served from 8 to 10 in the main dining room. Call for rates.

CAMPGROUNDS

Everglades National Park

Everglades National Park (1-800-365-CAMP) has two major campgrounds along the Main Park Road south of Homestead, at Long Pine Key (nearest the park entrance) and Flamingo (at the very end of the road). Reservations required Dec–Apr; otherwise, sites are first-come, first-served. (See also *Everglades National Park*.)

Homestead 33034

❦ You'll enjoy luxury when you hook up at **Goldcoaster** (305-248-5462 or 1-800-828-6992; www.goldcoasterrv .com), 34850 SW 187th Ave. In the heart of Food and Wine Country, the mobile home park offers a heated swimming pool and spa, a playscape, and laundry facilities. The high level of customer service is what keeps families coming back, so make your reservations early. Day ($44), week ($275), month ($750), and season ($2,150). Pets welcome.

Miami 33177

♿ ❦ The first-class **Larry and Penny Thompson Campground** (305-232-1049; www.miamidade.gov/ parks/Parks/larry_penny.asp), 12451 SW 184th St, is located next to the Miami Metrozoo. Dedicated to the memory of Larry Thompson, a popular columnist with the *Miami Herald*,

the campground was once part of the Richland Naval Station. A true destination location; you'll enjoy the natural setting with its 270 acres of nature, bridal, and hiking paths, including a 20-station fitness course. The campground has 240 sites for RVs and tent camping, and a choice of places to cool off. The large clear blue freshwater lake has it own white-sand beach, and three mammoth waterslides carved into a rock mountain empty into a heated pool. RV rates ($22 daily; $135 weekly; $400 monthly) include full hookup, water, and sewer. Tent sites are $10 nightly.

HOSTEL Ever wonder about staying at a hostel? Often thought of as inexpensive lodging for college kids, independent travelers of all ages are staying at these unique accommodations, many with resort-type features, for a fraction of the price. Most have a central entertainment area with community kitchen where you can cook your own meals. And you'll be required to pick up after yourself, which may include being assigned a small chore, such as sweeping. Plan to bring your own bedding, although they will often supply this if requested in advance.

Florida City 33034

❦ The **Everglades Hostel** (305-248-1122 or 1-800-372-3874; www .evergladeshostel.com), 20 SW Second Ave, is a great place to see if hostelling is for you. The clean, friendly hostel is in the heart of Florida City, where you can hop a bus and head to the Keys or Miami. The hostel also offers several types of tours into the Everglades, where you can wet walk in a cypress dome. They also rent canoes and bicycles so you can explore the area on your own. The hostel will nurture your mind and spirit, offering such amenities as a meditation gazebo, a whimsical tropical garden, and a glow-in-the- dark life-size chessboard. Guests often gather around the fully equipped kitchen to chat, lounge in the "living room" while watching the large-screen cable TV, or surf the Net with free web and wireless access. You'll also stay connected with free long-distance phone calls (within the United States). Office hours are 9–9, but once you check in you can come and go as you please. Camping in the garden with your own tent $12, dorm beds $19, private rooms $45. Discounts for Hostelling International (HI) members. Bring your own sheets or pay $2 for linen rental. Pets are welcome with prior management approval.

✳ Where to Eat

DINING OUT

Homestead/Florida City

At first glance you would think that the **Mutineer Restaurant** (305-245-3377), 11 SE First Ave, Florida City, was just another tourist trap. You'd be wrong. While tourists do flock here, they come for good reason. For lunch, serious seafood lovers should head straight to the all-you-can-eat seafood buffet ($10). Salads, sand-wiches, and burgers are priced from $5 to $11. This little gem really shines at night with appetizers such as she-crab soup—creamy lobster bisque served in a bread bowl ($5.25)—and seafood sampler for two ($30), which includes clams imperial with bacon, crabmeat, and cheese; oysters Rocke-feller with spinach, bacon, and Per-nod; mussels steamed in a spicy marinara sauce; and broiled shrimp

Kathy Wolf
DELIGHTFUL DESSERTS AT THE WHITE LION

and scallops. For landlubbers there's prime rib ($17–20). Make sure to save room for the Key lime pie and chocolate truffle mousse cake ($5). Decorated in a nautical theme, the chocolate walls and old-world drapes complement the cheery yellow polo shirts worn by the wait staff. Patrons can take their turn at the piano in the lobby, and you'll want to take the kids over to their petting zoo just for fun. Open 11–9:30 daily, and a bit later on the weekends in-season.

Prepare to be enchanted at the **White Lion Café** (305-248-1076; www.whitelioncafe.com), 146 NW 7th St, Homestead. The delightful restaurant features excellent food in a historic home, with comfortable sur-roundings that spill out into the lush garden patio. Dine in or out, or just come for dessert. The extensive bak-ery selection will be a hazard to your diet, but the goodies are worth it. Lunch 11–3 Mon–Sat. Dinner from 5 PM "until the fat lady sings," Tue–Sat. Lunch entrées $7–9, dinner entrées $9–$22. The open-air bar features live blues, jazz, and swing on Friday and Saturday nights.

Kendall

After several taste tests with my girlfriends, I'm convinced that **Punjab Palace** (305-274-1300), 11780 SW 88th St, ranks among the very best of Indian restaurants in the state. Featuring Punjabi cuisine, they serve authentic tandoori, including my favorite, chicken tikka masala. Order your spice with caution, as even the mild is fiery! Aromatic entrées run $11–17, with numerous vegetarian options, including a vegetable thali.

EATING OUT

Homestead/Florida City

It's worth traveling off US 1 to find **Alabama Jack's** (305-248-8741), 1500 Card Sound Rd, Key Largo. Located 13 miles southeast from Homestead, just before the toll, this eatery is a "must" for those heading to the Keys. The inexpensive pub food ($7–13) includes the *best* conch fritters in the region ($7). Country-western bands play on the weekends. Overlooking the canal, you'll enjoy watching huge mangrove snappers begging for treats. You'll feel like you are in the middle of nowhere, and you are, and it's worth it. Of course once you are there, you won't want to leave. Open 11–7 daily.

The historic **Capri Restaurant** (305-247-1542), 935 N Krome Ave, Florida City, has been open since 1958. While you'll find a great selection of Italian dishes, such as chicken, veal, and seafood pasta dishes ($12–22), or their certified Black Angus beef ($22–43), you'll also want to try one of their famous World Martinis, such as the Mango ($7), or a tropical drink, such as the West Indies Yellow Bird ($7). Open for lunch and dinner Mon–Sat.

❦ My sweet tea came garnished with lime at the **Farmer's Market Restaurant** (305-242-0008), 300 N Krome Ave, Florida City, where I had the best scallops in years, served up with a side of fresh mashed potatoes slathered in brown gravy. Set in the heart of a working farmer's market, this airy country kitchen is a popular stop for locals, where down-home cooking and fresh-as-it-gets seafood are the mainstays of a menu that doesn't break the bank. Dinner $8–15; breakfast and lunch served, too. Open 5:30 AM–9 PM.

Hiatari Sushi Bar (305-248-7426), 109 N Krome Ave, Florida City, offers a Japanese menu and a Thai menu with entrées ranging from $11–15. Or order by the piece from the sushi bar ($2–7). Open 11–11 daily.

Head to the **Key Largo Seafood House** (305-247-9456), 404 SW First Ave, Florida City, for their lump crab cakes ($11), grouper sandwich ($9), or famous lobster Reuben ($14). Entrées ($9–18), such as whiskey peppercorn snapper, come with a choice of two sides. The kid's Minnow's Menu ($5) covers even the pickiest appetite. All seafood is fresh from the Keys.

Fried gator tail, chunky chili, and a BLT with lots of thick bacon are just some of the treats you'll encounter at **Kim's Cupboard** (305-247-0844), 36650 SW 192nd Ave, Florida City. They also make boxed lunches to go. The cute little house is on the way to Everglades Alligator Farm and Everglades Outpost (see *Wildlife Rehabilitation & Zoological Parks*). Open 6–6 daily. Prices run from $3 to $8.

Don't leave the area without stopping at **La Panaderia Favorita** (305-245-0436), 337 West Palm Dr, Florida City. The tiny Mexican bakery is only

Kathy Wolf

KIM'S CUPBOARD

a couple of blocks west of US 1. They feature *epañada de calabaza,* and a wide variety of fresh-baked breads and pastries, such as sweet-cake. Their molasses cookies are as good as my Irish grandmother used to make! And the low prices are not much more than pocket change. Grab a hearty cup of coffee to go with it all.

The **Main Street Café** (305-245-7575), 128 N Krome Ave, Homestead, reminiscent of a 1960s coffeehouse, offers great music and a healthy menu. Try the teriyaki-salsa chicken wrap ($7), or the Krome Ave roast beef deli sandwich ($7). Vegetarians will enjoy the soy burgers, marinated tofu, and eggplant sandwiches ($5-7). The all-you-can eat salad and soup bar ($9) has homemade soups such as Russian borscht, Cajun black bean, and Caribbean stew. Open 11–4 Tue and Wed, 11–midnight Thu–Sat.

For eat-in or take-out Italian fare, call **Romano's Pizza** (305-246-7788), 110 N Homestead Blvd (US 1), Homestead. Twelve- to 18-inch pizzas ($6–16) and traditional entrées such as manicotti, lasagna, and chicken

parmigiana ($5–7). Open 10–9 Mon–Sat; delivery available 11 AM– 2 PM and 5–9 PM.

If you're looking for real Mexican food, then look no farther than **Rosita's Mexican Restaurant** (305-246-3114), 199 W Palm Dr, Florida City. The modest restaurant serves authentic Mexican food, such as huevos rancheros ($4) for breakfast and *mole rojo de pollo* (red mole—a spicy chocolate sauce—with chicken; $8) for dinner. Green enchiladas with chicken, cheese, or beef includes beans, rice, and salad ($5). I don't know why their Soda Mexicana from Honduras tastes so good, but it is the best cola I've every experienced. Shrimp rancheros ($8). Desserts only $2. Open 8:30 AM–9 PM daily.

Redland

Try the "secret recipe" campfire stew at **Redland Rib House** (305-246-8866), 24856 SW 177th Ave, a favorite around these parts for their St. Louis–style barbecued ribs, fresh-ground char-grilled burgers, black beans and corn, and homemade pies. Half a slab of ribs $10; a whole slab of baby backs $16.

✳ Entertainment

Most of the nightly entertainment is on the weekends at local restaurants. You'll find relaxing blues and jazz in the garden at **White Lion Café** (305-248-1076; www.whitelioncafe.com), 146 NW 7th St, Homestead. **Main Street Café** (305-245-7575), 128 N Krome Ave, Homestead livens things up with folk, country, blues, and classic rock on Saturday and Sunday nights, and open-mike night every Thursday. Open 8–midnight.

MIAMI METRO

✳ Selective Shopping
ANTIQUES, BOUTIQUES, AND SHOPS

Homestead

For 8 blocks along Krome Avenue in Homestead, you'll find an array of quaint antiques shops, art galleries, and restaurants. Or enjoy the wide selection of antiques and collectibles at **Jacobsen's** (305-247-4745; www.jacobsensantiques.com), 144 N Krome Ave, with 12 different dealers under one roof. The recently renovated **Historic Downtown** features turn-of-the-20th-century buildings, including the 1917 Town Hall.

Miami

A true hidden find, many of the pioneer buildings in **Cauley Square Historic Village** (305-258-3543; www.cauleysquareshops.com), 22400 Old Dixie Hwy (US 1), date to 1903, when millionaire farmer William Cauley shipped tomatoes on Henry Flagler's railroad (see *Palm Beach*). On the 10-acre site sit several pioneer homes and warehouses converted into quaint shops, an artisans' village, and a tearoom. You'll enjoy walking the lush tropical grounds as you explore more than a dozen reasonably priced

shops; many sell to the boutiques on South Beach. On weekends, live music is featured in the gardens. At **Stripes and Roses** (305-258-0449), you'll find Country French decor and attire. Divas will want to browse through **Wit & Style** (305-257-9377), featuring chic accessories and lotions. Antiques hunters will find **Unicorn Creations** (305-258-1047), a great place for antique, vintage, and exotic furniture, along with architectural elements. I love the little clay houses at **International Whimsy** (305-257-3548), and Stephanie Kondos's dollhouse miniatures (www.kondokreations.com) at **Paper Fetish** (305-257-1461), where you'll also find unique scrapbooking supplies. At **The Art Place** (305-258-0359), you might see artist Joaquin Godoy painting one of his commissioned portraits. When you're ready for break, a delicate luncheon can be found at the **Tea Room** (305-258-0044), where Belgium lace and Tiffany lamps surround you. The Village is open 10–5 Tue–Sat, noon–5 Sun.

MALLS AND OUTLETS Shoppers looking for brand-name bargains will want to head to **Prime Outlets at Florida City** (305-248-4727; www.primeoutlets.com), 250 E Palm Dr, Florida City. Open 10–9 Mon–Sat; 11–6 Sun.

PRODUCE STANDS, FARMER'S MARKETS, FISH MARKETS, AND U-PICK

Homestead/Florida City/Redland

Everyone gathers at the **Farmers' Market** (305-242-0008), 330 N Krome Ave, Florida City, for locally grown tropical fruits and fresh vegetables. Open 10–3 Sat.

DOWNTOWN HOMESTEAD

Kathy Wolf

You haven't been to South Florida if you haven't been to **Robert is Here** (305-246-1592; www.robertishere .com), 19900 SW 144th St, Florida City. At the young age of 7, Robert started his roadside fruit stand with a small table, a few fruits, and a sign that simply said, "Robert is Here," and has grown this "lemonade stand" into a modern-day success story. You'll find more than 20 different varieties of locally grown tropical produce with strange names such as anon (a sugar apple), atemova, canestel (egg fruit), mamey, monstera, and even "ugly fruit." The stand also has a huge selection of commonly known fruits and vegetables such as Florida oranges, grapefruit, and sweet onions. In addition to all the fresh fruit and vegetables, you'll find a large selection of honey, jams, marinades, and dressings such as Florida Orange Poppyseed, Key Lime Honey Mustard, Key Lime Caesar Peppercorn, and Creamy Vidalia Onion Cucumber. Unless he is in the fields, you'll probably find Robert behind one of the counters. Out back you'll enjoy the quirky zoo, an eclectic collection of rescued and abandoned animals, including emus, parrots, donkeys, and iguanas. At the observation hive you can view live bees making honey. The Southern Most Purple Martin House is as nice as any beachfront condo. Don't leave without one of Robert's famous Key lime milk shakes.

Laura Oswald used to sell fresh produce by the side of the road for 13 years, and then opened **The Tomato Lady's Hodgepodge** (305-251-1348), 20286 Old Cutler Rd, as a permanent location. Here, she offers bee pollen, fresh herbs, dried spices, and local veggies.

Tropical Fruit Growers of South Florida (305-401-1502; www.florida -agriculture.com/tropical), 18710 SW 288th St, Homestead, a coalition of one hundred South Florida growers, began in 1988. In this boutique industry, each grower harvests from farms under 100 acres, some as small as 3 acres. You'll hand pick tropical favorites such as lychee, carambola, longan, mamey sapote, guava, mango, banana, and green papaya and many other specialty fruits.

✳ Special Events

Second Saturday of every month: Walk through the studios of 35 fine artists while enjoying live entertainment at **ArtSouth** (305-247-9406; www.artsouthhomestead.org), 240 N Krome Ave, Homestead. The artists' community is set on 3½ acres in the heart of Homestead.

Last Sunday of every month: Divas are darling at the Hats & High Heels Party at **Cauley Square Historic Village** (305-258-3543; www.cauley squareshops.com), 22400 Old Dixie Hwy (US 1), Miami. The fun red-carpet-style event features prizes for

ROBERT IS HERE

Sandra Friend

LILY POOLS, FRUIT AND SPICE PARK

"Best Hat" and "Best High Heels."

First weekend in March: **Asian Culture Festival,** Fruit and Spice Park, Redland. Enjoy the sensory delights—music, dance, visual arts, food, plants, and more—of Asia during this celebration of cultures. Admission $6; children under 12 free.

April: The Fairchild Tropical Garden, Miami (305-667-1651), features the **International Orchid Festival,** where you'll see beautiful species of rare orchids amidst a tropical paradise.

Enjoy old-time fun with music, food, arts and crafts, and entertainment such as juggling and puppetry at the

Redland Natural Arts Festival (305-247-5727; www.fruitandspice park.org), Fruit and Spice Park, 24801 SW 187th Ave, Homestead.

Summer: In summer the Miami Metrozoo holds their annual **Big Cat-Nap Campout** (305-251-0400; www .zsf.org), 12400 SW 152nd Street, Miami. The special event allows children 6 and older to spend a night at the zoo. They'll learn about the animals through behind-the-scenes tours. Campers gather around a campfire, complete with s'mores, and wake to the sounds of lions and tigers. The event also includes complimentary zoo admission the next day, continental breakfast, and a commemorative T-shirt. Held 6 PM–8:30 AM. For members and nonmembers: adults $45–57, children $40–47, family of four $160–198.

October: One of Florida's wildest Halloween parties is **Metroboo** at the Metrozoo (305-251-0400; www.zsf .org), 12400 SW 152nd Street, Miami. A unique trick or treat for kids 12 and under, with costume contests, music, trick or treating, and fun prizes. Held 11–4. Adults 13+ $12, seniors $11, children 3–12 $7, under 3 free.

December: **Arts & Craft Show** at **Cauley Square Historic Village** (305-258-3543; www.cauleysquare shops.com), 22400 Old Dixie Hwy (US 1), Miami, features more than 50 vendors in a village filled with nostalgia and merriment.

The Florida Keys

UPPER AND MIDDLE KEYS

LOWER KEYS

KEY WEST

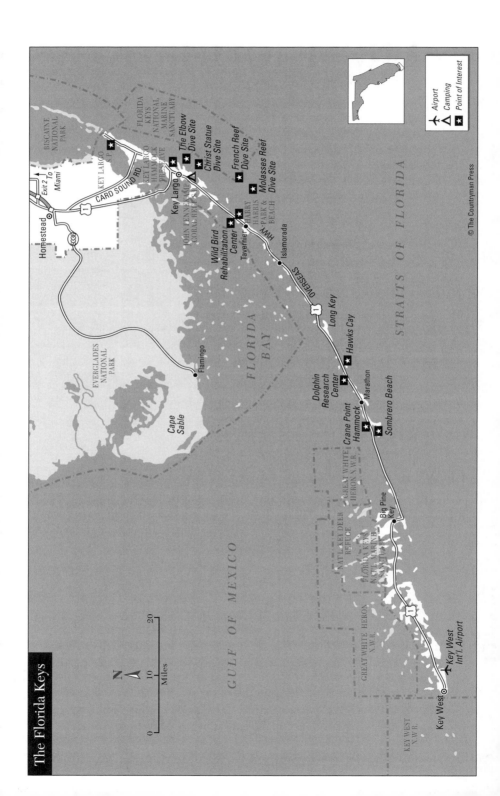

The Florida Keys

N

0 10 20
Miles

GULF OF MEXICO

EVERGLADES
NATIONAL
PARK

Cape
Sable

Flamingo

Homestead

Exit 2 To
Miami

CARD SOUND RD.

KEY LARGO
HAMMOCK
STATE

KEY SOUND RD.

Key Largo

BISCAYNE
NATIONAL
PARK

FLORIDA
KEYS
NATIONAL
MARINE
SANCTUARY

The Elbow
Dive Site

Christ Statue
Dive Site

French Reef
Dive Site

Molasses Reef
Dive Site

John Pennekamp
Coral Reef S.P.

Wild Bird
Rehabilitation
Center

Tavernier

HARRY
HARRIS
PARK &
BEACH

Islamorada

FLORIDA
BAY

OVERSEAS HWY.

Long Key

Hawks Cay

Dolphin
Research
Center

Marathon

Crane Point
Hammock

Sombrero Beach

GREAT WHITE
HERON N.W.R.

NAT'L KEY DEER
REFUGE

FLORIDA KEYS
NAT'L MARINE
SANCTUARY

Big Pine
Key

GREAT WHITE HERON
N.W.R.

KEY WEST
N.W.R.

Key West

Key West
Int'l. Airport

STRAITS OF FLORIDA

© The Countryman Press

✈ Airport
⛺ Camping
★ Point of Interest

THE FLORIDA KEYS

A string of pearls set in an emerald sea, the Florida Keys are connected by an amazing engineering feat—43 bridges that enable the Overseas Highway to island-hop more than 110 miles to reach one of Florida's oldest cities, Key West. With lush tropical foliage, expansive views of both shallow Florida Bay and the calm Atlantic waters, and the largest living coral reef in the United States, this is a special place, mostly disconnected from the rest of Florida and absolutely disconnected from the most of the world. Life is on "island time," people are friendly, and the atmosphere is casual virtually everywhere you go. It's no wonder authors have flocked to the Keys over the years, from luminaries such as Ernest Hemingway, Truman Capote, and Tennessee Williams to modern-day best-sellers such as Carl Hiaasen and James W. Hall. Artists, too—you'll find them here in profusion, with their roadside galleries, and musicians making a living working the endless supply of bars and restaurants up and down US 1. It's a different world, one that invites you to slow down and savor the sun, the breeze, and the coconut trees—the mellow world of the Keys.

A SUNSET TO SAVOR AT KONA KAI RESORT

Sandra Friend

UPPER AND MIDDLE KEYS

Many words have been written to praise the tropical beauty and splendor of the crystal-clear water around the coral reefs of **Key Largo.** For a landlubber like me, the island has one distinction that truly sets it apart—I know of nowhere else where you'll encounter a CROCODILE CROSSING road sign. The saline lakes of upper Key Largo are home to the last significant colony of American crocodiles in the world, protected by Crocodile Lakes National Wildlife Refuge. Key Largo is also the first dense outpost of truly tropical flora as you drive south, with protected thickets of some of the largest Caribbean trees on earth. It is the home of the most accessible coral reefs in the United States, where the first ever underwater preserve was established, and as such, is a mecca for divers and snorkelers alike. At 27 miles long, Key Largo is the largest of the Keys and includes the town of **Tavernier** at the Largo Sound end of the island. The first community on Key Largo was established at Rock Harbor in 1870.

Islamorada is where you first feel like you're driving in the tropics, where placid aquamarine waters stretch off to the horizon on both sides of the road as you drive the causeways connecting the islands. Called "the purple islands" (*morada*) by the Spanish explorers who sailed these seas, the islands sport lush foliage hiding a variety of small waterfront mom-and-pop motels and artist studios. Settlement began in 1907 with a subdivision called the "Townsite of Islamorada," and when the Overseas Railroad touched the islands, it adopted that name for the railroad station. The four major islands include Plantation Key, Windley Key, Upper Matecumbe, and Lower Matecumbe.

The largest of the island chains, **Marathon,** saw its first modern-day settlers in the 1830s, when Bahamian immigrants started a subsistence farming village on Vaca Key, near a source of fresh water; visit the remnants of Adderly Village at Crane Point Hammock. It wasn't until Henry Flagler's ambitious project hit this jumping-off point that the place fairly bustled with inhabitants, gathered here to engineer an amazing feat—crossing 7 miles of open ocean with a railway trestle. The marathon of work necessary to complete the railroad on Flagler's timetable gave the 13-island chain its name. Once completed, the piers of the Seven Mile Bridge created eddies that attracted tarpon, which in turn attracted anglers to the water's bounty, making Marathon another favored destination for sportsmen. The island is home to the only airport in the Keys outside of Key West.

GUIDANCE **The Florida Keys & Key West** (305-296-1552 or 1-800-FLA-KEYS; www.fla-keys.com), 1201 White St, Suite 102, Key West 33040, is your source for trip planning, and they have a number of excellent booklets and brochures to make it a breeze. Ask for information on a specific island or on a specific theme, such as diving, and they'll be happy to help. At MM 106, the **Key Largo Visitor Center** (1-800-822-1088; www.keylargo.org) is open 9–6 daily. The **Islamorada Chamber of Commerce** (305-664-4503; www.islamoradachamber.com), MM 82.5, has brochures and information on fishing the area. The **Marathon Visitor Center** (305-743-5417 or 1-800-262-7284; www.floridakeysmarathon.com), 12222 Overseas Hwy, is just before Vaca Cut.

GETTING THERE *By car:* The Overseas Highway, **US 1,** is the only way to drive the Keys.

By air: To reach the Upper Keys, use **Miami International Airport** (see the *Miami Metro* section). For the Middle Keys, a commuter flight to **Marathon Airport** (305-289-6060), 9400 Overseas Hwy, Suite 200, is in order.

By bus: **Greyhound** (305-871-1810; www.greyhound.com) stops all along the islands; call for specific pickup locations and rates.

GETTING AROUND *By car:* **US 1** connects the islands; destinations along the road are designated by mile markers, with directions generally expressed according to "MM."

By bus: Since **Greyhound** links the islands, it's possible to use the bus to island-hop.

By taxi: If you fly into Marathon Airport, you can get where you're going with **Action Taxi** (305-743-6800) or **Sunset Taxi & Transportation** (305-289-7422).

MEDICAL EMERGENCIES One of the most serious medical emergencies a diver can experience is the bends, and with all the diving going on in the Keys, the **Key Largo Recompression Chamber** (911 if emergency, 1-800-NO-BENDS for information) can be a lifesaver for those in need. General emergencies should head to **Fisherman's Hospital** (305-743-5533; www.fishermans hospital.com), 3301 Overseas Hwy, MM 48.7, Marathon, where there is a 24-hour emergency room, or **Mariner's Hospital** (305-852-4418), at MM 88.5.

❋ To See

ART GALLERIES

Islamorada
More than four hundred artists from around the country are represented in the fine work found at **Gallery**

AMERICAN CROCODILE

Theatre of the Sea

Morada (305-664-3650), 81611 Overseas Hwy—I was particularly taken by the citrus-colored, wheel-thrown "bowl sculptures" of Marge Marguiles, part of the vast array of "practical art" in the gallery. Open 10–6 daily.

The Rain Barrel, 86700 Overseas Hwy, MM 86, is a haven for artists, each with their own gallery space and working studios where you can look over their latest projects. Among them are the **Lawler Gallery** (305-853-7011), the studio of longtime artist Dan Lawler, who paints a variety of subjects, and the **John David Hawver Gallery** (305-852-9958), with seascapes and landscapes of the Keys in a variety of media.

Hidden away in Treasure Village at MM 86.7, **Spirit Dance—The Art of Truth** (305-853-2533; www.spiritdanceart.com), 86700 Overseas Hwy, exhibits spiritual works by Kelly Hostetler that draw on Native American traditions.

As the artist brought her massive works into Kona Kai for the gallery owners to look at, I was impressed by Stacie Krupa's bold, large paintings. You can look them over at **Stacie Krupa Studio Gallery** (305-517-2631; www.staciekrupa .com), 82935 Overseas Hwy, MM 83, where you may find her starting her next creative venture.

Inside a historic Conch home, the **Wellington House Gallery** (305-664-8913), 81599 Overseas Hwy, showcases the handmade furnishings, acrylics and water-colors, sculptures, and tapestries of local artists.

Key Largo
At **The Gallery at Kona Kai** (305-852-7200; www.g-k-k.com), on the grounds of Kona Kai Resort (see *Lodging*), view interpretations of South Florida as seen through the eyes of the finest artists—the pointillist ocean scenes of John Halver, the bold canvases of Stacy Krupa, Franco Passalauga's dreams of fish. It's also the only gallery in the Keys that represents Clyde Butcher's fine-art photography.

Marathon
The **Bougainvillea House** (305-743-0808), 12420 Overseas Hwy, is the local artist's collective, featuring 26 Keys artists. Some of the works you'll see here include Georgina Hosek's glazed mosaics of sea life, art photos of island scenes by Gayle and Mike Hewlett, and Diane Doran's fascinating clay-on-wood sculptures. Stop in for Art on the Porch exhibits the second Sat of each month. Closed Mon.

HISTORIC SITES

Islamorada
Swaying palm trees carved into tall slabs of coral rock are the centerpiece of the **Hurricane Monument** on Upper Matecumbe Key, a beautiful

HURRICANE MONUMENT, ISLAMORADA
Sandra Friend

but solemn reminder of the hundreds who perished when a tidal wave engulfed the islands of Islamorada during the 1935 Labor Day hurricane. You'll find the monument oceanside in a small park at MM 81.6. The **Pioneer Cemetery,** MM 82, is on the grounds of Cheeca Lodge in Islamorada; the angel statue here is one of the few objects that survived the hurricane. **Windley Key Fossil Reef Geological State Park** (see *Parks*) at MM 85.5 showcases historic quarry equipment used in Henry Flagler's day to slice coral rock from several quarries now encompassed by the park.

At **Indian Key Historic State Park** (305-664-2540), offshore between Tea Table and Lower Matecumbe in Islamorada, walk the streets of the original county seat of Dade County. Known to Spanish explorers in 1527 as the passage at the "Wells of Matecumbe," this coral rock island stands sentinel at a 2-mile passage between the reefs to Florida Bay that the earliest sailing ships could navigate. Yet more than three hundred ships wrecked within sight of the island within one year. A small wrecker's settlement established by renegade wrecker Jacob Houseman evolved into a trader's stop, where John James Audubon rested during his 1832 visit to the Keys. Houseman succeeded in having the settlement named the county seat in 1836 when Dade County was carved out of Mosquito County. In 1838 noted botanist Henry Perrine moved his family here and began to experiment with cultivating various tropical plants, particularly agave—which runs rampant on the island today. As the Second Seminole War dragged on, residents of the settlement feared an attack because of their well-stocked storehouses. It happened on August 7, 1840. When the Indians attacked, Houseman and his wife escaped; other residents hid in the post office and under tables. Perrine's first thought was for his family. Since their house sat above the water, he let them through a trapdoor to the turtle kraal below, and then turned to defend the exit by trying to reason with the Indians. Perrine was killed and the house set on fire. Fourteen-year-old Henry Jr. saved the rest of the family by sailing them to nearby Tea Table Key.

As you explore the island, note the foundations of the three-story warehouses, one with a "flushing commode" in the corner—the tide cleans out the hewn stone privy. The ruins of a cistern and post office are still here, as is Jacob Houseman's grave. A park ranger gives tours at 9 AM and 1 PM Thu–Mon; you must arrange your own transportation to the island. Use your own watercraft or check in at **Robbie's Marina** (see *Boating*) for the official state park ferry, which also serves **Lignumvitae Key Botanical State Park** (see *Parks*) on the opposite side of the channel.

Sandra Friend

INDIAN KEY

Key Largo

If you're a film buff, you have to stop at the **Caribbean Club Bar** (305-451-9970), MM 104 bayside; it's the only place in the Keys where scenes from the movie *Key Largo* were filmed in 1947, and the walls of the bar (yes, it's still a bar) are covered with memorabilia.

Marathon

Accessed from a visitors center at the southern tip of Marathon, **Pigeon Key** (see *Railroadiana*) was a work camp for workers on the Overseas Railroad, with historic homes, barracks, and outbuildings dating from the early 1900s. At **Crane Point Hammock** (see *Museums*), the **Adderly House** is hidden in the tropical forest along the hiking trails. On the National Register of Historic Places, it's the oldest remaining building on the island and was built of tabby in Bahamian style and completed in 1906. George Adderly's home became the focal point of a small African American settlement called Adderly Town, which persisted on Vaca Key through the completion of the railroad.

MARINE PARKS

Grassy Key

For more than 20 years, the nonprofit **Dolphin Research Center** (305-289-1121; www.dolphins.org), 58901 Overseas Hwy, has educated the public and performed noninvasive research on their colony of dolphins living in lagoons along Florida Bay. In 1958 it was Santini's Porpoise Training School, and then it became Flipper's Sea School, graduating dolphins that went on to movie and television fame. But the focus of the modern-day center is critical care for injured wild dolphins and as a retirement home for those old celebrities, including dolphins once seen on *Flipper*. There are 10 trainers for the 16 dolphins, with four programs daily. The center runs the region's Manatee Rescue Team to assist and rehabilitate injured and ill manatees spotted in Keys waters, and

1906 ADDERLY HOUSE, MARATHON
Sandra Friend

it works in partnership with other nonprofits to present weeklong dolphin-therapy sessions for human patients with special needs. The giant dolphin sculpture out front makes this stop unmistakable. Open 9–4 daily. Adults $19.50, seniors $16.50, children 4–12 $13.50. Extra fees apply for dolphin swim programs.

Islamorada

✐ At **Theatre of the Sea** (305-664-2431; www.theatreofthesea.com), 84721 Overseas Hwy, brick paths meander beneath a bower of tropical plantings, past gibbons and parrots and deep saltwater pools lined with coral rock where

At **Dolphin Connection,** at Hawk's Cay Resort (305-743-7000, ext. 1220; www.hawkscay.com) on Duck Key (see *Lodging*), I experienced the Dockside Dolphins 30-minute program, where you stay dry—well, sort of—and I got to meet up with "April" again. She gave birth to a cute little guy in 1992 while I was living at the resort, and she was the inspiration behind the Porto Cayo logo (see *Dining Out*). The 45-minute Dolphin Discovery program ($120 guest/$130 non–resort guest) puts you in the water on a platform where you can hug, kiss, and do a little training with the dolphins. For those who want more with the maritime mammals, the Trainer for a Day program ($275 guest/$285 non–resort guests) takes you behind the scenes for a unique hands-on experience. It's also the only place you can go to see the dolphins within 10 feet any time of day and watch the encounter without having to pay an admission. And whether young or old, you'll want to download the Echo and the Florida Keys coloring book ahead of your arrival from the Hawk's Cay web site (look under the "Activities" menu).

DOLPHIN ENCOUNTER AT HAWK'S CAY RESORT

Hawk's Cay Resort

loggerhead turtles and parrotfish glide. It was a step back in time to my childhood, as it's changed very little and grown more lush and interesting since Kenny McKenny opened these 17 acres as a tropical roadside attraction in 1946, created from old rock quarries left behind from the Overseas Railroad. The same family still owns and operates the park, and they pride themselves on being pioneers with marine mammal interaction. For an extra fee above park admission ($50–150), their special programs— Swim with the Dolphin, Wade with the Dolphin, Meet the Sea Lion, Swim with the Sea Lion, and Swim with the Rays—enable you to interact

Theatre of the Sea

SEAL ENCOUNTER, THEATRE OF THE SEA

with the residents of the park. Each program involves an educational class and orientation prior to your interaction. Trainer for a Day lets you tag along and assist with the care and feeding of marine mammals. If you're looking for a less structured experience, however, you'll find that here, too. Most of the animals here are either in rehabilitation from injuries or cannot be returned to the wild due to crippling problems such as blindness, and they live in enclosures scattered throughout the deeply shaded park. Walk around and make their acquaintance. The touch tanks let you examine conchs, starfish, and other creatures of the reef. Nature trails lead out to a beach and into the mangrove forest to introduce you to native habitats. But the real stars here are the marine mammals and their trainers. Educational programs are presented throughout the park, or you can just watch from the sidelines as other guests swim with the dolphins and snorkel with stingrays and colorful parrotfish. Open 9:30–4 daily. Adults $23.95, ages 3–12 $15.95. Reservations are essential for special programs, including several offshore cruises offered by the park.

MUSEUMS

Islamorada

Telling the story of the quest to explore beneath the sea, the **Florida Keys History of Diving Museum** (305-664-2784), MM 83 (mailing address: P.O. Box 897, Islamorada 33036), showcases artifacts from the long history of diving in the Keys. Founders Joe and Sally Bauer have been collecting historic diving artifacts for more than 30 years and claim the world's largest collection of this unique niche. The museum is brand new as of 2006. Donations appreciated.

Marathon

✍ Carved out of a dense tropical hammock, **Crane Point Hammock Museums & Nature Center** (305-743-9100; www.cranepoint.org), 5550 Overseas Hwy, has something for everyone. Administered by the nonprofit Florida Keys Land

Trust, this 63-acre preserve includes the last intact thatch palm hammock in the Keys. There are two museums on-site. In the Museum of Natural History of the Florida Keys, walk through a replica reef, see a six-hundred-year-old dugout canoe, and learn the gamut of Keys history, from its indigenous peoples through wreckers and "Flagler's Folly." In the Children's Museum, the kids will love the engaging outdoor exhibits that put them on the deck of a pirate ship or in an Indian village or railroad station, with touch tanks and an iguana house, too. But the beauty of this park is how it immerses you in the outdoors. Mulched trails lead through a lush primordial forest of ferns, where orchids hang high overhead; a boardwalk crosses a solution hole lined with mangroves. Butterflies flutter in a butterfly garden under the buttonwoods. Walk the trails to discover the Adderly House (see *Historic Sites*), the Marathon Wild Bird Center (see *Zoological Parks & Animal Rehab*), and a boardwalk out to Florida Bay. Open 9–5 Mon–Sat and noon–5 Sun. Adults $7.50, seniors $6, students 6 and up $4, children under 6 free.

RAILROADIANA After running his Florida East Coast Railroad the length of the Atlantic Coast in Florida in the early 1900s, Henry Flagler proposed the "Key West Extension," bridging 153 miles of open seas to reach the port at Key West. The newspapers derided it as "Flagler's Folly," yet Flagler had the deep pockets to make it happen. Thousands of workers swarmed into the Keys to blast coral rock, build support piers, and lay girders to make Flagler's dream come true, despite a 1910 hurricane that displaced part of the railroad in the Lower Keys. On January 22, 1912, Flagler stepped out of his private rail car to the cheers of half the population of Key West, officially inaugurating the **Overseas Railroad.** It was a hit with tourists, bringing eager sportsmen to previously undiscovered islands, and it encouraged commerce to and from the port of Key West. Then tragedy struck. In 1935 the Labor Day hurricane bore down on the Middle Keys. A 17-foot tidal wave struck the islands, toppling a train with more than five hundred World War I veterans who worked for the railroad into the sea. Miles of track and bridges were demolished. It was the end of the line for "Flagler's Folly," and much of the right-of-way was soon turned over to the transportation department to build the Overseas Highway, which began construction in the late 1930s. A large memorial on Matecumbe Key is dedicated to those who died in the storm. Remnants of **railroad trestles** (now used as fishing piers) and a **caboose** parked in Islamorada across from Matecumbe Station (which serves as the visitors information center) are some of the relics left behind.

✍ **Pigeon Key Historical Railroad Site** (305-289-0025), MM 48 on Knight's Key, oceanside before the Seven Mile Bridge, kicks right off

PIGEON KEY, A HISTORIC RAILROAD CAMP
Sandra Friend

with a bit of railroad history—the visitors center where you pick up the tram is "Old 64," a **Flagler railroad Pullman car** owned by George Kyle. A nonprofit organization, these folks run tours 10–4 daily (adults $8.50, ages 5–13 $5). Board the cute mock railroad tram, *Henry,* for a 2½-mile ride out on the old Seven Mile Bridge to Pigeon Key, a 4½-acre island that served as a work camp for workers on the Overseas Railroad. On the island, visit the **Pigeon Key Museum** for detailed background on the building of the Overseas Railroad and the original Seven Mile Bridge, which our tour guide asserted is better built than the one used by cars today; it's survived nine hurricanes. Several historic buildings, such as the Bridge Tender's House and the Paint Foreman's House, also tell the railroad's story. After the railroad's demise, the island became a stopping-off point for motorists crossing the Seven Mile Bridge and later passed into private hands before being acquired to tell its history. Open 9:30–4 daily; tours leave on the hour 10–3.

ZOOLOGICAL PARKS & ANIMAL REHAB

Key Largo

At the **Florida Keys Wild Bird Center** (305-852-4486; www.fkwbc.org), MM 93.6 bayside, wander a boardwalk through enclosures with wild hawks, osprey, roseate spoonbills, and other birds that could not be released after rehabilitation. The nonprofit center rescues and rehabilitates injured birds in the Upper Keys. Donations appreciated.

Marathon

✔ On the grounds of Crane Point Hammock, the **Marathon Wild Bird Center** (305-743-8382; www.cranepoint.org/bird.html) cares for injured and orphaned birds, particularly raptors, with the intent of rehabilitation to release them back into the wild. See ospreys, owls, and hawks in their flight cages, and pelicans that were injured by improperly discarded monofilament fishing line.

A nonprofit rescue mission for sea turtles, **The Turtle Hospital** (305-743-2552; www.turtlehospital.org) is the only state-certified veterinary hospital in the world that cares just for sea turtles. Working with donated medical equipment, experienced veterinaries stabilize, care for, and rehabilitate ill and injured sea turtles. Guided tours (adults $15, ages 4–12 $7.50) last 45 minutes and are offered daily at 10, 1, and 4. Guests at the Hidden Harbor Motel visit for free. Reservations are required; tours subject to cancellation due to turtle emergencies and/or weather.

✳ To Do

BICYCLING The **Florida Keys Overseas Heritage Trail** (see *Greenways*) provides miles of paved bike trail for you to roam, including the entire length of Key Largo and several long stretches in and around Islamorada.

BIRDING Along the **waysides of the Overseas Highway** and at any of the *Green Space* stops listed, you'll have the opportunity to view ibises, herons, and other wading birds. **Curry Hammock State Park** (see *Beaches*) boasts some of the best seasonal birding in the Keys—it's on the flyover route for most migrating raptors and has a tall observation tower for you to bring your binoculars and watch.

BOATING The folks are friendly at **Robbie's Marina** (305-664-9814; www .robbies.com), MM 75.5, Little Matecumbe Key, and you have lots of options for getting out on the water. Rent a boat, from a 15-foot skiff to a 26-foot Rendezvous, hop a boat out to the offshore state parks, arrange a snorkeling trip on a captained boat (see *Ecotours*), charter for offshore game fishing, head out fishing on the flats, or check in at adjacent **Florida Keys Kayak & Sail** (305-664-4878) for backcountry tours ($39 and up) and kayak or sailboat rentals. While you're there, walk out on the dock and feed the pet tarpon; it's amazing to see fish that big gathering in such a group. **Caloosa Cove Boat Rental** (305-664-4455), MM 73.5, is another option for renting a powerboat for the open waters, starting at $105 for a half day in a 16-foot Rivera with a 40 horsepower engine. For lengthier trips, stop at **Ray's Rentals** (305-743-9995; www.raysrentalboats .com) on Grassy Key, MM 59, to rent for a three-day minimum, starting at $380 for a 19-foot Carolina skiff.

DIVING

Key Largo
With the only living reef in the United States, the Florida Keys are a mecca for divers eager to enjoy the colorful underwater gardens of coral and to explore the many offshore wrecks. **Key Largo** is diver central, with dedicated dive resorts that cater to folks in wetsuits, dive shops, and charters to get you out on the reefs, which start 6 miles offshore.

A favorite for we snorkelers, **Keys Diver Snorkel Tours** (305-451-1177 or 1-888-289-2402; www.keysdiver .com), 99696 Overseas Hwy, makes a point of avoiding the crowds and provides top-notch gear for your experience out on the reef. Their small groups, safety-conscious practices, and responsible eco-snorkeling make them especially good for families and those a bit timid in the water. Since 1962, **Ocean Divers North** (305-451-0039; www.oceandivers.com), 105800 Overseas Hwy, has served visiting divers with a large stock of rental Scuba Pro equipment, PADI instruction, regulator repair service, and daily diving and snorkeling trips departing 8 AM and 1 PM. **Silent World Dive Center** (1-800-966-

DIVING ON KEY LARGO'S REEFS

Visit Florida

One of the favorite pastimes for nondivers visiting Key Largo is to grab a narrated tour on a glass-bottom boat over the reefs. At **John Pennekamp Coral Reef State Park** (see *Parks*), the official tour operator (305-451-6300; www.pennekamppark.com) runs three glass-bottom boat tours daily ($22 adults, $15 ages 12 and under) plus snorkeling ($29 adults, $24 ages 12 and under; plus equipment rental) and scuba tours ($45, plus equipment rental). As I'm not a diver, I opted to see the reef via the *Spirit of Pennekamp*. Forty years ago, they did this with a rowboat and a bucket. Today, it's a sleek modified catamaran (one of only five in the world) that can put on some speed as it snakes through the narrow mangrove-lined passages out to the open water of Largo Sound. It's a 6½-mile trip across the open ocean to Molasses Reef, so if your stomach is weak, take advantage of the Dramamine the staff offers you *before* you get on the boat. Once out at the reef, the captain drifts across the incredible walls of coral, a living garden of constant movement. Sea plumes wave like ferns in a breeze, and colorful rainbows form as a school of parrotfish flashes past. Our narrator, Matt, filled us in on all sorts of details about the reef, including the fact that coral spawns on the August full moon, spewing exploding volcanoes of luminous eggs and sperm. You could spend hours staring at the color and form of the tropical reef beneath you, and the trip is over too soon. Yes, the glass windows do tint the view—for true color, you'd need to dive or snorkel—but most visitors opt for this experience because of their lack of expertise with open water and a fear of sharks and barracuda, which are curious about divers, but rarely a problem.

DIVE; www.SilentWorldKeyLargo.com), MM 103.2 bayside, offers instruction and leads 14-passenger trips out to the reefs in Pennekamp and the Key Largo National Marine Sanctuary. At the Holiday Inn Marina, **Abyss Dive Center** (305-743-2126 or 1-800-457-0134; www.abyssdive.com), MM 54, offers instruction, rentals, and a dive boat to get you out on the reef. See *Dive Resorts* for other stay-and-play options. If you're an experienced diver and want a truly unique vacation, book **Jules Undersea Lodge** (305-451-2353; www.jul.com), 51 Shoreland Dr at MM 103.5; it's the world's first undersea hotel, boasting a two-bedroom, air-conditioned suite 30 feet below water in Emerald Lagoon, and yes, they offer room service.

Marathon

The Florida Keys National Marine Sanctuary Shipwreck Trail (www.fknms .nos.noaa.gov/sanctuary_resources/shipwreck_trail/welcome.html) commemorates five centuries of ships wrecked on the reefs surrounding the keys. Visit their web site or pick up a brochure at a visitors center to pinpoint where the wrecks are located.

Beginners dive at **Sombrero Reef,** a coral garden where parrotfish and
stingrays play, while advanced divers head out to the ***Thunderbolt,*** a sunken
research vessel that is home to barracuda, moray eels, and at least one goliath
grouper dubbed "Bubba."

ECOTOURS

Islamorada
At **Sea-n-Swim Tours** (305-664-5554), MM 77.5 at Robbie's Marina (see *Boating*), sign up to snorkel some of the nearby patch reefs (great for beginners like
me) or the 1733 *San Pedro* shipwreck, or take a sunset cruise out on Florida Bay.
Guided snorkel trips cost $49 adults, $29 for two and a half hours; sunset cruises
are $25 adults, $15 children and depart a half hour before sunset.

Key Largo
Hop a boat at **Captain Sterling's Everglades Tours** (305-853-5161 or 1-888-
224-6044), MM 102, for a guided tour on Florida Bay along the coastline of
Everglades National Park.

The ***Key Largo Princess*** (305-451-4655 or 1-877-648-8129) leaves the Holiday
Inn docks (MM 100) three times daily, offering trips to Molasses Reef and others at Pennekamp as well.

FISHING There are few better places than the Keys to spend your days fishing.
There are hundreds of places along US 1 where you can pull off and cast a line.
The waters of Florida Bay are shallow and clear for flats fishing, and on the
ocean side, the outer edge of the reef drops off into an abyss where some of the
best "big game" fish are found, including wahoo, sailfish, dolphin, kingfish, and
marlin. Flats fishing is especially popu-
lar because of the ease with which
you can catch the "Big Three"—
tarpon, bonefish, and permit. Tarpon
fishing is best Apr–Jun, and permit
and bonefish most common from
spring through fall. You'll find charter
boats and fishing guides at every
marina, because fishing is the lifestyle
of the Keys. Check at **Robbie's
Marina** (see *Boating*) because I know
they're nice folks; **Suzanne Fishing
Charters** (305-664-9202), Whale
Harbor Marina, Islamorada, to book a
deep-sea trip; at **World Wide
Sportsman** (see *Selective Shopping*)
for deep-sea fishing; and **Florida
Keys Anglers** (1-800-513-0799;
www.floridakeysanglers.com) for sight
fishing the flats.

FISHING THE FLATS

Hawk's Cay Resort

HIKING Most people don't associate hiking with the Keys, but in my research I've discovered great little walks that introduce you to the tropical habitats. You'll find two pleasant short nature trails at **John Pennekamp Coral Reef State Park,** a network of five short trails at **Windley Key Geological State Park,** and one of the best hikes in the Keys at **Long Key State Park. Curry Hammock State Park** has a new bayside loop trail, and **Crane Point Hammock** (see *Museums*) offers several miles of hiking trails in a dense tropical hammock. But the wildest place of all to hike is on Key Largo. Check in at Pennekamp's ranger station for a backcountry permit to go beyond the nature trail and wander the forest roads of **Key Largo Hammocks Botanical State Park,** which encompasses nearly 3,000 acres of tropical forest adjacent to Crocodile Lakes National Wildlife Refuge.

HOUSEBOATING Imagine drifting through the crystal-clear shallows of Florida Bay . . . on a houseboat! At **Barefoot Houseboat Rentals** (305-942-0045), 90511 Overseas Hwy, you can fulfill that dream of lazy days amid the mangrove islands on a 30- or 43-foot houseboat; three-day minimum.

LOBSTERING Aug 6–Mar 31 marks the annual **Florida lobster season,** when you're welcome to scuba or snorkel for your own dinner. Limits are 6 per day or 24 per boat, and specific areas, such as the waters of John Pennekamp Coral Reef State Park and Everglades National Park, are excluded. For the full list of rules and regulations, contact the Florida Marine Patrol (1-800-342-5367 or 1-800-ASK-FISH) or the National Marine Fisheries Service (813-570-5305 or 305-743-2437).

PADDLING Sea kayaking is the best way to explore the thousands of mangrove-lined passageways on Florida Bay, and you'll find plenty of outfitters ready to set you up on a paddling trip. At MM 104 on Key Largo, **Florida Bay Outfitters** (305-451-3018; www.kayakfloridakeys.com) offers instruction and rentals ($35 and up), with guided tours starting at $50; **Marathon Kayak** (305-743-0561; www.marathonkayak.com), 19 Sombrero Blvd at Sombrero Resort, has rentals and guided tours available. At Duck Key, **Hawk's Cay** (305-743-7000 or 1-888-443-6393; www.hawkscay.com), 61 Hawk's Cay Blvd, offers eco-kayak adventures for $35–40, or you can rent your own kayak for $20–30 per hour.

SAILING You'll experience the wind in your hair and the spray of the sea at **Colgate's Offshore Sailing School** (www.offshore-sailing.com) at Hawk's Cay Resort (see *Lodging*). Founded in 1964 by Olympic and America's Cup sailor Steve Colgate, the school offers a variety of courses to fit your schedule. The two-hour clinic gives you a chance to experience the thrill of sailing. The 3- to 6-day Learn to Sail courses on Colgate 26 sailboats combine classroom and offshore sailing, while leaving you enough time each day to enjoy the resort. You'll sail on 46-foot Hunters down to Key West on the Live Aboard Cruising course, while tacking, jibbing, reefing, learning about wind direction, what to do in weather conditions, and reading nautical maps. Or totally immerse yourself on the 10-day Fast Track to Cruising course, which includes both the Learn to Sail and Live Aboard Cruising courses, along with boat mechanics and how to plan your own sea adventure.

SCENIC DRIVES You don't have much of a choice—US 1 is the only highway linking the Keys, and it's one of the most scenic drives in Florida, often offering simultaneous views of the Atlantic Ocean and Florida Bay, especially through Islamorada south to Marathon. Relax and enjoy.

SPA THERAPY The **Indies Spa** at Hawk's Cay (305-743-7000 or 1-888-443-6393; www.hawkscay.com), 61

Sandra Friend

GETTING READY TO SET SAIL FROM JOHN PENNEKAMP STATE PARK

Hawk's Cay Blvd, nourishes your body after a long day in the sun. I've been to a lot of spas, and this one is most memorable. The yoga-inspired Thai Massage ($130–160) loosens tense muscles through a variety of stretches and relaxation techniques. Their signature Keys Style Margarita Salt Loofa treatment ($90) exfoliates you, starting with the tropical rain room, then continues with the Margarita Salt massage, followed by botanical tequila gel and their lime body lotion. Teens will love the Jazzy Island Manicure ($25) and Jazzy Island Pedicure ($30). Special teen massages are offered ($40) in the comfort of their bathing suit.

WATER SPORTS

Key Largo
Bay Dolphin Watersports (305-453-4554), 104000 Overseas Hwy, MM 104, offers sea kayak and WaveRunner rentals as well as snorkeling and scuba trips to the nearby reefs. There's lots to do at **Caribbean Watersports** (305-852-4707; www.caribbeanwatersports.com), 97000 Overseas Hwy, MM 97 at the Westin Beach Resort, where you can grab a Hobie Cat or a sailboard, or sign up for a sailing lesson or snorkeling trip. Lounge at their sandy beach, and kick back and enjoy the sunset. At **Key Largo Parasail** (305-747-0032), rise a thousand feet into the air on the sea breeze . . . if you dare!

Tavernier
H20 Adventures (305-853-0600) rents WaveRunners, Jet Skis, and powerboats.

✳ Green Space

BEACHES One little secret about the Upper and Middle Keys: Beaches are few and far between. The islands are mangrove lined, so when you find a stretch of natural beach, it's truly a delight. **John Pennekamp Coral Reef State Park** (see *Parks*) offers two small beaches, but you'll prefer swimming off the sandy beach at **Harry Harris County Park**, MM 92, Tavernier, or at **Founder's Park**, MM 86 in Islamorada. **Anne's Beach**, MM 73.5 between Islamorada and

Marathon, has a boardwalk through the mangroves and fishing areas as well as two small sandy beaches. On Marathon, check out **Sombrero Public Beach,** 2 miles south of MM 50 at the end of Sombrero Beach Road, where there's a playground, picnic tables, and rest rooms, and **Curry Hammock State Park** (305-289-2690), 56200 Overseas Hwy, which offers picnic tables, a brand-new campground, and a short nature trail.

GREENWAYS Making use of the remaining bridges and right-of-way of the Overseas Railroad, the **Florida Keys Overseas Heritage Trail** (305-853-3571; www.dep.state.fl.us/gwt/state/keystrail/default.htm), Three La Croix Court, Key Largo, is a paved path paralleling the Overseas Highway to enable bikers and pedestrians a safe way to travel through the Keys. Presently, a 9-mile segment on Key Largo and a 4-mile segment on Grassy Key are complete; other smaller segments are in the works, with plans to eventually extend the trail the full 106 miles between Key Largo and Key West.

PARKS

Islamorada

Offshore from Little Matecumbe Key, **Lignumvitae Key Botanical State Park** (305-664-2540) protects a rarity in these parts—a virgin tropical hardwood forest. A small part of the island was cleared for William J. Matheson, a wealthy Miami chemist, to build a caretaker's home in 1919; the stone structure is now the visitors center. Visitors must walk with a ranger to explore the botanical wonders, which include a gnarled lignum vitae tree more than two thousand years old. Tours start at the dock and are given twice daily, Thu–Mon; bring insect repellent and, if it isn't the dead of winter, a mosquito head net! Fee. Check at Robbie's Marina (see *Boating*) for daily tour boat times, which may vary.

✍ At **Windley Key Fossil Reef Geological State Park** (305-664-2540), MM 85.5, Henry Flagler's workmen quarried Key Largo limestone—a fossilized coral—to use in building structures along the Overseas Railroad. The quarry continued in active operation through the 1960s, producing decorative stone for building facades. Stop at the visitors center (open 8–5 Thu–Mon) to orient yourself to the history of this site, and then wander the trails to enjoy the shady tropical hammocks and to examine the incredible detail of fossils in the coral walls. There is a small picnic area on-site. Fee.

Key Largo

✍ The first undersea park in America, **John Pennekamp Coral Reef State Park** (305-451-1202), MM 103, offers landlubbers some fun as well. Start off at the visitors center to see the saltwater aquariums, including a 30,000-gallon tank, that orient you to the sea life found in this 70-nautical-square-mile park, and then explore the park's two nature trails. The Wild Tamarind Trail is a short loop through the dense tropical hardwood hammock—look closely at tree limbs to spot colorful tree snails. On the Mangrove Trail, walk a boardwalk through tunnels formed by the mangroves, with an observation deck over the meandering saline creeks. Keep alert for giant iguanas—nonnative, but nevertheless roaming the berm along the park road. There are two beaches for swimming and an underwater snorkeling trail. All this without getting on a boat! If you plan to visit the reef (and you should), the park concession (see *Ecotours*) offers diving, snorkeling, and glass-bottom boat trips. Fee.

Long Key

With its fine selection of oceanfront campsites, **Long Key State Park** (305-664-4815), 67400 Overseas Hwy, MM 67.5, has always been a favorite for tent campers, and you will enjoy exploring the mangrove-lined lagoons by kayak. But I love this park most for its hiking trail. **The Golden Orb Trail** loops only a little more than a mile, but it's one of the most fascinating hikes in the Keys, passing through five different plant communities, including the desertlike coastal berm, where salt-tolerant plants grow on layers of coral.

WILD PLACES In the Keys, it doesn't get wilder than out on and *in* the water. The **Florida Keys National Marine Sanctuary** (305-743-2437; www.fknms.nos .noaa.gov/welcome.html) encompasses 2,800 nautical square miles along the entire island chain. Both Florida Bay and the flats behind the Atlantic-side reefs have hundreds of small, uninhabited islands buttressed by mangroves and accessible only by boat. The sanctuary includes the waters of the Key Largo National Marine Sanctuary and John Pennekamp Coral Reef State Park.

Key Largo Hammock Botanical State Park (305-451-1202), CR 905 just north of US 1, offers a wild walk through the "land of little giants," the largest collection of the smallest National Champion trees in the United States, growing in the densest and largest tropical hammock in the country. Backcountry permits are available to allow you to roam more than 2,000 acres of tropical forest on forest roads. Avoid the temptation to go off-road unless you know your poisonous trees well. Fee. Adjacent **Crocodile Lakes National Wildlife Refuge** (305-451-4223; www.fws.gov/southeast/crocodilelake), covering nearly 7,000 acres, is not open to the public for good reason—it has the highest population of endangered American crocodiles on earth, and they need to be left undisturbed.

✻ Lodging

CAMPGROUNDS

Key Largo 33037

🐾 Shaded campsites are the norm at **Florida Keys RV Resort** (305-451-6090 or 1-866-784-6539), 106003 Overseas Hwy, a resort with full hookups ($35 and up), a pool and spa, and a 2-acre fishing lake.

🏄 **Key Largo Kampground and Marina** (305-451-1431 or 1-800-526-7688; www.keylargokampground .com), 101551 Overseas Hwy, has a handful of waterfront sites on the Atlantic Ocean, a boat ramp, and dockage. Two beaches and a pool make this a great family destination; full hookup and tent sites available, starting at $30.

Marathon 33050

Relax at **Jolly Roger Travel Park** (305-289-0404 or 1-800-995-1525; www.jrtp.com) along Florida Bay, where campsites are $30 off-season, $42–52 in-season.

Marathon 33050

🦞 ♿ On its own private island, **Conch Key Cottages** (305-289-1377 or 1-800-330-1577; www.conchkeycottages.com), MM 62.3, is a quiet retreat once known as Walker's Island, where some of the cottages date from the 1920s and have wonderful "old Conch" interiors with varnished wooden walls and ceilings. A path winds through the well-manicured grounds through tropical gardens to each of the cottages, which are painted in pastels and named after seashells. There are no phones to puncture the bliss of your stay, but use of a kayak comes with every unit. Rates run $74–147 for one bedroom, $163–215 for two bedrooms. Enjoy the pool tucked under the sea grapes, or swim at their own private beach.

DIVE RESORTS

Key Largo 33037

Amy Slate's Amoray Dive Center (305-451-3595 or 1-800-4-AMORAY; www.amoray.com), 104250 Overseas Hwy, is a dedicated dive resort with dive-stay packages, instruction, and underwater weddings; rates start at $75. Specializing in small, personalized diving expeditions, **Kelly's on the Bay** (305-451-1622 or 1-800-226-0415), 104220 Overseas Hwy, is a small family-owned resort with 32 bayside units ($70–175).

HOTELS, MOTELS, AND RESORTS

Duck Key 33050

Hawk's Cay Resort (305-743-7000 or 1-888-443-6393; www.hawkscay.com), 61 Hawk's Cay Blvd, encompasses 60 acres on a tropical island, just east of MM 61. Cross over the Venetian bridge to paradise. You'll think you've left the country at this Caribbean-style oasis in the Keys. I actually lived here for a few months while working on some graphic projects back in the 1990s. The staff remains as friendly today as they did back then, and their security rates high on my list. On one visit, I thought I had someone follow me back to my condo and quickly called the desk. Within seconds they had a team of security and the manager on duty checking inside and out. And they would have gladly moved me to another unit had I requested one. For accommodations you can choose from 161 guest rooms and suites in the main hotel or stay in one of their two-bedroom villas with living room and fully furnished kitchen. The Marina Villa is all on one floor, while the two-story Conch Villa has an optional tropical spa on your own private deck. For those needing more space or privacy, the Sanctuary Villa, at 1,750 square feet, comes with its very own private pool. All are tropically decorated and have a private porch or deck where you can watch the sun rise over the Atlantic Ocean or set on the Gulf. Once you've settled in, there's a lot to do. At the **Indies Club,** kids can splash around and "slide the plank" at the **Pirate's Ship** pool, complete with water cannons. The **Treehouse** features S-curve and rocket slides, monkey bars, a tire swing, and a climbing wall. Fun kids' activities also include the **Hermit Crab Derby** for the little ones and **Island Scavenger Hunt** for teens. Preteens and teens will love hanging out at **The Cove** (fee), where they can dance, sing karaoke, or play air hockey and Xbox. Couples will want to snuggle on the **Sunset**

Champagne Cruise ($35), and anglers will want to charter a boat and head to the backcountry flats ($325–675) or near the Gulf Stream for offshore or reef fishing ($550–1,300). Other water activities run the gamut from Jet Skiing ($59 and up an hour), wakeboarding ($89 and up per lesson), snorkeling ($35), and eco-kayaking tours ($35–45) to **Colgate's Offshore Sailing School** (see *Sailing*), where professional U.S. Sailing–certified instructors, under the direction of Olympic and America's Cup sailor Steve Colgate, teach you on Colgate 26 sailboats and 46-foot Hunters. Clinics run from two hours to 10 days. The **Dolphin Connection** gets you up close and personal with dolphins (see *Marine Parks*), and for those who want to lay back and relax, the resort has four pools and a saltwater lagoon. The **Indies Spa** (see *Spa Therapy*) takes you further into nirvana with their Pineapple Coconut Sugar Glow Body Treatment ($65) or their Tropical Breeze Escape Massage ($80–125). The Tropical Teaser ($216) pairs the two and adds a Mini-Botanical Facial for a full two hours of relaxation and rejuvenation.

Islamorada 33036

Chesapeake Resort (305-664-4662 or 1-800-338-3395; www.chesapeake -resort.com), 83409 Overseas Hwy, offers something for everyone: a place to relax with a view of the Atlantic framed by coconut palms, your choice of standard motel rooms or deluxe accommodations in spacious ocean-front rooms ($175 and up), and an oceanside pool and spa adjoining the sunning beach.

🦐 🛇 🐚 A gigantic retro sign on US 1 beckons you into **The Islander Resort** (305-664-2031 or 1-800-753-

6002; www.islanderfloridakeys.com), P.O. Box 766, MM 82.1, but there's nothing retro about this updated oceanfront resort. Every spacious room has high ceilings and a tiled floor; is decorated in shades of blue and white; and is sparkling clean, even the full kitchen. Walkways lead to the oceanfront, where you can enjoy two zero-entry pools or nearly a quarter mile of Atlantic Ocean beach. Your choices include studio lanai ($139–225), one-bedroom ($195–375), and two-bedroom ($295–495) units.

🛇 On Florida Bay, the tropical **Kon-Tiki Resort** (305-664-4702; www .kontiki-resort.com), 81200 Overseas Hwy, is a collection of 1960s-era villas with updated furnishings in spacious rooms; most have two bedrooms, full living room, dining area, and kitchen, and a screened porch ($110 and up, with discounts for weekly and monthly stays). Dockage is available for boats up to 25 feet long, but personal watercraft are not permitted.

🦐 🛇 🐚 "Think pink!" at the **Sands of Islamorada** (305-664-2791 or 1-888-741-4518; www.sandsofislamorada .com), 80051 Overseas Hwy, a charming little old-fashioned beach resort under the same ownership for 20 years. Dressed in bold tropical colors, the airy rooms and efficiencies ($105 and up) feature tile floors, high ceilings, full-size refrigerator, coffee-maker, and microwave. Relax in the pool or hot tub and listen to resident parrots Tela, Dolly, and Scootie squawk and squabble, or enjoy their beachfront on the Atlantic Ocean, where the water is crystal clear for snorkeling. A boat ramp and dockage are available for your craft.

Key Largo 33037

❦ Step between the carved wooden palms into another world at **Kona Kai Resort & Gallery** (305-852-7200 or 1-800-365-STAY; www .konakairesort.com), 97802 Overseas Hwy, where Joe and Ronnie Harris wrought magic on a 1940s seaside motel to transform it into one of the most intimate and relaxing resorts in the Keys, centered around a classy fine-art gallery. Tastefully decorated with art, the tropical gardens boast nearly 40 types of rare palms, a tropical fruit garden, and more than 400 species of orchids in Ronnie's orchid house—if you love tropical flora like I do, ask for a map. Each room is named for a tropical fruit: our one-bedroom Key Lime Suite ($177–489) included an incredible host of amenities, including a full kitchen with new appliances, glass-block accent walls, remote controls for the CD player and fans, island music and books, and original artwork decorating the rooms. Televisions are included, but no phones. The regular guest rooms ($189–331) are very spacious and include a mini fridge; there are one- and two-bedroom suites as well ($235–937). After watching the sunset from the dock on Florida Bay, we enjoyed a soak in the Jacuzzi and a swim in the pool. Guests have use of kayaks and paddleboats, too. Pampered? You bet. I can't wait to return.

Largo Lodge Motel (352-451-0424 or 1-800-468-4378), 101740 Overseas Hwy. Hidden in a palm hammock, this intimate resort caters to adults only, with rooms and cottages on the bay starting at $95.

✐ Several years ago I stayed at the **Marriott Key Largo Bay Beach Resort** (305-453-0000 or 1-866-849-3733; www.marriottkeylargo.com), 103800 Overseas Hwy, and was delighted by the size of my room ($199 and up) and its view of Florida Bay. Down at the lushly landscaped pool area, I grabbed a margarita at the tiki bar and relaxed with my favorite novel—the perfect end to a busy day of research. It's a large complex, with restaurants, meeting facilities, and a full-service spa, but still small enough to wander around in your sandals without feeling out of place.

✐ I've always found **Popp's Motel** (305-852-5201; www.popps.com), 95500 Overseas Hwy, a visually appealing destination. Owned by the same family since 1951, it offers 10 affordable "home away from home" cottages ($99–119) with kitchens, a boat ramp, and a private sand beach on Florida Bay.

Long Key 33001

& ✐ Nestled in a coconut grove along Florida Bay, the intimate **Lime Tree Bay Resort** (305-664-4740 or 1-800-723-4519; www.limetreebayresort .com), P.O. Box 839, has a waterfront pool, great snorkeling offshore, and an appealing selection of 33 motel rooms ($79 and up) and one- and two-bedroom suites ($200 and up), many with stunning views. With a family in tow, I'd go for the Zane Grey, a two-bedroom unit with island decor, a writing desk, wooden blinds, and wraparound windows with an awesome view of Florida Bay.

Marathon 33050

❦ & Hidden in a thickly canopied jungle of banana palms and other tropical plants on Marathon, **Banana Bay Resort & Marina** (305-743-3500 or 1-800-BANANA-1; www

.bananabay.com) is a retreat in itself. Enjoy clean, spacious guest rooms ($95–225) with continental breakfast served next to the oversized pool with adjoining whirlpool. While the marina, wedding chapel, and bayside tiki bar washed away with the Hurricane Wilma storm surge, we expect them to return. Meanwhile, it's still an appealing vacation destination.

✎ Settle into a cute cottage at **Crystal Bay Resort** (305-289-8089 or 1-888-289-8089; www.crystalbayresort.com), 4900 Overseas Hwy, a 1950s resort with updated interiors. The suites are large and open and make great use of the natural light. It's a perfect place to bring the family, with an on-site miniature golf course (go ahead, knock that ball into the gator's mouth!), a shaded playground, and a pool next to the bay as well as a marina and dock for Dad's boat. Cottages start at $85, efficiencies at $110, and suites at $140.

Retro rooms and a tiled pool make the charming **Flamingo Inn** (305-289-1478 or 1-800-439-1478; www.theflamingoinn.com), 59299 Overseas Hwy, a fun place to stay; it has curb appeal and basic accommodations for reasonable prices ($50–159).

✳ Where to Eat

DINING OUT

Duck Key
Hawk's Cay Resort (305-743-7000 or 1-888-443-6393; www.hawkscay.com), 61 Hawk's Cay Blvd. Three of the many restaurants on property are the **Palm Terrace,** where you'll enjoy a lavish gourmet breakfast buffet with super huge muffins and made-to-order omelets; **The Waters Edge,** at the marina, for steaks and seafood;

and **Porto Cayo,** for romantic fusion of Mediterranean and Floridian cuisine in elegant surroundings. Oh, and I was excited to see that Porto Cayo is still using my dolphin logo, which I created for them back in the 1990s when I was a commercial artist.

Grassy Key
Whole Roasted Duck à la Hideaway ($28) is the specialty at **The Hideaway** (305-289-1554; www.hideawaycafe.com), MM 57.5, US 1 South. Hosts Robert and Jackie serve excellent gourmet fare, such as chateaubriand ($31) and Seafood Puttanesca, which has shrimp, scallops, and shellfish in a spicy red sauce ($24). The romantic atmosphere comes complete with ocean view. Reservations required. It's tucked away at Rainbow Bend Resort, and you may want to call ahead for directions as the restaurant is tricky to find (hence "The Hideaway"). Open daily from 4:30.

Islamorada
Out on the docks behind World Wide Sportsman (see *Selective Shopping*), **Islamorada Fish Company** (305-664-9271; www.islamoradafishco.com), 81532 Overseas Hwy, has the perfect setting for savoring seafood. Entrées ($18–27) cater to seafood lovers, featuring tuna steak wasabi, dolphin chardonnay, and stuffed Florida lobster.

With all this fresh fish around, I was glad to come across **Kaiyo** (305-664-5556; www.kaiyokeys.com), 81701 Old Overseas Hwy, an upscale sushi bar with hardwood floors, beautiful mosaics, and a Zen garden out front. Relax in this fine bistro setting and enjoy Asian cuisine with Florida flair—Key lime lobster roll using fresh Florida lobster, pan-seared conch cake, and more. Open noon–10 Mon–Sat, closed Sun.

Squid Row (305-664-9865), 81901 Overseas Hwy, MM 81.9, serves up only-in-the-Keys conch burgers ($5) and offers serious Keys delights such as hearts of palm salad, conch salad, fresh Florida lobster, and their signature bouillabaisse, lobster thermidor, and steak Madagascar. Light fare can be had for under $10; a serious entrée will run you $14 and up.

Key Largo

🐚 A fish camp in the 1930s, **Ballyhoos** (305-852-0822), MM 97.8 in the median, is now a popular seafood grill with the catch of the day ($14 and up) served a dozen different ways and all-you-can-eat stone crab for $38. They also have daily specials for you landlubbers—try out the Cajun sausage with red beans and rice or open-face roast beef and mashed potatoes. Your salad comes accompanied with a unique bread I can best describe as a hot pretzel loaf, and the sweet tea (served in Mason jars) is perfect. I've eaten here several times and always enjoyed my meal.

Watch sunset turn the waters of Florida Bay from blue to gold from your table at the **Bayside Grille** (305-451-3380), MM 99.5 bayside, a classy restaurant with a view as romantic as they get. Dine on fresh yellowtail, grouper, dolphin, and jumbo shrimp; leave room for the luscious Florida orange cake. Open for lunch and dinner daily.

🐚 Kick back at **Calypso's** (305-451-0600), One Seagate Blvd, off Ocean Bay Dr at MM 99.5—hard to find, but worth it! Overlooking Ocean Bay Marina, this causal waterfront restaurant says "we know the music is loud and the food is spicy, and that's the way we like it!" Eat outdoors or in and enjoy specials such as coconut shrimp with raspberry jalapeño sauce or sautéed dolphin with mushroom caper cream sauce ($16 and up). The chef's signature dishes include coconut-crusted fish with butter pecan sauce, and horseradish-crusted yellowfin with velvety aioli. Okay, so it only *looks* like a fish camp, and if you order a sandwich you'll get paper plates and plastic utensils. You'll be delighted with your meal—but cash only, please.

Marathon

For a classy dinner out, visit **Annette's Lobster & Steak House** (305-743-5516; www.annetteslobster.com), 3660 Overseas Hwy, where dinner entrées ($14 and up) include dozens of exquisite selections, such as roast duckling, macadamia grouper, and rack of lamb. Reservations recommended.

Locals say the **Barracuda Grill** (305-743-3314; www.barracudagrill.com), MM 49.5, US 1 South past K-Mart and Home Depot (look for their yellow sign), is a *must*. The restaurant is owned and operated by Lance and Jan Hill and has a casual atmosphere with something for everyone: a variety of seafood, Angus beef, chops, and an interesting voodoo stew with seafood and veggies in a spicy tomato-saffron stock. Open daily from 6 PM, except Sun. No reservations are necessary.

Spectacular sunsets await you at **Cabots** (305-743-6442; www.cabots onthewater.com), US 1 South. Sit inside air-conditioned comfort or outside with views of the aquamarine Atlantic Ocean and Seven Mile Bridge. The Continental menu has everything from chicken to seafood at great prices ($10–27). Try the jumbo coconut shrimp or Island Popcorn Shrimp ($10) appetizers, and then move on to the Gulf grouper sandwich ($10), which comes grilled, blackened, or fried. The health-conscious will enjoy the veggie pasta ($11) with artichoke hearts, kalamata olives, shallots, garlic, capers, and chipotle pepper sauce. The yellowtail snapper Provençale, with marinated artichoke hearts, black olives, tomato, parsley, shallots, garlic, oregano, and lemon zest, is so fresh you'll think it jumped on your plate directly from the water. For landlubbers there's the 12-ounce New York strip ($27). Open 11–10 daily.

The **Key Colony Inn** (305-743-0100), US 1, is a classic—one that locals frequent and tourists return to. The extensive menu includes a bowl of salad presented tableside. A great dining spot for families. Open daily for lunch 11–2 and dinner 5–10. Reservations suggested.

EATING OUT

Islamorada
We tried a couple of times to eat at the **Hungry Tarpon Diner** (305-664-0535), in front of Robbie's Marina, MM 77.5, but it closes down between lunch and dinner, and we kept missing it. Nevertheless, I'm mentioning it here because no matter whom we asked, that's where they told us to eat. Small and unpretentious, it dates from the 1940s and serves real Florida cuisine, such as Grits and Grunts (two eggs, biscuits, grits or hash browns, and fried fish) for breakfast and fresh-as-it-gets hogfish, yellowfin tuna, and Florida lobster for dinner.

Boasting "the best breakfast in the islands," **Mangrove Mike's Café** (305-664-8022), MM 82.2 at the Sunset Inn, sports a 1950s motif and serves up People's Choice winners such as wraps, omelets, and hotcakes ($5–7) 6–2 daily.

If the sweet aroma of the smoker outside doesn't make you take a bee-line to **Time Out Barbecue** (305-664-8911), MM 81.5 on the Old Overseas Hwy, I hope this will—there's not a barbecue restaurant I can recommend more highly south of Lake Okeechobee. But I'm partial to Kansas City style, where the pulled pork is slow cooked in barbecue sauce and it comes out so succulent you don't need to add another drop of sauce. Daily lunch specials such as "Your Mama's" pot roast or fried catfish and hush puppies run $6, and their fish is fresh every day—"when it's gone, it's gone."

Key Largo
Giant biscuits! Great grits! You'll find them at **Harriette's Restaurant** (305-852-8689), 95710 Overseas Hwy, where Harriette Mattson and her trusty kitchen staff whip up a breakfast that'll keep you going until dinner. The menu includes a conch fritter burger, crab cakes Benedict, apple and peach crêpes, and breakfast burritos (real big ones); breakfast will run you $3–8. Open 6–2 daily; closed major holidays.

Marathon
After a long day on the water, grab a drink and a sandwich and watch the sun go down at local favorite **Burdine's Waterfront Chiki Tiki** (305-743-5317; www.burdineswaterfront .com), 1200 Ocean St, where you'll find huge burgers and fried Key lime

pie. At MM 47.5 at the end of 15th St.

An open-air restaurant along US 1, the **Cracked Conch Café** (305-743-2233; www.conchcafe.com), 4999 Overseas Hwy, serves conch in several unique preparations, including conch-stuffed chicken. Pronounced "konk," it's the soul food of the Keys, pulled from a shellfish found offshore, and it's also the proud nickname of the natives. Nightly specials include tropical dolphin and grouper Oscar, with entrées $12–23.

Locally caught seafood is abundant at the oldest fish market and restaurant in Marathon. **Fish Tales Market & Eatery** (305-743-9196; www.florida lobster.com), MM 54 oceanside at 117th St across from Vaca Cut Bridge, offers selections at the raw bar, salads ($6), sandwiches, or platters ($4–9), and draft beer by the glass or pitcher. The full-service fish house offers not only local seafood but also hand-cut aged choice and prime steaks, and homemade bratwurst. Open 11–6:30 Mon–Sat.

It's just a good old Keys fish market with real fresh food—**Herbie's** (305-743-6373), MM 51 on US 1 South, past the airport, has no pretensions with its picnic tables atop concrete floors. A local favorite since 1971, they serve up their famous conch fritters with a smile. The grilled conch sandwich makes a perfect lunch; sandwiches, salads, and platters $2–12. Open 11–10 Tue–Sat. Cash only.

You'll find the best prices for seafood straight off the boat at **Keys Fisheries Market & Marina** (305-743-4353; www.keysfisheries.com), MM 49 bayside, on the water. They're famous for their fresh lobster Reuben ($14),

or try their Key lime scallops ($15) or whiskey peppercorn snapper ($16).

Since 1954, the breezy **7 Mile Grill** (305-743-4481), 1240 Overseas Hwy, has been a great breakfast stop before you head south to the Lower Keys. Choose from nine different omelets (including fresh veggie), the 7 Mile muffin, eggs Benedict, blueberry hot-cakes, or just plan old eggs and grits ($3–7). Open for lunch and dinner, too.

COFFEE SHOPS AND SODA FOUNTAINS

Marathon

A giant coffee cup urges you to pull in to **Leigh Ann's Coffee House** (305-743-2001), 7537 Overseas Hwy at MM 51, where your favorite cup of Joe is an accompaniment to delectable fresh-made salads and pastries such as Sharon's Key lime éclairs along with daily lunch specials such as stuffed peppers.

✳ Selective Shopping

Islamorada

At **The Banyan Tree** (305-664-3433; www.banyantreegarden.com), 81997 Overseas Hwy, garden paths meander under the shade of gumbo limbo, sea grapes, and a large banyan tree, which also shades the shop full of antiques and home decor (look for Tiffany glass here), outdoor furniture, and plants and flowers.

In the front of **Hooked on Books** (305-517-2602), 82681 Overseas Hwy, you'll find plenty to read on maritime topics and the Florida Keys; an entire bookcase is devoted to Florida authors (hooray!). There's a mix of new and used books, many Ballantine and Penguin literary titles, and an entire room devoted just to children's literature.

You can't miss **Treasure Village** (305-852-2458), MM 86.7, not with the giant lobster out front. It's a mini mall of shops and galleries surrounding a shaded courtyard, where tropical birds twitter and squawk. Among the many selections are **Spirit Dance** (see *Art Galleries*); **Island Body and Sol,** with aromatic soaps and bath salts; and **Bluewater Potters.**

Ernest Hemingway's boat *Pilar* rests on the sales floor of **World Wide Sportsman** (305-664-3398 or 1-800-327-2880; www.basspro.com), 81576 Overseas Hwy, which is only one of many reasons to stop in and see one of the largest nautical outfitters in South Florida. This two-story department store of the outdoors focuses on fishing, befitting its location, with an excellent selection of technical wear, guidebooks, and tackle. Relax in the Zane Grey lounge, or ask about booking a deepwater charter trip; a full-service marina and waterfront restaurant are out back.

Key Largo
Stop in the **Book Nook** (305-451-1468), 103400 Overseas Hwy, where owner Joel keeps an outstanding stock of Florida guidebooks and local non-fiction on the front table. There's a full shelf of Florida mystery writers to choose from, as well as a nice selection of literary nonfiction, some genre paperbacks, and books on maritime history.

The **Florida Keys Gift Company** (305-453-4700), 102421 Overseas Hwy, has vibrantly painted fish from Jeannine Bean, beautiful gyotaku (Japanese fish prints) by artist Al Weinbaum, decorative art glass, hand-colored photos, and inspirational art,

including greeting cards with clever sayings like "Adventure without risk is Disneyland."

Great gifts await at **Largo Cargo** (305-451-4242; www.largocargo.com), 103101 Overseas Hwy, where the works of local artists include some very funky pottery, mermaids and palm trees, and seashore scenes—all that you expect in the tropics.

I love **Shell World** (305-852-8245), 97600 Overseas Hwy, because of its vast selection of tropical gifts, seashells, and coral. It's also the first large gift shop you see after leaving the mainland, and the massive coral strewn about outside will catch your attention. Their stock includes furniture and art imported from Indonesia, the usual T-shirts, and children's books and games.

Marathon
Food For Thought (305-743-3297; www.foodforthoughtinc.com), 5800 Overseas Hwy, mingles new books with health food.

It's not often a person gets cast as a character in a novel, but Charlie Wood, the owner of **Marathon**

PILES OF CORAL AT SHELL WORLD

Sandra Friend

Discount Books (305-289-2066), 2219 Overseas Hwy, and his store managed that distinction in one of Tim Dorsey's madcap tomes. Great selection of new fiction, books of regional interest, and especially—bless you—Florida authors. It's no surprise, since Charlie credits John D. Mac-Donald for luring him to the Keys. Browse rare books and used books as well as new books. Open daily.

Get your tropical gifts at **Marooned in Marathon** (305-743-3809), 7849 Overseas Hwy, a place with silly toys, whimsical playful sculptures, painted handbags in bold colors, and big papier-mâché blossoms. The owner is a city councilman/musician/ newspaperman, so you know this is a real Keys business. He and his wife have two other gift shops on the island: **Shipwrecked by Design** (305-743-3808) at Quay Village, MM 54, has nautical gifts, glass and metal art, lots of tropical Christmas ornaments, and treasure maps; and **Jules LaVernes Overseas Adventure** (305-743-2277) at Quay Village is full of unusual objects such as beaded balls, Buddha icons, and plastic flamingos.

Tavernier

With a spacious bistro feel, **Cover to Cover Books** (305-853-2464), 91272 Overseas Hwy, offers java with your James W. Hall. Books are displayed as if they were pieces of fine art—an author could not feel prouder to be included on these shelves. Open daily, until 9 Mon–Sat and 10 on Fri.

The Shell Man (305-852-8149), 92439 Overseas Hwy, has toys, a giant rooster, monkey-faced coconuts, and lots of shells and coral within a sprawling complex that includes a Christmas room.

FISH MARKET Buy it fresh at **Key Largo Fisheries** (305-451-3782), 1313 Ocean Bay Dr, Key Largo, where amberjack, snapper, swordfish, and mahimahi come in daily, and lobster and stone crab in-season. They'll ship it via FedEx anywhere!

✳ Special Events

February: **Florida Keys Chili Cookoff** (305-451-1302; www.key largorotary.org), second Sat, Key Largo. Sanctioned by the International Chili Society, it's a cookoff where everyone is welcome. Live bands and a petting zoo for the kids. Held at Rowell's Marina, MM 104.5 bayside.

Pigeon Key Art Festival (305-743-5176), second weekend. For more than a decade, artists have gathered here on historic Pigeon Key under the Old Seven Mile Bridge to showcase the fine arts.

March: Marathon Garden Club presents the **Annual Marathon House & Garden Tour** (305-743-4971), first Sat, 10–4, and has done so for three decades.

The Easter Bunny goes diving to host an **Underwater Easter Egg Hunt** (305-451-3020; www.floridakeysbest .com/florida_keys/kids_in_special_ situations.htm), last Sat, Key Largo, benefiting a local children's charity.

Enjoy the bounty of the surrounding seas at the **Original Marathon Seafood Festival** (305-743-5417; www.floridakeysmarathon.com), an annual celebration since 1982.

April: **Seven Mile Bridge Run** (305-743-8513), third Sat. More than 1,500 runners run across the longest segmented bridge in the world in this annual footrace, during which the Overseas Highway is closed to traffic.

May: **Marathon Offshore Grand Prix** (305-293-5115; www.keysoffshore.com), second weekend. The world's top high-speed powerboats race in the waters surrounding Marathon and the original Seven Mile Bridge.

Island Festival Featuring the Taste of Islamorada (305-664-4503), second weekend, Plantation Key. Enjoy music, art, and lots of food; presented by the Islamorada Chamber of Commerce.

July: **Key Largo Celebration of the Sea** (305-451-4747), last Sat. Concerts, scuba gear displays, and more.

October: Celebrate history at the **Indian Key Festival** (305-664-4087), first weekend, Indian Key, with living history and reenactments.

November: **Annual Island Jubilee,** first weekend, Harry Harris Park, Tavernier. Now more than 20 years old, this festival includes an arts and crafts show, barbecue, and a cardboard-boat regatta.

LOWER KEYS

The essence of the Lower Keys begins across the Seven Mile Bridge where the land widens and the Overseas Highway immediately takes a turn toward the west. For 30 or so miles you will be in the backcounty, where, among pine forests and secluded mangrove islands, a wealth of eco-opportunities exists. Your first clue that life as you know it is slowing down is on **Bahia Honda Key** at MM 37, where the Bahia Honda State Park (see *Beaches*) provides a wealth of natural activities on and off land. **Big Pine Key** is the central hub of shopping and activities, and the National Key Deer Refuge (see *Wild Places*). Spanish documents from 1627 show Big Pine Key's earliest name as Cayos de Cuchiaga, an Indian name cited by Hernando D'Escalante Fontaneda, a Spanish explorer who was shipwrecked in the mid-1500s and lived with the Calusa Indians for nearly two decades before his rescue in 1566. In 1678, it was found on Spanish charts as Cayo Pinero, or Pine Island—*pinar* means "grove of pines," and *pino* is "pine tree," of which there were many on the island. The British charts identified it in 1772 as New Castle Island, and in 1774 charts were again referencing "Pine Island" (Pinara Kays). The name Big Pine Island was specifically referenced in Ferdinand H. Gerdes's 1849 journals, which he wrote while doing reconnaissance of the Florida reef.

Continuing on, you'll drive several miles through residential keys such as Big, Middle, and Little Torch Keys; Summerland Key; Cudjoe Key; **Sugarloaf Key;** and Big Coppitt Key, where you can stop at the occasional roadside restaurant for a quick bite. While in the Lower Keys, you'll enjoy kayak tours where you may see a pod of dolphins or a nurse shark in the shallow waters. Discover skates, horseshoe crabs, colorful fish, and the occasional barracuda just a few feet off the sandy shores. Key deer are plentiful, and to protect them there is a speed restriction. I searched for years to see the dog-size Key deer, a subspecies of the Virginia white-tailed deer, until locals told me to go at dawn or dusk to the National Key Deer Refuge or on one of the quiet roads on No Name Key. Please don't feed this protected species; tame deer learn to come to the roadsides, where they get struck by cars.

Leaving the Lower Keys, you feel civilization returning as you cross over the Boca Chica Bridge and into Key West.

GUIDANCE The official contact for visitors to the Keys is **The Florida Keys & Key West** (305-296-1552 or 1-800-FLA-KEYS; www.fla-keys.com), 1201 White St, Suite 102, Key West 33040, where you will find information on all the Keys. The **Lower Keys Chamber of Commerce Visitor Center** (305-872-2411 or 1-800-872-3722; www.lowerkeyschamber.com), MM 31, 31020 Overseas Hwy, Big Pine Key 33043, offers great information specific to Big Pine Key.

GETTING THERE *By car:* Once you enter the Keys, one road links the islands— the Overseas Highway, **US 1.**

By air: To reach the Lower Keys, use **Miami International Airport** (see the *Miami Metro* section); **Marathon Airport** (305-289-6060), 9400 Overseas Hwy, Suite 200; or **Key West International Airport** (305-296-5439).

By bus: **Greyhound** (305-296-9072, 305-871-1810, or 1-800-231-2222; www.greyhound.com) stops all along the islands; call for specific pickup locations and rates.

By rail: **AMTRAK** (1-800-USARAIL; www.amtrak.com) takes you as far south as Fort Lauderdale. There, you can transfer to the Keys Shuttle.

By shuttle: Call 24 hours ahead for the **Florida Keys Shuttle** (305-289-9997 or 1-888-765-9997; www.floridakeysshuttle.com), which offers door-to-door service from Miami International Airport to numerous points in the Keys.

GETTING AROUND *By car:* **US 1** connects the islands; destinations along the road are designated by mile markers, shown as "MM."

By bus: Since **Greyhound** (see *Getting There*) links the islands, it's possible to use the bus to island-hop.

By taxi: If you fly into Marathon Airport, you can get where you're going with **Action Taxi** (305-743-6800) or **Sunset Taxi & Transportation** (305-289-7422). If you fly into Key West, take **Friendly Cab Co.** (305-292-0000).

PARKING Parking is readily available in the Lower Keys without charge.

MEDICAL EMERGENCIES General emergencies should head to **Fisherman's Hospital** (305-743-5533; www.fishermanshospital.com), 3301 Overseas Hwy, MM 48.7, Marathon, or **Lower Keys Medical Center**

SEVEN MILE BRIDGE

Visit Florida

(305-294-5531; www.lkmc.com), 5900 Junior College Rd, Key West. The **Key Largo Recompression Chamber** (911 if emergency, 1-800-NO-BENDS for information) is the closest resource for divers experiencing the life-threatening "bends."

✴ To See

ART GALLERIES Several talented local artists are shown at **Artists in Paradise Gallery** (305-872-1828), Big Pine Shopping Center, Big Pine Key.

ECOTOURS Take a five-hour island-hopping tour on glass-bottom boats with **Island Excursions** (305-872-9863 or 1-800-654-9560; www.strikezonecharter .com), 29675 Overseas Hwy, MM 29.5, Big Pine Key. Journey into the back-country along tidal flats and mangroves to seek out the elusive Key deer while dolphins swim nearby. The glass-bottom boats allow you to see starfish, sponges, tropical fish, and sea turtles up close. You will also have the chance to snorkel and do some light fishing while you learn about the history of the islands and its first inhabitants along with the local flora and fauna. The tour ($49) also includes the world-famous fish fry.

HISTORIC SITES The **Old Bahia Honda Bridge,** MM 37, in Bahia Honda State Park (see *Beaches*), was once part of Henry Flagler's Overseas Railroad and is listed on the National Register of Historic Places. During the Great Labor Day Hurricane, September 2, 1935, a 17-foot wall of water washed over the bridge, destroying the railroad. The bridge offers an excellent panoramic view of the area and an eerie reminder of what a hurricane's storm surge can do.

Surviving several hurricanes, the **Perky Bat Tower** on Sugarloaf Key has be-come somewhat of a legend. In 1929, Ricter C. Perky built the tower to reduce the island's mosquito population so that he could build a resort complex. Located

BAHIA HONDA STATE PARK

Sandra Friend

bayside down a side road directly off MM 17, the odd structure was supposed to be a welcoming home for bats, but the nocturnal creatures had other ideas. Today it stands as a tribute to Mr. Perky's good intentions.

WILDLIFE VIEWING **Blue Hole** (305-872-0074), a freshwater sinkhole on Key Deer Blvd, Big Pine Key, is an old quarry from the Flagler railroad days. In the heart of National Key Deer Refuge (see *Wild Places*), it offers excellent viewing opportunities for Key deer, alligators, turtles, and freshwater fish. The natural area contains an interpretive display, observation deck, and nature trails.

✳ To Do

BICYCLING Bicyclists will enjoy nearly a dozen miles of roads that run off MM 30, Wilder Rd, and Key Deer Blvd on Big Pine Key. Don't forget to cross over and explore No Name Key.

At **Big Pine Bicycle Center** (305-872-0103), MM 30.9, avid cyclist Marty Baird can tell you the best places to ride around Big Pine Key and No Name Key. His old-fashioned fat-tired cruisers make it easy for anyone to ride along the unpaved roads. Bikes rent for $6 per half day, $9 for a full day, and $34 a week, with second week at half price. Kids bikes are $5 per half day, $7 for a full day, and $26 a week, with second week at $13.

DIVING What better place to dive than in the Keys? From only a few feet offshore to ships sunk at depths of 110 feet, the Lower Keys are alive with underwater adventure. Dive boats can take you 5 miles offshore to Looe Key Reef (see *Coral Reefs*), where you can snorkel with colorful fish and coral, or 3 miles offshore down to the *Adolphus Busch*. The 210-foot-long ship is a great place for experienced divers, where they can swim through large holes cut in the sides of the ship, through the wheelhouse, and out the smokestacks. There are lots of tropical fish in the artificial reef, and lucky divers may even spot the gargantuan Jewfish, which weighs about 400 pounds. Sitting upright at 100 feet in crystal-clear water, the freighter's towers are only 40 feet down.

♿ Without a doubt, **Strike Zone Charters** (305-872-9863 or 1-800-654-9560; www.strikezonecharter.com), 29675 Overseas Hwy, MM 29.5, Big Pine Key, is the best when snorkeling or diving Looe Key Reef and the Lower Keys. Gayle and Mary, and their adorable chihuahuas, keep things safe on their 40- and 45-foot custom-built glass-bottom catamarans. On board you'll find things super clean and ship-shape. Tuck your belongings in dry storage and relax under the 350-foot canopy or grab some sun while motoring out to the dive site. So that you can explore with confidence, your guides will carefully go over instructions for a safe dive, and then the geography and ecology of the reef. At Looe Key Reef, you'll see a variety of colorful tropical fish, such as the bright orange clownfish and royal blue tang swimming among staghorn, elkhorn, piliar, and star corals to depths from just inches to up to 30 feet. Over at the HMS *Looe* wreck, those staying on board may even spot the smokestack through the boat's glass bottom. To ensure anyone can get in and out of the water with ease, they are even equipped to handle those with special needs. A freshwater shower is also available to rinse off the salt water after diving—or it can be used by those staying on board, who might want to cool off. Glass bottom $25; snorkel $30; scuba dive reef $40; scuba dive wreck $50.

FISHING **Strike Zone Charters** (see *Diving*) offers deep-sea and flats fishing in the warm blue waters of the Atlantic Ocean or in the sandy flats near and around the Keys. You'll fish for sailfish, tuna, snapper, and marlin on the deep-sea excursion and tarpon, bonefish, and shark on the flats charter. Deep-sea fishing: full day $595, half day $450; flats fishing: full day $425, half day $325.

PADDLING The best backcountry guided tours are by Bill Keogh's **Big Pine Kayak** (305-872-7474 or 1-877-595-2925; www.keyskayaktours.com), Big Pine Key, where you'll kayak or canoe through mangrove tunnels teeming with wildlife. Or rent your own boat and explore the mangroves and peaceful waterways on your own. You'll want to pick up Bill's book, the *Florida Keys Paddling Guide* by Countryman Press, to learn all about the wildlife and ecosystems that you'll encounter. Two locations are at the Old Wooden Bridge Fishing Camp and Parmer's Resort (see *Lodging*).

✳ Green Space

BEACHES Boasting one of the most popular beaches in the Keys, **Bahia Honda State Park** (305-872-2353), 36850 Overseas Hwy, also offers a full slate of recreational opportunities besides lolling in the sun. Walk the Silver Palm Nature Trail through the last significant silver palm hammock in the United States; rent a kayak and wind through the mangrove mazes and paddle offshore; camp or rent a cabin at one of the campgrounds; explore a portion of Henry Flagler's Overseas Railway; and stop in at the concessionaire, Coral Reef Park Company (305-872-3210), to arrange a snorkel trip to Looe Key Marine Sanctuary (adults $29, children $24, plus equipment rental).

CORAL REEFS Five miles off Big Pine Key, oceanside, is the beautiful coral formation **Looe Key Reef.** Under the protection of the Florida Keys National Marine Sanctuary, the refuge is named after the HMS *Looe*, a British ship that foundered on the coral in 1744 while towing a captured French ship. The reef is about 200 yards by 800 yards and formed in the shape of a U with several "fingers," so you can snorkel the high points or scuba in between. This is an amazing reef that you can spend an entire weekend exploring. Brightly colored tropical fish, such as those seen in the animated film *Finding Nemo,* swim with you and graze on the coral canyons below. You'll come face-to-face with yellowtail and sergeant majors while schools of angelfish swim nearby. Look closely to see moray eels hiding in more than 50 species of corals, such as staghorn, brain, and fire corals, some more than 7,000 years old. Listen carefully to hear parrotfish munching and crunching and shrimp crackling. This reef is large, and as such expect to see several barracuda and the occasional shark—none of which seemed interested in me when I was floating about, but novices and younger people may find it a bit unsettling. At times the water can be a bit rough, so check the surf report if this bothers you. For those not quite ready for such a large reef or the wide-open ocean, the reefs off Key Largo are smaller (see *Upper and Middle Keys*).

WILD PLACES Since the 1930s, the little-known **Great White Heron National Wildlife Refuge** (305-872-2239; www.fws.gov/southeast/Great WhiteHeron), managed by National Key Deer Refuge, has protected the Lower Keys's "backcountry," including more than 6,000 acres across hundreds of unpopulated mangrove

Sandra Friend
BLUE HOLE, NATIONAL KEY DEER WILDLIFE REFUGE

islands between Marathon and Key West. The islands are important nesting and roosting places for more than 250 species of birds. Access to the region is only by boat. Open dawn–dusk. Free.

North America's smallest deer roam in herds through the **National Key Deer Refuge** (305-872-2239; http://nationalkeydeer.fws.gov), 28950 Watson Blvd, MM 30, where 800 or so of the 2- to 3-foot-tall deer range across 8,500 acres of mangrove forests, tropical hardwood hammocks, and pine rocklands across the Lower Keys. On Big Pine Key, stop in at the visitors center in the Winn-Dixie shopping center off Key Deer Blvd for an orientation before heading out to look for deer. **Blue Hole** (see *Wildlife Viewing*), off Key Deer Blvd, is a good place to see deer at dusk and dawn coming to a rare freshwater water source. Farther up the road are two nature trails that wind through deer habitat. Open dawn–dusk. Free.

✳ Lodging
CAMPGROUNDS

Bahia Honda Key 33043
Bahia Honda State Park (305-872-2353; www.floridastateparks.org; reservations: 1-800-326-3521 or www.reserveamerica.com), 36850 Overseas Hwy, MM 37. Tent camping and smaller RVs (sites are typically 30–40 feet long). Beautiful beach and nature trail. The remnants of Henry Flagler's railroad offers excellent panoramic views. Rental boats, kayaks, bicycles, snorkeling and fishing gear. Eighty sites ($26 per night) come with water, some with electricity. Duplex cabins

LIGUUS SNAIL AT NATIONAL KEY DEER REFUGE

Sandra Friend

($120 per night) sleep six. No weekly or monthly rates. Maximum stay is limited to 14 days.

Big Pine Key 33043

One of the best campgrounds for kids is over at **Big Pine Key Fishing Lodge** (305-872-2351), MM 33, where you'll find a heated pool, shuffleboard, horseshoes, playground, and a game room. A boat ramp, dock, and marina area are also on-site, and you can charter a boat for saltwater fishing, or paddle the backcountry with Bill Keogh's Big Pine Kayak (see *Paddling*). Tent sites and full RV hookups. Call for rates.

Ohio Key 33043

The 75-acre private island is simply paradise at **Sunshine Key RV Resort & Marina** (305-872-2217 or 1-800-852-0348; www.RVontheGO.com), 38801 Overseas Hwy, MM 39, located just off Big Pine Key. The largest RV resort in the Keys, it boasts 400 RV sites and a 172-slip marina, and it has full amenities such as a heated pool, tennis, volleyball, laundry, marina café, dive shop, boat rentals, and more. In-season rates: $95/day, $570/week, $1,529/month. Off-season rates: $60/day, $360/week, $950/month. May be higher during events. Check the Internet for specials.

Sugarloaf Key 33044

Whether you want to tent camp, bring your own RV, or stay in one of their RVs, **Sugarloaf Key Resort KOA** (305-745-3549 or 1-800-562-7731; www.koa.com), 251 CR 939, MM 20, offers a chance to relax and unwind in tropical paradise. Only 20 minutes from Key West, it provides all the necessary amenities, including private beach, swimming pool, hot

tub, sauna, and waterfront pub. Call for rates.

FISH CAMPS

Big Pine Key 33043

The **Old Wooden Bridge Fish Camp** (305-872-2241; www.oldwoodenbridge.com), 1791 Bogie Dr, dates from the 1950s, when only six cottages provided fishing opportunities to wintering visitors. Located off the beaten path, the original building (circa 1943) still stands as the camp store at the base of No Name Key Bridge. Today you can camp out in 14 guest cottages along the shoreline of the Bogie Channel. The one- and two-bedroom cottages have been fully renovated to include modern luxuries such as a stove, refrigerator, microwave, cable television, and, of course, air-conditioning. The full bait and tackle store is also stocked with snacks and beverages, so you don't have to drive into town for supplies. Bill Keogh's Big Pine Kayak (see *Paddling*) departs to the backcountry from here. Rates: $150–190 per night; $945–1,190 per week.

HOTELS, MOTELS, AND RESORTS

Little Torch Key 33042

To get to **Little Palm Island Resort & Spa** (305-872-2524 or 1-800-343-8567; www.littlepalmisland.com), 28500 Overseas Hwy, MM 28.5 oceanside, you must first check in at the guest welcome station on Little Torch Key, where they immediately offer you fresh fruit and ice cold water, or you can order a PT 109, Gumby Slumber, or Jamaica Me Krazy drink while waiting for the ferry. You'll then board the historic *Truman* yacht for a short ride over to paradise. Leave your electronics behind, as this resort doesn't allow them, not even a cell phone, although there is a quaint phone booth if you have to reach the mainland. Once there, you'll be captivated by the peace and quiet as you walk under shady palms on your way to your own private, waterfront, thatched-roofed bungalow. There's lots to do on the 5-acre private island: play life-size chess under balmy palm trees; take a walk through the Zen garden and up to the full-service SpaTerre for a Javanese Lulur Royal Treatment ($250) or Tropical Essence Massage ($140–180); slip into the freshwater lagoon-style pool shaded under a canopy of palms; take to the water on one of the Windsurfers, day sailers, or kayaks; grab a chaise and stretch out along the beach; or swim out to the floating tiki hut. The poolside bar has a wide selection of top-line liquors, beer, and wines. At sunset enjoy a gourmet dinner pretty much anywhere you choose or in their elegant Colonial dining room. Listen to live music each night on the west side of the island, then gaze at the crystal-clear night sky before retiring to your own private bungalow or grand suite. Twenty-eight Bungalow suites ($700–$1,500 per night) come with king-size bed, living room, whirlpool bath, indoor and outdoor showers, and a private veranda. The two Island Grand Suites ($1,000–2,500 per night), also have his-and-hers bathrooms and an outdoor hot tub. Both Bungalow and Island Grand Suites require a two-night minimum stay. All money is handled over at Little Torch Key, so there's no need carry your wallet. Tipping is handled that way, too, with 10 percent added for staff, and an 18 percent gratuity for food or beverages. An optional two- or three-meal menu plan is available for an additional cost. Little Palm Island is a special treat for romantics or those who need some peace and quiet and extreme pampering.

Tucked away on 5 tropical acres, **Parmer's Resort** (305-872-2157; www.parmersplace.com), 565 Barry Ave, MM 28.5, offers quiet waterfront accommodations. The air-conditioned rooms, some with vaulted ceilings, come with cable TV and a private porch. Efficiencies have complete kitchens and come with one, two, or three bedrooms. Take a dip in the heated pool surrounded by lush tropical landscaping, and then walk down the garden paths to discover more than 70 exotic birds in their aviary. Rooms $75–135; efficiencies $105–350. Complimentary continental breakfast buffet is included.

Sugarloaf Key 33044
At MM 17 you'll find **Sugarloaf Lodge** (305-745-3211 or 1-800-553-6097), 17001 Overseas Hwy bayside, a welcome retreat. All rooms are waterfront at the fully equipped resort, complete with full restaurant, Pirate's lounge, and tiki bar. You'll find lots to do here, from tennis, mini golf, and shuffleboard to swimming in the heated pool or snorkeling in the crystal-clear ocean. Anglers will find all the necessary bait and tackle to land the big one. Rooms $95–145; efficiencies $110–150.

✳ Where to Eat
DINING OUT

Little Torch Key
You don't have to stay overnight at **Little Palm Island Resort & Spa** (305-872-2524 or 1-800-3-GET-LOST; www.littlepalmisland.com),

28500 Overseas Hwy, MM 28.5 oceanside, to enjoy their culinary delights, but you must have a reservation, and you won't be allowed to explore the island without an escort. Check in at the guest welcome station on Little Torch Key, and then you'll motor over on the historic *Truman* yacht. Breakfast, lunch, dinner, and exquisite Sunday brunch are held indoors in the elegant dining room or outdoors on the terrace or even the sandy beach. For breakfast try the lobster hash with red onions, green peppers, bacon, potatoes, egg any style, and chive hollandaise ($19); cinnamon French toast with blueberry or strawberry compote ($15); or buttermilk pancakes ($15). Brunch includes a host of items that change according to season. Wash it all down with a mimosa ($12) or Bloody Mary ($9). Lunch brings light fare such as the jumbo lump crab cake appetizer with frisée lettuce and saffron aioli ($22); shrimp wrap sandwich with tomatoes, spinach, shaved red onion, avocado, and chipolte-cilantro aioli ($17); and the mustard-crusted grouper entrée with tarragon-infused potatoes, baby carrots, snap peas, and tomato butter ($23). For those sunset dinners, try the seared scallop and duck foie gras appetizer with curried lentils and banana and orange ginger glaze ($24), and then the exquisite glazed mahi with marinated tofu entrée, served with edamame, baby bok choy, scallions, and lemon soy ($43). Worth the price to be romanced in paradise.

EATING OUT

Big Pine Key
My hiker buddies tell me the **Cracked Egg Cafe** (305-872-7030), 30739 Overseas Hwy, MM 31, is best

breakfast around and a welcome treat after logging long miles along the Overseas Highway.

Worth the drive off the beaten path, the **No Name Pub** (305-872-9115), N Watson Blvd, off MM 30 bayside, is a very cool place with lots of stories. The oldest pub in Big Pine Key, it was built in 1936 originally as a general store. It was rumored to have once been a brothel, and you have to see the way it's decorated to believe it. The owner, Doug, had me sample his Royal Pub Pizza ($17–22), Spicy Caribbean Wings ($9), and a bowl of his famous Pub Chili ($3). Each one was delish! With more than 60 types of beer to wash it all down with, it's a great place to sneak away just for the fun of it. Open daily.

Rob's Island Grill (305-872-3022), 31251 Ave A, is a really nice family sports bar with eight satellite connections, so no one needs to miss their hometown game. Rob has had a restaurant on the key since 1985, but this newly built one is only a few years old. Tucked back on a side street, bayside, watch for it or you'll almost miss it when coming from the north as you enter Big Pine Key. The restaurant offers a selection of sandwiches, sal-

NO NAME PUB

Kathy Wolf

ads, steaks, and seafood and will even cook your own catch. Vegetarians will also find this to their liking.

Cudjoe Key

A favorite of locals, the **Square Grouper** (305-745-8880), MM 22.5, is for those special occasions and those wanting excellent gourmet-type fare.

Little Torch Key

The waterfront **Parrotdise Bar & Grille** (305-872-9989; www.parrot disewaterfront.com), 183 Barry Ave, MM 28.5 bayside, offers fun and food for everyone. Kids will love the shark pool and tropical fish pond, while adults will enjoy the live music from acoustic guitar soloists to jazz festivals (see *Special Events*). For lunch you'll want to try their Lobster Reuben in Parrotdise ($15) and for dinner their Parrotdise Guava Shrimp, sautéed with a Key lime, guava, ginger, and cilantro sauce ($23). After your meal, take a walk on the dock and try to spot the many sea creatures that inhabit the shoreline, such as barracuda, crab, and even the occasional octopus. Then curl up in one of their beach hammocks or go back for some Key lime pie or chocolate pot de crème ($5). Open daily for lunch and dinner, with happy hour 3–7.

Ramrod Key

If you are looking for a party place, then head over to **Boondocks** (305-872-0020), MM 27.5 bayside, which features lively music, drinks, a raw bar, and light fare.

Saddlebunch Key

If you find your self jonesing for a cup of java, then pull over at MM 15 to **Baby's Coffee** (305-744-9866 or 1-800-523-2326; www.babyscoffee.com), 3178 US 1 oceanside. The roadside

café is housed in a 1920s building, and the story goes that the occupants had christened it "Baby's Place" after their youngest son. When New Yorkers Gary Tepinsky and Olga Manosalvas selected the site for their coffee shop, they adopted the name, and Baby's Coffee was born. Taking great care in creating the perfect cup o' joe, fresh beans are carefully selected and roasted to perfection in small batches to ensure consistency and are available in bags or through their mail-order business. A nice selection of fresh baked goods and logo items can also be found. Make sure to take particular note of the fine art on display. The talented Olga expresses herself through a mix of her Ecuadorian heritage and experiences from New York City and living in the Keys. Baby's Coffee is open every day except Christmas, and the coffee can also be found served at restaurants and inns throughout the Keys and up into Miami.

Sugarloaf Key

Not to be missed, **Mangrove Mamas** (305-745-3030), MM 20 bayside, is the place to stop for one of the best meals in the Keys. Locals come here for their light and airy conch fritters ($6), tempura fish ($17), and Black Angus steaks ($17–20). Lunch favorites are the teriyaki steak sandwich ($9) or the grouper sandwich ($7), which can be grilled, fried, blackened, or broiled. The intimate garden surroundings are a welcome retreat after days on the open ocean. Open daily, lunch and dinner.

Summerland Key

Pull over at MM 24.5 for some great seafood or pizza. **Fins 24** (305-745-3311), MM 24.5, famous for their seafood stews ($10–11), also offers a

STREET PERFORMER, MALLORY SQUARE

wide variety of salads, sandwiches, and burgers ($6–10), along with full dinners of fresh locally caught fish ($14–19) and a wide selection of Caribbean pizza ($11–20)—or try the Lotsa Meatsa ($9–21). Open for lunch and dinner, and they'll even deliver.

I could have hung out all day at **Montes Restaurant and Fish Market**, MM 25 bayside, where grouper sandwiches ($9) were served hot and tender, and the chocolate nut pie ($4) was to die for. The super-friendly staff and the relaxed atmosphere make it a must-stop for a quick bite at lunch or dinner. This seafood hangout also has an excellent fish market with everything from clams, crabs, and conch to lobster and Louisiana crawfish. Open daily.

✳ Entertainment

OPERA From serious to comic opera, the **Island Opera Theatre of the Florida Keys** (305-294-0404; www .islandopera.com), 16823 E Point Dr, Sugarloaf Key, presents repertory shows with local talent at several locations throughout the Keys. Their season runs Dec–Apr, with tickets around $20.

✳ Special Events

Contact the Lower Keys Chamber (305-872-2411 or 1-800-872-3722; www.lowerkeyschamber.com) to learn more about the following events.

April: Held at Parrotdise Bar & Grille in Little Torch Key (see *Eating Out*), the **Lower Keys Jazz & Art Festival** includes a juried art show and smooth jazz.

June: Anglers compete for $5,000 in cash and prizes at the **Big Pine & Lower Keys Dolphin Tournament,** Big Pine Key.

July: Everything happens below the surface at the unique **Underwater Music Festival.** The annual event broadcasts music for divers and snorkelers at Looe Key to promote reef preservation.

December: Fine arts and crafts are presented by local Keys artists at **WinterFest,** Big Pine Key.

KEY WEST

The Calusa people were the earliest inhabitants of Key West, but the island remained undiscovered until 1521, when Juan Ponce de León arrived, establishing a fishing and salvage village. Visited mainly by Spanish explorers, the island was first deeded to Cuba and called Cayo Hueso, meaning "Bone Island," and in 1815 the governor of Cuba transferred the island to United States. Because Key West was so remote, townies refused to recognize any nation and became a bit unruly. So, John Simonton, a large landowner, lobbied the U.S. government for a new naval base, hoping its presence would provide some order to the town. In 1823 Commodore David Porter of the U.S. Navy took charge and ran any rowdy residents out of town.

In 1982 the U.S. Border Patrol set up a blockade in response to the massive flotilla of Cuban immigrants seeking political asylum during the Mariel Boatlift, barring entrance to or exit from the entire Florida Keys. As such, Keys residents briefly declared their independence as the Conch Republic. You'll find souvenirs all over town with that moniker, along with sites relating to some of the more famous Key Westers, such as singer/songwriter Jimmy Buffett; Mel Fisher, the world's greatest treasure hunter; novelist Ernest Hemingway; Stephen Mallory, a U.S. Senator and Confederate Navy Secretary; President Harry S Truman; and playwright Tennessee Williams.

All over Key West you'll hear residents referred to as "Conchs" (pronounced "Konks"). The label began with early Bahamian immigrants and was adopted by all residents during the 20th century. Today a "Salt Water Conch" is a person born on the island; a "Fresh Water Conch" is born elsewhere but has been on the island so long they are considered a native.

GUIDANCE The official contact for visitors to the Keys is **The Florida Keys & Key West** (305-296-1552 or 1-800-FLA-KEYS; www.fla-keys.com), 1201 White St, Suite 102, Key West 33040, where you will find information on all the Keys. The **Key West Chamber of Commerce** (305-294-2587; www.keywest chamber.org), 402 Wall St, is another resource once you get to Key West.

GETTING THERE *By car:* Once you enter the Keys, one road links the islands— the Overseas Highway, **US 1.**

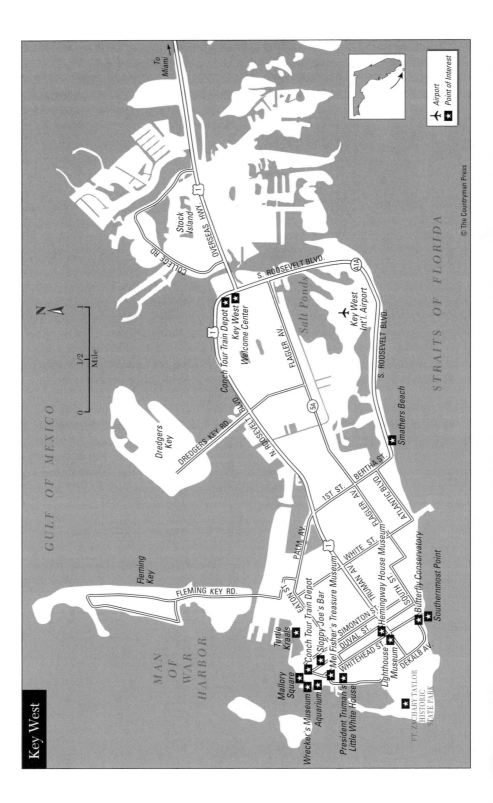

Key West

By air: To reach the Lower Keys, use **Miami International Airport** (see the *Miami Metro* section); **Marathon Airport** (305-289-6060), 9400 Overseas Hwy, Suite 200; or **Key West International Airport** (305-296-5439).

By bus: **Greyhound** (305-296-9072, 305-871-1810, or 1-800-231-2222; www.greyhound.com) stops all along the islands. Call for specific pickup locations and rates.

By shuttle: Call 24 hours ahead for the **Florida Keys Shuttle** (305-289-9997 or 1-888-765-9997; www.floridakeysshuttle.com), which offers door-to-door service from Miami International Airport to numerous points in the Keys.

GETTING AROUND *By foot:* The best mode of transportation in Key West is by foot. Everything is close by and parking is limited, so stretch your legs and work off all that Key lime pie.

By two wheels: Rent a bicycle or motorized scooter to ease your weary feet, especially on hot days. Vendors are located on almost every corner, and many lodgings provide these for free or for a nominal fee.

By car: **US 1** connects the islands; destinations along the road are designated by mile markers, shown as "MM." The hub of Key West's Old Town historic district is found around Duval, Eaton, Simonton, Green, Caroline, and Front Sts.

By bus: Since **Greyhound** links the islands, it's possible to use the bus to island-hop. Once in Key West, the **City Bus for Key West and Stock Island** (305-292-8165; www.keywestcity.com) and **City of Key West Transit** (305-292-8160) take you around the island. A **shuttle service to Key West's Old Town/Historic District** (305-293-6426) has stops along the entire route.

By shuttle: The **Bone Island Shuttle** (305-293-8710) runs daily 9 AM–10 PM to all locations around the island.

By taxi: You can get anywhere you're going with **Friendly Cab Co.** (305-292-0000).

PARKING Metered parking is free all over town for guests with handicapped tags.

Park and Ride Garages (305-293-6426) are at the corner of Caroline and Grinnell Sts. Get reduced rates with a validated shuttle ticket ($1 per hour with a $10 maximum). The open lot at Mallory Square ($3 per hour) has no maximum, so it can add up if you leave your car overnight. The lot at the Schooner Wharf ($2 per hour) on William St is another option if you're heading out on one of the sailing tours.

BASKET WEAVER

Kathy Wolf

MEDICAL EMERGENCIES For general emergencies head to **Lower Keys Medical Center** (305-294-5531; www.lkmc.com), 5900 Junior College Rd, Key West. The **Key Largo Recompression Chamber** (911 if emergency, 1-800-NO-BENDS for information) is the closest resource for divers experiencing the life-threatening "bends."

✴ To See

AQUARIUM ♿ ⊘ The first time I set foot in the **Key West Aquarium** (305-296-2051; www.keywestaquarium.com), One Whitehead St at Mallory Square, I was about six years old and scared to death of the giant fish they now call "goliath grouper," a docile native species that lives under piers and around the reefs. The aquarium opened in 1934 as the city's first tourist attraction. It's a must-see for its classic interior, including the *vero fresco* murals originally painted by Alfred Crimi in 1934 and retouched by local artists Gualberto Alfaro and David Laughlin in 1998. Historic photos of the aquarium and docks are suspended around the central room, which is ringed with tanks of native sea creatures, such as brilliant purple and yellow yellowcheek wrasse, chalk bass, and sergeant major. Staff members feed the stingrays and sea turtles and show off sharks that you're allowed to touch. The touch tank up front contains conchs, horseshoe crabs, and starfish. A pool rimmed with red mangroves shimmers with tarpon, rainbow parrotfish (who eat coral and excrete the beach sand you see in the Keys), bonnet head sharks, barracuda, and other common denizens of the deep. Open daily 10–6. Adults $10, ages 9–12 $5.

ART GALLERIES A bevy of art galleries can be found on Duval St, but you will also want to seek out other galleries sporadically located around town, such as

---

POLYDACTYL VERSUS POULTRY

Which came first in Key West, the chickens or the cats? According to historians, the cats arrived in the 1500s, escaping from anchored Spanish explorer ships, and later bred with a six-toed polydactyl (many-fingered) cat given to Ernest Hemingway by a visiting ship's captain, possibly from Boston, where the largest population of polydactyl cats can be found. The ubiquitous roaming chickens came later, in the 1800s, when early pioneers brought them down through the Keys for a food source. Now protected, both run amuck through the streets of Key West and are controlled to a certain extent through cat adoption clinics, spay/neuter programs, and "chicken lifts" that relocate some of the island's more than two thousand fowl to farms in central Florida. You'll find more than 50 descendants of the famous writer's cats lovingly cared for at Hemingway's house (see *Museums*), while feral cats are equally adored and never have to venture too far for a free meal. Chicken lovers should make sure to stop at the Chicken Store on Duval St (see *Selective Shopping*) and take part in the annual Chickenfest, a clucking good celebration held each June (see *Special Events*).

WYLAND AT WORK

Kathy Wolf

The Lemonade Stand Art Studio (305-295-6873), 227 Petronia St in Bahama Village; the **Harrison Gallery** (305-294-0609; www .harrison-gallery.com), 825 White St, which represents sculptor Helen Harrison along with other talented artists; the **Haitian Art Co.** (305-296-8932; www.haitian-art-co.com), 600 Frances St, which has been exhibiting a diverse collection of Haitian art since 1977; and **Mary O'Shea's Glass Garden** (305-293-8822; www .keywestglass.com), 213 Simonton St, the largest glass studio in the Florida Keys.

Back on Duval St you'll find **Alan S. Maltz Gallery** (305-294-0005; www .alanmaltz.com), 1210 Duval, which showcases the fine-art photography of this renowned artist; and you won't want to miss the infamous **Wyland Gallery** (305-292-4998; www.wyland.com), 719 and 102 Duval St, featuring the works of marine-life artist Wyland, along with other environmental artists. Wyland has painted more than 25,000 works since 1971, and his art is cherished by collectors in 30 countries around the world. Globally famous for his colorful large-scale Whaling Walls (see *Murals*), he has worked diligently to educate the world on environmental issues. You'll want to explore the "Wyland Kids, Save Our Blue Planet" section of his web site, where you can print out illustrations of marine animals for your little ones to color. And kids of all ages will fall in love with his new children's book, *Spouty and Friends.*

BUTTERFLY CONSERVATORY Known for his Wings of Imagination gallery on Duval St, artist Sam Trophia dreamed of a Victorian flower garden that evoked the sensory magic of stepping into an animated scene from a classic Disney movie. After many years of hard work with partner George Fernandez, the dream is now alive as the **Key West Butterfly Conservatory** (305-296-2988 or 1-800-839-4647; www.keywestbutterfly .com), 1316 Duval St, a half-acre tropical forest under glass where clouds of butterflies drift past as you stand mesmerized. Music adds a touch of magic as you watch blue morphos, giant

BUTTERFLIES SNACK ON BANANAS AT THE KEY WEST BUTTERFLY CONSERVATORY.

Sandra Friend

swallowtails, and heliconias settle down and feast on slices of fruit. Tiny colorful birds—honeycreepers, speckled tanagers, and paradise tanagers—flit about in search of fruit. In the Wings of Imagination Gift Shop (www.wingsofimagination .com), one room is devoted to the art of butterflies, where Trophia's creations include mounted butterflies that swirl like luminescent galaxies (see *Selective Shopping*). Open daily 9–5. Adults $10, senior citizens and military $8.50, ages 4–12 $7.50.

HISTORIC SITES Relive the building of the Key West extension of the Florida East Coast Railway at **Flagler Station** (305-295-3562), 901 Caroline St. While naysayers shook their heads, Henry Flagler started construction in 1905 on the first overseas railroad. Spanning 130 miles from the Florida mainland to Key West, "Flagler's Folly" was successfully completed seven years later, allowing the 84-year-old Flagler just long enough to see the first train arrive in Key West. Flagler fell down a flight of stairs at his home in Palm Beach, passing away May 20, 1913 (see Whitehall in *Central Palm Beach County*). Open daily 9–5. Fee.

At **Fort Zachary Taylor Historic State Park** (305-292-6713; www.florida stateparks.org/forttaylor/default.cfm), end of Southard St on Truman Annex, explore one of the United States's largest fortresses, built to protect the shipping lanes passing Key West. Construction of this massive masonry structure began in 1850. During the Civil War, Federal soldiers occupied the force, forcing Key West into Union hands. By the time construction was completed in 1866, the fort included a desalination plant and a row of latrines flushed out by the tides. During the Spanish-American War, the top levels of Fort Taylor were cut down to install modern weaponry; only in recent times has it been discovered that in doing so, the soldiers encased the largest known cache of Civil War–era cannons in concrete. As you tour the fort, notice the gothic styling within the various chambers. Fee.

Take a few moments to wander through the **Key West Cemetery,** where all the graves are above ground, and many have inscriptions such as I TOLD YOU I WAS SICK engraved on headstones. The 1847 historic cemetery is located in Old Town, bounded by Passover Lane and Frances, Olivia, Angela, and Margaret Sts, with the main entry gates open at the corner of Margaret and Angela. Several tours take you through or past the cemetery, or you can self-tour during the daylight hours.

IN THE RAMPARTS OF FORT ZACHARY TAYLOR
Sandra Friend

Open since 1997, the **Key West Historical Sculpture Garden** (www .historictours.com) is located in front of the Waterfront Playhouse (see *Entertainment*) near Mallory Square. The garden displays 36 bronze busts

of men and women who were instrumental in the development and evolution of
Key West. Plans to add an additional 36 busts are slated for the coming years.
The Wreckers, by Miami sculptor James Mastin, rises 25 feet at the entrance to
the garden and depicts the lives of these early pioneers.

The Sunset Celebration at **Mallory Square** is known the world over. Beginning
in the 1800s as a raucous port for pirates, the harbor was next a place for anti-
pirate demonstrations, and then the location from where American forces con-
vened for the Civil War, the Spanish-American War, and World Wars I and II.
In the 1960s hippies took to the docks to watch the sunset, and a carnival atmosphere began. By the 1980s the town felt they needed to regulate the somewhat
lawless partying, so in 1984 Key West Cultural Preservation Society, Inc., was
formed to manage the nightly event. Today you can join in the nightly festivities
where residents and tourists alike gather to watch the sun set into the west. Pre-
ceding sunset, the square comes alive with a unique collection of performing
artists, including fire eaters, jugglers, and magicians, while arts and crafts created
by local artisans are sold. So who was Mallory? Former Key West resident
Stephen Russell Mallory (1812–73) held a variety of governmental positions in
Key West in the 1800s. Having particular knowledge about naval affairs, he was
the Confederate Secretary of the navy during the Civil War, one of President
Jefferson Davis's most valuable cabinet members.

Mile Marker Zero (0) is located at the corner of Whitehead and Fleming Sts,
designating the beginning of US 1. The highway stretches 2,390 miles from here
along the U.S. eastern seaboard to its terminus in Fort Kent, Maine.

At 322 Duval St, the **Oldest House** in South Florida contains the **Wrecker's
Museum** (see *Museums*). Built in 1829 as a residence for Capt. Francis Watlington and his family, this six-room house with courtyard and outbuildings remained
a residence until 1973 and is on the National Register of Historic Places.

The stained-glass windows at **St. Paul's Episcopal Church,** 401 Duval St, are a
glorious sight to behold. So much so that Lloyd's of London insures them. You'll
want to be sure to visit this spectacular church (circa 1838), but you may not be
alone when you do. It's said that the ghost of John Fleming, who donated the
land the church rests on, wanders the grounds. When not on his ghostly rounds,
Mr. Fleming's earthly remains reside in the churchyard.

A popular photo spot is at the **Southernmost Point.** Located at the south end of
the island at the corner of Whitehead and South Sts, the site is marked by a huge
red, yellow, green, and white buoy (circa 1983). Standing 12 feet tall with a reach
of 7 feet wide, the buoy received a face-lift in 2005 only to be hammered later
that year with Hurricane Wilma. Still standing, it marks the southernmost point in
the continental United States that is accessible to the general public, and it is a
mere 90 miles from Havana, Cuba. The true southernmost point, on dry land
anyway, is within the U.S. Naval Base boundary, just a bit west of the buoy. The
actual southernmost point in the United States is on tiny Ballast Key, a federally
protected wildlife preserve with no public access. It is located a few miles southwest between Key West and the Marquesas Keys. While you can't step on the
southernmost island, you can fly over it on a tour (see *Airplane Tours*).

MURALS The **Coral Reef** wall at the Historic Seaport wraps around much of the building housing Waterfront Market and Reef Relief on William St. The mural, which showcases an impressive view of the Florida Keys's coral reef ecosystem, is one of **Wyland's Whaling Wall** projects (see *Art Galleries*). He was joined by artist **Guy Harvey,** best known for his painting of sport fish. Make sure to stop in at Reef Relief's Environmental Center & Gift Store.

You'll need to check in at the office at Glynn Archer Elementary School, 1302 White St, before viewing the mural painted by artist **William Hoffman.** The mural depicts the early years of Key West with Spanish explorers and the construction of the Overseas Railroad.

MUSEUMS At the **Audubon House & Tropical Gardens** (305-294-2116; www.audubonhouse.com), 205 Whitehead St, you'll experience the artistic works of John James Audubon. You'll see 28 first-edition pieces created by the world-famous ornithologist, along with an audio tour of the 1840s home, furnished with period pieces from the 1800s and built with architectural elements identified with wreckers and salvagers of the time. Enjoy a peaceful walk through the 1-acre tropical garden to calm your mind or enliven your spirits. Don't forget to browse through the gallery and gift shop for inspired and imaginative items. Open daily 9:30–5. Adults $10, students $6.50, children $5.

The Curry Mansion Museum (305-294-5349 or 1-800-253-3466; www.curry mansion.com), 511 Caroline St, built in 1899 by William Curry, a Bahamian immigrant who worked the shores of Key West as a salvager, is listed on the National Register of Historic Places. Curry started construction of the 25-room mansion in 1855, incorporating many design elements common to wreckers. Take particular note of the widow's walk and Tiffany glass door entry. Make your way up the stairs to the attic, where you'll find an array of antique toys and garments from the era. Throughout the mansion, each room is staged in Victorian elegance as if they were waiting for you to arrive. You can rest your head at the Curry Mansion Inn (see *Lodging*), which offers guest rooms and suites. Open 10–5 daily. Fee.

The Spanish colonial–style **Ernest Hemingway Home and Museum** (305-294-1136; www.hemingway home.com), 907 Whitehead St, is a National Historic Landmark. Built in 1851 by salvage wrecker Asa Tift, the home displays items collected by Hemingway during his world travels. A calm and creative environment, this is where Hemingway wrote most of his greatest novels and where you'll find more than 60 descendants of his famous polydactyl cats, who lounge throughout the elegant garden and stately home. Open daily 9–5 for tours. Adults $11, children $6, under 6 free.

THE HEMINGWAY HOUSE   Sandra Friend

At the **Heritage House Museum & Robert Frost Cottage** (305-296-3573; www.heritagehousemuseum.org), 410 Caroline St, you'll view a grand Caribbean colonial house (circa 1830s) with a variety of rare antiques and maritime memorabilia. The **Robert Frost Cottage,** located at the rear of the home, is often used for poetry conferences and can be viewed only from the outside during the tour. Open 10–4 Mon–Sat, with tours every half hour. The $15 admission also includes admission to the Oldest House and the Audubon House.

Key West Shipwreck Historeum (305-292-8990; www.shipwreckhistoreum .com), One Whitehead St. Your costumed guide, master wrecker Asa Tift, takes you on an engaging tour of the 1800s, when shipwreck salvaging was the means to untold wealth, albeit a perilous livelihood. Learn about the world of wreckers as he spins a tale of the 1856 sinking and recovery of the *Isaac Allerton,* the richest shipwreck in Key West history. See artifacts from this rich and colorful historical period, when wrecking was Key West's main occupation. Open daily 9–5. Adults $10, ages 4–12 $5, under 4 free.

Florida's only presidential museum is at the **Little White House** (305-294-9911), 111 Front St at the Truman Naval Station. Walk through rooms filled with history to see where President Harry S Truman spent 175 days at Quarters A while you listen to stories of historical meetings, elegant soirees, and how he kept the Secret Service on their toes. Modern moguls and CEOs should take note of the tiny desk where Truman signed important documents. Open daily 9–4:30. Adults $11, ages 5–12 $5, under 5 free.

At the **Mel Fisher Maritime Heritage Museum** (305-294-2633; www.melfisher .org), 200 Greene St, you'll see an outstanding collection of shipwreck salvage. Donated in large part (more than $20 million in treasure and historical artifacts) by the man who "saw the ocean paved with coin," founder Mel Fisher has established an incredible exhibit. You'll see such items as the "poison cup" gold chalice, an emerald-studded gold cross, gold and silver bars, thousands of silver coins, and other treasures from the 1622 shipwreck of the Spanish galleon *Nuestra Señora de Atocha.* Check out the second floor, where you'll learn more about pirates and life at sea. The Trade Goods museum store features authentic Spanish "cob" coins made into jewelry pieces, and replicas of doubloons and ancient weaponry. Free.

Inside the **Oldest House Wrecker's Museum** (305-294-9502; www.oirf.org/ museums/oldesthouse.htm), 322 Duval St, enjoy a tour of the Watlington house (see *Historic Sites*), built in 1829. Each room is decked out with period paintings, furnishings, and extensive exhibits that evoke the age of the wrecker, an old and storied career in the Conch Republic. In the back of the home, the office of Capt. Francis Watlington (circa 1870) features a "landlubber's tilt," with the windows and boards at a slant. Step out into the shaded courtyard and explore the outbuildings, the kitchen and a former carriage house with exhibits on the wreckers of the Keys. Artifacts include a book from 1836, fragments of a china doll tea set, and a giant turnbuckle for the iron struts supporting the 1853 Sand Key lighthouse. Open 10–4 daily for self-guided tours. Fee.

The bizarre and unnatural can be found at **Ripley's Believe It or Not** (305-293-9939; www.ripleyskeywest.com), 108 Duval St, where more than 13 themed galleries include everything from to a prehistoric mastodon skeleton to a shrunken torso reputed to have belonged to Ernest Hemingway. Open daily 9:30 AM–11 PM. Adults $15, ages 5–12 $12, under 5 free.

By far one of the most famous homes in Key West is the 1896 **Southernmost House Grand Hotel & Museum** (305-296-3141; www.southernmosthouse .com), 1400 Duval St. Tours take you through the former home of Judge J. Vining Harris, where you'll see 43 original U.S. Presidential signatures, along with other documents dating from 1486. The tour provides you with the rich history of the home and the politics of the time. When Truman snuck out of the Little White House, this is where the Secret Service would find him. The home is also a bed & breakfast (see *Lodging*). Open for tours 10–6 daily. Adults $8, children under 12 free.

At the **Turtle Kraals Museum** (305-294-0209), 200 Margaret St, you'll learn about the turtle-rehabilitation program of this former turtle canning facility. Open daily 11:15–4:15. Donation.

RAILROADIANA At the **Flagler Station Overseas Railroad Historeum** (305-295-3562), 901 Caroline St in the historic Key West Seaport, take a journey into the past through the movie *The Day the Train Arrived,* commemorating Flagler's disembarkation on the first train to Key West on January 22, 1912. Walk through a Florida East Coast railroad car with photographs and artifacts, and listen to storytellers describe one of the most awesome engineering feats of the last century. Fee.

WILDLIFE REHABILITATION The **Reef World Educational Facility and Environmental Center** (305-294-3100; www.reefrelief.org), 201 William St at the historic seaport, offers free activities about reefs, turtles, dolphins, and sharks, and what you can do to help protect living coral reef ecosystems. At their gift shop there is a great variety of educational materials and books for young and old on this fragile marine environment, and there is also a selection of eco-relevant clothes, gifts, and posters.

Housed in a corner of the Sonny McCoy Indigenous Park (see *Parks*), **Wildlife Rescue of the Keys** (305-294-1441; www.seabirdsanctuary.org/KeyWest .htm), 1801 White St, cares for sick and injured wildlife in the Lower Keys, particularly shorebirds, with an emphasis on rehabilitation and release. Dedicated volunteers have rescued crocodiles and assisted with whale strandings. Wander through the enclosures to visit with permanent residents such as pelicans, seagulls, and osprey that cannot be returned to the wild. Open 9–5 daily. Donation.

✳ To Do

AIRPLANE TOURS Let the wind blow through your hair as you and one other person share the adventure of a lifetime on **Island Aeroplane Tours** (305-294-8687; www.islandaeroplanetours.com), 3469 S Roosevelt Blvd, located at the Key West Airport. You'll fly in a 1941 open cockpit WACO UPF7 biplane as you soar only 500 feet off the ground and over the water. Different tours show you the sites of Key West and nearby islands. For a quick tour take the 15-minute Island Shipwreck Tour ($120) to see the Old Town District and shipwrecks in the Fleming Key Channel. You'll spot sharks and stingrays swimming below in the 35- to 40-minute Coral Reef/Boca Grande Key Tour ($275), which covers 34 nautical miles over Key West and nearby uninhabited islands. The 50- to 55-minute Grand Island Reef Tour ($325) takes in all the sites from Hemingway's famous Stilt House to Ballast Key, the true southernmost point in the United States. The super-adventurous can do loops, rolls, and spins in their 1999 Pitts Special aerobatic airplane ($250). All prices are per plane for two people. Call for reservations.

BIRDING Visit the **Key West Tropical Forest & Botanical Garden** (see *Botanical Gardens*) during the month of September for "Migration Mania," as migratory birds stop en masse at freshwater Desbiens Pond to drink deeply before setting off to Central and South America. Our feathered friends also flock to the freshwater pond near the White Street Pier at **Sonny McCoy Indigenous Park** (see *Parks*).

CRUISING You'll find golf cart–type electric cars for rent at the four locations of **Electric Cars of Key West** (305-294-4724 or 1-800-800-8802): Truman and Duval, Caroline and Grinnell, Caroline and Duval, and 2001 S Roosevelt Blvd. These two- and four-seaters range from $60 to $190, starting from two hours to three or more days.

Monarch Custom Carts (305-292-2229), 1020 Duval St. Cruise the streets of Key West in style in a customized electric cart. These cute two- to six-seater cars are modified to look like mini versions of the model T and muscle cars of the 1950s. Rates: 3 hours $95–155, 8 hours $145–205, 24 hours $190–240, 3 or more days $130–160 per day.

ECOTOURS Kayak Eco-Tours (305-294-8087; www.blue-planet-kayak.com) will take you paddling through a wildlife refuge or under the full moon. Guided tours are two and a half to four hours long ($40 and $50). Or you can rent a single or tandem kayak for a full day ($40–50) or a half day ($30–40) and explore on your own.

Lazy Dog Island Outfitters & Adventure Company (305-294-7178; www.mosquitocoast.net), 5114 Overseas Hwy, located at the Hurricane Hole Marina at MM 4.2. Lazy Dog takes you on sea kayaks through the backcountry on wildlife and snorkel tours. Rate is $55 per person and includes snacks, bottled water, and mask and snorkel sets.

GHOST TOURS You'll have a spooktacular time with **The Ghosts & Legends of Key West** (305-294-1713 or 1-866-622-4467; www.keywestghosts.com), where you'll learn about the ghouls that inhabit Victorian mansions, and secret voodoo rituals. Ninety-minute tours are at 7 and 9 nightly, starting at the Porter Mansion at the corner of Duval and Caroline Sts. Adults $18, ages 8–14 $8.

♿ You'll be led by lantern through the dark and narrow streets of historic Old Town for about 90 minutes with **Ghost Tours of Key West** (305-294-9255; www.hauntedtours.com), where you'll learn about the legends of pirates, wreckers, and former Key West inhabitants. The nightly 0.5-mile tour begins in the lobby of the Crowne Plaza La Concha Hotel at 430 Duval St and covers such sites as St Paul's Episcopal Church and cemetery (see *Historic Sites*) and Captain Tony's Saloon (see *Eating Out*). Founded in 1996 by the author of *Ghosts of Key West,* David L. Sloan, this nightly haunt has been featured on numerous television shows, including the History and Discovery channels. Two tours leave at 8 and 9 PM. Adults $15, ages 4–12 $10, under 4 free.

HOCKEY Families skate free at the **Southernmost Hockey Club** (www.keywest hockey) on Friday night. Bring your own inline skates to the corner of Bertha St and Atlantic Blvd. Call the YMCA of Key West at 305-296-YMCA for more information.

SAILING TOURS The 80-foot *Schooner Liberty* and 125-foot *Schooner Liberty Clipper* set sail morning, afternoon, and sunset for two hours on the **Liberty Fleet of Tall Ships** (305-292-0332; www.libertyfleet.com), 245 Front St. You'll enjoy the festive Caribbean barbecue during the season on the *Schooner Liberty Clipper.* Ships depart from Schooner Wharf at the historic seaport. Morning and afternoon sails: adults $35, children 12 and under $25; drinks available for purchase. Sunset sails: adults $49, children $35; includes complimentary drinks. Two-and-a-half-hour-long Caribbean barbecue dinner cruise: adults $75, children $55.

On **Sunny Days Catamarans** (305-292-6100 or 1-800-236-7937; www.sunny dayskeywest.com), at the foot of Elizabeth and Greene Sts, you can choose from a variety of catamaran tours, from snorkeling tours ($35–45) to a full-day excursion to Dry Tortugas National Park (see *Parks*) on their *Fast Cat* ($110) (reduced prices for children and seniors). Rates include a continental breakfast, buffet lunch, soft drinks, water, snorkeling gear, and a guided tour of the fort.

The 130-foot **Western Union** (305-292-1766; www.historictours.com), 202 William St at Schooner Wharf, is the last tall ship constructed in Key West and is the last sailing cable ship found anywhere. The *Western Union,* launched in 1939, spent the next 35 years laying cable off the shores of the Keys before being used in the Mariel Boatlift and in a program for troubled teens. Now back home, it is heralded as the "Flagship of Key West." On two-hour, fully narrated afternoon and sunset tours, you'll enjoy sailing on one of the few authentic coasting

SCHOONERS COMING INTO PORT

Kathy Wolf

schooners still in sailing condition. Step aboard the vanished mahogany decks, and relax as the ship moves gently out through the shipping lanes while soft music plays. On their 90-minute Stargazer Cruise ($45) you'll discover the mystery of the night sky as astronomer Joe Universe (www.keyweststargazer.com) provides you a bit of history and folklore, then uses a green laser beam to show you the stars and constellations overhead. Use your binoculars for a closer inspection of the band of animals that makes up the zodiac. Now owned by Historic Tours of America, the *Western Union* is on the National Register of Historic Places. You'll also enjoy their other sailing ship, **Schooner America** (305-292-7787; www.historictours.com), which also departs from Schooner Wharf in the historic seaport. Day sail $49, sunset sail $69, stargazing sail $49; reduced prices for children.

The **World Famous Glass Bottom Boats** (305-296-6293; www.seethereef .com), Two Duval St, is a great way to see the reef without getting wet. Adults $30, ages 6–13 $15, under 6 free.

TRAIN & TROLLEY TOURS Get your ticket for **The Conch Tour Train** (305-294-5161; www.historictours.com), 303 Front St in Mallory Square, and then board from Mallory Square or from Flagler Station, 901 Caroline St. Narrated tours depart every half hour and are 90 minutes long. This tour is the best way to learn about Key West before you explore on your own. Adults $25, ages 4–12 $12. **Old Town Trolley Tours** (305-296-6688 or 1-800-868-7482; www.historic tours.com) is operated by the same company, but this one gives you the option of hopping on and off at nine locations around town to spend a few minutes or hours at each location. Adults $25, ages 4–12 $12. Those with longer legs may be more comfortable on the trolley.

▼ The **Gay & Lesbian Trolley Tour** (305-294-4603; www.gaykeywestfl.com), operated by Key West Business Guild and Historic Tours of America, bears the rainbow flag during the 70-minute tour each Sat at 11 AM. You'll learn about the influence the gay and lesbian culture has had on the politics and economy of Key West, along with historical sites of specific interest to gay travelers. Call for departure location. Rates are $20 per person.

WALKING TOURS **Duval,** the main street of historic Old Town, stretches for 1 mile from the Atlantic Ocean (on the quiet side) to the Gulf of Mexico (on the spirited side), ending at Mallory Square (see *Historic Sites*). You'll find many art galleries, boutiques, restaurants, pubs, and lively music along this well-populated boulevard. Those attempting the "Duval Crawl" (one drink in every bar on Duval St) should have a designated driver, or at least someone who can carry you home.

✳ Green Space

BEACHES My sister got married on the beach at **Fort Zachary Taylor** (see *Historic Sites*), so in my mind, it's a romantic destination. It's a popular one, too, for watching the sunset and the cruise ships sailing past. Enjoy snorkeling or sunbathing on the coral rock sand; amenities include picnic tables, a bathhouse, and

ON THE BEACH IN KEY WEST

Visit Florida

a light-refreshment stand. Fee. On the Atlantic, **Smathers Beach** on S Roosevelt Blvd has shallow water great for the kids, and water sports including parasailing, Jet Skiing, and windsurfing. Free. At the White Street Pier, **Higgs Beach** is a popular family destination for its picnic tables and grills under the coconut palms. 🐾 **Gable Beach,** at Vernon St and Waddell Ave, is the one dog-friendly beach on the island. And for those who let it all hang out, **Atlantic Shores Resort,** 510 South St, features a private nude beach.

BOTANICAL GARDENS ♿ In 1936 the Works Progress Administration created a 55-acre botanical garden on Stock Island. But during World War II, pieces of the garden were sacrificed for an army hospital and other public works until the forest was whittled down to 8 acres and eventually abandoned. Thankfully, a group of dedicated volunteers has brought this botanical wonder back to life as the **Key West Tropical Forest & Botanical Garden** (305-296-1504; www.key westbotanicalgarden.org), 5210 College Rd, MM 4.25. Start your tour at the visitors center, which has a film about the biodiversity of the Keys, and pick up a map to walk any of the three self-guided tours through what is one of the top 25 biological hot spots of the world. Duke University students recently documented the flora of the forest, which includes a dwarf lignum vitae tree, the National Champion Cuban lignum vitae tree, *thrinax* palms more than a century old, and the oldest wild cinnamon tree in the Keys. Endangered white-crowned pigeons nest in the canopy, and thousands of migratory birds drop in for fresh water from Desbiens Pond, where the endangered mud-striped turtle lives. "The pond is like a turnpike stop on the flyway," said Carol Ann Sharkey, president of the nonprofit. At least 30 endangered species live in this last remnant of truly tropical forest on Key West. Plans are to finish removing invasive plants from the existing 8 acres and restore a new 8-acre tract (the former site of the army hospital) back to a formal botanical garden, and establish a medicinal plants research center on the site. The forest and gardens are open 10–5, closed Wed and during September. Donation.

For a relaxing break from Duval St, seek out **Nancy Forrester's Secret Garden** (305-294-0015), One Free School Ln (off the 500 block of Simonton St). This private paradise features lush tropical landscaping with orchids; an art gallery hides deep in the forest. Open 10–5 daily. Fee.

PARKS Seventy miles off the coast of Key West sits the **Dry Tortugas National Park** (www.nps.gov/drto). Named after its abundance of sea turtles (*tortugas* is Spanish for "turtles"), the area is a great location for snorkeling, but it is best known for the largest fort in coastal America—**Fort Jefferson.** Several tour boats and seaplanes offer transportation to the area with tours of the fort. Park entrance fee; primitive camping is available on Garden Key for a nightly fee. Call the campground at 305-242-7700.

Protecting the last 5.5 acres of natural Key West, **Sonny McCoy Indigenous Park** (305-292-8157), 1801 White St, encompasses the largest freshwater pond on the island and is home to Wildlife Rescue of the Keys (see *Wildlife Rehabilitation*). This is a hot spot for birders, as you can see warblers in migration and various raptors, including swallow-tailed kites. A boardwalk leads to natural-surface trails that take you through a forest of silver buttonwoods and thatch palms and a grove of gumbo limbo to an observation deck on the pond. There is a shaded picnic pavilion and rest rooms. Open 7–4 Mon–Fri; tours by arrangement. Free.

PRESERVES **Key West Nature Preserve** (305-809-3700), Atlantic Blvd. Meander the trail through this strip of natural coastal hammock, where sea grapes crowd the edge of a mangrove swamp and giant land crabs dig holes in the footpath. A boardwalk leads through a bower of nickerbean to an observation deck with a view of the pier and the wrack line on the beach. Open sunrise–sunset daily; no swimming. Free.

✳ Lodging

The zip code for all Key West accommodations is 33040.

BED & BREAKFASTS Curl up in a romantic atmosphere at the **Curry Mansion Inn** (305-294-5349 or 1-800-253-3466; www.currymansion .com), 511 Caroline St. The elegant 22-room mansion, built in 1899 by Florida's first millionaire family, is open for daily for historical tours (see *Museums*), which are free to guests. Rooms and suites are decorated with wicker or antiquities from the period, such as graceful canopy beds, and have private baths, wet bars, air-conditioning, ceiling fans, and cable television. You'll enjoy the close proximity to Duval St for shopping and dining, or relax any time of day at the swimming pool and hot tub, open 24 hours. Accommodations include a full deluxe breakfast and daily open bar. Rooms and suites range from $165 to $335.

🐾 ♿ 🐕 Settle into romance at **The Frances Street Bottle Inn** (305-294-8530 or 1-800-294-8530; www .bottleinn.com), 535 Frances St, where colorful antique bottles adorn the windows and walls of this 1879 home. Innkeepers Mary Beth, Dennis, and Marketa create a comfortable atmosphere with bright pastels and

ANTIQUE BOTTLES

Sandra Friend

🦐 ♿ I never felt more relaxed than at **Cypress House** (305-294-6969 or 1-800-525-2488; www.cypresshousekw.com), 601 and 613 Caroline St. The Bahamian Grand Conch mansion (circa 1888) is listed on the National Register of Historic Places and is lovingly cared for by an attentive staff and two adorable and very well-behaved Schipperkes, Ben and Gabi, who are never too far away from innkeeper Dave Taylor. (If you're lucky, Lady Bug, the resident cat, will honor you with her presence.) Just a block from all the activities on Duval St, the property is comprised of three buildings: the main Cypress House; the Simonton House, built for the original owner's daughter (circa 1908); and the Cypress House Studios, built in 1895.

Rooms are decorated with an eclectic mix of antiques, with modern amenities such as in-room refrigerators, air-conditioning, ceiling fans, cable TV, Wi-Fi, and phones with voice mail. And you can use the microwave in the kitchen to warm up leftovers. Rooms in the three-story main Cypress House are grand, airy, and spacious, with some as large as 20 by 14. A number of rooms contain private baths, while some share a bath.

Rooms 1 and 2 are located on the first floor and share a small bath. I stayed in Room 1, which opens out through double doors onto the veranda, and I was quite comfortable sharing with my "bathroom buddy," whom I finally met out by the pool on my third night. Readers will enjoy Room 2, the former library, fully stocked with a variety of books. The best part of Rooms 1 and 2 is that they are near the kitchen, so you'll wake up to the smell of freshly baked breads, and you won't need to climb any stairs after an evening on the town.

Romantics will want to check into the Blue Room (Room 5). This honeymooners' favorite was the former master bedroom of the house and still contains the original hand-painted blue and white floral ceiling. You'll find both luxury and romance: mini fridge, comfy sofa, private veranda, king-size bed, and super-huge private bath with walk-in glass shower, cozy corner tub, and double sinks.

wicker, bookshelves lined with books in the common areas, a quiet garden with a hot tub, and a wraparound veranda on both floors under the poinciana and palms. Over the years, the inn has worn many cloaks—from a private home to a general store, a Presbyterian church, and the starring role in the Fox TV series *Key West* in the 1990s. Each of the seven units ($89–199) has private baths and televisions; there is a phone and data port hookup in the lobby, where breakfast is served from 8 to 10. I especially appreciate their Green policy, which includes recycling, low-flow toilets,

The least-expensive rooms, 6 and 7, are located on the third floor, have double beds, and share a bath.

In the Simonton House, Rooms 11 and 12 comprise a two-bedroom suite sharing the living room, kitchenette, and bath and open into a lush tropical garden—a great option for families or couples traveling together. Three doors down at the Cypress Studios you'll find four well-appointed guest suites and rooms, all with private baths, and an outdoor hot tub. The Honeymoon Suite (Room 21) has a queen-size bed and opens onto the front porch overlooking Caroline St. Room 25 is ADA compliant and opens through an extra-wide door to a deck near the hot tub.

All guests have access to the 40-foot heated pool at the main house. Cypress House requires a minimum stay for all their rooms: five nights during season, three nights off-season, and seven nights during Fantasy Fest (see *Special Events*), but you'll want stay longer, so they'll give you a discount for week-long stays. The minimum stay is actually a benefit, as you'll have a chance to meet the other guests and share your adventures at the sumptuous continental breakfast by the pool, or later in the day at the not-to-be-missed nightly complimentary happy hour, which includes hot and cold hors d'oeuvres, beer, wine, and mixed drinks. Many guests come and go from this lush tropical oasis, where cold water, iced tea, Key Lime Coolers, and good times can always be found poolside. You'll find that guests become longtime friends here at Cypress House. Dave introduced me to two other women vacationing alone, and soon we were planning activities together, including an impromptu, and hilarious, "water ballet" at the pool. We still keep in touch and look forward to another "Key West Chicks" retreat at Cypress House.

Rates $139–400, depending on season and room. For parking, there are meters out front for quick trips, but ultimately you'll want to park your car and leave it at the covered public garage, only a few blocks away on Caroline St. Cypress House offers reduced-rate 24-hour access cards for guests. You'll find everything only a few blocks from the property, and with street parking difficult at best, you'll want to navigate Key West on foot or rent one of their bicycles.

and third-day bed-linen changes on your longer stays.

GUEST HOUSES The Eden House (305-296-6868 or 1-800-533-KEYS; www.edenhouse.com), 1015 Fleming St, is nestled on a side street within a short walk to all the activities on Duval. Built in 1924, the art deco–style inn has been lovingly cared for by owner Mike Eden since 1975. The attention to detail is everywhere, from the warm greeting and cool beverage you'll receive on your arrival to the lush tropical gardens, boardwalks, and hammocks found throughout the property. The fun and funky guest house feels like a beach house at times, and at others a quaint country inn. One thing is for sure—their knowledgeable staff knows the best places to eat and play on the island. But you'll want to spend some time right here on-site. Sun lovers will want to bask by the heated pool and Jacuzzi, or up on the elevated sundeck, while those with delicate skin will want to curl up under a canopy of palms in one of the property's eight hammocks, while listening only to the sounds of a waterfall. Enjoy a glass of wine or a chilled drink at the complimentary happy hour from 4 to 5. The comfortable rooms are very clean and efficient, with French doors leading out onto your own porch, some with swing. As this is a guest house, not a bed & breakfast, you'll have to venture out for breakfast; however, they are planning to open an on-site restaurant, Café Med, for breakfast. In the meantime, coffee and tea are available in the lobby at all times. Rates range from those for rooms with shared bath ($90–125) to the deluxe conch house with full kitchen ($225–350) and every imaginable configuration in between. Free parking available on-site.

HOSTELS Seasoned hostelers will find comfort at the **Key West Youth Hostel** (305-296-5719 or 1-800-468-5516; www.keywesthostel.com), Seashell Motel, 718 South St. Strict rules make this a no-party place. Only 2 blocks from the beach, in Old Town, the hostel is never closed and offers 92 beds, free wireless Internet, kitchen facilities, and a courtyard. Rates $28 per night for hostel members; $31 for nonmembers. Bikes are available for rent.

HOTELS, MOTELS, AND RESORTS
& Stay in style on an 1830s estate at the **Key Lime Inn** (305-294-5229 or 1-800-549-4430; www.keylimeinn .com), 725 Truman Ave, vintage motor-court cottages arranged around a central treed courtyard and swimming pool, with a grand 1854 Bahamian British colonial–style home of Walter C. Mahoney. The units include the fully renovated and comfortable cottages, built in 1939 by a former circus performer, and a handful of units in the historic home; Rooms 10 and 12 have access to the upper-story porch. There are 36 one-bedroom units and king rooms with a porch or patio and a country bed. Rates run $109 and up in the off-season, $149–229 during the high season, with surcharges for special events.

We weathered hurricane at the **Southernmost Hotel** (305-296-6577, 1-800-354-4455; www.southernmostresorts .com), 1319 Duval St, one of four related properties at the end of Duval St near the Southernmost Point, and to me, that's the real test of a hotel—do I feel safe? The answer is yes. We watched the Weather Channel as the storm howled and palm trees bent to the ground. Standard motel rooms ($89–250) with furnishings that evoke the islands are centered on two courtyards with swimming pools set in tropical gardens. There is a concierge on site, along with visitor information and bicycle and moped rentals; guests have access to the beach at the Southernmost on the Beach across the street.

✳ Where to Eat

DINING OUT Food and art meet at **Mangos** (352-292-4606; www .mangoeskeywest.com), 700 Duval St, an upscale restaurant featuring floral art from Piero Aversa, sculptures by John Martini, and plaster art from Sergio deVecchi. Infused with music, light, and the aromas from the kitchen, this is a delightful place for a meal. Executive Chef Paul Orchard oversees creations such as passion yellowtail snapper, which came dusted with toasted coconut and drizzled with a sour spicy mango-passionfruit sauce. The white conch chowder was luscious and creamy, and the tomato bisque tart had a hint of cheese. Choose from a tempting selection of desserts, including a crème brûlée, delicate and silky with a lingering cappuccino taste, a perfect accompaniment to that after-dinner coffee. Perfection doesn't come cheap—expect to drop $75 for a meal for two.

Pisces "A Seafood Place" presented by Café Des Artistes (305-294-7100; www.pisceskeywest.com), 1007 Simonton St. Same owner, same chef—different name. Café Des Artistes began in 1982 and underwent renovation in 2002. Much of the architecture of the original building (circa 1892) was restored, setting the stage for an incredible meal. Owner Timothy Ryan thought that with a fresh new look, the restaurant needed a new name, and Pisces was chosen to reflect the "fruits from the sea" concept. Buttery walls accented with plum drapes surround tables set with crisp white linens placed with half wall dividers, so intimate conversations can be held in private. Walls are decorated with original signed Andy Warhol prints, from owner Timothy Ryan's personal collection, framed within architectural arches. You'll especially enjoy the portraits of Marilyn Monroe and Mick Jagger, along with the famous *Campbell's Tomato Soup* and *Cow 1971*. Chef Andrew

Berman creates magic with seafood, and as a former Maine resident who has eaten her fair share of lobster, I give two thumbs up and then some for his famous Lobster Tango Mango—shelled Maine lobster flambéed in cognac with shrimp in saffron butter, mango, and basil. You'll also want to try the Aphrodite Pisces, lobster, shrimp, and sea scallops baked in puff pastry with lemon tarragon butter; Yellowtail Snapper Atocha, with lemon brown butter, avocadoes, mint, and peas; and house favorite Raspberry Duck. Save room for the flambéed Rhum Baba, with white chocolate mousse, fresh berries, and mango sauce ($9) or chocolate fondant, an upside-down chocolate soufflé with pistachio and warm Valrhona chocolate sauce ($9). A glass of late-harvest dessert wine ($9–15) is a great way to finish it all off. Appetizers $8–25; entrées $27–45. Reservations strongly recommended.

EATING OUT Savor a glass of cabernet while Dino croons at **Abbondanza** (305-292-1199), 1208 Simonton St, a comfortable Italian restaurant that offers all the classic dishes—even my

PISCES SEAFOOD RESTAURANT

Pisces Seafood Restaurant

favorite, spaghetti *calabrese,* with peppers, onions, and spicy sausage, and linguine *pescatore,* with shrimp, scallops, clams, and mussels. Entrées $9–18.

At **Alonzo's Oyster Bar** (305-294-5880), 700 Front St, oysters are the thing—brought in fresh and prepared fresh. I enjoyed the Dixie Oyster Spinach Salad, with fried oysters, bacon, hard-boiled egg, and mango touched with passionfruit vinaigrette atop a bed of baby spinach, and I was tempted by oysters prepared with spinach Parmesan, andouille, or Key lime garlic. The oysters come from around the country; daily raw selections are listed on the chalkboard. Entrées $14–19.

Since 1851, **Captain Tony's Saloon** (305-294-1838; www.capttonys saloon.com), 428 Greene St, has been the favorite watering hole of thirsty souls, from wreckers to writers. In the early 1900s it was a cigar factory, bordello, and favorite speakeasy. From 1928 to 1939, Ernest Hemingway met his friends here faithfully every afternoon at 3:30 while he was working on such books as *Death in the Afternoon* and *To Have and Have Not.* Hemingway's bar stool is still on view. The 1970s brought Jimmy Buffett and the Coral Reefer Band to the pub for impromptu sessions, and today you'll find a variety of talent, with music and a bit of mayhem nightly.

For the best Cuban con leche, head over to **The Five Brothers Grocery** (305-296-5205), 930 Southard St, at the corner of Grinnell. This tiny corner grocery store goes through 24 pounds of coffee a day and is a great place for Cuban sandwiches.

You come to the **Green Parrot** (1-800-901-9552; www.greenparrot.com),

corner of Whitehead and Southard Sts, to drink, not eat. With lots of ice-cold beer and tropical concoctions, you won't go thirsty. This legendary landmark, the last bar on US 1, pumps out great music all the time, and the must-see, one-of-a-kind watering hole has been serving great drinks, darts, and pool since 1890. The bar bills itself as "a sunny place for shady people," but don't be hesitant to scope it out—it really isn't as scary as it looks. Can't wait to see it? There's a live web cam on their web site. For those who want to poke their heads in just to say they were there, there's a great gift shop on-site for souvenirs.

Jimmy Buffett's Margaritaville Café (305-292-1435; www.margarita ville.com), 500 Duval St, is a must-stop for the infamous Cheeseburger in Paradise ($9), served just like the song says, or my favorite, the broiled yellowtail snapper sandwich ($10). Wash it all down with one of seven fresh fruit margaritas ($6), such as passion fruit or banana, or order up the original Margaritaville Gold Margarita ($6).

At **Sloppy Joe's** (305-294-5717), 201 Duval St, their namesake sandwich is big, drippy, and sweet, and the chili comes tomato-thick with a bit of a kick. The sliced potato salad is something right out of my childhood. But most folks don't come here for the food; they're here for the legendary drink, from margaritas and Rum Runners to a one-and-a-half-ounce pour on your favorite liquor. Touting themselves as Hemingway's favorite bar, they've been here since 1937, and they're still here for you to have a good time.

St. Main-stage shows run Tue–Sat at 8 PM. Advanced tickets $27, opening night $30; senior citizens, military, and students receive a 10 percent discount.

At the **Tennessee Williams Theatre** (305-296-1520), 5901 College Rd, you'll enjoy great theatrical perform-ances along with art exhibitions, festi-vals, fund-raisers, and community events. Indoors, the 480-seat theater has added 250 seats in their new Grand Foyer, allowing for intimate recitals and poetry readings. The Grand Foyer can also be converted to bistro seating for cabaret shows. Out-doors overlooking the water, perform-ances can accommodate 2,500 guests.

You'll find Florida's oldest continuous-ly running theater over at Mallory Square. **The Waterfront Playhouse** (305-294-5015; www.waterfrontplay house.com), 310 Wall St, has been presenting live theater since 1940, with an array of productions. You may see such musical productions as *Little Shop of Horrors*, dramas such as *A Streetcar Named Desire*, and innova-tive works such as *Naked Boys Singing*. Tickets $30–35.

✳ Selective Shopping

When traveling in and out of Key West, make sure to pull over at MM 15 to **Baby's Coffee** (305-744-9866 or 1-800-523-2326; www.babys coffee.com), 3178 US 1 (oceanside), Saddlebunch Key, for a great cup of coffee and bakery snacks. (See *Eating Out* in *Lower Keys*.)

The best Key lime pie is found at **Blond Giraffe** (www.blondgiraffe .com), where owners Roberto and Tania Madeira serve a variety of edible Key lime delights, such as the

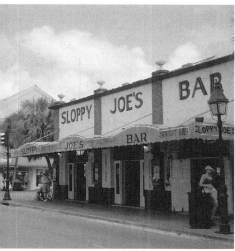

Sandra Friend

SLOPPY JOE'S, A LANDMARK

BAKERIES, COFFEE SHOPS, AND SODA FOUNTAINS If you love ice cream, you must not miss **Flamingo Crossing** (305-296-6124), 1105 Duval St, where their homemade fla-vors range into the tropical, including sour sop, guava, papaya, mango, and passion fruit. Their Rum Runner sor-bet is like a water ice, satisfying and light; the coconut ice cream is a thick sweet cream bursting with flavor. Not since Penn State's fabled Creamery have I encountered such rich and per-fect ice cream.

At the **Key West Ice Cream Factory** (305-295-3011), 507 South St, enjoy homemade ice cream flavors packed with fresh tropical fruit, premium tropical smoothies, and their original-recipe Key lime pie ice cream.

✳ Entertainment

THEATER Professional theater, live comedy, drama, music, and cabaret shows are presented Nov–Jul at the **Red Barn Theatre** (305-296-9911; www.redbarntheatre.com), 319 Duval incredible Key lime pie wrapped in chocolate served on a stick. You'll also find a nice selection of bath products, such as their Key Lime Goat Soap. Three locations: 629 Duval St, 305-293-6998; 1209 Truman Ave, 305-295-6776; and their factory store at 107 Simonton St, 305-296-9174.

You'll find an elegant and sophisti cated, but not stuffy, boutique at **Blue** (305-292-5172; www.blueisland store.com), 718 Caroline St. It has a great mix of casual and dressy wear, and I was able to find the neatest, super-soft T-shirts, along with some elegant cocktail outfits. The shop spe-cializes in smart, wearable women's clothing, shoes, purses, and hats. Open daily.

❤ Pet lovers go crazy browsing through the great selection of gifts, jewelry, and people clothing at **The Blue Cat** (305-293-9339), 291 Front St, which has as many items for dogs and dog lovers as it does for cats. Check out the Blue Cat logo T-shirt for a unique souvenir.

Playful and satirical chicken-related gifts line the shelves at **The Chicken Store** (305-294-0070; www.the ChickenStore.com), 1227 Duval St, which is home to the Rooster Rescue Team. For a donation, you can slip into a cottage filled with rescued gypsy chickens, part of Key West's long legacy of foraging fowl. Open 10–5 daily.

Cigar aficionados will want to check out **Conch Republic Cigar Factory** (305-295-9036; www.conch-cigars .com), 512 Greene St; **Cuban Leaf Cigar Factory** (305-295-9283), 310 Duval St; and **Key West Havana Cigar Company** (305-296-2680), 1121 Duval St.

An otherworldly gift shop awaits you at **Ghost Tours of Key West** (305-294-9255; www.hauntedtours.com), 423 Duval St, located at the Crowne Plaza La Concha Hotel. (See *To Do* for more information about the ghost tours.)

At the **Helio Gallery Store** (305-294-7901; www.heliographics.com), 814 Fleming St, you'll find great designs inspired by nature, such as botanical prints, pillows, table run-ners, totes, and textiles decorated with large banana leaves, coconut palms, butterflies, and more. Open 10–6 Mon–Sat or by appointment.

You can spend hours in **Island Books** (305-294-2904), 513 Fleming St, immersing yourself in the stacks and shelves. In the front of the store, they showcase local-interest and Florida authors. In the back, look for a rare-book room and a large cooking sec-tion. The mystery/horror genre is tucked in an appropriately dark cor-ner, and one large room is devoted to new overstock books.

From doorstops and footstools to pil-lows and purses, you'll find great stitchery over at **Island Needlework** (305-296-6091; www.islandneedle point.com), 527 Fleming St, where owner and designer Julie Pischke fea-tures her award-winning tropical needlepoint designs. Open Tue–Sat.

The colors will astound you at the **Key West Butterfly & Nature Bou-tique—Wings of Imagination Gift Shop** (see *Butterfly Conservatory*), where hundreds of butterflies are mounted in display cases from minus-cule to mural size. Nature lovers, put your mind at ease: The butterflies are harvested only after their natural life cycle is complete, which is about two to three weeks.

Don't leave Key West without something from **Key West Handprint Fabrics** (305-292-8965 or 1-800-866-0333; www.keywestfasions.com), 201 Simonton St, where you'll find colorful, original hand-print fabrics by local Key West artists. Ladies can select from dresses, skirts, capris, shorts, and assorted jewelry, and men will go wild for their tropical parrot shirts. Girls will want an outfit from their "Mommy & Me" collection. For those who love to sew, fabrics by the yard are $16–26, with quilting squares also available to commemorate your trip.

Since 1976, the **Key West Kite Company** (305-292-2535; www.key westkites.com), 408 Green St, has made the skies more colorful with their large selection of kites, windsocks, banners, flags, and more. You find an array of single lines, deltas, and parafoils, along with radical frameless stunt kites for kite surfing.

Enjoy unique wines at **The Key West Winery** (305-292-1717; www .keywestwinery.com), 103 Simonton St. The Key Limen wine tastes like a margarita, while the Category 5 white sangria honors hurricanes with a blend of their Key Limen, pineapple, mango, watermelon, and passion fruit wines. You'll also find edible Key lime treats and wine accessories. Open daily, with free wine tastings.

Everyone on land and sea seems to be wearing **Kinos Sandals** (305-294-5044; www.kinosandalfactory.com), 107 Fitzpatrick St. Walk into the small factory shop and you'll see busy shoemakers assembling these comfortable and durable flip-flops. It all began in 1966 with Cuban refugees Roberto "Kino" and Margarita Lopez. Roberto had a shoe factory back in Cuba, and he longed to continue his business, but first he needed to save for it. After years as a handyman, he finally had enough to open his factory, and it has been a local favorite ever since. These affordable sandals never seem to wear out. I've had my "Chain" ($10) sandal for three years, and they still look like the day I bought them, despite traipsing through South Florida storms. The "Lili" is the most common style seen on the docks, and it comes in a half dozen colors and in both women's ($10) and men's ($12) sizes. They also have one style for kids ($8). You'll need to check back often, as not all styles and sizes are on hand all the time.

Nellie & Joe's Key Lime Juice (1-800-LIME-PIE; www.keylimejuice .com) is the maker of the original Key West Lime Juice. Beginning 30 years ago in their kitchen, Nellie & Joe's can now be ordered through the Internet or picked up at a variety of stores throughout the United States. You'll find a great selection of their products at **Kermit's Key West Key Lime Shoppe** (305-296-0806; www .keylimeshop.com), 200A Elizabeth St, where you can also enjoy a hot cup of coffee and a fresh slice of Key lime pie outside in the beautiful garden. Make sure to stop by during the holidays, as Kermit festively decorates the outside of the store into an award-winning gingerbread house. Kermit is also known for his support of local organizations in the area, such as the Monroe Association for Retarded Citizens, Inc (www.marchouse .org). He pays his staff a fair wage, so they donate 90 percent of all tips received toward this worthwhile organization.

Whitehead Street Pottery (305-294-5067), 322 Julia St, specializes in stoneware, porcelain, and raku-fired containers. Open 10–5; closed Tue.

✳ Special Events

For information on the following events, contact the **Key West Chamber of Commerce** (305-294-2587; www.keywestchamber.org) and check out www.fla-keys.com for additional contact numbers.

January: Big-name sailing skippers compete for five days in North America's largest midwinter yachting races at the **Acura Key West Regatta.**

Now more than 20 years old, the **Key West Literary Seminar** (1-888-293-9291; www.KeyWestLiterarySeminar .org), held midmonth, brings in authors from around the world who hold workshops and readings for the likes of you and me, aspiring novelists and fans alike. This two-week festival celebrates the island's long-standing love affair with literature, from the plays of Tennessee Williams to the short stories of John Hershey—and, of course, the Hemingway classics.

You'll see exquisite homes on the **Old Island Days House and Garden Tour** (also offered Feb and Mar).

February: Over at Fort Zachary Taylor Historic State Park, the **Annual Civil War Heritage Festival** (305-295-3033) re-creates the Civil War with a mock land and sea battle.

More than one hundred artisans showcase their talents at the **Annual Old Island Days Art Festival,** held in the historic Old Town district along Whitehead St from Greene to Caroline Sts.

You'll get a chance to tour gingerbread-style Victorians and contemporary homes on the **Old Island Days**

House and Garden Tour (also offered Jan and Mar).

March: You won't want to miss the **Annual Conch Shell Blowing Contest,** an island tradition. Contestants compete in an attempt to make music on the fluted conch shells.

Check out extraordinary architecture and gardens at the **Old Island Days House and Garden Tour** (also offered Jan and Feb).

April: Attend the poetry-writing workshop to hone up on your lyrical skills at the **Annual Robert Frost Poetry Festival,** held at the Heritage House Museum (see *Museums*).

For more than two decades, the **Conch Republic Independence Celebration** has been held to commemorate the Conch Republic, which was founded in 1982 after response to the U.S. Border Patrol road-blocking traffic in and out of the Keys. Events include parades, bed races, and, of course, lots of partying.

The **Taste of Key West** presents the area's best culinary delights for the annual benefit held at the Truman Waterfront.

May: Offshore captains will want to seek the $15,000 prize at the **Annual Dolphin Masters Invitational.**

Musical sounds are heard at the **Key West Songwriters Festival,** where you can see some of America's best songwriters performing in intimate surroundings.

June: Ladies get a chance to catch the big one at the **Annual Conch Republic Ladies' Dolphin Tournament,** with prizes totaling $7,500.

Hispanic customs and cultures are brought to life at the **Annual Cuban American Heritage Festival.**

Celebrating the island's most loved and hated fowl, **Chickenfest,** held midmonth, is four days of fun that include arts and crafts, food, the Poultry in Motion parade, and lots of crazy events, such as the Shake Your Feathers chicken show, Chicken Soup for the Conch Soul, Chicken Scratch Nine-Hole Miniature Golf Tournament, and the Fowl Follies.

The **Key West Gator Club Dolphin Derby** chases down the colorful fish while raising money for college scholarships.

▼ The annual **Pridefest** celebrates the alternative lifestyle with parades and events throughout the city.

July: The **Del Brown Permit Tournament** celebrates the angling pioneer who fly-fished more than five hundred of these hard-fighting fish. The most challenging fish in fly-fishing, permit can be found in grass and sandy flats, searching for their favorite food—crabs.

Anglers fish in the tropical shallows at the **Flats Slam Event of the Key West Fishing Tournament Series.**

You'll think you're seeing double at the **Hemingway Days Festival,** where "Papa" seemingly is spotted throughout town at this annual event celebrating the author and his lifestyle. Bearded men compete at the look-alike contest over at Sloppy Joe's Bar on Duval St. The festival also includes the **Drambuie Key West**

Marlin Tournament, the top event for the mightiest of the offshore species, with $250,000 in prize money.

With a focus on preservation, the annual **Reef Awareness Week** offers a variety of ecotours and environmental education. Call Reef Relief at 305-294-3100 or log on to www.reefrelief .org to learn more about the delicate coral reefs just offshore.

September: ▼ The women take over the city at **WomenFest,** a lesbian-oriented event, which presents a variety of art, comedy, and fun in the sun.

October: The one, the only, not-to-be-missed event is **Fantasy Fest,** where for 10 days the town is packed with costumed participants in the mother of all costume competitions. Features a lavish, and R-rated, parade.

The two-day **Goombay Festival** pours into the streets of Key West's historic Bahama Village with island-style food, fun, and frolic.

November: "Go fast" powerboats race in the **Key West Offshore World Championships.** The annual event is described as the Indianapolis 500 of powerboat racing.

December: The Bahama Conch Community Land Trust presents the **Annual Key West Island Kwanzaa** festival the week between Christmas and New Year's. Events include African-themed ceremonies, rituals, and feasts.

THE A TO Z ON TIPPING

To tip or not to tip? And how much? South Florida is one area where it seems everyone is looking for a handout, from tip jars to valets. Some hotels even have a "resort fee" added. You'll feel your vacation dollars stretched thin if you haven't planned ahead for this inescapable add-on. In defense of the service workers, they hold some of the most underpaid and underappreciated careers. Worse yet, they are taxed on "estimated" tips, whether they received them or not. Years ago when I worked in the food service industry, it was not unusual for me to receive a negative paycheck, meaning I didn't make enough regular wages to cover taxes and social security deductions, so I ended up owing my boss money! Something to think about the next time you are wondering whether you should leave a tip or not. At restaurants, make sure to always read the bottom of your check before tipping. The general rule is any party of more than six should expect the gratuity to be automatically added in. Due in part to the large number of European tourists who are not accustomed to tipping, you'll find almost all the restaurants and bars in the beach areas to automatically add in the gratuity. Some hotels, resorts, and even bed & breakfasts, mainly along the southeast coast and into the Keys, have begun adding a daily resort fee that covers all the housekeeping and recreation services. Before you book your reservation, always ask about this fee, as it may add as much as $40 a day to your bill. After paying $269 for my room, I found that a bit obscene for a quick dip in the pool. If you do not intend to use any of the recreational equipment, you may be able to get all or part of this fee waived. We found one resort that automatically did this for handicapped travelers. At most spas, the tip is usually included on full-service treatments—ask when you book your appointment. After speaking with many of my travel buddies and service staff throughout South Florida, I have come up with the following general guidelines. As always, keep several single dollar bills handy.

Airport shuttle vans/buses
$2 per person to or from hotel.

Bartenders and cocktail servers
10–15 percent or $1 a drink. 15–20 percent in Palm Beach and South Beach.

Some bars, especially the trendier areas, have already added the gratuity to the bill, so check carefully before paying.

If you have drinks before dinner, try to settle up before going to your table. Some restaurants require the waiter to tip the bartender and cocktail servers a percentage of their tips. This is often done to keep things moving smoothly and so that the customer has to handle money only once. First ask the bartender if you can settle up. If not, it's okay to ask if she will get a cut from the waiter; e.g., "Does the waiter take care of you?" If they don't, then by all means, tip her—and generously. She'll tell your waiter that you're a good tipper, and you'll almost always be assured great service. And if your bartender has been exceptionally cordial, then it's still nice to leave her a few dollars.

Bed & breakfasts

Many bed & breakfasts have a no-tipping policy, so ask before you arrive or upon check-in. I always like to leave something anyway, as it's often a local teenager or college kid who cleans the rooms, and they can always use a few extra bucks. Some bed & breakfasts pool and split tips between the maids, cooks, and pool attendants. For those places, tip a little more than you would at a hotel, or about $5 per person per day.

Bellmen/bellhops

$1–2 per bag upon delivery to your room (arrival and departure). Many of the better hotels will show you to your room, open your door, and detail the amenities of your room or suite. It's nice to add a few dollars if they do this. If you need to hold your luggage before or after check-in, then consider tipping $1 per bag when they put your bags in storage and again when they retrieve them.

Buffets and cafeterias

First look to see if the tip was included. Tipping is not usually expected in self-serve eateries, but some are adding it to the bill. If you have a server who brings you things, clears dishes, or keeps your drinks refilled, then tip 10–15 percent. If he just refills drinks, then $1–2 is sufficient.

Busboys

Busboys are taken care of by the wait staff, but if they did something extra, like cleaning up that mess your darling child made, then give them $1–2.

Casino staff

Like food servers, casino workers make most of their income from tips. While it is not necessary to tip when you are losing, it *is* customary to tip a percentage of your winnings. For craps, blackjack, poker, and roulette dealers, tip a $5 chip or more per session or 10 percent of your winnings. For slot machine attendants, tip a $1–2 chip when they repair your machine. And cocktail servers should get at least a $1 chip per drink. Remember, at casinos, drinks are usually free or very cheap.

Complimentary breakfasts

If it is self-serve, then tip nothing. But if you sit down and are waited on, then tip $1–2 per person or estimate the price of the breakfast and tip 15–20 percent of that total.

Concierges

A good concierge can score you hard-to-get theater tickets, restaurant reservations, or put your name at the top of the hottest nightclub list, so make sure to tip her $5–10 for each service, or you can give her an envelope covering all your services at the end of your trip. Ask at the front desk which is preferred, as your favorite concierge may have the day off when you check out. If you have been conversing with a concierge before you arrive, then it is also nice to bring her a token gift from your hometown, such as candies, jams, or soaps, along with the gratuity, of course.

Doormen
Hailing a cab, $1–2. Hauling your bags in or out of your car, 50 cents to $1 a bag. Sometimes doormen do double duty as bellmen, so tip $1–2 per bag if they carry your bags all the way to the room. Tip the same as a concierge if they are helpful with directions or recommendations. No tip is necessary if they just open the door.

Golf caddies
$15–25 on top of the fee for the caddy.

Guides
Some companies have a no-tipping policy. Check when you book the trip. Other operators derive most of their income from gratuities. In most instances, you'll always be safe with 10–15 percent of the cost of the activity. For one-hour tours, such as on airboats and at historical sites, they'll be delighted with $1–2 per person. For three-hour tours, such as ecotours, horseback riding, and day cruises, tip $5–10 per person. For lengthier tours, such as half- or full-day kayaking and fishing charters, tip 15 percent of the cost of the excursion.

Limo/Town Car service
10–15 percent (arrival or departure). 20 percent if you have the driver at your beck and call for a block of time.

Maid service/housekeeping
$1–2 per person per day, with a little extra on the day you check out. Tip more if you're traveling with kids and/or pets or if you and your golf buddies have tracked half of the green into the room. You'll want to leave your tip daily because there may be a different maid each day. And make sure it is obvious that the money is for them; you'll often find an envelope on the dresser for this purpose. Personally, I like to leave it in the bathroom on the tray where they put the soap and shampoo. That always seems to ensure that they replenish it. Anytime you ask a maid or someone from housekeeping to come to your room, such as to deliver a hair dryer or for turndown service, always tip $1–2 per item.

Maitre d's
Nothing is expected, unless they reserve you a special table or squeeze you onto the "reservation-only" list. Then give $5–10, or more.

Massage therapists

10–15 percent if they come to your home or hotel room. Ask in advance if this is automatically included in the price. (See also *Spa treatments*.)

Musicians

$2–3 for special requests. If the mariachi band is walking around, tipping is optional. For pianists tip $1–5 at the end of your meal or their performance, whichever is first.

Nightclub servers

It is not necessary to grease the palms of the bouncer at the door. (See *Navigating Nightclubs* in the *South Beach* section of chapter 7, *Miami Metro*.) I've heard of people tipping $50 and up, and that still didn't get them in any faster, so don't bother. Once inside, tip bartenders and cocktail servers 15–20 percent. Don't tip on the cover charge if one is included in your bill.

Porters/skycaps (airport baggage handlers)

$1–2 per bag.

Resort/recreation fees

Resort fees can run the gamut from $5 to $40 a day per room. It is important to ask when you book your reservation so as not to be surprised. This fee may cover anything from free use of beach cabanas, snorkel equipment, paddleboats, kayaks, sailboards, sailboats, tennis courts, a round of golf, or simply the use of their swimming pool. For those who plan to vacation entirely at the resort, it may be a bargain.

Rest room attendants

A dying breed, these silent sentries are usually found at the trendiest nightclubs and restaurants. And you'll be especially grateful at the nightclubs as the night wears on. Attendants pay for the bevy of hairspray, perfume, tissues, and assorted touch-up makeup, so if you use any of it, please leave them $1 per visit.

Room service

Most hotels add the gratuity. If nothing is added, then tack on 15 percent to the total charge.

Spa treatments

15–20 percent for a full-service treatment. Most spas add this in automatically. If none is included, then tip at the end of the service and make sure to leave $2–5 for locker room and lounge attendants.

Swimming pool/beach attendants

If you want them to hold the same deck chair or cabana every day, then tip $2–3 per chair and $5–10 per cabana beginning the first day. It is not necessary to tip the keeper of the towels, unless he passes you a fresh one as you get out of the pool; then $1–2 is a nice gesture.

Take-out

If one of the wait staff takes your order and packages the food, then tip $1–2 or up to 10 percent. No tip is necessary for drive-up.

Taxis

15 percent of total fare (add more if the driver helps you with your bags).

Tip jars

It seems tip jars are popping up everywhere: coffee shops, gas stations, and even fast-food restaurants. Ugh! Do you leave something or not? It's just inappropriate for any food service establishment that doesn't actually bring you food and replenish your drinks to ask for a gratuity. The flip side is that these workers are generally paid only minimum wage, so if you're feeling generous, drop your change in the bucket.

Valets

You'll find valet parking your car hard to avoid. South Florida is "valet central," especially in the beach areas, and many places have mandatory valet. Expect to pay $7–15 for parking and to tip $1–5 when you pick up your vehicle. The recent trend is also to tip when dropping off. Note that the valets are often separate concessionaires and not employees of the restaurant or hotel, so liability may be limited.

Wait staff (full-service restaurant)

Wait staff in Florida are paid only a few dollars an hour and are taxed on all of their sales, so they expect 15–20 percent of the bill. Make sure to figure tips before coupons and discounts are applied. And always check your bill to see if the gratuity was automatically added.

Wine stewards

10–15 percent of wine bill, only if you used their services.

INDEX

K